This volume
of

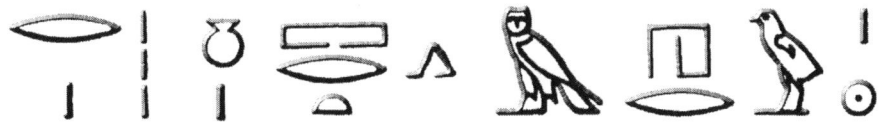

The Mystic Chapters of
The Rau nu Prt M Hru:
The Ancient Egyptian Book of
Enlightenment

Is for

Asar _____   _____
(first and last name of the owner of this book)

Cruzian Mystic Books
P.O. Box 570459
Miami, Florida, 33257
Tel./Fax: (305) 378-6253

First U.S. edition 2000

©2000-2005 By Reginald Muata Ashby

Publisher's Cataloging-in-Publication
(Provided by Quality Books, Inc.)

Ashby, Muata.
  The Egyptian book of the dead : the book of coming forth by day: mysticism of the Pert m heru : the ancient Egyptian book of enlightenment / by Muata Abhaya Ashby; edited by Karen Vijaya Ashby. -- 1st ed.
    P. cm.
    Includes bibliographical references and index.
    ISBN: 1884564283 (soft)
    ISBN: 1884564526 (hard)

  1.   Book of the dead. 2. Yoga. 3. Incantations, Egyptian. 4. Egypt--Religion. 5. Philosophy, Egyptian. I. Title.

BL2441.2.A84 2001   299'.31
                           QBIOO- 1 082

Sema Institute of Yoga
Cruzian Mystic Books and Music

Edited by Karen "Vijaya" Clarke-Ashby

Invocatory Prayers to be Read Prior to the Study of This Text

Adorations to the Divine in the form of the Rising Sun (Ra-Khepri)

Dua	**Ra**	**Cheft**	**Uben**	**F**	**em**	**aket**	**abdet**	**ent**	**Pet**
Adorations to Ra		when	rises	he	in	horizon	eastern	of	heaven

Anetej	**hra-k**	**iti**	**em Khepera,**	**Khepera**	**qemam**	**neteru**
Homage to Ra, coming forth as Khepera ,				Khepera, Creator of the gods and goddesses		

Cha – k	**uben**	**– k**	**pesd**	**Mut – k.**	**Cha**	**ti**	**em**	**suten**	**neteru**
Rising thee, shinning	thee,		lighting up thy mother.		Rising as Lord, king of the gods and goddesses				

Plate 1: The Crescent Moon, symbol of the divinities Asar, Djehuti and Khonsu.

Adorations to the Divine in the Form of the Moon (Asar)

Dua	**Asar**	**Un-Nefer**	**Neter Aah**	**Her Ab**	**Abdu**	**Suten**	**Heh**	**Neb Djetah**	**Sebeby**	**Heh**
Adorations to Asar	Un-Nefer	Divinity Great,	personality (in)	heart (of)	Abdu	King	eternity,	Lord of Forever	travelling (for)	eternities,

M	**aha -f**	**sa**	**dep**	**n**	**chat**	**Nut**	**utet**	**n**	**Geb**	**rpat**	**neb**
(in) form	raised he.	Son	primary	of	body (of)	Nut,	engendered	by	Geb	master	lord (of the),

Ureret	**qai**	**hed**	**ity**	**neteru rmteg**
Ureret crown	exalted	white crown	prince	(of) gods and goddesses (and) people

3

DEDICATIONS

To the Asar in All, To Goddess Maat and Her Sister, To Swami Jyotirmayananda, To Dja, To Atum-Ra, Asar, Aset and Heru!

About the Cover

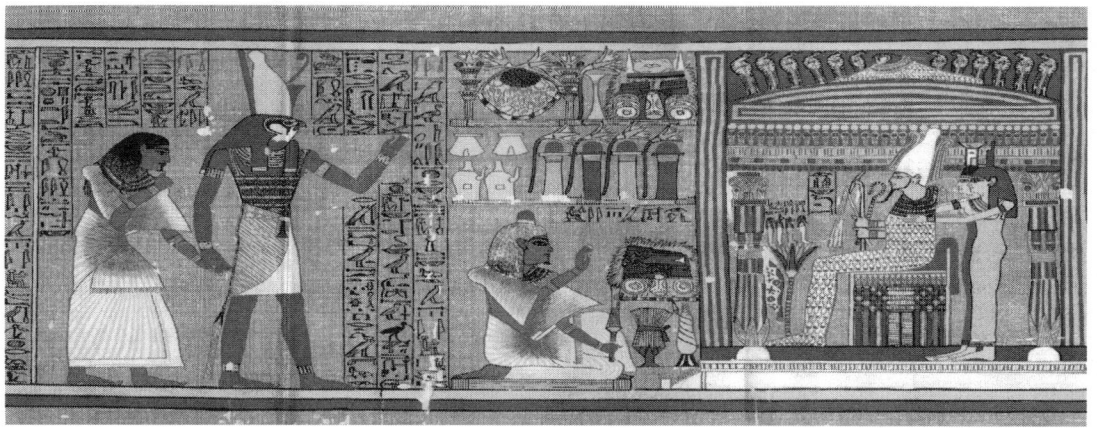

Plate 2: Pert M Hru of Ani (18th Dyn.)

Sema Institute of Yoga

Sema (☧) is an Ancient Egyptian word and symbol meaning *union*. The Sema Institute is dedicated to the propagation of the universal teachings of spiritual evolution which relate to the union of humanity and the union of all things within the universe. It is a non-denominational organization which recognizes the unifying principles in all spiritual and religious systems of evolution throughout the world. Our primary goals are to provide the wisdom of ancient spiritual teachings in books, courses and other forms of communication. Secondly, to provide expert instruction and training in the various yogic disciplines including Ancient Egyptian Philosophy, Christian Gnosticism, Indian Philosophy and modern science. Thirdly, to promote world peace and Universal Love.

A primary focus of our tradition is to identify and acknowledge the yogic principles within all religions and to relate them to each other in order to promote their deeper understanding as well as to show the essential unity of purpose and the unity of all living beings and nature within the whole of existence.

The Institute is open to all who believe in the principles of peace, non-violence and spiritual emancipation regardless of sex, race, or creed.

ABOUT THE EDITOR

The Ancient Egyptian Book of the Dead: The Book of Coming Forth By Day
Mysticism of the Prt M Hru: The Book of Enlightenment
was edited by
Dr. Karen "Dja" Clarke-Ashby

Figure 1: A female Scribe from Ancient Egypt

ABOUT THE EDITOR:

Karen Clarke-Ashby "Vijaya" is the wife and spiritual partner of Dr. Muata Ashby. She is an independent researcher, practitioner and teacher of Yoga, a Doctor in the Sciences and a Pastoral Counselor, the editor of the Egyptian Yoga Book Series. Dr. Ashby has engaged in post-graduate research in advanced Jnana, Bhakti, Karma, Raja and Kundalini Yogas at the Yoga Research Foundation. She is a certified Yoga Exercise instructor, and a teacher of health and stress management uses of Yoga for modern society, based on the Indian and/or Kemetic yogic principles. Also, she is the co-author of The Egyptian Yoga Exercise Workout Book, and author of Yoga Mystic Metaphors for Enlightenment.

A WORD FROM THE AUTHOR, ABOUT THE EDITOR:

Dr. Karen "Vijaya" Ashby has been an ardent supporter of the Kemetic teachings, and it was due to her devotion and strength of will that this volume was made possible in the manner in which it has come forth. As an editor, or rather, scribe, she exceeds the ordinary qualifications for this job because she is an Initiate as well. Her keen insight into the philosophy is derived not only from her study of the teachings, but living them as well. This has been an invaluable asset, because she is not only able to correct typographical and grammatical errors, but also to make comments, suggestions and raise questions which allow the teachings to be expressed in a very accessible format. Therefore, I offer my obeisance to her for her service to me and to humanity.

God always plans the best circumstances for all, and I feel especially blessed to have been granted the opportunity to have a partner who is dedicated to the path of enlightenment and upliftment of humanity, for there is no better human being that one can associate with than a person who is virtuous and devoted the Divine. It has been my honor to experience the good association of her company, input and suggestions which enrich the projects I have produced. It is rare for people to discover The Divine, and also rare for people to discover The Divine in their partner, so there can be no mistaking the glorious mission we have embarked upon and which has found unqualified success, as the Egyptian Yoga Book Series has found worldwide readership. Her support, encouragement, suggestions and dedication have made this possible. This great soul is in every way the embodiment of the philosopher and Kemetic Priestess. Her skills as a scribe are unsurpassed. May God continue to bless us with her presence in life, vitality and health for many years to come.

-Dr. Muata Ashby

ABOUT THE AUTHOR

Dr. R. Muata Abhaya Ashby, holds a Doctor of Philosophy Degree in Religion, and a Doctor of Divinity Degree in Holistic Health. He is also a Pastoral Counselor and Teacher of Yoga Philosophy and Discipline. Dr. Ashby received his Doctor of Divinity Degree from and is an adjunct faculty member of the American Institute of Holistic Theology. Dr. Ashby is a certified PREP Relationship Counselor. Dr. Ashby has been an independent researcher and practitioner of Egyptian, Indian and Chinese Yoga and psychology as well as Christian Mysticism. Dr. Ashby has engaged in Post Graduate research in advanced Jnana, Bhakti and Kundalini Yogas at the Yoga Research Foundation under the direction of Swami Jyotirmayananda. He has extensively studied mystical religious traditions from around the world and is an accomplished lecturer, musician, artist, poet, screenwriter, playwright and author of over 25 books on yoga and spiritual philosophy. He is an Ordained Minister and Spiritual Counselor, and also the founder the Sema Institute, a non-profit organization dedicated to spreading the wisdom of Yoga and the Ancient Egyptian mystical traditions.

Dr. R. Muata Abhaya Ashby began his research into the spiritual philosophy of Ancient Egypt and India and noticed correlations in the culture and arts of the two countries. This was the catalyst for a successful book series on the subject called "Egyptian Yoga." Now he has created a series of musical compositions which explore this unique area of music from Ancient Egypt and its connection to world music.

Figure 2: A male Scribe from Ancient Egypt

OTHER BOOKS BY MUATA ASHBY

EGYPTIAN YOGA VOLUME I: THE PHILOSOPHY OF ENLIGHTENMENT

EGYPTIAN YOGA VOLUME II: THE SUPREME WISDOM OF ENLIGHTENMENT

INITIATION INTO EGYPTIAN YOGA

BLOOMING LOTUS OF DIVINE LOVE

MYSTICISM OF USHET REKHAT

EGYPTIAN PROVERBS

THEF NETERU: THE MOVEMENT OF THE GODS AND GODDESSES

THE CYCLES OF TIME

THE HIDDEN PROPERTIES OF MATTER

THE WISDOM OF ISIS: GOD IN THE UNIVERSE

THE MYSTICAL TEACHINGS OF
THE AUSARIAN RESURRECTION

THE WISDOM OF MAATI

THE SERPENT POWER

EGYPTIAN TANTRA YOGA

MEDITATION: THE ANCIENT EGYPTIAN PATH TO ENLIGHTENMENT

(For additional titles by Dr. Ashby see the back section of this book
and send for the free catalog.)

Check out the latest books, audio and video presentations on Egyptian Yoga and seminars, classes and courses now
on the World Wide Web!

INTERNET ADDRESS:

http://www.Egyptianyoga.com

E-MAIL ADDRESS: Semayoga@aol.com

Tel. (305) 378-6253 Fax. (305) 378-6253

P.O. Box 570459
Miami, Florida, 33257

This book, *The Egyptian Book of the Dead: Mystic Chapters of The Rau nu Prt m Hru: The Book of Enlightenment* is a continuation in the series of books on the Ancient Egyptian mystical religious path based on the Anunian (based on Ra) and Asarian (based on Asar) tradition. It is very important to understand the Asarian Resurrection Myth in order to gain a deeper understanding of the Book of the Dead. The following book is essential to understanding the mythological and mystical basis of the Mystic Chapters of *The Ancient Egyptian Book of Enlightenment.*

 NEW EDITION

ASARIAN RELIGION
The Path of Mystical Awakening and The Keys to Immortality

The ancient Sages created stories based on human and superhuman beings whose struggles, aspirations, needs and desires ultimately lead them to discover their true Self. The myth of Isis, Osiris and Horus is no exception in this area. While there is no one source where the entire story may be found, pieces of it are inscribed in various ancient temples walls, tombs, steles and papyri. For the first time available, the complete myth of Osiris, Isis and Horus has been compiled from original Ancient Egyptian, Greek and Coptic Texts. This epic myth has been richly illustrated with reliefs from the temple of Horus at Edfu, the temple of Isis at Philae, the temple of Osiris at Abydos, the temple of Hathor at Denderah and various papyri, inscriptions and reliefs.

The ancient religion of Osiris, Isis and Horus, if properly understood, contains all of the elements necessary to lead the sincere aspirant to attain immortality through inner self-discovery. This volume presents the entire myth and explores the main mystical themes and rituals associated with the myth for understating human existence, creation and the way to achieve spiritual emancipation - *Resurrection*. The Osirian myth is so powerful that it influenced and is still having an effect on the major world religions. Discover the origins and mystical meaning of the Christian Trinity, the Eucharist ritual and the ancient origin of the birthday of Jesus Christ.

Soft Cover ISBN: 1884564-27-5 $24.95 U.S.

TABLE OF CONTENTS

LIST OF FIGURES

LIST OF TABLES

Preface

"The Egyptians neither entrusted their mysteries to everyone, nor degraded the secrets of divine matters by disclosing them to the profane, reserving them for the heir apparent of the throne, and for such of priests as excelled in virtue and wisdom."

—Clement of Alexandria (150?-?220)

The Three Levels of Religion and the Mysteries

⌐🕊️ *Sheta* (Mystery), ⌐ *Sheta* (Hidden)

The first and most important teaching to understand in our study surrounds the Ancient Egyptian word "Sheti." Sheti comes from the root *Sheta*. The Ancient Egyptian word *Sheta* means something which is *hidden, secret, unknown*, or *cannot be seen or understood, a secret, a mystery*. What is considered to be inert matter also possesses "hidden" properties or *Shetau Akhet*. Rituals, Words of Power (Khu-Hekau, Mantras), religious texts and pictures are S*hetaut Neter* or *Divine Mysteries*. *Shetat* or *Seshetat* are the secret rituals in the cults of the Egyptian Gods. *Shetai* is the *Hidden God, Incomprehensible God, Mysterious One,* and *Secret One*. One name of the soul of the Ancient Egyptian god Amun is *Shet-ba* (The One whose soul is hidden). The name Amun itself signifies "The Hidden One," *"Shetai." Sheti* (spiritual discipline) is to go deeply into the mysteries, to study the mystery teachings and literature profoundly, to penetrate the mysteries. *Nehas-t* signifies: "resurrection" or "spiritual awakening." The body or *Shet-t* (mummy) is where a human being focuses attention to practice spiritual disciplines. When spiritual discipline is perfected, the true Self or *Shti* (he who is hidden in the coffin) is revealed.

Shetaut Neter
(Secrets about the Divine Self)

The *Book of Coming Forth By Day* represents the second level of Shetaut Neter. Shetaut Neter means "the way or wisdom of the hidden Divinity which is behind all Creation." Religion has three levels of practice. The first is the myth, which includes the traditions, stories and everything related to it. The next stage is the ritualization of the myth. The final stage is the metaphysical philosophy behind the teachings given in the myth. The book *The Ausarian Resurrection,* presented the complete myth of Asar (Ausar or Osiris), Aset (Isis) and Heru (Horus). The *Book of Coming Forth By Day* represents stage two, the ritualization of the myth of Asar, and through the practice of the rituals contained in the book it is possible to feel, think, act and ultimately experience the same fate of Asar, spiritual enlightenment. Thus, a spiritual aspirant is to understand that {he/she} has incarnated on earth and has been dismembered by egoistic thoughts and actions. However, by gaining an understanding of the hidden mysteries, it is possible to reach a state of beatitude and resurrection, just as Asar.[1]

Therefore, a serious spiritual aspirant should see every aspect of {his/her} life as a ritual in which the soul within them (Asar) is struggling to be reborn again. This spiritual rebirth is accomplished by the practices of listening to the teachings, practicing them and meditating upon them. With the understanding of the hidden knowledge, you can see that all of nature around you is Divine. This includes plants, animals, planets and stars, food, other people, etc. So, through your understanding of the myth and how it relates to your life, and by living your life according to this understanding (ritual), you can lead yourself to discover and realize (mystical experience) the deeper truth behind your own being. This is the true practice of religion. If you understand the superficial teachings of a religious myth, and you practice its rituals blindly without understanding the deeper implications, you will not obtain the higher realization. Your practice will be at the level of dogma. This is why there is so much religious conflict in the world

---

[1] See the book *The Mystical teachings of the Ausarian Resurrection: Initiation Into the Third Level of Shetaut Asar* by Muata Ashby

today. At the level of dogma, each religion has different myths and rituals and therefore, little if any, common ground upon which to come together. The results of this misunderstanding and ignorance have been personal disillusionment and wars. Yet, at the mystical or metaphysical level, all religions are actually pointing towards the same goal, that of spiritual realization.

A NEW TRANSLATION OF THE PRT M HRU

Why do we need a new translation of the *Ancient Egyptian Book of the Dead*?[2] If you have picked up a Christian Bible lately, you will notice that you do not have the original text. In fact, the present versions are centuries removed from the original scriptures which comprised the original texts. The Bible is one of the primary sources containing information regarding the beliefs of the Christian faith. It is a compilation of selected portions of writings[3] by different authors, written over a period of 1,000-2,000 years (1,500 B.C.E.- 200 A.C.E.). It is composed of two main sections, the Old Testament and the New Testament, which are made up of smaller books. The original form of the Old Testament is in the ancient Hebrew language. Later, about 250 B.C.E., the Old Testament was translated into Greek. The original form of the New Testament is in the ancient Aramaic, Greek and Hebrew. These forms serve as the primary "original" texts of the Bible. However, since most of the people of the world do not understand ancient Aramaic, Hebrew or Greek, it became necessary to make translations of the Bible into forms that people of modern times could understand. Translations of the Bible pose important problems because the church and religious scholars admittedly[4] do not understand the meanings of some of the ancient Hebrew words in part or at all. Present day English speaking people would not even be able to understand the original King James Version of the Bible which was written only 387 years ago, much less scriptures that were written over 1,700 years ago. However, the essence of a teaching can be discerned and brought forth by those who are initiated into the correct understanding and practice of religious philosophy in its three steps[5]. This is why updates to the translations are necessary.

However, at the same time, the necessity for translations opens the door to corruption and misunderstanding, as some translators may want to present a certain view of the scriptures to prove their own points or to mislead others, or they simply may not produce a correct translation because they do not understand the philosophy which the original Sages were trying to impart. Many people do not see the spiritual scriptures as books of spiritual principles being imparted through metaphors. Rather, they insist that they are to be believed word for word or not at all. If this is the case, and if certain words, customs or ideas cannot be understood by theologians and scholars, as they have already admitted, there is bound to be some misunderstanding. For example, people in modern industrialized countries live with modern plumbing and aqueducts. Their concerns are different than people thousands of years ago worrying about the annual Nile flood or rains for watering their crops. Since ancient spiritual scriptures are most often enveloped in mythology which has been blended with historic events and personalities, these will inevitably contain some information related by expressions that only people living in those times would understand. If the scriptures are interpreted strictly in historical or literal terms, they will become the object of many different interpretations and consequently, arguments and misinterpretation as well. For this reason, the religious beliefs of the translator of the particular text in question may or may not be in agreement with the original scriptural meaning, and may consequently influence the translation. Therefore, the reader should exercise caution when choosing a translation to use for study. Another important consideration is that the translator should be a practitioner of the philosophy as well, that is, one who is involved with the culture of the text. In this way, by living the teachings, they can draw from the feel of the teaching and thereby bring to bear the inner insight which comes from the Divine source.

Since languages and culture change over time, it becomes necessary to update translations on a regular basis. Another important factor is that there are new discoveries that arise from time to time which alter

---

[2] Pert m Hru-Book of Coming Forth By Day

[3] The Bible does not include the entire group of scriptures that were written in biblical times. See the book *Christian Yoga* by Muata Ashby

[4] By general admission; confessedly.

[5] Myth, Ritual and Metaphysical (Mysticism).

the understanding of the use of some terms or elucidate a new meaning of the old text, which in turn affects the understanding of the meaning of the teachings. Although revision work has been incorporated into this volume, its most important contribution relates to the interpretation of the scriptures from the point of view of a living mystical tradition.

Unlike the Bible whose original texts were translated into many languages, the *Ru Pert Em Heru (Prt m Hru)* has not suffered removal from its original form, but from convention to suit modern culture. What I mean is that the pervasiveness of the Bible and its various versions has caused a situation in which many people, including scholars, have come to believe the Bible as being historically accurate, and the final authority on spiritual teachings. They also view the modern versions as being true to the original versions. While the study of the *Prt m Hru* has been mostly confined to scholars and a limited number of interested people, it has suffered from being interpreted by scientists instead of religious scholars and practitioners of the philosophy. Thus, the translations, while being accurate in many respects, have lost the deeper meaning which was originally intended. Yet, this meaning is as real today as it was seven thousand years ago when the *Pyramid Texts* were carved in stone, but it can only be discovered if the translation and interpretation has a spiritual basis.

Plate 3: An Ancient Egyptian tomb entrance at Sakhara (the land of Seker-Asar).

Author's Foreword

WHO WERE THE ANCIENT EGYPTIANS AND WHAT IS YOGA PHILOSOPHY?

The Ancient Egyptian religion (*Shetaut Neter*), language and symbols provide the first "historical" record of Yoga Philosophy and Religious literature. Egyptian Yoga is what has been commonly referred to by Egyptologists as Egyptian "Religion" or "Mythology," but to think of it as just another set of stories or allegories about a long lost civilization is to completely miss the greatest secret of human existence. Yoga, in all of its forms and disciplines of spiritual development, was practiced in Egypt earlier than anywhere else in history. This unique perspective from the highest philosophical system which developed in Africa over seven thousand years ago provides a new way to look at life, religion, the discipline of psychology and the way to spiritual development leading to spiritual Enlightenment. Egyptian mythology, when understood as a system of Yoga (union of the individual soul with the Universal Soul or Supreme Consciousness), gives every individual insight into their own divine nature and also a deeper insight into all religions and Yoga systems.

Diodorus Siculus (Greek Historian) writes in the time of Augustus (first century B.C.):

> "Now the Ethiopians, as historians relate, were the first of all men and the proofs of this statement, they say, are manifest. For that they did not come into their land as immigrants from abroad, but were the natives of it and so justly bear the name of autochthones (sprung from the soil itself), is, they maintain, conceded by practically all men..."

> "They also say that the Egyptians are colonists sent out by the Ethiopians, Asar having been the leader of the colony. For, speaking generally, what is now Egypt, they maintain, was not land, but sea, when in the beginning the universe was being formed; afterwards, however, as the Nile during the times of its inundation carried down the mud from Ethiopia, land was gradually built up from the deposit...And the larger parts of the customs of the Egyptians are, they hold, Ethiopian, the colonists still preserving their ancient manners. For instance, the belief that their kings are Gods, the very special attention which they pay to their burials, and many other matters of a similar nature, are Ethiopian practices, while the shapes of their statues and the forms of their letters are Ethiopian; for of the two kinds of writing which the Egyptians have, that which is known as popular (demotic) is learned by everyone, while that which is called sacred (hieratic), is understood only by the priests of the Egyptians, who learnt it from their Fathers as one of the things which are not divulged, but among the Ethiopians, everyone uses these forms of letters. Furthermore, the orders of the priests, they maintain, have much the same position among both peoples; for all are clean who are engaged in the service of the gods, keeping themselves shaven, like the Ethiopian priests, and having the same dress and form of staff, which is shaped like a plough and is carried by their kings who wear high felt hats which end in a knob in the top and are circled by the serpents which they call asps; and this symbol appears to carry the thought that it will be the lot who shall dare to attack the king to encounter death-carrying stings. Many other things are told by them concerning their own antiquity and the colony which they sent out that became the Egyptians, but about this there is no special need of our writing anything."

The Ancient Egyptian texts state:

> "Our people originated at the base of the mountain of the Moon, at the
> origin of the Nile river."

"KMT" "Egypt," "Burnt," "Black people," "Black Land"

24

In describing the Ancient Egyptians of his time, Herodotus (Greek historian c. 484-425 BC) said: *"The Egyptians and Nubians have thick lips, broad noses, wooly hair and burnt skin... ...And the Indian tribes I have mentioned, their skins are all of the same color, much like the Ethiopians... their country is a long way from Persia towards the south..."* Diodorus, the Greek historian (c. 100 B.C.) said the following, *"And upon his return to Greece, they gathered around and asked, "tell us about this great land of the Blacks called Ethiopia." And Herodotus said, "There are two great Ethiopian nations, one in Sind (India) and the other in Egypt."* Thus, from these accounts we gather that the Ancient Egyptian peoples were of dark complexion, i.e. of African origin and they had close ties in ancient times with the peoples of India. **Where is the land of Egypt?**

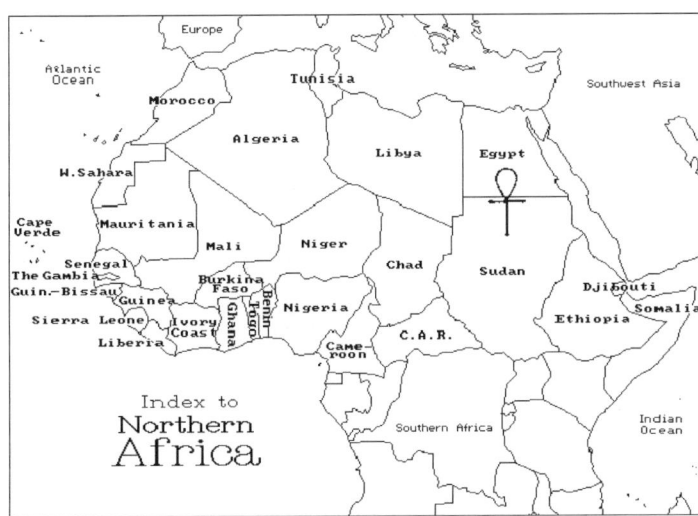

Figure 3: A map of North East Africa showing the location of the land of *Ta-Meri* or *Kamut,* also known as Ancient Egypt.

The Ancient Egyptians lived for thousands of years in the northeastern corner of the African continent in the area known as the Nile Valley. The Nile river was a source of dependable enrichment for the land and allowed them to prosper for a very long time. Their prosperity was so great that they created art, culture, religion, philosophy and a civilization which has not been duplicated since. The Ancient Kamitans (Egyptians) based their government and business concerns on spiritual values and therefore, enjoyed an orderly society which included equality between the sexes, and a legal system based on universal spiritual laws. The *Prt m Hru* is a tribute to their history, culture and legacy. As historical insights unfold, it becomes clearer that modern culture has derived its basis from Ancient Egypt, though the credit is not often given, nor the integrity of the practices maintained. This is another important reason to study Ancient Egyptian Philosophy, to discover the principles which allowed their civilization to prosper over a period of thousands of years in order to bring our systems of government, religion and social structures to a harmony with ourselves, humanity and with nature.

Christianity was partly an outgrowth of Judaism, which was itself an outgrowth of Ancient Egyptian culture and religion. So who were the Ancient Egyptians? From the time that the early Greek philosophers set foot on African soil to study the teachings of mystical spirituality in Egypt (900-300 B.C.E.), Western society and culture was forever changed. Ancient Egypt had such a profound effect on Western civilization as well as on the native population of Ancient India (Dravidians) that it is important to understand the history and culture of Ancient Egypt, and the nature of its spiritual tradition in more detail.

The history of Egypt begins in the far reaches of history. It includes The Dynastic Period, The Hellenistic Period, Roman and Byzantine Rule (30 B.C.E.-638 A.C.E.), the Caliphate and the Mamalukes (642-1517 A.C.E.), Ottoman Domination (1082-1882 A.C.E.), British colonialism (1882-1952 A.C.E.), as well as modern, Arab-Islamic Egypt (1952- present).

Ancient Egypt or Kamit, was a civilization that flourished in Northeast Africa along the Nile River from before 5,500 B.C.E. until 30 B.C.E. In 30 B.C.E., Octavian, who was later known as the Roman Emperor, Augustus, put the last Egyptian King, Ptolemy XIV, a Greek ruler, to death. After this Egypt was formally annexed to Rome. Egyptologists normally divide Ancient Egyptian history into the following approximate periods: The Early Dynastic Period (3,200-2,575 B.C.E.); The Old Kingdom or Old Empire (2,575-2,134 B.C.E.); The First Intermediate Period (2,134-2,040 B.C.E.); The Middle Kingdom or Middle Empire (2,040-1,640 B.C.E.); The Second Intermediate Period (1,640-1,532 B.C.E.); The New Kingdom or New Empire (1,532-1,070 B.C.E.); The third Intermediate Period (1,070-712 B.C.E.); The Late Period (712-332 B.C.E.).

In the Late Period the following groups controlled Egypt. The Nubian Dynasty (712-657 B.C.E.); The Persian Dynasty (525-404 B.C.E.); The Native Revolt and re-establishment of Egyptian rule by Egyptians (404-343 B.C.E.); The Second Persian Period (343-332 B.C.E.); The Ptolemaic or Greek Period (332 B.C.E.- c. 30 B.C.E.); Roman Period (c.30 B.C.E.-395 A.C.E.); The Byzantine Period (395-640 A.C.E) and The Arab Conquest Period (640 A.C.E.-present). The individual dynasties are numbered, generally in Roman numerals, from I through XXX.

The period after the New Kingdom saw greatness in culture and architecture under the rulership of Ramses II. However, after his rule, Egypt saw a decline from which it would never recover. This is the period of the downfall of Ancient Egyptian culture in which the Libyans ruled after The Tanite (XXI) Dynasty. This was followed by the Nubian conquerors who founded the XXII dynasty and tried to restore Egypt to her past glory. However, having been weakened by the social and political turmoil of wars, Ancient Egypt fell to the Persians once more. The Persians conquered the country until the Greeks, under Alexander, conquered them. The Romans followed the Greeks, and finally the Arabs conquered the land of Egypt in 640 A.C.E to the present.

However, the history which has been classified above is only the history of the "Dynastic Period." It reflects the view of traditional Egyptologists who have refused to accept the evidence of a Predynastic period in Ancient Egyptian history contained in Ancient Egyptian documents such as the *Palermo Stone, Royal Tablets at Abydos, Royal Papyrus of Turin,* the *Dynastic List* of *Manetho,* and the eye-witness accounts of Greek historians Herodotus (c. 484-425 B.C.E.) and Diodorus. These sources speak clearly of a Pre-dynastic society which stretches far into antiquity. The Dynastic Period is what most people think of whenever Ancient Egypt is mentioned. This period is when the pharaohs (kings) ruled. The latter part of the Dynastic Period is when the Biblical story of Moses, Joseph, Abraham, etc., occurs (c. 2100? -1,000? B.C.E). Therefore, those with a Christian background generally only have an idea about Ancient Egypt as it is related in the Bible. Although this biblical notion is very limited in scope, the significant impact of Ancient Egypt on Hebrew and Christian culture is evident even from the biblical scriptures. Actually, Egypt existed much earlier than most traditional Egyptologists are prepared to admit. The new archeological evidence related to the great Sphinx monument on the Giza Plateau and the ancient writings by Manetho, one of the last High Priests of Ancient Egypt, show that Ancient Egyptian history begins earlier than 10,000 B.C.E. and may date back to as early as 30,000-50,000 B.C.E.

It is known that the Pharaonic (royal) calendar based on the Sothic system (star Sirius) was in use by 4,240 B.C.E. This certainly required extensive astronomical skills and time for observation. Therefore, the history of Kamit (Egypt) must be reckoned to be extremely ancient. Thus, in order to grasp the antiquity of Ancient Egyptian culture, religion and philosophy, we will briefly review the history presented by the Ancient Egyptian Priest Manetho and some Greek Historians.

The calendar based on the Great Year was also used by the Ancient Egyptians. The Great Year is based on the movement of the earth through the constellations known as the precession of the Equinoxes and confirmed by the History given by the Ancient Egyptian Priest Manetho in the year 241 B.C.E. Each Great Year has 25,860 to 25,920 years and 12 arcs or constellations, and each passage through a constellation takes 2,155 – 2,160 years. These are the "Great Months." The current cycle or year began around the year 10,858 B.C.E. At around the year 36,766 B.C.E., according to Manetho, the Creator, Ra, ruled the earth in person from his throne in the Ancient Egyptian city of Anu. By this reckoning our current year (2,000 A.C.E.) is actually the year 38,766 based on the Great Year System of Ancient Egyptian history.

Figure 4: The land of Ancient Egypt

Egypt is located in the north-eastern corner of the African Continent. The cities wherein the theology of the Trinity of Amun-Ra-Ptah was developed were: A- Anu (Heliopolis), B-Hetkaptah (Memphis), and C-Waset (Thebes). The cities wherein the theology of the Trinity of Asar-Aset-Heru was developed were A- Anu, D-Abydos, E- Philae, F- Edfu, G-Denderah, and H- Ombos.

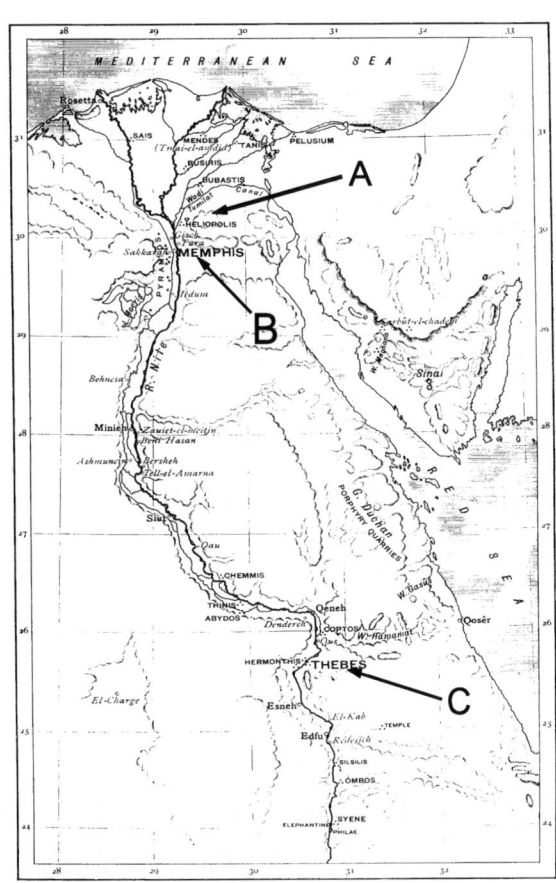

WHO AM I?

Who am I? What is this mind which perceives? What is this universe made of? Is there a God?

Throughout history, these and many other questions have followed humanity from generation to generation. The need of human nature to experience, to evolve and understand has led to the invention of philosophies which assist the human mind in grasping the realities it seems to perceive in the world as well as those which it seems to perceive with the heart, but which remain intellectually unknowable. In ancient times these philosophies developed as myths, religions, yoga systems and in modern times they have taken the form of sciences called psychology, physics and non-religious philosophies such as Marxism and existentialism. Yet with all the developments of the past, humanity as a whole remains in search of the answers to happiness, health and peace. Has religion and science failed? Most importantly, throughout all the teachings embodied in religions and the discoveries of modern science, has humanity missed out on the benefits of religion and science? Is there anything useful in these endeavors for humankind? A deeper study into the history, meaning and practice of ancient teachings reveals a remarkable concordance with modern scientific discoveries. In essence, modern sciences such as Quantum Physics are leading scientists to contemplate life and our understanding of reality in terms which ancient philosophers and Sages espoused thousands of years ago. Science is a discipline which professes to shun non-rational thoughts, a common feature to both mythology and religion. So how is it possible that it would lead to the same conclusions about existence as mystical religions and Yoga philosophy?

Two of the most important areas we will look into are psychology and mythology. We will look at these from a yogic or mystical-symbolic point of view rather than a rational, literal or logical way. The reasons for doing this will become clear as we progress through the study. Mythology and spiritual symbolism were never intended to be understood as factual events which occurred in a particular place in time exclusively. Rather, they are to be understood as ever recurring principles of human life which need to be understood in their deepest sense in order for them to provide humanity with the benefit of their wisdom.

Psychology has been defined as the study of the thought processes characteristic of an individual or group (mind, psyche, ethos, mentality). In this work we will focus on religious mythology as a psychological discipline for understanding the human mind, its development and transformation. Mythology can be understood as a language, however, it is a unique kind of language. Certain languages are similar because they are part of a family of languages. For example: Italian and Spanish. This similarity makes it possible for a person whose native language is Spanish to understand the meanings of some Italian words so as to somewhat be able to follow along a conversation in Italian. Mythology is much more intelligible than an ordinary human language. Mythology is more akin to music in its universality. If the key elements of this language are well understood, it is possible to understand and relate any mythological system to another and thereby gain the understanding of the message being imparted. Setting up your own personal spiritual program will require that you develop a profound understanding of the psychological principles upon which ancient mythology is based in order to discover your special path on the spiritual journey.

In order to gain insight into the *"Psycho-Mythology"* or psychological implications of religious and spiritual mythology which promote the psycho-spiritual transformation of the individual leading to the attainment of Enlightenment, we must first define what is meant by the terms psycho and mythology. Here, the term *psycho* must be understood as far more than simply that which refers to the mind and its thoughts. We will be using *psycho* to mean everything that constitutes human consciousness in all of its stages and states. *Mythology* here refers to the codes, messages, ideas, directives and beliefs which affect the psyche through the conscious and unconscious mind of an individual, specifically those effects which result in transpersonal or transcendental changes in the personality as well as those which constitute anti-yogic, anti-transcendental movements.

While our study begins with Egyptian Mythology, Religion and Yoga Philosophy, it also necessarily relates to all mythologies, religions and philosophies around the world. Briefly, Egyptian religion is the oldest recorded religion in this historical era and in our book, *Egyptian Yoga*, we compiled the correlations between the religion which developed in Egypt and those which developed later around other parts of Africa as well as in Asia.[6] It becomes evident that what has been called Egyptian Mythology is in reality a highly sophisticated and advanced system of Yoga Philosophy. Yoga is a system of personal transformation by which we are able to discover our true Self wherein lies the answers to all of our questions about the purpose of our existence, who we are, how to overcome adversity and promote prosperity, and why we are in the situations of life in which we find ourselves. Most importantly, the idea is not to amass mountainous amounts of wisdom teachings but to discover their meanings and how to apply them in ordinary life to rise above it, as a lotus rises above the muddy waters without retaining a single drop of the dirty water on its petals. If this does not occur, then one is not practicing philosophy, religion or yoga, but something else. Initiation is therefore the process of coming into a philosophy and way of life which allows you to become free of any restrictions or impediments to your happiness. It is also a process of discovering how to end pain and suffering in life. Thus, it is a process of becoming established in your own inner support and inner peace without depending on the world.

What is Human Existence and What is its Purpose?

Human life is a process in which a human being experiences various situations, ranging from pain and suffering to happiness and pleasure, between the time span of birth and death. From a yogic point of view, all human situations are painful because they are distractions from the true source of bliss and abiding happiness within the heart. Attachment to objects and relationships outside of oneself seems like the normal course of human life, but the masses of people adopt this mode of existence out of ignorance. Ignorance of what? Ignorance of their deeper Self. If they had knowledge of the deeper Self within, there would be no need to seek personal fulfillment through worldly achievements, worldly possessions or worldly relationships. This endless search leads every ignorant human being to engage in various situations and entanglements, which in the beginning seem to hold the possibility of bringing about a happy circumstance, but which invariably leads to pain, suffering and frustration. A mature human being discovers that ordinary human life cannot satisfy the inner need of the soul because it is unpredictable and transient. So what should one live for? Did not the Ancient Egyptians build wondrous monuments and innovations in science, medicine, government, social order, etc.? They did not withdraw from the world, but they did not seek spiritual fulfillment through the world either. This is the first key to understanding Ancient Egyptian culture and spiritual philosophy.

You do not have to turn on the television or read a newspaper to see the miserable condition of most people. Think about your own life. Has there been any situation where happiness was abiding? Have you experienced any relationship with someone who never disappointed you or caused you pain? Has there been any possession you acquired which did not lose its power to bring you happiness or that you did not become bored with, even though it made you happy to possess it in the beginning? Even those people who say they are happy with life as it is are deluding themselves into believing that the happy moments balance the painful ones. This is not true because even the happy moments are setting you up for some painful disappointment in the future, because all worldly situations and relationships come to an end. Thus, by living in accordance with the ignorant philosophy of life, your happy moments cause longing for more happy moments, and when these are not possible, there is disappointment and frustration. The longing and frustration does not end at the time of death. When the body dies, the mind continues to hold the deep rooted desires for worldly fulfillment and this causes the soul to be impelled toward countless new lifetimes of karmic entanglements in search of worldly fulfillment. All of this occurs out of ignorance of one's true Self.

> "The visible world is ephemeral, the spirit world is forever; gain strength from this since nothing physical can destroy you."

> "Labor not after riches first, and think thou afterwards wilt enjoy them. He who neglects the present moment, throws away all that he hath. As the arrow passes through the heart, while the warrior knew not that it was coming; so shall his life be taken away before he knoweth that he hath it."

> "There is no happiness for the soul in the external worlds since these are perishable, true happiness lies in that which is eternal, within us."

---

[6] The term Asia includes Europe.

FROM: THE STEALE OF ABU: "Be chief of the mysteries at festivals, know your mouth, come in Hetep (peace), enjoy life on earth but do not become attached to it; it is transitory."
—Ancient Egyptian Proverbs

Becoming free from the clutches of ignorance is not as simple as learning about its cause. Even if you are honest and truly believe in the philosophy of yoga and mystical spirituality, all of your mental efforts to negate the ignorance will fail in the beginning. This is because your mind has spent many hours over a period of days, months, years, lifetimes and eons, believing in the illusion of human life. Even if you were to understand that it is your worldly attachments which are causing you mental agitation and suffering, the process of attaining Enlightenment is not as simple as saying, "O.K. since my possessions are distracting me and causing me agitation and worry, I will give them up and have peace." Even if you were to find yourself without possessions, your mind would be grieving over their loss, or preoccupied with how to regain them or how to survive without them.

Even if you give everything up and go to a distant cave away from civilization, you cannot escape from the world. There will still be ants and mosquitoes to bite you, cold weather, rain, wild animals, and the restless wandering of your mind thinking of the life you left! Initiation into spiritual life is the process of learning an art of living which leads to freedom even while involved in the world. Your goal is to become as the lotus which rises up from the muddy waters, able to exist in the world without being soiled by it, and having discovered the bliss of inner spiritual discovery, always abiding in that wondrous glory in any situation which life presents to you. Once the teachings of spirituality are understood and you have a firm conviction as to their reality, then you can begin the process of making them your reality. Spiritual realization requires sustained effort over a period of time wherein spiritual disciplines are directed towards overturning the mountainous creations, which the mind has produced in the past due to ignorance. The mind is like a river. Ignorant ideas are like logs, rocks, branches and dams in the river which block, divert or distort the flow of water. With the correct equipment (correct understanding and practice of the spiritual disciplines) and through sustained effort, the obstacles to spiritual realization can be removed allowing the river of the mind to flow freely toward the ocean of self-discovery. As the second stage in the practice of religion (ritualism), the *Prt m Hru* also encompasses the disciplines of spiritual practice which are in modern times recognized by the name "Yoga," especially the Yoga of Righteous action. These will be discussed in detail later.

If you have developed enough spiritual sensitivity to understand that there is no abiding peace or happiness to be found in ordinary human existence, you are qualified to study the deeper mysteries of spiritual life. This is the process of Initiation, which leads from ignorance to Enlightenment and self-discovery. It is the process by which a human being living an ordinary life is taught how to lead an extraordinary life and to attain superhuman expanded (enlightened) consciousness. Where is there an inexhaustible source of bliss and happiness, which does not depend on external factors? Where is it possible to find unending peace and tranquillity and a joy which is not subject to external conditions of either prosperity or adversity? The initiatic process shows the way.

In order for the teachings of mystical spirituality to come true in your life, you must make them the central force in your life. You must center your life around them and infuse them into every aspect of your life. In this way you will become transformed into the ideal of what the teachings describe: an Enlightened human being. It is not possible to gain higher spiritual understanding of the practices in any other way except to live them. Thus initiation is a way of life and not a single event. It is a continuous process which leads to greater and greater awareness and expansion, culminating in the highest levels of Self-Knowledge, Stage Three of Religion.

Before proceeding with the main body of this work, it would be helpful to establish some working definitions for the disciplines which will be discussed in order to provide a common basis for understanding the journey we will undertake. These terms will be further defined and explored throughout the course of this work.

Philosophy

Philosophy has been defined as the speculative inquiry concerning the source and nature of human knowledge and a system of ideas based on such thinking. In this work, the idea of philosophy will be confined to the modes of thinking employed for the purpose of transforming the human mind, leading it to achieve transpersonal states of consciousness. In its original sense, philosophy is a mental discipline for leading a person to enlightenment. In modern times this lofty notion of philosophy has come to be regarded as unscientific speculation or even as an opinion or belief of one person or group versus another. Specifically, we will look at Kemeticism[7] as a philosophy of psychological transformation.

> "Never forget, the words are not the reality, only reality is reality; picture symbols are the idea, words are confusion."[8]

> "The Self {ultimate reality} is not known through study of scriptures, nor through subtlety of the intellect, nor through much learning; but by him who longs for it is it known."[9]

One caveat which any true philosophy must follow is the understanding that words in themselves cannot capture the ultimate essence of reality. Words can be a trap to the highly developed intellect. Therefore, we must always keep in mind that words and philosophical discourse can only point the way to the truth. In order to discover the truth, we must go beyond all words, all thoughts, and all of our mental concepts and philosophies, because the truth, as *Hermetic* and *Vedanta* philosophy would say, can only be experienced; it cannot be encapsulated in any way, shape or form.

The study of philosophy in its highest form is to assist the student in understanding {his/her} own mind in order to be able to transcend it, and thus, experience the "transcendental" reality which lies beyond words, thoughts, concepts and mental notions. Mental conceptions are based on our own worldly experiences. They help us to understand the world as the senses perceive it. However, clinging to these experiences as the only reality precludes our discovery of other forms of reality or existence which lies beyond the capacity of the senses. A dog's olfactory sense and the vision of a hawk are much superior to that of the human being.

However, the human has one advantage which is superior to all senses and scientific instruments, the intuitional mind when it is purified by the practice of Yoga philosophy and disciplines. Ancient mystical philosophical systems have as their main goal the destruction of the limited concepts and illusions of the mind. In essence, the philosophies related to understanding nature and a human being's place in it were the first disciplines which practiced what would today be called Transpersonal Psychology, that is, a system of psychology which assists us in going beyond the personal or ego-based aspects of the psyche in order to discover what lies beyond (trans) the personal (relating to the personality).

Metaphysics

Metaphysics is the branch of philosophy that systematically investigates first causes of nature, the universe and ultimate reality. The term comes from the Greek "*meta physika*," meaning "after the things of nature." In Aristotle's works, he envisioned that the first philosophy came after the physics. Metaphysics has been divided into *ontology*, or the study of the essence of being or that which is or exists, and *cosmology*, the study of the structure and laws of the universe and the manner of its creation. From time immemorial, philosophers, such as those who wrote the Ancient Egyptian Creation myths, to Greek philosophers such as Plato and Aristotle, to more modern philosophers such as Whitehead and Kant, have written on metaphysics. Skeptics, however, have charged that speculation which cannot be verified by objective evidence is useless. However, these skeptics do not realize that what they consider as "objective reality" is not objective at all, since objectivity is based on the perceptions of the senses, and as just discussed, modern science itself has proven that the human senses cannot perceive the phenomenal universe as it really is. Further, the objective information that can be gathered by scientific instruments is only valid under certain conditions. This makes it relative and not absolute information. Thus, what

---

[7] Term coined by the author to signify Kemetic, based on the ancient words Kemet or Kamit, used in Ancient Egypt to describe the land and inhabitants of North-East Africa, meaning Ancient Egyptian- related to Ancient Egyptian culture, religion and mysticism. *"KMT" "Egypt", "Burnt", "Land of Blackness", "Land of the Burnt People."* This term is most appropriately used to refer to the religion of Ancient Egypt in order to relate it to the culture of ancient times. Another term, "Egyptian Yoga" meaning Smai Tawi, has bee introduced previously. Howevber, the proper name of Ancient Egyptian Religion is "Shetaut Neter," meaning "the hidden way of the Divine Self" (i.e. God).

[8] Hermetic proverb. Hermeticism is the later development of Kemetic Philosophy.

[9] Indian Vedantic proverb.

people ordinarily consider to be real and abiding is not. Einstein's proof of relativity confirms this. There must be something real beyond the phenomenal world which sustains it. The search for that higher essence is the purpose of philosophy and metaphysics. Therefore, the value of metaphysical and mystical philosophy studies is evident.

Psychology

Psychology, as used by ordinary practitioners of society, has been defined as the study of the thought processes characteristic of an individual or group (mind, psyche, ethos, mentality). In this work we will focus on Kemeticism as a psychological discipline for understanding the human mind, its source, higher development and transformation. However, Mystical Psychology in reality does not relate only to the mind since a human being is composed of several complex aspects. The term personality, as it is used in Yoga, implies mind, body and spirit, as well as the conscious, subconscious and unconscious aspects of the mind. Therefore, the discipline of psychology must be expanded to include physical as well as spiritual dimensions. Once again, modern medical science has, within the last twenty years, acknowledged the understanding that health cannot be treated as a physical problem only, but as one which involves the mind, body and spirit. Likewise, spiritual teaching must be related as a discipline which involves not only the soul of an individual, but the mind and body as well – in other words, the entire human being.

Yoga

The literal meaning of the word Yoga is to *"yoke"* or to *"link"* back. The implication is to link back individual consciousness (human personality) to its original source, the original essence: Universal Consciousness. In a broad sense Yoga is any process which helps one to achieve liberation or freedom from bondage to the pain and spiritual ignorance of ordinary human existence. So whenever you engage in any activity with the goal of promoting the discovery of your true Self, be it studying the spiritual wisdom teachings, exercising, fasting, meditation, breath control, rituals, chanting, prayer, etc., you are practicing yoga. If the goal is to help you to discover your essential nature as one with God or the Supreme Being, Consciousness, then it is Yoga.

Yoga (Sanskrit for "union") is a term used for a number of disciplines, the goal of each being to lead the practitioner to attain union with Universal Consciousness. Present day Indian Yoga philosophy is based on several Indian texts such as the *Upanishads, Bhagavad Gita* and the *Yoga-sutras* of Patañjali, and several other Yoga treatises developed in India. The practice of Yoga generally involves meditation, moral restraints, and the awakening of energy centers (in the body) through specific postures (asanas) or physical exercises, and breathing exercises. All Yoga disciplines are devoted to freeing the soul or individual self from worldly (mental) restraints. They have become popular in the West as a means of self-control and relaxation.

The specific form of *"yoking"* or to *"linking"* back that was practiced in Ancient Egypt was called "Smai Tawi" or union of the two lands, i.e. the opposites, the Higher and lower aspects of self or soul and Spirit.

Religion

All religions tend to be deistic at the elementary levels. Most often it manifests as an outgrowth of the cultural concepts of a people as they try to express the deeper feeling which they perceive, though not in its entirety. Thus, deism is based on limited spiritual knowledge. Deism, as a religious belief or form of theism, holds that God's action was restricted to an initial act of creation, after which he retired (separated) to contemplate the majesty of his work. Deists hold that the natural creation is regulated by laws put in place by God at the time of creation and inscribed with perfect moral principles. A deeper study of religion will reveal that in its original understanding, it seeks to reveal the deeper essential nature of creation, the human heart and their relation to God, which transcends the deistic model or doctrine. The term religion comes from the Latin *"Relegare"* which uses the word roots *"Re"* which means *"Back"* and *"Ligon"* which means *"to hold, to link, to bind."* Therefore, the essence of true religion is the same as yoga, that is, of linking back, specifically, linking the soul of its follower back to its original source: God. So, although religion in its purest form is a Yoga system, incorporating the yoga disciplines within its teachings, the original intent and meaning of the religious scriptures are often misunderstood, if not distorted. This occurs because religions have developed in different geographic areas. As a result, the lower levels of religion which are mixed with culture (historical accounts, stories and traditions) have developed independently, and thereby appear to be different from each other on the surface. This leads to confusion and animosity among people who are ignorant of the true process of religious movement. Religion consists of three levels: *myth, ritual and mystical experience.* If the first two levels are misunderstood or accepted literally, the spiritual movement will fail to proceed to the next higher level. In order for a religious experience to lead one to have a mystical experience, all three levels of religion must be completed. This process will be fully explained throughout the text of this volume.

Mysticism

Mysticism is a spiritual discipline for attaining union with the Divine through the practice of deep meditation or contemplation, and other spiritual disciplines such as austerity, detachment, renunciation, etc. In this aspect, Mysticism and Yoga are synonymous.

Dualism

Similar to Deism, Dualism is the belief that all things in nature are separate and real, and that they exist independently from any underlying essence or support. It is the belief in the pairs of opposites wherein everything has a polar counterpart. For example: male - female, here - there, hot - cold, etc. While these elements seem real and abiding to the human mind, mystical philosophers throughout history have been claiming that this is only an outer expression of the underlying essence from which they originate. In reality, the underlying essence of all things is non-dual and all-encompassing. It is the substratum of all that exists. Modern science has been confirming this view of matter. The latest experiments in quantum physics show that all matter is composed of energy. Most importantly for this study, dualism is a state of mind that occurs at an immature level of mental understanding of reality. It is akin to egoism and egoistic tendencies which tend to make a person see {himself/herself} as separate and distinct from the world and from other living beings. Through the study and practice of mystical spiritual teachings, dualism is replaced with non-dualism and salvation, spiritual enlightenment, then occurs. Therefore, salvation or resurrection is related to a non-dualistic view of existence and bondage and death are related to dualism and egoism.

A dualistic view of life can lead to agitation, suffering and even catastrophic events in human experience because the mind is trained to see either good or evil, acceptable or unacceptable, you or me, etc., and not the whole of creation composed of many parts. In the dualistic state of mind, the attitudes of separation and exclusivism are exaggerated. These render the mind agitated. Mental agitation prevents the mind from achieving greater insights into the depths of spiritual teachings. Thus, agitated people are usually frustrated and unable to discover inner peace and spiritual fulfillment.

When societal institutions such as the church rationalize and even sanction dualism, then egoistic sentiments hold sway over the heart of human beings. In this sense, dualism and egoism go hand in hand. When universal love and humility are replaced by egoism and arrogance, then it becomes possible to hurt others and to hurt nature. When we forget our common origin and destiny, we easily fall into the vast pit of egoism. We see ourselves as an individual in a world of individuals, fighting a battle of survival for wealth in order to gain pleasures of the senses, rather than seeing ourselves as divine beings who are made in the same image, with the same frailties and potential. This degraded condition opens the doors to the deep-rooted fears and sense of inadequacy which translate into anger, resentment, hatred, greed and all negative tendencies in the human personality. The concept of dualism is the basis of the atrocities and injustices that have been committed in the history of the world. Under its control, human beings seek to control others and nature, and to satisfy their inner urges through violence because they cannot control themselves and express their deeper needs in constructive ways. In the Indian Vedantic tradition, duality or *dvaita* is seen as the greatest error of the human mind. For this reason all of the disciplines of Vedanta, Shetaut Neter, Yoga, Buddhism, Taoism and other forms of creation-centered spirituality are directed toward developing a correct understanding of human existence. When the underlying unity behind the duality is discovered, there can be no violence or ill will against others. This is the basis of non-violence. Harmony and spiritual enlightenment then arise spontaneously. Egoism now gives way to universal love and peace.

Spiritual Transformation

Transformation here is to be understood as not merely a change in specific behavior patterns or a change in feeling based on temporary circumstances, but as a complete re-orientation of the psychology of the individual. This re-orientation will lead to a permanent improvement in behavior and genuine metamorphosis of the innermost levels of the mind. Specifically, we will focus on Kemeticism as a system for psychological transformation wherein the individual ceases to be a limited individual, subject to the foibles and follies of human nature, and attains the state of transcendence of these failings.

Mythology

Most people hold the opinion that mythology is a lie, an illusion, fiction or fantasy. Mythology can be best understood as a language. However, it is a unique kind of language. An ordinary language is sometimes similar to another because it is a part of a family of languages. For example, Italian and Spanish words are similar. This similarity makes it possible for a person whose native language is Spanish to understand the meanings of some Italian words and somewhat follow along a conversation in Italian. Even so, mythology is much more intelligible than this. Mythology is more akin to music in its universality. If the key elements of this language of mythology are well understood, then it is possible to understand and relate any mythological system to another and thereby gain the understanding of the message being imparted.

Enlightenment

Enlightenment is the central topic of our study and the coveted goal of all practitioners of Yoga and Religion. Enlightenment is the term used to describe the highest level of spiritual awakening. It means attaining such a level of spiritual awareness that one discovers the underlying unity of the entire universe as well as the fact that the source of all creation is the same source from which the innermost Self within every human heart arises.

All forms of spiritual practice are directed toward the goal of assisting every individual to discover the true essence of the universe both externally, in physical creation, and internally, within the human heart, as the very root of human consciousness. Thus, many terms are used to describe the attainment of the goal of spiritual knowledge and the eradication of spiritual ignorance. Some of these terms are: *Enlightenment, Resurrection, Salvation, The Kingdom of Heaven, Christ Consciousness, Cosmic Consciousness, Moksha or Liberation, Buddha Consciousness, One With The Tao, Self-realization, Know Thyself, Heruhood, Nirvana, Sema, Yoga,* etc.

YOGA PHILOSOPHY AND THE WORLD RELIGIOUS PHILOSOPHIES DEFINED

Yoga philosophy and disciplines have developed independently as well as in conjunction with religious philosophies. It may be accurate to say that Yoga is a science unto itself which religions have used and incorporated into their religious philosophies and practices by relating the yogic principles to symbols such as deities, gods, goddesses, angels, saints, etc. The following is a brief description of yoga philosophy in comparison to the philosophies which developed along side it.

Yoga Philosophy

Human consciousness and universal consciousness are in reality one and the same. The appearance of separation is a mental illusion. Yoga is the mystical and mindful (thoughtful, aware, observant) union of individual and universal consciousness by integrating the aspects of individual personality, thereby allowing the personality to be purified so that it may behold its true essence.

Vedanta Philosophy

Spiritual Philosophy of Mystical Psychology of Ancient India.

1- Absolute Monism: Only God is reality. All else is imagination.
2- Modified Monism: God is to nature as soul is to body.

Monotheism

Monotheism means the belief in the existence of a single God in the universe. Christianity, Judaism, and Islam are the major monotheistic religions. It must be noted here that the form of monotheism espoused by the major Western religions is that of an exclusive, personified deity who exists in fact and is separate from creation. In contrast, the monotheism of Ancient Egyptian, Hindu and Gnostic Christian traditions envisions a single Supreme Deity that is expressed as the Supreme Deity of all other traditions, as well as the phenomenal world. It is not exclusive, but universal.

Polytheism

Polytheism means the belief in or worship of many gods. Such gods usually have specific attributes or functions.

Totemism

Totemism is the belief in the idea that there is a relationship between kinship groups and specific animals and plants. Many scholars believe that religions which use these symbols are primitive because they are seen as worshipping those animals themselves. However, when the mythology behind the beliefs is examined more closely, the totems are understood as symbols of specific tutelary deities which relate the individuals to a group, and also to the greater workings of nature, and ultimately, to God.

Pantheism

1- Absolute Pantheism: Everything there is, is God. God and Creation are one.
2- Modified Pantheism: God is the reality or principle behind nature.

Panentheism

Term coined by KC F. Krause (1781-1832) to describe the doctrine that God is immanent in all things but also transcendent, so that every part of the universe has its existence in God, but He is more than the sum total of the parts.

Kemeticism: Shetaut Neter: Ancient Egyptian Philosophy - Egyptian Yoga

1-Monotheistic Polytheism - Ancient Egyptian religion encompasses a single and absolute Supreme Deity that expresses as the cosmic forces (gods and goddesses), human beings and nature.

Hinduism and Mahayana Buddhism
1-Monotheistic Polytheism.

THE TREE STAGES OF RELIGION

While on the surface it seems that there are many differences between the philosophies, upon closer reflection there is only one major division, that of belief or non-belief. Among the believers there are differences of opinion as to how to believe. This is the source of all the trouble between religions. This is because ordinary religion is deistic, based on traditions and customs which are themselves based on culture. Since culture varies from place to place and from one time in history to another, there will always be some variation in spiritual traditions. These differences will occur not only between cultures, but even within the same culture. An example of this is Christianity with its myriad of denominations.

Therefore, those who cling to the idea that religion has to be related to a particular culture and its specific practices or rituals will always have some difference with someone else's conception. In the three stages of religion, Myth, Ritual and Mysticism, culture belongs to the myth stage of religious practice, the most elementary level.

Myth → Ritual → Mysticism

An important theme, which will be developed throughout this volume, is the complete practice of religion, that is, in its three aspects, *mythology, ritual* and *metaphysical* or the *mystical experience* (mysticism - mystical philosophy). At the first level a human being learns the stories and traditions of the religion. At the second level rituals are learned and practiced. At the third level a spiritual aspirant is led to actually go beyond myths and rituals and to attain the ultimate goal of religion. This is an important principle, because many religions present different aspects of philosophy at different levels, and an uninformed onlooker may label it as primitive or idolatrous, etc., without understanding what is going on. For example, Hinduism and Ancient Egyptian Religion present polytheism and duality at the first two levels of religious practice. However, at the third level, mysticism, the practitioner is made to understand that all of the gods and goddesses being worshipped do not exist in fact, but are in reality aspects of the single, transcendental Supreme Self. This is evident in the Prt M Hru.

In the area of Yoga Philosophy and the category of Monism, there are little, if any, differences. This is because these disciplines belong to the third level of religion wherein mysticism reaches its height. The goal of all mysticism is to transcend the phenomenal world and all mental concepts. Ordinary religion is a part of the world and the mental concepts of people, and must too be ultimately transcended.

SELECTED SPIRITUAL PHILOSOPHIES COMPARED

The Sages of ancient times created philosophies through which it might be possible to explain the origins of creation, as we saw above. Then they set out to create disciplines which could lead a person to discover for themselves the spiritual truths of life and thereby realize the higher reality which lies beyond the phenomenal world. These disciplines are referred to as religions and spiritual philosophies (mysticism-yoga). Below is a basic listing of world religious and spiritual philosophies.

TABLE 1: RELIGIOUS PHILOSOPHIES

Shetaut Neter	Vedanta	Samkhya	Buddhism	Yoga
Non-dualist metaphysics. God manifests as nature and cosmic forces (neteru). Union with the Divine through wisdom, devotion and identification with the Divine.	Non-dualist metaphysics. God alone exists. Union with the Divine through wisdom, devotion and identification with the Divine.	Dualist Philosophy. Discipline of understanding what is real (God) from what is unreal (transient world of time and space).	Union with the Absolute through extinction of desire.	Mystical tradition: union of individual consciousness with the Absolute Consciousness (God) through cessation of mental activity by wisdom, devotion and identification with the Divine. Example ↓ Egyptian Yoga Indian Yoga Christian Yoga Buddhist Yoga Chinese (Taoist) Yoga

TABLE 2: RELIGIOUS CATEGORIES

Theism	Atheism	Ethicism	Ritualism	Monism
Belief in a God which will save you.	Salvation by doing what makes you happy. There is no God, only existence, which just happened on its own without any help.	Salvation by performing the right actions.	Salvation by performing the correct rituals.	Salvation by understanding that all is the Self (God).
↓ Example	↓ Example	↓ Example	↓ Example	↓ Example
Orthodox Christian Orthodox Islam Orthodox Judaism	Epicureans Charvacas Atheists Existentialists Stoics Humanists	Zoroastrianism Jainism Confucianism Aristotelianism	Brahmanism Priestcraft	Taoism Spinoza Cabalism Sufism Idealism Christian Science Gnosticism Gnostic Christianity Vedanta Shetaut Neter Buddhism

Part I

Chapter 1: Origins and Basis Of Mysticism in the Rau nu Pert em Hru

Plate 4: Scene from the *Prt m Hru* of Lady Taameniu

INTRODUCTION TO THE PHILOSOPHY OF THE *PERT EM HERU*

What is The *Rau nu Pert em Hru?*

The scriptures presented in this volume come from the extensive body of texts known as the *Egyptian Book of the Dead.* These texts span the entire history of Ancient Egypt, beginning with the *Pyramid Texts* in the early Dynastic period. These were followed by the *Coffin Texts*, which were followed by the late dynastic texts which were recorded on a variety of different media, of which the most popularly known is papyrus.

The teachings of mystical spirituality are contained in the most ancient writings of Egypt, even those preceding the Dynastic or Pharaonic period (4,500 B.C.E.-600 A.C.E). The most extensive expositions of the philosophy may be found in the writings, which have in modern times been referred to as "The Egyptian Book of the Dead."

It was originally known as "Rau nu Prt M Hru" or "Rau nu *Pert Em Heru*" or "Reu nu *Pert Em Heru.*"

> ***Rau*** = words, teachings, liturgy, ***nu*** = of, ***Prt*** or ***Pert*** = going out, ***em*** or ***m*** = as or through, ***Hru*** or ***Heru*** = Spiritual Light or Enlightened Being (the God Heru). This may therefore be translated as: ***"The Word Utterances for Coming into the Spiritual Light (Enlightenment) or Becoming one with Heru."***

Thus, the *Rau nu Pert Em Heru* is a collection of words used to affirm spiritual wisdom and to direct a human being towards a positive spiritual movement. Each *Rau* or *Ru* contains affirmations of mystical wisdom that enables a human being to understand and experience that particular aspect of Divinity. The collection of these verses has been referred to as "Chapters," "Utterances" or "Spells" by Egyptologists. While the teachings presented in the *Rau nu Pert Em Heru* may be thought of as being presented in Chapters and referred to as such, they must also be thought of as special words which, when understood, internalized and lived, will lead a person to spiritual freedom. In this volume we will refer to the groupings of subjects as "Chapters" which may be better defined for our usage here as: a collection of Hekau -words of power- which impart a spiritual teaching and affirm that teaching, and by their repeated utterance make it a reality. The term "Ru" may be used as a shortened version of "Rau." It was not until after 1,500 B.C.E. that the collections of Ru were compiled in the form of papyrus scrolls and standardized to some degree. However, this process of standardization was not as rigid as the canonization of the books of the Bible, which had been separate scriptures relating to Christianity and Judaism prior to around the year 350 A.C.E.

In Egyptian mythology, Hru is not only a reference to the god who is the son of Aset and Asar (Isis and Osiris), but Hru also means "Day" and "Light." In fact, Day and Light are two of the most important attributes of the god Heru who is understood as the highest potential of every human being. Therefore, the title may also read as **"The Book of Coming Forth by (into) the Day," "The Guide for Becoming Heru," "The Chapters for Coming into the Light,"** or **"The Book of Enlightenment."** The writings were named "The Egyptian Book of the Dead" by modern Egyptologists who obtained them from the modern day dwellers of the area (northeast African Arabs) who said they were found buried with the Ancient Egyptian dead. In the interest of simplicity and consistency, the name *"Pert Em Heru"* will be used throughout this text.

The *Pyramid Texts* and the *Book of Coming Forth By Day* are similar in scripture and purpose. It is correct to understand that the texts referred to as the *Book of Coming Forth By Day* evolved out of the *Pyramid Text* writings. This is because the *Pyramid Texts* are the early form of the well-known texts, which have been called the *Book of Coming Forth By Day.* The *Pyramid Texts* are hieroglyphic writings contained in the pyramid tombs[10] of the kings of the early Dynastic period. Both are collections of utterances, originally recorded in hieroglyphic, which lead the initiate to transform {his/her} consciousness from human to divine, by purifying the mind with wisdom about the neteru (gods and

---

[10] Not to be confused with the Pyramids in Giza.

goddesses, divine forces in the universe), and through the practice of rituals which promote personality integration and thus, spiritual transformation. Each of these constitute major treatises of Ancient Egyptian philosophy and together constitute an advanced, holistic system of spiritual development. All of these have as the main purpose to effect the union of the individual human being with the Transcendental Self. This philosophy of spiritual transcendence and enlightenment did not begin with the dawn of the Dynastic period in Ancient Egypt. The evidence from ancient texts and the history of Manetho show that the Ancient Egyptian history, which is known about, is only the descendent of a much more ancient era of Egyptian civilization.[11]

ANCIENT EGYPTIAN RELIGION AS YOGA

The Ancient Egyptians Practiced Yoga

yo·ga (yō′gə) *n*. **1.** Also **Yoga**. A Hindu discipline aimed at training the consciousness for a state of perfect spiritual insight and tranquillity. **2.** A system of exercises practiced as part of this discipline to promote control of the body and mind. **--yo′gic** (-gĭk) *adj*.

—American Heritage Dictionary

Most people have heard of Yoga as an exercise, however, Yoga is a vast science of human psychology and spiritual transformation which includes physical and mental health as the prerequisite for further progress. Yoga, in all of its disciplines, was practiced in Ancient Egypt (Kemet, Kamut, Kamit or Ta-Meri) and is the subject of the Ancient Egyptian Mysteries. Yoga, as it was practiced in Ancient Egypt, included the disciplines of virtuous living, dietary purification, study of the wisdom teachings and their practice in daily life, psychophysical and psycho-spiritual exercises and meditation. Practitioners of Indian Yoga, Buddhist Yoga and Chinese Yoga (Taoism) today refer to all of these disciplines as Yogic disciplines. Therefore, the Ancient Egyptians were the first practitioners of Yoga Philosophy in our history. Through a process of gradually blending these in the course of ordinary life, an individual can effect miraculous changes in {her/his} life and thereby achieve the supreme goal of all existence, the goal of Yoga: Union with the Higher Self.

The Term "Egyptian Yoga" and The Philosophy Behind It

Egyptian Yoga is what has been commonly referred to by Egyptologists as Egyptian "Religion" or "Mythology," but to think of it as just set of stories or allegories about a long lost civilization is to completely miss the greatest secrets of human existence. As previously discussed, Yoga in all of its forms was practiced in Egypt earlier than anywhere else in our history. This unique perspective from Africa provides a new way to look at life, religion and the discipline of psychology. Perhaps most importantly though, Egyptian mythology, when understood as a system of Yoga, gives every individual insight into their own divine nature. This is its true worth.

The teachings of Yoga are at the heart of *Prt m Hru*. As explained, the word "Yoga" is a Sanskrit term meaning to unite the individual with the Cosmic. The term has been used in certain parts of this book for ease of communication since the word "Yoga" has received wide popularity especially in western countries in recent years. The Ancient Egyptian equivalent of yoga is: *"Smai."* *Smai* (Sma, Sema, Sama) means union, and the following determinative terms give it a spiritual significance, at once equating it with the term "Yoga" as it is used in India. When used in conjunction with the Ancient Egyptian symbol which means land, *"Ta,"* the term "union of the two lands" arises.

Smai Tawi

---

[11] See the book *Cycles of Time* by Muata Ashby

(From Chapter 4 of the *Prt m Hru*)

In Chapter 4[12] and Chapter 17[13] of the *Prt m Hru,* a term "Smai Tawi" is used. It means "Union of the two lands of Egypt," ergo "Egyptian Yoga." The two lands refer to the two main districts of the country (North and South) In ancient times Egypt was divided into two sections or land areas. These were known as Lower and Upper Egypt. In Ancient Egyptian mystical philosophy, the land of Upper Egypt relates to the divinity Heru (Horus), who represents the Higher Self, and the land of Lower Egypt relates to Set, the divinity of the lower self. So ***Smai Taui*** means "the union of the two lands" or the "Union of the lower self with the Higher Self. The lower self relates to that which is negative and uncontrolled in the human mind, while the Higher Self relates to that which is above temptations and is good in the human heart. Thus, we also have the Ancient Egyptian term ***Smai Heru-Set,*** or the union of Heru and Set. So Smai Taui or Smai Heru-Set are the Ancient Egyptian words which can be translated as "**Egyptian Yoga.**"

Above from left to right are the symbols of Egyptian Yoga: *Sma, nfr, nkh, and htp.* The Ancient Egyptian language and symbols provide the first "historical" record of Yoga Philosophy and Religious literature. The Indian culture of the Indus Valley Dravidians and Harappans appear to have carried it on and expanded much of the intellectual expositions in the form of the Vedas, Upanishads, Puranas and Tantras, the ancient spiritual texts of India.

The hieroglyph Sma, "Sema," represented by the union of two lungs and the trachea, symbolizes that the union of the Higher Self and lower self leads to the One.

The hieroglyph, nfr, "Nefer," close in pronunciation to "Neter" (God), expressed by the union of the heart and the trachea symbolizes: That which is the most beautiful thing, the highest good, and the greatest achievement.

The hieroglyph, nkh, "Ankh," symbolizes the union of the male (cross-temporal) and the female (circle-eternal) aspects of oneself, leading to the transformation into an androgynous being. Thus, the two become One. The Ankh was also later used in Christianity and Hinduism as a symbol of divinity. Therefore, the Ankh is the unifying symbol, which links Egypt, India and Christendom.

The hieroglyph htp, "Hetep," symbolizes supreme peace, the final abode of all who satisfy the desire of their soul, union with its Higher Self: YOGA. Egyptian Yoga encompasses many myths and philosophies, which lead to the reunion of the soul with its Higher Self. Ancient Egyptian religion involves three major theological branches based on the Trinity (Amun-Ra-Ptah) which emanates out of the Hidden and nameless Transcendental Divinity. This Divinity is variously known under the following names: Nameless One, Nebertcher or Neberdjer, Tem, Neter Neteru, Amun, Asar, Ra, Kheper, and Aset. These names are to be understood as being synonymous. They refer to the same idea of an Absolute Supreme Being or transcendental reality from which the phenomenal world arises, as land rises out of an ocean.

The central and most popular character within Ancient Egyptian Religion of Asar is Heru, who is an incarnation of his father, Asar. Asar is killed by his brother Set who, out of greed and demoniac (Setian) tendency, craved to be the ruler of Egypt. With the help of Djehuti, the God of wisdom, Aset, the great mother and Hetheru, his consort, Heru prevailed in the battle against Set for the rulership of Kemet (Egypt). Heru's struggle symbolizes the struggle of every human being to regain rulership of the Higher Self and to subdue the lower self. With this understanding, the land of Egypt is equivalent to the {Kingdom/Queendom} concept of Christianity.

---

[12] Commonly referred to as Chapter 17
[13] Commonly referred to as Chapter 176

The most ancient writings in our historical period are from the Ancient Egyptians. These writings are referred to as hieroglyphics. Also, the most ancient civilization known was the Ancient Egyptian civilization. The proof of this lies in the ancient Egyptian Sphinx, as previously discussed. The original name given to these writings by the Ancient Egyptians is *Metu Neter,* meaning "the writing of God" or *Neter Metu* or "Divine Speech." These writings were inscribed in temples, coffins and papyruses and contained the teachings in reference to the spiritual nature of the human being and the ways to promote spiritual emancipation, awakening or resurrection. The Ancient Egyptian proverbs presented in this text are translations from the original hieroglyphic scriptures. An example of hieroglyphic text is presented on the front cover.

Egyptian Philosophy may be summed up in the following proverbs, which clearly state that the soul is heavenly or divine and that the human being must awaken to the true reality, which is the Spirit, Self.

"Self knowledge is the basis of true knowledge."

"Soul to heaven, body to earth."

"Man is to become God-like through a life of virtue and the cultivation of the spirit through scientific knowledge, practice and bodily discipline."

"Salvation is accomplished through the efforts of the individual. There is no mediator between man and {his/her} salvation."

"Salvation is the freeing of the soul from its bodily fetters, becoming a God through knowledge and wisdom, controlling the forces of the cosmos instead of being a slave to them, subduing the lower nature and through awakening the Higher Self, ending the cycle of rebirth and dwelling with the Neters who direct and control the Great Plan."

The Ancient Egyptian Symbols of Yoga

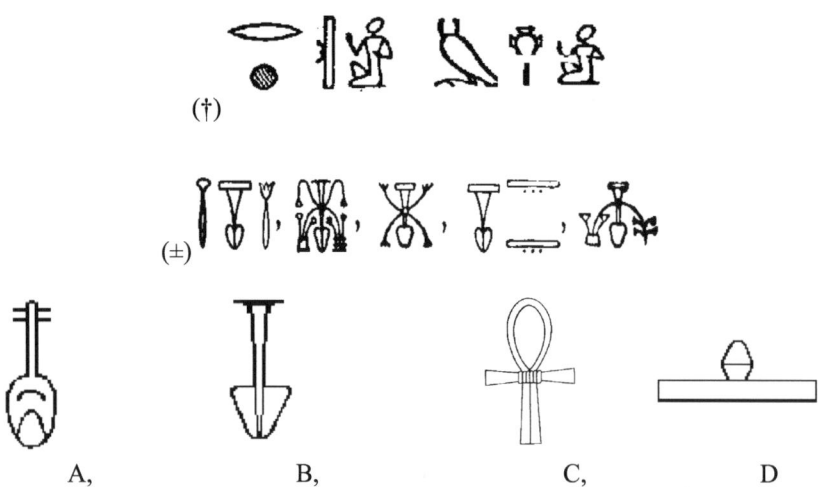

A,   B,   C,   D

The theme of the arrangement of the symbols above is based on the idea that in mythological and philosophic forms, Egyptian mythology and philosophy merge with world mythology, philosophy and religion. The hieroglyphic symbols at the very top (†) mean: ***"Know Thyself," "Self knowledge is the basis of all true knowledge"*** and (±) abbreviated forms of ***Smai taui,*** signifies "Egyptian Yoga." The next four below represent the four words in Egyptian Philosophy, which mean ***"YOGA."*** They are: (A) ***"Nefer"***(B) ***"Sema"*** (C) ***"Ankh"*** and (D) ***"Hetep."***

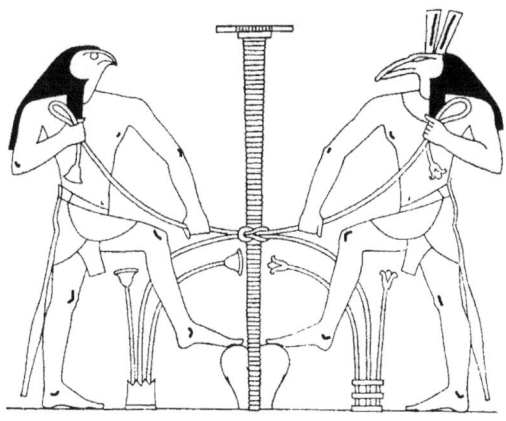

Figure 5: Above: Smai Heru-Set,

Heru and Set join forces to tie up the symbol of Union (Sema –see (B) above). The Sema symbol refers to the Union of Upper Egypt (Lotus) and Lower Egypt (Papyrus) under one ruler, but also at a more subtle level, it refers to the union of one's Higher Self and lower self (Heru and Set), as well as the control of one's breath (Life Force) through the union (control) of the lungs (breathing organs). The character of Heru and Set are an integral part of the *Pert Em Heru*.

THE STUDY OF YOGA

The study and practice of Yoga involves three distinct phases. These are: *Listening to the wisdom teachings, Reflecting on those wisdom teachings and making them an integral part of your life, and Meditation, the art of transcending ordinary human awareness and consciousness.* Since a complete treatise on the theory and practice of yoga would require several volumes, only a basic outline will be given here.[14]

When we look out upon the world, we are often baffled by the multiplicity, which constitutes the human experience. What do we really know about this experience? Many scientific disciplines have developed over the last two hundred years for the purpose of discovering the mysteries of nature, but this search has only engendered new questions about the nature of existence. Yoga is a discipline or way of life designed to promote the physical, mental and spiritual development of the human being. It leads a person to discover the answers to the most important questions of life such as Who am I?, Why am I here? and Where am I going?

As stated earlier, the literal meaning of the word *Yoga* is to *"Yoke"* or to *"Link"* back, the implication being to link the individual consciousness back to the original source, the original essence, that which transcends all mental and intellectual attempts at comprehension, but which is the essential nature of everything in Creation, termed "Universal Consciousness. While in the strict sense, Yoga may be seen as a separate discipline from religion, yoga and religion have been linked at many points throughout history and continue to be linked even today. In a manner of speaking, Yoga as a discipline may be seen as a non-sectarian transpersonal science or practice to promote spiritual development and harmony of mind and body thorough mental and physical disciplines including meditation, psycho-physical exercises, and performing action with the correct attitude.

The teachings which were practiced in the Ancient Egyptian temples were the same ones later intellectually defined into a literary form by the Indian Sages of Vedanta and Yoga. This was discussed in our book *Egyptian Yoga: The Philosophy of Enlightenment*. The Indian Mysteries of Yoga and Vedanta

---

[14] See the book *Egyptian Yoga: The Philosophy of Enlightenment* by Muata Ashby

represent an unfolding and intellectual exposition of the Egyptian Mysteries. Also, the study of Gnostic Christianity or Christianity before Roman Catholicism will be useful to our study since Christianity originated in Ancient Egypt and was also based on the Ancient Egyptian Mysteries.

The question is how to accomplish these seemingly impossible tasks? How to transform yourself and realize the deepest mysteries of existence? How to discover "Who am I?" This is the mission of Yoga Philosophy and the purpose of yogic practices. Yoga does not seek to convert or impose religious beliefs on any one. Ancient Egypt was the source of civilization and the source of religion and Yoga. Therefore, all systems of mystical spirituality can coexist harmoniously within these teachings when they are correctly understood.

The goal of yoga is to promote integration of the mind-body-spirit complex in order to produce optimal health of the human being. This is accomplished through mental and physical exercises which promote the free flow of spiritual energy by reducing mental complexes caused by ignorance. There are two roads which human beings can follow, one of wisdom and the other of ignorance. The path of the masses is generally the path of ignorance which leads them into negative situations, thoughts and deeds. These in turn lead to ill health and sorrow in life. The other road is based on wisdom and it leads to health, true happiness and enlightenment.

Our mission is to extol the wisdom of yoga and mystical spirituality from the Ancient Egyptian perspective and to show the practice of the teachings through our books, videos and audio productions. You may find a complete listing of other books by the author, in the back of this volume.

The Discipline of the Yoga of Wisdom is imparted in three stages:

1-<u>Listening</u> to the wisdom teachings on the nature of reality (creation) and the nature of the Self.
2-<u>Reflecting</u> on those teachings and incorporating them into daily life.
3-<u>Meditating</u> on the meaning of the teachings.

Note: It is important to note here that the duplicate teaching which was practiced in the Ancient Egypt Temple of Aset[15] of **Listening** to, **Reflecting** upon, and **Meditating** upon the teachings is the same process used in Vedanta-Jnana Yoga of India of today. **The Yoga of Wisdom** is a form of Yoga based on insight into the nature of worldly existence and the transcendental Self, thereby transforming one's consciousness through development of the wisdom faculty.

The Egyptian Yoga Perspective on Death and its Influence on Gnostic Christianity

Egyptian Yoga is the philosophy and disciplines based on Ancient Egyptian mysticism which promote spiritual enlightenment. Spiritual enlightenment means a movement towards transcending death. In this context, death is not regarded as a miserable event, but a transition into a higher form of being if one's earthly life had been lived in accordance with the teachings of Maat. In ancient times, the Ancient Egyptians were often referred to by people in neighboring countries as "the most religious people of all the world" because they seemed to constantly affirm spiritual principles in every aspect of their lives. This is not to be considered as a fanatical existence, the way we would look at cults or obsessed fundamentalist religious groups of our time. The Ancient Egyptians recognized the fact that there is a higher reality beyond the physical. Since all living beings must die some day, and move into that other reality, it makes sense to seek to understand, and become comfortable with death, and to revere the Supreme Divinity which was discovered to be the author and sustainer of all creation. Therefore, death should not be viewed as a pathetic event, but as an inevitable occurrence for which one should be prepared, and can even look forward to.

The creators of Ancient Egyptian mythology and religion recognized that if people live their lives independent of spiritual acknowledgment, life will lose its focus and human beings will lose their way.

---

[15] See the book *The Wisdom of* Aset by Dr. Muata Ashby

They will get caught up in the pettiness of human life and their egoism will lead them to untold sufferings both in life on earth as well as beyond. Therefore, life should be a process of affirming the spiritual reality, and even a worship of the Divine. In this manner life itself becomes a spiritual movement towards enlightenment, a process of promoting prosperity and peace. For more insights into the nature of death in light of *Prt m Hru* philosophy, see the sections of this book entitled "Readings for the Guidance of the Dying Person and their Relatives" and "Readings for the Guidance of the Spiritual Aspirant."

Ba ir pet Shat ir ta
"Soul is to heaven, body is to the earth"
From the Prt m Hru of the *Pyramid Texts* (3,200-2,575 B.C.E.)

The passage above shows that the fundamental teaching from the ancient period of Ancient Egyptian mystical philosophy never held a hope for a "physical resurrection." This understanding was carried over into Gnostic Christianity, which developed in Ancient Egypt during the Roman Period, and became a source for controversy between the Gnostic Christians and the Orthodox Christians. The main difference between Orthodox Christianity and other religions seems to have been the insistence on a physical resurrection from the dead. While other religions proclaimed a spiritual transformation of some kind, the Orthodox Christians fervently believed and still believe in a mysterious bodily resurrection from the grave. The Gnostic *Gospel of Philip* strongly refutes the Catholic view of a bodily resurrection, calling these notions ridiculous and misunderstood by the orthodox community. The following excerpt from the Gnostic *Gospel of Phillip* brings home this point.

> "Those who say that the Lord died first and then rose up are in error, for he rose up and then died. We are to receive the resurrection while we live."

Many Egyptologists have suggested that the Ancient Egyptians embalmed their dead with the idea that the dead person would attain immortality, and that the Ancient Egyptians believed that the physical body, which was mummified, would rise up again some day. This idea spurred many Hollywood[16] movies. The statements above, from the early and late periods of Ancient Egyptian culture, clearly show that the Ancient Egyptians never sought a bodily resurrection or eternal life in the physical body. They understood death as a passageway to the next existence, and just as the physical body needs nourishment, the spiritual body was also provided for by means of the subtle essence of the solid food that was buried with the mummy.

The Catholic Christian Church Fathers gradually moved away from a mystical interpretation of Christianity and formed a religious doctrine based on a bodily resurrection from death, leading to one's existence in heaven at the right hand of the Father. The Gnostic Christian leaders disagreed with this view. The same predicament was experienced in Islamic countries during the years immediately following the death of Muhammad (also Mohammed).

The problem of human existence is the forgetfulness of the Divine essence of the Self and the identification with the body as the Self. Through concern with the body and its needs and desires, the true Self becomes identified with worldly concerns and the fulfillment of desires of the body, mind and senses. This is the development of the ego and individual soul. This identification with the desires of the body is what leads the soul to further ignorance of its true Self. It is the pursuit of desires that keeps the mind occupied with worldly thoughts such as the fear of disease and death of the body, the pursuit of pleasure and happiness, and the eradication of things which cause displeasure.

Gnosticism, Hinduism, Buddhism, Taoism and Ancient Egyptian Religion all emphasize the need to practice detachment and dispassion toward the body. These disciplines relieve the pressure of the lower desires, which impel a person to run after the illusions of life. These traditions hold that only through detachment is it possible to calm the mind enough for it to perceive the transcendental reality.

---

[16] Hollywood, Calif., area of greater Los Angeles known throughout the world as the home of the US movie industry.

The constant preoccupation with the body is incessantly reinforced through many years of living with family and others in society. Such body consciousness leads to the conviction that the psychophysical complex (mind and body) is indeed the Self. It is this idea that is to be dispelled through the spiritual discipline of constantly turning towards the Divine (through the various disciplines of Yoga) instead of to the body and to the world of illusion.

This process becomes easier to understand through reflection on the fact that the body is composed of physical elements, which are themselves, transient. The body you have today is not the same as the one you had nine years ago. Every cell in your body has been regenerated. Even your bones are different. As surely as people are born, just as surely their body will some day cease to exist. Is it wise to hold onto something that you will definitely lose at some point in time? Impermanence is a given fact of life. Flowers grow, live and die. Insects grow, live and die. Yet people accept these changes. Why is it that people do not cry when the flower dies, or when a leaf falls from a tree and dies or for every creature in nature that has died? The fact is that it is not only death that causes fear, but attachment to that which died and has met the "unknown." So fear of death is due to ignorance of one's true nature.

Likewise, people hold on to life, no matter how miserable a situation they may be in, because they don't know any other way of thinking or acting, and also because they have the illusion that there is a chance they may find happiness someday or they may somehow come into some money. Wealth is a big illusion. You can read the papers and see how wealth destroys a person's peace of mind through the endless worries associated with acquiring, investing and protecting it.

Matthew 19
23. Then said Jesus to his disciples, Verily I say to you, That it is hard for a rich man to enter into the kingdom of heaven.
24 And again I say to you, It is easier for a camel to go through the eye of a needle, than for a rich man to enter into the Kingdom of God.

—Christian Bible

"Labor not after riches first, and think thou afterwards wilt enjoy them. He who neglects the present moment, throws away all that he hath. As the arrow passes through the heart, while the warrior knew not that it was coming; so shall his life be taken away before he knoweth that he hath it."

—Ancient Egyptian Proverb

An even greater illusion comes into play when a person tries to figure out which part of the body contains the soul. There is no body part which contains the soul or which can be considered to be the "Self." No body part can be called "me," yet somehow the conglomerate of thoughts, memories, physical body and senses is understood to be "me." This error or misunderstanding is the cause of human misery and pain because it involves the soul in the mishaps and troubles of the mind-body complex and its attending desires. If the mind and senses were transcended, these problems along with individual identification with the body-mind would cease, and the true Self would be discovered to be infinite and eternal. This is the discovery of the Saints and Sages. For this reason they have proclaimed that the soul has been overtaken by ignorance of its true Self, and due to this ignorance, it is subject to experience the pain of human existence.

A simple philosophical study of the body reveals the error in thinking that the body is the Self. If the senses fail to perceive, or a limb or organ ceases to operate, consciousness is still there. The awareness of being alive remains even if the perceptions of the senses or nerves fail. The practice of spirituality involves discovering that which transcends the body, as well as learning how to become attached to that transcendent reality as the truth, rather than remaining attached to the physical body and its desires and impulses, as well as to one's emotions throughout the ups and downs of human existence.

The world of unenlightened human existence is likened to being out in the middle of the ocean when there is a raging storm. The desires are the waves thrashing the mind about. Spiritual practice is the boat, which allows a person to weather the storm of the world with its ever-changing situations. It gives the power to move forward in life and not be disturbed by the choices, desires and unpredictability of the world-process.

THE STAGES OF HUMAN SPIRITUAL EVOLUTION AND ASPIRATION

The Format of this Book

This book is written in a format which follows the manner prescribed for human spiritual evolution. Therefore, the following section will detail the ancient teachings of spiritual evolution and aspiration so that the reader may consciously be aware of the process which this book is striving to engender. The scribes of ancient times did not have a set order for the Utterances of the *Books of Coming Forth By Day*. They were prepared in accord with the needs, special inclinations and interests of those who requested that one be made for them. Many translators of the various Chapters or Utterances of Coming Forth By Day in modern times have also placed the utterances in accordance with their own understanding of the intent of the priests/priestesses. What follows is a compilation of the most important mystical utterances. It is a special sequence which is synchronous with the universal principles of spiritual evolution. The chapter numbers given by traditional Egyptologists will be provided as footnotes preceding each chapter for easy reference.

In Yoga philosophy, spiritual evolution is described as follows: Listening, Reflection and Meditation. All of the five major categories of yoga described before (Yoga of Wisdom, Yoga of Devotional Love, Yoga of Meditation, Tantric Yoga and Yoga of Selfless-Righteous Action.) can be found in the *Ru Prt m Hru*. A spiritual aspirant listens to the teachings, reflects upon their meaning and then enters into deep meditation on them.

Table 3: The Stages of Spiritual Evolution

The Stages of Spiritual Evolution	In the Shetaut Neter (Egyptian Yoga) system, there are three stages of spiritual evolution.
1- *Aspiration*- Students who are being instructed on a probationary status, and have not experienced inner vision. The important factor at this level is awakening of the Spiritual Self, that is, becoming conscious of the divine presence within one's self and the universe by having faith that there is a spiritual essence beyond ordinary human understanding.	1- **The Mortals:** *Students who were being instructed on a probationary status, but had not experienced inner vision.*
2- *Striving*- Students who have attained inner vision and have received a glimpse of Cosmic Consciousness. The important factor at this level is purgation of the self, that is, purification of mind and body through a spiritual discipline. The aspirant tries to totally surrender "personal" identity or ego to the divine inner Self which is the Universal Self of all Creation.	2- **The Intelligences:** *Students who had attained inner vision and had received a glimpse of Cosmic Consciousness.*
3- *Established*- Students who have become IDENTIFIED with or UNITED with GOD. The important factor at this level is illumination of the intellect, that is, experience and appreciation of the divine presence during reflection and meditation, Union with the Divine Self, the divine marriage of the individual with the universal.	3- **The Creators or Beings of Light:** *Students who had become IDENTIFIED with or UNITED with the light (GOD).*

The three steps of spiritual practice (myth, ritual and mystical philosophy and experience) which complete the practice of religion, follow the formats described above closely. Many students of Ancient Egyptian religion have focused on the religious stories of Ancient Egypt as mythical fables or superstitious rantings from a long lost civilization. In the Egyptian Yoga Book Series, we successfully show how the teachings of mystical spirituality were carefully woven into and throughout Ancient Egyptian Mythology. Ancient Egyptian Religion centers around the understanding that every human being has an immortal soul and a mortal body. Further, it holds that creation and the human soul have the same origin. How can this momentous teaching be proven and its reality experienced? This is the task of Mystical Spirituality (religion in its three phases and/or the practice of Yoga disciplines).

Thus, it is evident that the *Ru Prt m Hru* utilizes the universal principles of mystical spirituality and mystical religion. The *Prt m Hru* lays heavy emphasis on Ritual, Spiritual Wisdom and the Mystical Union with the Divine. One more subheading may be added, that is, Mythology. The spiritual wisdom is to be studied and deeply reflected upon, and this will lead to a transformation in one's personality. This process constitutes the journey that a spiritual aspirant must follow in order to go from mortality to immortality. However, in ancient times, the first level of religion, the myth, was well known by all people in Ancient Egyptian society. So the first Yogic step of listening to the teachings or the first step of religion, learning the myth, was more part of the socialization of the culture. A person would learn it as they were growing up and would not require an introduction such as has been presented in the first part of this book. Therefore, their practice would be more advanced than a present day aspirant. They would go right into the practice of the rituals, and begin to learn the mystical implications of these as they relate to the myth of Asar, Aset and Heru, which they already knew so well. Thus, we will combine the universal principles of mystical spirituality and mystical religion and arrange this volume in accordance with the following criteria. Part 1 will treat the following subjects: Presentation of the myth upon which the *Prt m Hru* is based, Gloss on the Myth, Gloss on the Philosophy behind the Myth and the *Prt m Hru.* Part 2 will present the translated scripture of *Prt m Hru* as follows: Awakening, Wisdom and Ritual, Transformation-affirmations for reflection and advancement, and Mystical Union.

THE EVOLUTION OF THE BOOK OF COMING FORTH BY DAY

Phases of Ancient Egyptian Literature

MYTHS
(*PRE-DYNASTIC PERIOD*)
Shetaut Asar-Aset-Heru
The Myth of Asar, Aset and Heru

SHETAUT ATUM-RA
The Myth of Creation

PYRAMID TEXTS
(C. 5,000 B.C.E. OR PRIOR)

Pyramid of Unas
Pyramid of Teti,
Pyramid of Pepi I,
Pyramid of Mernere,
Pyramid of Pepi II

WISDOM TEXTS
(C. 3,000 B.C.E. – PTOLEMATIC PERIOD)
Precepts of Ptahotep
Instructions of Any
Instructions of Amenemope
Etc.

COFFIN TEXTS
(C. 2040 B.C.E.-1786 B.C.E.)

PAPYRUS TEXTS

(C. 1570 B.C.E.-Roman Period)[17]
Books of Coming Forth By Day
Example of famous papyruses:

Papyrus of Any
Papyrus of Hunefer
Papyrus of Kenna
Greenfield Papyrus, Etc.

MONUMENTAL INSCRIPTIONS AND THEOLOGICAL TREATISES

Example: Temple of Seti 1. Temple of Aset, Temple of Hetheru, Shabaka Inscription, Stele of Djehuti Nefer, Hymns of Amun, etc.

HERMETIC TEXTS

---

[17] After 1570 BC they would evolve into a more unified text, the Egyptian Book of the Dead.

The Origins of the Scriptures of Prt m Hru

As mentioned earlier, the texts which comprise the *Rau nu Prt m Hru* originate in the far distant past. In the form of the *Pyramid Texts* they were codified as utterances which when understood and practiced could lead the practitioner to reach expanded levels of consciousness. This was symbolically referred to as gaining power over the gods and goddesses and becoming a Glorified Soul. The antiquity of the scriptures is attested to by some of the rubrics used on some chapters. For example, the rubrics for some of the versions of Chapters 31 and 36 state that they *were originally found* (not created) *by Hertataf at Khemenu, the city of the god Djehuti, while on a tour of inspection of the temples of Egypt.* Some variants assign the finding to *Semti,* who was a king in the first Dynasty. For this and other reasons it can be said that the scriptures originated in Pre-dynastic times, but were codified in Dynastic times.

The common view of the *Pyramid Texts* is that they are the earliest known versions of the "Book of the Dead." They seem to be compositions of scripture which refer to a king who is part of a ritual wherein offerings are given in the temple and spells are uttered or chanted for the purpose of attaining power or control over the spirits of the dead and over the gods and goddesses. This has been the traditional interpretation by Egyptologists and others who have not had the opportunity to study and practice the mystical teachings from around the world. If these studies are entered into with an open mind and if one is willing to read the texts within the context of mysticism, and an expanded belief in the potential of human experience, a much different understanding arises from the literal interpretations which have been provided thus far. From a mystical perspective, it must be understood that the utterances of the "*Prt m Hru*" were not only for individuals as they were approaching the time of death or who had already died, but they also incorporated rituals designed to engender a mystical experience in the participants. These initiates were not waiting or just preparing for the time of death to use the knowledge in the Netherworld. They were interested in discovering the mysteries of the other world even while still alive. Thus, the book is not for the dead, but for those who truly want to become alive. Therefore, earliest known versions of the texts are compositions of scripture which refer to an initiate who is part of a ritual wherein offerings are given and special words are recited, uttered or chanted for the purpose of transforming the consciousness of that individual, to attain power or control over the spirits of the demons (the egoistic tendencies) and over the gods and goddesses (virtuous qualities).

We will not attempt to provide a literal translation of the texts since this would lead to intellectual stagnation. It would be like reading a poem and trying to apply its meaning literally and critiquing it on its grammatical merits. Mystical literature should be understood as a grand metaphor which seeks to explain the origins of creation and humanity, along with providing an understanding of the transcendental modes of consciousness and the human experience. These modes may be termed as *Higher Consciousness, God, The Supreme Being, Universal Soul, Supreme Consciousness, etc.*

So a mystical teaching, while existing in an historical context, is in reality not concerned with history or ordinary human reality, since these are, in the end, transient, illusory and irrelevant to the attainment of higher consciousness. Therefore, while certain historical information is needed to set a context for our study in relation to world history, an emphasis will be placed on revealing the mystical meaning contained in it, because it is this meaning alone that will lead the spiritual aspirant to attain the goal of mysticism, that of transcending ordinary human consciousness and discovering the deeper realities that lie within the heart. In this sense the *Prt m Hru* is absolutely true and factual in every detail. Mystical teachings are primarily concerned with the here and now as well as the transcendental wisdom, and not specifically with any particular historical event. The use of mythological stories and ritual traditions should not be confused with history. Myths are used by Sages in order to convey mystical teachings about the human condition and the mysteries of the human heart. Thus, any study which does not affirm the transcendental nature of a myth is relegated to understanding only the superficial (exoteric) meaning of a teaching.

In the earlier times, the teachings of the Metu Neter (Divine Speech- Egyptian Mysteries) and Shetaut Neter (The Secret Way of the Spirit) were inscribed in the mortuary pyramids of the wealthy nobles. These texts are called *Pyramid Texts.* Later, the texts were inscribed on the mortuary coffins themselves.

These texts are referred to as *Coffin Texts*. The next evolution in the codification of the Ancient Egyptian teachings was the use of papyrus paper.

The versions of the *Prt m Hru* which were recorded in the later periods of Ancient Egyptian history are not exactly the same as those which were inscribed in the earliest periods. While most of the teachings of the later versions can be traced to earlier origins, many new utterances were added by different priests and priestesses. Therefore, the exposition of the teachings represents an evolution in mystical thought which in many ways was refined and expanded over a period of more than 5,000 years.

Thus, the later versions are a combination of ancient, original teachings and more modern expansions and additions to the teachings, which were not part of the original. The earlier texts did not include vignettes. The addition of vignettes is an important evolution in the transmission of the teaching since it adds a new dimension to the visual quality of the scripture. The vignettes first appear in the *Coffin Text* period.

Certain scriptures, such as Chapters 16 and 143, were always included in a vignette (illustrated, embellished with pictures) form, and never included text. Along with this, it should be understood that the teachings presented in the book itself are implicit, meaning that there is a certain amount of understanding which one must already have in order to fully understand the book even before picking it up for the first time. Also, once the book is picked up and studied it must be understood that its wisdom is not only transmitted by words, but also through the visual or pictorial nature of the scripture itself. The process of initiation serves to provide the student with information about the symbols and the subtle meanings or nuances of the philosophy. This is why, with the exception of Chapter 4[18], there are few explanations or glosses in the text itself. Certain Chapters, such as Chapter 33[19], are like compilations and refinements of earlier concepts. While containing their principles, there are no groupings of utterances in the earlier works which compile the *Negative Confessions* or *Precepts of MAAT* and the concepts or laws which must be followed in order to be pure of heart, as found in the later papyrus versions of the *Prt m Hru*. This aspect of the later versions does not represent a new concept or innovation, but a refinement and an expansion of that which was present at the inception of the teaching and first recorded in the form of the *Pyramid Texts*.

Plate 5: Coffin of Hent-Mehit, Singer (Chanter) of Amun, 21st dynasty showing anthropoid (human) features, texts and vignettes.

The Order of The Chapters

The collection of writings in the *Prt m Hru*, dedicated to spiritual enlightenment, are separate but complementary passages which may or may not relate directly to each other. The original format of the texts which are now referred to as the "Book of the Dead" was a collection of related texts which may be described as injunctions, admonitions or affirmations, hymns, litanies and chants related to promoting and bringing into reality the spiritual enlightenment of the individual initiate. These early texts are now known as the *Pyramid Texts*. These passages may be accurately referred to as "Chapters" or "Utterances." However, the ancient term was "Rw" (**roo** or **rau**, meaning "group of words to be spoken"). It is notable that the text and illustrations within the various papyri do not always

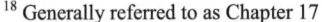

[18] Generally referred to as Chapter 17
[19] Generally referred to as Chapter 125

coincide and that different scrolls contain the same utterances in different orders. This points to the fact that there is no correct order in which the utterances must be presented nor is there a prescribed number of utterances which must be included in a volume in order for it to be considered a complete book. Also, the hieroglyphic scripture could be written in either a vertical or horizontal form, from right to left or left to right, and some chapters have variants, making their length variable. Some chapters, like Chapter 10, even obtain special instructions expressing the need to copy the texts as it is found, when making new scrolls of the *Prt m Hru*. Thus, some chapters like 4 and 31, have a short and long version. Consequently, there was no set length for a papyrus scroll of the *Prt m Hru*. Its length could range from a few feet to 70 or 80 feet or more in length. In ancient times certain chapters would be chosen by individuals in accordance with their feeling or the direction of their spiritual preceptors (priests and priestesses).

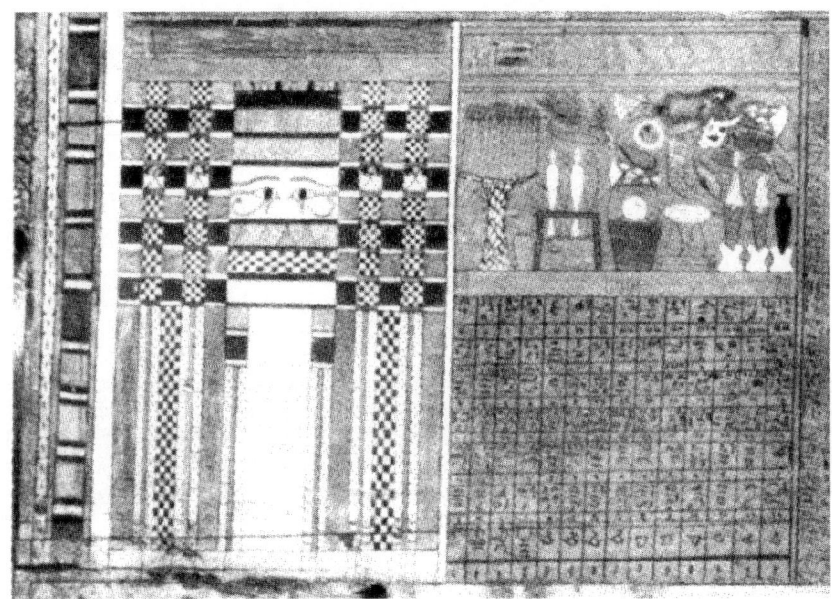

Plate 6: Above: Earliest chapters which include vignette, from coffin of 12th dynasty, showing the table of offerings (Hetep), a false door and the Sekhet Hetep (Chap. 18 of the *Prt m Hru*)

ba   àr   pet   śat   àr   ta
Soul   to   heaven,   body   to   earth.
Prt m Hru from *Pyramid Texts* (3,200-2,575 B.C.E.)

pet   χer   ba - k   ta   χeri   tut - k
Heaven   hath   thy soul,   earth hath   thy body.
Prt m Hru from *Papyrus Texts* (332 B.C.E.- c. 30 B.C.E.)

As the hieroglyphic scriptures above show, there are some concepts which existed in the earliest era of Kamitic culture which were maintained, over a period of thousands of years, down to the very late era. There are some utterances, chapters and concepts, which appear in most or all of the surviving copies. Some of these include Chapter 1, which pertains to coming forth by day, Chapter 9[20], which pertains to being triumphant over the enemies and understanding the deeper mystical wisdom about the nature of the

---

[20] Generally referred to as Chapter 17

Divine, and Chapter 36[21] which pertains to coming forth into the ultimate light, implying transformation from mortal human life into immortality and oneness with the Divine.

This presentation represents a new look at the *Prt m Hru,* the Ancient Egyptian compilation for scriptures dedicated to the purpose of attaining spiritual enlightenment, more fully translated: Ancient Egyptian Book of Coming Out of the World and Into Spiritual Enlightenment. It is the fruit many years of research into the mythology, mystical philosophy and culture of Yoga in Ancient Egypt. Also, it is the fruit of inner work by the author in the form of meditation on and spiritual practice of the teachings contained in the *Prt m Hru*. It is highly recommended that the reader should study the following volumes by the author first, before reading the *Prt m Hru* text in Part 2 of this volume. This advice is given because the teachings for coming into enlightenment which are contained in the *Prt m Hru* were not designed to be read by those who have not been initiated into the philosophy of Maat and Shetaut Neter. Therefore, it is suggested that the reader study the extensive introduction in Part 1 of this volume and also acquire the following volumes by the author as a further introduction to the mystical wisdom teachings of Ancient Egyptian Yoga Philosophy: *The Ausarian Resurrection, The Ancient Egyptian Bible* and *The Mystical Teachings of the Ausarian Resurrection.* The translation presented here is original, by the author, based on the original hieroglyphic texts. It is not intended as a literal, word for word treatise but as a prose translation in common English for better understanding. This format will better convey the meaning in terms that people in modern culture can more easily comprehend.

The *Rau nu Prt m Hru* is not a Bible, in the strict understanding of the term, from a religious-mythological point of view. As previously mentioned, religion has three levels of practice. First, there is the mythology upon which the religion is based. The text(s) that presents the story and basic beliefs of the religion is what constitutes the Bible of the particular religion. For example, in Christianity the religion is based on the myths related to the story of Jesus. This is what is presented in the Christian Bible, the myth. The words that are uttered in the church mass every Sunday are later developments of the tradition based on the myth. They represent the second stage of religion, the *Ritual* stage. In the same way, the myth that the *Ru Prt m Hru* is related to the story of Asar, his incarnation on earth, his death and resurrection but the myth is not told in the *Prt M Hru* texts themselves. The scripture which relates the story of Asar is the Bible, proper, of Ancient Egypt.[22] Therefore, the Bible of Ancient Egypt is the collection of scriptures containing the myth(s) related to the divinity. These were compiled in the book *The Ausarian Resurrection: The Ancient Egyptian Bible.* However, the utterances contained in the *Prt M Hru* book deal with the rituals related to the myth, i.e. the resurrecting Asar, the central teaching of the myth of Asar. This was explained in the books *The Ausarian Resurrection: The Ancient Egyptian Bible* and *The Mystical Teachings of the Ausarian Resurrection* also by the author. The *Prt m Hru* constitutes the utterances that are to be read, recited or chanted as a means of taking the teachings of the myth to the next level of practice, the ritual.

As occurs with the *Christian Bible, The Bhagavad Gita* and other texts, many people do not see the *Prt m Hru* as a book of spiritual principles and affirmations for transforming the mind. Rather, they insist that it is to be believed word for word. If this is the case, and if certain words, customs or ideas cannot be understood by theologians and scholars the *Prt m Hru,* it will become the object of many different interpretations and consequently, arguments. For this reason, the religious beliefs of the translator of the texts, which may or may not be in agreement with the original scriptural meaning, may influence the translation and therefore, the reader should exercise caution when choosing a translation to use for study. In the case of the *Prt m Hru,* scholars have consistently attempted to deny and downplay any mystical significance that may be found in the texts. This has served to minimize the understanding of the text and degrade the overall meaning of the spiritual philosophy behind it.

Another factor is that since languages change over time, it is necessary to update the translations on a regular basis. Present day English speaking people would not be able to understand the original King James Version of the Bible which was written only 387 years ago, much less scriptures that were written over 1,700 years ago. However, the essence of a teaching can be discerned and brought forth by those

---

[21] Generally referred to as Chapter 30

[22] See the book *The Ausarian Resurrection: The Ancient Egyptian Bible* by Muata Ashby.

who are initiated into the correct understanding and practice of religious philosophy in its three steps[23]. This is why updates to the translations by qualified scholars are necessary. Another important factor is that there are new discoveries that arise from time to time which may alter the timelines of the *Prt m Hru*, the Christian Bible and other texts or elucidate a new meaning of the old text, which in turn may affect the meaning of the teachings. This has been a major task which this volume, **Mysticism of the Prt m Hru: The Book of Enlightenment,** has attempted to perform in reference to the scriptures presented.

The question and struggle is to determine how best to provide a translation without reinterpreting the text. Some translators provide a word-for-word translation which means that each word is translated individually, but this is often difficult to understand since the nuances of the culture, inflections and grammar of ancient times is pretty much alien to modern society. Some translators work individually, while others work in committees. It is thought that committees would do a better job since its individual members would be less susceptible to deviation from the original texts. Some translators work individually, but their work is checked by a committee. In contrast to the Christian Bible, the *Prt m Hru* has been translated relatively few times (a few dozen) in the last 175 years. However it faces some of the problems that the Biblical scriptures face. There are several thousand Christian Bibles produced for people in various languages. Unfortunately, some of these Bibles were produced by translators who were not checked by any committee. Others could not even read the original texts, but gave their rendition anyway, and still others were simply paraphrased by people who thought they were conveying a meaning, but instead deviated from the original texts substantially. Some may want to promote a conservative agenda or a liberal agenda. Others may want to highlight a particular doctrine or political view over another, etc. So under these circumstances, it is not surprising that in the days of slavery in America, when Christian slave owners wanted to justify their ownership of slaves, some Bibles were produced espousing interpretations of scriptures and commentaries on those scriptures which promoted sexist and racist ideas. Paraphrases can convey the meaning of certain texts more easily than the word for word translations, but can also more easily reflect the doctrinal viewpoints of the translators. Therefore, it is important to know who has produced the book and if they have or had any ulterior motives or hidden agendas in their work. Many people feel that when they pick up a Christian Bible, they are holding the "Word of God." This idea has been engrained in the minds of many people for so many years that most do not question the contents of the Bible they are reading, and even become hostile when their illusions are challenged. They brand anyone who deviates from the concepts they have accepted as blasphemers or worse. All the while they are filling themselves with ignorance which will hurt their own spiritual evolution and accordingly, humanity as a whole.

Like the Christian Bible translations, the the translations of the *Ancient Egyptian Book of Coming into Enlightenment* poses important problems because the meanings of some of the ancient symbols are not understood in part or at all by the scholars. This is due, in part, to the fact that the use of the hieroglyphic language died out in the middle of the first millennia of the common era (around 500 A.C.E.). This break in the initiatic tradition accounts for some of the loss in terms of the meanings of rare glyphs. However, just as modern language adopts new terms and allows others to fall out of usage, the Ancient Egyptian language as it is understood today can still convey the teachings with remarkable lucidity.

The third level of religion is mysticism. This level requires that the practitioner of the rituals understand the myth and its ultimate purpose. Thus, this volume contains a compendium of the myth. However, there is no substitute for the complete text with reproductions of the vignettes prepared by the Ancient Egyptian Sages themselves which have been compiled in the book *The Ausarian Resurrection: The Ancient Egyptian Bible*. Along with that volume it is recommended that the serious student study the detailed commentary of the myth in the book, *The Mystical Teachings of the Ausarian Resurrection* as well as the lecture series on the Ausarian Resurrection, available on audio tape by Dr. Muata Ashby.

The Versions of the *Prt m Hru*

The Ancient Egyptian scriptures today referred to as the "Book of the Dead" evolved through at least three phases, stages or editions. These are referred to by most Egyptologists as "recensions" or "versions"

---

[23] Myth, Ritual and metaphysical (Mysticism).

(editions). This classification generally follows a historical outline of the development of the central universities of Ancient Egypt. In ancient times there were four main centers of philosophical scholarship. These were the main Temple in the city of Anu (Greek-Heliopolis), the main Temple in the city of Waset (Greek-Thebes), the main Temple in the city of Hetkaptah (Greek-Memphis) and the Temple in the city of Abdu, the center of the worship of Asar. Anu, Waset and Hetkaptah were the capital cities of the country in different historical periods. These were the schools attended by the Greek students of philosophy, Pythagoras being one of the most famous. Abdu remained as the spiritual center of Ausarian worship throughout history.

The *Pyramid Texts* are regarded by Egyptologists as being the first versions of the *Prt m Hru*. This is known as the **Anunian Recension,** and it is regarded as containing 759 utterances (chapters). These are regarded as belonging to the *Old Kingdom Period,* (cultural period of development- Dynasties 1-5). The next grouping of writings of the *Prt m Hru are referred to as Coffin Texts.* They are regarded as belonging to the *Middle Kingdom Period* (Dynasties 11-12). They were inscribed on wooded coffins and include complete utterances from the *Pyramid Texts* along with completely new ones. These texts are regarded as containing 1,185 invocations (utterances, chapters). In the city of Waset the priests/priestesses created a new version of *Prt M Hru.* These are usually referred to as the **Wasetian (Theban) recension** of the *Prt m Hru.* The **Wasetian Recension** adopted several texts from the older recension but added many more new ones. This recension is found on papyrus scrolls and one of its principal features are the extensive vignettes. In the very late period (after 600 B.C.E.), most papyri included a possible total of 192 chapters. These are usually referred to as the **Saite Recension** (Greco-Roman Period). This edition was written in hieratic text, including vignettes and contained only a few Hymns and sections of Chapter 33 which concern the Great Judgment and the Confessions of Innocence (42 principles of Maat).

The entire panorama of Ancient Egyptian theology can be thought of as a university system. Within a university, many colleges may be found. Each may specialize in a particular aspect of a subject while working harmoniously with other subjects presented in the other colleges within the university system. Likewise, the theology of Ancient Egypt emerged all at once but aspects of it were developed in different periods, by different schools or colleges which emerged within Ancient Egyptian history with the purpose of emphasizing and espousing particular perspectives of the theology, thereby popularizing certain teachings and divinities at different times. The earlier edition of the *Prt m Hru* originated in the College of Anu and was based on the Supreme Being in the form of "Ra." The next important edition developed in Waset. It was based on the Supreme Being in the form of "Amun" or "Amun-Ra." Both the Anunian and Wasetian teachings are to be regarded as emphasizing more of a devotional aspect of spiritual practice. They are referred to as "Theban Theology." The College of Hetkaptah (Memphis) developed a tradition that was based on the Supreme Being in the form of "Ptah." The Memphite teachings are referred to independently as "Memphite Theology" and are to be regarded as emphasizing more of a philosophical and psychological aspect of spiritual practice and were not used in exactly the same manner as the writings now referred to as the collection of chapters known as "Book of the Dead." The teachings of the Temple in the city of Abdu are a direct extension of the Anunian teachings, as they deal with the mythology related to the grandson of Ra, i.e. Asar. The later editions will be discussed at length in the following sections, as well as in the glosses and notes throughout this book.

The **Anunian edition** was inscribed in the pyramids of the early kings of Ancient Egypt in hieroglyphics. It is thus known as the *Pyramid Texts*. Some parts of it were inscribed in coffins, papyri, tombs, and steles. It should be noted that while this period roughly corresponds to 5,000 B.C.E.- 3,000 B.C.E., this is only the period in which the writings were codified (set down in hieroglyphic text). There are archeological and anthropological indications that the teachings existed prior to this period, in the vast reaches of so called "pre-history" referred to as the "Pre-dynastic" period.

The **Wasetian edition** (Theban-cultural period of development- Dynasties 18-20) can be found on papyri in hieroglyphics. The writings were partitioned into chapters with titles, but were still not given any definite order in the collection. These texts can be found after the cultural period of the 20th dynasty in hieroglyphic text as well as hieratic text.

Another version is recognized, called ***Saite*** or ***Ptolemaic edition.*** The Ptolemies were the Greek descendents of one of Alexander the Great's generals who took control of Egypt after Alexander had died. It is the latest cultural period of Ancient Egyptian history in which the country was besieged by outside conquering nations (Persians, Greeks, and especially the Romans) as well as internal social disintegration due to wars, breakdowns in social order and periods of civil unrest, martial law or the absence of government order altogether. In this edition, the chapters were arranged in a definite order and were written in hieroglyphics as well as hieratic text. However, this order was not absolutely rigid, nor did all the papyri follow what might be considered a sequential pattern for reading and studying purposes. It was considered sufficient that the chapters be present in the scroll (Ancient Egyptian book form).

The texts used for this present translation rely on the older versions (*Pyramid Texts* and *Coffin Texts*) in reference to the general themes of Kemetic spirituality content and as a method of determining the proper order of the collection of writings. Since the papyrus versions are summaries of the writings of the *Coffin Texts*, which are themselves expansions on the *Pyramid Texts*, the later versions (papyrus versions) are good sources in reference to the titles and format of separation of the chapters as well as the presentation of vignettes and the conciseness of writing in the presentation of certain concepts, for in the later versions, there is to be found a refinement of the verses which appeared in the earlier texts. The collection presented in this volume represent the most mystical chapters taken from all versions of the *Prt m Hru*. In this volume, when discussing writings from the *Pyramid Texts,* they will be referred to as "utterances." When discussing writings from the *Coffin Texts,* they will be referred to as "invocations," and when discussing the Papyrus Texts they will be referred to as "chapters." It should be noted that the use of the words *invocations, utterances*, or *chapters* can be confusing since in the *Pyramid Text* and *Coffin Text* writings, utterances can be as short as one sentence or as long as a long essay akin to the chapters of the later texts.

Due to the lack of diligence in transcribing the texts in ancient times, some of the chapters were duplicated within the same scroll, sometimes exactly the same way and at other times with grammatical errors, errors in meaning or minor changes that are inconsequential to the overall mystical importance of the teaching. In later papyruses, many innovations and expansions and sometimes even embellishments on the scripture can be found. These are not always in keeping with the intent of the original scriptures, those at the inception of the teaching. In these cases the errors, duplications or concepts not in keeping with the original scriptures and which may even be considered degradations in the philosophy, such as the *ushabti*[24] (*Coffin Text* 472) teachings or the predilection to remain in the Sekhet Hetep (enjoying heavenly pleasures) as opposed to moving forward into the Sekhet Yaru and on to discover and become one with Asar, have been either repaired, incorporated into one chapter or omitted altogether. Some of these discrepancies can also be accounted for by the vast periods of time since the scriptures were created, and also the intervening periods of social disturbances which have occurred. Keeping this in mind, it is remarkable that despite the minor discrepancies, the scriptures of Coming Forth from the early period of the *Pyramid Texts* to the Late period of the *Papyrus Texts* in the Ptolemaic and Roman Conquest Periods, display a faultless concordance of mythology and yogic mystical philosophy.

The occurrence of errors in the *Prt m Hru* should not be surprising to the student of Ancient Egyptian scripture. In fact, all scriptures from around the world including the Bible, the Koran, Bhagavad Gita, The Tao, and others, in themselves or their related scriptures, contain errors, both grammatical and/or contradictions in meaning. This is due to the vast amount of writing as well as the vast intervening periods of time between the writings, the versions, compilations etc., of the same scripture. The refinement of any scripture, as any book, depends on not writing, but rewriting. Those scriptures written independently and by different personalities at different times are bound to display inconsistencies. These should not be a basis for viewing that scripture in a negative light, but should promote understanding and a keen eye which knows how to sift truth from untruth. Added to these issues is the fanatical reverence of some aspirants. Some people have developed the opinion that simply because a text is ancient, that it must necessarily be correct in every detail. Further, many people believe that if a text is not ancient, it cannot be authentic or correct. This of course translates to the implication that modern day Sages are not to be revered as the Sages in ancient times. These are of course, misconceived ideas of the ignorant. In fact, the

---

[24] See the section of this book entitled "The choice of chapters" in Part II of this volume.

teachings are to be imparted by living spiritual teachers and authentic spiritual teachers have always updated and interpreted the teachings. This was true in ancient times and continues to be true today.

A true spiritual aspirant is not like an orthodox, narrow-minded personality who must believe that every single word in a particular scripture is "exactly" correct, or otherwise wrong and must be discarded altogether. An Ancient Egyptian proverb admonishes that true spiritual aspirant goes to the "essence of the meaning" without being distracted by minor concerns in grammar or correspondences of unimportant aspects of the scripture which have little bearing on the essence of the teachings.

"Strive to see with the inner eye, the heart. It sees the reality not subject to emotional or personal error;
it sees the essence. Intuition then is the most important quality to develop."

"Never forget: the words are not the reality, only reality is reality;
picture symbols are the idea, words are confusion."

"It takes a strong disciple to rule over the mountainous thoughts
and constantly go to the essence of the meaning; as mental complexity increases,
thus will the depth of your decadence and challenge both be revealed."

—Ancient Egyptian Proverbs

Language, Pronunciation, Spelling and Meaning

The authors of all of the world's scriptures were divinely inspired, however, they worked with the limited instrument of the human personality, which is in itself prone to error. This was true in ancient times as it continues to be true in modern times. The pursuit of perfection in life is not found in a perfectly written scripture. In any case, none exist, for one person's perfection can be another person's garbage. What is good for one person is not necessarily good for another. People have different tastes, opinions, etc., because they come from different walks of life, and not because one thing is intrinsically better than the other. Therefore, while one person likes one scripture over another, this does not mean that one is better than another. It simply means that one scripture appeals to one person's sensibilities, based on their cultural background, personality inclinations, etc. Further, just as it is impossible to know the exact pronunciations of words in old English, and yet it is possible to understand what writers like Chaucer and Shakespeare meant, it is unnecessary to know the exact pronunciations of Ancient Egyptian words where the meaning is well established. The teaching of the Ancient Egyptian *Myth of Ra and Aset*[25] bears out the importance of the essence of meaning as opposed to the spoken words. Further, since Ancient Egyptian language experienced at least three major periods of evolution (Old Kingdom, Middle Kingdom and New Kingdom), when determining pronunciations, like the spellings, we are faced with period differences, regional differences and personality differences. Some texts have different spellings for the same word within the same papyrus. Add to this the differences between colloquy[26] and script, the ever-changing regional accents and expressions, and the question then becomes which pronunciations are we talking about, the ancient or late ones, the ones of the north or those of the west, etc? Remarkably, the hieroglyphic texts underwent less changes than one might expect given the excessively long period of time for its usage, the longest in the world at over 5,000 years! Consider that it has only been since the beginning of the eighteenth century that western culture "standardized" language. Were it not for this, modern English speaking people might not understand the English speeches and writings of George Washington. Pronunciations can be approximated in many ways: correlating to Greek words, which correspond to the Ancient Egyptian, correlating to Coptic words derived from Ancient Egyptian, extrapolating from known words, etc. However, these will always be approximations and a spiritual aspirant should not spend too much time with this issue, but rather on understanding the philosophy behind the words, for no matter how they are pronounced or spelled, the essence remains intact and effective, and the essence is the meaning. The following Hermetic[27] proverbs give insight into the feelings of the Ancient Egyptian Sages on the question of pronunciation and meaning.

"Keep this teaching from translation in order that such mighty Mysteries might not come to the Greeks and to the disdainful speech of Greece, with all its *looseness and its surface beauty*, taking all the strength out of the solemn and the strong - the energetic speech of Names."

Ancient Egyptian literature has its own style and feeling, and the *usage* of the Kemetic language is exhorted above other languages because it is precise and more importantly, concise in its descriptions and terms, with a minimum of flowery language (*looseness and surface beauty*) while achieving a certain poetic sentiment. The absence of superfluous parts of speech in a language will consequently allow the language to be more direct and concise and thus, less subject to misinterpretation. This injunction is relating the idea that Kemetic grammar, the system of inflections, syntax, and word formation of the language, is simple, containing a minimum of prepositions[28] and adjectives to embellish a subject. Many Greeks who came to Ancient Egypt were not interested in changing their ways to suit the teaching, but rather wanted to suit the teachings to their lifestyles without making the fundamental changes that are necessary to attain enlightenment. In modern times, many people use Kemetic symbols and may even utter certain Ancient Egyptian words, but do so without true feeling or insight because they do not *live* the culture. In essence, they continue to be worldly people while appearing to adopt some spiritual philosophy, and therefore, their efforts fall far short of what is necessary to make the teachings effective.

---

[25] See the book Mysticism of the Goddess by Dr. Muata Ashby

[26] **col·lo·quy** (kŏl'ə-kwē) *n.*, *pl.* **col·lo·quies**. **1.** A conversation, especially a formal one. **2.** A written dialogue.

[27] Ancient Egyptian philosophy in the Greek-Roman period.

[28] In some languages, a word placed before a substantive and indicating the relation of that substantive to a verb, an adjective, or another substantive, as English *at, by, in, to, from,* and *with*. (American her. Dic.)

Thus, it is all right to translate the word *Asar* (Kemetic) into *Osiris* (Greek), as long as the meaning remains intact. However, this can only occur if one is deeply involved in the culture and if one is led by an authentic spiritual teacher. The objection above is not on the basis of pronunciation, but that in translating it the Greeks apparently wanted to make the terms into something other than what they were supposed to be. Thus, just as it is virtually impossible for a twentieth century English speaking person to communicate with a ninth century English speaking person, it would be more than likely that an Egyptologist of our time could not communicate verbally with an Ancient Egyptian person, but could communicate by writing hieroglyphs back and forth. The meaning, which transcends words and their time period of usage, is higher than the words themselves.

This is emphasized in the second proverb below where the objection is raised, because when the translation is made into Greek, the meaning is often lost. The language is taken but not the teaching (*the teachings keepeth clear the meaning of the words*). The meaning gives value to the words and thus, any words are useful in describing the transcendental essence. For example, the word "Neberdjer" from Ancient Egypt, "Brahman" from India, "Tao" from China, etc., have the same meaning, the Transcendental Absolute. A Chinese person using the word "Tao" will discover the same truth as the person who follows Kemetic Philosophy using the word "Neberdjer." Thus, meaning is more important than grammar or pronunciation since the mind assigns meaning first and pronunciation afterwards. Further, the medium of words cannot fully capture the perfection of thought because it is a limited medium. The fullness of the true essence of the Divine cannot be captured by any concept and words cannot capture the totality of any idea. However, sound and pronunciation do have legitimate purposes and uses in spiritual study and especially in the study of the Kemetic language.

The Language of Names

"Unto those who come across these words, their composition will seem most simple and clear; but on the contrary, as this is unclear, and has the true meaning of its words concealed, it will be still unclear, when, afterwards, the Greeks will want to turn our tongue into their own - for this will be a very great ***distorting and obscuring*** of even what has heretofore been written. Turned into our own native tongue, ***the teachings keepeth clear the meaning of the words***. For that its very ***quality of sound, the very power of Egyptian names***, have in themselves the bringing into act of what is said."

The Kemetic language is special in many ways because it reflects many universal cosmic principles of sound. An example of this is the Ancient Egyptian word "*mut.*" Mut means mother and it is reflected in "mata" of the Hindu language, "madre' of Spanish, "mother" in English, etc. The "m" sound is a universal "seed sound" principle of motherhood. However, this is not an absolute rule because other words are used as well. The use of names in the Kemetic language is important because they act as keys to unlocking the mysteries of life, but this is true only for those initiated into the philosophy. In Kemetic philosophy, words are seen as abstract representatives of phenomenal reality. Since the mind is the only reality and the external world only reflects a conceptualized form based on an idea in God's mind, words are a higher reality when compared to the physical world and all Kemetic words are names for objects and/or concepts. In fact, Creation is a concept given a name and not an absolute, abiding reality in and of itself.

By studying the phonetic and pictorial (Kemetic language is not only phonetic, but also illustrative) etymology (the origin and development of a linguistic form) and etiology (the study of causes or origins) of names and applying the initiatic science, it is possible to decipher the mysteries of Creation by discovering the teachings embedded in the language by the Sages of Ancient Egypt.

For example, the Kemetic word "Pa" is central to understanding the deeper essence of nature, divinity and the gods and goddesses of the *Prt m Hru*. In the study of the word "Pa," philosophy as well as pictorial and phonetic associations must be considered. Along with this, the variations in spellings act to expand the possible associations and thereby also the appropriate meaning in the given usage. Sometimes the very same words may be used, but its usage in different texts denotes a slight difference in the nuance of the meaning in accordance with the usage. This aspect of assigning the proper meaning of a word which is used even with the same spelling but in different contexts in different or even the same Kemetic scriptures, is an artistic development which comes to a translator with time. Thus, there is no right or wrong interpretation, but there is greater and greater approximation to the higher intended truth behind the teaching as research moves forward. Also, it should be remembered that research here implies not only studying books, but also meditation and introspection, as well as living in accordance with the philosophy.

Table 4: Study of the Kemetic Word "Pa"

The Etymological, Etiological, Phonetic and Pictorial Study of the Kemetic word "Pa"	Meaning
A-	A- **Pa**- demonstrative, this, the, to exist
B-	B- **Pau** - Primeval Divinity- The Existing One
C-	C- **Paut**- Primeval time - remote ages- beginning time
D-	D- **Paut**- stuff, matter, substance, components which make something up.
E-	E- **Pauti**- The Primeval God; Primeval Divinity who is self-Created; Dual form relates to rulership of Upper and Lower Egypt
F-	F- **Pauti-u**- Primeval Divinity with male or female determinative - source of all multiplicity in Creation.
G-	G- **Pat** (paut) **n Neteru**- Company of gods and goddesses
H-	H- **Pauti**- Company of nine gods and goddesses
I-	I- **Pau** or **Paut** -human beings, me, women

The Ancient Egyptian words and symbols related to the Company of Gods and Goddesses (Pauti) indicate several important mystical teachings. The root of the Ancient Egyptian word Pauti is *Pa* (Figure A). Pa means "to exist." Thus, Creation is endowed with the quality of existence as opposed to non-existence. *Pau* (Figure B) is the next progression in the word. It means the *Primeval Divinity*, the source of Creation. *Paut* (Figure C and D) is the next evolution of the word, Pau, meaning *primeval time* and *the*

The Ancient Egyptian words and symbols related to the Company of Gods and Goddesses (Pauti) indicate several important mystical teachings. The root of the Ancient Egyptian word Pauti is *Pa* (Figure A). Pa means "to exist." Thus, Creation is endowed with the quality of existence as opposed to non-existence. *Pau* (Figure B) is the next progression in the word. It means the *Primeval Divinity*, the source of Creation. *Paut* (Figure C and D) is the next evolution of the word, Pau, meaning *primeval time* and *the very substance out of which everything is created is the one and the same*. *Pauti* is the next expression of **Pa** and it has two major meanings. It refers to the *Primeval Divinity* or Divine Self (God) (Figure E). *Pautiu* refers to *Pauti* but in plural, as well as being a gender specific term implying, *the Divinity as the source of the multiplicity in creation*. In the Ancient Egyptian language, like Spanish for example, all objects are assigned gender. Also, Pauti refers to the deities who comprise the *Company of Gods and Goddesses* (Figure G and H). *Paut* (men) or *Pautet* (women) also refers to *living beings*, especially *human beings* (Figure I).

Pa ➔ Pau ➔ Paut ➔ Pauti ➔ Pautiu ➔ Paut and Pautet

Therefore, the most important teaching relating to the nature of Creation is being given here. The gods and goddesses of the creation are not separate principles or entities. They are in reality one and the same as the Primeval Divinity. They are expressions of that Divine Self. However, they are not transformations of or evolutions from the Divine Self, but the very same Divine Self expressing as Creation. So even though God is referred to as a primordial deity who did something a long time ago or set into motion various things, in reality God and Creation are one and the same. Ra is the "God of the primeval time" as well as the gods and goddesses of Creation which sustain it all the time. With this understanding, it is clear to see that God is not distant and aloof, observing Creation from afar. The Divine Self is the very basis of Creation and is in every part of it at all times. This is why the terms *Pa-Neter* and *neteru* are also used to describe the Divine. Pa-Neter means "The Supreme Being" and neteru means "the gods and goddesses." Also, the word "neteru" refers to creation itself. So neter-u emanates from Neter. Creation is nothing but God who has assumed various forms or neteru: trees, cake, bread, human beings, metal, air, fire, water, animals, planets, space, electricity, etc. This is a profound teaching which should be reflected upon constantly so that the mind may become enlightened to its deeper meaning and thereby discover the Divinity in nature.

The Divine Self is not only in Creation but is the very essence of every human being as well. Therefore, the substratum of every human being is in reality God as well. The task of spiritual practice and Yoga is to discover this essential nature within your own heart. This can occur if one reflects upon this teaching and realizes its meaning by discovering its reality in the deepest recesses of one's own experience. When this occurs, the person who has attained this level of self-discovery is referred to as having become enlightened. They have discovered their true, divine nature. They have discovered their oneness with the Divine Self.

In conclusion, it must be understood that Kemetic language is synonymous with Kemetic philosophy. As such, when speaking, one must adhere to truth. The ultimate truth is, that when we speak of objects, we are in reality speaking about principles, deeper basis of which is the Divine Self. When words are spoken, they immediately take on the first level of reality as they engender an image in the mind of the listener. When a listener acts upon what has been heard, the speech takes on a reality in the physical plane. Therefore, the speech is a reflection of an idea, a concept, and the physical reality is a reflection of speech. The cause underlying the concept is the real name of a thing, its higher reality, and this essence has no name or form in its potentiality, but only in its relative manifestation. This relative manifestation is the world of time and space and all living and non-living objects in it. Therefore, we have three levels of reality, the thought, the word and the actual object existing in the physical world. However, these are only relative realities since they are all ephemeral in nature and not abiding. The creative essence (God-transcendental consciousness) which gave power to the thought, the concept, is the source and substratum which lends temporary reality to the projection (thought, the word and the actual object).

Flowery and imprecise language as well as language that praises worldliness as opposed to the Divine (ex. language that promotes arrogance, pride and the illusion that human existence is abiding) distracts the mind away from this great practice. Thus, it becomes an agent of ignorance and confusion, fostering and sustaining a deluded notion of reality. This is the higher teaching which is otherwise espoused as *Maakheru* –"Truth of Speech." Therefore, truth is a higher reality in relation to words, language or symbols, etc. Thus, while one should endeavor to be as accurate as possible, understanding the meaning of the words and their teaching is more important than their pronunciation or spelling. The following Ancient Egyptian proverbs extol the ideals just introduced.

"If you are in authority, then you should do perfect things, those which will be remembered by posterity. Never listen to the words of flatterers or words that fill you with pride and vanity."

"Words cannot give wisdom if they stray from the truth."

"Words are not the reality, only reality is reality; picture symbols are the idea, words are confusion."

As one can imagine, studying the phonetic and pictorial etymology of names can be an extensive discipline and learning the Kemetic language entails much more than it would appear on the surface. Exploring this aspect of Kemetic culture could take an entire lifetime and would fill several volumes. In fact, the Egyptian Yoga Book Series is the fruit of such researches, exploring the essential basis and practice of Kemetic mysticism, and more will come in future years. In this sense it is like no other language. It is a world in and of itself, apart from the spoken verbalizations used to communicate in ordinary human situations. It is a language of the soul and of the cosmos, mystical philosophy and spiritual enlightenment. It is a language designed to take the mind beyond words.

New Terms

This volume will introduce new terminology to describe certain aspects of the writings contained in the *Prt m Hru*. The reason for this is, the terms that have been used by traditional Egyptologist have become outdated, and in order to have a clearer understanding, we must now progress to the use of terms and definitions which more closely approximate the meaning for our modern understanding. This is necessary because many of the terms which have been used are merely conventions devised by Egyptologists to account for Ancient Egyptian words and ideas, which have no direct translation in other languages. Therefore we must begin to study the terms and gain a new understanding and feel for these in their own language.

The pursuit of perfection in life does not come from discovering a grammatically perfect scripture, for there is none. It is gaining understanding from a scripture that speaks to us based on our karmic makeup (personality inclinations) as to the essence of our human existence, the Higher Self. In this sense, all the world's spiritual scriptures are perfectly capable of promoting spiritual enlightenment, for those to whom they appeal, if they are correctly understood and if allowances are made for human frailties. This is why a spiritual preceptor is so important on the spiritual path. That person can steer the mind when it is caught up in the petty issues of spiritual practice. That person is a guide to let the aspirant know how to deal with issues that on the surface seem like insurmountable contradictions or obstacles, which can bring an aspirant's spiritual evolution to a halt, but which are in reality insignificant misunderstandings to be out-stepped.

As stated earlier, in some cases, later versions of the *Prt m Hru* were refined or expanded and sometimes modified by the priests/priestesses or scribes of the later time. An example of this is the refinement of the concept of the neteru or gods and goddesses and their relationship to the initiate. In Utterances 273-274 of the *Pyramid Texts*, the concept of assimilating the neteru is put forth using the metaphor of eating the gods and goddesses and even cooking them as well. In Chapter 27 of the papyrus versions, the concept is refined to direct statements affirming knowledge of the true nature of the neteru and thus, the idea of becoming those same gods and goddesses by self-discovery. This concept is related to the original Kemetic concept of the consecration[29] idea (receiving and consuming the eye of Heru) which is contained in both the earlier texts (*Pyramid Texts*) as well as the later texts (papyrus versions) of

---

[29] This is the prototype for the Christian Eucharist ritual of consecrating items such as bread and wine in the Mass Ritual..

the *Prt m Hru*. Where these additions and changes were in harmony with the earlier, original texts and added to the spiritual importance and understanding of the text, they were retained.

Ancient Kemetic Terms and Ancient Greek Terms

In keeping with the spirit of the culture of Kemetic Spirituality, in this volume we will use the Kemetic names for the divinities through which we will bring forth the Philosophy of the Prt M Hru. Therefore, the Greek name Osiris will be converted back to the Kemetic (Ancient Egyptian) Asar (Ausar), the Greek Isis to Aset (Auset), the Greek Nephthys to Nebthet, Anubis to Anpu or Apuat, Hathor to Hetheru, Thoth or Hermes to Djehuti, etc. (see the table below) Further, the term Ancient Egypt will be used interchangeably with "Kemit" ("Kamit"), or "Ta-Meri," as these are the terms used by the Ancient Egyptians to refer to their land and culture.

Table 5: Kemetic Names of the main Gods and Goddesses of Ancient Egypt and the Greek translation in common use.

Kemetic (Ancient Egyptian) Names	Greek Names
Amun	Zeus
Ra	Helios
Ptah	Hephastos
Nut	Rhea
Geb	Kronos
Net	Athena
Khonsu	Heracles
Set	Ares or Typhon
Bast	Artemis
Uadjit	Leto
Asar (Ausar)	Osiris or Hades
Aset (Auset)	Isis or Demeter
Nebthet	Nephthys
Anpu or Apuat	Anubis
Hetheru	Hathor (Aphrodite)
Heru	Horus or Apollo
Djehuti	Thoth or Hermes
Maat	Astraea or Themis

How To Study The Mystical Teachings Of The *Prt m Hru*

The Papyrus of Ani, as it has come to be known, is an excellent example of the *Prt m Hru* text as it existed in the New Kingdom Dynastic period of Ancient Egypt. The hieroglyphic texts of Ancient Egypt, the teachings of Egyptian mystical spirituality are called "Khu" or "Hekau," meaning *utterances* or *words of power,* and are collectively known as "Metu Neter," Words of The God or Neter Metu - Divine Speech. Modern Egyptology, the scholarly study of Ancient Egyptian civilization from the early nineteenth century to the present, has labeled these *utterances* as *spells* or *incantations.* In a way this assessment is correct because these utterances are to be understood as words which, when spoken with meaning and feeling, can have a transforming effect on the mind, allowing expansion of consciousness. However, the Hekau should not to be understood in the context of Western magic or witches spells or voodoo, etc. To do so would be a grievous error of intellectual laziness and cultural egoism, trying to make simple correlations to lower forms of spiritual practice. This form of treatment would yield the conclusion that the Ancient Egyptian religion is merely a myriad of conflicting stories and the presumption that Ancient Egyptian spirituality is a conglomerate of idol worshipping and occult nonsense.

In ancient times, Ancient Egyptian spirituality drew followers from all corners of the world. Those who came from far away recognized the greatness of Egypt, which was the fruit of the Temple system of education. The Temple was a formidable power for human mental, physical and spiritual development, healthcare and social government.

Any study of mystical spirituality needs to be carried out from the perspective of the present. This means that the teachings need to be understood in the context of today and how it affects one's life right here and right now. What good would it do to know all about the history of what a Sage, such as Ptahotep, did and taught 5,000 years ago if it is not understood in the context of a teaching which can be used in the present? As the reader, whether or not you believe and practice the teachings or are simply interested in understanding them, you should look upon them from the perspective of something which is alive and viable for today. The following instructions are included for those who wish to seriously integrate the teachings into their lives for the purpose of discovering their deeper meaning and their power to transform the human mind.

Before undertaking this study, we need to establish the parameters by which we will explore the teachings. Many people do not realize that mystical spirituality is like an advanced form of psychotherapy, incorporating not only a keen understanding of psychology, human emotion, and social relationships, but also the relationship between individual human consciousness and Cosmic Consciousness. Unlike the discipline of Western psychotherapy or the psychological treatment of mental, emotional, and nervous disorders, mystical spirituality or psychology is not just concerned with the mentally insane and how to bring them back into the mainstream of society or normal human life. This is because this so called "normal" social structure cannot be so normal if it turns out psychotics or those who suffer from any of a class of serious mental disorders in which the mind cannot function normally and the ability to deal with reality is impaired or lost. These mental illnesses and psychoses include: anger, hatred, greed, lust, envy, jealousy, depression, schizophrenia, sadism, manic depressive psychosis, and paranoia. The structure of modern society is conducive to the development of social stresses, based on passion, greed and lust, as well as both physical and mental disease, due to pollution of the environment and the mind. The ordinary practice of religion does not incorporate a mystical aspect. This shortcoming is the source of strife and dysfunction in family relations, social relations and spiritual relations of in modern culture. Mystical spirituality integrates and develops not only the intellect, but also the emotions to deal with practical life and the will power capacity of the personality, all the while leading the soul to ultimate spiritual self-discovery. It promotes harmony in society, harmony with nature and harmony between humanity and the Divine. Therefore, mystical psycho-spiritual counseling is more powerful than ordinary psychoanalysis.

Mystical teachings should be studied in the context of a transpersonal discipline which not only seeks to promote the ordinary standards of "normalcy," but also to transcend these in order to achieve a supernormal mental, physical and spiritual level of health. This element is what differentiates ordinary thinking in psychology, sociology and medical science from the ideals of mystical teaching. The ordinary discipline seeks to settle for a worldly reward in the form of what is commonly accepted as peace and joy, but which is in reality, limited, ephemeral, fragile and illusory. Mystical psychology seeks to go beyond the ordinary and to discover the that which is to be known and which upon knowing, all is known, the Absolute, which transcends time and space. This idea is extremely important because ordinary human life cannot satisfy the inner need of the heart of a human being since it is transient, ephemeral and unpredictable. So no matter how well integrated ordinary psychology may help a person to become, they will be missing the spiritual dimension wherein lies the abiding fulfillment of the human being.

Figure 6: Above: Forms of the God Djehuti

The Creator of Hieroglyphic Text and Author of Medu Neter (Divine Words-Speech)

Figure 7: Below: Forms of the Goddess Maat/Maati

The embodiment of truth, justice, regularity and harmony.
She is the bestower of Maak-heru (Spiritual Enlightenment)

Chapter 2: The Myth Behind The Rau nu Prt m Hru

UNDERSTANDING THE AUSARIAN RESURRECTION MYTH: A SUMMARY OF THE AUSARIAN RESURRECTION

In order to understand the *Prt m Hru,* it is necessary to have a working understanding of the concept of the levels of religion, the concept of God, the Ancient Egyptian Creation Myth and the Myth of Asar, Aset and Heru.

Religion, metaphysics, mysticism and yoga have been intimately related throughout history. Central to all of them is the idea that each of us is related to a higher existence, and that we can learn to use our higher divine faculties once we have purified our minds and bodies. In perfecting ourselves we are able to rise above our mortal human existence and partake in divine wisdom and bliss. This is the true purpose of all religions. The Egyptian *Prt m Hru* represents the metaphysical act and realization of the mystical teachings hidden in the Asarian Myth. Therefore, it represents the next step in the process of religion: the process of realizing or having a direct experience of the underlying truths of the myth.

The Mind and Philosophical Concepts

In the earliest times, God was conceived of as anonymous, immanent, and all pervasive. It is a concept akin to the Eastern pantheism and panentheism of the Hindus. However, when the mystical implications of the teaching are well understood, they reveal a different picture behind the outer edge of the symbols and scriptures. While it is true that the Supreme God without form was given zoomorphic and anthropomorphic forms in later times, the transcendental idea was never lost. It remained in the background, for those who had the interest and intellectual understanding to grasp the concept that the symbols given by the Sages are like masks which are created for the initial understanding of the mind. This is useful in the beginning stages of religious practice when the mind needs something concrete to hold onto. This is why the Supreme Being was given names such as Amun, Ra, Ptah, Asar and Aset. However, when spiritual knowledge and aspiration increases, the mind is gradually strengthened by the practice of the teachings and the increasing understanding of the principles which are represented by the symbols. Then it is possible to leave behind the images and concepts of the mind in order to explore what lies behind them. In this context, the images and symbols are like roadmaps and pointers to the absolute truth, and the absolute transcendental truth is the real destination of the spiritual journey.

The mind needs concepts in order to understand the world around it. Therefore, the Sages of every religion have constructed concepts and images of spirituality to aid the mind to understand gradually increasing levels of higher reality. It is unfortunate that some people become stuck in the concepts and images and try to fix these into a concrete historical context. In doing so they deprive themselves from the richness of the deeper experiences of their religion because it is rooted in the past, instead of the present. Therefore, when we speak of a "creation," it should not be understood as an event which occurred only in the distant past, but as a mystical metaphor of that which underlies all reality. In fact, all mystical symbols should be treated in this manner. In so doing, the hidden meanings of the mystical teachings reveal themselves readily and easily.

Philosophy is the discipline of thinking which leads the mind to understand the essence of existence. The study of philosophy in its highest form is to assist the student in understanding {his/her} own mind in order to be able to transcend it, and thus, experience the "transcendental" reality which lies beyond words, thoughts, concepts and mental notions. Mental conceptions are based on our own worldly experiences. They help us to understand the world as the senses perceive it. However, clinging to these experiences as the only reality precludes our discovery of other forms of reality or existence which lies beyond the capacity of the senses. A dog's olfactory sense and the vision of a hawk are much superior to that of the human being. The world of a dog or hawk is much different because they have an expanded range of sensitivity in their senses. Human beings use instruments such as telescopes and microscopes to expand the capability of the senses, but these are also limited and cannot capture reality as it truly is. If the human senses cannot even perceive the atoms which scientists tell us comprise all material objects in creation, how can they be expected to perceive that which is even subtler than the atom, the spirit of the Divine Self?

However, the human has one advantage which is superior to all senses and scientific instruments, the intuitional mind when it is purified by the practice of Yoga philosophy and disciplines. Ancient mystical philosophical systems have as their main goal the destruction of the limited concepts and illusions of the mind. In essence, the philosophies related to understanding nature and a human being's place in it were the first disciplines which practiced, what is now referred to as Transpersonal Psychology, that is, a system of psychology which assists us in going beyond the personal or ego-based aspects of the psyche in order to discover what lies beyond (trans) the personal (relating to the personality).

The Concept of God

The following is a synthesis of important Ancient Egyptian aphorisms on the nature of "God."

"GOD is the father of beings. His Unity is Absolute. He is One and alone. GOD is the eternal One... infinite and endures forever. GOD is hidden and no man knows GOD's form. No man has been able to seek out GOD's likeness. GOD is hidden to Gods and men... GOD's name remains hidden... It is a mystery to His children, men, women and Gods. GOD's names are innumerable, manifold and no one knows their number... though GOD can be seen in form and observation of GOD can be made at GOD's appearance, GOD cannot be understood... GOD cannot be seen with mortal eyes... GOD is invisible and inscrutable to Gods as well as men."[30]

The concepts of God are only concepts and not realities. The correct study and practice of mystical philosophy lead a person to discover the transcendental nature of the Divine. This is the objective of the *Prt m Hru*, to realize the teachings contained in the myth of Asar, the Ausarian Resurrection.

God and The Female Aspect

The writings of *Prt m Hru* affirm the gender-less nature of the Divine. While the Divine may be referred to as the male aspect, God, it may also be referred to as Goddess. Thus, we have striven to correctly translate the word "Neter" as "Divinity" instead of "God," and "neteru" as "gods and goddesses" instead of just "the gods." In Ancient Egypt women enjoyed complete equality in society. They had the same rights as men. This cultural righteousness was reflected in the practice of religion as well or it might be said that the practice of righteousness in religion supported the practice of righteousness in society. The importance of equality between the sexes cannot be overstated in our times. Sexism and the subjugation of women through government decrees, laws, culturally entrenched prejudices and male delusions of superiority, have led to a world in which the fabric of society, marriage and family are disintegrating and causing interpersonal strife, stress and anxiety in society. These conditions cause an intensification of egoism and the bondage to the world for both men and women, and lead to mental and physical disease, frustration and even violence as well as spiritual stagnation. Therefore, it must be clearly understood that since the *Prt m Hru* texts were written for men and women alike, it has been prepared with the least amount of gender references in regards to the Initiate for whom it is written. It thus becomes a working texts for anyone, the way it was originally intended. In those instances where the word god or goddess is used, their use relates to the time and space manifestation of the transcendental Divine Self, which is beyond gender.

---

[30] Portions from: Egyptian Ru *Pert Em Heru*, Hymns of Amun and the Papyrus of Nesi-Khensu

A COMPENDIUM OF THE AUSARIAN RESURRECTION MYTH

The Creation

The process of creation is explained in the form of a cosmological system for better understanding. Cosmology is a branch of philosophy dealing with the origin, processes, and structure of the universe. Cosmogony is the astrophysical study of the creation and evolution of the universe. Both of these disciplines are inherent facets of Ancient Egyptian philosophy through the main religious systems or companies of the gods and goddesses. A company of gods and goddesses is a group of deities which symbolize a particular cosmic force or principle which emanates from the all-encompassing Supreme Being, from which they have emerged. The Self or Supreme Being manifests creation through the properties and principles represented by the *Pauti* Company of gods and goddesses-cosmic laws of nature. The system or Company of Gods and Goddesses of Anu is regarded as the oldest, and forms the basis of the Asarian Trinity. It is expressed in the diagram below.

Ra-Tem
⇩
Hetheru – Djehuti - Maat
⇩
Shu ⇔ Tefnut
⇩
Geb⇔Nut
⇗ ⇩ ⇘
Set — Nebethet   Asar ⇔ Aset   Asar ⇔ Nebethet
⇩   ⇩
Heru   Anpu

The diagram above shows that *Psedjet* (Ennead), or the creative principles which are embodied in the primordial gods and goddesses of creation, emanated from the Supreme Being. Ra, also referred to as Ra-Tem or Ra-Atum, or Atum-Ra, arose out of the *"Nu,"* the Primeval waters, the hidden essence, and began sailing the *"Boat of Millions of Years"* which included the Company of Gods and Goddesses. On his boat emerged the "neters" or cosmic principles of creation. The neteru of the Ennead arising from Ra-Atum are Shu, Tefnut, Geb, Nut, Asar, Aset, Set, Nebethet and Heru Ur. Hetheru, Djehuti and Maat represent attributes of the Supreme Being as the very *stuff* or *substratum* which makes up creation. Shu, Tefnut, Geb, Nut, Asar, Aset, Set, and Nebethet represent the principles upon which creation manifests. Anpu is not part of the Ennead. He represents the feature of intellectual discrimination in the Asarian myth. "Sailing" signifies the beginning of motion in creation. Motion implies that events occur in the realm of time and space, thus, the phenomenal universe comes into existence as a mass of moving essence we call the elements. Prior to this motion, there was the primeval state of being without any form and without existence in time or space.

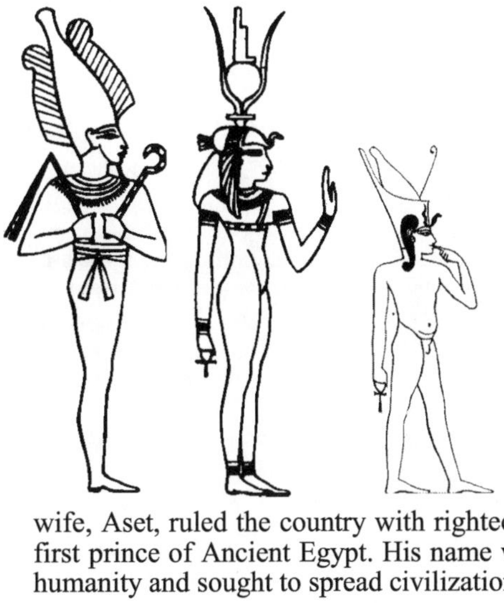

Figure 8: Asar, Aset and Heru

Asar was the first human king of Ancient Egypt. He and his wife, Aset, ruled the country with righteousness and compassion. Together, they engendered a child, the first prince of Ancient Egypt. His name was Heru. Asar and Aset dedicated themselves to the welfare of humanity and sought to spread civilization throughout the earth, even as far as India and China.

69

During the absence of Asar from his kingdom, his brother Set had no opportunity to make innovations in the state, because Aset was extremely vigilant in governing the country, and always upon her guard and watchful for any irregularity or unrighteousness.

Upon Asar's return from touring the world and carrying the teachings of wisdom abroad, there was merriment and rejoicing throughout the land. However, one day after Asar's return, through his lack of vigilance, he became intoxicated and slept with Set's wife, Nebethet. Nebethet, as a result of the union with Asar, begot Anpu.

Set, who represents the personification of evil forces, plotted in jealousy and anger (the blinding passion that prevents forgiveness and understanding) to usurp the throne and conspired to kill Asar. Set secretly got the measurements of Asar and constructed a coffin. Through trickery, Set was able to get Asar to "try on" the coffin for size. While Asar was resting in the coffin, Set and his assistants locked it and then dumped it into the Nile river.

The coffin made its way to the coast of Syria where it became embedded in the earth and from it grew a tree with the most pleasant aroma in the form of a Djed. The Djed is the symbol of Asar's Back. It has four horizontal lines in relation to a firmly established, straight column. The Djed column is symbolic of the upper energy centers (chakras) that relate to the levels of consciousness of the spirit.

The king of Syria was out walking and as he passed by the tree, he immediately fell in love with the pleasant aroma, so he had the tree cut down and brought to his palace. Aset (Auset, Ast), Asar's wife, who is the personification of the life giving, mother force in creation and in all humans, went to Syria in search of Asar. Her search led her to the palace of the Syrian king where she took a job as the nurse of the king's son. Every evening, Aset would put the boy into the "fire" to consume his mortal parts, thereby transforming him to immortality. Fire is symbolic of both physical and mental purification. Most importantly, fire implies wisdom, the light of truth, illumination and energy. Aset, by virtue of her qualities, has the power to bestow immortality through the transformative power of her symbolic essence. Aset then told the king that Asar, her husband, is inside the pillar he made from the tree. He graciously gave her the pillar (Djed) and she returned with it to Kamit (Kmt, Egypt).

Upon her return to Kmt, Aset went to the papyrus swamps where she lay over Asar's dead body and fanned him with her wings, infusing him with new life. In this manner Aset revived Asar through her power of love and wisdom, and then they united once more. From their union was conceived a son, Heru (Heru), with the assistance of the gods Djehuti and Amon.

One evening, as Set was hunting in the papyrus swamps, he came upon Aset and Asar. In a rage of passion, he dismembered the body of Asar into several pieces and scattered the pieces throughout the land. In this way, it is Set, the brute force of our bodily impulses and desires that "dismembers" our higher intellect. Instead of oneness and unity, we see multiplicity and separateness which give rise to egoistic (selfish) and violent behavior. The Great Mother, Aset, once again set out to search, now for the pieces of Asar, with the help of Anpu and Nebethet.

After searching all over the world, they found all the pieces of Asar's body, except for his phallus which was eaten by a fish. In Eastern Hindu-Tantra mythology, the god Shiva, who is the equivalent of Asar, also lost his phallus in one story. In Egyptian and Hindu-Tantra mythology, this loss represents seminal retention in order to channel the sexual energy to the higher spiritual centers, thereby transforming it into spiritual energy. Aset, Anpu, and Nebethet re-membered the pieces, all except the phallus, which was eaten by a fish. Asar thus regained life in the realm of the dead.

Figure 9: Above center; The birth of Heru. Aset gives birth to Heru, assisted by Djehuti and Amun

Figure 10: Above left; Goddess Uadjit and the God Saa adoring the newborn Heru

Figure 11: Above right; Goddess Nekhebit and the God Hu adoring newborn Heru

Heru, therefore, was born from the union of the spirit of Asar and the life giving power of Aset (physical nature). Thus, Heru represents the union of spirit and matter, and the renewed life of Asar, his rebirth. When Heru became a young man, Asar returned from the realm of the dead and encouraged him to take up arms (vitality, wisdom, courage, strength of will) and establish truth, justice and righteousness in the world by challenging Set, its current ruler.

The Battle of Heru (Horus) and Set

The battle between Heru and Set took many twists, sometimes one seeming to get the upper hand and sometimes the other, yet neither one gaining a clear advantage in order to decisively win. At one point, Aset tried to help Heru by catching Set, but due to the pity and compassion she felt towards him, she set him free. In a passionate rage, Heru cut off her head and went off by himself in a frustrated state. Even Heru is susceptible to passion, which leads to performing deeds that one later regrets. Set found Heru and gouged out Heru's eyes. During this time, Heru was overpowered by the evil of Set. He became blinded to truth (as signified by the loss of his eyes) and thus, was unable to do battle (act with Maat) with Set. His power of sight was later restored by Hetheru (goddess of passionate love, desire and fierce power), who also represents the right Eye of Ra. She is the fire spitting, destructive power of light, which dispels the darkness (blindness) of ignorance.

When the conflict resumed, the two contendants went before the court of the Pasedjed (Ennead) gods and goddesses (Company of the nine gods and goddesses who ruled over creation, headed by Ra). Set, promising to end the fight and restore Heru to the throne, invited Heru to spend the night at his house, but Heru soon found out that Set had evil intentions when he tried to have intercourse with him. The uncontrolled Set also symbolizes unrestricted sexual activity. Therefore, all sexual desires should be pursued in accordance with moral and intellectual principles, which dictate rules of propriety that lead to health, and personal, societal and spiritual order (Maat). Juxtaposed against this aspect of Set (uncontrolled sexual potency and desire) is Heru in the form of ithyphallic (erect phallus) Min, who represents not only control of sexual desire, but its sublimation as well. Min symbolizes the power which comes from the sublimation of the sexual energy.

Through more treachery and deceit, Set attempted to destroy Heru with the help of the Ennead, by tricking them into believing that Heru was not worthy of the throne. Asar sent a letter pleading with the

71

Ennead to do what is correct. Heru, as the son of Asar, should be the rightful heir to the throne. All but two of them (the Ennead) agreed because Heru, they said, was too young to rule. Asar then sent them a second letter (scroll of papyrus with a message) reminding them that even they cannot escape judgment for their deeds; they will be judged in the end when they have to finally go to the West (abode of the dead).

This signifies that even the gods cannot escape judgment for their deeds. Since all that exists is only a manifestation of the absolute reality which goes beyond time and space, that which is in the realm of time and space (humans, spirits, gods, angels, neters) are all bound by its laws. Following the receipt of Asar's scroll (letter), Heru was crowned King of Egypt. Set accepted the decision and made peace with Heru. All the gods rejoiced. Thus ends the legend of Asar, Aset, and Heru. The Resurrection of Asar and his reincarnation in the form of Heru is a symbol for the resurrection which must occur in the life of every human being. In this manner, the story of the Asarian Trinity, of Asar, Aset and Heru and the Egyptian Ennead holds hidden teachings, which when understood and properly practiced, will lead to spiritual enlightenment.

Figure 12: Heru as King of Kamit (Egypt)

Chapter 3: The Principal Gods and Goddesses of the Prt M Hru

"When therefore, though hearest the myths of the Egyptians concerning the Gods - wanderings and dismemberings and many such passions, think none of these things spoken as they really are in state and action. For they do not call Hermes "Dog" as a proper name, but they associate the watching and waking from sleep of the animal who by Knowing and not Knowing determines friend from foe with the most Logos[31] like of the Gods."

–**Plutarch** (c. 46-120 AD)

INTRODUCTION

THE MAIN GODS AND GODDESSES OF ANCIENT EGYPT AND THE PERT EM HERU

Table 6: The Great Trinity of Ancient Egypt

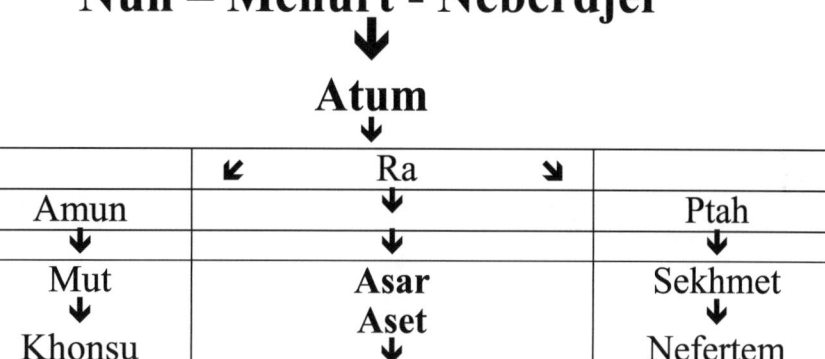

This table is provided to show the relationship between the main divinities of the *Prt m Hru* in the context of the overall scheme of Ancient Egyptian mythology. It should be noted that the hierarchy presented above should not be taken as an order of importance, but as an order of emergence in the prominence of the Divinity in the culture of Ancient Egyptian religious practice. There are four main Trinity systems which became prominent in Ancient Egypt. All the deities emerged at the same time, but their prominence as individually worshipped divinities occurred at different times in Ancient Egyptian history. *Amun-Ra-Ptah* is first. Arising out of each of these, a new Trinity of male (father), female (mother), and child emerges. Thus, we have: *Amun-Mut-Khonsu, Asar-Aset-Heru*, and *Ptah-Sekhmet-Nefertem*. Khonsu and Nefertem are aspects of Heru. The main Trinity system related to the *Prt m Hru* is based on Ra, *Asar-Aset* and *Heru*. When dealing with Wasetian Theology, the main Trinity system and mythology is related to *Amun-Mut-Khonsu*. When dealing with Hetkaptah Theology, the main Trinity system and mythology is related to *Ptah-Sekhmet-Nefertem*. Thus, it is clear that while each divinity system has a clearly defined mythology and mystery teaching related to it, they all are in effect related to each other in the broad context of an all encompassing set of complementary principles which together are more than the sum of their parts, i.e. when put together they transcend any polytheistic concept and produce a picture of universal wholeness. Indeed, they represent a harmonious family, whose members are all descended from the same ancestor. This is why the reader may notice that sometimes references are made to other divinities in related Trinities. Also, the divinities are presented in similar iconography, for example, Atum-Ra, Ra, Amun, and Asar have Divine Boats. They are used virtually interchangeably because their underlying origin and symbolism are so closely related. The differences

---

[31] Divine creative intelligence expressed through the divine speech and manifest in all objects in creation.

presented in the myths and the icons are for the purpose of introducing and elucidating varying aspects of the Divine, just like in a modern big business, the marketing department may have several executives highlighting and promoting different aspects of the same company. As they coordinate their work, they produce in the mind of the people, a view of the company, from different angles, creating a total view of the company. In a sense, the Sages of Ancient Egyptian mythology created a mythology with different names and forms to teach the masses about the glory and diversity of the Divine so as to show them the grandeur of the Spirit.

In this context, Atum-Ra is the Primordial Divine Principle which emanated from the Primeval Waters (Nun-Mehurt) to engender Creation. Thus, Ra is the Supreme Being, and Asar is his incarnation, an avatar (divine incarnation on earth), much like Jesus is an incarnation of God the Father in Christianity, and Krishna is an incarnation of the god Vishnu in Hinduism. Further, after he is killed by Set, he incarnates as his son, and through him he ultimately attains victory over the forces of chaos, ignorance and egoism. So, although all of the gods and goddesses are related, the story of Asar was the most powerful in terms of popular appeal. It is upon the teachings related to Asar that the entire teaching of the *Prt m Hru* is primarily based.

The religion of Ancient Egypt revolved around four major Trinities of gods and goddesses who emanated from the one Supreme Being. These Trinities had major centers of worship in ancient times. They were Amun (city of worship-Thebes or *Waset*), Ra (city of worship-*Anu* or the city of the sun), Ptah (city of worship-*Hetkaptah*) and Asar (city of worship-*Abdu*). Along with these divinities, their female counterparts and their sons also had centers of worship. For example, Aset, the companion of Asar and mother of Heru, had a worship center at the island of Philae. Heru had a worship center in the city of Kom Ombo. However, it must be clearly understood that all of these divinities were related. They emanated from Pa Neter or Neberdjer, the Supreme Being, and therefore, must all be considered as brothers and sisters.

The idea of classifying the neteru or gods and goddesses comes about as the Sages of ancient times sought to explain the manifestations of the Divine in nature as well as in human psychology. However, they should not be understood as divinities, but as cosmic forces and principals, their forms denoting the special qualities of those forces. The Ancient Egyptian word "neteru," which is loosely translated as "gods and goddesses" therefore actually means "cosmic forces engendering creation" – it is the etymological origin of the Latin word "natura," and Anglo words "nature" and "natural." The neteru (plural) emanate from Neter (singular-meaning "Supreme Being-Supreme essential power). Thus, the neteru have mythical references to nature and mystical references to human psychology which lead to greater understanding of the origins and destiny of human existence. We will begin our survey of the neteru with the primordial ocean, Nun.

This section of the book is designed as a brief introduction to the neteru for use with the Prt M Hru scripture which follows in Part II of this book.

THE NETERU, THEIR SYMBOLISM AND FUNCTIONS

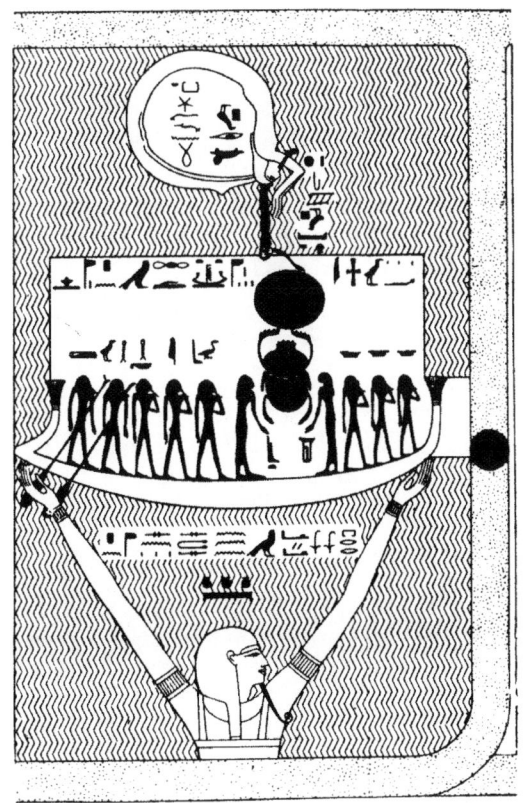

NU OR NUN

Figure 13: The Primeval Waters of Creation

In the particular scene above, taken from the sarcophagus of Seti I, the Primeval Waters of Creation, Nun, pushes the Boat of Atum-Ra, who emerges as Khepri (Scarab) onto the waves. Behind Khepri are the Divinities Geb (Earth), Shu (Space, Air, Ether), Heka (The Divine Creative Word), Hu (Divine sense of taste) and Saa (Divine Understanding). Assisting him are Aset and Nebethet. There are three divinities standing in the bow of the boat with the *aa*, ⬄, doorway symbol on their head. They symbolize the three worlds or planes of creation that are engendered and sustained by Khepri. In the text, it is said that Khepri is the Creator aspect of Asar. Thus, they are in reality one and the same. This interpretation is supported by the following vignette from the Papyrus of Ani, where the souls of Ra and Asar are shown meeting in the mystical city of Djeddu.

Khepri pushes the sundisk into the arms of Nut, who is standing on the head of Asar in order for her to receive it. She in turn passes it into the area encircled by the body of Asar himself, i.e. the Duat (Netherworld).

Since the texts which compose the exposition of the Kemetic teachings come from various tombs, papyruses and inscriptions, the depictions of the gods and goddesses are not always uniform. This is because the priests and priestesses were describing different aspects of the same teaching. For example, in the boat above there are ten divinities accompanying Khepri, a form of Ra, the Neter, as the Creator. In the boat below, there are ten divinities including Ra, i.e. nine neteru (gods and goddesses) and one Neter. The initiate looks on from the bow of the boat.

In Ancient Egyptian mystical philosophy, Creation is explained as an emanation which came from a primeval mass of undifferentiated matter called Nu or Nun. From this mass arose Atum-Ra in the form of Khepri, the Scarab on the Divine Boat. The boat below shows Ra and his main retinue which includes the king himself in the last position, symbolizing his divinity and the fact that he is righteously following the divine path.

Figure 14: The Boat of Ra

As Ra sails in his boat he establishes Maat (order) and sustains Creation. The figure below shows Ra in his boat with his daughter Maat sitting in the bow, breaking through the waters and thus making the way for him. Ra brought with him a Company of Gods and Goddesses, and through them (the neteru or cosmic forces of Creation, who are the primeval ocean itself), he manages Creation.

Figure 15: Ra in his boat with Maat at the bow.

NEBERTCHER

(Neberdjer): Amun-Ra-Ptah
(The Transcendental Self and the Sacred Trinity)

There are several Trinities in Ancient Egyptian mythology, each conveying a special message through the symbolic references and relationships of the symbols. The Trinity of Ra-Nut-Geb, representing the three basic principles of existence: Spirit (God-Supreme Being), Heaven and Earth, is possibly the oldest to be found in the Dynastic period of Ancient Egyptian history. As the evolution of the understanding of the Supreme Being progressed, its exposition through the medium of theology and mystical philosophy was refined. This refinement, which occurred over a period of 5,000 to 10,000 years, led to the teachings of the Asarian Trinity of Asar, Aset and Heru, and those of Nebertcher: Amun-Ra-Ptah.

NEBERDJER

Figure 16: Neberdjer, the All-encompassing Divinity

The Ancient Egyptian Trinity composed of Amun, Ra and Ptah was formally known as:

"Neberdjer: Everything is Amun-Ra-Ptah, three in one."

The following passage from the *Hymns of Amen* (*Amun*) sums up the Ancient Egyptian understanding of the Trinity concept in creation and that which transcends it.

33. He whose name is hidden is Amun, Ra belongeth to him as His face, and the body is Ptah.
34. Their cities are established on earth forever, Waset, Anu, Hetkaptah.

The gods of the Egyptian Trinity of Amun-Ra-Ptah, arise from the nameless Supreme Being known as Nebertcher or Neter Neteru. Therefore, the Trinity is in reality describing one Divinity which expresses in three aspects. Thus, in the Egyptian system of gods and goddesses, we have Amit-Rai-Sekmet as consorts to Amun-Ra-Ptah, representing their dynamic power of manifestation.

In the creation story involving the Asarian Mysteries, Asar assumes the role of Khepera and Tem, while at the same time giving insight into the nature of Neberdjer:

"Neb-er-djer saith, I am the creator of what hath come into being, and I myself came into being under the form of the god Khepera, and I came into being in primeval time. I had union with my hand,

and I embraced my shadow in a love embrace; I poured seed into my own mouth, and I sent forth from myself issue in the form of the gods Shu and Tefnut." "I came into being in the form of Khepera, and I was the creator of what came into being, I formed myself out of the primeval matter, and I formed myself in the primeval matter. My name is Asar.

Neb-er-tcher (Neberdjer)

Neberdjer Speaks:

I was alone, for the gods and goddesses were not yet born, and I had emitted from myself neither Shu nor Tefnut. I brought into my own mouth, *hekau* (the divine words of power), and I forthwith came into being under the form of things which were created under the form of Khepera."

These passages all point to the fact that while the name of the Supreme Being has changed under the different priesthoods, these are merely different expressions of the same principles and teachings which even use the same wording, therefore, there is no discontinuity or confusion within the theology. More importantly, the last passage reminds us that all of the names and forms are merely outward expressions of the Supreme Being, *Neb-erd-jer,* in its physical manifestation. Nebertcher, as previously discussed, is a name which signifies the all-encompassing meaning of the collective members of the Trinity. Nebertcher includes all male and female aspects of the Trinity, and is therefore to be understood as the androgynous and primordial being from which arose all names and forms, all gods and goddesses, all creation and all opposites in Creation (male and female, hot-cold, etc.)

THE MYSTERIES OF ANU

Atum (Tem)

The sun and the moon were incorporated into the Ancient Egyptian worship from the most ancient times. The moon was symbolically associated with Asar, Aset and Djehuti, while the sun was symbolically associated with Ra, Ptah and Amun. According to the ancient creation story, the Supreme Being took the form of the sun god and arose out of the Primeval Ocean. According to one version, Ra arose in His boat along with the Ennead of gods and goddesses. According to another story, the Supreme Being arose in the form of a primeval hill or piece of solid land in the form of Atum, Tum or Tem. Thus, the Supreme Being who manifests as the rising sun out of the Primeval Ocean is known by various names. These are: Atum, Tum or Tem, Ra-Tem, Atum-Ra or Asar and Ptah. Atum is also one of the first god symbols to be depicted in human form. The priesthood of Anu developed an elaborate cosmology incorporating the concept of Tem into the creation myth, thereby merging human existence with the Divine. First we will review an outline of the theology of Anu, and then we will examine the mystical implications for human psycho-spirituality.

The *Pyramid Texts* of *Pepi II* determines the Company of Gods and Goddesses of Anu to be: Tem, Shu, Tefnut, Geb, Nut, Asar, Aset, Set and Nebethet. In the *Pyramid Texts* of *Pepi II,* the following account is given about the emergence of Atum (or Tem, Tum):

> He who was born in the Nu (primeval waters),
> before the sky came into being,
> before the earth came into being,
> before the two supports* came into being,
> before the quarrel** took place,
> before that fear which arose on account of the Eye of Heru existed...
> *(Shu-Tefnut)
> **(quarrel between Heru and Set)

Figure 17: The Forms of Ra

From left to right: Two forms of Kheperi: Morning Sun (Creator), Ra: Noon Sun (Sustainer of the Day), Tem: Sunset (dissolver of the Day)

The idea of the Primeval Ocean (Nu) and the original primeval spirit which engendered life in it occurs in several myths. The earliest occurrence of the idea of the primeval waters is found in the Egyptian religion which predates the Asarian Resurrection Myth. This pre-dynastic (10,000-5,500 B.C.E.), pre-Asarian, myth spoke of a God who was unborn and undying, and who was the origin of all things. This deity was un-namable, unfathomable, transcendental, gender-less and without form, although encompassing all forms. This being was the God of Light which illumines all things, and thus was later associated with the sun, the forms of *Ra* or *Tem,* and with *Heru* who represents *that which is up there,* i.e., the Divine. Tum, Tem or Temu is an Ancient Egyptian name for the deep and boundless abyss of consciousness from which the phenomenal universe was born. *Khepera (or Khepri),* the dung beetle, represents the morning sun which is becoming. This form is also associated with the young Heru, *Heru in the Horizon,* also known as *The Sphinx.* Ra ☉ represents the daytime sun which sustains Creation. Tum comes from the root *tem* ⌂⊱⌐♭⊑⌐ "to be complete," "fullness" or *temem* ⌂⊱⊐⋀⌐, which means "to make an end of." Also Tum is regarded as the evening or setting sun in the western sky, symbolizing the completion, the end of the journey. This is why the initiate wishes to go to the *beautiful west* upon completion of the span of life. The beautiful west is the abode of Asar. Tum was analogous in nature to the Babylonian *Tiamat,* the Chaldean *Thamte,* the Hebrew *Tehorn,* and the Greek *Themis.*

 Sundisk (Symbol of Ra)

The story related in the Papyrus of Nesi-Amsu is that the primeval God laid an egg in the primeval chaotic waters from which the God {him/her}self emerged. While this primordial God, who emerged out of the waters, created or emanated Ra, the Sun or Life Force, Djehuti, the word or creative medium, and Maat, the principle of cosmic order and regularity, the underlying emphasis was on all of these, as well as human beings and the phenomenal world, being essentially emanations from that same Primeval Ocean. Other stories tell of how the creator masturbated and engendered life through and within *Himself.* The papyrus of Nesi-Amsu further discusses the emergence:

> "When Atum emerged from Nun, the primordial waters, before the sky and earth were born and before the creation of worm or reptile, he found no place to stand..."

Tum, therefore represents the first emerging thought which contemplated its own existence in the vast ocean of undifferentiated consciousness which was devoid of names and forms, devoid of tangibleness, solidification, coagulation and grossness.[32] All that existed was subtle matter, the Primeval Ocean. The *Pyramid Texts* continue, explaining how Atum continued the process of creation by emitting the other principles of creation in the form of the gods and goddesses as follows.

> "Tum (Atum) is he who came into being (through Himself) in Anu. He took His phallus in His grasp that he might create joy in Himself, emitting the twins Shu (air, dryness, space, ether) and Tefnut (moisture)..."

Figure 18: Tem in the Solar Boat wearing the double crown, sitting within the sundisk.

In this manner, the various qualities of matter emanated from Tum and gave form to the Primeval

---

[32] Capable of being touched; material; something palpable or concrete.

Ocean, and continue to give and sustain its form at every moment. Geb is the son of Shu and Tefnut and represents the solid earth. Nut is the daughter of Shu and Tefnut and represents the sky and the heavens, and is the mother of Asar, Aset, Set and Nebethet.

In a creation story involving Khepera (Ra in the aspect of the rising sun, the creation of a new day), he says he rose up from Nu and:

> "I found no place there whereon I could stand. I worked a charm upon my heart, I laid a foundation in Maa*, and then I made every form. I was one by myself, {since} I had not yet emitted from myself the god Shu, and I had not spit out from myself the goddess Tefnut; there was no other being who worked with me." (*referring to Maat-truth, righteousness)

Tm, (Tem, Tum, Atum, Atum-Ra), therefore, is the ultimate source and cause of Creation. From Tm arises Khepri who transforms into Ra and finally, Ra reverts back to the original essence, Tm.

RA AND THE TRINITY OF ANU

In the myth of Ra and Aset, Ra says: "I am Kheperi in the morning, and Ra at noonday, and Temu in the evening." Thus we have *Kheper-Ra-Tem,* ☉◯⚊⚘⁊, as the Anunian Triad and hekau. In Chapter 4 of the *Prt m Hru,* the initiate identifies {him/her}self with Tem, symbolizing that {his/her} life as a human being with human consciousness is coming to an end. Instead of an awareness of individuality and human limitation, there is now a new awareness of infinity and immortality, even though the physical body continues to exist and will die in the normal course of time. The initiate will live on as a "living" soul and join with Tem (individual consciousness joins Cosmic Consciousness):

> "I am Tem in rising; I am the only One; I came into being with Nu. I am Ra who rose in the beginning."

This passage is very important because it establishes the mystical transcendence of the initiate who has realized {his/her} "oneness" and union with the Divine. In other papyri, Tem is also identified with the young Harmachis (young Heru,

the solar child) as the early morning sun. Thus, Kheperi-Ra-Temu are forms of the same being and are the object of every initiate's spiritual goal. Being the oldest of the three theologies, the Mysteries of Anu formed a foundation for the unfoldment of the teachings of mystical spirituality which followed in the mysteries of Hetkaptah, through Ptah, and the Mysteries of Thebes, through Amun. With each succeeding exposition, the teaching becomes more and more refined until it reaches its quintessence in the Hymns of Amun.

THE COMPANY OF GODS AND GODDESSES OF ANU

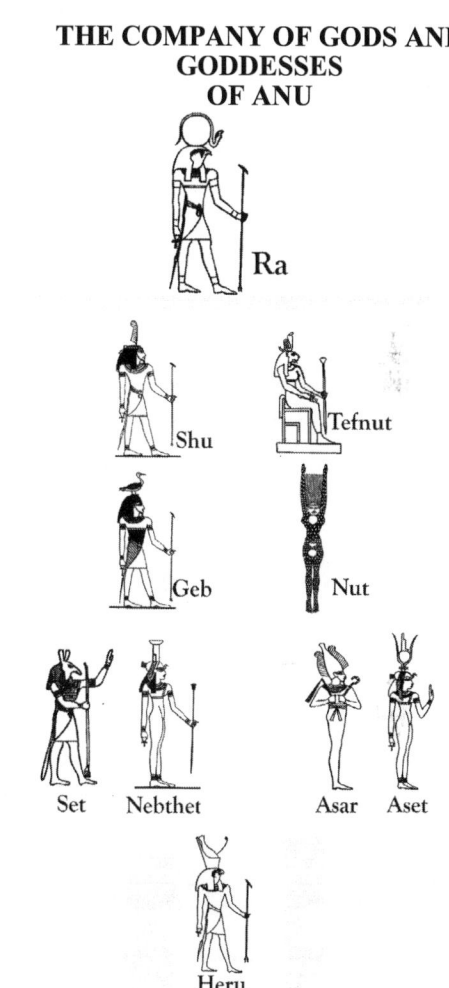

Figure 19: The Company of Gods and Goddesses of Anu

The characters of the Myth of Creation and their various forms of interaction with each other are in reality an elaborate mystic code relating to understanding what Creation and God are, as well as the nature of human consciousness. The first thing that is noticed when the deities of the Ancient Egyptian Creation, based on the teachings of Anu, are placed in a hierarchical fashion based on their order of Creation by Ra, is that they arise in accordance with their level of density. Density here refers to their order of subtlety of the elements in Creation. Ra is the first principle which emerges out of the Primeval Waters. He is the subtle, singular principle of Creation, the focus of oneness in time and space. The ocean itself transcends time and space and is beyond existence and non-existence. Ra is the first principle to emerge out of the Absolute and his emergence signifies the beginning of existence.

The second important idea derived from the Pauti (Company of Gods and Goddesses) is that they represent a whole number, 10 (Ra plus the nine gods and goddesses), and thus convey the idea of a special symmetry. The iconography has been likened to that of a tree and indeed, comparisons have been made to the Kabalistic Tree of Life as the study of the Kemetic gods and goddesses reveals a subtlety of wisdom which leads to the discovery of the Divine Self, as symbolized by Ra. This Kemetic tree, like the tree mentioned in the Hindu Bhagavad Gita, has its roots above, in the heavens with the Supreme Being, and its branches below, in the phenomenal universe with the gods and goddesses.[33] The highest level, Ra, is juxtaposed against the lowest level of the Pauti with the image of Heru. So at one end we see the perfect singularity of the Supreme Self and at the other we see the perfect combination of Spirit and Matter in the form of Heru. Ra is perfection in the Transcendental Realm, Asar is perfection in the Astral Realm and Heru is perfection in the Physical Realm. While the figure above may be understood as a reference to a "higher" and a "lower" idea, in reality the figure is not to be understood as a teaching of something that is above or better and something that is below or lesser. It is a teaching which expresses the essence of Creation, containing subtle as well as grosser objects which all emanate from the same source. The Ancient Egyptian teaching states: That which is above is the same as that which is below. If the "Above and Below" teaching is to be applied, it should be understood as referring to the idea that everything in Creation is a reflection of the spiritual essence which transcends physicality. The physical universe is an emanation from the spiritual essence and as such, is sustained by it. The very matter

which constitutes Creation is in reality spirit in a condensed form, just as when a person falls asleep their dream world is condensed out of their own consciousness. Nun is the underlying primordial consciousness of Creation. Ra may be seen as the Soul of Creation and Djehuti may be seen as the Cosmic Mind of Creation, Hethor may be seen as the Vital Life Force of Creation and Maat may be seen as the underlying order of Creation. Djehuti, Hetheru and Maat are the underlying principles which sustain the Pauti.

The figure above displays the Pauti of Creation along with the underlying principles which sustain them, as these are inherent in the attributes of the gods and goddesses themselves. As explained earlier, the Pauti refers to Creation itself. The deities of the Pauti are nine in number and include Shu, Tefnut, Geb, Nut, Asar, Aset, Set, Nebethet and Heru. Maati, Hethor and Djehuti are not part of the Pauti itself. They are subtle principles which support its existence. While Heru is a product of the union of Soul (Asar) and Intuitional Wisdom (Aset). Anpu (Anubis) is a production of Soul and mortal life. He also is not part of the Pautti. So he is a new principle emanating from Creation itself, representing the mental faculty of discernment.

TEFNUT

Figure 20: Tefnut

In the creation story involving the Asarian Mysteries, Asar assumes the role of Khepera and Tem while at the same time giving insight into the nature of Neberdjer:

"Neb-er-djer saith, I am the creator of what hath come into being, and I myself came into being under the form of the god Khepera, and I came into being in primeval time. I had union with

---

[33] Bhagavad Gita: Chapter 15 Purushottam Yogah--The Yoga of the Supreme Spirit – Verses 1-3

my hand, and I embraced my shadow in a love embrace; I poured seed into my own mouth, and I sent forth from myself issue in the form of the gods Shu and Tefnut."

In the form of Tefnut, the goddess is the consort of Shu and she represents the life force that is contained in air. She also symbolizes moisture and every form of watery substance as well as the power of water. In these capacities she is directly related to Sekhmet and Bast, as the feline aspect of the goddess is a linking technique used throughout Kemetic mythology.

SHU

Figure 21: The Forms of Shu

Shu is the first born son of Ra as he emerged in the Boat of Millions of Years, from the Primeval Ocean. He represents air, space or ether. Ra commanded that he separate Geb and Nut, who were in a sexual embrace. Since then, he sustains Nut, the sky, and separates her from Geb, the earth, so that Creation may continue to exist, for human interactions cannot occur without space and air. Shu is as well, the king of the gods and goddesses, able to lead aspirants to the Divine.

Shu and Tefnut are also known as the Akeru (leonine) divinities. That is, they are the lion and lioness who guard the Akhet (horizon) which is entrance to the Netherworld, i.e. they are the boundary between the Netherworld and the Physical World, depending on which perspective is used. The lions are symbolic of the mountains flanking the valley through which the dead and the sun must pass.

Figure 22: Akhet, the horizon, with the sundisk.

From the point of view of creation, they are the first physical entities created by Ra and are thus the passageway of the spirit into the realm or plane of matter, time and space. This is why they are associated with the Akeru, who represent yesterday and tomorrow, i.e. the principle of duality.

Plate 7: Akeru, the lion gods of Yesterday and Tomorrow

The sun traverses between the Akeru, i.e. the past and the future. Therefore, always remaining in the eternal present. This is deeper mystical teaching for every spiritual aspirant to understand, how not to get caught up in the pettiness of life and the tension, and anxiety over what happened in the past and the tension, and anxiety over what is desired in the future. In *Pyramid Texts* 796, 1014 and 1713 it is stated of the righteous soul: *the gates of Aker are opened for you.* The eternal present is the pathway between the physical plane and the astral plane. The past and the future do not exist. Only eternity is real.

GEB AND NUT

Figure 23: Geb and Nut

Geb and Nut are the earth and the sky (heavens). They are the children of Shu and Tefnut, and they are also the physical universe in which human interaction takes place. After their father, Shu, separated them, Nut who was pregnant, gave birth to Asar, Aset, Set, Nebethet and Heru Ur. It is from these neteru that all other neteru and human beings are descended. Geb is considered as the king of the earth, as well as a beneficial force on behalf of all spiritual aspirants. Nut is the mother goddess, and she lifts up all righteous aspirants into heaven, to take their place on her body as a shining spirit (star). One version of the Creation story tells how Ra traverses over Nut's back in his boat (sundisk), and every evening she consumes him and every morning she gives birth to him as the morning sun.

AMUN

Amun, the Self, is the "hidden" essence of all things. The Sun (Ra) is the radiant and dynamic outward appearance of the hidden made manifest and also the light of Cosmic Consciousness, the cosmic mind or that through which consciousness projects. In this aspect, Ptah represents the physical world, the solidification or coagulation of the projection of consciousness (Amun) made manifest. These manifestations are reproduced symbolically on earth in the cities of *KMT* (Egypt), *Anu* (city of Ra), *Waset* (city of Amun), and *Hetkaptah* (city of Ptah). Waset (Weset) or Newt was known to the Greeks as Thebes, who knew it also as *Diospolis* (heavenly city). Thebes is the city identified in the Old Testament as *No* (city), *No-Amon* (city of Amon).

Figure 24: Amun as the Ram headed man and a man with double plumed crown.

(The Symbols of Amun)

In the form of Amun-Ra, the evolution of the concept of the Divine takes on an emphasis of the subtle and hidden qualities of divine consciousness. This teaching found its greatest expression in the city of Waset, called Thebes by the ancient Greeks. As a ram headed man, the iconography emphasizes the qualities of the ram (virility, leadership and the astrological period of the ram as it relates to the Great Ancient Egyptian Year). The human headed form emphasizes all-encompassing, non-dual divinity as symbolized by the double plumes (Aset and Nebethet) uniting in one being.

The concept of Amun is the central theme of not only Ancient Egyptian religion and mystical philosophy, but also of every world religion and of modern physics as well. The idea of Amun has been mythologized by Sages in such a fashion that the study of myths reveals increasingly more profound layers of the mystery of life. The outer layers are shed through intuitive understanding of the philosophical ideas and teachings revealing the core wherein lies the discovery of the true essence of mystical religious philosophies.

The name *Amun* appears in the remotest times of Egyptian history and came to prominence in the ancient city of Waset, Egypt. The mysteries of Amun represent a quintessence of Ancient Egyptian philosophy concerning the nature of the un-manifest aspect of all existence and the understanding of human consciousness. This teaching speaks of God as an un-manifest, nameless, formless, *Being of Light* which is the source of all that is manifest. The formless *Being of Light* later became known as the *Watery Abyss* and Amun. In the Shabaka Inscription, this teaching was espoused with *Ptah* assuming the role of the manifestation of the un-manifest Self, and from him emanate the neteru in the form of an Ogdoad (eight) of neteru.

PTAH

Ptah is the third member of the great Ancient Egyptian Trinity. He figures prominently in the *Prt m Hru* in Chapter 11 of Opening the Mouth (expanding the Mind) ceremony. The name of Ptah is written in hieroglyphic as a human form supporting heaven and earth. The name *Ptah* is composed of the following parts:

Ptah Nunu (left) and Ptah Tanen (right).

The third member of the Trinity, Ptah, as the Creator emerging from the primeval waters, Nun, and as the primeval hill, Atum (Tanen).

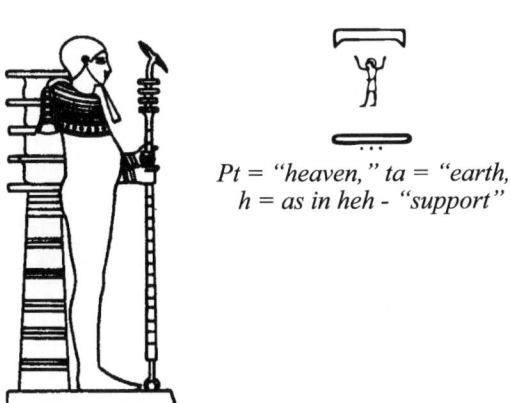

Pt = "heaven," ta = "earth," h = as in heh - "support"

"Ptah conceived in His heart (reasoning consciousness) all that would exist and at His utterance (the word - will, power to make manifest), created Nun, the primeval waters (unformed matter-energy).

Then, not having a place to sit Ptah causes Nun to emerge from the primeval waters as the Primeval Hill so that he may have a place to sit. Atom (Atum) then emerges and sits upon Ptah. Then came out of the waters four pairs of gods, the Ogdoad

Ptah is known as the *Overlord of the two lands,* referring to Lower Egypt and Upper Egypt, also material existence (manifest) and spiritual (un-manifest). *Htp* (Supreme Peace) is also the name of *Ptah (Pth)* if written backwards. He is also known as *Hetepi*. Thus, Ptah (Neter, God, Heru) is the support of heaven and earth and the supreme abode of peace which transcends the realm of time and space and the pairs of opposites. In this aspect, Ptah is associated with *Shu,* the God of air and breath, who is therefore, the sustainer of heaven and earth or the soul and the body.

Mut

The goddess Mut is the counterpart of Amun. She is nature itself, and she exemplifies its capacity to recycle. Her main symbol is the vulture. Just as vultures eat carrion and turn it into life, so too the goddess takes in death, and brings forth new life for the spiritual aspirant.

Figure 25: Important Forms of Ptah

Figure 26: Mut as the vulture goddess and consort of Amun.

THE GREAT TRINITY: AMUN-RA-PTAH

Figure 27: The Great Trinity: Amun-Ra-Ptah

Creation manifests as three aspects. This teaching is expressed in the Ancient Egyptian statement: "I was One and then I became Three,"

and "Nebertcher: Everything is Amun-Ra-Ptah, three in one." Nebertcher (Supreme Being, a name of Asar) manifests as Amun-Ra-Ptah. In this teaching, Amun represents the witnessing consciousness, Ra represents the mind and senses, and Ptah represents matter and all physical manifestation. Therefore, the Trinity owes its existence to the one. The realization of the

underlying unity, the oneness behind the multiplicity of the Trinity, gives profound insight into the true nature of the Divine and the way to discover the Supreme Self. When you begin to understand that the underlying basis behind Creation, meaning your consciousness or identity, your senses and mind, your perceptions of the physical universe, is in reality the One Supreme Spirit, you begin to turn away from the world of ordinary human existence, to discover the Self within, and to *Know Thyself.* [34]

The God/Goddess Hapi

Figure 28: Hapi

The divinity Hapi represents the androgynous Life Force which sustains all life and manifests as the Nile River. In ancient times as well as modern times life and prosperity, feast or famine in North East Africa is dependent on the existence of the Nile. The iconography of Hapi is the mans body with large female breasts. These symbolize not only the burgeoning sustenance of mother Tefnut, who symbolizes the power of water, but also there is a teaching whereby Hapi sustains and unifies the duality (symbolized by two streams and two breasts) of life in the form of Upper and Lower Egypt. Metaphysically speaking, Hapi sustains the body as ell as the spirit which inhabits it and make civilization possible.

---

[34] For more details on the teachings of the Ancient Egyptian Trinities see the book *Egyptian Yoga Vol. 2* by Dr. Muata Ashby

ASAR-ASET-HERU

Figure 29: Asar-Aset-Heru

Figure 30: Asar

From a mystical standpoint, the Trinity of Asar-Aset-Heru represents the movement of the Spirit as it manifests in Creation. As we have seen through the story as well as the iconography associated with them, in reality it refers to the deeper principles of human, as well as super-human, existence. Asar becomes the silent Spirit who is the source and support of Creation in his names Asar-Dua, meaning Asar, the Begetter (in the Duat), and Asar-Neb-Heh[35], meaning Asar, Lord of Eternity. Aset is Creation itself. Heru is the dynamic manifestation of the Spirit (of Asar) which moves in and interacts with Creation (Aset). Thus, Asar expresses as Creation (in the form of Aset) as well as the dynamic forces (in the form of Heru) within it. This teaching is also expressed in the idea of the Trinity concept and the birth of God into human form (Avatarism).

Asar and Seker

Asar is also an Avatar, a divine incarnation into time and space, the incarnation of the Higher Self, the Soul, into the realm of time and space.

In the Creation myth, Asar is the son of Geb and Nut, who are in turn the offspring of Shu and Tefnut, who are themselves children of Ra. In another Creation myth of Asar, it is said that Asar uttered his own name, *"Asar!!,"* and thereby brought the world and all life within it into existence. This is the process of Divine incarnation whereby the Supreme Being becomes the universe. Asar, *Lord of the Perfect Black,* is the personification of the blackness of the vast un-manifest regions of existence. Asar is the essence of all things, and the very soul of every human being as the Higher Self, who, through ignorance, has become involved in the world, has been slain by its own ego (represented by the god Set), and struggles to regain its original state of perfection. Asar also symbolizes the fragmented ocean of consciousness which has been cut into pieces by the lower self. No longer is there the vast all-encompassing, all-knowing, all-seeing consciousness. The Divine has become limited in association with the human mind, body and senses, due to the desire to experience human feelings and egoistic sentiments. Instead of looking at the universe through the cosmic mind, the Divine now expresses {him/her}self through billions of life forms whose bodies, minds and senses are too limited to see the vastness of Creation.

---

[35] The term "heh" meaning eternity, relates to the divinity Ptah as the last letter-symbol in his name Pet-Ta-Heh, symbolizes "heh" eternity and sustainer of Creation.

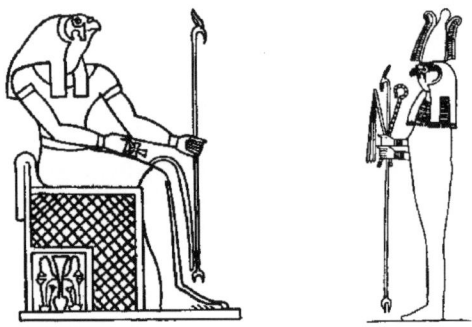

Figure 31: Asar Seker- King in the Netherworld

Seker is Asar's title when he is resurrected and he takes his place in the Netherworld as the king. In this aspect he presides over the judgment of the heart of the aspirant.

The union with Aset symbolizes the achievement or striving for spiritual salvation or resurrection while the union with Nebethet symbolizes bondage, suffering and the cycles of birth and death, known as reincarnation.

Aset

Figure 32: Aset, Mistress of Wisdom and Words of Power, Love, Cosmic Consciousness and Intuitional Wisdom.

In the temple of Denderah, it is inscribed that Nut gave birth to Aset there, and that upon her birth, Nut exclaimed: *"As"* (behold), *"I have become thy mother."* This was the origin of the name Ast, Aset, later known to the Greeks and others. It further states that *"she was a dark-skinned child and was called Khnemet-ankhet"* or the living lady of love. Thus, Aset also symbolizes the "blackness" of the vast un-manifest regions of existence, Asar. In this capacity she is also the ultimate expression of the African ideal prototype of the Christian Madonna, especially in statues where she is depicted holding the baby Heru in the same manner as Mother Mary later held baby Jesus. Her identification is also symbolized in her aspect as *Amentet,*[36] the Duat, itself. Therefore, Amentet (Aset) and the soul of Amentet (Asar) are in reality one and the same. In her aspect as Amentet, Aset represents the subtle substance of nature, the astral plane.

The devotional love of Aset was instrumental in discovering and putting the pieces of Asar's dead body back together. The two most important features which Aset encompasses are love and intuitional wisdom. Aset's undying love and devotion to Asar transcended her loss of him twice. Her love also caused the resurrection of her son, Heru, as well. This divine devotion led her to discover the pieces of Asar's dead body. This is the devotion of the initiate which leads him or her to the Divine. All that is needed to attain spiritual enlightenment is a deep, ardent love for the Divine.

In her name, *Rekhat,* Aset also represents *rekhit* or wisdom. She is the patroness of all *rekht* or Sages. Aset represents the kind of wisdom which transcends all intellectual knowledge. She is at the same time, Creation, and Amentet, the ultimate reality of that Creation. Thus, it is said that she veils herself and that "no mortal man has unveiled her." The wisdom of Creation or knowing Aset in her full essence means becoming one with her in consciousness. When this unity occurs, one transcends ordinary human consciousness, so in this sense, no worldly human can discover her. The wisdom of Aset refers to that profound understanding of the essence of the Divine which is devoid of any kind of ignorance in reference to the Transcendental Self. This wisdom is the intuitional realization, which comes from pondering the nature of the Divine. Pondering implies repeated reflection and meditation on the Divine, trying, with sincerity and humility, to understand and become one with the Divine.

---

[36] This aspect of the goddess will be discussed later.

Figure 33: The Goddess Aset, Suckling baby Heru

Aset is also a healer. She healed the body of Asar even after it had been dismembered into several pieces. As a goddess she assists all those who pray to her, bestowing health and well being. She manifests in the form of love, motherhood, valor, devotion to God and intuitional realization of the Higher Self, Enlightenment.

Asar and Aset were worshipped throughout the ancient world. In the first century B.C. E. Aset was one of the most popular goddesses in the city of Rome. Her temples were filled with altars, statues, laves, obelisks, etc., brought from Egypt, and orders of priestesses were endowed to perform the "Mysteries of Aset" and other Egyptian miracle plays in the great temples of the Eternal City. From Rome, the cult of Aset spread to Spain, Portugal, Gey, Gaul, Switzerland, and by way of Marseilles, to North Africa. In a manner similar to which Aset was identified with many other goddesses in Egypt and Nubia, in foreign lands she was given the attributes of other goddesses such as Selene, Demeter, or Ceres, Aphrodite, Juno, Nemesis, Fortuna, Panthea, etc.[37]

The Name "Asar" and the name "Aset"

Asar

The goddess, who symbolizes creation itself, the physical universe, supports the incarnation of the soul (Asar). In this way, the physical (Aset) supports the spirit (Asar). This symbol of the goddess herself is the throne, and this is why the throne seat, 𓊨, is where Asar is shown seated. The name Asar is spelled with the throne symbol, the eye symbol, 𓁹. And the male determinative, 𓀭. The eye symbol written in this manner means "to make," "create," "to do" or "engender." Therefore, the mystical symbolism of the name Asar is the essence, which procreates or comes into existence through Aset.

Aset

The symbols of the name of Aset are the throne seat, 𓊨 "as", the phonetic sign for "t", ◠, the determinative egg, 𓆇, symbol of motherhood, and the female determinative, 𓁦.

This manner of reading of the name of Asar is supported by the myth of Asar and Aset as well as their epithets and their iconographies. The name Asar is intimately related to the name Aset. Asar and Aset are often referred to as "brother" and "sister." This relates to the idea that they come from the same parent, i.e. the same spiritual source. In ancient times men and women who married were also referred to as brother and sister. This had no relation to their parentage. Rather, this epithet relates to the mystical origins of all human beings. Essentially, we are all brothers and sisters. As our true nature is not man and woman but soul, and our parent, the Universal Spirit.

Through the myth of the Asarian Resurrection, we learn that Asar and Aset are Avatars, divine incarnations, sent to earth to lead souls, incarnating as human beings, towards righteousness, prosperity and spiritual enlightenment. In a higher sense, Asar represents the soul of every human being which comes to earth and must struggle to overcome the lower nature, who is symbolized by Set.

---

[37] For more on the teachings of the Temple of Aset- the Yoga of Wisdom, see the book *The Wisdom of* Aset by Dr. Muata Ashby.

NEBETHET

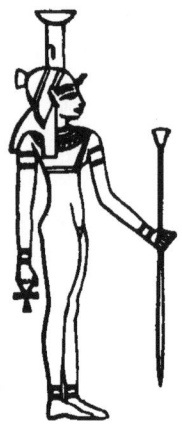

Figure 34: Nebethet "Mistress of the House"

Nature, Worldly Consciousness and Death.

Nebethet is the sister of Asar and Aset. She represents the gross aspect of nature and the natural phase of life called death. Nature is what the Spirit impregnates with its life giving essence. Therefore, nature (Nebethet) is the recipient of Asar's seed (spirit). According to natural law, anything that is born must be subject to the laws of nature and ultimately die. In his original form, detached from nature, Asar was timeless, immortal, and untouched by the passions and frailties of human nature. As an incarnation of the Divine, Asar becomes intoxicated with nature, his own Creation, and becomes associated with it through intercourse with Nebethet. In the myth of the Asarian Resurrection, the sexual union between Nebethet and Asar produced the deity Anpu.

Asar, as a symbol of the human soul, is a stark example of the fate of human existence. His situation embodies the predicament of every individual human being. This is why the Ancient Egyptian Pharaohs and all initiates into the mystery of Asar are referred to as Asar and Heru, and are considered to be the daughter or son of Aset. Every human being assumes the role of Heru, the champion, and once the battle of life is won and the body ceases to function, the initiate now becomes of Asar. Just as Asar became intoxicated with his own Creation, so too the human soul becomes involved with nature and thereby produces an astral body composed of subtle elements, and a physical body composed of an aggregate of gross physical elements (water, earth, fire, air), which exist within Shu (ether-space). In this capacity, Nebethet represents the lower nature

of matter or the binding, fettering and condensing aspect, which dulls the intellect and intoxicates the mind and senses.

There is deep mystical symbolism in the images and teachings surrounding the Triad or Asar, Aset and Nebethet. In the temples of *Denderah, Edfu* and *Philae,* there are sculptured representations of the Mysteries of Asar. These show *The Asar* (initiate) lying on a bier (ritual bed), and Aset and Nebethet, who stand nearby, being referred to as the "two widows" of the dead Asar. Aset and Nebethet are depicted as looking exactly alike, the only difference being in their head dresses: Aset ⌡, Nebethet ⍰ or ⌂. However, the symbols of these goddesses are in reality just inverted images of each other. The symbol of Nebethet is the symbol of Aset when inverted ⌡➔⌂. Aset also means throne or abode. Nebethet means all-encompassing physical domain. Therefore, each is a reflection of the other. So Aset symbolizes the subtle spiritual essence of existence while Nebethet symbolizes the material substance of existence, two aspects of the same reality. Thus, it can be said that both life and death are aspects of the same principle.

The bodies and facial features of Aset and Nebethet are exactly alike. This likeness which Aset and Nebethet share is important when they are related to Asar. As Asar sits on the throne, he is supported by the two goddesses, Aset and Nebethet. Symbolically, Asar represents the Supreme Soul, the all-encompassing Divinity which transcends time and space. Aset represents wisdom and enlightened higher consciousness. She is the knower of all words of power and has the power to resurrect Asar and Heru. Nebethet represents temporal consciousness or awareness of time and space. She is related to mortal (worldly-physical existence) life and mortal death. This symbolism is evident in the sistrums which bear the likeness of Aset on one side and of Nebethet on the other, and the writings of Plutarch where he says that Aset represents "generation" while Nebethet represents "chaos and dissolution." Also, in the hieroglyphic texts, Aset is referred to as the "day" and Nebethet as the "night." Aset represents the things that "are" and Nebethet represents the things which will "come into being and then die." Thus, the state of spiritual enlightenment is being referred to here as Aset, and it is this enlightened state of mind which the initiate in the Asarian Mysteries (*Asar Shetaiu*) has as the goal. The Enlightenment of Asar is the ideal state of consciousness in which one is aware of the transient aspects of Creation (Nebethet) as well as the transcendental (Aset). Aset represents the transcendental aspect of matter, that is, matter when seen through the eyes of wisdom rather than through the illusions produced by the ego. So, an enlightened personality is endowed with dual consciousness. To become one with Asar means to attain the consciousness of Asar, to become aware of the transcendental, infinite and immortal nature (Aset) while also being aware of the temporal and fleeting human nature (Nebethet).

SET

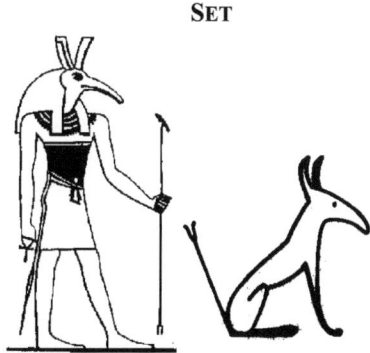

Figure 35: Set and the Set animal

Set represents the unbridled lower self of all human beings. His impulsiveness and reckless passionate pursuits are the ever present enemy of the aspirant or anyone else who is striving for control over the urges of the mind, body and senses. The lower self is represented by the desires of the mind which lure the soul into the varied situations of pain and pleasure in the world of time and space (the relative existence). These desires lead to a degraded mental capacity which manifests in the forms of selfishness, greed, hatred, anger, lust and other human failings. These faults or mental complexes are termed *fetters*. The fetters of the mind prevent the soul from discovering peace, harmony and oneness with the universe. Out of greed and jealousy, Set killed Asar. He represents the ego consciousness in a human being which kills the higher expression of the soul. If the ego is mastered, it can be a great servant to the Divine Self. This is symbolized by Set protecting the Boat of Ra from the demon serpent of chaos depicted in the following figure from Ancient Egyptian Mythology.

Figure 36: Set protecting the boat of Ra

HERU

Figure 37: Heru, Son of Aset and Asar

Heru represents the rebirth of the spiritual life - aspiration for freedom, the new life of the resurrected soul, the union between spirit (Asar) and creation (Aset). However, unlike Anpu (Anubis), who also represents the union of Spirit and Matter, Heru represents the higher aspect of this union because Aset is the embodiment of wisdom and truth while Nebethet is the embodiment of nature and the grosser physical elements. In this aspect Heru represents the subtle spiritual realization of spirit and matter united and seen as one.

89

BEHDETY OR UR UADJIT

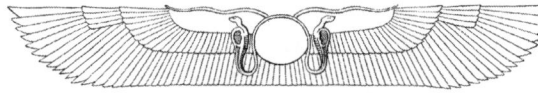

Figure 38: Behdety or Ur Uadjit

The Winged Serpent, also: Winged Sundisk,
composed of two serpents (Aset and Nebethet),
a sundisk symbolizing Ra manifesting as the dual
principles (Uadjut -Aset and Nekhebet - Nebthet)
and the wings Heru.
This is an important symbol of Heru,
meaning "All-Encompassing Divinity."

Heru is the rebirth of the Spirit. This rebirth is
not a physical birth from the womb, but a rebirth of
higher spiritual aspiration in the mind as the desire
for enlightenment. No longer is there interest in
worldly pursuits which are empty and shallow.
Instead, there is a burning desire to face and
conquer the lower self and regain the original glory
and freedom of knowing and becoming one with
the Higher Self. This is symbolized by Heru
regaining the throne of Upper and Lower Egypt. In
doing so, he has regained mastership of the higher
and the lower states of consciousness. Thus, Heru
represents the union and harmonization of spirit
and matter, and the renewed life of Asar, his
rebirth.

Heru is the God of Light. Before Heru is
victorious in the Asarian myth, he is a symbol of
the "Dual Nature of Humankind." Heru in this
aspect represents the opposite forces that are
within each of us, the animal nature (passionate
behavior as demonstrated by cutting off Aset's
head) and the Divine. Therefore, the real battle is
within each of us and not in the outer world of time
and space.

Asar-Seker, Heru and Ra utilize the symbol of
the hawk, 𓅃, an animal which is swift and
possesses sharpness and clarity of vision. Thus, the
symbol of the hawk refers to the quality of a highly
developed intellectual capacity to see what is real,
true and abiding versus that which is false, fleeting
and illusory. It is because of this quality of
discriminative intellect that Anpu is considered as
an aspect of Heru. The principles of mystical
spirituality as represented by Aset, Maat and
Djehuti (order, justice, peace, love, contentment,
righteous action, study and reflection on the
teachings, meditating on the Divine, etc.) are
leading toward the truth while the egoistic values
of society, as represented in the character of Set
(greed, hatred, anger, lust, restlessness, etc.), lead
to falsehood, pain, suffering, disappointment and
frustration.

The picture of Heru-Set (below) shows us that
the "enemy" or foe of truth (Maat) is inside each of
us. Set, the symbol of evil, is actually a part of
Heru that must be conquered and sublimated. In
this aspect, Set represents the "beasts" or
"demons" we must conquer within ourselves:
ignorance, passions, desires, restlessness of the
mind, temptation, lust, greed, depression,
insecurity, fear and pain. Through the journey of
life, a battle rages on between the Higher Self and
the lower, and only by living a life of virtue can the
"God of Light" inside come alive and vanquish the
unrighteous lower nature. This is the underlying
theme of the Asarian Resurrection myth and the
prerequisite for anyone who wishes to gain the
higher benefit of reading the Prt m Hru texts.

HERU AND SET

Figure 39: Heru-Set

(also known as "He who has two faces")
The Struggle between the
Higher and the Lower Self

When aspiration arises, the practice of Maat ensues until spiritual sensitivity is perfected. This process of virtuous living based on spiritual principles (Maat) serves to cleanse the heart (mind) of the impurities of the lower self and place the aspirant on the road to spiritual victory (enlightenment).

ANPU (APUAT)

Figure 40: Anpu (Apuat)

Discernment and Discriminative Knowledge of What is Real and What is Not Real.

Anpu is the son of Asar and Nebethet. He is the embalmer of the deceased (spiritual aspirant) and symbolizes the guide to the initiate, the trained intellect of the aspirant, who is dead to the wisdom of divine reality and hopes to be resurrected (to discover divine reality). This implies the ability to discipline one's mind and body so as to not get caught up in the illusions or emotions of the mind. When the mind and its wavelike thought vibrations are under control, the way is open to spiritual realization in an atmosphere of peace and harmony. This peace and harmony do not necessarily imply an outer situation of calm. It does imply an inward peace which comes from understanding the implications of the wisdom teachings. Anpu represents the dawn when darkness turns to light. He watches over the balance (scales) in the hall of judgment of the *Prt m Hru* with extreme diligence, and in the aspect of *Apuat*, he is the *Opener of the Ways* who leads souls to the *Elysian Fields in the Great Oasis.* Therefore, his great quality of *discriminative*

knowledge allows the aspirant to *diligently* watch the mind in order to promote thoughts which are divinely inspired (*Shemsu Hor* - follower of Heru), instead of those which are egoistic (Setian) and tending toward nature and its perils (life, death, pain, pleasure, etc.). Anpu, as the son of Nebethet and Asar, is therefore, a combination of gross nature (Nebethet) and the Spirit (Asar).

It is Anpu who leads the souls to the abode of the Supreme Being in the *Prt m Hru* by constantly urging them to awaken from the dream of the world process and its illusions. Thus, in this aspect, Anpu should be considered as the original *Angel of Death.* The reliefs and hieroglyphs of *Anpu sitting atop the ark containing the inner-parts of Asar* are found at the entrance or purification area of the burial chamber (chest or ark) of the initiate, 🐕. In the *Prt m Hru*, it is stated that Anpu appointed the *Seven Spirits, the followers of their lord Sepa, to be protectors of the dead body of Asar.* Sepa is the name of the chief of the Seven Spirits who guarded Asar, and *seven* is the number of spiritual energy centers in the subtle spiritual body (Serpent Power - Kundalini Chakras). There are also seven cows of Creation, which serve Asar as the "Bull of Creation." Anpu is an aspect of Heru, and Heru is the Higher Self. Therefore, the true enlightener of the Self is the Self. In this manner, it is your innermost Self who is enlightening you through your desire to practice spiritual discipline.

The struggle between Heru and Set is the struggle of every human being to control the mind with its erratic desires, longings, unfulfilled expectations and disappointments. This struggle is not avoidable by anyone who is not enlightened. Some people succumb under the weight of the lower self and its desires for fulfillment. This is a pathetic condition which those people have allowed to develop due to their own indulgence in the sensual desires of the body, and also due to their ignorance of their true divine nature which is buried deep within, under the weight of egoistic thoughts and unconscious ignorant feelings.

DJEHUTI

Figure 41: Forms of Djehuti

Djehuti is the symbol of right reason, the link to the Higher Self. When the determination to pursue the Divine arises, the struggle becomes a holy war against ignorance and illusion within one's consciousness. If this process is not understood as a struggle to overcome anger, hatred, greed, bigotry, jealousy, etc., within one's self, the energy of the struggle becomes directed to the world outside of oneself in the form of political, religious, social, ethnic, gender, etc., conflicts.

The struggle between Heru and Set does not end with either destroying the other. Heru pursues the path of reason seeking counsel with the wisdom of Djehuti. Wisdom follows the exercise of reason, and reason follows the practice of studying, questioning, reflecting and inquiring into the nature of truth. Set, the lower self, refuses to abide by the decree of wisdom but he is eventually sublimated through his own humiliation and ignorance. In the end, when the aspirant is aligned with all the divine forces, the lower self can no longer struggle. The overwhelming force of the Divine pushes the lower self into a position of service rather than of mastership. This is its rightful place.

NET

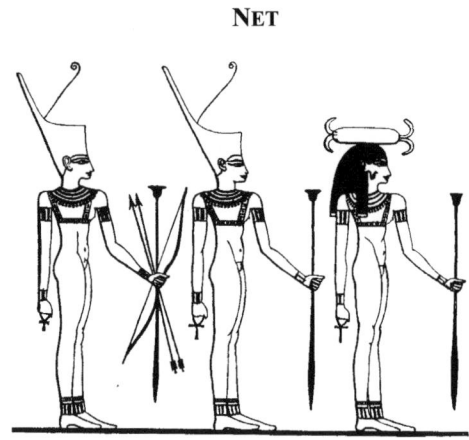

Figure 42: Forms of Net (Neith)

Net is the goddess of creation and war as well as honor and decisive action. Her attributes are the bow, shield and arrows. She is androgynous (neither male nor female, but including both), and was known to watch over Asar's ceremonial bed when he lay dead, along with Aset and Nebethet. She assisted Djehuti in bringing justice for Heru in the Asarian myth.

SELKET (Serket)

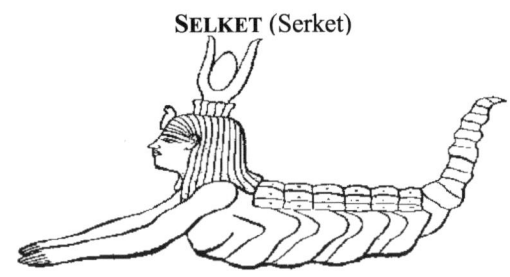

Figure 43: SELKET (Serket)

The Goddess Selket assisted Aset in her time of sorrow over the death of Heru and Asar. She protected Aset and Heru from the evil of Set and was the voice of reason in the time of mental anguish.

HERU-UR

Figure 44: Heru-Ur

The neteru of the Ennead arising from Ra-Atum are Shu, Tefnut, Geb, Nut, Asar, Aset, Set, Nebethet and Heru Ur.

Heru-Ur means "Heru the Elder" or "Heru-The Great" and also "Heru of the Future." He represents the perfection of Ra in Creation. In reference to the Asarian Resurrection myth, he represents Heru after he had challenged Set and reestablished order and harmony in the land of Egypt.

MIN (AMSU-MIN)

Figure 45: Min (Amsu-Min)

(Self-control - Sex-sublimation)

In the *Book of the Dead* (Chap. 4[38]), the initiate identifies with Amsu-Min and says:

"I am Amsu in his movement. This is true; he has given to me his plumes and they are on my head now. Who is this person that is being spoken about?

As for Amsu it is Heru, the ***redeemer of his father***. As for his movement it is his birth. As for his plumes on his head they are the actions of goddess Aset and Nebethet. They give of themselves to his person. They will be his protectors."

Min is the aspect of Amun manifesting as Heru in the form of the victorious savior (vindicator) of his father's (Asar's) honor. Hetheru is his companion and female aspect, whose passion and restorative influence provides healing and strength to allow Heru to continue the struggle against Set. Both of them represent the idea of aroused and sublimated sexual energy. In this capacity Amsu-Min (Amun) he is known as "Bull of his mother," i.e. generator of his own coming into being. In other Kemetic texts it is explained that the two plumes on the head of Min are Aset and Nebethet. The passage above also shows that Aset and Nebethet are the forces of life and death which manifest the power of Amsu (Heru).

The state of "Heru-Min" consciousness, when Heru is victorious, is the goal of all spiritual efforts. It is the ultimate objective of all spiritual-religious traditions. It means being triumphant over ignorance in the form of egoism and the fetters of Set (anger, hatred, greed, lust, selfishness, desire, elation, depression, conceit, etc.). At this stage, there is no possibility for the lower nature to sway the mind of a person. Now the lower self is like a slave to the Higher Self. The freedom from the fetters allows the mind to experience boundless *Sekhem,* Life Force energy-power, and to be at peace, Hetep, ▵. This peace and harmony allows the mind to see beyond the veil of ordinary human consciousness, in effect, to behold the Divine Self, Asar.

---

[38] Generally referred to as Chapter 17

THE EYE OF RA AND THE EYE OF HERU

There are several Ancient Egyptian myths relating to the *"Eye."* One tells that the Eye (individual soul) left Ra (Divine Self) and went into Creation and was lost. Ra sent Djehuti (wisdom) to find the Eye and bring it back. It was through the *magic* (wisdom teachings) of the god Djehuti that the Eye realized who it was and agreed to return to Ra. Upon its return, however, it found that Ra had replaced it with another. In order to pacify it, Ra placed it on his *brow* in the form of a *Uraeus serpent, where it could rule the world.* One variation to the story holds that the Eye left Ra and went to Nubia in the form of a lioness (Hetheru, in her aspect as destroyer of evil and unrighteousness). When Ra heard this, he sent the Nubian god *Ari-Hems-Nefer,* a form of Shu and Djehuti to bring the Eye back. They took the form of baboons (symbol of wisdom) and soon found the Eye near the Mountain of the Sunrise, where Asar was born. The Eye refused to leave because it had learned to enjoy its new existence. It was destroying those who had committed sins (plotted against Ra) while on earth. Djehuti worked his magic on the Eye and brought it back to Ra. Another variation of the story holds that Ra sent *Shu* and *Tefnut* in search of the Eye. The Eye resisted, and in the struggle, shed tears, and from the tears grew men. This is a clever play on words because the word for "tears," Remtu, ⬭𓂝𓏏𓇗, (that fell from the eyes of Ra) and the word for "men," Reth or Rethu, ⬭𓂝𓏏𓏥, have similar sounds in Ancient Egyptian language. This play on words sustains the idea that human beings came forth, figuratively speaking, out of the sorrow of God as he saw souls leaving him and becoming human beings, i.e. forgetting their true nature. The implication is that the tears (physical substance) of Ra and his rapture (feeling-passion) become vessels for the souls to exist in the embodied state, i.e. as human beings.

The relationship of "tears" to "men" symbolizes the idea that humankind is the expression of the desire of the Divine Self to have experiences in the realm of time and space. Further, "tears" are a symbol of human experience. It implies that human experience is a sorrowful condition because consciousness has degraded itself to the level of gross, limited human experience in the form of an individual ego as opposed to its expansive, limitless Self. This contraction in consciousness is what allows the ego to emerge as an individual and distinct personality out of "nowhere," just as a dream personality emerges out of "nowhere." Instead of knowing itself as the immutable soul, the soul sees the ego and the world of time and space as the reality. This development would be like the ocean forgetting that it is the ocean and believing itself to be one of the waves. Therefore, instead of seeing itself as encompassing all the waves, it is concerned with its transient experience, as an individual wave, and with comparing itself to other waves.

Life is "sorrowful" from the standpoint of wisdom because even conditions that appear to be pleasurable are in reality setting the individual up for disappointment and frustration later on, because no positive situation can last indefinitely. Also, the pursuit of worldly pleasure and pain sets up mental impressions that will survive the death of the body and lead the soul to further incarnations in search of fulfillment. Therefore, the Sages say that *all life is painful to the wise.* This is why Yoga philosophy emphasizes going beyond both pleasure *and* pain in order to transcend the bondage to time and space. This can be accomplished by turning away from the world which is illusory and seeking to discover the Self.

The masses of people who do not have spiritual sensitivity put up with the world and its ups and downs due to lack of reflectiveness. Having been taught from their youth by family and society to look for happiness in the world, they do not know any better. Through the development of wisdom and reflection, the aspirant can develop an intuition which transcends pleasure and pain and move beyond the world of ordinary human experience as a source of happiness.

Through the story of the Eye, very important mystical teachings are being conveyed. The Eye, *Udjat,* is a symbol of intuitional vision. Also, it represents the desire of the Divine to go into itself (Creation) and the subsequent forgetfulness that ensues. The resistance of the Eye to return to the divine abode is a symbol of the predicament of ordinary people who, through ignorance and intense desire, detest the idea of even considering the spiritual values of life because their hearts (minds) are consumed with passion. They are consumed with the desire to experience the pleasures of material existence. Ra sent the Eye (consciousness) into Creation. Consciousness then became "lost" in Creation, symbolizing the souls of human beings and all life forms, forgetting their true nature. The Eye, lost in Creation, is the human soul which is caught up in the cycle of birth-death-birth (reincarnation) due to forgetfulness and distraction (ignorance of its true nature). The Supreme Being (Ra) sent out the messenger of wisdom (Djehuti) in the forms of *Metu Neter* (ancient scriptures of wisdom) and *Sbai* (spiritual preceptor-Guru) to instruct the Eye in reference to its true nature. Having "remembered" who it was in reality, the Eye then returned to its rightful place.

The same teaching of the Eye is to be found in the story of Heru and Set where Set (ego) tore out Heru's Eye. It is Djehuti who restored the Eye through the power of magic (wisdom teaching). In this context, the whole teaching of wisdom which Djehuti applies (*Hekau*) to the Eye causes it to remember its essential nature and its glory as the Eye of Heru. Upon its return, the Eye provided Heru with the strength of will he needed to overthrow Set. This story mythologizes the journey of the human soul and its eventual redemption wherein it achieves the sublimation of the ego and attains *Self-realization.*

In this aspect, the plight of the Eye and its subsequent restoration through the teachings of Djehuti in the *Udja Hetheru* text as the transmitter of wisdom, embodies the principle of the teacher-disciple relationship though which spiritual knowledge is transmitted. We saw this same principle in the initiation of Heru by Aset, in the *Asar Uhem Ankh* (Asarian Resurrection) text and it is also found in Gnostic Christianity in the teachings Jesus gave to his disciples, as well as in the Indian Hindu Vedantic principle of the Guru-Disciple relationship, such as that which existed between Lord Krishna and Arjuna in the *Bhagavad Gita* text and Vasistha and Rama in the *Yoga Vasistha* text. In these two scriptures, two aspirants are reminded of their divine essential nature by the Gurus who are themselves, one with the Divine Self. Gradually, they are led to realization of the Self through a process which involves the classical teachings of Yoga (wisdom, reflection and meditation). These texts are highly recommended for any serious student of Yoga scriptures. Djehuti is the master teacher who initiates the aspirant on the spiritual path of wisdom. In teaching others, the priest or priestess assumes the role of Djehuti. Djehuti is the *Spiritual Preceptor* of the Eye.

When Heru's Eye (the moon) was torn out and thrown away by Set, the god Djehuti who presides as the moon found it and turned it into the Moon. When the parts of the Eye of Heru are added up, it gives the answer 63/64 which approximate the whole number 1. One is the number which symbolizes oneness, wholeness, all sight, all knowing, the Supreme Being, The Absolute. As long as the soul is involved in creation (matter), there will remain some small separation between the individual Ba and the Universal Ba, the ONE. In order to become completely unified, merged into infinity, the individual soul of the enlightened person dissolves into the Universal soul at the time of death; this is complete Oneness with the divine. The missing part of the Eye of Heru, 1/64, is added by Djehuti through his magic, i.e. the magic of purified intellect.

The Eye is therefore, the quintessential symbol of the creative power of the Divine. Also, it is the cardinal principle of power which can be directed against evil and unrighteousness, primarily in the form of demoniac qualities in nature or in human beings. This is why the Eye symbol was used so profusely in ancient times and why the Eye symbols were used on coffins to signify awakened consciousness which will not be defeated by death. In ancient times the mummy was placed in the coffin, lying on the left side and as if looking out through the two eyes. The mystical symbolism is that attaining the transcendental and unitary qualities of the two eyes, a human being thus attains the capacity to transcend death, i.e. to look out on eternity.

Figure 46: Coffin of Khnum-Hotep

The Eye of Ra is the Goddess of Creation

An Ancient Egyptian Creation myth holds that all came into existence out of a Primeval Ocean of unformed matter, the Duat. The teaching of the fullness of the Primeval Ocean is to be found in the *Prt m Hru* (Chapter 4; Chapter 21). The hekau-utterance in Chapter 4 gives an exact description of the concept of "fullness" and of the female nature of the Primeval Ocean. The initiate says:

"It is my seeing Ra, born as yesterday. As concerns the hinder parts of goddess Mehurt, she is his vitality and she is my vitality also, binding, strengthening and surrounding me. Who is this person that is being spoken about?

It is the primeval waters of heaven. Another way to understand this is: It is the image of the Eye of Ra on that morning of his birth which is every day. As to Mehurt, she is the Divine Eye of Ra who is on his face."

Being the Eye of transcendental consciousness (*Divine Eye of Ra*), Mehurt is the fullness of the spirit from which the world proceeds. Thus, the Eye of God is the source of creation and the root of existence. The spirit has boundless potential (vitality) to create and Mehurt is that essence. The initiate is to discover {her/his} own identity with that fullness of being by discovering Mehurt, i.e. the Eye of Ra. In this capacity, Mehurt is the female aspect of the creator divinity, on a par with Tem, and with the primeval waters itself as the primeval being who emerged from the Primeval Waters, the Nun.

MEHURT – HETHERU

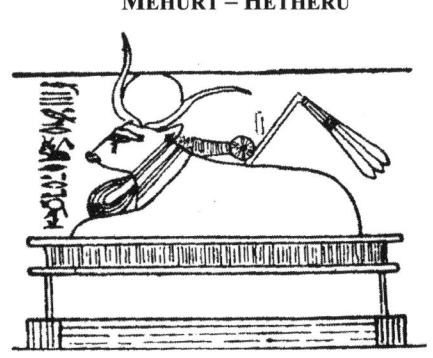

Figure 47: Mehurt - Hetheru

The Goddess of Creation

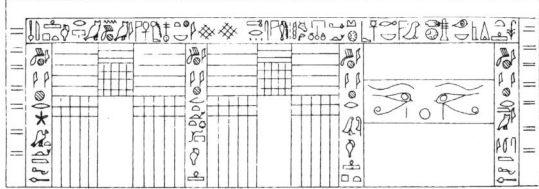

Related to the goddess Hetheru, Mehurt was originally the female embodiment of the watery matter, the Primeval Ocean from which the substance of the world was formed and from which Ra emerged. In other versions of the Creation story, the Primeval Ocean is referred to as Nu, a male form. Thus, the Primeval Ocean is seen as an *androgynous* essence from which all arose in the form of opposites. Mehurt, ⟨hieroglyphs⟩, means "mighty fullness." She was the infinite source of matter which was impregnated by the male spirit. This is one of the reasons why one of the symbols of Amun is a pregnant woman ⟨glyph⟩. Of course, the female primeval matter and the male spirit are both aspects of the same energy. This is expressed in the last line of the utterance where it is explained that Mehurt herself is the "image" of the "Eye of Ra." The Eye of Ra is His own daughter, Hetheru. Mehurt is depicted as a cow goddess brimming with life giving essence. The symbol of the cow is common to Hetheru, Nut and Aset. The cow goddess is often referred to as a "seven fold deity" known as the "seven Hetherus" who preside over the life of each individual[39] and the course of Creation. This title refers to the further differentiation of the three primordial principles of the Trinity (Asar-Aset-Heru) which is expressed as the phenomenal universe through a series of sevens. This number, *seven*, is expressed in all levels of Creation. It is expressed in the seven levels of the human subtle anatomy with the seven spiritual centers[40], and also as the seven primary colors of the rainbow. This principle of sevens translated into the Gnostic Idea of the "seven planetary spirits," and the Christian Archangels, known as the *Heads of the Celestial Host,* were titled the "Seven Archangels of the Presence."

Aset-Hetheru in Ancient Egypt symbolized the source of Creation. The *Milky Way* was produced

---

[39] The Seven Hetheru's are the origin for the concept in Greek and Roman mythology of the *"Fates."* They were three goddesses, Clotho, Lachesis, and Strops, who control human destiny.
[40] see *Egyptian Yoga: The Philosophy of Enlightenment* and *The Serpent Power*

by her udder and she was "the Great Cow which gave birth to Ra, the Great Goddess, the mother of all the gods and goddesses...the lady who existed when nothing else had being, and who created that which came into being." The cow is therefore a prominent representation of Aset and Hetheru. In her form as seven cows, Hetheru, an aspect of Aset, symbolizes the seven energies which course through the universe and which are sired by the *Bull* (Asar-male aspect of the Supreme Being). The *Bull* is a metaphor for the spirit. Just as the bull on a farm sires many cows, so to the "Bull" (Supreme Spirit) engenders all life in Creation.

In Indian Mythology, the cow holds a similar symbolism as that of Ancient Egypt. The cow is known as the "fountain of milk and curds." In a mystical sense, the world is a curd of the milk which emanated from the Celestial Cow (God). When the giant serpent of the Primeval Ocean moves, it churns the waters and thereby causes the waters to take on various shapes and forms just as churning milk causes it to turn into curds and butter. Curds are the part of milk that coagulates, i.e. goes from liquid to solid. The world is a curd in the ocean of consciousness, i.e. a coagulated thought of God, just as, when asleep, a dream is a coagulated manifestation of subconscious human desire.

HETHERU (HET-HOR, HATHOR)

Figure 48: Hetheru

(Spiritual Power and Sexual Energy)

The Hieroglyphic symbol, [glyph], for the name of the goddess means [glyph], *Het (house) and Heru,* [glyph], *(the god of light).*

In a text from the Temple at Dier al-Medina, Hetheru is referred to as having the same divine attributes as Heru. She is described as *The Golden One* and *The Queen of the Gods.* Her shrines are even more numerous than those of Heru. Hetheru or Het-Heru, meaning *The House of Heru* or *The House Above* (heavens), became identified, like Heru, with the salvation of the initiate. In the *Egyptian Prt m Hru,* she is the one who urges the initiate to do battle with the monster *Apep,* the symbol of egoism which spurs negativity and evil, so as not to lose {his/her} heart as she cries out: "Take your armor." In a separate papyrus, the initiate is told that she (Hetheru) is the one who "will make your face perfect among the gods and goddesses; she will open your eye so that you may see every day... she will make your legs able to walk with ease in the Netherworld, Her name is Hetheru, Lady of Amenta."

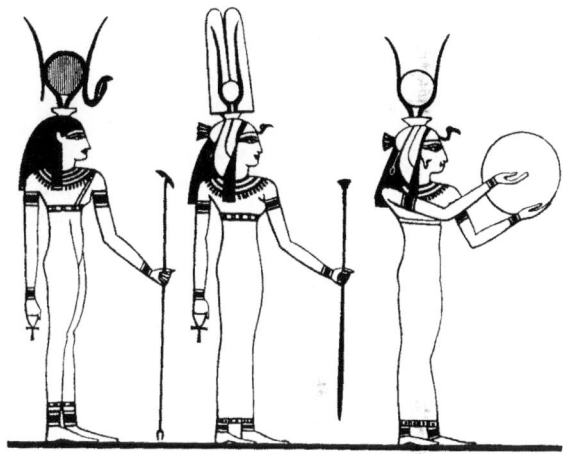

MORE FORMS OF HETHERU

In Chapter 24[41], the role of Hetheru in the process of salvation is specified as the initiate speaks the words which will help {him/her} become as a lotus:

"I am the lotus, pure, coming forth out into the day. I am the guardian of the nostril of Ra and keeper of the nose of Hetheru. I make, I come, and I seek after he, that is Heru. I am pure going out from the field."

The lotus has been used since ancient times to symbolize the detachment and dispassion that a

---

[41] Generally referred to as chapter 81

spiritual aspirant must develop. The lotus emerges everyday out of the murky waters of the pond in order to receive the rays of the sun. The spiritual aspirant, a follower of the goddess, must rise above egoism and negativity (anger, hatred, greed, and ignorance) in life in order to gain in wisdom and spiritual enlightenment. Hetheru and Heru form a composite archetype, a savior with all of the complementary qualities of the male and female principles, inseparable, complete and androgynous.

Hetheru represents the power of Ra, the Supreme Spirit, therefore, associating with her implies coming into contact with the boundless source of energy which sustains the universe. Therefore, making contact with Hetheru implies developing inner will power and vitality which engenders clarity of vision that will lead to the discovery of what is righteous and what is unrighteous. A mind which is constantly distracted and beset with fetters (anger, hatred, greed, conceit, covetousness, lust, selfishness, etc.) cannot discern the optimal course in life. It becomes weak willed because the negative emotions and feelings drain the mental energy. Thus, unrighteous actions and sinful thoughts arise and the weak mind cannot resist them. Unrighteous actions lead to adverse situations and adverse situations lead to pain and sorrow in life. In this sense Hetheru comes to human beings in the form of adversities to urge them to reflect on their unrighteous actions and challenge them to sublimate their ego. However, those who are not very reflective might view it as punishment, since they do not have a higher philosophical understanding.

MESKHENT

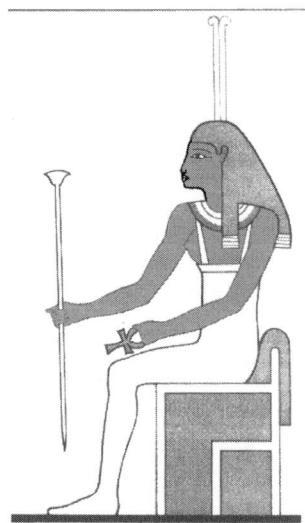

Figure 49: Meskhent

Along with her associates, the goddesses *Shai, Rennenet* and *Meskhent*, Maat encompasses the Ancient Egyptian teachings of *Ari* (karma) and reincarnation or the destiny of every individual based on past actions, thoughts and feelings. Thus, they have an important role to play in the judgment scene of the *Prt m Hru*. Understanding their principles leads the aspirant to become free of the cycle of reincarnation and human suffering and to discover supreme bliss and immortality. If a person is ignorant about their higher essential nature, they will only have knowledge of human existence. At the time of death their soul will wander and experience either heavenly or hellish conditions in much the same way as one experiences good and bad dreams. Spiritual enlightenment means discovering your essential nature as one with the Supreme Self, and when this is achieved, there is no more hell or heaven; there is a resurrection in consciousness. This is what the goddess urges every aspirant to achieve through study, reflection and meditation on her teachings, and it is the central theme in the *Ausarian Resurrection* myth.[42]

---

[42] See the Book *The Wisdom of Maati* for more on Maat philosophy.

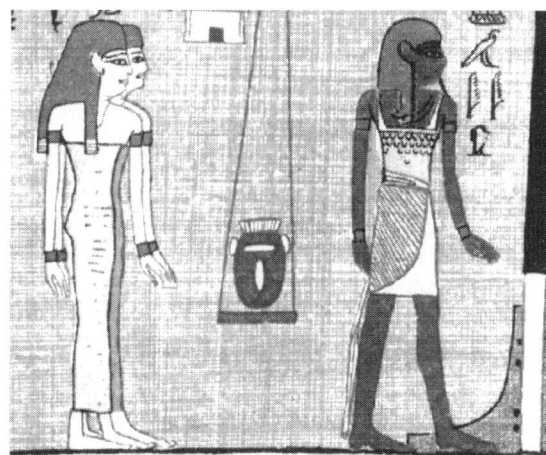

Figure 50: Above (left): the goddesses Renenet and Meskhenet, right- Shai (From the Papyrus of Ani-see Chapter 33)

The hands of Djehuti (God of wisdom) are the God "Shai" which means "destiny" and the Goddess "Renenet" which means "Fortune and Harvest." The implication is that we reap (harvest) the result of our actions (destiny) according to our level of wisdom. Djehuti, one's own wisdom capacity through higher intellectual understanding, bestows control over one's Shai (Fortune) and Renenet (ability to reap one's fortune) and therefore one's <u>Meskhenet</u> (Destiny - Karma). Therefore, one's karmic destiny depends on one's reasoning capacity, i.e. *intellect*.

Underlying the principles of Shai and Renenet is goddess "Meskhenet." She is the one who determines where the next birth (karmic fate) of the soul will take place. Therefore, the teachings of Ari (Karma) and reincarnation are an integral part of Kemetic Philosophy.

AMENTET

Ament means "hidden." It is a specific reference to the female form of the astral plane or Netherworld known as *Amenta* or the Duat. Aset was known as the dark-skinned daughter of Nut. Like Asar, her husband, who was known as the "Lord of the Perfect Black," Aset was the Mistress of the Netherworld known as Amentet (Amentat). Thus, Aset also symbolizes the "blackness" of the vast unmanifest regions of existence. Her identification is also symbolized in her aspect as *Amentet,* the Duat, itself. Therefore, Amentet

(Aset) and the soul of Amentet (Amen-Asar) are intimately related. Upon further reflection into the mythology, it becomes obvious that since Asar is the Duat, and since the goddess Amentet, the goddess, is also Ament or the realm of Asar, they are in reality one and the same (both the realms and the deities).

Figure 51: Amentat

Thus, Aset and Asar together form the hidden recesses of Creation. In essence they are the source of Creation and are therefore both simultaneously considered to be the source of the Life Force which courses through Creation.

SEKHMET-BAST-RA

Sekhmet-Bast-Ra, The All - Goddess

Figure 52: Sekhmet-Bast-Ra, The All - Goddess

Another important form of the Goddess is known as *Sekhmet-Bast-Ra*. Sekhmet-Bast-Ra is a composite depiction of the Goddess encompassing the female head, lioness head, and vulture head, symbolizing all of the attributes of the goddesses as well as the attributes of the gods. This is a recognition that all things in Creation are not absolutely female or male. All of Creation is a combination of male and female elements. Therefore, since Creation is androgynous, so too Divinity and the human soul are also androgynous. This understanding is reflected in the following instruction from Aset to Heru in the Ausarian Resurrection, verse 125:

> Heru asked: "O Divine Mother, how are male and female souls produced?" Aset answered: "Souls, Heru, son, are of the self same nature in themselves, in that they are from one and the same place where the Creator modeled them; nor male nor female are they. Sex (i.e. gender) is a thing of bodies, not of souls."

Arat (ART, AART, ARATI)[43]

Figure 53: Arat (The Serpent Form of The Goddess)

The Serpent form of the Goddess represents several important teachings related to the Life Force energy (Sekhem) permeating Creation. Emanating from the Divine Self, it enlivens and sustains all of Creation. It also refers to the internal Life Force energy which lies dormant within every human being. This Life Force energy is known in

modern times as Arat Sekhem, the Serpent Power or Kundalini.

Art **(Goddess)**

The symbol of the serpent is used because it is the perfect metaphor to represent the serpentine mode of movement which characterizes the Serpent Power energy. In the teaching of the Temple of Aset from Ancient Egypt, the Serpent Power (Arat) was symbolized as the image of a serpent with three and a half coils. Later in history, the same image was used in India to represent the same teaching.

THE FELINE ASPECT

Figure 54: Sekhmet

One important element of the goddess is the feline aspect. In nature, cats have an inimical relationship with serpents. In Ancient Egyptian mythology, the *Serpent of Darkness* is seen as the embodiment of ignorance and evil which threatens the movement of the Boat of Ra and which prevents the spiritual aspirant from attaining enlightenment. Therefore, the goddess in the form of a cat (Bast) or the lioness (Tefnut - Sekhmet) is seen as the warrior and champion of the gods (Asar and Heru) as well as the aspirant. She is the one who paves the way for spiritual evolution by destroying the evil of ignorance and sinfulness in the human heart.

---

[43] For more on the teachings of the Serpent Power and the spiritual disciplines related to its development for the purpose of promoting spiritual evolution, see the book *The Serpent Power* by Dr. Muata Ashby.

PTAH-SEKER-ASAR

Figure 55: Ptah-Seker-Asar

Ptah-Seker-Asar is the triune divinity, a form of the three divinities Ptah, Seker and Asar, which together epitomize the Ancient Egyptian capacity to mythologically and philosophically mix and equate the forms of the Divine. This shows the underlying concept that all of the divinities are in reality aspects of each other. Otherwise, these iconographical combinations would not be possible.

MAFDET

Figure 56: The Leopard Goddess Mafdet cutting the head of the Demon serpent Apep.

The Leopard Goddess Mafdet was associated with Sekhmet, the Eye of Ra and with Hetheru. She is the embodiment of the destructive force that can be unleashed on the negative impetus, symbolized by the serpent demon Apep. Mafdet is also identified with the execution blade itself.

Figure 57: (left) Sem Priest making an offering.

Figure 58: (right) Ancient Egyptian Priestess.

The Sem (officiating) priest wears a leopard skin, as a symbol of the power to dispel the evil of death and to open the mouth (mind) of the initiate.

THE ICONOGRAPHY OF THE HAWK AND THE TRIUNE FORM OF HERU

Ancient Egyptian iconography, the pictographic elements of scripture, can independently provide deep mythological, religious and philosophical teachings by themselves. This is one of the greatest strengths of Kemetic scripture and art. This is because the reading process need not be limited to the deciphering of letters, but it can also derive meaning from pictures used in the language (pictures used as letters).

One of the most important iconographies of Kemetic religion involves the Hawk icon. The hawk is an animal which flies high above the earth and whose visual acuity allows it to survey vast regions while being able to focus on minute objects. Also, it is able to fly at high speeds. These qualities are what motivated the Ancient Egyptian Sages to use it as a symbol for the basis of the entire system of Anunian mythology which blends the concept of

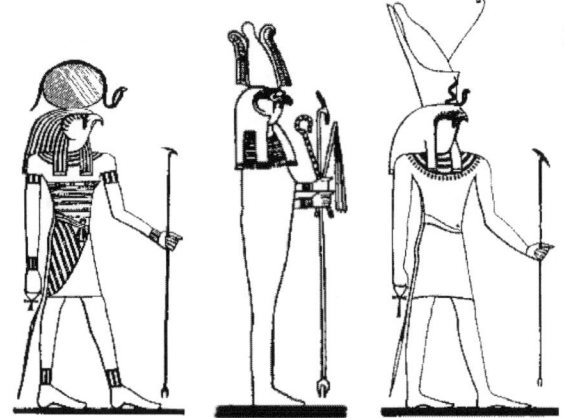

Tem, the singular essence which emerged out of the Primeval Void (Primeval Ocean) with the concept of Heru, the Supreme Divinity. The Hawk theme runs through the mythology of Tem as Atem-Ra or Ra-Tem, as well as that of Asar and that of Heru.

Figure 59: The Hawk Trinity: Ra, Seker and Heru

Left- Ra Herakti, Center-Asar Seker, Right- Heru, son of Asar and Aset, Lord of the Two Lands.

The Hawk motif unites and binds the mythology of Ra, Asar and Heru in a very strong way, and we are to understand that we are indeed looking at the same divinity who is manifesting in different aspects and operating in different realms or planes of existence. Ra represents perfection in the heavens or the transcendental, Asar Seker represents perfection in the Netherworld and Heru represents perfection in the Physical plane.

THE GODS OF THE SENSES

Figure 60: Above-Relief showing the gods of the senses (from the Temple of Heru at Edfu).

The senses are seen as instruments of the personality, used for perceiving information which in turn is transferred to the mind. The gods of the senses are, from left to right, *Saa* (touch, feeling and understanding) and *Hu* (taste and divine sustenance), *Maa* (sight) and *Sedjem* (hearing). *Hu* and *Saa* were known to serve as bearers of the Eye of Heru (enlightened consciousness). They were also considered to be the tongue and heart of *Asar-Ptah* (the Self). Thus, they represent the vehicles through which human beings can experience and understand the teachings of moral and spiritual wisdom about the Self, i.e. the faculties of speech and intuitional understanding.

Chapter 4: A Gloss On The Philosophy of *The Rau nu Prt m Hru*

THE GODDESS MAAT AND MAAT PHILOSOPHY

Figure 61: Goddess Maat

Order, Righteousness, Justice, Balance, Harmony, Truth

*"Those who live today will die tomorrow, those who die tomorrow will be born again;
Those who live Maat will not die."*

WHO IS MAAT?

Even though the figure of goddess Maat is not usually seen in the *Rau Prt m Hru,* her presence is the most strongly felt of all. Her name is mentioned more than any other goddess and indeed, she is said to be an aspect of the all-goddess, Aset. Therefore, in order to understand the *Prt m Hru,* we must have a working knowledge of the goddess and her philosophy. When Ra emerged in his Boat for the first time and creation came into being, he was standing on the pedestal of Maat. Thus the Creator, Ra, lives by Maat and has established Creation on Maat. Who is Maat? She is the divinity who manages the order of Creation. She is the fulcrum upon which the entire Creation and the Law of Cause and Effect or Karma, functions. Maat represents the very order which constitutes creation. Therefore, it is said that Ra created the universe by putting Maat in the place of chaos. So creation itself is Maat. Creation without order is chaos. Maat is a profound teaching in reference to the nature of creation and the manner in which human conduct should be cultivated. It refers to a deep understanding of Divinity and the manner in which virtuous qualities can be developed in the human heart so as to come closer to the Divine.

Maat is a philosophy, a spiritual symbol as well as a cosmic energy or force which pervades the entire universe. She is the symbolic embodiment of world order, justice, righteousness, correctness, harmony and peace. She is also known by her headdress composed of a feather which symbolizes the qualities just mentioned. She is a form of the Goddess Aset, who represents wisdom and spiritual awakening through balance and equanimity.

In Ancient Egypt, the judges and all those connected with the judicial system were initiated into the teachings of Maat. Thus, those who would discharge the laws and regulations of society were well trained in the ethical and spiritual-mystical values of life, fairness, justice and the responsibility to serve and promote harmony in society as well as the possibility for spiritual development in an atmosphere of freedom and peace, for only when there is justice and fairness in society can there be an abiding harmony and peace. Harmony and peace are necessary for the pursuit of true happiness and inner fulfillment in life.

Maat signifies *that which is straight*. Two of the symbols of Maat are the ostrich feather ($\int$) and the pedestal ($\longrightarrow$) upon which God stands. The Supreme Being, in the form of the god *Atum, Asar*, and *Ptah*, are often depicted standing on the pedestal.

Maat is the daughter of Ra, the high God, thus in a hymn to Ra we find:

> *The land of Manu* (the West) *receives thee with satisfaction, and the goddess Maat embraces thee both at morn and at eve... the god Djehuti and the goddess Maat have written down thy daily course for thee every day...*

Another Hymn in the Papyrus of Qenna (Kenna) provides deeper insight into Maat. Qenna says:

> *I have come to thee, O Lord of the Gods, Temu-Heru-khuti, whom Maat directeth... Amen-Ra rests upon Maat... Ra lives by Maat... Asar carries along the earth in His train by Maat...*

Maat is the daughter of Ra, and she was with him on his celestial boat when he first emerged from the primeval waters along with his company of gods and goddesses. She is also known as the *Eye of Ra, Lady of heaven, Queen of the earth, Mistress of the Netherworld and the lady of the gods and goddesses*. Maat also has a dual form or *Maati*. In her capacity of God, Maat is *Shes Maat* which means *ceaseless-ness and regularity* of the course of the sun (i.e. the universe). In the form of Maati, she represents the South and the North which symbolize Upper and Lower Egypt as well as the Higher Self and lower self. Maat is the personification of justice and righteousness upon which God has created the universe, and Maat is also the essence of God and creation. Therefore, it is Maat who judges the soul when it arrives in the judgment hall of Maat. Sometimes Maat herself becomes the scales upon which the heart of the initiate is judged. Maat judges the heart (unconscious mind) of the initiate in an attempt to determine to what extent the heart has lived in accordance with Maat or truth, correctness, reality, genuineness, uprightness, righteousness, justice, steadfastness and the unalterable nature of creation.

WHO IS MAATI?

Figure 62: The Two Maati goddesses preside over the judgment of the heart in the Prt m Hru

Who are the Maati goddesses? In the segment above we introduced the idea of opposites in creation. The Hall of Maat, known as the hall of judgment for the heart, is presided over by two goddesses known as *Maati.*

The goddesses Aset and Nebethet have a special relationship to the Maati goddesses. The Ancient Egyptian texts reveal that these two goddesses are none other than Aset and Nebethet. As stated earlier, Aset and Nebethet are depicted as looking exactly alike, the only difference being in their headdresses: Aset 𓊽, Nebethet 𓎡 or 𓎼. However, the essential meaning of their symbols is inverted, that is, the goddesses are in reality just inverted images of each other. Thus, they are complementary goddess principles which operate to manifest life-death-life or the cycle of birth-death-rebirth known as reincarnation.

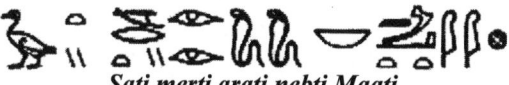

Sati merti arati nebti Maati
The two daughters, goddesses {Aset and Nebethet} of all righteousness and truth.

Aset and Nebethet are also known as *Rekhtti,* the two goddesses. They manifest in the Judgment hall of Maat in the *Egyptian Book of Coming Forth By Day* as *Maati* or the double Maat goddesses who watch over the weighing of the heart of the initiate (*The Asar*) in their name as *Sati merti arati nebti Maati.* Aset and Nebethet are the basis of the judgment of the soul and the criterion which decides its fate in life as well as after death.

WHAT IS TRUE VIRTUE?

In order to understand what true virtue is and all of the elements that drive a human being and cause him or her to be the way {he/she} is, we must begin by understanding the teachings of *ari* (karma) and *uhem ankh* (reincarnation). The human being is not simply a mind and body which will someday cease to exist. In fact, every human being's mind and body are in reality temporal emanations or expressions of their eternal Soul. One's identification with the mind and body as being who they are is referred to as delusion. It is only this aspect of the human being, the ego-personality, which is temporal and mortal. The soul is immortal and perfect while the ego-personality is subject to error, confusion and the consequences of these. If a human being is aware of the deeper soul-reality, this state of being is known as the state of *Enlightenment.*

However, if a human being does not have knowledge and experience of their Higher Self, then they exist in a condition of ignorance which will lead to sinful behavior, pain and sorrow in life. The ego-personality is subject to the forces of time and space and will suffer the consequences of its actions. This is the basis for the teaching of karma. When the ego-personality dies, the soul moves on. If the human being has discovered {his/her} Higher Self by purifying the heart (mind and body), then the soul moves forward to unite with the supreme Self (God). If the ego in a person is fettered by ignorance, then the soul moves in an astral plane until it finds another ego-personality about to be born again in the world of time and space, so that it may have an opportunity to have experiences that will lead it to discover its higher nature. This is the basis for the teaching of reincarnation.

"He delivers whom he pleases, even from the Duat (Netherworld)."
"He saves a man or woman from what is
His lot at the dictates of their heart."

The utterances above are directly referring to Ari-Meskhenet or karma and reincarnation. Many people believe that karma is equal to fate or destiny, however, this interpretation could not be further from the original understanding of the ancient Sages. The etymology of the word, karma, comes from the Sanskrit "karman" which means deed or action. In Yoga philosophy, karma refers to one's actions. These actions lead to certain experiences and consequences. In Ancient Egyptian philosophy, the word karma is *Ari* or *Iri*, meaning "action," (karmic action) and is presided over by the goddesses Maati, Rennenet and Meskhenet.

Figure 63: Above: Goddess Meskhent as the "birthing block" overlooking the karmic scales of Maat in the Judgment scene of Papyrus Ani.

Meskhenet presides over the birth circumstances and life experiences of every individual. She is the one who carries out the decree which has been ordained by Djehuti after the judgment of the heart in the hall of Maat. It is Djehuti who records the deeds (actions) or karmas of every individual and then decrees the proper Shai (destiny) and Rennenet (harvest or fortune) which are fitting for that particular individual.

Figure 64: Above: The "Ab" heart-container being weighed in the karmic scales of Maat in the Judgment scene of Papyrus Ani.

The Ancient Egyptian hieroglyphic symbol of the heart is a heart shaped vase, ♉, referred to as the *ab*. The vase is a container which may be used for holding water, beer, wine, milk, etc. Likewise, the human heart is seen as a vessel which contains thoughts, feelings, desires and unconscious memories. In mystical terms, the heart is a metaphor of the human mind including the conscious, subconscious and unconscious levels. The mind is the reservoir of all of your ideas, convictions and feelings. Therefore, just as these factors direct the path of your life, so too they are the elements which are judged in the Hall of Maati by the two goddesses, Aset and Nebethet, along with Asar. The heart then is the sum total of your experiences, actions and aspirations, your conscience or *ari* (karma), and these are judged in the balance against the feather of Maat.

Thus, ari or karma should be thought of as the total effect of a person's actions and conduct during the successive phases of {his/her} existence. But how does this effect operate? How do the past actions affect the present and the future? Your experiences from the present life or from previous lifetimes cause unconscious impressions which stay with the Soul even after death. These unconscious impressions are what constitute the emerging thoughts, desires, and aspirations of every individual. These impressions are not exactly like memories, however, they work like memories. For example, if you had a fear in a previous lifetime or the childhood of your present lifetime, you may not remember the event that caused the fear, but you may experience certain phobias when you come into contact with certain objects or certain people. These feelings are caused by the unconscious impressions which are coming up to the surface of the conscious mind. It is this conglomerate of unconscious impressions which are "judged" in the Hall of Maat and determine where the soul will go to next in the spiritual journey toward evolution or devolution, also known as the cycle of birth and death or reincarnation, as well as the experiences of heaven or hell. The following segment from the Ancient Egyptian "Instruction to Meri-ka-Ra" explains this point.

> *"You know that they are not merciful the day when they judge the miserable one..... Do not count on the passage of the years; they consider a lifetime as but an hour. After death man remains in existence and his actions accumulate beside him. Life in the other world is eternal, but he who arrives without doing wrong, before the Judge of the Dead, he will be there as a neter and he will walk freely as do the masters of eternity."*

The reference above to "his acts accumulate beside him" alludes to the unconscious impressions which are formed as a result of one's actions while still alive. These impressions can be either positive or negative. Positive impressions are developed through positive actions by living a life of righteousness (Maat) and virtue. This implies living according to the precepts of mystical wisdom or being a follower of Heru (*Shemsu Hor*) and Aset. These actions draw one closer to harmony and peace, thus paving the way to discover the Self within. The negative impressions are developed through sinful actions. They are related to mental agitation, disharmony and restlessness. This implies acts based on anger, fear, desire, greed, depression, gloom, etc. These actions draw one into the outer world of human desires. They distract the mind and do not allow the intellect (Saa) to function. Thus, existence at this level is closer to an animal, being based on animal instincts and desires of the body (selfishness), rather than to a spiritually mature human being, based on reason, selflessness, compassion, etc.

(Purification of the heart)

How then is it possible to eradicate negative karmic impressions and to develop positive ones? The answer lies in your understanding of the wisdom teachings and your practice of them. When you study the teachings and live according to them, your mind undergoes a transformation at all levels. This transformation is the "purification of heart" so often spoken about throughout the *Egyptian Book of Coming Forth By Day*. It signifies an eradication of negative impressions, which renders the mind pure and subtle. When the mind is rendered subtle, then spiritual realization is possible. This discipline of purifying the heart by living according to the teachings is known as the Yoga of Action or Maat.

The philosophy of Maat is a profound teaching which encompasses the fabric of creation as well as a highly effective system of spiritual discipline. In creation stories, God (Neter Neteru) is said to have established creation upon Maat. Consequently it follows that Maat is the orderly flow of energy which maintains the universe. Further, Maat is the regularity which governs the massive planetary and solar systems as well as the growth of a blade of grass and a human cell. This natural process represents the flow of creation wherein there is constant movement and a balancing of opposites (up-down, hot-cold, here-there, you-me, etc.).

Most people act out of the different forces which are coursing through them at the time. These may be hunger, lust, fear, hatred, anger, elation, etc. They have no control over these because they have not understood that their true essence is in reality separate from their thoughts and emotions. They have *identified* with their thoughts and therefore are led to the consequences of those thoughts and the deeds they engender. You, as an aspirant, having developed a higher level of spiritual sensitivity, are now aware that you have a choice in the thoughts you think and the actions you perform. You can choose whether to act in ways that are in harmony with Maat or those that are disharmonious. You have now studied the words of wisdom and must now look beyond the level of ritual worship of the Divine to the realm of practice and experience of the Divine.

In ordinary human life, those who have not achieved the state of Enlightenment (the masses in society at large) perceive nature as a conglomeration of forces which are unpredictable and in need of control. However, as spiritual sensitivity matures, the aspirant realizes that what once appeared to be chaotic is in reality the Divine Plan of the Supreme Being in the process of unfoldment. When this state of consciousness is attained, the aspirant realizes that there is an underlying order in nature which can only be perceived with spiritual eyes.

The various injunctions of Maat are for the purpose of keeping order in society among ordinary people, people without psychological maturity and/or spiritual sensitivity, meaning that they lack an awareness of spiritual principles and moral - ethical development. Also, they provide insight into the order of creation and a pathway or spiritual discipline, which when followed, will lead the aspirant to come into harmony with the cosmic order. When the individual attunes his or her own sense of order and balance with the cosmic order, a spontaneous unity occurs between the individual and the cosmos, and the principles of Maat, rather than being a blind set of rules which we must strive to follow, become a part of one's inner character and proceed from one in a spontaneous manner.

This means that through the deeper understanding of cosmic order and by the practice of living in harmony with that order, the individual will lead him or herself to mental and spiritual peace and harmony. It is this peace and harmony which allows the lake of the mind to become a clear mirror in which the individual soul is able to realize its oneness with the Universal Soul.

THE PHILOSOPHY OF KARMA IN ANCIENT EGYPT

An action is repaid by its like, and to every action there is a consequence.
—Sage Meri-ka-Ra[44]
From the Ancient Egyptian Wisdom Texts

From ancient times, the cause and effect aspect of people's actions was well understood. Actions based on egoism and ignorance of the Divine lead a human being to frustration and the inability to discover true joy and peace. Actions based on truth and natural harmony lead to inner and outer peace and contentment. This "Hetep" or peace allows a human being to discover the higher nature or Self. Otherwise, egoistic actions lead one to bolster the lower self and ignorance. Actions based on the lower nature are characterized by egoistic desires (passion, greed, lust, envy, hatred, jealousy, anger, etc.). These actions inevitably lead to strife, violence and discontent. Actions based on Maat (righteousness-truth, selflessness, sharing, compassion, devotion to God, etc.) promote inner peace, social harmony and contentment. This is a proper environment for spiritual evolution. People who are constantly running after worldly desires will never be able to rest while those who affirm righteousness and peace will discover the real joy of life which cannot come from wealth, conquests, fame, hurting others, etc. By turning one's mind towards righteousness and selflessness a human being can evolve to discover the greater or deeper essence of their own being. This is referred to as "Nehast" or what modern day Christians call "The Resurrection."

MAAT AS THE SPIRITUAL PATH OF RIGHTEOUS ACTION

Maat is equivalent to the Chinese concept of the *Tao* or "*The Way*" of nature. This "*Way*" of nature, from the *Tao-te-Ching*, the main text of Taoism, represents the harmony of human and Divine (universal) consciousness. Also, Maat may be likened with the Indian idea of *Dharma* or the ethical values of life and the teachings related to *Karma Yoga,* the yogic spiritual discipline which emphasizes selfless service and the attitude that actions are being performed by God who is working through you instead of your personal ego-self. God is working through you to serve humanity, which is also essentially God. All Buddhist Monks utter the prayer *I go to the Buddha for refuge. I go to the Dharma for refuge. I go to the monastic order for refuge.* The Buddhist aspirant is admonished to take refuge in the *Buddha* (one's innate *Buddha*

---

[44] These are the teachings of King Kati to his son Meri-ka-Ra, and are referred to by this author by the son's name since they denote his royal and spiritual enlightenment.

Consciousness), the *Dharma*, and the *Sanga* (company of enlightened personalities). The following statement from Chapter 9 of the Bhagavad Gita shows how Lord Krishna admonished his followers to seek sanctuary in him as, Jesus did to his disciples hundreds of years later.

> 32. O Arjuna, those who take refuge in Me, whether men born in a lowly class, or women, or
> Vaishyas, or Shudras, even they are sure to attain the highest goal.

Jesus also exhorted his followers to bring him their troubles "and I will give them rest." Dharma is understood as the spiritual discipline based on righteousness, order and truth which sustains the universe. In the same way, the Ancient Egyptian Initiate was to lean upon Maat in order to purify his or her heart so as to uncover the virtuous character which leads to Divine awareness.

> "There are two roads traveled by humankind, those who seek to live Maat, and those who
> seek to satisfy their animal passions."

—Ancient Egyptian Proverb

Figure 65: The offering of blind Maat by the king (Waset (Thebes)).

The offering of blind Maat is an extremely important ritual displayed in papyruses and carved on the temples. because it symbolizes the legitimacy of the ruler to aspire to divine consciousness. Maat is the prerequisite to all spiritual evolution. Without righteousness in life no order and peace can be possible. The first responsibility of the king, i.e. anyone who aspires to become one with the gods and goddesses, is to uphold Maat objectively, without egoistic bias, i.e. "blind."

From Worldly Action to Divine Action

Ari
"Action," "to do something," "things done"
(From Chapter 33 of the *Prt m Hru*)

It is important here to gain a deeper understanding of what is meant by action. In primeval times, before creation, the primordial ocean existed in complete peace and rest. When that ocean was agitated with the first thought of God, the first *act* was performed. Through the subsequent acts of mind or efforts of divine thought, creation unfolded in the form of the various gods and goddesses who form the "companies of gods and goddesses." They represent the qualities of nature (hot-cold, wet-dry, etc.) in the form of pairs of opposites. When the first primeval thought emerged from the Primeval Ocean of pure potentiality, immediately there was something other than the single primordial essence. Now there is a being who is looking and perceiving the rest of the primordial essence. This is the origin of duality in the world of time and space and the triad of human consciousness. Instead of there being one entity, there appears to be two. The perception instrument, the mind and senses, is the third factor which comprises the triad. Therefore, while you consider yourself to be an individual, you are in reality one element in a triad which all together comprise the content of your human experiences. There is a perceiver (the real you), that which is being perceived (the object) and the act of perception itself (through the mind and senses).

With this first primordial act, God set into motion events which operate according to regular and ceaseless motion or action. This is the foundation upon which the universe is created and it emerges from the mind of God. Therefore, if one is able to think and act according to the way in which God thinks and acts, then there will be oneness with God. Human beings are like sparks of divine consciousness, and as such, are endowed with free will to act in any given way. This free will, when dictated by the egoism of the individual mind, causes individual human beings to feel separate from God. This delusion of the mind leads it to develop ideas related to its own feelings and desires. These egoistic feelings and desires lead to the performance of egoistic acts in an effort to satisfy those perceived needs and desires. This pursuit of fulfillment of desires in the relative world of the mind and senses leads the soul to experience pain, sorrow and frustration, because these desires can never be 100% satisfied. Frustration leads to more actions in search of fulfillment.

The fleeting feelings which most people have associated with happiness and passion are only ephemeral glimpses of the true happiness and peace which can be experienced if the source of true fulfillment within you was to be discovered. Maat shows a way out of the pain and sorrow of human existence and leads you to discover Asar within you, the source of eternal bliss and supreme peace. The negative impressions rise up at given times in the form of uncontrolled desires, cravings, unrest, and the other forms of self-torment with which human life abounds. If you choose to act according to your own will (ego), then you will be in contradiction with Maat. This means that you are contradicting your own conscience, creating negative impressions which will become lodged in the heart (unconscious mind), making it heavy, i.e. out of balance with the scale Maat[45] and will cause continuous mental agitation while you are alive and hellish experiences for yourself even after death.

One's actions carry on even after death in the form of impressions lodged in the deep unconscious mind, witnesses to how we have led our lives. Further, it is these impressions that lead us to our fate based on our own faculties since the divinities who act as judges in the Prt m Hru, Anpu (right mind), Djehuti (intellect) and Maat (righteousness), are merely aspects of our own personality. Therefore, we are the determiners of our own fate while on earth as well as beyond, as the following Maatian proverbs affirm, in support of the mystical iconography and the interrelationships of the divinities of righteousness and action.

---

[45] See the Judgment scene.

"This instant is thine; the next is in the womb of futurity, and thou knowest not what it may bring forth; maturity of the unborn is in the keeping of the Law. Each future state is that thou has created in the present."

"The impious Soul screams: I burn; I am ablaze; I know not what to cry or do; wretched me, I am devoured by all the ills that compass me about; alack, poor me, I neither see nor hear! This is the Soul's chastisement of itself. For the Mind of the man imposes these on the Soul."

It is important to understand that when the soul is attuned to a physical body, mind and senses, the experiences occur through these. Thus, the experiences of pleasure and pain are regulated by how much the body, mind and senses can take. If there is too much pain the body faints. When there is too much pleasure the mind and senses become weakened and swoons into unconsciousness or sleep. If there is too much pleasure, there develops elation and the soul is carried off with the illusion of pleasure, which creates a longing and craving for more and more in an endless search for fulfillment that is in reality a cycle of frustration and ultimate disappointment.

However, after death, there is no safety valve as it were. Under these conditions the soul will have the possibility of experiencing boundless amounts of pleasure or pain according to its karmic basis. This is what is called heaven and hell, respectively. Therefore, if you have lived a balanced life (Maat), then you will not have the possibility of experiencing heaven or hell. Rather, you will retain presence of mind and will not fall into the delusion of ignorance. Therefore, the rewards of developing a balanced mind during life continue after death. This mental equanimity allows you to see the difference between the truth and the illusions of the mind and senses, in life as well as in death.

Arit Maat
Work rightly, lead life of integrity, in accordance with Maatian principles-righteous offerings

Thus, if you choose to act in accordance with Maat, you will be in a position to transcend the egoistic illusions of the mind and thereby become free from the vicious cycle of actions which keep the mind tied to its illusory feelings and desires. When the mind is freed from the "vicious cycle,"[46] the soul's bondage to the world of time and space is dissolved because it is not being controlled by the mind, but has become the controller of the mind. When the practice of Maat is perfected, the mind becomes calm. When this occurs, the ocean of consciousness which was buffeted by the stormy[47] winds of thoughts, anxieties, worries and desires, becomes calm. This calmness allows the soul to cease its identification with the thoughts of the mind and to behold its true nature as a separate entity from the mind, senses, feelings and thoughts of the ego-self. The soul is now free to expand its vision beyond the constrictive pettiness of human desires and mental agitation, in order to behold the expansion of the inner Self.

Actions are the basis upon which the Cosmic Plan of creation unfolds. In human life, it is the present action which leads to the results that follow at some point in the future, in this life or in another lifetime. Therefore, if you are in a prosperous situation today or an adverse one, it is because of actions you performed in the past. Thus, both situations, good or bad, should be endured with a sense of personal responsibility and equanimity of mind (Maat). From a transcendental point of view, the soul looks at all situations equally. This is because the soul knows itself to be immortal and eternal, and untouched by the events of human existence which it has witnessed for countless lifetimes. It is the ego, which is transient, that looks on life's situations as pressing and abiding, and therefore either tries to hold onto situations which it considers to be "good" or to get away from or eradicate situations which it considers to be "bad." All situations, whether they are considered to be good or bad by the ego, will eventually pass on, so they should be viewed as clouds which will inevitably pass on, no matter how terrible or how wonderful they may seem to be. When life is lived in this manner, the mind develops a stream of peace which rises above

---

[46] Actions based on vices.
[47] See Chapter 4 of the Prt M Heru *... at the time of the storms...*

elation and depression, prosperity and adversity. By looking at situations with equal vision and doing your best regardless of the circumstances, you are able to discover an unalterable balance within yourself. This is Maat, the underlying order and truth behind the apparent chaos and disorder in the phenomenal world. In doing this, you are able to attune your mind to the cosmic mind of the innermost Self, which exists at that transcendental level of peace all the time.

This means that if you are, deep down, indeed the Universal Self, one with God, and if you have come to your current situation in life of bondage to the world of time and space due to your own state of mental ignorance, then it follows that if you undertake certain disciplines of knowledge (studying the teachings) and daily practice (following the teachings), those same actions will lead you to liberation from the state of bondage. Ignorance of your true Self is the root cause of your bondage to the karmic cycle of life-death-reincarnation-life-death-reincarnation, etc.

Actions must be performed by everyone. Even breathing is an action. Therefore, nobody can escape actions. No one can say: "I will go far away from civilization and escape all actions and then my actions will not lead me to a state of ignorance about my true Self." This form of thinking is a fallacy because, as just discussed, breathing, eating, drinking, sleeping, sitting, and walking are actions. The process of liberation requires more than just removing yourself from the field of physical actions (physical plane). You could go to a quiet cave, temple or church and you would still be plagued by the unruly thoughts of the mind which cause distraction from the Self. Thoughts are subtle forms of actions. Therefore, an action performed in thought can be equally significant and cause as much karmic entanglement as an action performed with the body. An action first originates in the mental field (astral plane) of consciousness which is stirred by desires rising from the unconscious mind (causal plane). This agitation prompts the mind toward thoughts and actions in an attempt to fulfill the desires of the unconscious, but those actions and thoughts create more desires and more future agitation. This is the state of bondage which is experienced by most people and it continues for lifetimes without end. This cycle continues until there is a discovery that desires cannot be fulfilled in this manner. Therefore, the root of desire, ignorance, must be eradicated in order to end the desires of the mind and achieve true peace and balance.

You need to develop subtlety of intellect and profound insight into the nature of the universe and of your innermost Self. The best way to achieve this goal is to practice a blending of wisdom and action in your personal spiritual discipline in order to harmonize your mental and physical qualities. In this process, you must understand that the ancient Sages have given guidelines for which thoughts and actions are in line with the scales of Maat, and which actions and thoughts are not. The 42 precepts of Maat constitute the focus of the Prt m Hru, however, throughout the book, many more injunctions are given. Their purpose is to cleanse the heart of the aspirant.

"The wise person who acts with Maat is free of falsehood and disorder."
–Ancient Egyptian Proverb

The practice of Maat signifies wisdom in action. This is to say that the teachings are to be practiced in ordinary day to day situations, and when the deeper implications of this practice are understood, one will be led to purity in action and thought. In order to become one with the Divine, you must become the Divine in thought and deed. This means that you must spiritualize your actions and your thoughts at all times and under all conditions. Actions which present themselves to you in the normal course of the day, as well as those actions which you have planned for the future, should be evaluated by your growing intellectual discriminative quality (Anubis and Saa), and then performed to your best capacity in a selfless manner. Now action has become a living offering to the Divine. This is the way to spiritualize action so as to move constantly towards the Divine. This is what the East Indian Yoga practitioners call Karma Yoga, or the Yoga of Action, the performance of action in such a manner that they lead to spiritual enlightenment instead of more entanglements in the world and more spiritual ignorance.

Arit Heru
The Eye of Heru, perfected action, movement towards the Divine.
(From Utterance #78 of the Ancient Egyptian *Pyramid Texts*)

From the beginning of the *Prt m Hru* scriptures in the period of the *Pyramid Texts* to the end with the Papyrus versions, there is a teaching of the Eye of Heru as being the various offerings (bread, incense, wine, etc.) to Asar. Each offering is considered to be the "Eye." Also, an offering, in the form of the Eye is given to the initiate. It is the Eye of divine action (Ari m hetep), now turned inward and upward towards the Divine, i.e. sublimated, in the form of Heru. This offering is given to the spiritual aspirant, but not as a new item that has never been known, but as something that was lost or taken away as it were, by Set (egoism). In other words, one's own righteous actions have allowed one to rediscover that which was lost, the Eye of intuitional vision, the Eye of Heru. In this manner the Eye is given in ritual fashion as an item to be consumed such as bread, wine, etc. In consuming these, the aspirant consumes Divinity. The Eye (bread, incense, wine, etc.) received by the initiate is the consecrated offering which has now become the essence of Heru. Consuming it means assimilating Heru into one's system, just as with any other food item. It is the highest possible action a human being can perform, as it is an acceptance of one's divine nature and one's self-sustenance, i.e. one's living off of oneself. The acceptance of this Eye in this manner is a direct reference to acceptance of oneself as being the Divine. There are several references to this teaching presented in the Prt m Hru. One passage, from Chapter 4, is presented below. As we know the saying, "you are what you eat," thus, by consuming the Eye offering one is to become Heru. This is the prototype for the same concept in Christianity, which called the offering the *Eucharist.* So a spiritual aspirant must offer Divine Actions and in return receives Divinity.

> I am the god great who came into existence out of himself, Nun. I created my own name
> and the Company of Gods and Goddesses, as I am The God. Who is this person that is
> being spoken about? Ra this is, Creator of the names of his own body parts.

Adversity in Life

Why is there adversity in life? Wouldn't it be nice if there was no misfortune to hamper your movement in life? Human life abounds with adversity. Even the very rich experience adversity. In fact, no matter who you are, you will experience adversity of one form or another as you progress through life.

Adversity is a divine messenger. Imagine how life would be if you could do anything you wanted to do. You would indulge every desire and whim. You would only seek to satisfy your desire for pleasure, and you would not accomplish anything significant in life. In the end you would be frustrated and disappointed because, no matter how hard you try, it is not possible to ever completely satisfy your desires for the pleasures of the senses.

Adversity is a form of resistance which life places on all beings for the purpose of engendering in them a need to strive to overcome it. When adversity is met with the correct understanding and with the right attitude, it can become a great source of strength and spiritual inspiration. However, if adversity makes you hardhearted, insensitive, selfish, cold and bitter, then you will lead yourself deeper into the quagmire of negativity and pain. Adversity is God's way of calling your attention away from negative ways of life and toward the basic elements of life. Often when people succeed in acquiring some object they desired, they develop conceit and vanity. They look down on others and feel proud of their accomplishment. However, when they lose what they desired, they fall into the valley of adversity, despair, violence and anger. They blame others for their misfortune and seek to hurt others for their loss.

Many of those people who have experienced the most adversity in history include Sages and Saints. Why should God allow those who are trying to be closest to the Divine be plagued with adversity? The answer lies in an Ancient Egyptian proverb:

"Adversity is the seed of well doing; it is the nurse of heroism and boldness; who that hath enough, will endanger himself to have more? Who that is at ease, will set their life on the hazard?

–Ancient Egyptian Proverb

Have you noticed that it seems as though the people who are most righteous and deserving of prosperity are the ones who suffer the most in life? In families, the child who is most obedient gets the most attention and disciplinary control. People who are loving and compassionate suffer illnesses and pain from others. This is because nature has been set up by God to create situations which challenge human beings so as to provide for them opportunities to discover their inner resources which give them the capacity to overcome the trouble, and thereby grow in discovery of their deeper Self. Those who suffer most are in reality those who have drawn more attention from the Divine, indeed, chosen for more intense spiritual testing. This testing process of nature allows every soul the opportunity to face trouble with either boldness and faith or with fear and negativity. The rewards of adversity faced well are increased strength of will and an increased feeling of discovery of the Divine within. When adversity is faced with negativity and ignorance, it leads to pain, sorrow and more adversity. Therefore, adversity cannot be understood and successfully faced with negativity (anger, hatred, hardheartedness, etc.). Adversity can only be overcome with wisdom and virtue, and virtue is the first and most important quality to be developed by all serious spiritual aspirants.

From a spiritual perspective, what is considered to be prosperity by the masses of ignorant people is in reality adversity, and what is considered to be adversity by the masses is in reality, prosperity. The masses consider that becoming rich and being able to indulge the pleasures of the senses through food, drink, drugs and sex is the ultimate goal, yet is there anyone who has discovered true peace and contentment because of billions of dollars? Having the opportunity to indulge the pleasures of the senses creates an opportunity for the mind to become more dependent on the worldly pleasures. This process intensifies the egoistic feelings and draws the soul away from discovering true peace within. There is increasing agitation and worry over gaining what is desired, and then preoccupation with how to hold onto it. Not realizing that all must be left behind at the time of death, people keep on seeking worldly fame, fortune and glory, and in the process never discover true happiness. They have duped themselves into believing that material wealth brings happiness, because the greedy corporations, the media and popular culture reinforce this message. In reality it is a philosophy of ignorance based on lack of reflection and spiritual insight. Adversity is a call to wake up from this delusion which will eventually result in pain and sorrow, and those who are experiencing the worst conditions are receiving the loudest call. Therefore, adversity is in reality prosperity because it stimulates the mind, albeit through suffering, so that it may look for a higher vision of life and discover the abode of true happiness, peace and contentment which transcends worldly measure.

This exalted vision of life is the innate potential of every human being. What is necessary is the dedication and perseverance to seek a higher understanding of the divine nature of creation and the divine nature of the innermost heart. It has the power to absolve and redeem all negativity. This is the highest goal of all human beings and the most difficult. However, as you gain greater understanding and greater will to act with virtue, your vision of the divine will increase and draw you closer and closer to the Higher Self. This is the glory of virtue and its power to vanquish and eradicate vice from the human heart.

Where Do Sin and Negativity Come From?

When a child is born, does that child know anything about the associations and acquaintances it will make? Does it know about either the good or bad people it will meet? Does it know about the negative things it will do in the future? There are many factors which determine the actions which an individual will perform in their lifetime. The most important of these is the tendency it carried forth from its previous lifetimes. You are not a finite, mortal human being. In reality you are an eternal soul, wandering in the realm of physical nature as you take birth again and again in search of true happiness and peace. Your search has led you to past lives wherein you experienced prosperity and adversity as well as degrees of sinfulness and virtue. If there was a tendency to negative thoughts in the past lifetime, there may be a tendency for more negativity in this lifetime if it is stimulated and not opposed.

The most important thing to remember now is that your present effort can overcome any and all of your past negativity if you apply yourself with earnestness and resolve to become fully established in virtue. This means that you must decide to dedicate your life to discovering and facing all shades of vice and negativity within you and in so doing, never fall back into the pits of ignorance which lead to pain and sorrow.

Having forgotten your eternal nature, you have been wandering through many lifetimes, meeting many other souls in the form of friends, relatives, etc., who are also wandering travelers, seeking the same thing you are: peace and contentment. However, when the soul forgets its eternal nature, it becomes indoctrinated by society and takes on the values and beliefs of society. If society says that money is most important, then the masses of ignorant people do whatever they can to get money. Those who cannot do it legally do it by any other means, because they have lost the connection to their fellow souls due to the delusion of ignorance caused by the pressure of desires and mental agitation. If those around them call them bad, they begin to think "I am a bad person" and then proceed to think of themselves as evil, unconsciously generating thoughts of anger, hatred, envy, etc., which cause them untold miseries though many lifetimes.

In reality, there is no real "badness" in the true you, the deepest part of you. Your Soul is in reality pure, and full of love which is waiting to be discovered. However, your ego is like a blanket of dust which has settled on a piece of glass and obstructs the light from passing through. When you live according to the precepts of virtue, the dust of ignorance, shame, desire, hatred, anger, lust, envy, greed, etc., are removed from your being. Then it is possible for you to discover the treasure which lies within your own heart. Thus, there is in reality no such thing as a criminal heart, only hearts which are clamoring for freedom from the bonds of ignorance and fear.

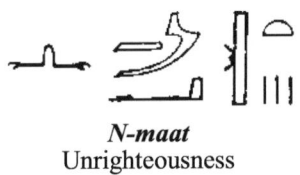

N-maat
Unrighteousness

In the Ancient Egyptian Myth of Asar, there is a teaching in reference to the god named Set. Set is the embodiment of evil, greed, lust, hatred envy, etc. He killed his own brother (Asar) to steal his Kingdom (Egypt). Heru, Asar's son, confronts Set and a battle ensues. Heru eventually overcomes Set through virtue. However, at the end it is revealed that Heru and Set are in reality not two personalities, but indeed one and the same. So the idea behind the teaching is that the true enemy is not outside of you, but within your very own personality, and it exists there in the form of negative qualities which in effect fetter your higher vision of spiritual reality. They cloud your intellect and deteriorate your willpower, so they allow for sinful and unrighteous thoughts to control you and direct your actions. However, the love, sweetness and wisdom of the Divine is also there within you, and this divine essence is equipped with immense spiritual force which can be discovered and used for developing a positive vision which can eradicate all negativity and reveal the true you, as the sun is revealed when the clouds disperse after a storm.

From Where Does True Happiness Come?

In reality, happiness does not and cannot come from objects that can be acquired or from activities that are performed. It can only come from within. Even actions that seem to be pleasurable in life cannot be considered as a source of happiness from a philosophical point of view, because all activities are relative. This means that one activity is pleasurable for one person and painful for another. This leads to the realization that it is not the activity itself that holds the happiness, but the individual doer who is performing the action, and assigning to it a value which she or he has learned from society or past karmic mental impressions, to assign. Therefore, if it was learned that going out to a party is supposed to be fun, then that activity will be pursued as a source of happiness. Here action is performed in pursuit of the fruit of the action in the form happiness; a result is desired from the action. However, there are several negative psychological factors which arise that will not allow true happiness to manifest. The first is that the relentless pursuit of the action renders the mind restless and agitated. The second is that if the activity is not possible, there will be depression in the mind. If the activity is thwarted by some outside force, meaning that something or someone prevented you from achieving the object or activity you saw as the "source of happiness," you develop anger and frustration. If by chance you succeed in achieving the object or activity, you become elated. This will cause greed in the mind and you will want more and more of it. When you are not able to get more at any particular time, you will become depressed and disappointed. Therefore, under these conditions, a constant dependence on outside activities and worldly objects develops in the mind which will not allow for peace and contentment. Even though it is illogical to pursue activities which cause pain in life, people are constantly acting against their own interests as they engage in actions in an effort to gain happiness, while in reality, they are enhancing the probability of encountering pain later on. People often act and shortly thereafter, regret what they have done. Sometimes people know even at the time of their actions that they are wrong, and yet they are unable to stop themselves. This is because when the mind is controlled by desires and expectations, the intellect, the light of reason, becomes *clouded* and *dull*. However, when the mind is controlled by the purified intellect, then it is not possible to be led astray due to the *fantasies* and *illusions* of the mind. When the individual is guided by their purified intellect, only right actions can be performed no matter what negative ideas arise in the mind. Such a person cannot be deluded into negative actions, and when negative actions (actions which lead to future pain and disappointments) are not performed, unhappiness cannot exist. In addition, a person who lives according to the teachings of non-doership (performing righteous action without desires or expectations for the future results of their actions) lives a life of perpetual peace and happiness in the present.

True peace and inner fulfillment will never come through the pursuit of actions when there is an expectation or desire for the fruits of those actions. Any action performed by a person will produce a result. This is due to the cause and effect nature of the physical plane. However, a human being, though working with an attitude to promote success in a project, should not depend on or expect a specific result from their actions, because the world is unpredictable. If a person does so they are succumbing to the lower nature, the animal instincts and desires that drive the ignorant. Rather, while fruits or results of actions may be promoted for practical reasons such as sustaining oneself, acquiring the necessities for progressing in life or for advancing the public good, an aspirant should perform actions with the internal awareness that the fruits of actions (results) will not produce abiding happiness. Further, an aspirant should primarily view actions as a means to promote purity of heart since actions give an opportunity to practice Maat. Living by Maat means going against the ego-desires. Maatian actions are necessary if the ego-personality is to be sublimated. So the Yoga of Action is an integral and crucial part of every spiritual aspirant's journey towards enlightenment.

The belief in objects or worldly activities as a source of happiness is therefore seen as a state of *ignorance* wherein the individual is caught up in the *illusions*, *fantasies* and *fanciful notions* of the mind. However, happiness and peace can arise spontaneously when there is an attitude of detachment and dispassion towards objects and situations in life. If actions are performed with the idea of discovering peace within, based on the understanding of the philosophy outlined above, and for the sake of the betterment of society, then these actions will have the effect of purifying the heart of the individual. The desires and expectations will dwindle while the inner fulfillment and awareness of the present moment will increase. There will be greater and greater discovery of peace within, a discovery of what is truly stable and changeless within as opposed to the mind and outer world which are constantly changing and unpredictable.

Keeping The Balance

"Neither let prosperity put out the eyes of circumspection, nor abundance cut off the hands of frugality; they that too much indulge in the superfluities of life, shall live to lament the want of its necessaries."

"See that prosperity elate not thine heart above measure; neither adversity depress thine mind unto the depths, because fortune beareth hard against you. Their smiles are not stable, therefore build not thy confidence upon them; their frowns endure not forever, therefore let hope teach you patience."

Ancient Egyptian Proverbs

As the proverbs above suggest, equanimity is one of the most important qualities that a spiritual aspirant must develop in order to practice virtuous living. Virtuous living requires strength of will because life is constantly tempting the mind and body toward the pleasures of the senses and toward egoistic desires. When the mind is constantly agitated, swinging back and forth, becoming elated and exuberant in prosperous conditions and angry and agitated during adversity, the mental energy is drained and dispersed. It becomes hard to concentrate, to act with clarity, to distinguish between right and wrong and to fulfill the duties of life. This is why in the *Prt m Hru,* the initiate is constantly saying that {he/she} has *"Kept the Balance"* and is worthy to enter into the divine realms.

Undue mental agitation is the source of angry thoughts wherein people say and do things they would not otherwise do. They get caught up in a pattern wherein they are easily provoked to anger by others who can "push the right buttons." When the mind is in control and always aware of the thoughts within as well as the world outside, it is impossible for this mind to fall prey to the provocation of others or to despair or fear. This is the ideal of equanimity that is to be reached by living a virtuous life through the study and practice of the teachings of mystical spirituality.

A Synopsis of Maat Philosophy Based on the Kemetic Hieroglyphic Text

The Path of Maat: Right Action

Ari
"Action," "to do something," "things done"

Arit Maat
Work rightly, lead life of integrity, in accordance with Maatian principles.

Ari em hetep.
Work contentedly, with peace and contentment, without egoistic desire or expectations.

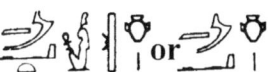

Maat Ab
Thus attain Purity of Heart

Maakheru
Become true of Speech, Spiritually enlightened.

Arit Heru
Receive the Eye of Heru, perfected action, the eucharist, the act of becoming one with the Divine
(the highest action).

117

The Mysticism of Duality and Non-duality

Figure 66: Left-The front of the typical Temple of Egypt-Africa.

Figure 67: Above- The Kemetic Caduceus: The god Asar, embraced by Aset and Nebethet with Khepri above.

The front of the typical Temple of Egypt-Africa, the facade entrance showing two Pylons and the single opening. In an inscription at Edfu the pylons are referred to as Aset and Nebethet, the two goddesses of Asar who raise him up to attain resurrection and immortality. The single opening symbolizes non-duality and singularity of consciousness. Thus, on entering into the Temple, there is a symbolic ritual-meditation leading toward a spiritual movement out of the world (duality – Aset and Nebethet) and into the shrine wherein the underlying oneness of the universe is to be explored and discovered. Thus, the temple is a place wherein the duality and multiplicity of human existence can be transcended. Therefore, the architecture of the temple, in and of itself, is a meditation on spiritual enlightenment and nonduality.

The Mysticism of the Three Realms of Existence

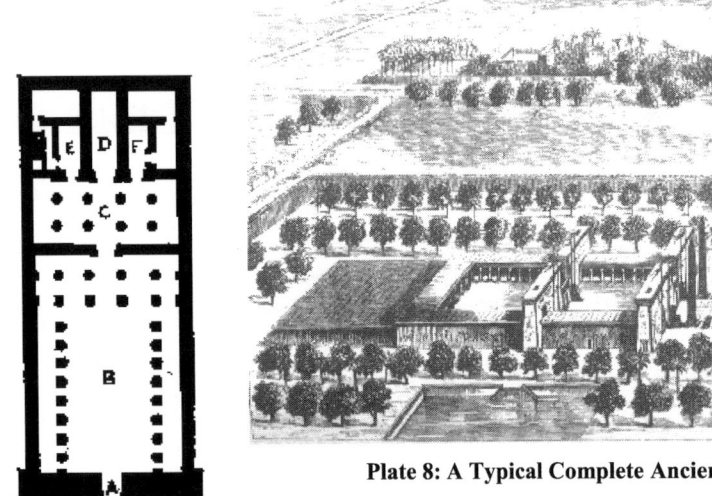

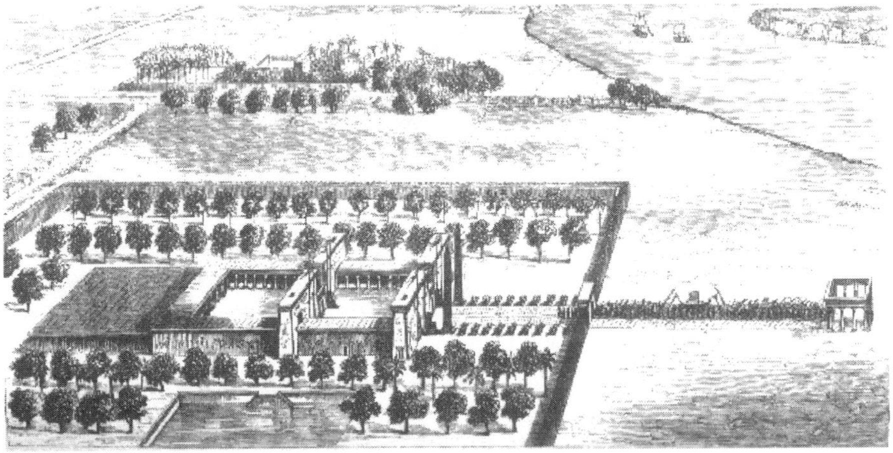

Plate 8: A Typical Complete Ancient Egyptian Temple Complex.

118

In the earliest Dynastic period, commonly known as the *Archaic Period,* the *House of God* or *hwt ntr* was composed of three parts. These were: (1) The sanctuary (holy of holies), (2) The Hypostyle hall (structure resting on pillars), (3) The courtyard. The sanctuary held the Divine image and was the scene of the innermost rituals for discovering the essence of the Divine. The sanctuary was not open to outside light. The further away from the sanctuary the other rooms were, the wider and taller they were. Also, they were more open to outside light. The pylons at the entrances were known as Aset and Nebethet, who *raise the Sun (i.e. God) who shines on the horizon.*

Plate 9: A diagram of the Temple of Amun-Ra at Karnak, Egypt.

The diagram (floor plan) shows the Pylons (A), the Court (B), the Hypostyle Hall (C), the Chapel of Amun (Holy of Holies - D), the Chapel of Mut (E), the Chapel of Chons (F).

The Temple is a symbol of the universe. The bottom part represents the earth. From the earth sprout three plants: the papyrus, the lotus and the palm. These were depicted in the form of columns. The ceiling was vaulted (an arched structure, usually of masonry, forming a ceiling or roof) and painted or carved with forms of heaven, depicting stars and divine representations. Thus, the temple was a microcosm of the universe in the same way as the human being is a microcosm of the universe. In the temple, initiates and spiritual preceptors gathered for the purpose of intense initiatic studies and spiritual practice as well as to provide a focus for the education and management of society.

Thus, the construction of the Ancient Egyptian Temple follows the format of creation, reflecting the Trinity and Triad aspect of the phenomenal universe, and the triune aspects of human consciousness through the three segments of the temple structure and the three sprouting columns. Out of the duality (earth-heaven) come the three aspects of consciousness, subject-object-interaction. This same duality (Aset-Nebethet) acts as an enlightening factor which resurrects the initiate (i.e. the Sun, the Divine essence within the human being).

The Mysticism of the Journey of the Divine Boat

The typical Ancient Egyptian Temple was aligned on an east-west axis. In this manner the sun would symbolically rise and set between the pylons. Therefore, the pylons are the Akhet (horizon) of the temple, the doorway to the Netherworld and eternity. The two pylons at the entrance represent the two mountains in between which the sun travels (see hieroglyphic symbol below) in order to reach *Manu,* the passage to the Netherworld in the west, the abode of the blessed. Luxor Temple and Denderah Temple, however, have a north-south axis.

Figure 68: The Divine Boat From Papyrus Nu

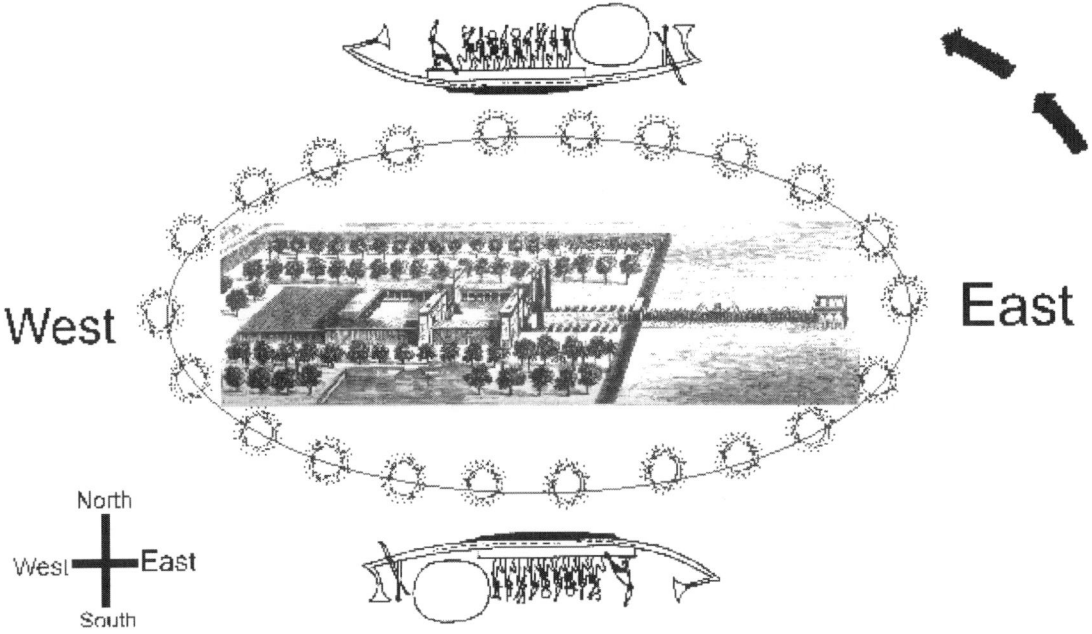

Plate 10: The Journey of the Divine Boat over temple.

Figure 69: Far Left and Center- Akhet- The Horizon as Manu, the west.

Figure 70: Far Right- The front of the Ancient Egyptian temple with the sun setting behind it, i.e. over the Holy of Holies.

The Place Where Nothing Grows

There is a special realm in the Duat that is shrouded in the deepest darkness, and it is untouched by the myriad of cries, dismemberments and sufferings of unrighteous souls (the enemies of Ra and Asar) being experienced based on their bad deeds (actions) of the past, as well as the cries of happiness and pleasure of the righteous souls who are experiencing heavenly or pleasurable conditions according to their good deeds (actions) of the past. This part of the Duat is composed of the seven *Arits* or Halls. It transcends time and space as well as the mind and thoughts. It is absolute existence. The rest of the Duat as well as the physical world is relative reality. In this special realm, there is no growth of any kind. There is no birth, no death and no passage of time, just eternity. This is the meaning of the following hekau-utterance from *The Egyptian Prt m Hru,* Chapter 33:

> "I come to you through the great path, to see thy beauties. With my two arms I adore you in your name, Maa. I have come through this exalted spiritual path and I find that it is a primordial path. The ash tree had not come into being, nor was the shed tree born yet; the ground was not yet created nor were there any plants or vegetation either. As to myself, I go into the abode of Hidden Existence. I speak words with Set. I breathe in odors. Comes close to me the clothing which is upon those who prostrate upon the hidden things there."

That which is in the place where nothing grows, **n-rutef,** is the place of absolute stillness **Urti-hat**. It is a region that is devoid of forms or mental concepts of any kind. It is the primeval or celestial waters from which creation arises. It is the place which is "hidden" from that which is in motion, the relative reality. Therefore, it is hidden to those whose minds are in constant motion due to desires, cravings, emotional attachments, greed, etc. That which is relative or temporal emanates out of that which is absolute and eternal. The relative reality emanates from this hidden place of stillness. It is to this place of stillness where one must go and have "communion" with God. When this occurs, that which is hidden is revealed.

Blackness and Nothingness and the Body of Asar

Figure 71: Asar's body bent in a circle surrounded by the Primeval Ocean of Creation.

Above: The body of Asar (God) is the eternal (symbolized by the circular form of his body) Life Force, which sustains Creation. The body of Asar itself is the heart of the Duat or Astral Plane and the supreme abode of Asar as well as the goal of all spiritual practice.

This deepest and most dark realm of the Duat is Asar, Himself, and this is why Asar is referred to as the "Lord of the Perfect Black" and is often depicted as being black or green of hue. The black color refers to deep consciousness and the green refers to the engendering life force in all vegetation. It is also why Nut, Aset, and Hetheru are also described as "dark-skinned."[48] They are emanations from this realm

---

[48] From an inscription in the temple of Denderah, Egypt.

of blackness which is described as a void or "*nothingness*" in the hieroglyphic papyrus entitled *The Laments of Aset and Nebethet*. This notion of nothingness is akin to the Buddhist notion of *Shunya* or the "void," which refers to the area of consciousness which is devoid of mental concepts and thoughts. When there are no thoughts or forms in the mind, it is calm, expansive and peaceful. When there are thoughts in the mind, the mental awareness is narrowed and defined in terms of concepts. If the mind is confined to these concepts and narrow forms of thought, then it is confined to that which is limited and temporal. If it eradicates its desires, cravings and illusions, then it becomes aware of the innermost reality and realizes its connection to the entire cosmos. However, the words nothingness" and "blackness" should not convey the understanding of a black color or darkness when the lights are turned off, for these are concepts also. It is a transcending of all experiences that can be defined in terms of ordinary conceptualization or perception with the physical or astral mind and senses. In fact, deep down there is a light but not like that of a light bulb. It is a mystic light which transcends even the sun. This is Heru, the luminous Divine Self which is the objective of all spiritual aspirants. Thus, the teaching of the Duat (Amentet, Re-Stau, etc.) gives insight into the nature of the human mind. It is a description of the mental landscape, its demons, gods and goddesses (everything that leads to ignorance and mental agitation) as well as the way to discover the abode of the innermost Self (everything that leads to peace, harmony and wisdom). Therefore, the task of a spiritual aspirant is to eradicate the concepts, agitation, desires and cravings in the mind and to discover the "hidden" innermost reality which is Hetep (Supreme Peace), eternal and pure.

In the Asarian Resurrection Myth, Asar was killed by his brother and resurrected by his sister and wife, Aset. While his spirit resurrected and became the lord of the West, his body became the sustaining essence which causes vegetation to grow. This is the reason why Asar is depicted as having green hue. In a mystical sense, Asar is the very sustenance of life. All food that is eaten is therefore Asar also. This idea is also expressed in the benediction of the Ancient Egyptian doctors, who upon administering medicaments would speak the special words of power *si neter iri mettu wadj,* "may God make the vascular system flourish." The Kemetic term for flourish is "greening." So one is order to become healthy one is to become green like Asar. This is the source of the Eucharist teaching. Thus, Asar is the sustenance of the Duat (Astral) as well as the Ta (earth) realms.

Figure 72: Asar, with vegetation growing from his body, being watered by the farmer. From a bas-relief at the Temple of Aset.

From a higher level of understanding, the Duat is the unconscious mind and Asar is that level which transcends the thinking processes, its deepest region. It is the level of consciousness that is experienced during deep dreamless sleep. Therefore, it is the "Hidden" aspect of the human heart, and thus, it is also known as Amun.

The East and The West: Reincarnation and Heaven

Another very important teaching in reference to the Duat or "Beautiful West" comes from the following Hymn to Amen-Re. The hymn to Amun-Ra instructs us in the wisdom that those who are judged by God to be unrighteous will not attain the coveted goal of reaching the abode of the Supreme Divinity. Instead they will be directed toward the "East." This is a clear reference to reincarnation. The "East" implies the dawn and a new life for the sun in the form of Khepri. In effect, it symbolizes the rebirth of the sun through Nut and concurrently, the rebirth of the soul as well. Reincarnation is the continuous cycle of birth-death and rebirth into a new body which the soul undergoes over a period of millions of years until it is purified enough to discover and return to its original source, the Supreme Divinity. In ancient times, the Greek historian, Herodotus, recorded that the Ancient Egyptians were the first to understand and teach the wisdom in reference to reincarnation. Therefore, in order to reach the West, it is necessary to be pure of heart which implies having lived according to the principles of Maat as well as having developed reverence and devotion toward, and wisdom about, the Divine. This implies that one has lived life based on studying, reflecting, meditating and practicing the spiritual teachings.

> "Amun-Ra who first was king,
> The god of earliest time,
> The vizier of the poor.
> He does not take bribes from the guilty,
> He does not speak to the witness,
> He does not look at him who promises,
> Amun judges the land with his fingers.
> He speaks to the heart,
> He judges the guilty,
> He assigns him to the East,
> The righteous to the West."

Having explored this most hidden region of the Duat (unconscious mind) through the practices of yoga and meditation, the initiate can now affirm that {he/she} has had experience of the Divine. Those who attain this experience are called Sages and/or Saints. Those who are established in this state of awareness, meaning that they have a continuous divine awareness based on this experience, are called enlightened Sages. Due to their mystical experience, anything that an enlightened Sage says is considered to be directly inspired by the Divine. Thus, they are considered to be "enlightened human Beings." This is the meaning of the following hekau-utterance from the *Prt m Hru,* Chapter 33:

> "It is I who have entered into the house of Asar and I have clothed myself with garments of the one who is within. It is I who have entered into Rastau (1) and I have seen the secrets (2) which are within. Hidden was I, but I found a way (3). It is I who went into Yanrutf (4). I put on the clothing, which was there, over my nakedness. Given to me was unguent of women by encompassing the earth of humankind. Truly, he (5) has spoken to me about himself."

The mystical meaning behind the hekau just presented is very important to the understanding of what is meant by the terms "enlightenment" and "mystical experience." (1) Rasta or Restau refers to the site of the grave of Asar, the passageway to the Netherworld; (2) "Secrets" of course refers to the Shetai or Hidden Supreme Being who is known as Asar-Amun, (3) Here, the initiate discovered that {he/she} was able to find the boundary and to discover the abode of the "Hidden One." The initiate was able to discover the difference between what is real and what is illusion, and was therefore able to traverse the illusory Duat and discover the special location wherein there is supreme peace and immortality. (4) Yanrutf (Nerutef) refers to the mythological site of the grave of Asar or the innermost shrine. (5) This line imparts the wisdom that God {him/her}self (Asar) is the one who ultimately gives the highest wisdom about God. All of the teachings of the scriptures are only incomplete and indirect descriptions of God because God transcends any and all mental concepts. Even though the spiritual scriptures are given by Sages and Saints who are in communion with God, the medium of communication, words and concepts, remain in the realm of the mind (relative reality). Therefore, the study of the scriptures and various rituals cannot in and of themselves confer enlightenment or the mystical experience of union with the Divine. For this to occur, it is necessary to actually experience the Divine and in order for this to occur, it is necessary to discover one's true essence as one with God, for only by becoming one with something can that thing be known. In this form of knowing, there is experience, unlike intellectual knowledge which does not confer experience. If a teacher tells you about China, you have "intellectual knowledge." If you visited China, you have "experience."

"There is no life for the soul except in knowing, and no salvation but doing."
—Ancient Egyptian Proverbs

There is no way to describe the kind of knowledge that is gained through actual experience. Therefore, in order to truly have knowledge of the Divine, it is necessary to commune with the Divine. All other forms of knowledge are incomplete and will not lead to abiding peace, **Menu hetep,** either while living on earth or in the Duat. This does not mean that acquiring intellectual knowledge is not important. Before you can harvest fruits, you must first plant the seeds. Before you plant the seeds, you must clear the land and prepare the soil. Intellectual knowledge tills the soil, removing the weeds and shrubs of mental agitation, egoism, selfishness and negativity. A seed planted in this fertile soil will grow into the tree of the subtle, purified intellect. Then it is possible to harvest the fruits of intuitional realization of the Self or Enlightenment. Shai and Rennenet are found in the judgment scene in the Hall of Maat wherein Djehuti records the result of a person's deeds and level of spiritual understanding. The hands of Djehuti (god of wisdom) are the goddess "Shai" which means "fate" or "destiny" and the goddess "Rennenet" which means "fortune and harvest." The implication is that you reap (harvest) the result of your actions (destiny) according to your level of wisdom. Thus, you yourself are the determiner of your own actions, the judge of your own actions and the determiner of your own fate and fortune or the fruits you will reap for those actions.

"The choice of the earthly condition is made by the soul itself, and very generally it differs from what it has been in the preceding term of life in this world. The cause is in him who makes the choice and the divinity is without blame in the matter.
—Ancient Egyptian Proverbs

THE SCALES OF MAAT AND THE PSYCHOSPIRITUAL ENERGY CENTERS

Figure 73: The Greenfield Papyrus (left) and the Kenna Papyrus Sales of Maat (right).

The Serpent Power System of Energy Centers from Ancient Egypt is depicted clearly in the judgment scenes of certain papyri. The Serpent Power, known as Kundalini energy and as Prana in India, Chi in China, and Ra-Sekhem in Ancient Egypt, flows throughout thousands of *nadis* or subtle energy channels in the subtle (astral) body. If any of the energy channels are blocked or over-sensitized, a dis-balance can arise, causing illness in the mind and physical body. There are three most important channels through which the Serpent Power flows. In India these are known as: *Sushumna, Ida and Pingala.* These are represented by the Egyptian Caduceus of Djehuti which is composed of a staff which has two serpents

124

wrapped around it. Thus, in the Kemetic mystical system, the three main channels of Life Force energy of the Serpent Power may be understood as being presided over by three divinities: Asar as the central shaft, and Aset and Nebethet as the solar and lunar channels, respectively. In reference to the Scales of Maat, goddess Maat, in her non-dual form becomes the central shaft, and in her dual form as the Maati goddesses (Aset and Nebethet, also known as Uraeus Serpent Goddess), assumes the role of the solar and lunar channels. During the ceremonies connected to the mysteries of the Uraeus Serpent Goddess *Uatchet* (Udjat), the priest addresses the initiate:

The Goddess Uatchet cometh unto thee in the form of the living Uraeus (Arat), to anoint thy head with their flames. She riseth up on the left side of thy head, and she shineth from the right side of thy temples without speech; they, (Arati), rise up on thy head during each and every hour of the day, even as they do for their father Ra, and through them the terror which thou inspirest in the holy spirits is increased, and because Uatchet and Nekhebet rise up on thy head, and because thy brow becometh the portion of thy head whereon they establish themselves, even as they do upon the brow of Ra, and because they never leave thee, awe of thee striketh into the souls which are made perfect.

The preceding scripture from the Ancient Egyptian embalming ceremonies is echoed in the *Book of Coming Forth By Day*. The state of enlightenment is further described in Chapter 26 where the initiate realizes that the seven Uraeus deities or bodies (immortal parts of the spirit) have been reconstituted:

"The seven Uraeuses are my body... my image is now eternal."

These seven Uraeuses, *Iarut,* are also described as the *"seven souls of Ra"* and *"the seven arms of the balance (Maat)"* and they are also the seven Cow Goddesses[49].

The Process of Human Evolution

In mystical philosophy, the process of human evolution is often referred to in terms of levels of spiritual evolution. The idea of describing and using the seven states of consciousness was recognized by the Ancient Egyptian Sages long before any other civilization adopted the concept. This teaching became an integral part of the philosophy of Maat because it is indeed this aspect of a human being, which is being judged in the Hall of Maat. The level of consciousness is equal to the level of purity of heart. Therefore, the heart (subconscious and unconscious mind) may be classified into one of the seven states of evolution, and this classification will determine its fate. It is important to note here that all souls are responsible for their own state of consciousness and that each soul will judge itself and thereby determine its own fate. Through your own actions and beliefs you are fashioning the content of your own mind. This, your own creation, will lead you to varied experiences during life and after death.

The development of the Life Force energy within every human being was practiced in ancient times by the Egyptians and then the mystery schools of Mediterranean cultures, the mystery schools of Asia Minor, and the Yoga practitioners of China and India. The Ancient Egyptian Papyruses of Kenna and Greenfield are examples of the Serpent Power in Ancient Egypt. The Ancient Egyptian deity *Arat (serpent goddess)*, who was known as the Uraeus goddess by the Greeks, presides over the Life Force energy known as Ra or Sekhem. This same Arat is an aspect of Hetheru who is the scorching, fiery eye of Ra and which is also the right eye of Heru. Within this brief explanation you can see the interrelated nature of all deities as they refer to the various facets of spiritual development of a human being.

The Psycho-spiritual evolution of a human being has been symbolically represented as an unfoldment of psycho-spiritual energy centers in the spiritual body of a human being. The Psychic Energy Centers in the spiritual or etheric body are distributed throughout the subtle spine going up from the base of the spine to the Crown of the head: *The Uraeus.* Each one of these centers are called *Chakras* or vortices of energy. In Egyptian symbolism they are depicted as circles or links in a chain in the Karmic scales of Maat, used to judge the initiate. In Indian symbolism they are portrayed as a *padmas* or Lotuses, symbolizing psycho-spiritual principles of human consciousness. By understanding these and removing

---

[49] See Chapter 20.

obstacles to them, Kundalini energy is freed. When your consciousness is freed you can move toward the divine essence of your being.

Mental and emotional complexes, egoistic sentiments, desires and ignorance constitute the main obstacles and blocks to the Serpent Power, one's own spiritual consciousness. Through physical exercises, physical cleansing through diet and lifestyle changes, and meditation on the psycho-spiritual implications of each center, Serpent Power Yoga is effected.[50]

Figure 74: The Ammit Monster

The monster/demon of the judgment scene; one third hippopotamus, one third lion and one third crocodile.

Maat philosophy encompasses the highly mystical teachings related to the psychospiritual energy centers and the Serpent Power or Arat. In India, this system of spiritual philosophy is known as Kundalini Yoga. The Life Force energy is latent in the spiritual body of every human being. As it is awakened, by following the teachings of Maat, it leads a person to awaken in spiritual consciousness. Maat presides over the scale as it determines the level of righteousness of the heart of the person in question, which relates to their level spiritual of evolution. There are seven spiritual centers which operate in the subtle body of a human being. They are represented by seven spheres or chain links (fig. 73). Each represents a psychospiritual principle which must be mastered in order to evolve spiritually. Those who have not yet evolved beyond the third center are symbolically devoured by the Ammit monster. That is to say, they experience hellish conditions as a punishment for wrong doings in life. The first center represents fear and the basic necessities of life (eating and elimination). The second center represents creativity and sexuality. The third center represents ego control over others (negative will power) and personal energy. The fourth center represents selfless love. The fifth center represents self-control and positive will power. Ther sixth center represents the Eye of Heru, intuitional vision of the spirit world as well as the phenomenal world. The seventh center represents transcendental vision and becoming one with God. Spiritual evolution implies growing beyond the first three lower centers. The masses of people are entangled with the world due to their egoism, desires and worldly concerns. This is what the lower three centers represents. The upper four centers represents the process of spiritual evolution and self-discovery.[51]

The energy centers of the subtle body are likened to a tree, which the aspirant climbs through personality integration, which leads {him/her} to intuitional realization of the transcendental self. In the process of creation, the creative energy manifests in the form of six planes of consciousness. This is the realm of phenomenal reality including physical, astral and mental existence. Most people function on the level of the first three energy-consciousness levels. The goal of this Yoga (Serpent Power) is to unite the six phenomenal consciousness centers with the seventh or transcendental realm of consciousness, the Absolute. This Absolute is what various religions refer to by different names such as the Kingdom of Heaven, Asar, Krishna, Brahman, the Tao, God, Higher Self, Goddess, Christ, Buddha, etc.

---

[50] See the book *Initiation Into Egyptian Yoga* by Dr. Muata Ashby.
[51] See the book "The Serpent Power" by Dr. Muata Ashby.

The previous picture from the Papyrus of Kenna shows Ammit, the monster who devours the unrighteous. Notice that he is biting the scales of Maat between the third and fourth circles. These circles indicate levels of spiritual evolution or psycho-spiritual energy centers. The Greenfield Papyrus shows the centers as a chain with seven links. These centers refer to the judgment of the heart of the initiate. Centers 1-3 indicate immature human beings who live to seek sensual pleasures and centers 4-7 indicate individuals who are progressing on the spiritual path. The Ancient Egyptian symbol of the serpent and/or vulture at the level of the brow indicates the energy consciousness at the level of the sixth energy center and the serpent on the top of the head refers to the energy center at the crown of the head, meaning that the energy-consciousness has reached the Transcendental Self.[52]

---

[52] For more on the Ancient Egyptian Teachings of the Life Force (Serpent Power) see the book *The Serpent Power*.

The Serpent Power of India
and
Serpent Power of Ancient Egypt in the Prt M Hru

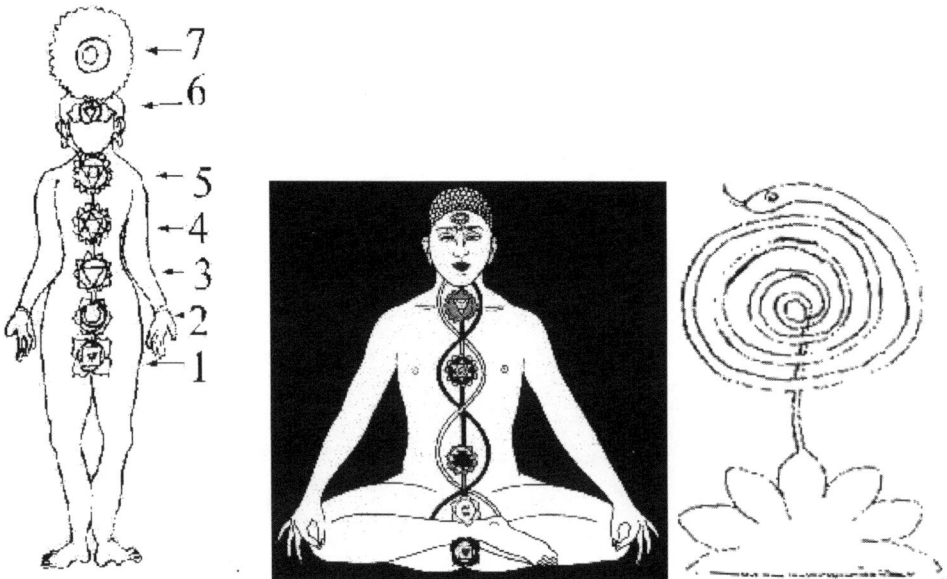

Figure 75: The Indian Iconography of Kundalini Life Force Mysticism

Left: Picture from Indian Kundalini Yoga showing the location of the energy centers. Center: Picture showing the two opposing life force energies as two serpents intertwining the central shaft.
Right: Kundalini Serpent with the classic 3 ½ turns, symbolizing the journey through the energy centers and a return to the primordial state of consciousness, i.e. spiritual enlightenment.

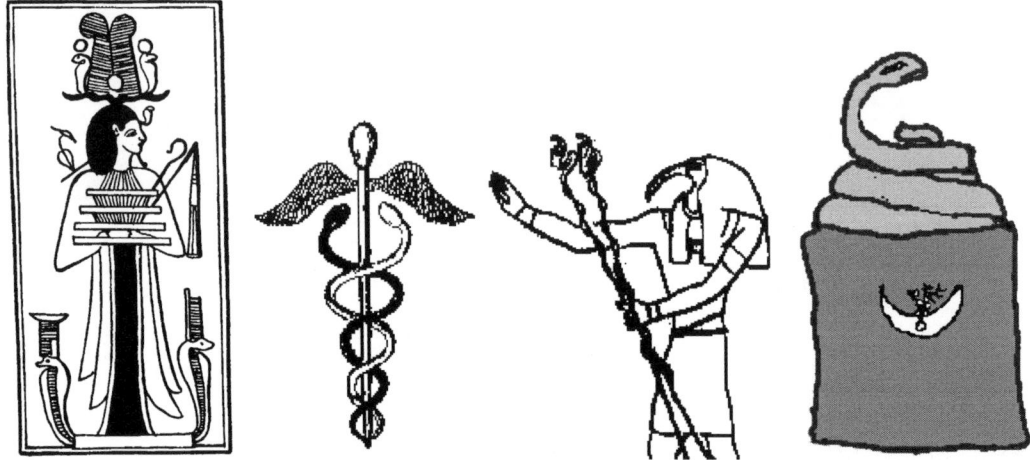

Figure 76: The Kemetic Iconography of Kundalini Life Force Mysticism.

Left: The God Asar from Ancient Egypt displaying the four upper psycho-spiritual energy centers. The serpents represent Aset and Nebethet, together, forming an anthropomorphic caduceus. *Center:* the god Djehuti holds the ancient form of the caduceus staff. To his left is the caduceus of the Hermetic Period, still used by medical doctors and veterinarians in modern times. *Right*: the "Basket of Aset" showing the Arat "Serpent Power" with the classic 3 ½ turns.

128

ONE ULTIMATE , ABSOLUTE ABODE, TWO PATHS LEADING TO IT: NON-DUALISM IN ANCIENT EGYPT

Figure 77: (right) Another example of the Kemetic Caduceus, with Atum-Ra, symbolizing the central shaft, attended on by goddesses Nebethet and Aset.

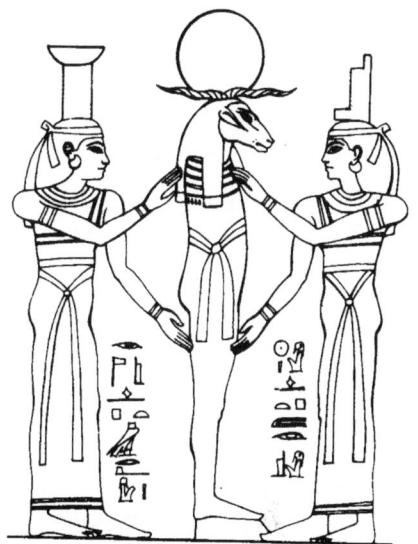

After the millions of years of differentiated creation, the chaos that existed before creation will return; only the primeval god[53] and Asar will remain steadfast-no longer separated in space and time.

–Ancient Egyptian *Coffin Texts*

The passage above concisely expresses the powerful teaching that all creation is perishable and that even the gods and goddesses will ultimately dissolve into the primordial state of potential consciousness. Therefore, it behooves a human being to move towards the Divine since that is the only stable truth that exists as an abiding reality. This is known as the Absolute, from which all has emanated and into which all will dissolve. *Tm* (Tem, Tum, Atum, Atum-Ra) is the Absolute, from which Creation arises and into which Creation will dissolve. A righteous person has the choice to go to the Djed and abide in Asar, to merge with him, or they can await the time when Ra traverses through the Duat, the eternal journey described earlier, illuminating it as He passes in his Boat. If they choose Ra, they will be picked up and be loaded unto the boat where they will merge with Ra and experience peace, bliss and happiness for all time. The *Book of Amduat* discusses the Duat with the followers of Ra in mind, while the *Prt m Hru* and the *Book of Gates* discusses the Duat with the followers of Asar in mind. If they choose to stay in the Duat, they will lead a life in the astral plane similar to that on earth for a certain period of time but with very important differences. These differences are outlined in Chapter 8 of the Ancient Egyptian *Book of Coming Forth By Day*. The same transcendental and non-dualist philosophy evident in the passage above from the *Coffin Texts* can be found in the Indian *Upanishads*[54].

Before creation came into existence, Brahman (the Absolute) existed as the Unmanifest. From the Unmanifest was created the manifest. From himself he brought forth himself.
Hence he is known as the Self-Existent.

—Taittiriya Upanishad

The Ancient Egyptian concept of Nun is powerfully expressed in the following passage from the *Coffin Texts*.

I am Nu, The Only One, without equal and I came into being at the time of my flood...I originated in the primeval void. I brought my body into existence through my own potency. I made myself and formed myself in accordance with my own desire. That which emanated from me was under my control.

Once again, the initiate is to discover that the Divine Self is the substratum of manifest creation and that {his/her} deeper essence and the deeper essence of all humanity is that same Self-existent Divinity which brought the entire creation into being by the power of her own will and desire. Nun is an aspect of Tem. In this aspect, it is to be understood as a formless potential matter which can convert itself into any form and any element (earth, water, fire, metal, etc.). This process may be likened to how temperature affects water. For example, very cold water becomes ice, and ice can have any shape. When very hot, the water evaporates and becomes so subtle (vapor) as to be "unmanifest." At room temperature, he same water is visible but formless.

---

[53] Referring to the Supreme Being in the form of Atum-Ra
[54] Mystical spirituality texts of India.

All matter is like the water. All matter is composed of the same essence which takes on the form of various objects, just as clay can take many forms. However, the forms are not abiding but temporary. God has assumed the forms of Creation just as an actor assumes a part in a play. When the play is over, the actor's mask is stripped away and the true essence of the actor's identity is revealed, just as ice melts to reveal water. The Divine Self is the substratum of all that is manifest. The same philosophy, and using almost the same exact language, is evident in the Indian *Upanishads*.

> *...In the beginning there was Existence alone—One only, without a second. He, the One, thought to himself: Let me be many, let me grow forth. Thus, out of himself he projected the universe; and having projected the universe out of himself the universe he entered into every being.*
>
> —Chandogya Upanishad

Ultimately though, in reality there is only one abode for the soul, and that is, the Divine Self, which transcends even Tem, that being from which rises Ra, Asar and all Creation. This is confirmed in all versions of the *Prt m Hru* and is perhaps most succinctly expressed in the *Coffin Texts,* where it is explained that there is an even more subtle essence beyond Atum, that is unknown by men, and nameless. The initiate, reading the following passages, is to make the following realizations.

> *I am the Double Lion (i.e. eternal), older than Atum.*

> *I am Ra, who is exalted forever, I am Atum, more of a spirit* (i.e. subtler) *than the other spirits.*
> *I am the Lord of Eternity.*

> *I am the Only One, who journeys over the Primeval Void.*
> *I am the One whose name is not known by human beings.*

This means that essentially, Asar and Ra are actually one being. This is most clearly demonstrated by the depiction of Asar, in a Divine Boat (Neshmet). This is one reason why the moon was chosen as a symbol of Asar. It is said that Ra has the Moon and Sun as his eyes, and either works as a passageway to the deeper transcendental Self, just as the eyes of a human being act as a window into the inner Self. This idea of the oneness of the Supreme Being is stated again directly in the image above which reads: *This[55] is Asar resting in Ra, Ra resting in Asar.* The two great goddesses Nebethet and Aset attend on Atum Ra as he stands on the pedestal of Maat. Once again, the image of the Trinity is given with one male aspect and two females aspects, symbolizing non-duality (one God, one Spirit) and duality (two goddesses), respectively. The concept of two paths is evident in the very decision to present the culmination of the spiritual journey in the form of two chapters wherein the spiritual aspirant can join Ra (Chapter 35) or Asar (Chapter 36). This presentation points to the highly advanced philosophical view that the Ancient Egyptian Sages were putting forth, that the gods and goddesses (Neteru) are merely images for worship, and are not to be seen as ultimate or absolute realities in and of themselves. They are to be understood as windows into the transcendent, avenues by which the energies of the mind and body may be channeled towards a higher, spiritual goal in life. Not until Vedanta philosophy emerges in India, is there another form of mysticism like it in the world.

bes Visible image of god

The Ancient Egyptian word "bes" implies the concept of "image" or "manifestation" and clearly delineates between the essence and image of something-. Therefore, the understanding of the concept is that the idol or image, while being composed of God as all matter is, does not encompass God. It is only one of an infinite number of images that can be chosen.

---

[55] The Creator, *Atum-Ra*

The Non-dualist Philosophy of Akhenaton

Akhenaton was at the same time, a king and mystical philosopher. He introduced not a new religion, but a form of worship, which was highly philosophical and abstract, and thus less suited for the masses and more appropriate for the monastic order. The tenets of his hymns can be found in hymns to other Ancient Egyptian gods such as Amun (Amen), Asar (Asar), and Ra, which preceded those to Aton. However, the form of their exposition brings forth a new dimension of Ancient Egyptian philosophy, which is unsurpassed in some ways, even by the Hymns of Amun[56]. However, he was not able to reconcile the worship of Aton with the pre-existing forms of worship in Ancient Egypt. Also, he was not able to balance the duties of kingship with those of his position as High Priest. While he was not able reconcile these issues, he did bring forth the most advanced exposition of Ancient Egyptian philosophy. Scholars of religious studies have classified him as the first monotheist, before Moses, but his contributions to religion go much deeper than the simple monotheistic concept put forth by Moses.

Upon closer study, the philosophy, which Akhenaton espoused, is comparable to the most advanced spiritual philosophies developed in India, known as Vedanta philosophy. In Vedanta, two important forms of spiritual philosophy developed. They are expressions of non-dualist philosophy known as Absolute Monism. The Hymns to Aton, which also espouse Absolute Monism, were recorded at least 579 years before its exposition in India through the Hindu Upanishads which are considered to be the highest expression of Hindu mystical philosophy. Akhenaton's teachings were given less than 200 years before the supposed date for the existence of Moses. However, Moses' teaching was not understood as Absolute Monism, but rather as monotheism. Therefore, whether the Jewish Pentateuch was written by a person named Moses or by Jewish scribes much later, as most modern biblical scholars now agree, the influence of Akhenaton's teachings would have been foremost in the instruction of Moses. Remember that the Bible says Moses learned the wisdom of the Egyptians (Acts 7:22). While all of the attributes of Yahweh, the Hebrew God, are contained in the teachings related to Aton, the Hymns to Aton go farther in espousing the nature of God and God's relationship to Creation and humanity. They are based on Monism. Absolute Monism means that there is a recognition that there is only one reality that exists: God. All else is imagination. This means that everything that is perceived with the senses, thoughts, etc., is a manifestation of God. Modified Monism views God as the soul of nature, just as the human body also has a soul, which sustains it.

The next form of philosophy present in Akhenaton's hymns is Pantheism. There are two forms of Pantheism, Absolute and Modified. Absolute Pantheism views God as being everything there is. In other words, God and Creation are one. Modified Pantheism is the view that God is the reality or principle behind nature. Panentheism is the doctrine that God is immanent in all things but also transcendent, so that every part of the universe has its existence in God, but God is more than the sum total of the parts. God transcends physical existence. Aten or Aton was represented not as a human being, but as the sun, from which extended rays that terminated with hands which bestowed Ankhs (Life Force), to all Creation. This image was used exclusively and constituted a non-personalized form of Divine iconography pointing towards the abstract and transcendental nature of the Divine as a principle, as opposed to a personality. This was not a departure from Ancient Egyptian philosophy, but an attempt to reinforce elements, which were already present in the very early forms of worship, related to the formless, nameless *God of Light* teaching. The following exerted verses from the Hymns to Aten approved by Pharaoh Akhenaton exhibit the most direct exposition of the philosophies mentioned above.

---

[56] See the book "Egyptian Yoga Volume II" by Dr. Muata Ashby.

Figure 78: Akhenaton with his family, receiving Life Force from Aten through the sun's rays.

One God, like whom there is no other. Thou didst create the earth by thy heart (or will), thou alone existing, men and women, cattle, beasts of every kind that are upon the earth, and that move upon feet (or legs), all the creatures that are in the sky and that fly with their wings, [and] the deserts of Syria and Kush (Nubia), and the Land of Egypt.

Thou settest every person in his place. Thou providest their daily food, every man having the portion allotted to him; [thou] dost compute the duration of his life. Their tongues are different in speech, their characteristics (or forms), and likewise their skins (in color), giving distinguishing marks to the dwellers in foreign lands... Thou makest the life of all remote lands.

Oh thou Lord of every land, thou shinest upon them...

Thou hast made millions of creations from thy One self (viz.) towns and cities, villages, fields, roads and river. Every eye (i.e., all men) beholdeth thee confronting it (the objects of the world).

These statements by Akhenaton in his Hymns to Aton follow the transcendental and tantric philosophy that originated in the *Pyramid* and *Coffin Texts,* and much later, in the Gnostic Gospels which was espoused by Jesus.[57] Nature itself and all objects including people are a manifestations of the Divine.

"The Kingdom is spread upon the earth but people do not see it!"

−Jesus in the Gnostic Gospel of Thomas from Egypt

In the New Testament *Gospel of Luke* 17:21 we find the following statement:

"The Kingdom of God is in the midst of you (within thee)."

−Jesus in the Christian Bible

---

[57] See the book *Christian Yoga* by Muata Ashby.

THE ELEMENTS OF THE HUMAN PERSONALITY

It is important to understand the architecture of the human constitution. The *Prt m Hru* makes a distinction between these because the human personality is a conglomerate or composite of several aspects or levels of existence. These elements are not readily discernible to the ordinary person due to the lack of spiritual sensitivity. Further, one element may not be effective in all planes of existence. For example, the Ka may not be discernible in the Ta or Physical Plane, while the Khat may not be discernible in the Pet or Heavenly Plane. It is necessary to know about these, because in knowing them, one gains greater insight into the higher planes of existence and the teachings of the *Prt m Hru*. This section will concentrate on the subtle human anatomy and the anatomy of all existence. It will discuss the Physical, Astral and Causal planes of existence and their inner workings as they relate to the elements that compose the human personality. First we will review the themes and essential wisdom developed in the book *Egyptian Yoga: The Philosophy of Enlightenment*. Then we will proceed to look into the nature of the subtle spiritual Self with more detail and depth. The Ancient Egyptian concept of the spiritual constitution recognized nine separate but interrelated parts that constitute the personality of every human being.

Pa Neter

Neberdjer

Net

The Transcendental Self

Akhu

Ba

Sahu

Khaibit

Ab

Sekhem

Ka

Ren

Khat

Figure 79: A two dimensional depiction of the elements of the personality.
The diagram above shows the Kemetic concept of the elements of the personality (bodies) with the grossest (human body) at the center, and the subtlest (Spirit, God) at the outer edge.

(1) THE KHU OR AKHU:

The Khu or Akhu

The hieroglyph of the word Khu is the "crested ibis." The ibis is representative symbol of Djehuti, the god of reason and knowledge. As such it relates to the pure spiritual essence of a human being that is purified by lucidity of mind. The Khu or Akhu is the spirit, which is immortal; it is associated with the Ba and is an Ethereal Being. The Khu is also referred to as the "being of light" or "luminous being." The Khu illumines the personality and without this light, the personality and the mind cannot function. It is the light of consciousness itself.

(2) THE BA:

The Ba

The hieroglyphic symbol of the Ba is the Jabiru bird. The Jabiru is a stork. It symbolizes the nature of the soul to spread its wings and take flight, and exist apart from the body. The Ba is the heart or soul which dwells in the Ka with the power of metamorphosis. Sometimes described as the "Soul" and "Higher Self," it is seen as a spark from the Universal Ba (God). The Ba may be dialogued with and can be a spiritual guide to the developing individual. It is the equivalent of the Hindu "Atman." It is the indestructible, eternal and immortal spark of life. It is not affected by anything that may happen to the senses, body, mind or intellect (higher mind).

Through the mind, the Ba (soul-consciousness) "projects" and keeps together an aggregate of physical elements (earth, air, water, fire) in a conglomerate that is called the psycho-physical personality. When the soul has no more use for the physical body, it discards it and returns to the Universal Ba if it is enlightened. If it is not enlightened, it will tune into another aggregate of elements to make another body (reincarnation).

(3) THE SAHU:

The Sahu

The hieroglyphs of the word Sahu are the door bolt, meaning consonant "s" or "z," the arm, meaning the guttural sound "ain," the intertwined flax - consonant "h," the chick is the vowel "u," the determinative cylinder seal, meaning "treasure" or "precious," and the determinative of the "corpse" or "body." The Sahu is therefore sometimes referred to as the "glorious" spiritual

body in which the Khu and Ba dwells. When the elements of a person are integrated (i.e., person moves towards or reaches enlightenment), the spiritual and mental attributes of the natural body are united and deified. The Sahu is the goal of all aspiration. It is the reason for human existence – to become Godlike while still alive by spiritualizing one's physical aspects and thereby allowing these to become proper vessels for the higher aspects of the personality to unfold.

(4) THE KHAIBIT:

The Khaibit

The hieroglyphs of the word Khaibit are the "sunshade" and the consonant "t." The sunshade produces a shadow when the light is reflecting on it. Similarly, the shadow of a person, their personality, is produced when the light of their true essence (Akhu) is shining on the aspects of the personality. The Khaibit is therefore, an outline of the soul that is illumined by the light of the Spirit, which reflects in the mind as a subtle image of self (ego). In Chapter 31 of the *Prt M Hru*, it is stated *I* (as the sundisk) *fly away to illuminate the shades* (in the Duat). The shades are the subtle reflection of the soul, which are not self illuminating and which therefore exist only due to the presence of light and an object. In this case, the object is the Soul. The Khaibit is a subtle manifestation of the elements of the personality that acts somewhat as the resistor in an electronic component. A resistor causes a shadow in a manner of speaking, when it is placed in an electric circuit. In the same manner, the Khaibit and the other elements of the personality consume spiritual energy from the spirit and produce a particular image thereafter referred to as the individual personality of a human being. The Khaibit or Shadow is associated with the Ba from which it receives nourishment. It has the power of locomotion and omnipresence.

135

(5) THE AB:

The Ab

"The conscience (Ab) of a man is his own God."

The Ab or conscience is the source of Meskhenet (Ari, Karma) and the mother of reincarnation. The Ab represents the heart. It is the symbol of the deep unconscious mind, the conscience and also the repository of unconscious impressions gathered in past experiences from the present life and previous lives. As desires can never be fulfilled by experiences or from objects in the world of time and space, at death, the ignorant soul will harbor impressions of unfulfilled desires which will lead to further incarnations in search of fulfillment. This point is described in Chapter 36, from the *Egyptian Book of Coming Forth by Day:* *"My heart, the mother of my coming into being."* The mind is seen as the source of incarnation (coming into being) because it contains the desires and illusions which compel a human being to be born to pursue the fulfillment of those desires. In the judgment scene from the *Book of Coming Forth By Day,* the Ab undergoes examination by Djehuti, the god of reason. In other words, one's own reasoning faculty will be the judge as well as that which is being judged. The heart (mind) itself metes out its own judgment based on its own contents. It is one's own heart which will fashion (*mother*) one's own fate (*come into being*) according to one's will and desires, which are based on one's understanding (wisdom) about one's true Self. Thus, the new embodiment is fashioned in accordance with what a person has done during previous lives and what they desire for the future. A desire for worldly experience will cause embodiment. A desire to go to the west and join with God will bring spiritual enlightenment.

(6) THE SEKHEM:

The Sekhem

Sekhem is the Life Force or Power that exists in the universe. The symbol of Sekhem is the hand held staff pictured above. When used in worldly terms it refers to a scepter that means physical power, authority and strength. In spiritual terms, the Sekhem is the power or spiritual personification of the vital Life Force in humans. Its dwelling place is in the heavens with the Khus, but all life draws upon this force in order to exist. Sekhem also denotes the potency, the erectile power or force used in fashioning one's own glorious new body for resurrection.

(7) THE KA:

The Ka

The hieroglyph of two upraised arms that are joined is the Ka. It is the abstract personality or ego-self. It is the source from which subconscious desires emerge. It is also considered to be the ethereal body possessing the power of locomotion. It survives the death of the physical body. It is the ethereal double containing the other parts of the personality. The concept of the Ka was known in India, and the word was also known. The Indian God Brahma had a Ka (soul-twin). This teaching of the Ka in Ancient Egypt and in India shows that there is a keen understanding of the reflective quality of the personality. In reality the physical personality is a reflection or more accurately, a projection of the astral body. The Ka is associated with the Sekhem in that it is the dynamic aspect of a person's personality in the Astral Plane. It is the dynamic aspect of the vital force in the body of a human being.

(8) THE REN:

The Ren

The Ancient Egyptian word Ren means "name." The name is an essential attribute to the personification of a being. You cannot exist without a name. Everything that comes into existence receives a name. This is an essential quality of that which comes into the realm of time and space. The Ancient Egyptian symbols that signify name are the "mouth" and "water." The name is sometimes found encircled by a rope of light called a cartouche, which is associated with the Shen (a symbol of eternity), the top part of the Ankh Symbol. The cartouche represents a rope of sunlight or Life Force harnessed into the form of a circle. It is the most impregnable structure to protect one's name against attack. The ⬭, means mouth.

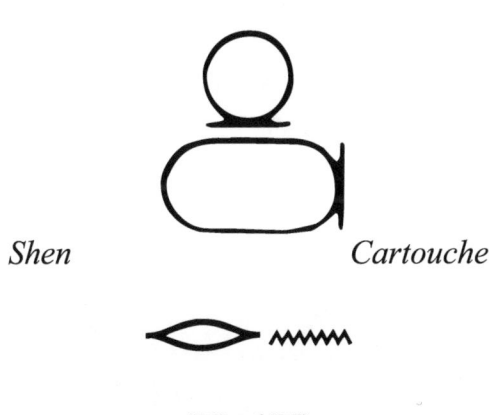

Shen   *Cartouche*

"R" and "N"
or "REN"

The symbol of the mouth is of paramount importance in Ancient Egyptian Mystical wisdom. The symbol of the mouth refers to the consonant sound "r," and it is a symbol of consciousness. It is the mouth which is used in two of the most important mystical teachings of Ancient Egyptian Yoga, *The Creation* and the *Opening of the Mouth Ceremony* of the *Book of Coming Forth By Day*. God created the universe by means of the utterance of his own name. In the *Book of Coming Forth By Day,* the mouth is manipulated so as to promote enlightenment. Why is the mouth so important to this mystical symbolism? This issue is discussed in more detail in the following section entitled "More Mystical Implications of the Name"

(9) THE KHAT:

The Khat

The hieroglyphs of the word Khat are the fish meaning "dead body" and the consonant "k," the vulture meaning the vowel "a," the symbol of "bread" and the consonant "t," the egg-like determinative symbol of "embalming" and the determinative symbol of the "mummy," "corpse" or "body." The Khat is the concrete personality, the physical body. It refers to the solid aspect of a human being (bones, skin, blood, sense organs, etc.) which is transient and mortal.

MORE MYSTICAL IMPLICATIONS OF THE NAME

Consider the following. When you think of anything, you attach words to your thoughts. In fact, it is difficult to think without words. Therefore, words are the symbols that the human mind uses to group thoughts and which constitute intellectual forms of understanding. However, thoughts are conditioning instruments. This means that when you think, you are actually differentiating. The differentiation process allows the mind to be conscious or aware of differences in matter. It labels these differences with different names based on the form or function of the object or the relationship it has to it. The mind learns to call objects by names. For example, a chair is an aggregate of matter just like a rock. However, the mind has learned to call it a particular name and associate the name "chair" with a particular kind of object which looks in a particular way and serves a particular function that is different from the rock.

When the mind goes beyond words, it goes beyond thoughts and thereby experiences undifferentiated consciousness. This is the deeper implication of the opening of the mouth ceremony. It signifies opening the consciousness and memory of the undifferentiated state of existence. At a lower state of spiritual evolution, consciousness appears to be differentiated, even though the underlying essence is undifferentiated. However, when intuitional realization or spiritual enlightenment dawns in the human mind, words are no longer viewed as differentiating instruments, but merely as practical instruments for the spirit to operate and interact with the world through a human personality. This is the difference between a human being who is spiritually enlightened and one who is caught in the state of ignorance and egoism.

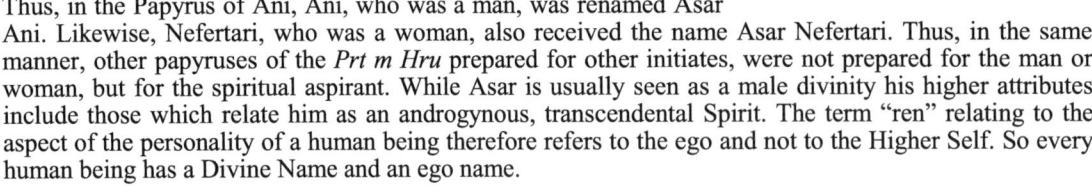

The vocal capacity in a human being is intimately related to the unconscious level of the mind. This is why those who do not practice introspection and self-control often blurt out things they do not wish to say, and later regret. For this reason, the teachings enjoin that a spiritual aspirant should practice the disciplines of virtue which lead to self-control through right action and righteous living. In this manner, one's speech becomes *maakheru,* the highest truth. When one's speech becomes truth, one's consciousness is truth. When one's consciousness is truth, it is in harmony with the transcendental truth of the universe which is symbolized by the Ancient Egyptian goddess Maat. Thus, becoming true of speech is a primary goal for every spiritual aspirant. It is synonymous with coming into harmony with the universe and thus, refers to spiritual enlightenment itself.[58]

The symbol of the water recalls the image of the Primordial Ocean of Consciousness. Thus, Ren relates to consciousness manifesting through names, words and sound itself.

The Importance of the Spiritual Name

Plate 11: (right) Queen Nefertari as initiate Asar.

The hieroglyphic inscription reads *"Asar Nefertari, the great queen, beloved of goddess Mut and Maakheru (spiritually victorious) is in the presence of Asar, the Great God"*

In Ancient Egyptian Asarian mysticism, all initiates were given the spiritual name *"Asar"* regardless of if they were male or female. Thus, in the Papyrus of Ani, Ani, who was a man, was renamed Asar Ani. Likewise, Nefertari, who was a woman, also received the name Asar Nefertari. Thus, in the same manner, other papyruses of the *Prt m Hru* prepared for other initiates, were not prepared for the man or woman, but for the spiritual aspirant. While Asar is usually seen as a male divinity his higher attributes include those which relate him as an androgynous, transcendental Spirit. The term "ren" relating to the aspect of the personality of a human being therefore refers to the ego and not to the Higher Self. So every human being has a Divine Name and an ego name.

---

[58] For a detailed examination of the principles embodied in the neteru or cosmic forces of the company of gods and goddesses, the reader is referred to the books *The Hidden Properties of Matter, The Ausarian Resurrection* and *The Mystical Teachings of The Ausarian Resurrection* by Dr. Muata Ashby.

What is the deeper implication of this? This is a very important mystical teaching relating that the deeper Self within Ani is Asar, the Divine Self. That is, his true identity is not the birth name, but the Divinity which transcends mortal existence. In modern times, John would be Asar John, Cynthia would be Asar Cynthia, etc. It is an affirmation and acceptance of one's Divine true essential nature not only as an expression of God, but as God in fact. Thus the entire journey of self-discovery revolves around your discovering that the deeper reality within you is God. This does not contradict other religions. In Buddhism, the deeper reality a Buddhist is looking for is Buddha Consciousness. Thus, in Ancient Egyptian terms as related in the *Book of Coming Forth By Day,* the deeper reality to be sought is Asar. So as you live your life, see your existence as a journey of discovery. Feel that you have come from a divine source and that as you practice the teachings, you are drawing ever closer to discovering that source. See your entire life as a ritual. When you wake up in the morning reflect on the majesty of the Sun (Divine) just as Ani does with his prayer. When you eat, see this as an offering to the Divine Self within you.

There are essentially three important elements being imparted in the *Prt m Hru*. The first is the message that righteousness leads to spiritual realization. The second is that the process of purification is acting with righteousness. The third message of the text is the wisdom about the Divine. By learning about the nature of the Divine, acting, feeling and thinking as the Divine, it is finally possible to become one with the Divine. The spiritual name is an essential and powerful force linking the initiate to that spiritual source as well as a constant reminder of the true glory of the Higher Self.

THE MYSTICAL AND COSMIC IMPLICATIONS OF THE ELEMENTS OF THE PERSONALITY

This section will provide a more detailed classification of the human being in an attempt to understand the underlying origin and cause of human existence. Also, it will seek to bring forth a deeper understanding of how the Cosmic Forces operate through the human constitution at gross and subtle levels.

As discussed earlier, the Universal Soul, God, Pure Consciousness, emanates Creation and all that is within it, all that is. The human being is like a ray of that emanation which refracts into several parts composing all of the levels of existence. Human consciousness may be compared to a reflection of the sun in a pool of water. Human consciousness is a reflection of divine consciousness in the pool of the mind which operates through the brain and nervous system. This idea is also reflected in the relationship between the parts of the spirit called BA and AB.

BA ⇔ AB

The Ab is the heart or seat of the mind, and it is in the mind where the soul, Ba, reflects. So the mind has no independent existence without the soul's sustaining life force and consciousness, and the individual human soul has no independent existence without the Universal Soul.

Universal Ba ⇨ Individual Ba ⇨ Individual Ab[59]

These levels of existence transfer into the four states of consciousness and various levels of psycho-spiritual psychology related to the Uraeus-Serpent Power system.[60]

The Universal Ba or Soul, or in other words, the consciousness of the Supreme Being, emanates and sustains each individual human being through the various parts of the human spirit. There are three basic parts to the human being. These are further broken down into more specific parts.

---

[59] Human heart and mind.
[60] See the book *The Serpent Power* by Dr. Muata Ashby

Table 7: The Three Bodies of Men and Women and of God

The three basic parts of the human being are the Causal Body, the Astral Body and the Physical Body. They may be viewed in a increasing order of density as follows. These bodies also relate to the bodies of the universe:

Neberdjer (Universal Self) ↓	**Universal Self** ↓
Heaven (Ament)[61] ↓	**Causal Body** ↓
Duat ↓	**Astral Body** ↓
Earth	**Physical Body**

Sages of ancient times who were able to discern, through their intuitional vision (spiritual eye), the different levels of vibration and psychology within all human beings, have set forth this teaching about the constitution of the human being. An important point to note is that each of the lower three states involves duality while the highest state involves non-duality. The human soul is a projection of the divine into the realm of duality (causal -astral- physical planes). The human soul forgets its divine origin and believes itself to be a creature among other creatures; hence, the idea of duality arises. The ignorant human being is not aware that {he/she} is at all times most intimately connected to the Universal Self, as are all objects and all other human beings. Just as each wave in the ocean is essentially the same as the ocean, each wave-like human personality and all the objects in Creation are essentially the Primeval Ocean, the Self. Ignorance of this then gives rise to the various egoistic feelings. The ignorant human being, not aware of {his/her} storehouse of innate potential to experience fullness and peace within, goes on seeking for fulfillment in the worlds of duality instead of seeking to know and experience the only source of true fulfillment, the Universal Self, which encompasses all other realms. Non-duality is experienced as absolute oneness and interconnectedness with all that exists. There is no feeling of you and me, here and there, male or female; there is no desire for objects because all objects are one with the Self. There is only the experience of awareness of the Self. Human words and concepts are not capable of describing the actual experience of oneness with the Self, therefore, all mystical descriptions are transcended in the actual experience. They are like a map, but you must take the journey and arrive at the destination by your own will and self-effort. Thus, they serve as guides, to lead the mind toward the understanding of yogic philosophy. --

The nine major elements or parts of the human personality espoused by the Ancient Egyptian Sages may be classified as follows within the three basic bodies for the purpose of study and understanding, as illustrated below. God is also understood to have three bodies: Universal Causal Body, Universal Astral Body, Universal Physical Body, the three aspects of universe or planes of existence. Within these bodies are the constituent elements, totaling nine in number. God also has nine elements. However, unlike those of the human being which are limited and characterized by their individuality, the divine elements are universal and all pervading in their respective level of existence. Thus we are told in the Ancient Egyptian scriptures that God has a Universal Ba, a Universal Sahu, a Universal Khu (Akhu), a Universal Khaibit, a Universal Ka, a Universal Sekhem, a Universal Ab, a Universal Khat, and a Universal Ren. Thus, the individual elements that compose the personality of each individual human being emanate from the same Supreme Being.

---

[61] In Kemetic Philosophy there are two heavens, a lower physical heaven wherein the lower aspects of the personality (Khat, Ren, Sekhem, Ab) reside and a higher heaven wherein the higher aspects of the personality such as the Akhu, Sahu, and Ba reside.

Table 8: The Nine Aspects of the Human personality and of God.

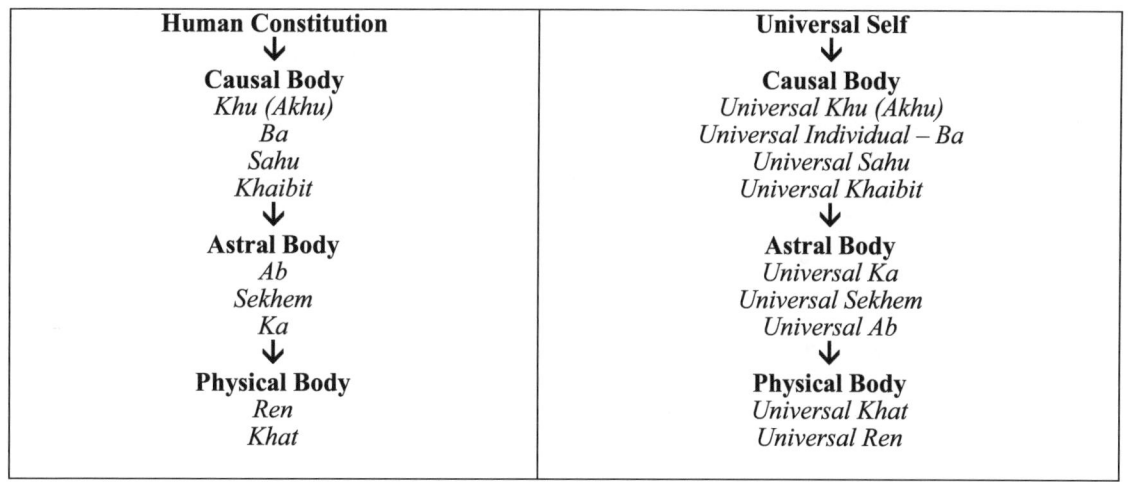

Human Constitution	Universal Self
↓	↓
Causal Body	**Causal Body**
Khu (Akhu)	*Universal Khu (Akhu)*
Ba	*Universal Individual – Ba*
Sahu	*Universal Sahu*
Khaibit	*Universal Khaibit*
↓	↓
Astral Body	**Astral Body**
Ab	*Universal Ka*
Sekhem	*Universal Sekhem*
Ka	*Universal Ab*
↓	↓
Physical Body	**Physical Body**
Ren	*Universal Khat*
Khat	*Universal Ren*

Ren = Name
Khat = Form

(Name and form are the basis of physical existence on the earth plane.)

It should be noted that while the gross elements of the ego-personality are evident at the level of the physical body, the original cause of the existence of the individual and {his/her} separation from the Divine occurs at the level of the Causal Body. Many people erroneously think of their soul as existing within their physical body. However, the opposite is true. The soul emanates from the Self. It in turn creates the other parts of the personality. All of this creation occurs within the Divine Self and not the body. The Causal Body is where the slightest tendency towards thought and desire occurs. It is here where the deep unconscious impressions cause the other parts of the body to emerge. When the physical body of an un-enlightened person dies, the gross elements of the ego (name and personality used in a particular lifetime) also die. The Astral and Causal bodies survive with the unconscious impressions collected from that lifetime. Through these bodies the soul continues the pursuit of fulfillment of desire (unconscious impressions lodged in the Astral-Causal mental subtle matter). The pursuit of fulfillment of desires may continue in the Astral plane (Duat-Netherworld) for a time, where the individual experiences of pain or pleasure (heaven or hell) according to {his/her} Meskhenet (karmic basis composed of impressions gathered from feelings, actions and desires of many lifetimes).

The task of an aspirant is to cleanse the Physical, Astral and Causal planes of the mind so as to regain conscious perception of the Universal Self. Since the Universal Self is non-dual, immortal, eternal and the source of all planes and all objects within those planes, the union with the Universal Self bestows omniscience and a boundless vision of infinity, immortality and a feeling of non-duality and connectedness to all things great and small. The correct practice of the various yogic disciplines are designed to accomplish this cleansing process. If successful, the soul comes into communion with the Self (Universal Ba, Asar, Ra, Aset, etc.) while still alive, and after death the soul of the enlightened person dissolves in the ocean of pure consciousness from whence it came originally. This is the meaning behind the teaching of *merging with the maker* presented in the Ancient Egyptian story known as *The Story of Sinuhe.*[62]

Earlier we discussed the fact that in the process of embodiment, the Universal Ba itself becomes the individual Ba of every human being due to its association and identification with the feelings of the emotional body, *Ka,* and the cravings of the physical body, *Khat.* If this is true, then how is it possible that the Universal Self (*Ba*) is also non-dual, meaning without a second, one and alone, all-encompassing

---

[62] See Egyptian Yoga: The Philosophy of Enlightenment (Egyptian Yoga Volume I)

as well as transcendental? At this more advanced level you must understand that all of the parts of the body are merely emanations from that same divine Self, just as you emanate a dream in your sleep or an idea in your Waking State, out of the depths of your consciousness.

In the same way this entire universe and everything in it is nothing but the emanation of God's consciousness. All that exists is ethereal, subtle matter, the Self. The process of thought has the effect of coagulating matter in a form as directed by the thought. In this way you have created your body and mind along with all of the other parts of your individual existence. In reality these parts are nothing more than subtle energy held together by your thoughts and ultimately, every one of those parts are not yours, but are parts of the Self. Thus, nothing exists outside of the Self, God. Therefore, even though there appears to be many objects, colors and differences in creation, the underlying essence of it all is the Self. Think about it. If there was something other than the Self, then the Self could not be all-pervasive, all-encompassing and all-powerful. Its movements would be restricted. The idea that there is a devil or some evil being who is the nemesis of God is erroneous because there can be no other being outside of the Self. The Self is the soul or substratum of all that is.

The idea of a "devil" who is a counterpart or nemesis of God who is "all good" was a development out a dualistic way of understanding life and mythology. This dualistic view is contrary to the teachings of mystical spirituality. It is the basis for egoism and misunderstanding in the practice of true religion. True religion means that you look for a connection, a oneness between yourself and God. For this to be possible you need to discover that your ego-personality is only a superficial expression of your deeper reality which is God. When you discover the depths of your own being, you realize that you are not an individual, separate from the universe and God. You discover that underneath the apparent separation there is oneness. A dualistic view looks for differences and affirms that there is a separation between God, creation and humankind. Thus, a practitioner of dualism prays to God, looks to God for salvation and believes he exists as an individual while the non-dualist practices the teachings that lead to the understanding that the innermost reality in the heart is God. God is in all things everywhere, and nothing exists besides God.

If you were to let go of your thoughts related to your body consciousness, you would discover that you are separate from your body. In the advanced stages, you could dematerialize and materialize it at will as well as perform other feats that are considered as miracles or psychic powers. The parts of the spiritual body are in reality like layers of clothing on your true Self. Therefore, in the *Gospel of Thomas,* Jesus exhorts his disciples to strip without being ashamed and on that day they will see him (Christhood, Enlightenment).

42. His disciples say to him: "On what day wilt thou appear to us, and what day shall we see thee?" Jesus says: "When you strip yourselves without being ashamed, when you take off your clothes and lay them at your feet like little children and trample them! Then {you will become} children of Him who is living, and you will have no more fear."

All of the elements of the personality come together and create a conglomerate which collectively makes up likes and dislikes, opinions, feelings, thoughts, and desires of an individual. All of them constitute a conditioning[63] of the individual consciousness. This conditioning is referred to as egoism. The ego must be dismantled and stripped from the mind. When this occurs you will discover that what seemed so real and concrete (astral body, physical body) is nothing more than condensed thoughts. This discovery will free you from them as a bird is freed from a cage. When you take them off, what is left is the true Absolute you. All Creation has that same Absolute Self at its core. Therefore, you must seek to transcend all of the layers of ethereal matter so as to discover your true Self. This is accomplished by the practice of all of the disciplines of yoga presented here and in the Egyptian Yoga Book Series.

When we speak of "conditioning" we are referring to the conditioning of consciousness into the forms of the parts of the spirit in the same way that consciousness becomes conditioned into various forms (subjects, objects and interactions) in a dream. What is holding it all together? Desire born of ignorance of the Higher Self, which is transcendental and independent of concepts, and is whole, or free from

---

[63] See also Egyptian Yoga: The Philosophy of Enlightenment (Egyptian Yoga Volume I)

fragmentation. The subtlest parts of the body: *Khaibit, Individual - Ba, Sahu,* and *Khu or Akhu,* are the deepest levels of the unconscious mind. Contained in them is the cause of separation between the individual soul and God. This individuation principle is called *ignorance.* Therefore, ignorance, based in the causal body, is the primary "cause" of the astral and physical bodies (ego) coming into being. This is why it is called the causal body. It causes the other bodies to come into existence. When this ignorance is removed, all of the bodies become as if transparent, as when you wake up in a dream even when you are still asleep. The dream continues, but you "know" it is a dream, so you witness it as a dream and not as reality. Upon waking from a dream you discover that even while things seemed to be so real, they were not. You were not even moving; you were placidly lying on the bed. In the same way, a Sage discovers that the Self is not moving; only the thoughts, senses and body controlled by those thoughts can be said to be moving. Does a dream move? No. In the same way, the real you is not located in the body and is not moving. Therefore, you are the "Unmoved Mover." You are Atum, the creator who causes movement but itself does not move. This is the reason why the Sages consider the body and the phenomenal world as an "illusion." Plato and Aristotle elaborated on this idea in later years, but it originated in Memphite Theology, which they studied as initiates of the Ancient Egyptian mystical teachings. Essentially, the teaching explains that while the world exists and is characterized by movement and change, it has a deeper basis that is unchanging and undisturbed. This is the support or unmoving cause that supports the existence of Creation. This teaching can also be found in the great Indian Yoga text known as the Bhagavad Gita. It states that a Yogi who has become established in the awareness of the Self becomes indifferent, unmoved by the changes that seem to appear in matter, the senses no longer interested in the illusion created by ignorance.

Gita 14

23. Seated like one indifferent, he is not disturbed by the gunas; he knows that the gunas[64] alone operate and not the Self, and thus, being established in the Self, he moves not.

Thus, the Sage looks on the body as a marionette, created with thoughts by the Self, or as a projection as in a dream. Having awoken from the dream, when the physical body dies, the Sage who has discovered {his/her} oneness with the Self remains as the Self and does not create any more bodies to further incarnate. This is because {he/she} has discovered {his/her} essential nature and there are no more desires for experiences as a human being. Thus, there is no cause for the creation of a new ego-personality. This is the state that Sages experience with respect to the waking world of ordinary human beings. They are no longer caught up in the illusion of the world. This is called Liberation, Salvation, Heruhood, Waking up, Meeting Asar, Resurrection, Nirvana, etc. This is the loftiest goal of human life.

"Knowledge derived from the senses is illusory. True knowledge can only come from the understanding of the union of opposites."

–Ancient Egyptian Proverb

If you look at yourself objectively, you will realize that every cell in your body is changing from moment to moment, and that you are never the same as you were a moment ago. Even solid objects are changing and decaying, albeit at a slower rate, but eventually they will decompose into their constituent elements. In much the same way, the human body is changing and constantly moving towards extinction. But is this real? Is this change a quality of your inner Self? Upon closer examination, the real you is not changeable; the real you is Pure Consciousness and one with the Supreme Being who is eternal. Remember the teaching: *"The Great God inside the common folk"* from Chapter 17 of the *"Prt m Hru."* This is what it means. Your inner Self is one with the Divine Self. Initiatic science shows that the real you, the innermost Self, is unchanging.

What is it that is constantly moving, constantly restless from the time you wake up until the time you go to bed again? This is the thinking mind with all of the worries, all of the desires, all the beliefs, all of the ambitions and all of the regrets. These thoughts, worries, desires, beliefs, ambitions and regrets

---

[64] Note- Gunas are the three qualities of matter: Rajas-active (agitation), Tamas-passive (dullness), and Sattwa-harmony (lucidity.)

constitute your mental conditioning, your personality, and your ego-self concept. Through the process of your human experience in the world, your mind has become conditioned to expect to see reality in a certain way and therefore, it perceives life according to its conditioning. This conditioning, your ego, is what is holding you back from being able to realize your innermost Self, which is all encompassing, all-knowing, and all-blissful contentment and peace.

Your ego-personality is like a movie character that emerges at the beginning of a movie and fades away at the end. The movie screen remains in order to receive images from other movies. In the same way your personality emerged out of your mental conditioning at the time of your birth and since then, it has never stopped changing, moving, craving and searching for fulfillment. Egoism is the feeling of separation from the Self and attachment to an illusory personality that arises out of the dream quality of consciousness. It is intensified by the distractions of the mind due to the pursuit of fulfillment of sensual desires. At the time of your death, the gross aspects of your personality (Khat and Ren) will cease to exist, but the impressions created through these in the unconscious will leave you still craving for the unfulfilled desires. This is because the deep unconscious mind with its conditioned impressions of desire, survives death and follows you into the Duat (astral plane) until you finally are born again in the earth plane to once again continue seeking fulfillment.

"Get thyself ready and make the thought in you a stranger to the world-illusion"

–Ancient Egyptian Proverb

The concept of relativity of time is expressed in the hieroglyphic text entitled, *The Songs of The Harper*. In one verse, the relativity of the passage of time is explained as follows:

"The whole period of things done on the earth is but a period of a dream."

This formula of the Harper, when put together with the *Coffin Text* formula given previously about the nature of Atum Ra (*after the millions of years of differentiated creation, the chaos that existed before creation will return; only the primeval god* [65] *and Asar will remain steadfast-no longer separated in space and time*) form an exceedingly powerful combination which should act as a fuse to ignite the mind's deeper insight into the nature of Self. The "period of millions of years" mentioned in the *Coffin Texts* is in reality the same as the period of a dream, and as you know, a long period of time can be experienced in a dream, but in reality nothing has happened, except that your consciousness has emanated a dream world. But as you also know, the dream world comes to an end and dissolves back into consciousness. In the same manner, God has emanated this world and will some day dissolve it back into the Primeval Ocean of potential consciousness. Consider your dreams. They may seem to occur over a period of hours. You may even experience the passage of years within your dream, and yet upon waking up you realize that the entire time you were in bed asleep for a few hours. In the same way, the entire period of the existence of the universe is nothing but the span of a short dream in the mind of God.

From an advanced perspective, neither time nor space can be said to exist as something that is real, just as time, space, matter or physical objects within a dream cannot be called "real." The entire dream world exists in the mind and does not require real time or space. The phenomenal world, which is experienced in the Waking State of consciousness, is also not real and does not exist except in the mind of God. This teaching is not only confirmed by the *Hymns of Amun*,[66] but it is also a primary teaching of Memphite Theology that is presented in the *Shabaka Inscription*.[67] In reality only eternity is real, and God is eternity. Since all matter is in reality constituted of the thought energy of God, and the changes in matter are called time, it must be clearly understood that God is the only reality that exists.

God is eternity itself. The limited perceptions of the unenlightened human mind and senses are what human beings refer to as "time" and "space" awareness. However, the perception of time and space is due to the limitations and conditioning of the human mind and body. If it were possible to perceive the entire universe, then you would discover that there is only oneness, an eternal view that is not restricted to time

---

[65] Referring to the Supreme Being in the form of Atum-Ra
[66] See the book *Egyptian Yoga Volume II* by Dr. Muata Ashby
[67] See also Egyptian Yoga: The Philosophy of Enlightenment (Egyptian Yoga Volume I)

and space. This is the view that God has towards Creation. The task of the spiritual aspirant is to grow out of the limitations of the mind and body and discover the Cosmic Vision that lies within. When this is accomplished, there is a new perception of the universe. This represents the death of the human being and the birth of the spiritual life in the human being.

God has assumed the form of the neteru or Pautti. These "neteru" are cosmic forces, energies that sustain the universe and which constitute "physical matter." Therefore, this "physical" universe is in reality the body of God and everything in it is Divine, from the smallest atom to the largest celestial bodies in the heavens. It must be emphasized that in this process, *The Universal Ba*[68] itself becomes the individual Ba of every human being, due to its association and identification with the feelings of the emotional body, *Ka,* and the cravings of the Physical body, *Khat.*

By practicing the disciplines of Maat, the initiate is able to curb the wanton desires of the ego and thereby strengthen the will of the intellect. The science of practicing virtue in life will serve to assist the aspirant to purify the heart (mind), to cultivate peace of mind, and thereby to develop insight into the innermost Self. At this stage, the movement or vibration in the Primeval Waters which caused the world to be, subsides. Just as a calm lake reflects a pure image, the purified mind will reflect the clarity of the Cosmic Soul. The waves, caused by movements of the mind, would once again become just as the waves in the Primeval Ocean before creation, silent, at rest, at peace.

Your innermost Self, the Cosmic Soul, is constantly interacting with the world through the mind. If you had yellow sunglasses on, when you look at anything you would see a yellow tinge. In the same way, when you look at the world through your conditioned mind and senses, your vision reflects the tinge of egoism and divergent thoughts, but most of all, ignorance of your true Self which causes body identification. If you were to eradicate your mental conditioning, you would see a different reality. This is the goal of the various disciplines of mystical spirituality, to purify the intellect, **Saa**. By developing your higher intellectual ability to cut through the illusions of life with the ax of wisdom, you purify your subconscious mind from all of the conditioning. It is this purification of Saa which can lead you to awareness of the Higher Self.

The philosophy of the four states of consciousness (waking, dream, dreamless sleep, undifferentiated (transcendental concsiousness) is of paramount importance for the spiritual aspirant. A profound understanding of this teaching will lead you to develop subtlety of intellect in discerning the reality of the thoughts in your own mind as well as that which is real around you. In the book *The Cycles of Time,* we explored in depth, the practices of how this teaching is applied in everyday life in order to realize its significance at the deepest levels of the mind through virtuous living, the practice of Maat.

Maat philosophy provides us with a guideline for determining what is real and what is not. This is crucial to the correct operation of the mind because the mind supports whatever reality it believes to be true. You experience the world through your mind and senses. You have learned that these are valid criteria to determine the validity of the world and of your inner experience. Everything must be known through your rationalizing mind once it has been perceived by your senses. However, as we showed in the books *Egyptian Yoga: The Philosophy of Enlightenment* and *The Hidden properties of Matter*, what is normally considered to be real and abiding, solid matter, is nothing more than energy in its grosser states of being. It must be clearly understood that mental perceptions are not direct perceptions of matter. Your hand which you use to hold an object is itself a swirling mass of energy which is connected to other masses of energy conduits that lead to the brain. Sensual stimulus is an interaction between different forms of energy that registers in the brain centers in a specific manner. The mind perceives these stimuli by reacting to the centers and then acknowledges a perception. Therefore, perception occurs in the brain itself and not in the hand. Consider for a moment the situation of a paralyzed person or your own experience if a limb has fallen "asleep." In these eventualities, there is still a limb, but there is no perception. Why? Because the perception media, the senses, are incapacitated. Consider the possibility of the paralyzed limb coming into contact with an object. Did any interaction occur? From the standpoint of the observation yes there was some sort of interaction between two objects, but not from the standpoint of the person with the disability.

---

[68] The terms: The Universal, World Ba, Pa Neter, Amun, Nebertcher are to be understood as being synonymous.

Now consider the Dream State of consciousness. When you have dreams you perceive various objects, you touch them and you may even feel you own them. They appear to be real and "feel" very solid and true. However, upon waking you realize that they did not exist and never did. They were simply energy forms, which you created out of the subtle astral matter and perceived through the deluded mind. They were fleeting masses of subtle energy that arose out of your own mind and were perceived by your own mind. You developed an illusory triad of consciousness during your Dream State and from this arose an entire world. Your waking ego self-concept dissolved and you became a new subject. This "new" you used the subtle senses to perceive objects which you yourself imagined to exist. This is the triad of *seer, seen and sight.* When you woke up, this triad dissolved into your waking consciousness as if it never existed. However, upon waking up, you did not wake up into a reality, but rather you moved into another form of triad.

The *triad* of human consciousness arises out of your inability to perceive reality without the mind and senses. The mind and senses along with your soul form the three elements of the triad. If you were to transcend the mind and senses, you would perceive reality directly through your soul. Only through direct perception is it possible to know the truth or reality. The teaching of the triad is expressed in the symbolism of the Divine Trinity, which arises out of the Primeval Ocean.

The whole idea here is that the world you perceive as real is illusory. The senses, which you use to perceive the world are illusory, and the mind which you use to perceive the world is also illusory. Therefore, there is only one factor left which qualifies as real. That factor is the *witnessing consciousness* that perceives all of the different states. Through spiritual practices (yoga of wisdom, yoga of action, yoga of devotion and yoga of meditation) you can gradually lead your mind to deeper and deeper levels of perception of the truth until you discover the Absolute Truth beyond all of the illusory layers of the mind.

This essay has been presented so that the practitioner may begin to understand the visualization that is desired by the *Prt m Hru* texts, when it is written that the initiate is to say statements such as the following ones below. They are mystic formulas designed to awaken the innermost memory of one's true and ultimate identity as one with the Divinity who has brought all into existence and who will also dissolve it. This is the ultimate discovery, coveted by all mystics of the world. In other words, the temporary mortal existence is not the ultimate reality.

The Importance Of The "I Am" Formula

There is a special teaching contained in all mystical religious systems and yogic traditions. It is the "I Am" formula. In the philosophical disciplines, a formula is a set of words or symbols which contains a representation of the composition or structure of a complex idea or philosophy. It contains a recipe as it were, describing the ingredients that are necessary to produce the desired product. In this case the desired product is spiritual enlightenment. The "I am" formula holds the key to understanding the entire philosophy, if properly understood and practiced.

When people become deluded and feel they belong to a certain group or culture with particular customs, language and opinions, they begin to separate from others. The separation is emotional, philosophical, etc., but it is not real otherwise. This is not a desirable situation from a spiritual point of view. Culture and language should not be seen as a person's identity. A human being cannot transcend the world as long as {he/she} holds onto the idea that {he/she} is of a particular group or other ("I am German," "I am American," "I am Spanish," "I am Jewish," "I am Christian," etc.). While living in a culture, a spiritual aspirant should assert: "I am a spirit living as a German man," "I am a spirit living as an American woman," "I am a spirit living as a Spanish man," etc. Likewise, a person should not identify with a particular religion either. A spiritual aspirant should assert: "I am practicing this religion to lead me to enlightenment. I might have been born as a Christian, a Hindu or a Muslim in a previous incarnation, but now I am a practitioner of the Kemetic mystical spirituality and I will use its wisdom to lead me to God, the goal of all religions." This attitude promotes harmony, understanding and peace between religions. This atmosphere of peace will allow for the exchange of spiritual wisdom between them. This exchange will lead to greater spiritual awareness and evolution instead of strife, distraction and unrest between them.

In modern times people often confuse their identity with their job roles and get so caught up in that false identification that they cannot find happiness without it. The executive dresses up in executive clothing, works in an executive office, drives an executive car, comes home to the executive neighborhood to the executive wife to be greeted by the executive children, and so on. If {he/she} is not treated in an executive manner, {he/she} will get upset. If others do not live up to {his/her} social standing, they are chastised. There are many forms of delusion which can arise when a person begins to identify with their occupation, birthplace, ethnicity, gender, etc. A person may feel "I am an American and all other countries are primitive" or "I was born in the city and I am sophisticated and not like you country people" or "I am a man and I'm stronger, so you women are inferior." The soul, identified with the personality as a woman, may feel, "I cannot enjoy life unless I become a mother." As a result, she will proceed to get pregnant whether or not she is healthy, can financially take care of the child, or is at a stage in life where she can handle the responsibilities, etc. This happens because ignorance, lack of will, and desire have deluded the mind and the ability to reason has been impaired. Indoctrination with ideas like "life is for having babies and becoming a mother" or the pressure from society with ideas like "if you don't get pregnant you are not worth anything" hold sway in the weak and ignorant mind. When the soul is caught up in such mental delusion, one forgets that one's role (mother, father, boss, employee, etc.) in life is only a vehicle for spiritual discovery, and not an end in itself. It is not who *you* are. What would you say about an actor who gets off the stage but continues to play the role when they go home, to the market, church, etc? You would call them insane! Yet people are constantly playing roles, in their ordinary lives, based on their erroneous notions of reality, and these ignorant notions are constantly being reinforced by society at large (government, media, misguided religious people).

The predominant form of Yoga practiced in Orthodox religion is a limited form of Devotion, while the predominant form of Yoga practice in mystical religion is a combination of Gnosis or Intuitional Wisdom and Devotion. Orthodox religion is limited because it takes a person only part way in the realization of the objective of devotion in spiritual practice. Orthodoxy admonishes a person to love the image or symbol God, as opposed to promoting an awareness of God as an internal experience. For example, Gnostic (mystical) Christianity not only admonishes a person to love Jesus and God and follow their example, but also leads a person to allow that devotion to reach full expression. This means that a true devotee unites with the beloved and thereby becomes one with the beloved. This is the true meaning of Jesus' statements "I and The Father are One" and "Know ye not that ye are gods." The Orthodox Church would consider it blasphemous for a Christian to say "I am God," but Yogic mystical religions such as the Kemetic religion would consider any statement to the contrary as a misunderstanding of the higher truth and a reinforcement of spiritual ignorance.

The Egyptian *Book of Coming Forth By Day* is a text of wisdom about the true nature of reality and also of *Hekau* (chants, words of power, utterances) to assist the initiate in making that reality evident. These chants are in reality wisdom affirmations which the initiate recites in order to assist him or her in changing the consciousness level of the mind. The hekau themselves may have no special power except in their assistance to the mind to change its perception through repetition with understanding and feeling in order to transform the mind into a still and centered state. Through these affirmations, the initiate is able to change {his/her} consciousness from body consciousness ("I am a body") to Cosmic Consciousness ("I am God"). This form of affirmatory (using affirmation in the first person) spiritual discipline is recognized by Indian Gurus as the most intense form of spiritual discipline. However, there must be clear and profound understanding of the teachings before the affirmations can have the intended result. It is also to be found in the Bible and in the Gnostic Gospels as we will see. Compare the preceding statements in the Indian Upanishads and the Christian Bible to the following Ancient Egyptian scriptures (*Metu Neter,* Sacred Speech) taken from the *Egyptian Book of Coming Forth By Day* (c. 10,000-5,000 B.C.E.) and other hieroglyphic texts:

Table 9: Essential "I Am" Formulas from the Upanishads, Bible and Prt m Hru

| Vedanta Philosophy is summed up in four *Mahavakya*s or *Great Utterance*s to be found in the Upanishads:

1- **Brahman, the Absolute, is Consciousness beyond all mental concepts.**

2- **Thou Art That** (referring to the fact that everyone is essentially this Consciousness).

3- **I Am Brahman, the Absolute** (I am God); to be affirmed by people, referring to their own essential nature).

4- **The Self is Brahman** (the Self is the essence of all things). | Compare to the Bible:

On the essence of God: *"God is everywhere and in all things."* (Deuteronomy 4:7)

On the name of God: **"I Am That I Am."** (Exodus 3:14)

Jesus speaks of his own origin and identity: **"I and the Father (God) are ONE."** (John 10:30) | Compare the preceding statements in the Indian Upanishads and the Christian Bible to the following Ancient Egyptian scriptures (*Metu Neter*, Sacred Speech) taken from the *Egyptian Book of Coming Forth By Day* and other hieroglyphic texts:

Nuk Pu Nuk. *("I Am That I Am.")*

In reference to the relationship between God and humankind:

Ntef änuk, änuk Ntef. *("He is I and I am He.")*[69] |

Vedanta philosophy has been called *The Heart of Hinduism* since it represents the central teachings upon which Hindu philosophy is based. Just as Christianity has many denominations, there are many traditions in India which follow different gods or goddesses. However, like the gods and goddesses of Ancient Egypt, the deities of India all emanate from the same Supreme Being and this is acknowledged in all of the different systems, thus leading people to the same goal, although sometimes under different names. This is why Vedanta is referred to as the end of the Vedas, "end" implying distillation or an extraction of the purest essence of the Vedas, the raw mystical philosophy which underlies all of the systems. Therefore, the Upanishads are the principal *Vedantic* texts. The Indian Vedantic text Yoga Vasistha Vol. II describes the ego as follows:

When the Self (transcendental-Absolute consciousness) develops identification with the limited body, it assumes the form of *ahamkara* (egoism), which expresses in this manner: "I am this body. I am this mortal individual." This egoism is the true root of all evil.

Pride, vanity, conceit, narcissism, vainglory, superiority, insolence, presumption, arrogance, disdain, haughtiness, hauteur, loftiness, selfishness, lordliness, superciliousness, etc., represent various forms of intensification of the ego. Through the intensification of body-consciousness and through the pursuit of selfish acts in the hopes of fulfilling personal desires, the ego idea of self becomes inflated. The mind is more and more intensely turned towards the individual self, the body and the world for fulfillment, rather than towards the transcendental Self, the spirit within.

The characteristics mentioned above are considered to be demoniac or satanic forms of behavior. On the other hand, selfless service, charity, inward renunciation of possessions, etc., represent saintly or virtuous qualities, which lead to the Divine because they cause effacement of the ego. This effacement leaves the soul free of the troubles, needs, concerns and sufferings of the ego-self and gives rise to the Christ-Self. It is this ego-body consciousness idea of self which produces the major obstacle to spiritual evolution. It is this very problem that mystical wisdom and the ceremony of the Christian and Kemetic Eucharist are directed to solving.

In the following statements we are to understand that God, as represented by the deity Krishna, is himself the light. Further, a new parallel to the character of Jesus emerges with the *"I Am"* formula in which Jesus

---

[69] From the Ancient Egyptian Book of Coming Forth By Day (Book of the Dead).

declares that he is, or from a Gnostic perspective, what he represents, is Christhood, the teaching, the light of wisdom itself.

Gita: Chapter 7 Jnana Vijnana Yogah—the Yoga of Wisdom and Realization

8. O Son of Kunti! I am the taste in the waters, I am the light in the sun and the moon; I am Pranava (Om) in the Vedas, the sound in the Ether element, and manliness in men.

9. I am the pure fragrance in earth, I am the effulgence in fire,[70] I am the life in all living beings, and I am the austerity in the ascetics.

10. O Partha, know Me to be the eternal seed of all beings. I am the intellect in the wise, the valor of those who are valiant.

11. O Best of the Bharatas! Among the strong, I am their strength that is devoid of lust and passion. Among all beings I am the desire that is not opposed to Dharma (the ethical law).

Compare the statements in the Gita to the following "I am" statements from the traditional New Testament. Using the Yogic principles inherent in mystical Christianity, it is clear to see that these statements are referring to the same mystical ideal.

Revelations 1
8 I am Alpha and Omega, the beginning and the ending, saith the Lord, who is, and who was, and who is to come, the Almighty.

John 1:23
23 He said, I [am] the voice of one crying in the wilderness, Make straight the way of the Lord, as said the prophet Isaiah.

John 6:35
35 And Jesus said to them, I am the bread of life: he that cometh to me shall never hunger; and he that believes on me shall never thirst.

John 9:5
5 As long as I am in the world, I am the light of the world.

John 10:14
14 I am the good shepherd, and know my [sheep], and am known by mine.

John 11:25
25 Jesus said to her, I am the resurrection, and the life: he that believes in me, though he were dead, yet shall he live...

John 14:6
6 Jesus saith to him, I am the way, and the truth, and the life: no man cometh to the Father, but by me.

Compare the previous statements to the following Egyptian Hermetic teaching. The *I am* statement in all of them is pointing to the same mystical truth.

"I am the Mind - the Eternal Teacher. I am the begetter of the Word - the Redeemer of all humankind - and in the nature of the wise, the Word takes flesh. By means of the Word, the world is saved. I, Thought - the begetter of the Word, the Mind - come only unto they that are holy, good, pure and merciful, and that live piously and religiously, and my presence is an inspiration

---

[70] Fire of worldly desire.

and a help to them, for when I come, they immediately know all things and adore the Universal Spirit. Before such wise and philosophic ones die, they learn to renounce their senses, knowing that these are the enemies of their immortal Souls.

The idea of the *Word* or *Logos* being the savior of the world existed before Christianity. The main difference in Orthodox Roman Christianity was that the *"word"* or saving wisdom became flesh in the personality of Jesus, the man. This was an idea that Gnostic Christianity and other mystery religions rejected. The more ancient idea holds that the *word* itself is not only the Divine Presence, but its power of manifestation as well. With this understanding, the entire universe, including the human personality, body and mind are all manifestations of the *"Living Word"* itself—not just Jesus. The new Christian idea that emerged sees the *word* as being embodied in the person of Jesus himself and nowhere else. This is a more egoistic view. Jesus is a symbol of the potential realization of the divine word or essence in every human being.

In relation to the term *"word,"* another Biblical term, *"Dabhar,"* is of interest. This word implies creation, deeds, actions, and accomplishments as opposed to talk. It relates to the creative power of the Divine, of which human beings partake. Biblical scholars have often confused the meanings of these terms. However, a thorough understanding of the writings of the Hellenistic period known as *"Hermetic"* and the more ancient writings of Egypt reveal the correct interpretation. The following verses come from various chapters throughout the Egyptian *Book of Coming Forth By Day*, which show the initiate's gradual realization that the gods are in reality aspects of {him/her}self. This is the earliest known form of the *"I am"* formula used in philosophy. Thus, the *I am* (God) is the source of all action and all existence. In this respect the *I am* is related to the ancient Kemetic teaching of *Un*. Un means existence or that which is, i.e. the principle of *beingness* or abiding nature behind the changing way of Creation. This is one of the main titles of the god Asar in his aspect as Un-Nefer, or Beautiful (good) Existence. Further, the initiate understands {his/her} true nature and its power:

"I am the Great God, the self created one, Nun...I am Ra...I am Geb...I am Atum...I am Asar...I am Min...I am Shu...I am Anubis...I am Aset...I am Hathor...I am Sekhmet...I am Orion...I am Saa...I am the Lion... I am the young Bull...I am Hapi who comes forth as the river Nile..."[71]

In the following segments from Chapter 23 of the Ancient Egyptian *Book of Coming Forth By Day*, the initiate, having understood his oneness, and having identified with God in the form of Asar, exclaims the following:

"I am yesterday, today and tomorrow. I have the power to be born a second time. I am the source from which the gods arise."

This is the moment of great realization to which the entire religious system of the Ausarian Resurrection was directed. The aspirant or initiate was to understand his identity with the transcendental reality properly before death, but if not, then on the way through the Duat (after-death state or astral plane of mind). As with the Gnostics, the Ancient Egyptians considered those who had not had this mystical experience as *"Mortals"* while those who had it were called *"Sons of Light."*
And I am that God, the Great one in his boat, Ra, I am.
–From *Prt m Hru* Chapter 1

I am the god Tem as I am One. I became thus from Nun; I am Ra in his rising in the beginning of time, the prince.
–From *Prt m Hru* Chapter 4

It has been decreed for millions of millions of years of duration. It is given to me to send the old ones. After that period of time I am going to destroy all created things. It is the earth that came forth from Nun, now coming forth into its former state.
–From *Prt m Hru* Chapter 8

---

[71] Selections from various chapters of the Prt M Hru.

I am beyond your grasp because I am one with God. I am the Single One, who is in the Primeval Water of Creation... I am that same God, the Supreme One, who has myriad of mysterious names. I was born of Temu, the first divinity that came into existence. I know this! I am one possessing the knowledge of the innermost truth.

–From *Prt m Hru* Chapter 9

I am Ra, coming forth from Nun, the Divine Soul, and Creator of his own body parts.

–From *Prt m Hru* Chapter 22

I am the substratum of all the gods and goddesses.

–From *Prt m Hru* Chapter 26

I am Ra! I am one whose name is unknown[72], Lord of Eternity...

–From *Prt m Hru* Chapter 27

---

[72] One of the most ancient and mystical names to describe the transcendental Divinity, "Nameless One." This term also refers to the Primeval being who arose from the Primeval Ocean, bringing Creation into existence, i.e. Atum.

Part II

Translation of the Mystic Chapters of Rau nu Prt m Hru

INTRODUCTION:

Medut Neter
"Speech (words) of the Divinity"

Neter Medut
"Divine Speech"

MODE OF SPEECH AND GRAMMAR IN THE *PRT M HRU*

Ancient Egyptian writing is called Divine Speech, *Medu Neter,* because it is said to have been brought down to humanity from the heavens by the god Djehuti. This very name, that was given by the Ancient Egyptians themselves, gives us insight into the nature of the hieroglyphic texts and the manner in which one should go about studying it and trying to understand it. First you must understand that ancient hieroglyphic writing is not a system like any other writing. It is not just literal like English, because there are several different levels of meaning. The glyphs can have a phonetic meaning, pun meaning, literal meaning, mythological meaning, etc., because they use pictures and because they are essentially mystical writings. This means that learning the technical aspects of reading the glyphs is not enough to understand the true meaning of what is being said.

Any person can learn to read the glyphs to a level of basic understanding of their mundane meanings. This is the exoteric (outer) practice, but not everyone can learn to understand their deeper meaning. A true reader of the glyphs must be well versed in the mythology behind them as well as the mystical teachings within them. Therefore, your study cannot be just academic memorization, because the glyphs relate to the higher aspect of the mind, the intuitional knowledge of the Self. Therefore, a true reader must be on the spiritual path of enlightenment.

This book will give you insight into the esoteric meaning of various glyphs and thereby allow you to unlock the mythological and philosophical meaning of the texts for yourself, a process which is in reality the discovery of your own Higher Self. Thus, the study of Ancient Egyptian hieroglyphs is actually the practice of self-discovery if it is conducted in the proper manner, otherwise it falls short of this lofty goal and is no different than any other subject of study. While some degree of technical accuracy is required for success in any endeavor, artistic freedom is necessary in order to allow the inner spirit to have input as well. Therefore, the objective is not to be able to read fluently or with perfect pronunciation, but with understanding. You could conceivably spend an entire day researching and discovering the meaning of one single glyph, because the meanings are so deep. So realize that this is a lifelong study and not an ordinary discipline.

Many important elements have been incorporated into the grammatical structure of the translation which follows. The tone and meter of Ancient Egyptian writing is unique in and of itself, and should not be completely changed when translating it into a different language, so as to keep some of the feel of the writing. Feeling is an important aspect of education, especially spiritual education. Grammar and modes of speech are closely tied to culture, and culture is the mask of philosophy. Therefore, in order to understand Kemetic Philosophy, it is necessary to understand something about the culture which created it and not just grammar. In other words, some of the grammar and original names should be retained because they bring with them some essential elements of culture in their very utterance. They evoke images and ideas which one's own language cannot effectively translate. Western grammar is closely tied to Western Culture.

Western Grammar may commonly appear as follows:

1- the subject
    2- particle
        3- the verb
            4- adverbial modifiers (prepositional phrases, indirect object, etc.)
            5- the direct object

In contrast to Western grammar, the basic structure of Ancient Egyptian writing is as follows:

1- particle
    2- the verb
        3- the subject
            4- the direct object
            5- adverbial modifiers (prepositional phrases, indirect object, etc.)

I have tried to incorporate this structure wherever possible so as to give the writing a closer feel to the original text, but not too much so as to confuse the reader by making the text alien to the conventions they are used to. Also, Ancient Egyptian writing often had a poetic quality and very often used punning. Punning, or a play on words, sometimes on different meanings of the same word and sometimes on the similar meaning or sound of different words, was used to indicate deeper, more subtle meanings, like a hidden teaching underneath the surface story or word, and not only verbal punning was used, but also pictorial punning. Since Ancient Egyptian hieroglyphs constitute a pictorial language, it follows that using the same pictures for different words can denote a depth to the original meaning by adding the meaning or feel of the pictorial characters from other words.

While striving to retain some of the feeling and flavor of the original poetic style and grammatical structure of the text, this translation will make use of the prose style of writing, since its aim is to explain the mystical teachings contained in this wonderful and most ancient scripture from Africa, in easy terms. Also, there will be many explanatory footnotes to clarify new terms and important teachings. However, to reiterate, it is recommended that the serious student of the *Prt m Hru* first read the book, ***The Ausarian Resurrection,*** to gain a deeper insight and background into the philosophy and culture of Kemetic Mysticism before attempting to understand the teachings that will be presented here. Also, one must never forget that there is no substitute for studying any spiritual scriptures directly under the guidance of a qualified Spiritual Preceptor.

THE CHOICE OF CHAPTERS

As stated earlier, in ancient times there was not a set order for the Utterances or Chapters of sayings for Coming Forth Into The Light (attaining enlightenment), although they did follow a certain wisdom. Beginning with the *Pyramid Texts*, the wisdom of Coming Forth By Day was inscribed. Additional texts were added later, causing the collection to grow in the form known as the *Coffin Texts*. In the late period of Ancient Egyptian history, the Sages and Saints saw fit to codify the Chapters, and a general order was adopted. However, the idea of inclusion of all Chapters to complete one book was not adopted. Chapters were compiled in accordance with the determination of the priests and priestesses, taking into account the personality of the aspirant and other spiritual factors. Therefore, the choice of Chapters is open and not rigid. Also, some of the Chapters were created with the prevailing religious notions in mind, and therefore varied somewhat from period to period. One example of this is the inclusion, in the later period, of the teachings related to **ushabti**, the images of the deceased to work for {him/her} in the afterlife.

The Chapters for this compilation have been chosen in the traditional manner which was practiced in ancient times. Some Chapters were seen as more important than others, and others were routinely omitted. This shows that while the core of the teachings contained in the *Prt m Hru* were consistent, they were also flexible and responsive to the times. With this in mind, the present translation takes into account modern history, and the psychology of modern day human beings. This process of moving with the times is essential in keeping the teachings alive for each new generation. The expression of the teachings may change, but the essence must always stay the same. This will insure that each generation will receive the same wisdom, but in a manner that they can relate to it. Otherwise, a teaching which may have been so meaningful to one generation will fall out of touch with the next, and may even fall out of favor, and even worse, repudiated.

The following selection was compiled by the author with the following questions in mind. Which order most coherently and succinctly expresses the meaning of the mystical process of spiritual enlightenment? Having studied the available Chapters of the *Prt m Hru*, which ones are most important for promoting spiritual evolution and the most important spiritual goal of all: the attainment of spiritual resurrection (enlightenment, liberation, nirvana, etc.)? The order of the Chapters has been presented in a series of sections which relate to every aspect of the spiritual journey.

In modern times, many people have been disillusioned with religion and ritualism, the practice and/or belief in religion but without understanding its deeper meaning. This book seeks to present the mystical wisdom contained in the Chapters, and thereby omits the Chapters that deal with issues that might have been more specifically created with contemporary issues in mind, but which no longer apply to our times.

The following Chapters contain the essential wisdom of coming forth. In fact, there are certain key Chapters which should be known well. These are Chapter 1, the Hymns, Chapter 4, Chapter 8, Chapter 18, Chapter 31, Chapter 33, and Chapter 36. If nothing else is done, these Chapters should be studied well, if possible, under the guidance of a qualified spiritual preceptor.

SEGMENTS FROM THE PYRAMID TEXTS AND COFFIN TEXTS

Plate 12: Pyramid Tomb of Ancient Egypt-Middle Kingdom Period-city of Abdu-not to be confused with the Great Pyramids at Giza

Distributed among the Chapters of the later period texts, the reader will find readings from the Ancient Egyptian *Pyramid Texts* and *Coffin Texts*, which are the progenitors of the Chapters of the *Prt m Hru*. They are placed at appropriate places where they relate to the text of the Chapters they precede. This is done to show the continuity of thought between the older texts and the Papyrus Texts, and to show heretofore unrealized aspects of the teachings, in other words, to reveal a depth to the teachings so as to promote better and more profound understanding.

NOTES AND THE STUDY OF MYSTICAL PHILOSOPHY OF THE *PRT M HRU*

The notes have been provided with a two-fold purpose in mind. First to clarify certain terms used and secondly, to provide insight into the philosophy of the teachings. I tried to be brief but certain areas demand philosophical elucidation in order to benefit from the scripture and to update its meaning. However, I will be treating these scriptures fully in the upcoming lecture series (beginning 12/5/1999) which will be recorded and available to all who desire fuller understanding of the mysticism of the *Prt m Hru,* which is the text's heart and soul.

Plate 13: Interior of coffin showing spiritual texts. The female figure inside, as if receiving the body of the aspirant, is goddess Nut.

Rau nu Prt m Hru- The Book of Enlightenment

Section 1: From Death to Life. Awakening of the Spiritual Self

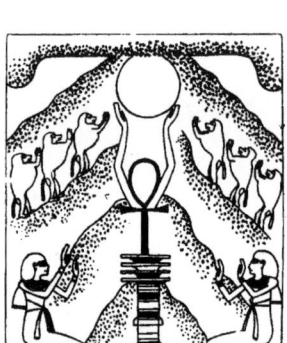

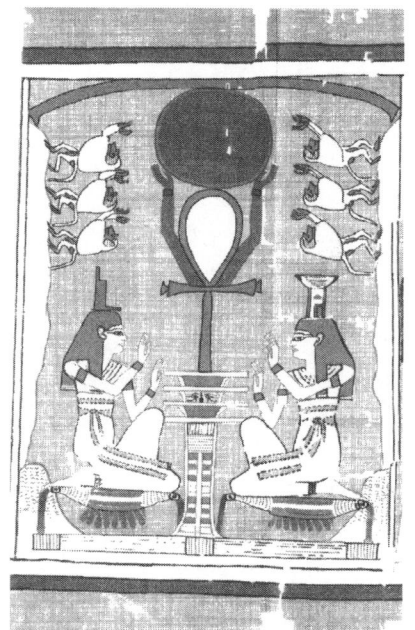

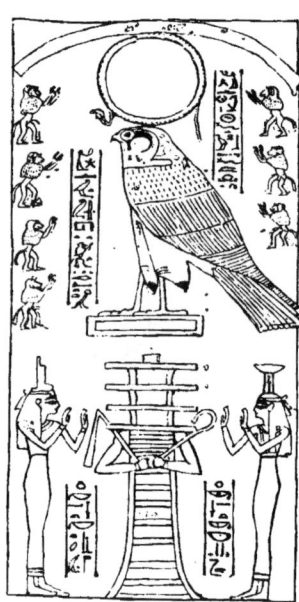

Figure 80: (left) Chap 1 Vignette of the rising sun - Papyrus Kenna.

Plate 14: (Center) The Kemetic Caduceus- Chap 1 Vignette of the rising sun from papyrus Ani accompanying the Hymn to the Rising Sun – The Solar disk rises from the Pillar of Asar and is embraced by its ankh. The goddesses Aset and Nebethet, kneeling on the symbol of gold, support, attend on and praise the event of the rising sun. The six baboons represent the spirits of the dawn.

Figure 81: (right) Chap 1 Vignette of the rising sun - Papyrus Hunefer

Ha	em	reu	nu	pert	em	heru	setjesu
1- Here begin	the	words	for	going	into	light,	praisings

Sakhu		pert	hait	em	neter-khert	akhu	em
glorifications		coming out	going in	through	Lower-astral-plane		in

Amentet	nefert	djedtu	heru	n	qeres	aq	em chet	pert
Amentet	beautiful.	2-Words to say	day	of	burial	going in	cocoon	coming out.

Djed in	Asar	Any	Asar	Sesh	Any :	Inetedj her-k	Ka
3-Words by	Asar	_____	Asar's	scribe	the initiate:	Homage to thee,	life force

Amentet	In	Djehuti	Suten	heh	im – i	nuk	Neter	aaa
Amentet.	4- Hail	Djehuti,	king	eternity	in – me,	I am	God	Great

nem	depet	ahay		ni	her-k	nuk	ua	m	nenu	n nen
in	boat,	fought	5- I		for thee	I am	one	of	those	burgeoning

Neteru	udjaudjau		se-maak-heru	Asar	er	cheftau-f		heru
Gods and goddesses	magistrates	allow to become spiritually victorious	Asar	as to	enemies- his		day

puy	n	udjad	medutu	Nui	imtu-k		Asar!	Nuk	ua
that	of	weighing	words.	6- I am	advocate – yours		Asar!	I am	one

M	enenu	n	neteru	mesu	Nut	semaaiu	cheft	nu
in	those	of	gods and goddesses,	children	Nut	slayers	enemies	of

Asar	chnr	sebiu		her	f	nu	imtu	k	Heru
Asar	restrain	fiends		person	his	7- I am	advocate	yours	Heru

Prt M Hru Chapter 1 Part 1

1. This is the beginning of the words by which a person can come forth into the light, that is, become an enlightened[74] being. They are praises, glorifications and wisdom teachings for going into the Netherworld,[75] that beautiful land, Amentet[76].

2. These words are to be said on the day of burial of the body and its cocconing and the going forth of the soul out into the light, but are also to be known even when one is still alive.

3. In my name of Asar[77]_____, I say "Homage to you, Oh Asar, Divine One who are the bull whose power sustains Amentet[78] and all Creation.

4. Behold, Djehuti[79], you great divinity of reason, the wise king of eternity is within me! And I am that God, the Great one in his boat, Ra, I am.

5. I am one of those burgeoning gods and goddesses, who are the magistrates, whose decree makes Asar to be victorious in respect to his enemies on the day when the words are weighed.[80]

6. Hear this, oh Divine One, I fought for you. When Set and his evil fiends killed you and dismembered you out of greed and hatred. I am one of those divine beings[81], the children of goddess Nut, who destroy the enemies and tie up the demons who try to hurt Asar on that day when the words and deeds are weighed in the balance of Maat, the final judgment of how people have lived in accordance with Truth and Justice.

7. I also support and believe in Heru, your son who redeemed your name after Set murdered you[82].

8. I am verily the god Djehuti, your vicar, who made maak-heru your name against the accusations of your enemies on the day of judgment, which took place in the great temple of your father, Ra, who dwells in the city of Anu[83], the first place on earth.

9. Hear me well, I declare that I am Djedy[84], one who is established in you, who are my Higher Self. I am the son of that same Supreme Self. My mother conceived me in that same divine essence and she gave birth to me there in all glory.

---

[74] Someone who has attained Self-realization, Self-discovery, Spiritual resurrection, discovery of the Higher self, oneness with God, etc.

[75] Astral Plane

[76] Glorious abode of the blessed- The "Hidden Place wherein God is established" -Land of the blessed, Netherworld, Kingdom of Asar, final resting place of righteous, enlightened souls after death.

[77] The initiate speaks.

[78] Netherworld (Astral Plane).

[79] Aspect of the mind (intellect) of Ra, i.e. Cosmic Mind. Recorder of the results of the judgment of the soul in Utterance 19.

[80] Referring to the great judgment in the hall of Maati.

[81] Primordial gods and goddesses.

[82] See the Ausarian Resurrection by Muata Ashby

[83] City of Ra, where he emerged from the Primeval Ocean and ruled bodily as the God-king of Egypt in the most ancient times-before the Dynastic period-See the book *Cycles of Time* by Muata Ashby.

[84] This was the name of two towns in Ancient Egypt. In mystical terms it refers to being firmly established in the Netherworld. The Ancient Egyptian word **Djedu** refers to "steadfastness" or "stability" as well as to the pillar of *Asar*. This is also being referred to in the following line from the *Egyptian Ru Pert Em Heru*, Rau (Chapter I):

nuk Djedi, se Djedi au am-a em Djedu Mesi - a em Djedu "I am Djedy (steadfast), son of Djedy (steadfast), conceived and born in the region of *Djedu* (steadfastness)."

Plate 15: **The Sorrow of death is depicted in this vignette from the Papyrus of Any. The words are an invocation for a movement of resurrection, (Papyrus of Ani-Chap.1).**

10. At the same time, I am also with the men and women who lament over your passion[85]. I am also the one who proved your words to be true in my heart. I proved this before all your accusers and detractors.

11. Thus, Ra, the Supreme One, ordered Djehuti to exonerate you from the accusations of your enemies because you are true of words and deeds.[86] Those accusations were proven to be false and malicious.

Plate 16: The funerary procession moves on with the corpse being taken to the tomb and the funerary sled is in the form of the Divine Boat, making the journey to the West. (Papyrus of Ani-Chap.1)

12. So too it is with me. As you are righteous, I am righteous. Therefore, as it was done for you in ancient times, let it be done for me also. Let Djehuti vindicate my words and actions as well.

13. One am I in Heru on the festival day when the dismembered body of Asar is to be made whole and clothed.

---

[85] Murder and dismemberment- see the *Ausarian Resurrection* by Muata Ashby
[86]MAAK-HERU

14. I make to flow the hidden waters so that the period of resting of the heart of Asar, my innermost Self, may be washed and purified.

15. I unbolt the doors of the innermost shrine in the innermost region of Lord Seker, who is Asar as the king of the Netherworld[87] and ruler over those who have passed to the afterlife.

16. I am the priest/priestess who performs the ceremonies of opening the mind to the higher spiritual truths.

17. One am I in Heru, as protector of the left shoulder[88] of Asar in the place of power[89]. I go in and I come out as one who is in God on the day of defeating the demons in the city of power.

18. I am with Heru on the day of the festivals of Asar, doing offerings on the sixth day of the festival of Denat in the city of Anu.

19. I am pure in the Djedu, powerful in the house of Asar raising up with exaltations, the earth.

20. I see all the secrets in Rastau[90]. My path to glory is clear.

21. I am the reader of the Holy Books of the soul in Djedu. I am the Sem[91] priest/priestess carrying out the duties of my office. I am the great power, the controller of my constructions on the day that the sacred Hennu boat, the symbol of your celestial journey as Seker, moves into its place of balance.

22. I have received the shovel on the day of digging the earth in Suten Henen[92].

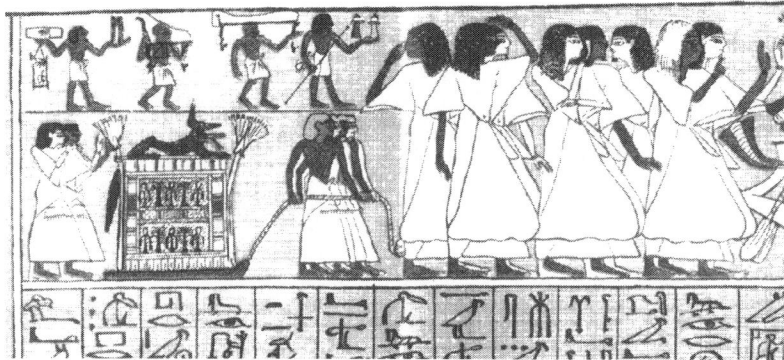

Plate 17: The funeral continues as male mourners follow the sled bearing the body. Behind them are servants drawing a funerary shrine atop which is Anpu. They also bring articles to be buried with the deceased.

---

[87] Astral Plane.

[88] See Figure 26

[89] Sekhem- Life Force energy- similar to the concept of Prana in India and Chi in China,

[90] Entrance to the Netherworld of Seker (Asar as king of the Astral Plane). The use of the word "Rastau" (Restau) is also related to the god Ra. In some texts refers to the Netherworld.

[91] Officiating priestly rank.

[92] The mythical city from which Ra ruled when he was on the earth.

Chapter 1 Part 2

23. Hail! Ye gods and goddesses who cause perfected souls to go into the House of Asar. Allow the soul of this follower of Asar, which is found to be righteous[93] and free from all wrong doing, wrong thinking and wrong speaking, who is already one with Asar, to enter into Asar's house.

24. Let {him/her} hear as you hear; may {he/she} see the things that you can see; let {him/her} stand up as you stand up and may {he/she} sit as you sit.

Plate 18: Offerings and readings are made in the hopes of resurrecting Asar. (Papyrus of Ani-Chap.1)

25. O you exalted ones, who give food and drink to the perfected souls who dwell in the house of Asar[94], give food and drink to this Asar[95]_____[96] whose heart is pure and vindicated[97] before[98] the gods and goddesses and before you as well.

26. Hail to you, who open the ways and roads to spiritual fulfillment for the perfected souls who dwell in the house of Asar, open up a way for Asar _____. Open up a road for this soul of Asar _____, who is righteous with you. May this Asar enter into the house of Asar with fearlessness and may Asar_____ come forth with contentment.

27. May there be no opposition to Asar_____ and let there not be any repulsion to the Asar_____ from that place.[99]

28. May this Soul[100] go in with the favor of Asar, the Supreme One. And may it come forth with gladness at being accepted as being truthful,[101] honorable and just in the sight of God.

---

[93]MAAK-HERU

[94] The God

[95]The person for whom this text has been written, i.e. the initiate.

[96] The blank space, here and henceforth, after the Divine name "Asar" is where the name of the reader, i.e. the initiate, should be spoken.

[97]MAAK-HERU

[98] In the presence of…

[99]The house of Asar.

[100]The person for whom this text has been written, i.e. the initiate.

[101]MAAK-HERU

29. Having been accepted in the House of God and becoming one with God, let the commands of Asar_____ be performed in the House of Asar.

30. May the commands of this Soul be effective as those of God are effective. May this Spirit[102] be glorified along with yours (God's), and may there be found no fault of any kind in the Soul of Asar_____ so let the balance scales of justice be cleared and may the trial of Asar_____ be ended.

Figure 82: Funerary scene from the tomb of Neferhotep.

The barges transport priests/priestesses, mourners, the body and coffin to the western shore of the Nile river in the city of Waset (Thebes) where the cemeteries are located, symbolically moving towards the "Beautiful West"
(Ament),
the final abode of the blessed.

---

[102]The person for whom this text has been written, i.e. the initiate.

GLOSS ON CHAPTER 1: ITS MEANING AND MYSTICAL SIGNIFICANCE

There are several important teachings contained in Chapter One. The opening invocation begins by stating the purpose and method of use for the text that follows. The *Pert Em Heru* is a mystical text. Mysticism relates to the union of the individual human being to the Higher Consciousness, sometimes referred to as the Supreme Being, God, Goddess, The Self, The Absolute, etc., as well as by several specific deity names such as Asar, Christ, Buddha, Krishna, etc. It is not a historical treatise. It relates to the fulfillment of the myth of Asar in the Ausarian Resurrection Myth and this, to the spiritual evolution of each individual human being.

> "It is evident that the religious rites and ceremonies were never based on mere myths or superstitions; they were created with the aim of promoting the morality and the happiness of those whose duty was to respect them."
> —Plutarch (c. 46-120 AD)

The text of the *Pert Em Heru* is essentially a set of wisdom teachings and rituals which are designed to help a person to transform their mind in order to discover the higher form of consciousness. Thus, the text is not only to be studied, but also recited and lived. This is the higher implication of the understanding of the concept behind rituals. Many people think of rituals as a set of activities to be carried out in some specific order within the confines of a church or temple. In Ancient Egyptian Religious Philosophy, rituals had also the purpose of reinforcing virtue in the masses as well as the spiritual aspirants. The practice of Maat or the cultivation of virtue was seen as a prerequisite for the maintenance of a well-ordered society and as a pre-qualification for the priests and priestesses, who were the shepherds of the society. Therefore, in the broader sense, religious rites or rituals are a part of everyday life and should be directed at promoting purity of heart, harmony and truth. People ritualistically attend activities they enjoy. Other rituals are eating at lunch time, watching a favorite television show at the same time daily or weekly, etc. If the rituals are leading a person to discover the higher consciousness within themselves then they are to be considered as rituals which are leading to the revelation of the mysteries of life. This is the purpose of the rituals contained in the *Pert Em Heru*. Through songs and praisings, a person propitiates the Divine in order to seek the grace of the Divine in the form of spiritual enlightenment. This is to be carried out by means of one all-important discipline referred to as Maak-heru or truth of speech.

The term MAAK-HERU has several important implications. It means vindicated, righteous of speech, spiritually victorious, purity of heart and strong of will in speech. This most important word means spiritual victory through living a life of righteousness and physical, mental and moral purity which includes truthfulness of thought, word and deed. It is the perfection of virtue in life, and the character of Heru who wins the battle against Set, the evil one, symbolizes it most prominently. Thus, it is a term relating to spiritual enlightenment, resurrection and rebirth of the spirit.

This chapter also introduces an important aspect of spiritual philosophy, Faith. In verse #7 the aspirant proclaims the belief in God and it is this faith that opens the door to spiritual realization. For it is faith that allows one to carry on in times of adversity and it is faith that promotes spiritual awakening even when the mind does not fully understand the spiritual philosophy. Therefore, faith is the first step on the latter of spiritual realization and wisdom or the understanding of what one has faith in, is the fulfillment of faith. If there is no understanding there can only be blind faith and blind faith does not lead to enlightenment but to confusion and conflict. Faith can move mountains only when it is leading to purity of heart and right action in peace and non-violence. Otherwise it is faith in the ego that is being practiced, that is, faith in the lower nature and not in God. All the problems between religions and those who consider themselves faithful to them arise due to the lack of real faith in and understanding of who God is. Therefore, faith must be followed by righteous action and this leads the personality in a process of personality integration and sublimation of the ego which promotes spiritual enlightenment, i.e. "coming into the light."

Asar is addressed as the "Bull of Amentet." He is referred to as a bull because on a farm the bull can sire many cows. As we will see, Asar is referred to later on and depicted as the bull who services the

seven cows which constitute aspects of creation. Thus, God is the source which engenders and sustains life in the seven realms of creation.

Asar Ani propitiates the gods and goddesses by declaring that he has upheld the truth against the enemies of Asar. The enemies of Asar are anger, hatred, greed, jealousy, hypocrisy, violence, disharmony, etc. They are symbolized by Set and his fiendish friends who murder Asar and steal the throne of Egypt away from Asar and Heru. Asar Ani (the initiate) positively affirms that he worked to uphold truth and righteousness in life on behalf of God. When you seek to live a life of righteousness, you are actually upholding the Divine Will; you are serving God. The reward for this form of service is purity of heart, inner peace, and spiritual enlightenment, all of which constitute Maak-heru or truth-speaking. He also states that he is related to Asar. He also states that he is related to Heru. But what is the nature of this relationship? Ani actually means that he is one with them, that he is actually an expression of them. This is further elaborated in the verse relating to his origins and birth in Djed.

You might expect Asar Ani to say that he was conceived in some city of Ancient Egypt by a human man and a human woman, but he does not say anything of the kind. Instead he states: "Nuk Djeddi se Djeddi au am - a em Djedu mesi - a Djedu." Translation: "I am Djedi, the son of Djedi. My mother conceived me in Djedu, and gave birth to me in Djedu." The teaching may be more easily understood as follows: "I am steadfast, son of steadfast, conceived and born in the region of steadfastness." Asar Ani states emphatically that he is steadfastness. Since Asar (the God) is steadfastness itself, this teaching must be understood as a ritual identification of Asar Ani and Asar. Ritual identification relates to the understanding that your identity is not the limited body, but that your true identity is one with the Supreme Being (Asar). This teaching is also imparted by the name of the initiate. Ani is no longer referred to as "Ani" but instead as "Asar Ani," meaning that his true identity is the Divine, and that his personality is only a manifestation of that divinity. Therefore, all human beings who practice the teachings of the *Pert Em Heru* are referred to as being "Asar."

In the Ausarian Resurrection Myth, Djehuti interceded on behalf of Asar when he was wronged by Set, so as Asar, Ani seeks to be redeemed and vindicated as Asar was. Asar Ani, through his spiritual discipline of righteousness (Maak-heru) has opened the water-springs of knowledge and spiritual upliftment. The unbolting of the door of the Shetai Shrine in Ra-stau relates to the Holy of Holies, not in the temple, but of the unconscious mind within himself. Asar Ani's purity has allowed him entry into the hidden (Shetai) realms wherein God is to be found. Thus, he is not obstructed by the flames of passion and desire which distract the mind and prevent a person from discovering the transcendental realms of consciousness.

Although Asar Ani is described as a scribe at the beginning, he is now described as the priest who is pouring libations and officiating the rituals of glorification and praisings of the Divine. He is achieving divine vision of the hidden mysteries and he is reciting the liturgy (these chapters) which are allowing him to view the Supreme Being (Soul-God in Djedu).

Asar Ani is continually referred to as the one "whose word is true" throughout Chapter One. This signifies that a person who is able to attain the higher spiritual vision must achieve purity of heart by living in accordance with Maat (the precepts of righteousness).

Having affirmed his righteousness and worthiness, Asar Ani closes Chapter One with an invocation to the spirit guides who open the way to self-discovery and lead the soul to the abode of Asar (the God). He also prays that there should be no opposition to his movement in the transcendental realms of existence and that he may not be sent back from those heights of spiritual experience. These final requests raise many important questions. What is the nature of the opposition to self-discovery and what does the "sending back" imply?

These questions denote a keen understanding of the concepts of Karma and Reincarnation. The obstructions to spiritual evolution are the enemies of the Divine (ignorance, egoism, anger, hatred, greed, lust, etc.) which degrade the mind and cause a person to live sinfully and egoistically, drawing them away from discovering the divinity within themselves.

The sending back implies the idea that those who do not seek entry into the divine realm of existence (Djedu) will be turned back and will have to take birth again in order to have another chance to act righteously and thereby purify their heart. Righteousness is the most important aspect of spirituality because it allows a person to discover inner peace and freedom from worry. When there is no worry and the mind is peaceful, it can understand the teachings and it can see the divine essence within just as the bottom of a lake can be seen when there are no waves. Therefore, Maat leads to clarity of vision and this is all under the term Maak-heru. So Maak-heru may be defined as becoming established in righteousness (Maat) of the Higher Self (Heru).

CHAPTER 2[103]
THE BEGINNING OF THE WORDS TO BE UNDERSTOOD FOR ATTAINING ENLIGHTENMENT

1. These are the words, which when spoken and understood, lead a human being to become spiritually enlightened. They are words for living after the death of the body. The Asar_____, the noble aspirant, should say joyfully:

2. Hail, Only One,[104] who shinest in the moon. Let me come forth from the masses of people who live in ignorance upon the earth. Let there be established for me a place among the shining spirits who have transcended death. Open for me the Netherworld, which lies beyond this physical universe. Let me as well be allowed to go out among the living to do what I would like to do among the living.

Plate 19: The initiate walks towards the Western Horizon and sees the Divine Heru standing on the symbol of the West which is between the symbol of the horizons, representing yesterday and today.

PYRAMID TEXT UTTERANCE 50: ADORATIONS TO THE RISING SUN

(Utterance 50-line1-Pyramid of Unas)

Hail Ra! You dawn in the heavens for Asar _____, Lord of All and to yourself all things belong. To the Ka of Asar _____ all things belong, and a sacred altar is raised.

Plate 20: Vignette from Papyrus Nekht-Adorations to Asar. Text above is the Hymn to Ra.

---

[103]Based on the Papyrus of Ani.
[104]God, the Supreme Being (Asar).

GLOSS ON CHAPTER 2: ITS MEANING AND MYSTICAL SIGNIFICANCE

Chapter Two is a very short chapter which contains some powerful teachings referring to the fate of the masses of people and to the need for directing the mind to a higher goal of life. First Ani addresses Asar as the one who shines from the moon. This refers to Asar as a lunar deity. Asar in his aspect as the moon symbolizes the mind. In ordinary astronomical observation, it is obvious that the moon shines because it is illumined by the sun. Essentially what human beings see as the light of the moon at night is in reality the light of the sun which is shining on the moon and reflecting onto the earth. In mystical philosophy the moon symbolizes the mind. The understanding is that the mind shines with awareness because the light of Universal Consciousness (God) is reflecting in it. Thus, the only reason why a human being can exist, think, be aware, awake, etc. is because the underlying consciousness is supporting their existence just like water is sustained in a glass because the glass is holding it and supporting it.

Next Asar Ani requests a special dispensation from the divine. He asks that he be singled out from among the rest of society and that he be allowed to enter into the place which is forbidden to most other people. This is an important teaching to understand.

Most people in society are consumed with the various worries and concerns of life. They are not concerned with spiritual matters until such time as when they experience some adversity in their lives. Then they turn to the church, temple or to prayer, hoping that God will help them in their time of need. This way of spiritual worship is egoistic and limited. It cannot help a human being to discover their true essence. It is like engaging in an activity which causes you to become filthy all day and then you just wash your hands and go along with your business. What happened to the rest of your body? In the same way, you cannot expect to attain spiritual enlightenment if you only pray when there is an adversity because this will only scratch the surface of your personality and like the body, your entire personality needs to be cleansed. This cleansing is called purity of heart.

The masses of people are ignorant of the higher spiritual teachings so they are caught up in the illusions of sensual pleasures and egoistic desires. Therefore, a spiritual aspirant, recognizing the error of the masses, must move away from the ignorance of the masses who do not progress spiritually, those who are "at the portal" but who are not able to go in.

So spiritual desires are positive desires because they lead you to liberation and self-discovery. Positive desires rather than worldly desires must be cultivated through study, reflection and practice of the teachings of Yoga and Mystical Spirituality, under the direction of a qualified spiritual preceptor. This is what makes the difference between a spiritual aspirant and the worldly masses.

Spiritual enlightenment leads to freedom, not only after death, but also while alive as well. When you are free from anxiety, anger, hatred, greed, jealousy, etc., you are able to achieve greatness in life. The demons of the lower self are the chains that bind a human being to negativity, worldly entanglements, sinful thoughts and activities. These negative aspects of the personality are what lead a person to experience untold sufferings in life as well as the hellish conditions they encounter after death.

167

HYMN 1[105]

ADORATIONS TO RA WHEN HE RISES IN THE EASTERN HORIZON OF HEAVEN.

1. Behold Asar_____ bringing divine offerings of all the gods and goddesses. Asar _____ speaks thus:

2. Homage to thee, who comes in the form of Khepri[106], Khepri the Creator of the gods and goddesses. You rise and shine, illuminating your mother, goddess Nut, the sky, crowned as king of the gods and goddesses. Your mother Nut worships you with her two arms. The western horizon receives you in peace and Maat embraces you at the double season. Give Asar _____ Glorious Spirit being[107], and spiritual strength through righteous speaking. Grant the ability to come forth as a living soul so that Asar _____ may see Heru of the two Horizons.[108] Grant this to the Ka[109] of Asar _____ who is Righteous of Speech in the presence of Asar, the Divine Self. Asar _____ says: Hail to all the gods and goddesses, weighers of the house of the soul, in heaven and on earth by means of the scales of Maat, who are givers of Life Force sustenance.

Plate 21: Ani stands before Ra who is in his Divine Boat. Ani is in the Duat in the adoration pose as he utters the Hekau of the Hymn to Ra.

3. Tatunen,[110] One, maker of men and women as well as the company of the gods and goddesses of the south, the north, the west and the east, i.e. all the neteru[111], grant praises to Ra, the lord of heaven, sovereign of life, vitality and health, maker of the gods and goddesses. Adorations to thee in your form as all goodness, as you rise in your boat. The beings up high praise thee. Beings in the lower realms praise thee. Djehuti[112] and Maat[113] have written for thee, who are shining forth, every day. Your enemies are put to the fire. The fiends are put down, their arms and legs being bound securely for Ra. The children of weakness disrespect and insurrection shall not continue.

4. The great house[114] is in festival time. The voices of the participants are in the great temple. The gods and goddesses are rejoicing. They see Ra in his glorious rising, his beams of light piercing, inundating the lands. This exalted and venerable god journeys on and unites with the land of Manu, the western horizon, illuminating the land of his birth every day and at the same time he reaches the province where he was yesterday.

---

[105] Generally referred to as Chapter 15

[106] Morning sun, solar child-Nefertem.

[107] i.e. allow the initiate to become an Akhu or Glorious Spirit.

[108] The All-Encompassing Divine Self in the form of Heru.

[109] Spiritual essence of the personality which holds a person's desires, impulses and impetus to incarnate; the Life Force which sustains the physical being.

[110] Creator -aspect of Ra, Atum, Asar, Khepri, Amun, Neberdjer, etc) who first arose on the primeval mound. Protector of the souls of Asar and Heru.

[111] Gods and goddesses

[112] Ibis headed deity, minister of Ra, originator of hieroglyphic writings and music.

[113] Goddess of righteousness, truth, regularity, and order.

[114] Royal family.

Figure 83: Set protecting barque of Ra from the giant serpent of disorder-(dissolution).

5. Be in peace with me! I see your beauties and I prosper upon the land; I smile and I defeat the ass fiend as well as the other fiends. Grant that I may defeat Apep[115] in his time of strength and to see the pilot fish of the Divine Boat of Ra, which is in its blessed pool.[116] I see Heru in the form as the guardian of the rudder. Djehuti and Maat are upon his two arms. Received am I in the prow[117] of the Mandet[118] Boat and in the stern of the Mesektet[119] Boat. Ra gives divine sight, to see the Aten[120], to view the moon god unceasingly, every day, and the ability of souls to come forth, to walk to every place they may desire. Proclaim my name! Find him in the wood board of offerings. There have been given to me offerings in the life-giving presence, like it is given to the followers of Heru[121]. It is done for me in the divine place in the boat on the day of the sailing, the journey of The God. I am received in the presence of Asar in the

land of truth speaking[122] of the Ka of Asar _____.

Figure 84: Heru spearing Apep who is in the form of a man.

---

[115] Leader of the fiends, second only to Set.

[116] The pool or lake is the symbol of the Primeval Ocean. In ancient times the temple complexes included a lake for ritually sailing the boat of Ra as well as for keeping fish, crocodiles and other animals as temple mascots.

[117] Front section of a ship's hull, the bow.

[118] The name of Ra's Divine boat when it is traveling from noon to midnight, i.e. the evening boat.

[119] The name of Ra's Divine boat when it is traveling from midnight to noon, i.e. the morning boat.

[120] The sundisk.

[121] In Kemetic Mystical Philosophy the principle of "Shemsu Heru" is very important. It may be likened to the disciples of Jesus in Christianity who were his "followers." It means living and acting like Heru, a life of truth and increasing spiritual enlightenment.

[122] Maak-heru.

GLOSS ON THE HYMNS TO RA: ITS MEANING AND MYSTICAL SIGNIFICANCE

The invocatory hymn of any scripture is an important part of the overall feeling of the spiritual tradition. Ra, of course, symbolizes the Higher Self, the Supreme Being, God. Thus, the invocation to God is a form of prayer, or devotional expression towards the Divine, but at the same time it is a form of propitiation. In essence, prayer can be understood as talking to God, but the hymn goes a step further. Most times in modern culture people pray in order to ask for something. Sometimes people want God to help them with a problem in their life. Sometimes the prayer is for good luck. Sometimes the prayer is asking for the right numbers to the lottery. At other times the prayer is for deliverance from some ordeal in life. But how often do people pray for deliverance from human life? How often do people ask God to show them the way to achieve spiritual enlightenment? This is the very objective of the Hymn to Ra.

The hymn opens with salutations and descriptive appellations of Ra, as he rises in the morning. This is not some distant God, but a familiar presence. Ra is a being who can be seen daily and who can be approached easily. He illumines all the earth and causes all life to be. Ra is the source from which all of the gods and goddesses, all life, all human beings, etc., emanate. He sustains Creation by establishing Maat (order) and Djehuti (reason) as he moves through Creation. It is especially acknowledged that Ra is not only the illuminer of the physical world, but also of the Netherworld, the Duat (kingdom of the dead). This signifies that Ra is not the sun itself. This is a very important point to understand. Ancient Egyptian mythology holds that there are three realms of existence. These are the Physical Plane (Ta), the Astral Plane (Duat) and the Heaven (Pet). Just as the universe has three realms, the human being has three bodies. These are the Physical Body, the Astral Body and the Causal Body. The physical realm is the place where human beings experience the physical body and the sense organs. The astral realm is where the mind and subtle senses operate. The Causal Body is the deep unconscious level of the mind where impressions related to one's past experiences and desires for the future are stored.

The three bodies are related to three states of consciousness within a human being or the mode in which consciousness manifests within the mind. The Physical Body relates to waking, day to day consciousness. The Astral Body relates to dream consciousness and the Causal Body relates to the unconscious level of mind. However, there is a fourth state of consciousness. This is the Transcendental Self (Neberdjer-Asar) which supports the other three (Amun-unconscious, Ra-dream and Ptah-waking). Deep within the unconscious mind lies the Self which transcends all bodies. This is the abode of Asar within every human being. If a person does not discover Asar within themselves by discovering the inner recesses of their own heart, they become caught in an endless search for fulfillment in the astral and physical realms through the astral and physical bodies. This is known as the cycle of birth and death or reincarnation. When the physical body ceases to exist, the soul of a human being goes to the astral realm in order to continue the journey of spiritual evolution.

If a person has acted with virtue and in accordance with the voice of their conscience, their soul will experience positive conditions in the astral realm. This condition is referred to as heaven. If a person acted according to their egoistic desires, selfishness and pride, they will experience pain and sorrow in the astral realm. This condition is referred to as hell. So the hymn goes on to invoke the grace of Ra. The astral realm is a subtle universe which is in a different plane than the physical. Ra passes through the astral realm just as he also passes through the physical. He passes through the physical realm in his Andetet Barque (boat), and through the astral realm in the Sekhet night barque. However, when he passes through the Duat, there are certain ropes which hang from his boat. The desire of the spiritual aspirant reading the text is that {he/she} may be able to see and grab hold of the ropes which are hanging from the boat.

The ropes symbolize divine compassion and divine love. God is extending his hand, as it were, to rescue the soul from the suffering that can occur outside of the boat. The boat itself is the innermost realm of God. It is the place of contentment and peace, being closest to the Divine. All other realms are as if a separation from that divine perfection that is in the boat. They represent a distancing from God, a separation from what is Divine.

The act of reaching out to grab the ropes is the act of spiritual aspiration and it signifies the practice of all of the spiritual disciplines (of Yoga) which enable a person to move towards their Higher Self as opposed to getting more deeply involved in the relative realms which are again, a separation from the Divine.

This is a beautiful hymn dedicated to the Divine, the Supreme Being, in the form of Ra. It contains much of the same feeling and dedications as in Plate 1 of the papyrus of Ani. However, it also has several important additional teachings which are important to the study of *Pert Em Heru*.

The idea of Ra emerging and "inundating the lands" with his life giving essence has special mystical significance. This teaching refers to the original creation when the entire universe and the forms of Creation were not yet in existence. The time prior to the dawn symbolizes the undifferentiated state of the universe as well as the human mind. In the beginning the universe was like a calm ocean and there was no differentiation in it. Everything looked the same. However, when Ra emerged from the ocean he caused waves, and these waves took on many different forms. These forms are what we refer to as elements or matter. Think of the time when you fall asleep. You lose consciousness of your waking personality and you are submerged in an ocean without forms. This is like the primeval ocean of creation. From it arises your dream world in which you are a character among other characters of your own creation. Thus, you are the Creator of your dream world and God is the creator of the dream of the universe.

God created the universe by causing vibrations in that primordial ocean of his own consciousness by uttering sound. Sound is the medium by which God ordains what happens in Creation from its inception to its end. The word manifests through the power and faculty of speech. Therefore, speech is related to Cosmic Consciousness and the ability to create in the world of time and space as well as in the astral realm. In the same manner, a human being can create his or her world according to the desire of the heart.

Thus, just as a human being must breathe air in order to sustain life, this entire universe must receive the breath of life from the Divine in order to be sustained. However, ordinary human beings (ignorant masses) only know of the physical air that sustains the physical body. A spiritual aspirant seeks to breath the air which sustains the elevated states of consciousness which are above the waking state of consciousness.

The hymn goes on to show that Ani praises the Divine at dawn and at eventide. This teaching relates to the necessity for devotional exercise such as prayers, chanting and recitation of the hekau or words of power which propitiate divine grace and promote spiritual knowledge and the kindling of spiritual feeling deep within the heart leading to purity and enlightenment. A person engages constantly in the world with its illusions. Thus, spiritual practice should be daily, encompassing every aspect of life, in order to overwhelm the worldly impressions produced by distraction, ignorance and the lower desires. The process of spiritual worship leads a human being to draw divine grace to {him/her} self. This is what is referred to as being one of the "favored ones" of God. This favored status is attained by becoming "one of those who worshiped thee upon earth" meaning while they were alive and in human form.

Many people mistakenly believe that the *Pert Em Heru* is a book of rituals only for people who have passed on to the next life, but in reality it is a discipline for those who are alive. The physical body is the best place to carry out a spiritual program, the practice of Yoga and Mystical Religion. This is because it is the place where the soul can experience an extended period of waking consciousness in which to consciously work on purifying the heart. The dream and dreamless sleep states or subconscious and unconscious levels of the mind are inconstant and minimal spiritual progress can be accomplished in these states.

HYMN 2 A HYMN TO ASAR

Plate 22: Above- Initiate and spouse in the "Dua" adoration pose facing Asar.

1. Glory to Asar Un-Nefer[1] , the great god within Abdu, [2] king of eternity, lord of everlastingness, who passeth through millions of years in his existence. Eldest son of the womb of Nut, engendered by Geb, the chief lord of the crowns of the North and South,[3] lord of the lofty white crown.[4] As Prince of gods and of men he has received the crook and the flail and the dignity of his divine father.[5]

2. Let thy heart which is in the mountain of Amenta be content, for thy son Heru is established upon thy throne. You are crowned lord of Djedu[6] and ruler in Abdu. Through thee the world waxeth green in triumph before the might of Neb-er-djer.[7] He leadeth in his train that which is and that which is not yet, in his name Ta-her-seta-nef; [8] he toweth along the earth in triumph in his name Seker. [9]

2. He is exceedingly mighty and most terrible in his name Asar.

3. He endureth forever and forever in his name Un-nefer.[10]

4. Homage to thee, King of Kings, Lord of Lords, Prince of Princes, who from the womb of Nut have possessed the world and have ruled all lands and Akert.[11] Thy body is of gold, thy head is of azure, and emerald light encircleth thee. O Anu[12] of millions of years, all-pervading with thy body and beautiful in countenance in Ta-sert.[13]

5. Grant thou to the Ka of Asar, the initiate, splendor in heaven and might upon earth and triumph in Neterchert;[14] and that I may, sail down to Djedu like a living soul and up to Abdu like a bennu;[15] and that I may go in and come out without being repelled at the pylons of the Duat. May there be given unto me loaves of bread in the house of coolness, and offerings of food in Annu, [16] and a homestead forever in Sektet-Yaru,[17] with wheat and barley therefor..." It has come to a good ending in Waset, the place of truth.

Special Notes On this Hymn To Asar

1. "The good and beautiful ever existing one," a title of the god Asar.
2. *Abdu* was the city which the Greeks called *Abydos*. It is also reputed to be the resting place of the body of *Asar*.
3. In ancient times Egypt was divided into two districts, north and south. Each had various kings and queens but the whole land was ruled by an emperor and or empress, i.e. the titles *Neb-Tawi* (ruler of the two lands), *Neb Nestu Tawi* (ruler of the crowns of the two lands).
4. The crown of Upper Egypt, the south and most ancient origins of the culture and civilization.
5. *Asar*, as the night sun (the moon) was also the son of Ra.
6. This was the name of two towns in Ancient Egypt. In mystical terms it refers to being firmly established in the Netherworld.
7. Nebertcher literally means "All Encompassing Divinity" or "Supreme Being."
8. The One who draws the world, i.e. Ra, the Supreme Being, who causes the world to exist by drawing it along in the movement of the Boat of "Millions of Years."
9. Seker is the divine form of the Supreme Being (*Asar, Ptah, Tenen*) as the night sun, symbolizing the period of death.
10. The "Beautiful Being" or the "Good Being," i.e. *Asar*.
11. The country of which Asar is the ruler. There was an Akert or burial ground on the western side of the Nile. This is where many important excavations have been conducted in recent times, uncovering the tombs of Kings, Queens and Nobles of Ancient Egypt.
12. A name of the sun god, i.e. Ra (*Asar*).
13. A name of the Netherworld.
14. Lower realm of (Amentet) Heaven, the first place where departed souls go and hope to leave there to reach Amentet, the land of the blessed.
15. Mythological meaning: Phoenix; Mystical meaning: Glorified Soul-enlightened human being.
16. The city of the sun, the first city which emerged with the creation, thus, the abode of Ra and the Ennead.
17. A section of the astral world. It is part of the *Sekhet-hetepu*, where souls of the blessed reap and sow.

CHAPTER 3[123]

A HYMN IN PRAISE OF ASAR, THE FOREMOST BEING IN AMENTET, THE UN-NEFER WHO IS WITHIN ABDU!

1. Asar _____ speaks: Oh my Divine Lord, who exists for all eternity, Lord of Lords, King of Kings and God of the gods and goddesses who live with you.[124] I have come to you as a one of the neteru[125] among men and women and I ask that you make for me a place in the foremost section of the Neterkhert where those divine beings live. They adore the images of your Ka. They arrive in your abode and remain there for millions and millions[126] of years. As concerns myself and that which is in the body and personality, they as well, may there not arise any holdup in Ta-Meri. Grant that they may all come to you, the great as well as the little, and likewise may there be granted entry and exit to the Duat for Asar _____.

GLOSS ON THE HYMNS TO ASAR (HYMN 2 AND CHAPTER 3): ITS MEANING AND MYSTICAL SIGNIFICANCE

In many ways the hymn to Asar is similar to that of Ra. The hymn to Asar affirms the supremacy of Asar. He is held in equal status as Ra. According to Ancient Egyptian Mystical philosophy, Asar is the son of Geb and Nut, who are the children of Shu and Tefnut, who in turn are the children of Ra. Thus Asar can be seen as the great grandson of Ra, but Asar is not to be thought of as having a filial relationship with Ra like ordinary human genealogy. The hymn to Asar has many important additional mystical teachings. In essence, all of the Ancient Egyptian gods and goddesses are to be understood as being emanations from the one Supreme Being. Thus all of them can be identified as "Supreme Beings" within their own system of theology. So if a spiritual aspirant has a particular inclination towards a god or goddess, they can follow the teaching of that particular god or goddess with the understanding that they are symbols of the higher divinity. So there is no contradiction in the teaching.

Asar wears the crown of Upper and Lower Egypt. This means that he is the lord who presides over duality, the lower self (the ego) and the Higher Self in a human being. Asar is the essence which sustain life in the two lands. He does so under the auspices of Neberdjer (Lord of the Utmost Limit). Neberdjer means Supreme Being, Transcendental Self, The Absolute. Thus, the teaching is being imparted that Asar, though being the High God, is also the symbolic form of the Transcendental Self which has no form but that is the absolute source of all power.

In most depictions, Asar is represented as a man wrapped with mummy swathings since he was killed by his brother, torn to pieces and then later re-membered and resurrected by Aset. In his form as Seker he is depicted as a being with the body of a human being and the head of a hawk. This relation to the hawk is of course a subtle way of saying that Asar is identified with Heru. Heru means, the "Most High," the spiritual light of consciousness. Heru is also identified with Ra. Asar, Ra, Heru, Neberdjer, Aset, Amun and Ptah are all Kemetic names of the Divine, symbolizing that which is eternal. This teaching of eternity is metaphorically referred to as henti periods or simply as "millions of millions of years." Thus, we are to understand that God is unfathomable existence, the source and sustenance of Creation, and the very source of all that is beautiful and good.

Asar is in possession of the crook staff and the flail staff. The crook is the symbol of leadership. This refers to the ability to lead oneself as well as others to what is righteous and good. The flail is the instrument used for separating the chaff from the seed. In modern times machines do this work. The thresher is an agricultural machine used to separate grain from chaff and straw. The first threshers were the feet of humans and animals or flails. The mystical implication is that a spiritual aspirant must separate themselves from egoism and ignorance in order to move from what is untruth to truth, from un-reality to

---

[123] This chapter is sometimes referred to as #185.

[124] Supreme Being.

[125] As one of the gods and goddesses.

[126] En heh en heh can mean millions of years or undetermined expanse of time, i.e. forever.

reality and from mortality to immortality. This process is accomplished as a person studies, practices and realizes the mystical teachings being imparted.

Foremost in the practice of the teachings is Maakheru (Maak-heru, truth-speaking). Truth speaking is a profound teaching which relates to the innermost reaches of consciousness. Human consciousness has three main realms just as the physical universe has three realms. This is derived from the teachings of the Ancient Egyptian Trinity of Amun-Ra-Ptah which emanates from Neberdjer, The Absolute Self. You may have noticed that sometimes you say things that are on your mind without even thinking about it. Sometimes you regret what came out and sometimes you are amazed at the wisdom which comes forth. This occurs because the mouth or the faculty of speech in a human being is directly linked to the unconscious level of the mind. As stated earlier, the Self abides in the unconscious of every human being. When a positive thought arises in a person's mind, it has emanated from the innermost Self. This is the voice of conscience within every human being. So if a person lives virtuously, in accordance with the dictates of truth, justice, peace, harmony, love, etc., they are speaking with truth. Then if a person is acting in accordance with truth, they are upholding Maat, the order and harmony of the universe which God has established. Therefore, speaking and acting with truth are the primary spiritual disciplines for attaining spiritual enlightenment or self-discovery. This is the basis of the famous Ancient Egyptian Proverb: *Know Thyself.*

When a person has perfected themselves in living righteously, they are referred to as *Maak-heru,* or "True of speech." This is the highest spiritual attainment because it means knowing truth from untruth and the Self from the not self. Righteousness includes studying the spiritual teachings and gaining an understanding of the mystical implications contained in them. It includes practicing the rituals which reinforce the teachings and lead to the unfoldment of the devotional feeling in the heart towards the Divine. It means practicing the teachings by offering one's actions to the Divine as a worshipper offers flowers at the altar of a deity. It means gaining insight into the fact that one is inexorably related to the Self. It means intense meditation on the nature of the Divine by calming the mind and senses to such a degree as to gain the ability to enter into the astral body and the causal body at will, in order to discover their nature and reveal the Hidden Self (Amun) which is one's true identity. Therefore, God has prepared the road for those who wish to lead themselves to attain spiritual enlightenment. All they need to do is practice righteousness (Maat).

One of the most important titles of Asar is "Un-Nefer." Un-Nefer means "Most Beautiful Being." In his aspect as the slain and resurrected king, Asar symbolizes the human plight of reincarnation and the ultimate possibility for resurrection and ascension into the higher planes of existence as ruler over death. As Un-Nefer, Asar represents the soul of all creation who causes the universe to exist for aeons.

This chapter contains a mystical description of the state of higher consciousness that is the objective of all spiritual efforts, to become a *Living Ba* and to take the form of the Bennu. The Ba is the soul, and one is not truly living if one only has awareness of the waking and dream state of consciousness. These only constitute the transient personality of a human being, the ego consciousness. The ego is illusory, being different in the waking state, different in the dream state and different in the unconscious. Therefore, it is necessary to transcend these three realms in order to achieve awareness or experience of the real Self.

The Bennu is the prototype of the Greek Phoenix. The Bennu is Ra, who is essentially one with Asar, being reborn or resurrected into the higher form of existence after having died to the lower form of existence. Chapter 26 expands on the Bennu teaching and a more extensive commentary will be offered in that section.

The final section of the Hymn to Asar relates to sepulchral offerings. These relate to offerings of bread, ale and other items. These are of paramount importance since they relate to one of the most important rituals contained in the *Pert Em Heru.* These offerings are so important that they occur in the Ancient Egyptian Pyramid Text and also in other chapters of the *Pert Em Heru.* They relate to the ritual identification of the initiate or spiritual aspirant with the Divine. This ritual was so powerful and important that it was adopted by the Christian church as the Eucharist. It will be further explained in Chapter 21 and elsewhere.

In closing, there is a supplication to the Divine that the initiate be allowed to attain a permanent residence in the Sekhet-Aaru or Divine realm and that the spirit be nourished therein. This signifies a desire to end the cycle of birth and death. This movement points to the development of dispassion and detachment in the mind. Many people practice the rituals of various spiritual traditions but they have one important obstacle; they are holding onto worldly desires, expectation and illusions (the not-self or ignorance).

As a spiritual aspirant you must realize that worldly objects cannot bring you happiness. The happiness you seem to feel from objects that you desire when you attain them is only the projection of your own internal feeling for them. You have learned to think that you will be happy if you attain them so you become attached to what you think is good in life. However, you will never be truly fulfilled with anything in this world. The teaching of dispassion and detachment requires a profound understanding of the nature of the universe. When this unfolds, a spiritual aspirant realizes that objects are illusory emanations from the Self and that they are perishable, like objects in a dream. Thus, you must learn to turn away from objects and people and attach to God and the spiritual disciplines which will allow you to attain Godhood. This teaching will be elaborated throughout this commentary.

Section 2: The Wisdom of Self Discovery and The Path of Righteousness

chem - not know, be ignorant of something

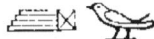

Saa - To not Know, is a weakness, an evil

Saa or ***Siaa*** -To Know, understand, Divine Knowledge

rech - become aquatinted with –know something

rch ren n neteru - to know the name of the gods and goddesses

rech - i   em   iab-i
Know   I   in   heart mine
("I know what is in my heart" or "I know myself")
From Chapter 13 of the *Prt m Hru*

177

CHAPTER 4[127]

THE WISDOM OF THE SECRET IDENTITY OF THE GODS AND GODDESSES

1.   This is the beginning of the praisings and glorifications for going out and coming into the Neterkhert, glorious in Amentet, the beautiful place. These words are for allowing one to go out into the light in all the forms that a person may desire, to play the Senet game in the resting booth, and to go forth as a living soul.

2.   These words are to be spoken by Asar _____ after arriving from the journey. It is a glorious thing to do on earth, the coming into these words, which bring completeness and spiritual enlightenment.

3.   I am the god Tem as I am One. I became thus from Nun[128]; I am Ra in his rising in the beginning of time, the prince. Who is this person that is being spoken about?

4.   It is that person, Ra in the beginning, in his rising in Suten Henen[129] as the king. At that time the sky had not been created and raised up by Shu[130]. He is upon the hilltop[131] within Khemenu[132]. I am the god great who came into existence out of himself, Nun. I created my own name and the company of gods and goddesses, as I am The God. Who is this person that is being spoken about?

Plate 23: Chapter 4- The Initiate and spouse play games as their souls look towards the Divine.

---

[127] Generally referred to as Chapter 17.
[128] The Primeval Ocean from which creation arose. It is also a god, first born of the Supreme Being.
[129] The mythical city from which Ra ruled when he was on the earth.
[130] Shu, the son of Ra and god of air and space-ether, and the husband of the goddess Tefnut.
[131] The Ancient Egyptian Creation states that god arose from the Primeval Ocean and created a hill upon which to stand.
[132] City of the Ogdoad of gods and goddesses, headed by the god Djehuti.

5. Ra this is, Creator of the names of his own body parts. These parts came into existence in the form of the gods and goddesses, i.e., the Company of Gods and Goddesses of Ra.[133] I am without obstruction among the gods and goddesses. Who is this person that is being spoken about?

6. Tem it is, whom, is being spoken about. He is within his Sundisk.[134] Another way to understand this is: It is Ra in his form as he shines at dawn in the eastern horizon of heaven. I am yesterday, I know tomorrow! Who is this person that is being spoken about?

7. As for the word "today," it refers to Asar. As for the word "yesterday," it refers to Ra on that day of putting down his enemies and those of Neberdjer[135]. He makes his son, the god Heru, the prince. Another way to understand this is: It is the day of the festival of becoming established in the Divine, of prostrations and binding[136] the mummy this of Asar by his father Ra. The gods and goddesses fought when it was decreed to us by Asar as Lord of Amentet, to do so. Who is this person that is being spoken about?

8. Amentet created the souls of the gods and goddesses when it was decreed in the Set-Amentet place. Another way to understand this is: Amentet is that which it verily is, the limit of me and Ra when go in the gods and goddesses all into it standing, fighting that person. It is I; I know this god who is in it! Who is this person that is being spoken about?

Plate 24: The initiate addresses the gods and goddesses and the souls of Ra and Asar (far- right) meet in Djedu of the Netherworld.

9. It is Asar. Another way to understand this is: Ra is his name as he copulates with his own phallus. I am the sacred bennu bird[137] which is in the city of Anu. I am the keeper of the records[138] of what is and what will be. Who is this person that is being spoken about?

10. It is Asar. Another way to understand this is: It is the corpse. Another way to understand this is: As to the excrements his, what will be, it is the body. Another way to understand this is: It relates to eternity with the fullness of time. As for that eternity, it is the day; as for that eternity, it is the night. I am Amsu in his movement. This is true; he has given to me his plumes and they are on my head now. Who is this person that is being spoken about?

11. As for Amsu it is Heru, the protector of his father. As for his movement, it is his birth. As for his plumes on his head, they are the actions of the goddesses Aset and Nebethet. They give of themselves to his person. They will be his protectors. They will protect his personality from all maladies that may befall him. Another way to understand this is: The two great and majestic serpent goddesses are within his forehead. Another way to understand this is: Those serpents are his eyes, his plumes on his forehead. Asar _____ will exist, making offerings in peace to all the gods and goddesses as a Spiritually Enlightened Being on earth in the city. Who is this person that is being spoken about?

---

[133] The Company of Gods and Goddesses of Ra is comprised of: Shu and Tefnut, Geb and Nut, Asar and Aset, Set and Nebethet and Heru-Ur. For more details on the mystical teachings of the Creation Myth see the book ***Mysteries of the Creation*** by Muata Ashby.

[134] Symbol of all the forms of Ra-the face of the sun ☉.

[135] All encompassing Divinity- The Supreme Being.

[136] Annual festival of symbolically putting the body of Asar back together, which was mutilated by his brother, Set.

[137] Sacred Phoenix of Ra.

[138] Knowledge and wisdom which transcends time and space.

12. It is the horizon of the Divine Father, Tem. I subdue the corruption in me. I destroy the evil in me. What is this that is being spoken about?

13. It is the cutting of the spine, that body part of Asar _____ who is maak-heru in the presence of all the gods and goddesses to make go away that evil in its entirety so that Asar _____ may be in control. What is this that is being spoken about?

14. It is the purification performed on the day of his birth[139]. Purified am I in my great and magnificent nesting place which is Suten-Henen. It is the day of sacrificial offerings by men and women to that great God who is in it. Who is this that is being spoken about?

15. It is Heh[140]. That is the name of the One. "The Green Lake" is another name. The pool of the nation together with the pool of Maat. Another way to understand this is: "Guide of eternity" is the name of the One, "Green Lake" is the name of the other. Another way to understand this is: "Begetter of eternity" is the name of the One and Green Lake is the name of the other. As for the Great God who is in Khert,[141] it is Ra himself.

Plate 25: The initiate and spouse extend worship to the Divine in the kneeling Dua (adoration) pose, playing the sistrum.

16. I move upon the path. I know Rastau[142], the Netherworld, that of the south land of Yanrutf[143] in the Duat, which is north of the tomb. As concerns the lower island of Maat, it is Abdu. Another way to understand this is: It is that road of the movements of the Divine Father, Tem upon it when he journeys to Sektet-Yaru, the place where birth is given to the sustenance of the gods and goddesses behind the shrine. As to the Khert in the Duat, it is the holy place where Shu raised the sky.[144] As to the wooden door in the north of the Duat, it is the gateway. Another way to understand this is: It is the great double-door that, of the journey of Tem himself, when he journeys to the horizon, eastern of heaven[145] in the Divine presence. Grant to me your two arms. I am the Divinity who comes into being among you. Who is this person that is being spoken about?

17. It is the blood, that which comes out from the phallus of Ra after his journey. As to the cutting of himself [146] which he did[147], it is the rising up and coming into being of the gods and goddesses that issue from Ra. Hu[148] and Siaa[149] will be following Tem in possession[150] of that day and every day afterwards.

---

[139] May be understood as a second birth into spiritual consciousness.

[140] The god of endless expanse of time-literally "Millions of Years," also associated with Shu.

[141] Khert Neter – (Neterkhert) The god of Neterkhert -lower part of heaven, the graveyard.

[142] Entrance to the Netherworld of Seker (Asar as king of the Astral Plane). The use of the word "Rastau" (Restau) is also related to the god Ra.

[143] *N-rutef, nerutef*; That which is in the place where nothing grows.

[144] In the creation myth, Ra ordered Shu to separate the sky, the goddess Nut, from the earth, the god Geb and to thereby create space and duality.

[145] Tem is the evening sun which journeys around to the east to start a new day, i.e. a new life as the morning sun, Khepri, the resurrection.

[146] The glyph used here includes the vertebrae, denoting the relation of the cutting or partitioning of Ra's own Life Force energy.

[147] In one Ancient Egyptian creation myth, Ra created human beings by cutting his own phallus. The bloodletting denotes Ra's female nature and the blood itself became living human beings and the gods and goddesses.

18. I experience fullness as Asar _____ and spiritual victory[151] for thee, the Divine Eye, after being sent and then failing[152] on the day of the fight between those two gods[153] within him. Set put excrement in the face of Heru. But then Heru took possession of Set's testicles. Then Djehuti took possession with his own fingers himself and in so doing lifted my hair at the time of the storms. Who is this person that is being spoken about?

19. It is the right Eye of Ra in its state of rampage after it was sent by him.[154] Behold! Djehuti raises the hair as he brings to him the Eye full of Life, Vitality and Health without any deficiency or impurity, to the Lord. Another way to understand this is: The eye, being sick, since it was in the face crying, was raised up by Djehuti. As concerns spit, I spit. It is my seeing Ra, born as yesterday. As concerns the hinder parts of goddess Mehurt[155], she is his vitality[156] and she is my vitality also, binding, strengthening and surrounding me. Who is this person that is being spoken about?

20. It is the primeval waters of heaven. Another way to understand this is: It is the image[157] of the Eye of Ra on that morning of his birth which is every day. As to Mehurt, she is the Divine Eye of Ra who is on his face. As to Asar _____ who is maak-heru, it is that person, one great among the gods and goddesses who are within the following of Heru. The speech about Asar _____ is: "That person is beloved by the Lord." Who are these persons that are speaking about Asar _____?

21. They are Mseti, Hapy, Duamutf, and Kebsenuf.[158] Homage to you Lords of Maat, divine beings behind Asar, givers of purity, the cutting away of wrongdoing to those who are within the following of Hetep-Sech-us[159]. Grant ye to me that I may come into your presence. Destroy all wrongs for me just as you did for those seven[160] Akhus in the following of their Lord Sepa[161]. Lord Anpu made a place for them on the day when they came to thee. Who are these persons that are speaking about Asar _____?

22. As to these all, Maat and Djehuti, they are with Isdesba[162] Lord of Amentet. As to the divine beings behind Asar, they are again Mseti, Hapy, Duamutf, and Kebsenuf. They are behind the Chepesh[163] in the northern heavens. As to the givers of cutting away of unrighteousness within the followers of goddess Hetep-Sech-us, it is the god Sebek who is within the primeval waters. As to goddess Hetep-Sech-us, she is the Eye of Ra. Another way to understand this is: She is the ever-present fire in the following of Asar and she makes the souls of his enemies to burn. As to the impurities, they are under the control of Asar _____ who makes offerings to all the gods and goddesses and who is maak-heru since coming down from {his/her} mother. As to those seven divine, glorious spirits, they are: Mseti, Hapy,

---

[148] Hu is an aspect of Ra, the sense of taste for divine food (glory, beauty, goodness, living on spirit-light, Righteousness-Liquor or Nectar of Maat)

[149] God of understanding-intellect.

[150] i.e. in control of.

[151] Maak-heru

[152] During the battle between Heru and Set in the myth of the Ausarian Resurrection, Heru's vision was damaged by Set.

[153] Heru and Set, who fought over the rulership of Egypt after Set killed Asar, Heru's father, the rightful king of Egypt.

[154] Refers to the myth of the Destruction of Evil Men and Women.

[155] Mighty Fullness.

[156] Mehurt gives birth to Ra and Asar _____.

[157] Fullness itself.

[158] The four sons of Heru, his foremost followers.

[159] The serpent goddess as the Eye of Ra in her aspect as destroyer of the enemies of Asar and whose purifying effect allows spiritual aspirants to enter Yanrutf.

[160] The god Anpu (Anubis) appointed seven spirits to follow and protect the initiate.

[161] Centipede god who has the power to prevent snake bites.

[162] A protector god in the Company of Gods and Goddesses of Djehuti.

[163] Big Dipper, common name applied to a conspicuous constellation in the northern celestial hemisphere, near the North Pole. It was known to the ancient Greeks as the Bear and the Wagon and to the Romans as Ursa Major (the Great Bear) and Septentriones (Seven Plowing Oxen). The seven brightest stars of the constellation form the easily identified outline of a giant dipper. To the Hindus, it represents the seven Rishis, or holy ancient Sages. "Big Dipper," Microsoft (R) Encarta. Copyright (c) 1994 Microsoft Corporation. Copyright (c) 1994 Funk & Wagnall's Corporation. See the gloss to this verse, also see "Opening of the Mouth" Chapter 11 and its Gloss.

Duamutf, Kebsenuf, Maa-itf,[164] Cherybqef,[165] and Herukhenty-maa[166]. They were set up by the god Anpu as protectors of the mummy of Asar. Another way to understand this is: they were set up behind the cleansing place of Asar. Another way to understand this is: the seven spirits are 1-Nedjhnedjh,[167] 2-Iaqeduqedu,[168] 3-Yanerdinefb-f Khentyh-h-f,[169] 4-Aqherimyunut-f,[170] 5-Dsher-maa-immyhetinesu,[171] 6-Ubensherperemtechtech,[172] and 7-Maaemgerhinnefemheru.[173]

23. As for the head of these divine beings, those who make possible the building of his binding together, it is Heru in his the title "Protector of his father." As to the day that of his coming within, the words to be said by Asar to Ra are "I come to thee in seeing your decree for me in Amentet. I am his soul, innermost in the nests."
Who is this person that is being spoken about?

24. It is Asar, who goes in to Djedu[174]. He finds there the soul of Ra, rising, embracing the soul of Asar. Another way to understand this is: They are the souls of Heru, the protector of his father, and Heru, the foremost seer.[175] Another way to understand this is: They are the souls of Shu and Tefnut and they come into being as the souls of the fledgling gods and goddesses.

25. I am like that cat in the dividing of the tree for him in the city of Anu on that night of defeating the enemies of Neberdjer in him. What then is it?

26. It is like the cat, the fledgling form of Ra, who is he himself and is called cat by the words of the god Siaa. He is like unto that cat which he brought into being. Another way to understand this is: The god Shu will be the person making the belongings of the god Geb for Asar. As for the dividing of the tree for him in Anu, that refers to the children of impotent revolt who have Maat done onto them. In regards to the night, that of fighting and their going into the eastern heaven, this means a rising and fighting in heaven and on earth in its entirety. Hail to you, "The One in his Egg," shining in the form of his sundisk, dawning in his horizon as the golden being in the sky, devoid of any double and yet as well as the gods and goddesses, sailing upon the supporting pillars of Shu who gives Life Force to his mouth and illuminates the two lands as the Glorious Spirit that he is. Protect thee Asar_____, the exalted one, from that god whose form is secret, and whose two arms are the scales[176] on that night of the reckoning by the goddess Auaadi.[177] Who then is it?

Plate 26: Scene from Chapter 4 of the Prt M Hru. The cat of Ra (goddess Bast) cuts off the head of the demon serpent.

---

[164] He who sees his father.

[165] He who is under the moringa tree.

[166] Heru the foremost seer.

[167] The Protector.

[168] The One who revolves.

[169] One who does not give to him a flame to he who is foremost in the eternal fire.

[170] The one who goes into him at the appointed time.

[171] The red eyed one who is in the house of red clothing.

[172] The one who shines going forth as after coming back.

[173] One who can see at night and what will be brought to him during the day.

[174] City of the double pillars of Asar.

[175] Two aspects of the god Heru, symbolizing spiritual principles that need to be developed by every spiritual aspirant.

[176] Scales of Maat, presented in the judgment scene of Utterance 19.

[177] Form of the goddess who settles the karmic (good and evil deeds) accounts in the maatian scale of balance.

27. It is the god "Bringer of the arm." As for the night of the reckoning, it is the goddess Auaadi in the night, that of the burning, of putting down the enemies and of giving punishment to the wrongdoers on his block for killing souls. Who then is this being spoken about?

28. It is Shemsu, the mutilator of Asar. Another way of putting it is: It is Apep[178] when he has one head with Maat. Another way of putting it is: It is Heru when he has two heads,[179] being one of them with Maat and the other being with unrighteousness. At that time he is the giver of wrong to the doer of Maat and to followers concerning it. Another way of putting it is: It is Heru the Great, the foremost powerful ruler; it is Djehuti. Another way of putting it is: It is Nefertem[180] in the form of Sept[181] who obstructs the wrongdoings of the wrongdoers towards Neberdjer. Save thee me from those chiefs who are administerers of pain with their powerful fingers full of sickness and who slay those who are in the following of Asar. They shall not have power within me. I will not go under their knives. Who then is this being spoken about?

29. It is Anpu, who is also Heru, the foremost seer. Another way of putting it is: The divine beings are the judges of the things related to the unrighteous people. Another way of putting it is: He is the Great Physician in the Sheniu chamber of Sekhem[182]. I will not go under their knives, which are for receiving torture since I know their names. I know who the oppressor is among them, of the house of Asar, shooting by the means[183] of the Eye, but whom is not seen he.

30. He surrounds the heavens by means of a flame that comes out of his mouth. He controls Hapy[184] but cannot be seen. I am full of vitality, first among those who are on earth, in the presence of Ra. I moor[185] joyously in the presence of Asar. Your offerings will not come through me; not will those offerings be placed upon their altars, for I am in the following of Neberdjer in accordance with the writings[186] of Kheperu. I fly as the Falcon God[187]! I cackle as the goose. I spend eternity like Nehebkau[188]. Who then is this being spoken about?

31. Those who are there on the day of making their offerings to the image[189] of the Eye of Ra together with the image of the eye of Heru. Hail Ra-Tem[190], Lord of the Great House, ruler of *Life, Vitality and Health*, and the gods and goddesses all. Save thee me from that god whose face is like a dog and whose eyebrows are like those of human beings. He lives by violence and he is the guardian of the paths, those of the lake of fire and he consumes bodies. He is the overwhelmer of hearts and breaths and putting out excrement. Yet, he is not seen. Who then is this being spoken about?

32. "Consumer of millions"[191] is his name and he is in the place of the earth. As for the place of fire, that is what is in Yanrutf and in the Sheny Building[192].

33. As for any unrighteous person who treads upon the mound, they fall victim to the knives. Another way of putting it is: His name is "Sharp Knives" and he is the guardian of the passages of Amentet. Another

---

[178] The evil serpent and foremost enemy of righteousness. Therefore, he is the enemy of Ra and Asar.

[179] Heru-Set, two gods in One.

[180] God of the primeval lotus blossom-symbol of creation, which arose from the Primeval Ocean. The sun god in the form of a newborn child-morning sun-creator-aspect of Heru.

[181] Form of Heru of the eastern Delta Region of Egypt-the newborn star Sirius.

[182] Life Force.

[183] Through-as a means to accomplish, etc.

[184] The god of the Nile river. This unseen force controls the Nile river, but yet it can be felt.

[185] Arrive and settle down as a boat arrives in port.

[186] Wisdom teachings, spiritual scriptures.

[187] Heru.

[188] Benign Serpent God.

[189] Symbol.

[190] Combination of the god name Ra and Tem as being one in the same.

[191] A close correlation occurs here between Kemetic mysticism and Indian Yoga Mysticism. In the Indian scripture, called the Bhagavad Gita, Lord Krishna reveals his form as the devourer of human beings.

[192] Where the Sheniu Chamber of Sekhem is located.

way of putting it is: "Controller of Time[193] is his name. Hail, Lord protector, captain of the Two Lands, Lord of blood, you of the block of slaughter, who live by eating the entrails. Who then is this being spoken about?

34. It is the guardian of the inner ways, those of Amentet. Who then is this being spoken about? It is the heart, that of Asar, that is in me, slaughtering all. The Ureret Crown has been given to him along with joy and rulership of Suten-Henen. Who then is this being spoken about?

35. It is the one to whom the Ureret Crown has been given along with joy as ruler of Suten-Henen; it is Asar. He is charged with rulership over the gods and goddesses on the day of the **Union of the Two Earths**[194] in the presence of Neberdjer. Who then is this being spoken about?

Plate 27: The goddess Mehurt resting before the Udjat Eye, from Chap. 4 of the Papyrus of Ani.

36. As for he who was charged with rulership of the gods and goddesses, it is Heru, son of goddess Aset. He was made ruler in the throne of his father Asar. As for the day that, of the *Union of the Two Earths*, it means complete wholeness of the two lands, these at the burial chamber of Asar _____, the living soul in Suten-Henen. The giver of Astral sustenance[195] and eradication of wrongdoing is showing Asar _____ the way to eternity. Who then is this being spoken about?

37. Ra it is himself. Protect thee me in the presence of The God Great, that taker of souls who slurps up putrefaction and who lives by putrefactions, the guardian of the night who is within the darkness. Feared is he by those in misery. Who then is this being spoken about?

---

[193] Herysep-f.
[194] Smai-Tawi-Egyptian Yoga.
[195] Sekhem, for the Ka.

38. It is Set, the slaughterer. As for the souls within the Tjafy,[196] that god, taking control of my soul, who consumes hearts and who lives on entrails and who is the guardian of darkness within the boat of Seker, fear him those people who have unrighteousness within themselves. Who then is this being spoken about?

39. It is Set. Another way of putting it is: He is the Great Bull, the soul of Geb. Hail Khepri, the innermost in his Sacred Boat with the gods and goddesses as his body. Save thee Asar _____ who is maak-heru from those who control those to be judged. Neberdjer has given to them the order to glorify Asar _____ and to protect against Asar's enemies, the slaughterers in the slaughterhouses, those who come out of their restraints. They shall not send their knives into me. No, they will not go into me!

40. As for their slaughterhouses, may I not linger there in great weakness, in their torture houses. May not be done to me anything disagreeable or hateful to the gods and goddesses because I am pure within the Meqet chamber[197]. I have brought to thee divine meals in faience[198] within the Tashent Chamber[199]. Who then is this being spoken about?

41. It is Khepri in his boat. Ra, it is himself. As for those guardians, the judges, they are baboons[200] and their names are Aset and Nebethet. As for those things hateful to the gods and goddesses, these are: putrefaction, moral corruption and falsehood. As for that one who passes through the purification chamber within Meqet, it is Anpu who is behind the sarcophagus which contains the body parts of Asar. As for the one giving the divine meals in faience within the Tashent Chamber, it is Asar. Another way of putting it is: As for the divine meals in faience within the Tashent Chamber, it is heaven and earth. Another way of putting it is: Shu forged the faience and it is the Arit (eye) of Heru. As for the Tashent Chamber, it is the shrine of union with Asar in his throne.

42. Tem's house is built now and founded by the Rereti[201] gods who arrive with medications to purify Heru, glorifying him. Set is purified at the same time.

43. I come to the land on my own two feet; my two feet being those of Asar _____ maak-heru, in the presence of Asar. I am Tem, I am in the city. Turn away lion, you bright mouthed one with the shining head. Go away from me because I am spiritually strong. Another way of putting it is: Turning away from the invisible watcher. Watch and guard me not, for I am Asar _____, Aset found me when the hair upon my mouth and forehead were scattered.[202] I was conceived by goddess Aset. Begotten was I through Nebethet. These goddesses cut the things that obstruct me. Fear and terror follows thee, and it is in his two arms. Bent for me are their two arms for a time period of Heh[203]. The common folk go around[204] me, worshiping me. My advocates destroyed, for me, all the unrighteous people who were my enemies. I seize the knowledgeable ones by their two arms. The two sisters[205] have given to me sweet things. I create what is in the city of Kheraha[206] and in the city of Anu. All the gods and goddesses fear me greatly, verily. Terrified of me is every god and goddess because whoever curses me receives arrows. I live as I will to live. I am Uadjit, mistress of the fires for those coming my way with evil intent. Who then is this being spoken about?

44. *"Secret of Forms Given by the God Menhu,[207]"* is the name of the shrine. *"He sees the face and hand"* is the name of the storm cloud. Another way of putting it is: It is the name of *"Slaughter Block."* As for

---

[196] Souls of Heru and Ra.

[197] Region of the outer world that one must pass through in order to get to the Sektet-Yaru.

[198] **fa·ience** also **fa·ïence** (fᵊ-äns," -ä's," fᵊ-) *n.* **1.** Earthenware decorated with colorful, opaque glazes. **2.** *Color.* A moderate to strong greenish blue.

[199] Room of pure offerings to the Divine.

[200] The baboon is the symbol of the god Djehuti because it is noticed to be a smart animal. Sometimes Djehuti presides over the judgment of the heart of the Asar in the form of a baboon and here he is related to the goddesses. Mythologically he is their uncle.

[201] Double lions-double powers- the lion and lioness are the symbols of physical power, vitality and strength.

[202] Dispersed or uncovered.

[203] Vast undetermined amount of time-millions and millions of years.

[204] In devotional worship in India there is a common practice of walking around the object of devotion (image of the god or goddess).

[205] Aset and Nebethet.

[206] An Ancient Egyptian city near the modern site of Old Cairo.

[207] The Slaughtering God.

"Bright Mouth Shining Head," it is the phallus of Asar. Another way of putting it is: it is the phallus of Ra. As for the spreading of the hair, I scatter the hair to uncover the mouth and the forehead, being Aset,[208] who secretly being there in the face, rubbed her hair therein. As for Uadjit, mistress of fires, it is the Eye of Ra.

Declaration

45. Whoever recites these words daily when they are in a state of purity, will go forth into the day and have the capacity to assume any form they desire. Whoever reads and studies this text while they are alive on earth will be benefited greatly. They will be foremost among human beings and no harm shall come to them. This is a matter a million times true. I can say this because I have experienced this myself in my own life!

---

[208] Here once more the scripture shows the tantric concept of transcending gender as the initiate affirms his identity with the female goddess of wisdom.

GLOSS ON CHAPTER 4: ITS MEANING AND MYSTICAL SIGNIFICANCE

Verse 1-9

Chapter 4 is one of the most important chapters in the Prt M Hru. There are two central reasons for this. Firstly, it is one of the few chapters which contains original glosses throughout which explain its meaning. Glosses are explanatory statements which are in this case introduced by the sage through the question "Who is this being spoken about?" This style of writing glosses later appears in Hindu texts wherein the questions are asked by the aspirant for the benefit of the readers, so they may receive more elucidation on the philosophical teachings being presented. Thus, the Ancient Egyptian writing itself contains an explanation of its own passages. Thus, we are being led by the sages of ancient times to the teachings of spiritual wisdom.

Secondly, this chapter establishes, without a shadow of a doubt, the identity of the gods and goddesses of Kemetic philosophy as well as their inter-relationships. We are led to understand their roles in the mythology, but most importantly, we are to understand that they are all emanations from the same Supreme Being. In other words, this chapter clearly establishes the Panentheistic (that God is immanent in all things but also transcendent) and Pantheistic (everything in existence is God) aspect of the philosophy. God and Creation are one, and God is the reality or principle behind nature in Kemetic Philosophy. This understanding is also known as monism. The gods and goddesses are in reality Ra, and this of course means that in a higher sense there is no other god but Ra. This is the "***One One***" teaching of Kemetic Philosophy, laid bare for our view. Thus, Chapter 4 is an exposition of this central teaching of mystical philosophy. The spiritual aspirant should meditate on this teaching until the realization is fully achieved.

In verse 4 the following statement appears: *I created my own name and the company of gods and goddesses, as I am The God.* This "creator" teaching must be meditated upon again and again in order to realize its magnitude. The entire universe is in a constant phase of creation at every moment. This is the essence of nature. All life, being part of nature, MUST therefore create in order to be in harmony with the universe. No one can escape this. Animals have little choice in the matter. They must follow the dictates of their instincts, which are backed up by an impetus from nature. There are three choices for human beings. If they follow the path of worldliness they will be compelled through ignorance and sensual desires, to create worldly relationships and entanglements. Those who follow the path of spiritual self-discovery create higher consciousness, expansion and glory. Those who are misguided, thinking they can withdraw from all action and do nothing, will eventually create adversity and insanity. The question is not can one be without action, but what should that action be? The sages of Ancient Egypt discovered that Maat is the key to the creation of social harmony, health and worldly as well as spiritual prosperity. Therefore, Maat is the path of creating virtue and enlightenment, the path that leads to discovering "I Am" The God!

Verse 4 is providing the highest wisdom teaching here as it shows the aspirant as One with the Creator, who arose from Nun. The term "Creation" implies that something "new" has come into existence that was not there before. As we examine Kemetic Philosophy more closely, we discover that the idea of Creator and Created are only used metaphorically. This understanding is revealed by the scripture itself. God created Creation by turning herself into Creation. God lives in her own Creation. Therefore, God is the Creator, Created, and the interaction between the two. If Creator and Created are one, this means that actually nothing has been "created." This may seem contradictory, but it is in fact an application of the highest philosophical thinking to the mythology, just as calculus is a higher philosophical concept applied to arithmetic. In a higher sense, the terms "creation" and "created" imply that something new has come into being that did not exist before. The teaching itself tells us that Creation arose out of the Nun or primeval essence, that already existed, and that Nun is God's own "body" and further, that the forms of Creation and the gods and goddesses emanated out of God herself. What is being given here is the teaching of non-duality behind the apparent multiplicity and variety of the universe. If one paints one's body, one may not look the same, and yet one remains the same. Only the appearance is different. Creation appears to be different from God when people look at the universe with the mental paint of ignorance and egoism. If all is One, then all is a manifestation of God. Another way to look at it is that there is no duality, no me, no you, no desire, no conflict and no ignorance, just awareness of the non-dual Self within and without, everywhere. This means that Creation is an illusion. This teaching is called Monism, a philosophy which up to now was thought only to have been espoused in the Sanskrit teachings of Indian Vedanta and Yoga philosophies, and here we have

it in ancient Kemet a full 2,500 years before the emergence of Indian culture and philosophy and a full 4,000 years before Judaism. This is the supreme realization, and if this is achieved, the declaration at the end of the chapter becomes effective. This chapter is so extensive that a full treatment would require a separate volume. Other important points presented in this chapter include the following.

Verse 9 gives us the Kemetic concept of Tantric Yoga. Tantrism is the philosophy of discovering the underlying unity behind the opposites of Creation. Sexuality is a primary means of metaphorically explaining the manner in which God begot Creation. In explaining it as a sexual act with himself, God is no longer just male, but also female. We are thereby led to understand that God transcends gender, while including both genders as she expresses as the genders within Creation itself at the same time. One Ancient Egyptian creation myth states that god engendered creation by masturbating and ejaculating in his  own hand, and his seed became Creation. His semen (seed) goes into his own hand and thereby he inseminates himself. Thus he is male and female at the same time. In another version of the creation myth, God in the form of Geb is seen swallowing his own ejaculate, thereby impregnating himself and bringing forth Creation and life on earth. In Amunian theology, the high priestess is referred to as "Amun's wife" and "god's hand" as she (female aspect) serves to facilitate his Creations.

Figure 85: From a papyrus in the British Museum #10,018

Verse 10

Amsu-Min is the form of Heru, which is associated with the god Amun. He is the "Avenger of his Father," who fought against Set after Set killed his father, Asar. His character is depicted as the ithyphallic god holding his phallus with the left hand and a flail in the right. The flail symbolizes mastery over the three worlds (Physical, Astral and Causal or Earth, Heaven and Netherworld). On his head there are two plumes symbolizing Aset and Nebethet and therefore, mastery over the serpent power and consequently duality as well. This symbolizes sublimation of the sexual energy and its mastery to use that force for spiritual redemption. The teaching of "excrement" is introduced here. It is written: *It is Asar. Another way to understand this is: It is the corpse. Another way to understand this is: As to the excrements his, what will be, it is the body.* One normally thinks of wonderful fragrances as being divine and holy while feces and putrefaction is unholy and loathsome. This verse explains that excrement is also God, because God manifests as all that exists and excrement is part of existence. In verse 18 it is stated that Set threw excrement in the eyes of Heru. Thus, excrement is at the same time divine and demoniac. How can this be? Since God created all, then the loveliest beauty and the ugliest grossness are products of the same Spirit. But this is only from the viewpoint of the human ego, for this is the aspect in a human being that assigns values based on egoistic desires. In fact, excrement is that which is created by the ego, not God, though it is composed of God matter, the Nun. So when the ego is present, there is use of raw materials and the production of excrement. When only the pure Spirit is present, there is only consciousness, no beautiful fragrance and no putrid odors. The concept of offensive odors and fragrant odors is based on ego-consciousness, not on universal consciousness, which encompasses all. Thus, both offensive objects and desirable objects are in reality divine. Therefore, if excrement is divine, it must be possible to discover this divinity within it and further, since excrement is part of nature and the purpose of nature is to lead aspirants to the Divine, how can excrement in life, that which is detestable, be a help to spiritual evolution instead of a source of disgust? This theme will be elaborated in the gloss on Chapter 25.

Verse 11

This verse introduces the teaching related to the Serpent Power, which is symbolized by a serpent(s) perched on the forehead. The two serpent goddesses, known as Ararti in Ancient Egypt, are part of the philosophy of the Serpent Power known as Kundalini Yoga in India. They are depicted as a serpent and/or a vulture emerging from the forehead. See the book *The Serpent Power* by Muata Ashby for more details. When the serpent power reaches the forehead, this symbolizes the opening of intuitional vision which destroys all unrighteousness which a person may experience due to ignorance and delusion. This verse is also related to Chapter 7, Sections 3 and 10.

Verse 13

Only when one's personality is purified from the negative aspects of the ego personality can it be said that the Higher Self is in control. Thus, people who are caught in the ignorance of life and who are led by their desires, passions and delusions about their true nature are not in control of their lives. The ego controls them.

Verse 18

This verse contains many important teachings. It includes the invocation of Maakheru, the spiritual invocation of all aspirants to successfully attain Cosmic Consciousness. Set is the ego aspect of the human consciousness. When a person lives egoistically, they are leading themselves to mental agitation. This blinds them to truth and the way to succeed in life and defeat adversity, so they suffer. This teaching is related to the mythology of the Asarian Resurrection myth wherein the Eye of spiritual vision of Heru was damaged in his fight with Set.[209] This verse also introduces the concept of castration which is based on an episode in the myth wherein Heru castrated Set, i.e. took control of his own sex desire and sublimated it in order to allow himself to become powerful enough to overcome Set who symbolizes egoism and disharmony. The lifting of the hair has two meanings, first as a metaphor for removing the obstruction to proper vision and secondly, in other papyri it refers to the unveiling of the third eye, the spiritual center between the eyebrows, related to the Serpent Power or Kundalini yoga. Mental agitation is likened to a storm. When the trials, tribulations, desires, frustrations as well as the lower aspects of personality (anger, hatred, greed, lust, envy, jealousy, elation, passion, etc.) affect the mind, it becomes clouded with thoughts which distract a human being from seeing truth. This state is called ignorance. Djehuti is the symbol of firm intellect. Taking hold of the testicles means the mind attaining firm control over the lower nature.

Verse 19

This reference to the Eye relates to the myth commonly known as the Destruction of Evil Men and Women. It is a version of the myth of Hetheru and Djehuti. Ra sent his Eye to burn up the unrighteous but it got lost and Ra made a new one to replace it. When it finally returned it was enraged. Djehuti calmed it, brought it back and restored it to its rightful place.[210]

Meh-urt means literally: "Mighty Fullness." She is the cow goddess from which the universe arose, according to one Ancient Egyptian creation myth. It is clear to see that while there are several Ancient Egyptian creation myths, they are all interrelated. The relationship as described in the scripture shows that the different gods and goddesses are in reality aspects or manifestations of the same creative and sustaining power. This important passage also shows the Ancient Egyptian conception that the creative principle behind the universe can also be seen as female, i.e. the goddess. In essence, Ra and Mehurt are aspects of the same creative principle.

Verse 22

Ancient Egyptian mythology, as well as that of Hinduism (Narayana) and Christianity (Genesis), holds that creation arose from an all-pervading ocean. Mystically, this ocean, called Nu or Nun in Kemetic Philosophy, refers to God's consciousness, which is vast and can become anything God chooses. The Chepesh has important mystical symbolism. Chepesh has a relation to the thigh of Asar. In Ancient Egyptian mysticism the thigh is the symbol of sexual potency. It symbolizes the male generative capacity and is one of the offerings of Hetep given in Chapter 36 (usually referred to as #30B) of the Pert M Heru.

Also, in ancient times the Chepesh symbol represented the "Northern path" of spiritual evolution. Since the constellation of the Ursa Major ("Great Bear" or "Big Dipper"), known to the Ancient Egyptians as "Meskhetiu," contains *seven* stars and occupied the location referred to as the "Pole Star," it does not move,

---

[209] See Chapter 2 for a summary of the myth or the book Ausarian Resurrection: The Ancient Egyptian Bible.
[210] See the book *Mysticism of Ushet Reckat: Worship of the Goddess* by Muata Ashby.

while all the other stars in the sky circle around it. This constellation, whose symbol is the thigh, ⌒, was thus referred to as "the imperishables" in the earlier Pyramid Texts: "He (the king-enlightened initiate) climbs to the sky among the imperishable stars."[211] The Great Pyramid in Egypt, located in the area referred to as "The Giza Plateau" in modern times, incorporated this teaching. The main chamber in the Great Pyramid incorporates two shafts that pointed in ancient times, to the Chepesh (Great Bear-Thigh) in the north sky and to Orion (Sahu or Sah), the star system of Asar (Osiris) in the southern sky. The imperishable constellation refers to that which is unchanging, absolute, transcendental and perfect. Time lapse photographs of this constellation show it as remaining in the center and other stars moving around it. Also, it does not sink below the horizon and become "reborn" in the eastern horizon each day as other stars. The Orion constellation refers to that which is changing, incarnating (rising in the east) and becoming. In this manner Asar is reborn through Sopdu (the star Sirius-Aset, Isis) in the form of Heru-Sopdu (Heru who is in Isis) also known as Sirius B. Therefore, mystically, the "Northern Path" is promoted as the path to immortality and enlightenment through the attainment of absolute consciousness which transcends the perishable and ever-changing nature of creation. The "Southern Path" is the process of reincarnation, renewal and repeated embodiment (*uhem ankh*), for the purpose of further spiritual evolution through self-discovery by means of human experiences. This teaching is also reflected in the zodiac inscription from the temple of Hetheru at Denderah and in the "Opening of the Mouth ceremony" where a symbol of the imperishable constellation, *Seb-ur* ⌒, is carried by the priest. The mystical intent is to open the mind, through mystical wisdom and disciplines, so as to render it *ur-uadjit*, [image], (universal and infinite, all-encompassing, unlimited) and beyond the fluctuations of egoism, i.e. mortal consciousness.

Verse 25

In mystical symbolism, the act of dividing relates to separating one's eternal part from one's ephemeral part. The tree is symbolic of the ever-growing entanglements of life. Thus, in this context it is a separating from the entanglements of life so as to discover the glory of eternity. This is an important passage, which clearly states that the enemies (fiends-demoniac aspects of personality- lower aspects of personality, i.e., anger, hatred, greed, lust, envy, jealousy, elation, passion, etc.), are "within" the personality of a human being and not outside as demons or devil.

Verse 26

The cat is a symbol of Ra since the cat has a natural animosity towards serpents. Ra's greatest enemy is the serpent of chaos. The cat is also a manifestation of his daughter, Hetheru, and is called Bastet. The children of impotent revolt refers to the unrighteous and rebellious aspect of personality, the demons of the mind, anger, hatred, greed, jealousy, lust, envy, etc., which cannot escape the truth.

Verse 28

In the Ancient Egyptian Ausarian Resurrection Myth, there was a great battle between Heru and Set. In actuality, as we are discovering from this chapter of the Pert M Heru, the battle was not between two gods but within one personality, i.e., between the lower self and the Higher, which is a metaphor that applies to all human beings. This important passage relates the understanding that duplicity in the human heart is the source of unrighteousness in life and in the world. In this state of mind one acts wrongly towards righteous people, thus, setting up disharmony by acting in contradiction with Maat.

Verse 29

Sekhem is the Ancient Egyptian conception of Life Force, which pervades and sustains the universe and all life in it. It is equal in most respects to the concept of Prana of the Hindu Yoga systems or Chi of the Chinese Martial Arts and Yoga systems. In modern times the movie "Star Wars" also popularized the concept as "The Force."

Verse 30

---

[211] Pyramid Texts 1120-23. *Egyptian Mysteries,* Lucie Lamy

Nehebkau is a Serpent God. His name means "He who harnesses the spirits." He is the son of the goddess Serqet, the scorpion goddess who assisted Aset in her escape from Set. He is an invincible force, which protects the spiritual aspirant against snakebites from the fiends-demoniac serpents. His power comes from the **seven** cobras, which he swallowed. Thus, Nehebkau is the male form of the Serpent Power or Kundalini Energy.

Verse 35-36

These two verses are extremely important to the concept of Kemetic Spirituality that The Sema Institute has sought for many years to bring forth and espouse. These verses contain the term *Smai Tawi* (*Union of the Two Earths*) which is in reality a metaphor symbolizing the union of the Higher Self and lower self. This is what the mystics of India call Yoga. Yoga is the science of promoting a union between the soul or individual consciousness and the Spirit or universal consciousness. All of the spiritual practices of all mystics everywhere in the world are to be considered as yoga practices. Therefore, yoga is a universal science, practiced by all cultures since the beginning of history, which commenced with Ancient Egyptian Culture.

Verse 40

The Meqet chamber is a region of the outer world that one must pass through in order to get to the Sektet-Yaru. This term contains a pun and relates to the words mes (child-born) and Meskhenet (goddess of birth and the fate of the next life, i.e. Iri or Karma and reincarnation). Thus, purity in the chamber affords the spiritual aspirant the opportunity not to be reborn in the world but to enter into the Divine realms instead.

Verse 41

The eye of Heru is the offering that is made and also this eye relates to purified consciousness. Further, there is a relation here between the Eye of Heru, the Divine Offerings and the body parts of Asar. This is, therefore, the source of the Eucharist idea in Christianity. The idea is to consume the body (parts of Asar's body) and consciousness (Eye) of God and thereby become one with God. The god Anpu is the protector of the contents of the coffin of Asar, i.e. his body, which makes the chest the most sacred artifact of veneration. This is similar in most respects to the idea of the Arc of the Covenant in Judeo-Christian mythology.[212] Finally, this verse contains a statement, which condenses the purpose of the entire Kemetic teachings of this and all other Asarian scriptures, *As for the Tashent Chamber, it is the shrine of union with Asar in his throne.* This line is so important because it states directly that the goal of the spiritual aspirant is to have a Sma (union) with Asar himself, that is, to become One with God. The direct translation of the term "Smai Tawi" is "Yoga Egyptian" or "Egyptian Yoga."

Verse 43

This verse also relates to back to Verse 18. It relates once again to the hair that has fallen over the forehead and is blocking (obstructing) the divine vision that occurs from the *third eye*, the psycho-spiritual center at the point between the eyebrows. Here the third eye is being uncovered, i.e. the obstructions are dispersed. The reference to the forehead relates to the opening up of the third eye, the eye of intuitional vision, the Eye of Heru, as well as the sixth spiritual consciousness center-located at the point between the eyebrows. The implication is that all obstacles are removed which were impeding the expansion of consciousness (metaphor of the mouth) and spiritual vision (forehead). This passage, and others like it in various texts, are the source for the teachings which became popular in the mysteries of Isis (Aset) during the Greek and Roman periods wherein the focus of the spiritual initiation and evolution were related as an "unveiling of Isis," i.e. the sight of Isis (truth) in its naked form. The reference to being conceived and begotten through the goddess is a clear relation to the divine birth, i.e. being "born again" in the form of Heru, the spiritual vision of life which has been resurrected (Asar) after it was mutilated by egoism (Set). It is a resurrection, from the ignorance and death of mortal existence and assuming the role of the divinity, Heru, who redeems the soul and leads one to spiritual enlightenment. It is also a reference to the Serpent Power. Aset and Nebethet are the goddesses of the Serpent Power. Being born of them means being born of elevated consciousness through the elevation of the serpent power, which is the innate Life Force, latent in every human being.

---

[212] See the book **Christian Yoga** by Muata Ashby for more details.

The goddesses Aset and Nebethet represent the two aspects which sustain human life, matter and spirit. They also manifest as the Maati goddesses and the serpent goddesses of the Kemetic caduceus, the pillar and the two serpents. There are two opposing energies in creation and these cause life to exist. One relates to cooling and the other to heating. Thus, there is an opposite to everything in creation (male-female, up-down, life-death, good-bad). However, it must be clearly understood that the opposites of creation are in reality illusions. The two serpents are in reality aspects of the one. Being attended on by these two divinities means having become one with Asar, because they serve him, and him alone. This verse clearly shows that the initiate is to identify {him/her} self with Asar in ritual, but later, in spiritual fact. This is the goal of self-discovery, to reveal one's own Asarian nature.

The movement of the Serpent Power (Egyptian- Art, Arart; Indian-Kundalini) opens up the mind like a drain opener unclogs a drain pipe. [213] In the last line of this verse the initiate proclaims I am Uadjit. Here once more the scripture shows the tantric concept of transcending gender as the initiate affirms his identity with the female cobra goddess of the Serpent Power or Kundalini Energy.

---

[213] See the book **Serpent Power** by Muata Ashby.

CHAPTER 5[214]

RECOGNITION OF GODDESS HETHERU AS THE POWER TO LIVE IN RIGHTEOUSNESS

1. Hetheru is the lady of Amentet. She is also the dweller in Urt,[215] and she is also the Mistress of the Exalted, Blessed Land[216].
2. She is the Eye of Ra and she dwells in his forehead,[217] which is the beautiful face in the boat of forever.
3. She is the seat of peace from which righteousness and truth can be done within the boat of the favored ones, the blessed beings. She makes it possible for the boat of the sun to make its journey in Maati.

Plate 28: The goddess Hetheru in the form of a hippopotamus presides over the Hetep offerings as she herself in the form of the Mehurt cow, looks on from the mountain of Amenta above the tomb. (Chap. 5)

CHAPTER 5B[218]

THE CHAPTER OF BEING IN THE PRESENCE OF GODDESS HETHERU PERPETUALLY

Plate 29: From Papyrus Nu- The Initiate Stands Next to Goddess Hetheru

1. These words are spoken to Asar _____. Behold, I am a pure traveler.
2. Behold O Ahi,[219] Let me be among those who follow the goddess Hetheru.

---

[214] Generally referred to as Chapter 186
[215] The great land or passageway.
[216] Egypt.
[217] The third eye, between the eyebrows.
[218] Generally referred to as chapter 103

GLOSS ON CHAPTER 5: COMMENTARY, ITS MEANING AND MYSTICAL SIGNIFICANCE

These chapters, though short, provide some important aspects of wisdom related to the goddess. Chapter five establishes the goddess' main attributes and her abode, dwelling in the forehead of Ra as his Eye (right eye), meaning that she is the power of the god. Further, it shows that she is the friend of all who practice righteousness and peace and that she is the means by which the movement of the boat of Ra is possible. Though this text uses the name Hetheru, the goddess aspect should be thought of in broader terms. The scriptures themselves support this, for the goddess in all her manifestations, is in reality a metaphor for all that which manifests. In other words, the God is the engenderer of manifestation, the spirit behind it, and the Goddess is the manifestation itself, the vehicle for the spirit to have experiences in the Creation. The cow aspect of the goddess, which is shared by all of the main goddess forms including goddesses Net, Aset, Mehurt and Hetheru, is the primary symbol in Kemetic Mystical Philosophy which refers to the vast manifestation of the spirit which is Creation.

Verse 3

This verse associates the goddess Hetheru with the aspect of Maati. Maati means the truth of the physical world and truth of the transcendental realms, above and below, i.e. the movement of the boat of Ra sustains Matter and Spirit and without this movement there can be no material or spiritual existence. The movement symbolizes vibration, and vibration is the force which sustains gross matter (physical-phenomenal universe and the subtle matter – spiritual realms, Astral Plane, etc.)

GLOSS ON CHAPTER 5B: ITS MEANING AND MYSTICAL SIGNIFICANCE

The word Hetheru literally means the house or dwelling place of Heru. Heru is the spirit living within Creation (Hetheru). She is the manifestation of Life Force emanating from Ra's brow, i.e. Creation is an effluence of God's very essence and he himself lives in it, therefore, God is everywhere and in all things. Knowing this truth brings spiritual strength and endurance to live in peace and righteousness.

Verse 1

Being close to the goddess means two things. First it is necessary to purify oneself from the fetters of the lower nature. This means that one must turn away from vices and towards virtues. These gross impurities (anger, hatred, greed, lust, envy, jealousy, vengefulness, etc.) act as fetters on the soul, dragging it to the depths of degraded thinking, feeling and acting, which in turn lead to adversity and frustration in life. One must turn towards the virtues which the goddess herself in the form of Maat, has laid out. These principles include all of the actions that lead to purity of heart. These are contained in the Precepts of Maat, discussed at length in Part I, Chapter 4 of this Volume. They are **Truth, Non-violence, Right Action, Self-control, Living in accordance with the teachings of Maat, Right Speech, Right Worship, Selfless Service, Balance of Mind - Reason – Right Thinking, Not-stealing, and Sex-Sublimation.**

Verse 2

Once the spiritual aspirant is purified, then it is possible for that person to practice true religion, authentic spiritual practice. This is because the unpurified mind is subject to error and confusion in understanding the teachings. This will lead to their misapplication of the teachings and the intensification of the aspirant's struggle, and possible failure.

In the practice of authentic spirituality, the highest goal is to be a true follower of the Divinity. This means being a devotee of whichever form of the Divine has been chosen, in this case, the goddess. Devotion to the Divine is the most secure path to spiritual awakening and realization, but there must also be wisdom and right action as part of the devotional practice. Following the Divinity implies living one's life with the prospect of

---

[219] One of the gods in the Judgment Hall of Asar.

discovering the Divinity everywhere, internally as well as externally and abiding with the Divinity perpetually. Following the Divinity therefore implies living with the idea that all is Divine. This means learning to see the Divinity in all things and adoring the Divine in all things, thereby dwelling with the Divinity wherever you are and also during whatever activity you may be performing. Thus, all your actions are performed as offerings to the Divinity. If this spiritual philosophy is understood and practiced, spiritual enlightenment, the goal of the entire text, is secured. Thus, in these small chapters, great spiritual principles have been embedded as formulas for spiritual realization and the upliftment of humanity.

CHAPTER 6[220]

RECOGNITION OF GODDESS ASET AS PROTECTOR AND BENEFACTOR

1. Goddess Aset came, she stopped at the town and sought out a hiding place for Heru when he came out of the marshes ... awoke in a bad state and painted his eyes in the god's ship.

2. It was commanded to him to rule the banks, and he assumed the condition of a mighty warrior, for he remembered what had been done, and he engendered fear of him and inspired respect.

3. His great mother protects him and erases those who come against Heru...

4. ...A matter a million times true!

GLOSS ON CHAPTER 6: ITS MEANING AND MYSTICAL SIGNIFICANCE

Chapter 6 shows the importance of knowing the myth of the Asarian Resurrection before embarking on the study of the Prt M Hru scriptures. This is why Chapter 2: *The Myth Behind The Rau nu Prt m Hru Understanding The Ausarian Resurrection Myth: A summary of the Ausarian Resurrection* was included in this volume. It is a gloss and summary of the most important episodes and issues presented in the Asarian Resurrection Myth which need to be understood in order to have a firm grasp of the philosophical issues brought out in the Prt M Hru. Chapter 6 is actually relating the events of the Asarian Resurrection Myth, namely, the death, resurrection, and the ensuing struggle and ultimate victory of Asar and Heru, which were all facilitated by the goddess, to the initiate who is now reading the text.

Actually, the initiate, the spiritual aspirant,, is Asar and Heru, and Aset is serving, protecting and enlightening {him/her} the way she did for Asar and Heru. Aset therefore, is the initiate's mother, spouse and sister. Thus, the important mystical key presented in Chapter 6 is the assertion that these teachings are not relating to some far off land long ago, but to the present embodiment of the Divine which is the initiate {him/her} self, who is in fact the embodied and slain divinity which is to be resurrected and enlightened.

---

[220] Generally referred to as chapter 157

CHAPTER 7[221] SECTION 3: DECLARATION OF ASET

1. Words spoken (to Asar _____) by Aset: I have come that I may be protector thine.

2. I blow on you, air to your face and the winds of the north to your nostrils, which come forth, out through Temu.

3. I have prepared for you your lungs.

4. I have granted that you might be like a Divinity[222]. Your enemies fall under your feet.

5. You have been made to be spiritually victorious in Nut,[223] and to be powerful along with the gods and goddesses.

Plate 30: The goddess Aset sits on her heels and holds the Shen, symbol of eternity.

GLOSS ON CHAPTER 7 SECTION 3: ITS MEANING AND MYSTICAL SIGNIFICANCE

Chapter 7, Section 3, is an expansion of the theme presented in Chapter 6. It states in no uncertain terms that Aset will indeed assist the aspirant on the spiritual quest. As she blew air on Asar in the Asarian Resurrection and thereby resurrected him, so too she will blow air on the spiritual aspirant. The ability to breathe air is understood as synonymous with being alive. Therefore, the goddess prepares one's lungs so that they may breathe the glory of eternity and immortality. This preparation entails the defeat of the poisons and toxins, which curtail the respiration. Just as with the physical lungs where too many toxins such as pollution, meat eating, smoking, act to close off the airways and in this manner obstruct the ability to breathe and experience peace, so too, vices and the negative aspects of the personality (anger, hatred, etc.) act to constrict the mind and spiritual consciousness, and thus, the ability to perceive the Divine.

The goddess grants the power to defeat these impurities by means of her wisdom and spiritual insight. With her intuitional wisdom teaching, the goddess led Heru to enlightenment and spiritual victory over his enemies, whereby he attained Godhood and the kingship of Kemet. This is the goal of every spiritual aspirant, which can be accomplished by following the path which the goddess has laid out. The path of Aset is the path of wisdom, with its three steps: listening and understanding the teachings, reflecting upon and practicing them in daily life and achieving a transcendental meditative mental process, which leads to spiritual enlightenment. For more on this path see the book *The Wisdom of Isis* by Muata Ashby.

---

[221] Generally referred to as Chapter 151

[222] God or Goddess

[223] i.e. in Heaven

CHAPTER 7, SECTION 10: DECLARATION OF NEBETHET

Plate 31: The goddess Nebethet kneels with hands on the Shen (eternity) symbol, uttering words from Chapter 7, Section 10.

1. These words are spoken to Asar _____ maakheru by goddess Nebethet: I have gone around, behind my brother Asar. I have come, I am your protection, behind you. The two lands make homage (to you) at your utterance.

2. You are maakheru in them. Your prayers have been heard by Ra. I have strengthened you, making you spiritually victorious over what is to be done with you.

3. Ptah has defeated your enemies for you. I am protecting you with my flame, warding off the one who is in the valley of the tomb where movement is hindered, warding off the one with sand at the feet.

4. I am the one embracing, protecting, Asar _____ who is Maakheru in Hetep and Maat.

GLOSS ON CHAPTER 7, SECTION 10: ITS MEANING AND MYSTICAL SIGNIFICANCE

Chapter 7, Section 10, is similar to Chapter 7, Section 3, but there is a subtle nuance of emphasis, which complements and augments Chapter 7, Section 3. In Chapter 7, Section 3, the emphasis from goddess Aset is on action and making the aspirant victorious and Divine. In this chapter the goddess Nebethet, the twin of Aset, but who represents the lower nature (time, space and mortality), declares that she will support and protect the Asar. The emphasis is on protection and the provision of a mystical flame, which sustains life.

The flame is a reference to the word oodja. The term, ⌡, oodja, the central sign in the Ancient Egyptian benediction, *Life, Vitality and Health,* gives us a very important teaching in reference to the process of human existence on earth. The sign signifies "fire drill" or an instrument used to start a fire or the commencement of the burning process. Used in this manner, the idea that is given is that the Divine Life Process, ☥ (Ankh), engenders a fire (*oodja,* vitality) which courses through the body and promotes health, ⌡, (*seneb*).

Vitality is what gives the impetus to life. It is the force which sustains and gives a person the will to live. If there is no vitality, the entire personality is depressed and there is no enjoyment of life. Vitality sustains the immune system and the immune system keeps external (bacteria, viruses, poisons, waste material, etc.) as well as internal agents (chemical, emotional, psychological and spiritual imbalances which deplete the immune system and make one vulnerable to disease) from disturbing the course of life. Vitality may also be referred to by the term "Life Force" or the Kemetic term "Sekhem." Therefore, the following formula may be applied to the understanding of the inner processes that sustain life: Vitality = immunity = health = life. For more on these important issues of health and vitality, see the book *The Kemetic Diet: A Holistic Guide to Food for the Body Mind and Soul* by Dr. Muata Ashby.

The embrace is an important mystical symbol of the goddess. It is the means by which the goddess extends her power to heal, protect and provide power to overcome obstacles in life. Thus, in a broader sense, this and the previous chapter signify the support of the two subtle spiritual principles of life, which the goddesses represent intrinsically. These are the earthly mortal nature (symbolized by Nebethet) and the heavenly, wise and immortal nature (symbolized by Aset). Their natures shall not be a hindrance to the spiritual realization of the Asar, but instead will be a help. Both the earthly, mortal parts as well as the heavenly aspect of a human being need to be harmonized and sublimated so that they may not obstruct the movement towards enlightenment. If the intuitional mind (Aset) is impaired, there can be no spiritual realization. Likewise, if the physical nature is wracked by pain, frustration and/or agitation from fear (especially fear of death), worldly desires, misunderstanding, negative emotions, illness, etc., there will also be no spiritual enlightenment.

So cultivating the goddesses within one's Self means promoting health of body, mind and soul through righteous action and righteous living. Also, it means the cultivation of the higher spiritual principles in life, the virtues. This is accomplished by virtuous living, studying the spiritual teachings and meditating upon them under the guidance of the goddess in the form of a spiritual preceptor.

![decorative border of lotus motifs]

CHAPTER 8[224]

A CONVERSATION BETWEEN ASAR _____ AND GOD IN THE FORM OF ATUM[225]

Plate 32: The initiate and spouse worship the god Djehuti

1. These are the words which when spoken and understood protect an aspirant from dying a second time. These words are to be spoken by Asar _____ who is Righteous of Speech.

2. Oh Djehuti! What is it that has come into being through the conflict of the children[226] of Nut?

3. They have engendered unrest, unrighteousness and have created fiends and they have slaughtered (themselves, animals and nature[227]). They have created (for themselves) fetters by their doings which render them weak.[228]

4. Give them, Oh Great Djehuti, a commandment of Atum so that their unrighteousness may not be seen, so that you will not experience that. Shorten their years; shorten their mouths because they have committed unrighteousness towards you in secret[229].

5. I am your pallet[230] and I even brought you the inkpot as well. I am not among those with hidden unrighteousness. There is no wrongdoing within me!

6. These words are spoken by me: "Oh Atum, I am Asar _____! Tell me, what place[231] is this that I have come to? There is no water here. There is no air and there is a great darkness."

---

[224] Generally referred to as chapter 175.

[225] This chapter is an evolution of Utterances that are found in the *Pyramid Texts* and the *Coffin Texts* which relate to Atum as the first primordial being. It is an instructional dialogue much in the Vedantic tradition of India wherein the god or goddess {him/her} self speaks to the spiritual aspirant directly. This chapter thereby shows that the later versions of the *Prt m Hru* incorporate and evolved the teachings of the earlier versions, since this form of dialogue is not found in the earlier versions.

[226] Nut is the goddess of the sky or heaven. Since all planets are as if given birth by the heavens, it follows that all things on earth, including plants, animals and human beings, are children of Nut. Also, Nut is the mother of the gods and goddesses: Asar, Aset, Set and Nebethet, and by association also, their progeny: Heru and Anpu. The conflict being alluded to here is he one between Asar and Set, and Set and Heru. See the book *The Ausarian Resurrection* by Muata Ashby . This question is very similar to one which occurs in the Bhagavad Gita of India where the question is asked: *Gita: Chapter Arjuna Vishad Yogah--The Yoga of Arjuna's Dejection 1. Dhritarashtra asked: O Sanjaya, what did my sons and the sons of (my brother) Pandu (the Pandavas) do, assembled in the holy place of Kurukshetra, eager to fight?*

[227] These specific infractions are mentioned in the Hermetic texts-See the book *The Ausarian Resurrection* by Muata Ashby.

[228] Maat Philosophy holds that leading a life of unrighteousness renders a human being spiritually weak and susceptible to temptations of the lower nature. See the book *Wisdom of Maati* by Muata Ashby.

[229] The secret nature of the offences against the Divine (Djehuti) relate to the sins committed by people of which only god is aware. While there may be no human witnesses, Djehuti, who symbolizes the cosmic intellect, is always aware of the acts of every personality.

[230] A tool used for printing or gilding letters on book bindings. This is a humble invitation to the Higher Self to be the guiding force in one's life as opposed to the ego and its unrighteousness that was referred to earlier. This verse points to the understanding that one must be not only free from committing unrighteousness, but also there must be righteousness in the heart as well (internal, mental righteousness). Here the initiate is to quash all egoistic notions and place {him/her} in the hands of God. A similar teaching occurs in Indian mysticism as the spiritual aspirant is asked to allow {him/her} to become the flute upon which God, in the form of Krishna, plays the divine melody of prosperity and spiritual salvation. This means giving oneself to God, the ultimate devotional gesture in any religion.

[231] The place refers to the Netherworld, the afterlife state.

7. In this plane you have no physical body, therefore, you may live here through peace of heart. Moreover, there is no sexuality here, in place of water, air, bread, beer and lovemaking, I have given you the opportunity to attain the state of Akhu[232] together with peace of heart.

8. Atum has decreed that my face should be seen and that I should not suffer the things that cause pain.

9. Every god is sending his throne to the leader of eternity. It is thy throne, given to thy son Heru. Atum, holding what was sent to him by the elder divinities commanded this. It is he who has been ruling thy throne. It is he inheriting the throne within the island of double fire.[233] Command that I may be seen, as I am his double and that my face may see the face of Lord Atum.

10. What is the duration of life?

11. It has been decreed for millions of millions of years of duration. It is given to me to send the old ones. After that period of time I am going to destroy all created things.

12. It is the earth that came forth from Nun, now coming forth into its former state.[234]

13. I am fated with Asar; done for me to become images of the serpents, not knowing they the people and not knowing the gods and goddesses the excellent beauty that I made for Asar which was greater than all the gods and goddesses. I gave to him the desert. His son Heru is his heir on his throne within the island of double fire.

14. I made, also, a divine ruling place for him in the Divine Boat of Millions of Years.

15. It is Heru, who is now established on the Serek[235] for those who are beloved and who are attaining sturdiness. Furthermore, the soul of Set, which is greater than all the gods and goddesses, was sent. It is given to me to make fettered his soul within the Divine Boat, for his desire is feared by divine body parts.

16. Hail father mine, Asar; do make for me what you did for thy father Ra, the achievement of long life on earth, achieving the throne, health, progeny and endurance for my tomb, and my loved ones who are on earth.

17. Grant that my enemies be destroyed, that the scorpion goddess may be on top of them, fettering them. Father mine, Ra make thee for me these things: Ankh, Udja, Seneb (*life, vitality and health*).

18. Heru is now firmly established[236] on his Serek. Give thee movement in course of time, that of advancing towards blessedness.[237]

---

[232] Glorious spirit status, i.e. spiritual enlightenment.

[233] The place of duality and consumption, i.e. human existence on earth.

[234] This passage relates to the dissolution of creation back into the primordial state, from the Nun, or primeval waters from which all things emerged in the beginning. This is an important teaching which shows that Ancient Egyptian mythology and philosophy recognized the concept that creation is not a linear event, having a beginning and an end, but it is akin to a cycle which recurs at given intervals, governed by Divinity.

[235] Royal standard. This symbol was used in ancient times prior to the cartouche for inscribing royal names.

[236] Heru underwent a struggle with Set over the rulership of Egypt. This is symbolic of the struggle of the spiritual aspirant with {his/her} lower self. When Heru is established, it means a spiritual victory, Maak-heru-Spiritual Enlightenment.

[237] Spiritual Enlightenment.

GLOSS ON CHAPTER 8: ITS MEANING AND MYSTICAL SIGNIFICANCE

This Chapter is one of the most important of the collection of the *Prt M Hru* because it presents several important teachings in reference to the disembodied state that is experienced in the Astral Plane. This wisdom allows the aspirant to expand the understanding beyond the ordinary mortal existence in order to understand what it means to transcend the body and mortal consciousness.

What does it mean to be without the body and to transcend body consciousness? What does it mean to live in one's Astral Body and what does it mean to transcend even this level of existence? The scripture explains that those in the Duat will lead a life similar to that on earth, but with very important differences. These differences are outlined in Chapter 8.

Verse 1-4

The chapter begins as a question, which opens up a dialogue on the profound questions of life. The initiate asks Lord Djehuti, the god of scripture and cosmic mind, what has happened as a result of the struggle between Asar, Aset, Set, and Nebethet, the children of Nut. This is of course a reference to the Asarian Resurrection saga. However, this epic story is also part of a greater issue, relating to the creation of human beings, for in the Creation Myth of Anu, the neteru are explained as elements of Creation. Ra is Fire, Shu is air, ether and the principle of duality, Tefnut is water, Geb is earth and the principle of solidity, and Nut is the principle of expansion. Nut and Geb's children are the composite elements that go to compose the personality of every human being. Asar is soul, Aset is wisdom (intuitional mind), Set is ego and Nebethet is physical body and mortality. Every human personality is a mixture of soul and ego. Egoistic human interactions, (i.e., human interrelations), lead to unrest and unrighteousness, and this has resulted in the conditions of present life. According to an Ancient Egyptian myth, the Story of Hetheru and Djehuti, which was further elaborated in the Hermetic texts, the elements of nature, seeing the unrighteousness of human beings, asked that God set limits for them. God instructed Djehuti to accomplish this task. This is why human beings cannot live beyond certain limits and their mental capacity is restricted, even though as science had discovered, most human beings only use 10% of the brain.

Verse 5

Next, the initiate, having accepted these facts, proclaims his allegiance or attachment to the Divine and his detachment from the world of ordinary unrighteous human existence. The initiate surrenders {him/her} self to the will of the Divine. The metaphor here is I am your pallet. Furthermore, the initiate not only makes {his/her} personality available to God so that she may do with it as she pleases, but also the aspirant brings the writing instrument. This teaching is similar in most respects to the Hindu ideal in the religious practice related to the god Krishna. Krishna is the master flute player, and his devotees are asked to allow themselves to be played like a flute, that is, that God should be the driving force behind one's life, as opposed to the ego. This teaching is called "surrender to God," and it is one of the direct pathways to spiritual enlightenment. It requires a keen understanding of the illusory nature of the world and a renunciation of it, as well as an understanding and turning towards the Divine, not only in name only or as a fanciful notion, but as a profound movement of giving one's self to the Divine.

This teaching is similar to the *"refuge doctrine"* which is found in both Christianity and Buddhism. The idea behind the refuge doctrine is that through the practice of placing one's trust, troubles, joys and sorrows in the hands of the deity, one's mind will be unburdened and exclusively directed towards the deity. The peace which can be gained from this way of living is immense. Through the increasing levels of peace and healing which can be gained, increasing levels of spiritual sensitivity are attained. This idea is strongly expressed in the following Christian statements:

Matthew 11
　　28 Come to me, all [ye] that labor and are heavy laden, and I will give you rest.
　　29 Take my yoke upon you, and learn from me; for I am meek and lowly in heart:
　　　　 and ye shall find rest to your souls.

The message of devotion is also an integral part of Buddhist philosophy in the following credo:

> I go to the Buddha for refuge.
> I go to the doctrine for refuge.
> I go to the monastic order for refuge.

The Buddhist aspirant is admonished to take refuge in the *Buddha* (one's innate *Buddha Consciousness*), the *Dharma* (Buddhist spiritual discipline), and the *Sanga* (company of enlightened personalities). Jesus also exhorted his followers to bring him their troubles "and He will give them rest."

The concept of refuge in the Divinity is also found in the Gita, Chapter 9:

> 32. O Arjuna, those who take refuge in Me, whether men born in a lowly class, or women, or Vaishyas, or Shudras, even they are sure to attain the highest goal.

The preceding statements are very important for spiritual as well as social reasons, because all four spiritual personalities, Atum, Jesus, Buddha and Krishna, are not only trying to free aspirants from ignorance about themselves, but also the erroneous notions about the social order which is fraught with injustices such as racism (caste system), economic disparity and sexism. Worry and preoccupation with worldly affairs are one of the principal obstacles to spiritual movement, therefore, one of the quickest paths to spiritual evolution would be by relieving one's burden by taking refuge in something greater than one's small and helpless human ego.

The refuge teaching may also be found in the Koran:

> 7:200 If a suggestion from Satan assail thy (mind), seek refuge with Allah; for He heareth and knoweth (all things).
> 113:1 SURA 113. Falaq, or The Dawn. In the name of Allah, Most Gracious, Most Merciful. Say: I seek refuge with the Lord of the Dawn...
> 114:1 SURA 114. Nas, or Mankind. In the name of Allah, Most Gracious, Most Merciful. Say: I seek refuge with the Lord and Cherisher of Mankind...

Verse 6

Now, having sought refuge in the Divine Self (Atum), the initiate asks the higher wisdom of the transcendental realm, the knowledge of its nature.

Atum explains that there is no body in this realm, and therefore, no need for food or sexuality. One important point here is that life goes on beyond the embodied state, that is, the Kemetic concept of Astral Existence. This is an advanced exposition of the understanding that there is a higher existence beyond the mortal physical existence. This existence is in and through the mind itself. Sexuality and the physical pleasures which human beings seek are activities, which can only be performed in the physical realm, when there is a physical body and the mind and senses with which to experience. The Sahu or Spirit-Soul (living-soul, enlightened) state is beyond physicality and beyond time and space. Thus, in order to achieve this level of consciousness, it is necessary to renounce and leave behind the ignorant and egoistic notions of the lower desires and the needs of the body. This process is outlined in the *Ausarian Resurrection Myth* as well as in the *Book of Coming Forth By Day*.

Verse 8-9

All human experiences occur in the mind. Think about it. When you experience a dream, everything occurs in the mind. When you experience the sense of touch, it is not your body which is experiencing it, but your mind. Your mind registers sensation via messages, which are sent to it through the nerves, which have their connection to the brain. The brain registers the sensations and the mind interprets them in a particular way according to its conditioning. For example, the sensation of touching something soft is understood as

softness because the mind has learned to interpret it as such. However, what are you experiencing when you are asleep having a dream? You are not using the senses or other parts of the body and yet there are sensations and feelings. In the Dream State, when you are sleeping or also when you are lost in a daydream, you are experiencing the Duat or the astral world. When you die you go to this world and have various experiences based on the life you led while on earth. If you were righteous, you will be led to heavenly experiences; if you were unrighteous, you will be led to hellish conditions.

In reality, you are the Spirit who is using a body to have physical experiences. Having forgotten about your true nature, you experience the pleasure and pain of the body, thinking that pleasure or pain is experienced because of something that the body does. In reality, it is your spirit, which enlivens the brain and nervous system and allows them to bring sensations which you call experiences. The body acts as a safety valve in reference to pleasure and pain. If there is too much pain, the body automatically swoons and there is a cessation of the experience. If there is too much pleasure or elation, then again the body swoons. However, when the body dies, the mind survives and has perception of the astral (mental) world in much the same way as you have various experiences tumbling from one dream to another during a night's sleep. In this condition, the soul is led to experience various situations of pleasure or pain according to its past history of good or bad deeds (ari, karma), and also according to its level of spiritual realization. This means that if you believe that you are the body, an individual personality, then you will continue to experience existence in that way. You will see yourself as an individual lost in a maze of situations, which the mind can create endlessly. These situations are based on your deep-rooted unconscious desires and your level of ignorance about yourself.

There is a big difference in the level of intensity with which the experiences of the Astral Plane are perceived. In the bodiless state there is no safety valve to control the levels of pain or pleasure, and therefore, it is possible to experience unimaginable levels of pain as well as pleasure. These are known as hell or heaven, respectively. In the bodiless state the unconscious mind and the subtle senses remain with the soul when a person has not reached the heights of spiritual enlightenment (complete detachment from mind and senses). The unresolved desires in the unconscious emerge to impel the soul to move on in the search for fulfillment of those desires even though they are unreal and unnecessary. Imagine if you could do whatever you wanted to do but without restriction. If you want to eat pizza, you can eat continuously without getting overweight or sick. If you want to do violence against certain people you will be able to do so in an unrestricted manner. If you want to indulge in any pleasures of the senses such as sex, music, beautiful sights, etc., you can do so. In so doing the intellect becomes overwhelmed, and therefore unused. Thus the intellect becomes weak and atrophied. The senses take control and direct the path of the soul. This is the antithetical movement to the surrender to the Divine, mentioned earlier. This is the path of egoism and reincarnation, not of enlightenment and Self-realization.

Verse 10-14

The important question here relates to the duration of life in the transcendental realm. In Kemetic Philosophy the term *millions of millions of years of duration* is often used, to symbolize an unfathomable amount of time, i.e. forever. But in mystical philosophy, forever relates to the span of time from the present, to the end of time, i.e. the end of creation, and not to eternity which transcends time. At some point the astral experience is exhausted and then the soul, with its remaining unconscious impressions, returns to the physical realm in order to once again gain experiences as a living human being. If enlightenment is not attained, this cycle of birth, death and astral experiences is repeated over and over again, indefinitely. This is why the process of yoga and mystical spirituality has as its primary goal to cleanse the unconscious impressions of the mind. In Ancient Egyptian terms this process, known as *Maak-heru* or "Purity of Heart," is the central mission presented in the *Prt M Hru.*

Verse 15-18

In this concluding portion of the scripture, we see that the initiate agrees with and accepts the wisdom of Atum, and in so doing becomes Heru. As we know, Heru was triumphant in his struggle against Set, who is his own ego or lower nature. The unenlightened aspects of a person's personality fear the power of the ego, but when this is controlled, there is a glorious peace that ensues. Thus, all good things accumulate onto the

initiate. Both success and prosperity upon earth are granted at the same time as spiritual enlightenment. This form of existence is known as Sagehood, to have both victory over the lower nature and victory in the heavenly worlds. This is the coveted goal of all spiritual aspirants in all mystical traditions from the beginning of time. This state is the glorious achievement, which gives life meaning and is the source of all good and wonderful things in life.

CHAPTER 9[238]

THE CHAPTER FOR REPULSING APEP WHOM IS THE EMBODIMENT OF EVIL.

Plate 33: The initiate holds three Divine Standards, Ibis, Hawk and Bull.

1. I Asar _____ speak now to Apep. You are the evil of unrighteousness, which strikes like a serpent and thereby draws human beings to their ruin. Listen, I have lived a righteous life and I have discovered my greatness. I am not like one of those weak people who are powerless against your schemes and tricks of temptation and delusion.

2. Your poison of desire, falsehood, hatred and fear cannot enter me. For I am so subtle, due to my purity[239], that I am as if hidden from you, like Amun[240], the Hidden Spirit which pervades all.

3. I am beyond your grasp because I am one with God. I am the Single One, who is in the Primeval Waters[241] of Creation. Thus, my essence is that of the gods and goddesses.[242]

4. I am that same God, the Supreme One, who has myriad of mysterious names. I am the God who depends on nothing but on whom all depends. I am the God who made this Creation and who dwells there for millions of millions of years.

5. I was born of Temu, the first divinity that came into existence. I know this! I am one possessing the knowledge of the innermost truth.

---

[238]Generally referred to as Chapter 7. Based on Papyrus in Turin museum.

[239] See Chapter 33: Affirmations of Innocence: The 42 Precepts of Maat- spiritual purity and the requirements for those who want to benefit from these scriptures.

[240]Amun literally means the Hidden Spirit, the witnessing consciousness, which underlies all awareness and the mind itself.

[241]The substratum from which all has emanated at the command of the Single One (God).

[242]The gods and goddesses emanate from God, the Supreme Being (Single One) and engender and support the existence of Creation (Physical universe), thus they are to be understood as cosmic forces.

GLOSS ON CHAPTER 9: ITS MEANING AND MYSTICAL SIGNIFICANCE

The vignette for this chapter gives insight into the qualities which must be developed in order to succeed in repelling evil (Apep) in the human personality. The initiate holds three standards, meaning that {he/she} supports, follows and adheres to those teachings and powers symbolized by them. From left to right the first standard is Djehuti, the god of writing and intellect. The second is Heru, the god of will power and spiritual aspiration. The third standard displays the Kha, bull. The sound of the words Ka (astral body – mind and senses) and Kha (bull-generative power) are a play on words because the Ka is the engenderer of the Khat or physical body. The bull is a symbol of sexual energy and the generative power of God, who produced all Creation. Therefore, an aspirant must develop the ability to understand the spiritual teachings by developing the reasoning capacity. The aspirant must also develop spiritual aspiration and devotion towards the Divine, which means promoting this practice of Maat (right action) and selfless service to humanity as a means of worship of the Divine. This also relates to studying the teachings under the guidance of a spiritual preceptor (Aset), that is, being a follower of Heru (Shemsu Hor). When the lower human qualities are placed in subjection, that is subdued, they become powerful forces in the personality that no longer lead a human being towards worldly desires, entanglements, as well as weakness in the face of temptations and vices, but serve to promote determination, stamina, will, detachment and unwavering pertinacity or intractability when it comes to resisting the forces of negativity, and success in the spiritual journey.

Verse 1-2

This chapter is one of those which constitute the hallmark of Kemetic Scripture. This is because it places the initiate in a strong position as opposed to a meek position, in reference to the demons. From the opening statement of this chapter, there is a tone of superiority and control over the demoniac forces, which are led by Apep, who is a lieutenant of Set, the general of the demoniac forces in Kemetic mystical religion. The aspirant asserts, in no uncertain terms, that {he/she} knows the demon and that said demon cannot exert its influence on the mind of the aspirant. This is of course an exalted position enjoyed only by the most advanced aspirants.

Verse 3-5

In the next verses the scripture explains why there is so much confidence and power. The initiate asserts "I am one with God." This statement in itself contains the key to the *Prt M Hru* scriptures as a whole. Its great significance overshadows all in its magnanimous implications. As in the Ausarian Resurrection myth when Heru defeated Set by becoming all-encompassing, i.e. One with God, the Supreme One, so too the spiritual aspirant gains power over the entire Creation by this attainment. This is because since the Supreme Spirit encompasses all, just as when a person is dreaming their mind actually encompasses everything in and anything that happens in the dream, the all-encompassing essence controls that which is within it. Therefore, becoming one with God is equivalent to encompassing all, and since nothing can escape the grasp of the all-encompassing consciousness, there can be no fear, no desire and no illusion. So, this is the source of all power, the supreme wisdom of the ages, which bestows spiritual enlightenment and all freedom to the aspirant who attains it. This Chapter closes with a statement summarizing the great realization, that the initiate is not an individual, mortal being, but indeed, the consciousness of every individual is actually one and the same as the Supreme Being of Primeval times. Therefore, every aspirant on the path of Atum discovers his true identity as that Divinity, encompassing all Creation and manifesting as the myriad of names and forms within it.

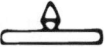

CHAPTER 10[243]

THE FOUR FLAMES MADE FOR THE KHU

Figure 86: Four men, holding torches, approach the mummy.

1. The fire comes to your Ka, Oh Asar _____!

2. Behold! The flame rises in Abdu and it comes to the Eye of Heru. It is set correctly in your brow, Oh Asar, ruler of Amentet. It is fixed on your shrine and it rises onto your brow. It is set on your breast Oh Asar _____ and it set on your brow. The Eye of Heru is protecting you. All your enemies fall before you.

3. The Eye of Heru is whole and powerful. It sends out rays like Ra. It puts down the threefold might of Set.

4. The four flames enter into your Ka, Oh Asar _____. The four flames enter into your Ka.

5. The Eye of Heru has avenged his father Asar and protected him.

6. This chapter should not be read and the ritual associated with it should not be performed for anyone, even your father or son or mother or daughter, except for yourself alone. This is a great mystical teaching of the Netherworld.

7. If this ritual is performed for someone each day, their spirit will go forth from every hall in the Duat and from the seven Arits of Asar, God. There will be no obstruction of any kind for such a spirit and there will be no negative verdict what the words are weighed.

8. This person's mouth should be opened with the traditional metal instrument and take care to record these words exactly as you found them for these are great mysteries of the Netherworld.

9. This chapter is to be recited over four flames and in the rays of Ra. Doing this will provide power for the Khu to be among the never setting stars.

10. If this chapter is recited the Khu will never, never falter and that person shall be a living soul for ever and the Khu will be as vigorous as that of Asar.

11. ...And behold, these things shall be performed by one who is clean and pure, a person who has eaten neither meat nor fish[244] and who has not had sexual intercourse[245].

---

[243] Generally referred to as chapter 137A.

[244] One who keeps a vegetarian diet. The scripture seems to mention both meat and fish separately as if to leave no doubt since there are many people who consider themselves as vegetarians but still eat fish, thinking that it is not a form of meat. Indeed, any form of animal flesh, including insects, reptiles and crustaceans (any of various predominantly aquatic arthropods of the class Crustacea, including lobsters, crabs, shrimps, and barnacles) is "meat."

[245] One who practices celibacy-control of sex desire.

12. Every Khu for whom this is read and performed will go forth unobstructed, as a follower of Asar, continually.

GLOSS ON CHAPTER 10: ITS MEANING AND MYSTICAL SIGNIFICANCE

Verse 1-5

The Eye of Heru is a metaphor of spiritual consciousness. Just as it was made whole in the Asarian Resurrection myth, so too the Eye of the initiate is also made whole. In this wholeness there is power, just as scattered rays of the sun become powerful when focused, but are harmless when shining indiscriminately. The god Ra is said to originate from an "isle of fire." The serpent on his brow (Hetheru) spits out venomous fire which destroys evil. Thus, fire is the symbol of purity, the force which drives off the demoniac agencies in nature and negative qualities in the personality. Set is known as the "great strength." As the threefold mighty one, his power in the three realms (Earth Plane, Astral Plane and Causal Plane) is overcome by the fire of the spirit (Ra). Also, Set presides over the three lower psychospiritual consciousness centers of the human personality with their qualities of fear, sex desire and egoistic will. These three lower aspects of the personality are sublimated and the initiate is able to develop the four higher principles (universal love, self control, inner vision and transcendental consciousness) that lead to spiritual enlightenment. In this manner, the power of Set, as the ego aspect of consciousness which troubles the spiritual aspirant by means of egoistic will, sex desire and ignorance, can be overcome. The four flames symbolize the fullness of Sekhem (Life Force) which is to be developed and raised to the point between the eyes (Third Eye). The four flames entering the Ka, which is constructed with a subtle fire (spirit energy), is symbolic of the four primeval divine forces which sustain Creation. There are four sons of Heru, four pillars of heaven, four canopic jars containing the organs of the deceased and four cardinal points, symbolizing physical existence, the number of Creation. Thus, on entering the Ka or Astral body, the fires nourish and strengthen its Life Force by their combined essence, encompassing the power of the physical realm, dissolving it into the astral body (the Ka, which is in the Astral Plane). In order for this process to begin, the fire of fullness must enter the Ka, that is, one's fullness of awareness must shift to the Astral body, the Ka. The Ka is the subtle aspect of the human personality comprised of the mind and senses. From here the awareness can be directed towards the higher aspects of consciousness, first the Third Eye, and then the Khu. Thus, the Third Eye opens the way to the Khu and the other higher aspects of the personality, the Ba, Sahu, Khaibit, etc.

Verse 6-7

When the fullness or wholeness of the Third Eye is achieved, there is no power that can withstand its force. This practice of affirming and asserting the true power that is within must go on daily and perennially so that it may have its full transformative effect on the mind. The mind is what the thoughts are. Therefore, positive affirmation and study of the teachings should be a daily practice until the fullness of the Eye is achieved. These teachings are not for the masses, nor are they to be studied or ritualized in front of others, even in a familial context. This teaching transcends all relations, including family, and constitutes a direct linking of the aspirant to the Divine Self. They are for serious and advanced students of the mystical philosophy who understand how to meditate on the Divine and the essence of their very existence.

Verse 8-12

This Chapter is also dedicated also to making the Glorious Spirit, the Khu or Akhu, brighter and stronger. The Khu is an aspect of personality, which becomes dim when a person indulges in worldly consciousness and becomes dull to the spiritual essence. The performance of this ritual bolsters the Khu so that it may become bright like a star in the sky, so much so that it remains shining perpetually, like the stars along the axis of the earth that do not move or change in any way. This is an internal attainment which is experienced by the aspirant and which manifests as a glow in the personality, the aura and the intellect. Verse 11 contains a most important injunction for spiritual practice, which will allow the great attainment to become effective. One must control the lower nature, working towards purity of heart and purity of the body through a vegetarian diet and the practice of celibacy. These disciplines are essential in promoting purity of mind and body which will allow one to defeat Set and discover the Khu, and thereby promote its fullness.

CHAPTER 11[246]
THE WORDS FOR OPENING THE MOUTH

Plate 34: Chapter 11, the priest assumes the role of Ptah, opening the mouth/eyes of the initiate with various instruments.

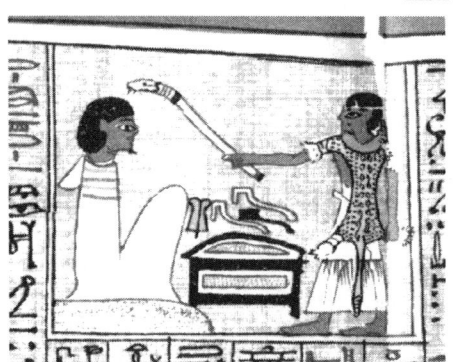

1. These words will open up the mouth[247] of Asar _____. Oh Ptah![248] Open my mouth! Loosen the heavy weight of the bandages[249] placed on my mouth by the god of my town. Come Djehuti, filled and equipped with words of power to loosen these double bandages of Set [250] which are shielding my mouth.

2. Atum repulses the obstruction of these fetters. My mouth is opening now. As for Shu,[251] he opened the mouth of the gods and goddesses with the iron harpoon of heaven.

3. I am Sekhmet. I rest upon the pedestal[252] in the great wind, the magnanimous sky I am.

4. I am the great Sah[253], the innermost of souls in Anu.[254] As for Hekau all, all words spoken against me, the company of gods and goddesses will stand up for me against those.

Pyramid Text Utterance 20-21 **[11-13]**: Opening of the Mouth and Eyes

"O Initiate, I have come in search of you, for I am Horus; I have struck your mouth for you, for I am your beloved son; I have split open your mouth for you... I have split open your eyes for you... with the Chepch of the Eye of Heru- Chepesh. I have split

---

[246] Generally referred to as Chapter 23.

[247] In Kemetic (Ancient Egyptian) mystical philosophy, the mouth is the symbol of consciousness. God created the universe by the utterance of his own name. Through words a human being can attain enlightenment (Maak-heru) or reach the depths of degradation (Set-Apep). Therefore the aspirant should always strive to expand (open up) their minds through virtuous living and righteous speech.

[248] Ptah: The third aspect of Neberdjer: Amun-Ra-Ptah, and head god of the city of Hetkaptah (Memphis). He is creator and sustainer of the universe with equal status to Ra, Tem, Asar, and Khepri. He in particular receives the invocations for opening of mouths from all spiritual aspirants. Ptah is a cosmic divinity who supercedes all minor divinities, the powers that bind human beings to human (worldly, physical) existence.

[249] The bandages are the mummy wrappings. Of particular interest are those placed over the mouth because these stifle the faculty of speech. This relates to a stunting of spiritual evolution.

[250] Set is the divinity or cosmic force of egoism and unrighteousness, which constantly seeks to stifle the soul. One's own unrighteousness is one's own spiritual enemy. In the Ausarian Resurrection myth Set battled against Heru for the throne of Egypt. His weapons were murder, lies, deceit, sexual depravity, lust, greed, etc. Heru overcame these to become King of Egypt, i.e. spiritually enlightened.

[251] Father of Asar, Aset, Set and Nebethet, god of the air (wind) and of space, husband of Tefnut (power of water).

[252] The gods and goddesses are often depicted standing on pedestals. The pedestal is a symbol of Maat, meaning that in order to be divine, one must stand (be established) upon truth and righteousness.

[253] Goddess-pun on Saa (Siaa) -Intelligence-knowledge-understanding.

[254] The city of Ra, where he first emerged from the Primeval Ocean, the origin of the gods and goddesses.

open your mouth for you... I have split open your eyes for you... with the adze of Upuaut..... with the adze of iron . . .

GLOSS ON CHAPTER 11: ITS MEANING AND MYSTICAL SIGNIFICANCE

The body or *Shet-t* (mummy) is where the soul focuses its dynamic existence. Your mummy is the condition of spiritual dormancy, which is prepared (embalmed) by Anubis for the practice of the mysteries. This preparation involves the development of mental discipline and the faculty of discernment between real and unreal. This is symbolized by the mummified figure of Asar (the soul). The bandages represent the fetters which bind the soul. The most important bandage is the fetters of Set.

Mysticism of Opening The Mouth of The Asar (The Initiate)

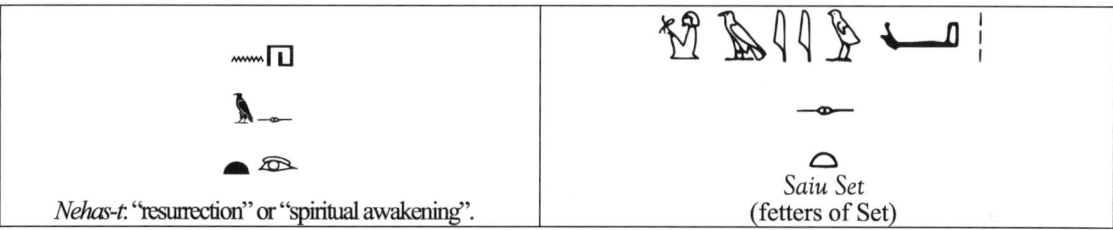

Nehas-t: "resurrection" or "spiritual awakening".	*Saiu Set* (fetters of Set)

These were the bandages placed over the mouth of the mummy. These fetters are most important to the initiate because the mouth symbolizes the memory of the initiate, however, this is a special memory of being one with the Divine. If the mouth is bound, there is no memory of the true Self because there is no expansion in consciousness. The mouth is the mystical symbol of consciousness. This is because the mouth is the means through which consciousness manifests. Have you noticed that sometimes you say something you did not realize was in your mind? The mouth is tied to the unconscious, and if there is vice, then the speech will be automatically evil. If there is virtue in the personality, the speech will be automatically harmonious and peaceful. Righteous speech promotes expansion in spiritual consciousness, while evil speech promotes constriction and bondage of spiritual consciousness. This is why the practice of following the precepts of Maat is so important in life. Also, for this reason there are hekau in the *Book of Coming Forth By Day*, Chapter 11, *Chapter of opening the mouth of Asar Ani*, directed toward opening the mouth. Once again, it is wisdom itself (Djehuti) which accomplishes the lifting of the fetter of ignorance (loss of memory).

The body is an essential element of spiritual practice because it is with the body that spiritual discipline must be performed. This is the center of the temple of the universe. It is the *Holy Land* to be sanctified and discovered. In a figurative sense then, the human mind is the heart of the shrine of the body, the holy of holies, where divine realization occurs. When spiritual discipline is perfected, the true Self or *Shti* (he who is hidden in the coffin) is revealed.

The opening of the mouth and eyes is a mystical teaching relating to expansion in expression (mouth) and awareness (open eyes). These factors (mouth and eyes) are the signs of the existence of consciousness or its absence. From the passages above we learn that the priests and priestesses "open" the mouth and eyes by toughing them with the ritual instruments which symbolize the eternal, the absolute, i.e. the expansion of consciousness immortality and spiritual enlightenment. Also, we learn that the adze instrument (ursa minor) is actually also the Eye of Heru, which is the greatest offering-eucharist of the Egyptian mysteries. The Eye symbolizes divine consciousness as it is one and the same with Heru, Asar and Ra. Therefore, being touched with these instruments means attaining god-consciousness. For more on the "Chepesh" and the mysticism of the opening of the mouth ceremony see the gloss to verse 22 of Chapter 4.

CHAPTER 12[255]

WORDS FOR ALLOWING A MAN OR WOMAN TO REMEMBER THEIR NAME IN THE NETERKHERT.[256]
Plate 35: Vignette of Chapter 12-the initiate sees {him/her} self.[257]

1. These words are to be said by Asar _____.

2. May my name be granted to me in the great house.

3. May I remember my name in the house of fire on that night when the years and months are counted[258].

4. I rest upon the eastern side of heaven.

5. As for any god or goddess that may advance behind me, I say their name as they come forth.

GLOSS ON CHAPTER 12: ITS MEANING AND MYSTICAL SIGNIFICANCE

One of the important teachings contained in this chapter is the idea of remembrance. Spiritual enlightenment is not something new that is added to a person. It is a gathering and making whole one's consciousness so as to discover one's true identity as One with the Divine. Thus, the initiate asks that they be given their name in the *Per Aah* or Great House. The Per Aah is the abode of the Divine Self, and only there can one be given one's true name, which is transcendental and unverbalizable. The myth of Aset and Ra explains this mystical point in great detail.[259] Thus, by means of this glorious spiritual discipline of remembrance and invocation for higher knowledge, it is possible for one to become aware of the doorway to eternity, the eastern side of heaven, which is the entranceway for all souls as well as the gods and goddesses. This being so, the knowledge of all beings entering the Netherworld is known by the power of one's own remembrance of one's Self which is the essence in all divinities. It must be understood that the eastern side of heaven is also the "western" side of Ta or the physical plane, and this is desirable for it leads to the divine abode. One should not want to go to the eastern side of the Ta, because this means reincarnation back into the world (Ta plane).

---

[255] Generally referred to as Chapter 25.
[256] Cemetery-lower divine realm as opposed to the Astral Plane and heaven which can be seen as higher realms of consciousness. The Neterkhert may be likened to the ancient Greek concept of the Netherworld but only in certain respects. It is not a hell dominated by a devil, etc.
[257] From - Chap 25 Auf-Ankh-Turin Papyrus.
[258] Reckoned up, i.e., the great judgment of the soul.
[259] See the books *The Wisdom of Isis* and *Worship of the Divine Mother* by Muata Ashby.

CHAPTER 13[260]
Words for giving a heart to Asar _____ in Neterkhert.

Plate 36: Vignette of Chapter 13- the initiate adores {his/her} own soul and holds {his/her} own heart in {his/her} hand, while propitiating it through the hekau.

1.   Heart mine in the house of hearts; heart mine be with me in the house of hearts. My heart is peaceful for me. I do not eat the cakes of Asar in the eastern lake, the boat sailing downstream or upstream. I do not go into the boat with you. It is I with my mouth and my words with my two legs for walking; and with my two arms for pulling down the enemies. Opened for me are the doors of heaven. Geb,[261] the chief of the gods and goddesses, has unbolted his jaws for me. My eyes, which were blinded, are opened and my legs stretch out freely. They are firmed up by the god Anpu and they extend forth for me, expanding as goddess Sekhmet.

2.   I am in heaven doing my will in the house of the Ka of Ptah.[262] I know my heart![263] I am powerful. I know I am powerful in my arms. Powerful am I in my legs. Powerful am I in my actions, which are desired by my Ka.

3.   My soul and body are not restricted at the portals[264] of Amentet in my going in, in peace, and coming out in peace.

GLOSS ON CHAPTER 13: ITS MEANING AND MYSTICAL SIGNIFICANCE

Chapter 13 relates to affirming self-control. Once again there is a negative reference to the east, the eating of cakes there, again, symbolic of desires and thoughts of worldly life and reincarnation. Most people do not have control of their lives. They are like a candle flame, which is constantly buffeted by wind, obstructing it from shining to its full potential. The heart is a metaphor for the mind. When the mind is overpowered by egoistic desires and by unrighteousness (negative behavior such as lying, stealing, cheating, hypocrisy, craving, lusting, longing, etc.), it is not able to envision the higher reality of the spirit. Thus, a person who is ignorant of the higher spiritual reality and who is led through life by their desires, longings, cravings and expectations will eventually encounter frustration and unrest. They will never discover inner peace or the

---

[260] Generally referred to as Chapter 26.

[261] God king of Egypt who ruled the land in ancient times, husband of goddess Nut, and father of Asar, Aset, Set and Nebethet.

[262] Mythologically, the city of Memphis (Het Ka Ptah-house of the ka of Ptah) has its correspondent in heaven.

[263] This is a reference to the Ancient Egyptian injunction "Know Thyself", i.e. "I Know who I am."

[264] Gates.

Divine presence within. They will be controlled by their desires and emotions rather than being masters of their desires and emotions.

Thus, Asar Ani does not want to end up with his spiritual movement obstructed because this obstruction leads to frustration and disappointment. When the human heart experiences frustration, it is a form of anguish for the soul, which expresses as anger, depression and grief. In the acute stages it expresses as hatred and violence. One becomes susceptible to negative feelings and emotions, as a victim as well as a perpetrator (criminal). Thus, losing control of the heart is against the positive spiritual movement towards self-discovery. Asar Ani therefore requests that the mummy wrappings be loosened from his body and that the heart-soul not be imprisoned in the body. The body here refers to mortal consciousness or the consciousness of the waking reality of the ego that excludes the higher states of consciousness.

Thus, Asar Ani affirms that he is in control of his heart and therefore, in control of his mind and the power to move wherever he pleases. In fact, he states that he is the master of the heart and that he knows how to use it. This implies the attainment of the faculty of discernment as symbolized by the character of Anpu, the jackal deity who embalmed Asar (the God) and who led him through the dangerous realm of the astral plane which has many demons (anger, hatred, greed, lust, etc.) which seek to enslave the soul. He expresses strong dislike for the idea of "eating the cakes of Asar in the eastern side of the lake of flowers." This reference relates to the understanding of life as related by the journey of Ra. Every day Ra in the form of the sun-disk is metaphorically consumed by Nut and she gives birth to him every morning. Therefore, the east represents rebirth, the new life or the process of reincarnation. In the same fashion, those who do not attain the ability to either join Ra in his barque or join Asar (the God) in Djedu (Amentet), are reborn again. Reincarnation implies having to once again be born in the world of time and space to suffer the limitations of youth, the trials and tribulations of adulthood, the pain of disease, old age, and death once again. Therefore, human life is to be understood as a separation from divine consciousness. (separation from the Divine), and is not to be seen as an auspicious, desirable existence.

It must be clearly understood that any pleasure which can be attained as a human being with the mind and senses through the ego and its desires and longings is infinitesimal in comparison to the peace and contentment that can be experienced upon discovering and joining with the Higher Self (God). Therefore, a spiritual aspirant is admonished to control the desires and to curb the restlessness of the heart as they study and practice the teachings of Maat. In so doing the heart is purified from the evil of ignorance and the aspirant is led to deeper and deeper levels of experience culminating in spiritual enlightenment or self-discovery.

About "Know Thyself"

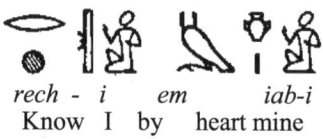

rech - i   em   iab-i
Know I   by   heart mine

"I know what is in my heart" or "I know myself"

The iab or heart is the mind of a person, and an aspect of the ego personality. It is the part of the human personality which contains the desires, feelings, and conscious, subconscious and unconscious thoughts. Thus to know one's heart is the great injunction of spirituality for to know this heart is indeed synonymous with knowing the innermost Self. Like the 42 injunctions of Maat, the teachings contained in the writings of the *Pert Em Heru* are given from the first person singular perspective, but are indeed meant as universal injunctions and therefore may be read:

"Do not lie" instead of "I have not lied" and likewise, "Know thyself" instead of "I know myself."

Further, Ani goes on to say he has gained control of his body and his soul will not be imprisoned. This clearly means that he has gained knowledge of his true, deeper, powerful Self, because he knows himself not

214

as Ani anymore, but as one with the Divine Self, and this gives him the power over his ego personality in the physical world as well as the Netherworld.

There are other passages in Chapter 4, Chap 31, as well as temple inscriptions with the same teaching that Socrates later popularized as "Know Thyself."

CHAPTER 14[265]

THE CHAPTER FOR NOT ALLOWING THE HEART TO BE TAKEN AWAY IN THE NETHERWORLD.

1. Asar _____ says: Hail you who take away hearts from people in the Netherworld and transform them in accordance with their actions while they were alive.

2. Offerings, prostrations and homage have been done to you, Hail to you, who are lords of eternity, possessors of forever, do not carry off the heart of Asar _____.

3. Do not cause to come into being any words, which may be harmful against it because that heart belongs to Asar _____.

4. Asar says: "I live upon righteousness,[266] I exist in it. I am Heru, who is pure of heart within a pure body."

5. This kind of heart belongs to one who is great of names and mighty of words which control Asar_____'s body. The heart obeys the command of Asar_____ and goes to the body and controls its organs and limbs.[267]

6. Pleasing is this heart to the gods and goddesses. Righteous is Asar _____ and being so has allowed Asar_____ to gain control over it. Asar _____ has gained power over his (or her) own members. The heart obeys Asar _____ and it rules over the body in the Netherworld.

7. Asar_____ is spiritually victorious, having attained hetep[268] in Amentet, the beautiful place in the horizon of eternity.

8. May I abide in the body of my father, Geb,[269] and my mother Nut.[270]

---

[265]Based on the Papyrus of Ani and Papyrus at Turin. Generally referred to as chapter 3.

[266]Maat.

[267] This passage relates to the idea that the higher, righteous Self (Higher Self) is controlling the body as opposed to the unrighteous ego self (lower self).

[268]Supreme Peace-contentment and fulfillment of spiritual enlightenment.

[269]Geb is the father of Asar, Aset, Set and Nebethet. See *the Ausarian Resurrection, The Ancient Egyptian Bible* by Dr. Muata Ashby.

[270]Nut is the mother of Asar, Aset, Set and Nebethet. See *the Ausarian Resurrection, The Ancient Egyptian Bible* by Dr. Muata Ashby.

GLOSS ON CHAPTER 14: ITS MEANING AND MYSTICAL SIGNIFICANCE

Ab (Purification of the heart)
The symbol of the heart is a clay vessel.

How is the heart taken away from a person? Every day the heart of every human being on earth is taken away from them and they accept this willingly. The heart is the mind, and the mind is consciousness of self. When you go to sleep every day, the consciousness of your waking self is taken away. This is a kind of forgetfulness wherein all the situations of life, good or bad, fade away for a time. Upon waking one remembers the situations of life. People are quick to remember their desires, but also quick to forget the unpleasant aspects of life, and in so doing, they are bound to make the same mistakes again and again. Firstly, forgetting that the world is more toil than fun reinforces the illusion that there is some abiding happiness somewhere in the world. Through this ignorance, people are unwittingly leading themselves to the same types of adversity and frustration they are trying to avoid in life, and ultimately they must reincarnate because they have not been able to remember the Self. This predicament, that is, being caught up in a world of illusion and being fed situations (fate) against one's will, is what the *Prt M Hru* terms "eating excrement" Chapter 25: *Evil doubly it is. Detestable, I do not eat excrement; I do not eat it! It is abominable to my Ka. It does not go into my body. I live in accordance with the knowledge of the gods and goddesses and the glorious spirit beings. I live and am empowered through their bread.*[271] *Powerful am I by eating it. Under the hair,*[272] *within Hetheru, my Lady, I make a great offering. I make bread in the city of Djedu*[273] *and oblations in the city of Anu.* The tendency towards satisfying one's desires and away from one's dislikes is an agitating mental movement that reinforces the ego consciousness, and thereby, the forgetfulness of what is truly important and worthwhile in life, virtue and spirituality. Thus, there is another more subtle forgetfulness that persists in worldly living. It is the forgetfulness of the Higher Self. However, at the time of death one does not come back to the same body.

King Djehutimes (Thuthmose) III called the Heart:

" A guide in my affairs...
the Conscience or HEART of a Human is his and her own GOD."

The deeper level of the mind is in contact with the soul, which is itself one with the Spirit of God. This soul is the aspect of a human being through which divine wisdom can be transmitted directly to a person if their mind is not cluttered with egoistic impressions and agitation. When the mind is calm, then it is possible to commune with the Divine directly through meditation. The path to calming the mind is through virtue, Maat.

What happens to the mind when a person dies? What happens to their identity, their self-consciousness? If the mind is unenlightened, certain aspects of the mind disintegrate while others linger and impel the soul to heavenly or hellish experiences in the Astral plane, and later on to reincarnation. The mind is the aspect of a human being that recalls one's identity and history. A person remembers their life based on the mental process. However, at the time of death as well as at the time of falling asleep, the waking identity is lost and the weakness of the mind allows the deep-rooted impressions in the mind to weave (Kemetic term *Mehenit*) a new identity in the dream world. This new identity is accepted as real, while the dream is happening, but at the time of waking up, this identity is dissolved and one once again recalls the waking identity, none of these identities are abiding.

---

[271] This is an allusion to divine sustenance, in some ways similar to the Christian eucharist bread. It is a metaphor referring to the divine light upon which spirit beings are sustained. When a human being consumes this divine food they too become Akhu (glorious spirit beings). This food is devotion to God, righteous living and wisdom about one's divine nature (i.e. to Know oneself).
[272] Hair is a metaphor for tree branches; mystically it relates to the Tree of Life which is the body of the goddess, from which she imparts sustenance and nourishment (physical and spiritual).
[273] Where the pillar of Asar is found, i.e. establishment of the spiritual aspirant in the Self-God.

The Ab or mind of a person constitutes all of the thoughts, desires and inclinations of that person's experience. The Kemetic symbol for the mind is a small pot, a container that holds the Ari or impressions of previous actions, which were experienced by that person. These impressions do not fade away at the time of death. They are like subtle seeds that remain and impel the personality to pursue other actions in the future.

The objective of the spiritual disciplines is to discover that identity which cannot be lost or taken away. This is the true identity of a human being, the identity as the Self behind all the transient identities. How is this abiding identity discovered? Verse 4 has this answer, by living upon and in righteousness (Maat), acting as Heru in one's day to day life and purifying the body and mind.

Living by Maat means leading a virtuous life of peace and nonviolence, seeing oneself as the instrument for God's work on earth, developing the feeling of one's actions as being offerings to the Divine, that should be done with a spirit of giving one's best work to God. Living by Maat also means refraining from engaging in negative thoughts, words or deeds. Those who live by these rules eradicate the egoism and thereby attain purity of heart.

Purity of heart means that the egoistic tendencies (anger, hatred, resentment, worry, anxiety, greed, lust, envy, jealousy, ignorance, etc.) of the mind have been cleansed, and therefore no longer weaken the mind, causing it to become deluded about life, or fearful of death, or ignorant as to the true nature of the Self. This achievement allows great will to develop in such a mind, and the soul thereby gains control over that mind as well as the body, since it is the mind that controls the actions of the body. This is called *Maakheru Khat*, victory over the body, i.e. the lower nature. It is an attainment that also means experiencing *Hetep*, Supreme Peace, due to the harmonizing of the opposites, the Higher (Soul) and lower (body). These attainments in themselves mean experiencing the beautiful Amentet. They are one and the same.

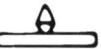

CHAPTER 15[274]

WORDS FOR NOT HAVING ONE'S HEART REPUDIATE ONE IN THE NETHERWORLD

Plate 37: Vignette for Chapter 15, Auf-Ankh, the initiate propitiates to the heart while adoring the four sons of Heru.

1. Heart mine! Of mother mine - Heart mine! Of mother mine!

2. My heart, which leads my existence, my director on earth in the capacity of witness concerning me in the great judgment in the presence of the Lord of the trial. Do not say concerning me: "See this person has done wrong concerning truth and righteousness." I declare, as I have done on earth, may it be done to me[275] in the presence of the Great God, who is the Lord of Amenta.

3. Homage to thee, heart mine, leader mine! Homage to thee, my inner organs and heart! Homage to you, gods and goddesses who oversee the balance,[276] august by your powers and your words of goodness to Ra, the Divine Self. May you cause prosperity for me before Nehebkau.[277] Behold thee him, joined he the earth in the inner part great, having been buried upon the earth but not dead in Amenta, but as a glorious being within it.

---

[274] Usually referred to as Chapter 27.

[275] This teaching of the *Pert M Heru* appears later in Christianity: **Golden Rule,** saying of JESUS, Luke 6:31 "As ye would that men should do to you, do ye also to them likewise."

[276] Judgment of souls.

[277] Serpent God: "He who harnesses the spirits." Benevolent god, male aspect of the Serpent Power (known as Kundalini in India) who protects the spiritual aspirant on earth as well as in the Netherworld (Astral Plane) See the book: *The Serpent Power* by Dr. Muata Ashby.

GLOSS ON CHAPTER 15: ITS MEANING AND MYSTICAL SIGNIFICANCE

This chapter is important because it elaborates on the teaching of Ari (karma). Ari is the sum total of the effect of one's actions. For example, if a person acts out of greed and seeks to satisfy their greedy urges, these actions set up impressions in the unconscious mind which become lodged there as seeds. They are not specific memories. They are more like urges or deep-seeded feelings. Whenever a person has the opportunity to pursue their greedy desires, these impressions will sprout into thoughts which will push the person to indulge in seeking to fulfill their desires. These will, in effect, take over or steal away a person's heart and lead them down the path of unrighteousness and egoism. The world is constantly putting people into situations where they are tested as to their virtuous qualities. Wealth is one of the strongest temptations. Many times people who were previously law abiding and generally decent become avaricious and greedy when they see an opportunity to gain wealth. This is of course a factor of spiritual ignorance. They have not learned that true happiness and wealth comes from the spirit, and not from money or material objects.

Thus, the judgment of the soul is how virtuous a life a person can live. The greater judgment occurs at the time of the death of the body because that is the time when the soul's own accumulated impressions lead it either to the realm of enlightenment or to reincarnation. This is the way in which the heart leads itself to its own fate. Therefore, a spiritual aspirant should exert great care to take in positive impressions and to eradicate the negative impressions in their mind. The positive impressions can be promoted by the study of the teachings such as the *Pert Em Heru* and other Yogic scriptures. The negative impressions can be purged by making sure that the present and future actions in life are virtuous, and that no negative memories or thoughts based on previous negative actions will be allowed. This means that one's thoughts and actions should be based on truth, justice, righteousness, etc. They should be based on what is correct rather than on what the ego desires. For example, if you know that it is wrong to overeat, then you need to exert your will to stop when you have nourished the body sufficiently. You should not continue to eat because you are enjoying the pleasure of the palate. Otherwise you will build up impressions of pleasure seeking and you will also cause the body to come out of its natural balance. Negative impressions are ego impressions, what the body and the mind with its egoistic feelings desire in the form of pleasures of the senses and sentimental concepts. Positive impressions come when you do not seek to go beyond the boundaries of necessity. Pleasure may be experienced as part of life just as pain may be experienced. Both of these are natural components of human life and Creation ordains them. However, when a person begins to hate discomfort and seek pleasure, this leads a person to be constantly distracted and restless. There is no situation in the world which is completely ideal, yet people constantly seek pleasure and to eradicate pain. This pursuit causes impressions of agitation wherein the mind is constantly in motion. Thus, the seeds of negative impressions constantly impel a person to egoistic actions in the world and consequently to lose control of the real means to achieve abiding happiness, inner peace and contentment.

Asar Ani declares emphatically that he has gained control over his heart, that he is the lord and master of it. Mastery of the heart signifies gaining control over the egoistic desires, expectations and selfishness of the mind. Self-mastery means being in control of one's emotions and being able to control the temper. It also means having the ability to concentrate and the will power to do what is right even when it is not what the ego wants. The control over the mind is what allows a person to *command* that the cosmic forces of the universe (neteru-the gods and goddesses) do their bidding. A person who has gained self-mastery can demand any duty or sacrifice from his or her mind and not be wavering between what their personal desires are and what righteousness dictates.

Such a person cannot be caught up in the illusions of the mind or in expectations of happiness from the world. He or she knows that true happiness comes when a person acts in accordance with truth, justice, righteousness and peace. Therefore, a self-mastered person does not depend on or look to material objects or worldly situations as sources for their happiness or fulfillment. Thus, they become masters over the objects. An ordinary person who is running after objects is in reality enslaved to them since the objects are their reason for living. The ignorant person is always running after the objects while the Sage is always serene in the presence or absence of objects. Therefore, the Sage's mind is always clear, peaceful and flowing with ideas to accomplish the most fantastic tasks without desiring, coveting or owning anything.

CHAPTER 16[278]

WORDS FOR NOT GOING INTO THE CHOPPING BLOCK

Plate 38: Vignette from Chapter 16- the initiate stands next to a chopping block.

1. These Divine words are to be said by Asar _____ :

2. It is my vertebrae[279] tied[280] up in my spine in heaven, guarded on earth by Ra. My spine was granted on the day of firming up as concerning any unrighteousness upon my legs on the day on the road of cutting hair.

3. It is bound, my spine, by Set. The company of gods and goddesses are in control of that. Strife will not come into being. Make me powerful by means of the slyer fathers. I have acquired power over the two lands.[281] Tied up is the vertebra by goddess Nut, seeing in the first time, seeing Maat. The gods and goddesses were not yet born into physical forms.
4. I am of Divine Birth! I am the heir of the great gods and goddesses, Asar _____ who is maak-heru.

---

[278] Generally referred to as Chapter 50.

[279] The vertebrae refers to the spine, the structure which sustains the physical body and allows human life to thrive. It also refers mystically to the Serpent Power or Kundalini Life Force energy which courses through the subtle spine and leads to spiritual enlightenment. See the book *Serpent Power* by Muata Ashby.

[280] Firmed up, strengthened.

[281] Upper and Lower Egypt together symbolizes holistic rule on the physical plane and whole consciousness (above and below) or spiritual enlightenment.

GLOSS ON CHAPTER 16: ITS MEANING AND MYSTICAL SIGNIFICANCE

This Chapter treats a very important subject in Kemetic Philosophy, the teaching related to the spine and spiritual evolution. In Kemetic Mysticism, the spine is important for two reasons. First, it is the means by which the physical personality is able to carry out actions in life. The human personality cannot live an effective life without a healthy spine. If a severe enough spinal cord injury occurs, the personality is effectively incapacitated, powerless and impotent. Therefore, care of the spine is important in order to have a fruitful life and a basis for spiritual practice.

Figure 87: The Kemetic Symbol of the spine.

Secondly, the subtle spiritual spine is the part of the personality wherein the Ka connects to the physical body. This is also the site where the Sekhem (Life Force) resides and where, if cultivated, it can rise to the point between the eyebrows and elevate consciousness. The body of Asar was mutilated in the Asarian Resurrection myth and likewise the personality of the initiate has also been mutilated by Set, their own egoism, which has caused their true identity, as being one with God, to be lost among the varied thoughts, desires and ignorance of the mind and unconscious impressions.

The binding up, firming up or tying up of the spine means its strengthening (physically) as well as the cultivation of the inner Life Force, the Serpent Power.[282] It should be understood here that while there are several special practices and disciplines to cultivate the Life Force, virtuous living, the practice of Maat, is a safe, gradual and effective means to do this also, and thus, the reference to Maat in verse three. As one lives in righteousness, the Serpent Power rises automatically to the higher energy centers and ultimately leads one to spiritual enlightenment.

When this firming up process occurs, there is no longer a danger of going to any chopping block, (i.e. the loss of consciousness, death, etc.). Rather, one becomes powerful enough to resist the onslaught of worldly ignorance, which is the chopping block to which most ordinary people go, willingly, like lambs in a slaughterhouse. Rather, there is a divine realization, *I am of Divine Birth! I am the heir of the great gods and goddesses,* which allows the aspirant to transcend all adversities and dangers in all planes of existence. For only those who identify with their body as being their identity can be susceptible to the dangers and adversities that can befall it at any moment. Those who have discovered their Divine lineage or ancestry are free from any such afflictions or misfortunes. Therefore, spiritual enlightenment has many practical benefits, undisturbed, inviolable peace on earth and abiding bliss in the worlds beyond.

---

[282] See the book *Serpent Power* by Muata Ashby.

CHAPTER 17[283]

AN APPEAL FOR NOT REINCARNATING AS A HUMAN BEING AGAIN

1.   Disgusting is this land of Abtet (the east), the going to the dwelling. Nothing will be done to me that is considered disgusting by the gods and goddesses because I am! I pass through, pure within, through the birthing place.

2.   Neberdjer granted to me his own glory on the day that of **unity of the two lands** [284] in the presence of the Lord of Things. As to the knowledge of these words, if they are yours as a glorified spirit, a perfected soul, you will be in Neterkhert.

GLOSS ON CHAPTER 17: ITS MEANING AND MYSTICAL SIGNIFICANCE

The Hymn to Amun-Ra

"Amun-Ra who first was king,
The god of earliest time,
The vizier of the poor.
He does not take bribes from the guilty,
He does not speak to the witness,
He does not look at him who promises,
Amun judges the land with his fingers.
He speaks to the heart,
He judges the guilty,
He assigns him to the East,
The righteous to the West."

This Chapter is important, first because it establishes the Kemetic teaching of reincarnation and secondly, because it establishes the means for avoiding it. The last three lines of the hymn above give an exact interpretation to the Kemetic concept of reincarnation which is being referred to in this chapter. Reincarnation is the repeated coming back of the soul, to experience existence as an individual human being over and over again. In this chapter of the *Prt M Hru*, reincarnation is described as a movement to the east. This is because all births follow the movement of the sun, which rises in the east and thereby creates the new day, and its rebirth allows all life to live again for another day. So moving to the east means rebirth while moving to the west, where the sun sets and ends the day, means moving towards the final resting place, the supreme abode and ultimate destiny of enlightened souls, which ends all future rebirths. This also means that the person going to the west has united {him/her} self with Asar. This is the Smai Tawi movement of enlightenment. This is the goal of Egyptian Yoga.

Uhem ankh – The hieroglyphic symbols meaning, "To Live again" - Reincarnation

The Ancient Egyptian word "Meskhent" is based on the word "Mesken." Mesken means birthing place. Thus, Meskhent is the goddess (cosmic force) which presides over the Mesken of newborn souls. She makes a person's desires and unconscious inclinations, their ari (karma), effective.

The term "embodied soul" needs to be understood correctly first. As an advanced aspirant, you need to realize that the soul is never in the body. This is a term used to help the beginning aspirant. The soul is

---

[283] Generally referred to as chapter 176
[284] Smai Tawi (Egyptian Yoga).

actually the Self, which has come to see itself (through ignorance-forgetfulness-dullness of mind), as a separate individual being. In order to sustain that illusory reality, the individualized soul uses energy (Sekhem, Prana, Chi, life force energy, etc.). It is actually the same kind of energy which is used to sustain a dream when you sleep at night. But as you know, you must at some time wake up from the dream. All thought has energy associated with it. You think and will to exist as an individual human being, therefore the energy of that thought (Life Force Energy) sustains that reality for a while. When the soul no longer wishes to continue with that thought, the energy is withdrawn from that particular individualized existence and the soul focuses on another idea, another personality and thus experiences a new dream (reincarnation into a new lifetime). This is called reincarnation. Actually the soul never entered the body, so it can never leave what it never entered. Incarnation is only a mental experience and not a reality. The soul never goes into any body; it is always transcendental and free. Caught only by its own idea of individuality, it is subject to the law that affects individualized existence (ari or karma). When a person discovers their true identity, they are free from all limitation (karma), and thus the energy that comes with the idea or reality of freedom is vast. They can do wondrous things, not only on the physical plane, but also beyond.

The details of the process of reincarnation are described as follows. The goddess Meskhent presides over the future birth of an individual, but she represents only the culmination of the process, which has come to be known as "reincarnation" in modern times. In reality it is the individual who determines {his/her} own fate by the actions they perform in life. However, the wisdom of the Ancient Egyptian Sages dictated that the process should be explained in mythological terms to help ordinary people better understand the basic concepts of the philosophy. The process works as follows:

The deities Shai and Rennenet govern an individual's fate or destiny and their fortune. These deities are the hands of the great god Djehuti (he symbolizes the higher intellectual development of a human being), and he inscribes a person's fate once they have faced the scales of Maat, that is, they are judged in reference to their ability to uphold Maat in life. A person's intellectual capacity reflects in their actions. Thus it is fitting for the intellect to judge its own actions. This is an objective judgment which only the individual is responsible for and it occurs at the unconscious level of the mind, beyond any interference from a person's personality or ego consciousness, which is on the surface level of the mind. The gods and goddesses are cosmic forces, which only facilitate the process, but from a mythological and philosophical standpoint, they are concepts for understanding the mystical philosophy of the teaching.

Once the judgment has been rendered, the goddess Meskhent takes over and appoints the person's future family, place of birth, social status, etc. This is not meant as a punishment, but as a process of leading the soul to the appropriate place where they can grow spiritually. If before you died you desired to be a musician, the goddess may send you to a country, family and circumstances where this desire can be pursued. If you were a mugger in a past life, you may end up in a place and situation where you will experience pain and suffering such as you caused others, and this experience will teach you to act righteously in the future, thus improving your future birth. What you do after that is within the purview of your own free will, and your actions in the new lifetime will engender and determine the next, and so on.

This is the process of repeated reincarnations. The objective is to lead oneself, by progressively becoming a more righteous personality each lifetime to increasingly better births, until spiritual aspiration dawns. Then one becomes inclined to seek the company of Sages and Saints, to find a spiritual preceptor who can lead one to self-discovery (Rech-iab). First, a person must become virtuous because this purifies the person's actions and thus, their karmic basis. Negative karma leads to bad situations, and also to mental dullness which makes it difficult if no impossible, to understand the teachings. There is a great deal of mental agitation and suffering. The positive karmic basis promotes birth into the family of spiritually minded people, harmonious surroundings, as well as the company of Sages, but most importantly, clarity of mind (lucidity) to understand the wisdom teachings. If the soul is judged pure in reference to Maat, it will not be led to reincarnation (Kemetic term *Uhem Ankh*), but to the inner shrine where it meets its own Higher Self, i.e. God, Asar. This meeting ends any future possibility of reincarnation. It means becoming one with the Divine Self. It is termed Nehast (Resurrection i.e. the Ausarian Resurrection). This is the only way to break the cycle of reincarnation.

So ari is not destiny, but the accumulated unconscious impressions from desires, thoughts and feelings of the past (in this and previous lives). A person can change their ari by their present actions. The individual is always responsible for their present circumstances by the actions they performed previously, which now has led them to the place they are today, etc. So one's karmic destiny is not set, otherwise people could not change. There would be no point to studying the teachings because they would be destined to suffer or be happy based on some perverse cosmic joke. Life is not like that. God has provided free will, and with it a person can have a glorious life full of wisdom and prosperity, or a life of strife, suffering and frustration based on egoism and egoistic desires. I have detailed this information in the following books: *Egyptian Yoga Vol. 1*, *Egyptian Yoga Vol. 2* and *The Wisdom of Maati*. The original Ancient Egyptian hieroglyphic texts containing this teaching are: *Ru Pert Em Heru* (especially Chapters 17, 125 and 125A), The Ancient Egyptian *Wisdom Texts of Ani* and The Ancient Egyptian *Wisdom Texts of Merikara, Temple of Aset* in Agylkia Island (formally at Philae) and the *Temple of Asar* in Abdu, as well as many other Kemetic texts.

CHAPTER 18[285]

THE CHAPTER OF DISCOVERING THE FIELD OF PEACE

Plate 39: The Seven Arits, each with a watcher, a gatekeeper and a herald from the Book of Am-Duat.

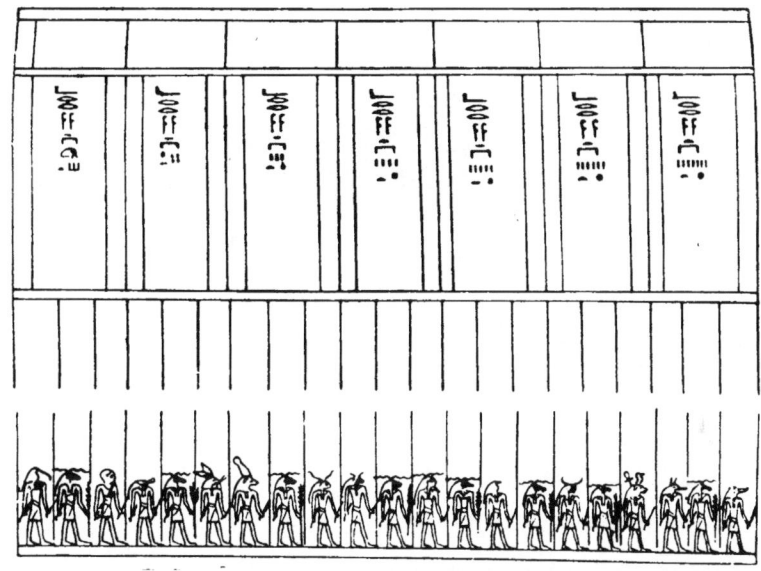

1. Here begin the words of Sekhet Hetep and the words of coming into the light and of going in and coming out through the Neterkhert and arriving in the Sekhet Yaru and then being in peace in the great city, the lady of winds.

2. I am powerful in there[286]; I am a glorious spirit in there; I plough in there also. I reap there. I eat there. I cause myself to drink therein and I make love therein. I do these things as they are done by those people who have physical bodies on earth.

3. Says Asar _____ Maak-heru, I have come here in peace and I make homage to you, divine ones in charge of food. I have come here in peace to receive divine food. Grant me also the ability to see the Great God every day so that I might partake in the offerings made to his Ka daily.

---

[285] Generally referred to as Chapter 110.
[286] The Sekhet Hetep region.

4. Says Asar _____: Set has carried Heru away, looking at what has occurred in the Sekhet Hetep. I have opened the winds upon the divine soul in his day within the Divine Egg. He has released Heru. I have crowned him in the house of Shu; it is the house of stars his. I behold peace in districts his!

5. He has made it through the *Meht* [287] district of the Company of Gods and Goddesses, his elders.

6. He pacifies the Divine Fighters[288] who are the overseers of life. He created what is good. Bringing an offering he makes peace between the Divine Fighters in their respective domains.

7. He cut off the crops[289] from the Combatants. He has brought to an end, strife from their children. He has removed the injury of the souls. I am powerful over it. I know it. I have sailed in its waters so that I may come forth to its towns. I am powerful in my speech, having been granted noble glorious spirit status. Other spirits will not have power over me, again, they shall not have power over me!

Plate 40: Sekhet-Hetepet-with Sekhet Yaru-Divine Boat with steps (lower left register)- lakes, the birthplace of the gods and goddesses-From Papyrus Auf-Ankh

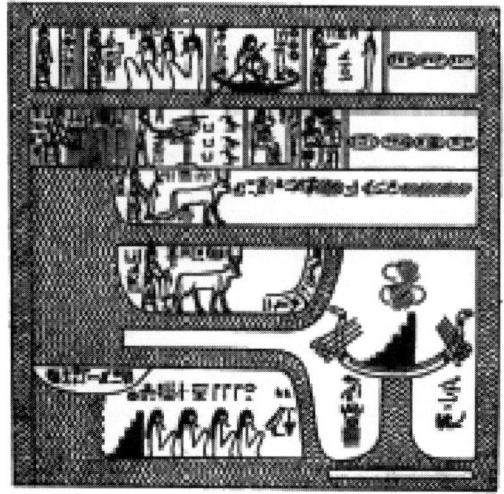

Plate 41: Sekhet-Hetepet-with Sekhet Yaru (lower register)-Divine Boat with seven steps, nine lakes (upper register)- Birthplace of the Gods-Papyrus Nebseni.

---

[287] Abode of the primordial gods and goddesses who were brought into being by Ra.

[288] Heru and Set from the Asarian Resurrection myth. The domain of Heru is the fertile land while the domain of Set is the barren desert.

[289] The spelling for the word used here "iakebu" (crops) is a pun on the word "iakebu" meaning hair. The difference is in the determinative that was used. This reference to hair recalls the Christian Biblical story of Samson and Delilah.

Plate 42: The Duat - Sekhet-Hetepet of Anhai from the *Prt m Hru of Initiate Anhai*.

1- Lady Anhai pays homage to her parents and divine beings (uppermost).
2- Anhai binds wheat into bundles, then praises exalted souls.
3- Anhai is seen ploughing.
4- The Celestial Boat in the form of a headrest containing a shrine with seven steps.

8. I am one who is known by the god Hetep[290]. O Hetep, I have attained this field of yours. I eat in it, I drink in it, I plough in it, I copulate in it. I do not perish in it for my speech is strong in it. I will not be agitated in it for I know the wooden post that is in Hetep. It is called Bqwtt. It was made steadfast with the blood of Shu and held fast by the sweetness of the day [291] when the years are separated.

---

[290] Here now referring to the god of the field of Hetep who is also called Hetep.
[291] Warmth, beauty and Life Force of the shining sun as an emanation of the Divine when he spreads himself and thereby creates time and space.

9. Hidden is my mouth, and silent is mouth his. The words his are secrets. His speech fulfills eternity, taking possession of everlastingness, existing as Hetep Neb Hetep.[292]

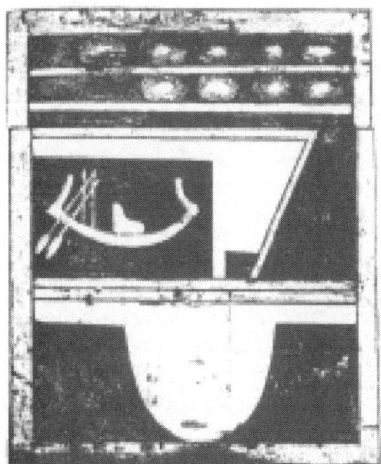

Plate 43: Sekhet-Hetepet-with Sekhet Yaru-Divine Boat-nine lakes-Birthplace of the gods and goddesses-Coffin of Sen.

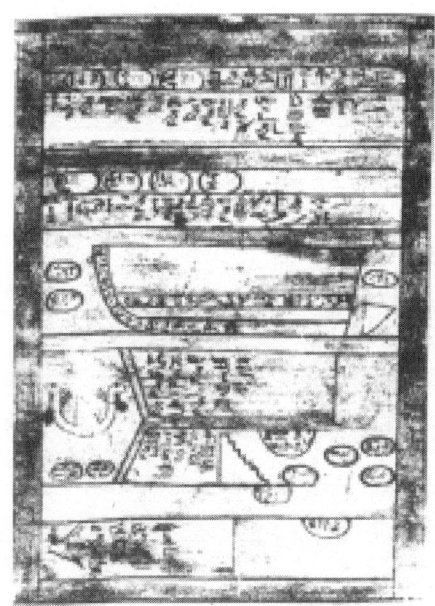

Plate 44: Sekhet-Hetepet-with Sekhet Yaru-Divine Boat-steps-nine lakes-Birthplace of the gods and goddesses-Coffin of Kau-de

---

[292] "Peace all peace"

227

GLOSS ON CHAPTER 18: ITS MEANING AND MYSTICAL SIGNIFICANCE

Architecture of Heaven, Hell and the Transcendental

While there is no Kemetic[293] scripture wherein this concept is discussed fully, it is described in various texts. Foremost among these are Chapter 18 of the various editions of the *Prt m Hru* and the *Book of Am Duat* (Book of What is in the Duat). The Ancient Egyptian concept of creation recognized three realms of existence, *Ta* (Earth), *Pet* (Sky-Heavens) and the *Duat* (Astral Plane), as previously discussed. The Duat is the realm where the nine primordial gods and goddesses of the Ennead were birthed, the residence of astral beings, the lower gods and goddesses as well as the demons and fiends that dwell there alongside the departed souls. It is also within this realm that Asar can be discovered. The Duat is to be understood as a parallel plane of existence in reference to the physical plane of ordinary physical human experience. It is a mental plane which human beings visit temporarily, during the dream state of consciousness or during meditation when experiencing a vision. Unlike a dream, at the time of death, there is no coming back to the waking state, of the previous birth, after death, the unenlightened remain in the "dream world" of their own making, which, while on the astral level of consciousness, is unconscious of the path to discover God. Due to ignorance, they are not able to discover the path to the Divine Self, but only experience situations (hellish or heavenly) based on their level of ignorance, and then return to the physical plane by being born again into another family (reincarnation). The conscious state of mind is a level used by a human being to experience the physical world. In order to experience the Duat or Astral plane consciously, it is necessary to enter into the subconscious levels of mind, which is within one. This is a deeper level of mind. Thus, as one explores the depths of mental existence, one goes gradually moving towards more subtle planes until one reaches the subtlest, God, the Divine Self. Thus, while these realms are understood as levels of Creation, they are also understood as planes of consciousness within the personality of a human being. Therefore, creation is a projection inward. A detailed view of the architecture of existence may look as follows. The physical plane is within the Astral, which is within the Causal, which is in turn within the Spirit (God) from the subtlest essence, the Spirit, to the grossest, the physical world.

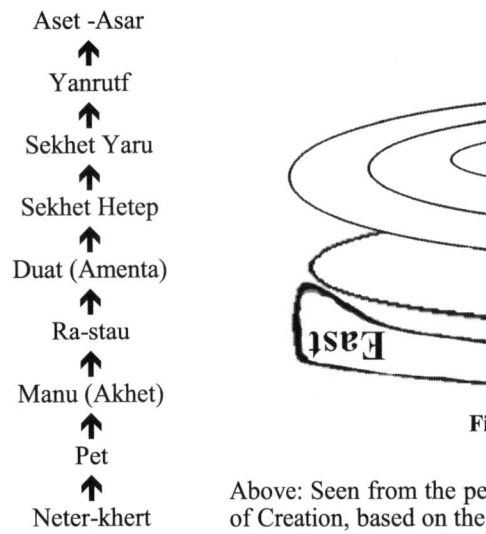

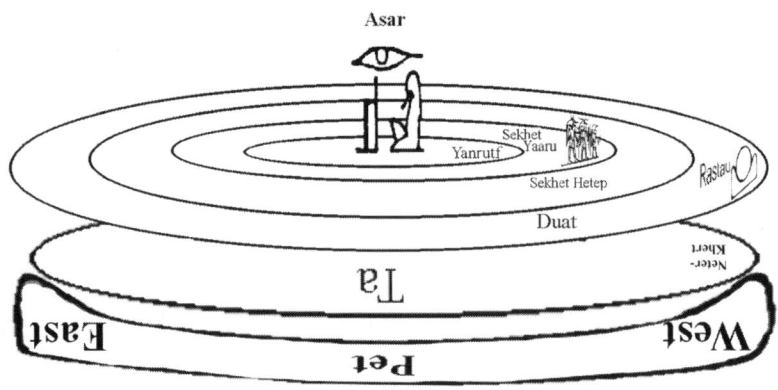

Figure 88: The Architecture of Creation.

Above: Seen from the perspective of the physical world, a three dimensional diagram of Creation, based on the teachings of the *Prt M Hru* (Book of the Dead) and the *Book of Am Duat* (Book of What is in the Duat). It contains the Ancient Egyptian concept of Creation which includes three realms. These are the TA, ⟨⟩ (Earth), Pet, ⟨⟩ (Heaven), and the Duat ⟨⟩ (the Netherworld). Notice that the earth plane is the smallest with the more subtle planes being larger, and that the abode (Aset) of Asar is in the center of Creation. Though depicted as a small object in the center of the

---

[293] Ancient Egyptian

228

Duat, it is actually all-encompassing (Asar, Neberdjer or Pa-Neter) of the other planes. The Physical Plane is a reflection of the Astral Plane, which itself is a reflection of the Sekhet Hetep, which is itself and emanation from God, who dwells in the Sekhet Yaru.

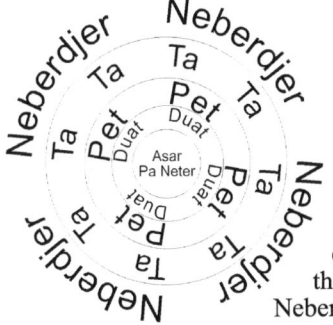

Figure 89: Below-right- Kemetic Concept of Existence when viewed as a movement inward.

The realms of existence within the Spirit: Ta or the Earth Plane, Pet or the Heavenly Plane, Duat or the Astral Plane (Netherworld) and Neberdjer, the All-encompassing Spirit. In this model of Creation the Neter-khert, Ra-stau, Amenta, Sekhet Hetep and Sekhet Yaru are all contained within the "Duat." Yanrutf, within which the transcendental Self is to be found, is the realm of Neberdjer, the Transcendental or Pa-Neter (The Divine Self.

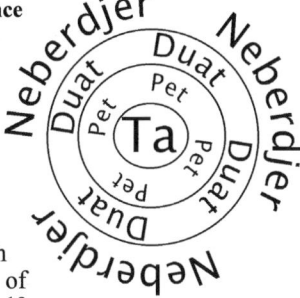

Figure 90: Left- Kemetic Concept of Existence viewed as a movement outward from God (Asar), while still encompassed by God (Neberdjer).

Goddess Nut and the Concept of Heaven

Goddess Nut holds special significance in the architecture of Creation as well as in the success of the spiritual movement of the aspirant. In the Pyramid Texts Utterances 1-6, there are special propitiations (devotional worship) made to goddess Nut, and she thereby recognizes the initiate as her beloved child Asar, gives the initiate the throne of Kemet, symbolizing the Ta (earth-physical) realm, and lifts the initiate up to the heavens to govern as Ra-Herakti (Ra-Heru), the form of Ra as the sustainer of Creation. Goddess Nut lifts the aspirant, now recognized as Asar, to take {his/her} place in the higher Astral Plane as an Akhu (Glorified Spirit), symbolized by the stars in the night sky, which is her own body as well as the reflection of the physical world. Thus, the initiate takes {his/her} rightful place in the Kemet "above." So, it is Nut, who represents expansion in consciousness, through identification with one's Asarian nature and Divine parentage, that elevates the spiritual aspirant into the higher planes of existence to take their rightful place. Nut extends from one end of the horizon to the other. As such, she receives all those going in or out of the Physical plane, including the sun, Ra-Herakti, on his divine journey through the Physical heaven (physical sky) in the Physical world and the Astral Heaven (higher sky located in the Astral world). It is one's Nut aspect that lifts one out from the Neterkhert and into the Duat, for in order to pass through the Akert and into the Ra-stau, one must pass through the limits of the lower heaven, the horizon, which Nut presides over.

The Amenta, The Beautiful West

In the context of Smai Tawi philosophy, the earth is set up in an order set by the sun, which is the sustainer of Creation, from east to west. In the east there is a beginning and in the west, an end, just as in life there is birth and death. The goal of life is to lead a life of righteousness and spiritual enlightenment, so as to enter into the western horizon, through the valley of Manu[294], into the Amentet ("hidden" region in the west), which is the final destination of the soul. The term Amentet (Ament, Amenta) may be understood as a region of the Duat or also as the Duat itself. Those who are enlightened and have come to understand their oneness with Asar, go to rejoin Asar in the *Beautiful West* (the Land of the Setting Sun- Ra) also known as Amenta, and become one with him. When you succeed in cultivating an intuitive intellect (*Saa* or *Sia*) which understands the nature of creation and the oneness of all things in the one "Hidden God," then you will achieve *Saa-Amenti-Ra,* the intelligence or knowledge of the Amenti of Ra, the hidden world. Those who do not achieve this level of spiritual realization are subjected to the various experiences which can occur in the

---

[294] Valley with horizon at the end of the earth-passage to the Duat-related to Aker, the symbol of the two lion divinities. The lion on the right is "Sef," Yesterday, and on the left is Duau, "Tomorrow."

Duat. Notice that the teaching of the Duat incorporates the main characters of the Ancient Egyptian religion, Amun, Ra and Asar, thus showing the uniformity of its understanding and the synchronicity of its teaching throughout Ancient Egypt. When the Ta (Physical Plane) and the Duat (Astral Plane) are placed end to end, the wisdom of the Kemetic conceptualization of the realms of existence can be seen. **Note:** The original drawings presented in this volume as well as those contained in the ancient versions of the *Prt m Hru* are given only as a means to promote understanding of the principles of Kemetic mysticism. They are not to be understood as actual locales, but rather as representations of psychological realms within the mind to assist the mind in finding its path to the Divine Self, the ultimate abode. Further, they should also not be understood as levels as in an ordinary educational system wherein a student must go to kindergarten, elementary, junior high, high school and then college. Rather, they are venues wherein the soul obtains experiences in time and space. The needs of the soul at a given point determine the realms of experience. Thus, the soul may have experiences on earth, and then in the Astral Plane, and then back to the earth again, and if enlightened at that point, jump to the Plane of Asar directly.

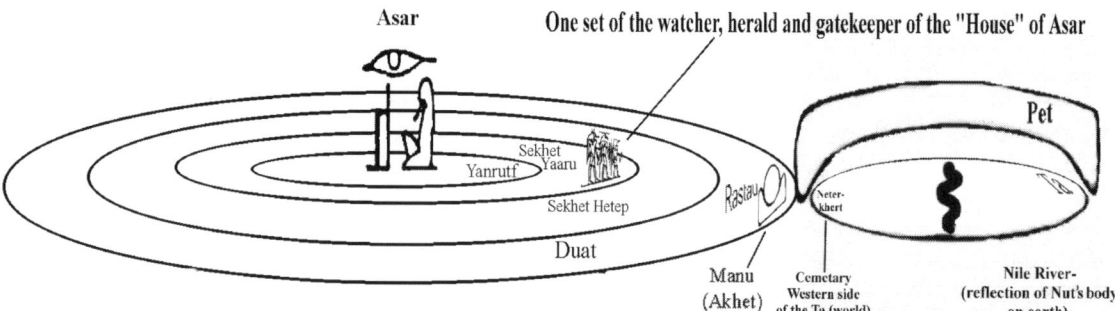

Figure 91: The Architecture of Creation when viewed two dimensionally.

The Sekhet Hetep

According to the Sarcophagus of Seti I, the Duat is the body of the god Asar, which is pictured as a man bending backwards into a circle, touching his toes with his hands. It is said to have fourteen Aats or regions.[295] The ultimate destination of all departed souls is the region of the Duat called *Sekhet Yaru*. Sekhet Yaru means "Field of Plants." It is located within the region called *Sekhet Hetep* or "Field of Peace." Hetep may be translated as peace and/or offerings which make peace. Each region is presided over by a divinity. The vignettes used for the depictions of the Sekhet Hetep come from several papyruses of the *Prt m Hru*. They vary in some ways, according to the particular writer (scribe) and the particular teacher (priest-priestess) who commissioned its illustration. However, the description used here encompasses the common elements of all of them and their mystical significance. In order to accomplish this, several chapters of the Sekhet Hetep from different papyruses[296] and *Coffin Texts*[297] have been combined to produce the translations of Chapter 18, which have been presented in this volume.

According to the *Prt m Hru*, the soul of an unrighteous person is given over to the demons for torture and suffering. The blessed (followers of Maat) are allowed to pass into the Sekhet Hetep, the kingdom of Asar. The Sekhet Hetep is a realm which resembles the physical world, in that the soul experiences life situations similar to those on earth, much like a dream world. These important teachings reveal that the experiences of a human being are not only confined to the field of the earth, but also occur in other fields or planes of existence as well. The difference between a dream and death is that after the dream, a person wakes up, but the waking up out of the dream is merely changing the focus of consciousness to a "different" field rather than to an abiding reality. In death one wakes up not to the physical existence, but to an astral existence. For those who are enlightened, there is no waking up, sleeping, astral experiences, or reincarnating into the

---

[295] This is a mystical teaching that the fourteen waning and waxing phases of the moon represents in the ritual of the Asarian mysteries.

[296] Papyrus of Any, Papyrus of Kerquny, Papyrus of Yauf Ankh, Papyrus of Nebseni.

[297] Coffin of Sen, Coffin of Kau-tep

physical world, because they have discovered their nature as one with the Divine Self. In this sense, everything emanates from the Supreme Divinity and all fields are to be viewed as relative realities in reference to the absolute reality, i.e. God. Just as in a dream, these experiences of the relative fields may be pleasant or uncomfortable in accordance with the workings of the ari or karma of the individual, just as in life some days are happy while others are frustrating.

Another important point, implied in the teachings of the ancient texts related to the Sekhet Hetep, is the understanding that the portrayal of the activities which one does in the Sekhet Hetep were based on the way of life as it was experienced in ancient times, and therefore, the depictions in the scriptures related to the Sekhet Hetep reflect those times. However, while the activities of modern life may be different in some ways, the principles of the experiences remain the same. This realm is a plane in which people can have various experiences, some being like those of the previous physical life. One may experience joyous or hellish conditions in accordance with one's character and previous life's actions. However, these experiences, like physical life experiences, are transitory. Like the Physical Plane, it is also a relative plane of existence and therefore, there is no abiding residence there. One must eventually move on if one is to discover the Divine Self. While the concept of the Sekhet Hetep, the existence of an Astral Plane, does apply in our times, the activities presented in the ancient vignettes would not. Rather, they would be based on life in present times. A person living in the twenty first century might be dealing with cellular phones, televisions, working at a computer store, etc., and these would be the activities experienced by that person in the Astral Plane. So therefore, it is not critical for our study to spend time examining the specific activities that apply to a different era, but rather we should explore and be well aquatinted with the principles of the journey of the soul through the various layers of creation (states of consciousness).

The Sekhet Yaru

More advanced souls traverse to the Sekhet Yaru. This is the paradise for the worshipers of Asar, also known as the "House of Asar." It is the realm of heavenly enjoyments. All creation is a manifestation of the spirit in a sevenfold manner. The Sekhet Yaru is composed of seven sections known as *Arits* or "Mansions." They may be thought of as rooms within rooms or dimensions within dimensions or planes of existence within successively higher planes of existence. They relate to the seven energy centers of the subtle body of each individual human being as well as the seven Hetheru Cows, which are sired by Asar. Thus, the Spirit (Asar) engenders the seven aspects of Creation (the cows).

Each Arit has a gate, and each gate has three attendants, a watcher, a herald and a gatekeeper. As an aspiring soul approaches the gate, the watcher takes notice, the herald announces that person's name and if the person knows the higher mystical truth, the gatekeeper allows entry. This teaching degraded in later times to the point where people began to think that by simply memorizing the names of the attendants, they would be allowed access. Rather, one must know the higher mystical truth which unites one with the dweller within the abode of the house, that is, one must know and be ready to experience one's identity with Asar.

Figure 92: The watcher, herald and gatekeeper.

Thus, throughout our study we have discovered the numbers 1, 3, 7, 14, 21 and 42. These numbers are important to the understanding of the abode of Asar. They include the number of entrances to the house, which are seven, the number of Aats or regions of the Duat, which are fourteen, and the number of principles to be transcended in order to gain entry at any entrance, three. The number 42 is a multiple of 7, and the number of precepts of Maat, as well as the body parts of Asar and the nomes (original cities of Ancient

231

Egypt). The supreme abode being entered into is the One, singular, supreme and transcendental essence, Asar himself. Asar is the singular divinity, the one, expressing as the seven openings, each of which manifest through three modes or a trinity or triad of existence. In total, there are seven trinities to be transcended because there are three personalities at each gate of the seven entrances, totaling 21 principles. However, this need not be a daunting task since all that is necessary is to understand the principle of the trinity itself. When this is accomplished, all trinities are transcended easily. This trinity may be likened to the teaching that is derived from the Kemetic teaching related to *Neberdjer: Amun-Ra-Ptah,* that is, the Absolute who manifests as the seer, the instrument of seeing and that which is seen.

The Watcher is that aspect which sees (seer) and takes notice, the witness. The Herald is the instrument of acknowledging what has been seen. The Gatekeeper is the element which is seen, and which needs to be satisfied that the aspirant is worthy of gaining entry. The Gatekeeper receives information from the Watcher, who takes notice of those approaching, and then, depending on the determination of the Herald who announces whether or not the person whom the Watcher has seen is authorized (worthy) to enter or not, takes the appropriate action. Each aspect of the trinity (Watcher, Herald and Gatekeeper) should be seen not as independent personalities, but as aspects of one, having the sense of sight, speech and organs of action (hands to open the gate). Knowing the truth about the singular being whose gate they are protecting, allows or legitimizes one to gain entry into the house. It is like when you go to the mansion of an important person, if you tell the guard that you personally know the person who lives there, once this is verified, you will be allowed entry without obstruction. Thus, by uniting the trinity into its underlying basic singularity, one enters into the abode of Asar, who is beyond the trinity.

Along with the knowledge of the trinities, a spiritual aspirant must know the principles inherent in each gate for they allude to the psycho-spiritual energy system known as the *Serpent Power* [298]. Each center is a pathway to the inner self that needs to be discovered, purified, explored and finally, transcended. Each pathway symbolizes certain aspects of the personality that must be transcended and certain aspects of the personality that must be cultivated.

In order to promote spiritual evolution, a spiritual aspirant needs to cultivate virtue in life, and it is for this purpose that the injunctions of Maat Philosophy were created by the Ancient Egyptian Sages. These injunctions are forty-two in number, exactly twice as many as the total number of personalities in each gate of the house of Asar (21). As a human being lives in accordance with Maat, they automatically purify their heart, thereby enabling them to see a glorious and magnanimous aspect of life that is not open to unrighteous human beings. This purifying and opening of the heart, that is, transcending lower psychological tendencies of the personality through virtuous living, is the prerequisite for being able to understand and transcend creation (the elements of physical existence) and the trinity (ego-delusion due to ignorance, passion and vice).

Having attained the ability to exist in the Sekhet Hetep is likened to living in the city of the king or the capital of the country. This locale is what ordinary orthodox religions refer to as heaven. In the city one can live an ordinary life, have a family, job, etc. However, the objective is to discover the king. Thus, in order to get closer to Asar, one must gain entry into the Aset (abode) of Asar, which is in the Yanrutf section or room of the Sekhtet Yaru (House of Asar). This is like living in the house of the king or president. In the house or palace of the king, one cannot live as ordinary people of the city. One is constantly reminded of the king and one's life is constantly in service to the king. Further still, the Yanrutf is like going to the throne room of Asar and putting on his clothes and looking like him, and there are no other thoughts but of the king. Now with the royal garb and acting like the king, sitting on the Aset (throne) of the Asar, one becomes the king. This is taking one's position in the Djed Pillar of Asar, that is, becoming established in the Divine Self. This process of establishment in the Divine is otherwise described in the Sekhet Hetep Chapter of the *Prt m Hru* as the discovery of the *Dept UnNefer,* boats with the throne of Asar. Some Sekhet Hetep illustrations have two boats, each having a throne. One boat is the Boat of UnNefer. Sometimes it is depicted with a snake headed prow and stern and a flight of seven steps, symbolizing the seven entrances to the abode of Asar, the seven energy centers of the psycho-spiritual body (Serpent Power-Kundalini energy), and the seven aspects of Creation (symbolized by the seven Hetheru cows). The other boat is the *Dept Ra,* the Boat of Ra. In some papyruses, the boats as well as the entire Sekhet Hetep are described in different ways. In some, only one

---

[298] See the book **Serpent Power** by Muata Ashby.

boat is depicted. However, what one must look for in determining the intent of the scripture is its overall consistency with previous scriptures, as well as its mystical mission. In this way, errors or omission of particular papyruses need not impede the overall understanding of the text and its spiritual meaning.

In Kemetic mystical philosophy, the Netherworld is associated with the afterlife state, and also with the Sleep and Dream states. This is shown through the various Ancient Kemetic parable teachings such as those related to Sa-Asar. Sa-Asar was a Sage who incarnated to give spiritual teachings. The following is the beginning section of the parable of *Sa-Asar*. The concluding portion will be presented in the gloss to Chapter 33. It relates that:

> *A man and a woman wanted to have a child, but could not conceive so the woman, named Mehusekhe, went to a temple to sleep there in the hope that a god or goddess would come to her and tell her what to do. A spirit came to her in a dream and told her to go to the place where her husband was, and to eat from a melon vine and embrace her husband in love and she would then conceive a child. She became pregnant and her husband, Setna, was very happy. In a dream, the spirit came to Setna and told him the child would be a boy and he is to be named "Sa-Asar," and that he will do great wonders in the land of Egypt.*

This parable shows the mystical philosophy related to the link between the dream state of human consciousness and the Astral Plane or Duat (Netherworld) where the gods and goddesses reside. Also, this realm is the medium through which the "living" can communicate and have interaction with the deceased and the divine. Therefore, the understanding that the subconscious levels of the mind are levels of higher consciousness within the human personality that are in contact with a higher plane, referred to as the Duat, was well known in Ancient Egypt, even by the *Rekhit* or "common folk."

Table 10: The States of Consciousness and the States of Matter

States of Consciousness	State of Awareness	Planes of Existence
Waking State	Conscious	Physical Plane
Dream State	Subconscious	Astral Plane
Deep Dreamless-Sleep State	Unconscious	Causal Plane

Table 11: Psychospiritual Centers and their Principles

Center number	Element of Creation to be Transcended	Worldly Principles to be Transcended	Psycho-Spiritual Virtues to be Cultivated
1	Earth	Fear, survival, worry, food dependency	Faith, stability, righteousness
2	Water	Sex desire, passion	Control of Sex urge
3	Fire	Egoistic desire, controlling others and the environment	Selfless Service Surrender to God
4	Air	Attached, sentimental love	Universal love
5	Ether	Evil speech, lies, cursing, talking too much	Silence, introspectiveness, self-discipline
6	Mind	Ignorance	Divine vision
7	(Beyond all elements)	Individuality	Transcendence

Asar, Ra and the Duat

"No one reaches the beneficent West unless their heart is righteous by doing Maat. There is no distinction made between the inferior and the superior person; it only matters that one is found faultless when the balances and the two weights stand before the Lord of Eternity. No one is free from the reckoning. Thoth, a baboon, holds the balances to count each one according to what they have done upon earth."

—Ancient Egyptian Proverb

The realms of existence are personified as neteru deities (See below). Ta is the earth or physical plane. The god of the earth is Geb (A). When Ra emerged from the Nun or Primeval Ocean (Primeval Waters or Pure Consciousness) being pushed up by the god Nu (B), he began a movement through creation which takes him across the sky which is his daughter Nut (C). He has a *Mandet* -day boat (D) and a *Mesektet* -night boat (E). The day boat is used for the journey through the physical heavens and over the physical world (Ta) and the night boat is used for the journey through the Astral Plane (Duat). Nut is said to eat the sundisk (day boat) at dusk and give birth to it every morning. The drawing below shows the daytime journey. The god Geb is leaning on the ground while the goddess Nut stretches across above him. The motion of the boat sustains creation. From this boat hangs certain tow lines which are the privilege and good fortune of every spiritual aspirant who can grab hold, because doing so means being pulled up onto the boat, out of the world (physical and astral planes) and being admitted to the boat which goes on for millions of years, i.e., eternity, to become one with Ra, one with God. The *Prt m Hru* explains that this desired spiritual evolution is made possible by living a life of righteousness and purity.

Figure 93: Ra in his boat, sails over the body of Nut while Shu holds her up and separates her from Geb.

So the Duat is the abode of the gods, goddesses, spirits and souls, and the realm where those who are evil or unrighteous are punished, but it is also where the righteous live in happiness. It is the "other world," the spirit realm. The aspect of the Duat as the realm Ra, as symbolized by the sun, traverses after reaching the western horizon, in other words, the movement of Ra between sunset and sunrise, i.e. at night, led some people to think that the Duat was under the earth, since they saw Ra traverse downward, around the earth and emerged in the east, however, this interpretation is the understanding of the uninitiated masses. The esoteric wisdom about the Duat is that it is the realm of the subconscious and unconscious human mind and at the same time, the realm of Cosmic Consciousness or the mind of God. Both the physical universe and the astral plane, the Duat, are parts of that Cosmic Consciousness.

West **East**

Figure 94: Ra in the Cycle of Eternity
(From the Papyrus of Khonsumes)

Above: Another conceptualization of the Journey of Ra through the Duat. Ra traverses through the body of Nut. From right to left: Nut holds him in an embrace and consumes him in the evening (head face down). Then Ra is renewed by three divinities, the first being named "Living years," then, "Living eternity," then "Forever," then goddess Maat (order, regularity, truth, etc.) and the god Hekau (Words of Power) assist him to be reborn again to create a new day as they adore him.

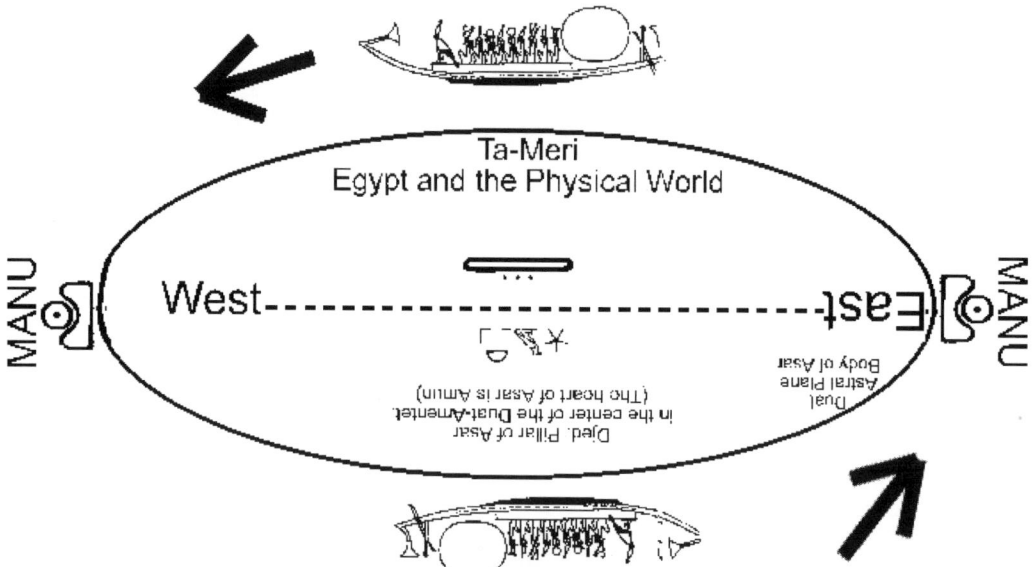

Figure 95: Two-dimensional rendering of the Physical plane and the Astral plane based on the Ancient Egyptian Mystical Teachings.

The physical world is a reflection of the Duat, and the Duat is a subtle projection of the Divine Self, which is sustained by the Divine Self. When the sun ends its journey through the world, it passes through the western horizon. This western Horizon, *Manu,* is the eastern horizon of the Astral world, the Duat, and when the sun reaches the western horizon of the Duat, it reaches the eastern horizon of the physical world once again. When the sun reaches the eastern horizon of the world, this signifies a rebirth, a reincarnation. The same thing applies to human beings. After death they live in the Astral plane for a time. This period is termed heaven or hell in accordance with their actions while on earth. According to the *Prt m Hru,* if they are allowed to mount the boat of Ra due to their righteous life, they avoid going to the east and being reborn in the world again.

236

Figure 96: Asar in his boat.

The figure above depicts Asar sailing over heaven, sustained by four pillar goddesses. On the right are three hawk gods and on the left, three jackal gods performing the Henu praise. Above is the Winged Scarab (Ra-Khepri). Following the boat are the eight primeval gods and goddesses of Creation, and on the far left is the four-headed ram of Amun as well as the ram headed hawk of Amun. Thus, the mythologies of Ra, Amun and Asar are neatly summarized as one whole, containing many aspects.

It is necessary to pass through all of these levels in order to reach the Supreme Abode. For this to be possible, the initiate must possess certain special knowledge about the passageways, as a gatekeeper, watcher and herald guard each passageway. They ask the initiate questions, and if answered correctly, they announce the new arrival and allow passage. As discussed earlier, the special knowledge consists of spiritual wisdom gained from the study of spiritual scriptures blended with meditative experience (the second and third levels of religious practice). This teaching is made plain in Chapter 31 where it is stated: ***I go out through the gate, which is Illumination of the heart.*** Thus, it is illumination of the mind ("enlightenment"), the discovery the hidden realms of existence which are aspects of one's own personality, is the hekau or word of power which opens the door to the House of Asar. This signifies that the whole idea of seven entrances to the abode of Asar are in reality avenues of psycho-spiritual awakening, the movement of opening the mind (heart) and leading it towards spiritual enlightenment. Of course, spiritual studies and meditative experiences are only possible when life is lived according to virtuous principles (Maat). Further, it should be understood that if the higher spiritual secrets are known, it is not necessary to know every specific name of the Arits or the gods and goddesses. In other words, if the names, functions and teachings of the highest gods and goddesses (Ra, Asar, Aset, Heru, Set, Maat, and Djehuti) are known, the lower obstructions cannot hinder the movement of that person.

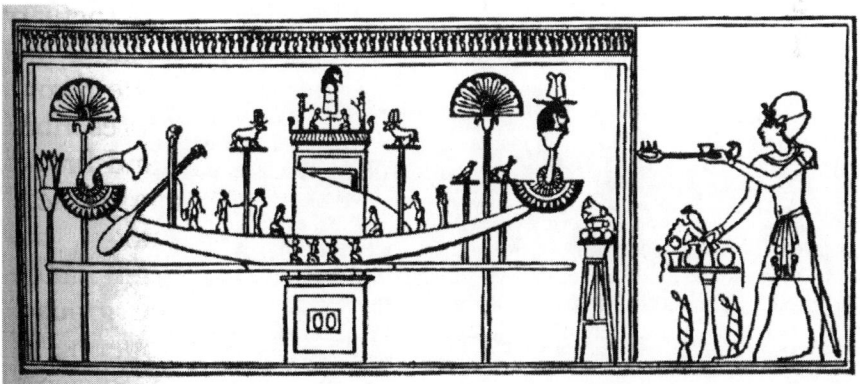

Figure 97: Asar in his Boat. King Seti I, making offerings to him in Abdu, the sacred city of Asar

Figure 98: Nut and Geb and the higher planes of existence.

The figure above depicts another conceptualization of the Netherworld, which is at the same time the body of Nut. At the bottom lies the earth god Geb in the plough (earth) posture. Above him are two Nut goddesses. The lower one symbolizes the lower heaven where the moon traverses, the physical realm. The higher one symbolizes the course of the sun (winged Sundisk) in its Astral journey. This shows a differentiation between the physical heavens and the Astral plane, as well as time and space and Astral time and space, i.e., the concept of different dimensions and levels of consciousness.

Synopsis:

It should be understood that the teachings related to the architecture of Creation are presented to the initiates so they may gain an understanding about the nature of existence. Those souls who are karmicaly directed to have astral experiences after death will do so as described. Those who have progressed to a certain point will move forward after death until they discover Asar or Ra, while those that were unrighteous while on earth will experience hellish conditions as described in the story of Sa-Asar (see the gloss to Chapter 33 for the complete story). Those who are virtuous, but not yet fully enlightened, achieve heavenly existence after death, and being protected by their virtuous karma, in time move through the various sections of the Duat and eventually discover the Divine Self in the form of Asar, Ra or Net. However, those who have attained enlightenment in life, upon the death of the body, will bypass these experiences or move past them without obstruction and go directly to the Divine Self. In reality, since they are already one with the Self, they are already there. In other words, upon becoming an enlightened being, one becomes aware of one's identity with God, and therefore, need not go anywhere after death, for one is already where one needs to be.

In actuality, a human personality exists on all the planes at the same time. A human being is in contact with the Divine (God), the Duat, etc., at all times. However, an unenlightened human being is not aware of this contact and sees {him/her} self as a separate, finite and mortal being. This contact eludes them because of their ignorance, mental agitation, worldly impressions in the unconscious level of mind which block their higher vision of the Higher Self, etc. An enlightened personality is aware of this contact and thereby understands {him/her} self to be one with God, and one with Creation itself. The task of every human being is to discover their deeper essence. This process is called spiritual evolution.

The Khat and Ren (physical body (form) and name), for example, exist on the Physical plane (Ta). The Astral body (Ka) together with the Sekhem (Life Force) and Ab (mind) exist on the Astral plane. The Akhu, Sahu, and Ba reside in the Causal plane. Therefore, in an advanced sense, spiritual enlightenment should not be understood as a journey through planes of existence, but rather, it should be understood as an awakening to the true nature of reality. If one were able to shift one's attention from the physical body and ego identity in the physical world one would immediately discover one's astral identity through the Ka, Sekhem and Ab. Likewise, if one were able to shift one's attention from the astral body and astral identity in the astral world, one would immediately discover one's causal identity through the Akhu, Sahu, and Ba. If one were to pierce through the veil of ignorance which keeps one identifying with one or more of the elements of the personality which operate in the relative planes (Physical, Astral or Causal), then one would immediately discover one's identity with the Divine Self, the subtlest essence within one's very own personality. This process is made possible through the mystical philosophy and the yogic disciplines [study of the wisdom teachings, Devotion to the Divine, Right Action (Maat) and practice of Meditation]. These disciplines allow one to shift one's attention to the other planes of existence and not

be bound only to the ignorance of thinking of oneself as only a physical being. In the diagram above, the Pet realm is actually part of the Physical plane since we are talking about the physical heavens. The astral heavens are part of the Duat or Astral plane.

In reality, the three states of consciousness that ordinary people experience are merely negative reflections of the positive states. Those who have practiced yogic disciplines and mystical philosophy discover the positive states of consciousness, and thus attain spiritual enlightenment. Therefore, the Dreamless Sleep State has its positive counterpart in the Lucid Causal Consciousness state wherein there is awareness of all-encompassing existence, but no thoughts or desires. The Dream State has its counterpart in the Waking (Lucid) Astral Consciousness wherein there is experience of the Astral plane and expanding consciousness. The ordinary Waking State has its opposite or positive in the Transcendental Self or enlightened state. This is the state of consciousness manifested by sages and saints who have attained the state of Maakheru.[299]

Table 12: The States of Consciousness and their relative experience in enlightened and unenlightened human beings.

Resurrection, spiritual Enlightenment-Nehast	Lucid Causal Consciousness	Lucid Astral Consciousness Visions and/or Awareness during the dream	Enlightenment in the Waking Consciousness	← Positive states of consciousness Enlightened
↗ GOD- THE SPIRIT MANIFESTS IN BOTH ENLIGHTENED AND UNENLIGHTENED HUMAN BEINGS ↘	Negative reflection of Lucid Causal Consciousness in the Personality manifests as: ↓↓↓	Negative reflection of Lucid Astral Consciousness in the Personality manifests as: ↓↓↓	Negative reflection of Enlightenment in the Personality manifests as: ↓↓↓	Spiritual Wisdom or Spiritual Ignorance are the cause of Enlightened or unenlightened consciousness Respectively
Dense Dull of heart- Wmet htp ab	Dreamless Deep Sleep without awareness of infinity or eternity	Dreams Without awareness of the fact that one is in a dream	Ignorance of one's true divine nature in the Waking State	← Negative states of consciousness Un- Enlightened

---

[299] For more on the philosophy of mystical psychology, see the book *Egyptian Yoga Vol. 2, The Supreme Wisdom of Enlightenment* by Muata Ashby.

Table 13: The States of Consciousness, the Meditative States and the Planes of Existence Experienced.

Ignorant States of Awareness {Negative} Ignorant- Khemn	Levels of Consciousness And the planes where they are experienced	Enlightened (positive) Meditative State experienced in meditation practice uaa "Meditation"	Aspect of the Personality Used to experience the state of consciousness	Kemetic Planes of existence experienced
Ego Principal - Duality	Transcendental Consciousness (Beyond time and space)	Nehast Resurrection, spiritual Enlightenment-	Khu (Akhu)	Aset Per (Asar)
Deep Dreamless- Sleep State	Unconscious Causal Plane Sekhet Yaru	Sahu-Seh Super-consciousness Ecstacy, religious	Causal Body Ba Sahu Khaibit	↑ Yanrutf ↑ Sekhet Yaru ↑
Dream State	Subconscious Astral Plane Duat- Sekhet Hetep	Ka- Resut Astral Vision Dream - vision	Astral Body Ka Sekhem Ab	Sekhet Hetep ↑ Duat ↑ Amenta ↑
Point between Physical (waking) and Astral (Dream) planes, half-sleep, swoon. Fall asleep, etc.	Intermediate	Manu	Aker- Duality urs - The Headrest	↑ Ra-stau ↑ Akhet
Waking State	Conscious Physical Plane Ta	Mauiu One Pointed Mind "to think, to ponder, to fix attention, concentration"	Physical Body and Name (name and Form) Khat Ren	Neter-khert ↑ Pet ↑ Ta

CHAPTER 19[300]

THE CHAPTER OF THE TREE OF LIFE: BREATHING AIR AND POSSESSING WATER IN THE DUAT

Plate 45: Vignette from Chapter 19- The tree of life is the symbol of the goddess. Through it she nourishes all life and in particular, she provides spiritual strength to the aspirant for success in the spiritual journey.

1. Words to be spoken by Asar _____ maakheru.

2. Hail to you great river[301] in the heavens, in thy name of "Traverser of the heavens"! Grant thee, power over the water to Asar _____ maakheru like Sekhmet[302] who protected Asar against the violence on the night and day of slayings. Lead Asar_____ maakheru to the abode where there is an abundance of water just as you led those other honorable persons who were slain and became a noble, blessed souls, knowing not, they the name of he who led him.

3. Asar_____ maakheru is opening up in Djed[303]. Asar _____ maakheru's nostrils are opening up in Djedu[304] in Hetep[305] the dwelling place in Anu, the house that was constructed by Sesheta[306], on which Knum[307] is standing.

4. If there is a north wind blowing, sit on the south side. If there is a south wind blowing, sit on the north side. If there is a west wind blowing, sit on the east side. If there is an east wind blowing, sit on the west side.

5. Lowering the eyebrows on the nostrils[308], Asar_____ maakheru enters into all places desired and resides therein.

---

[300] The translation for this chapter was based primarily on the Papyrus of Auf-Ankh and the *Papyrus of Ea* and is commonly referred to as #57. It is included here as representative of a genre of teachings found in similar chapters, specifically: Chapter 58: "Breathing Air and Possessing Water in Netherworld (Duat)"; Chapter 59 "Drinking Water in the Netherworld"; Chapter 60 "Another Chapter for the Same Purpose"; Chapter 61 "Another Chapter for the Same Purpose"; Chapter 62 "Another Chapter for the Same Purpose"; Chapter 63 "Drinking Water and Not Drying Up by Fire."

[301] Referring to the celestial Nile. Everything on earth is a reflection of what is above. The Great Pyramid complex in Giza has its counterpart in Orion and the star Sirius, and the nomes also have their counterparts in the star systems above.

[302] Lioness form of the goddess, especially associated with Hetheru (Hathor). She is the wife of the god Ptah, destroyer of demons and unrighteous personalities, purifier of hearts, and consequently, protector of righteous souls.

[303] The Pillar of Asar, metaphysically, the upper psycho-spiritual consciousness centers which awaken when a person becomes enlightened.

[304] The city of the Djed Pillar of Asar.

[305] Supreme Peace.

[306] Goddess of writing and counterpart of Djehuti. She is also the presiding deity over the seven psycho-spiritual consciousness centers of spiritual enlightenment of the Serpent Power, also known as "Kundalini energy" in India. She was also associated with the sacred *Persea Tree* on which the names of the kings were written at the time of coronation. She was the "Recorder of Deeds," "Mistress of Books," and "Reckoner of time." The Persea Tree was associated with the goddess in the feline form, who resided in the city of Anu (Heliopolis of the Greeks) and slew the demon serpent *Apophis,* who was the enemy of Ra and also of all souls.

[307] The god who created human beings on his potter's wheel, "The Fashioner of Men and Women." Also, this word means "union."

[308] This is a classic description used in yoga meditation practice to instruct the aspirant to practice concentration.

In this Chapter, the vignette is of special importance. It shows the goddess Nut in the form of a tree of life. In her form as the ***Tree of Life***, the goddess is the source of food and drink, mystically referred to as "breathing the air," which sustains life. The vignette above comes from the papyrus of Ani and is typical of other papyruses, which acknowledge the nourishing aspect of vegetation as the source of life for human beings. This is one aspect of the mystical teaching of the tree of life in Kemetic spirituality. Asar is the source, the Spirit, which enlivens all things. The goddess, is the conduit through which that life essence is transmitted to human beings. The goddess bestows food and drink to the aspirant. Other subtle implications of this vignette are the references in the text accompanying it to the food and drink as being the "breath" which sustains life, i.e., Life Force energy. Further, the fact that the aspirant obtains these directly from the goddess who is in the tree suggests that the best food is obtained by a direct contact with the goddess, that is, by picking fresh vegetables and fruits from plants directly.

This chapter is also an invocation that the food and drink obtained from the tree may bring strength and power to resist the slaying of the personality. This point was alluded to also in Chapter 16, where the initiate discovers protection from the chopping block. The idea is that this special food of the goddess leads to spiritual strength and enlightenment. It is actually referred to as the air which when breathed allows one to become a blessed Soul, to reside in peace in Anu, the first and foremost city.

The last line in the chapter holds the key to how this divine food is to be obtained. The instruction is given to lower the eyebrows onto the nostrils. This is the classic instruction given to every practitioner of meditation. It means to concentrate on one point, while at the same time watching the breath. This practice is also augmented by the repetition of Hekau (Mantras, Words of Power) as chants. Using the words from this chapter can be an especially powerful means to practice concentration and meditation. If this practice is understood and implemented properly, it will lead to the expansion of consciousness and the opening up of all the secrets of existence, and in so revealing, the meditator discovers {his/her} essence there as the Divine Self.[309]

---

[309] For more details on the art and practice of Kemetic meditation, see the books *Meditation the Ancient Egyptian Path to Enlightenment, The Glorious Light Meditation Technique of Ancient Egypt, The Wisdom of Isis* and *The Serpent Power* by Muata Ashby.

CHAPTER 20[310]

MAKING A RIGHTEOUS APPEAL TO GOD FOR BEING GIVEN SUSTENANCE IN THE NETHERWORLD AND SPIRITUAL ENLIGHTENMENT

Plate 46: Vignette for Chapter 20- The initiate adores Asar Seker. Behind him are the seven Hetheru goddesses and the Divine Bull, Asar.

1.   These words are to be said by Asar _____ in Spiritual Victory.[311]
"Homage to you, my God, in your form as the Sundisk, you who are the Lord, sovereign of Maat.[312] You are that One, Lord of all eternity and Creator of time.

2.   See that I have come to you, my Lord, Ra. I have made the offerings to the Lord of the divine cow goddess, those seven manifestations of the Divine, which are impregnated by the Great Bull, with life essence.

3.   My God, you who sustain the spirits with divine food, which is made up of your very own essence, give my soul the blessing of being with you."

4.   The seven cow goddesses are:

5.   **I**-Dwelling place (house) of the essence of God, Lord Neberdjer (All-encompassing Self).

6.   **I I**-Mistress of the Universe, Dwelling in her Abode

7.   **I I I**-Storm Cloud-One who Blows Wind Keeping the God Aloft

8.   **I I I I**-Beloved one with Red Hair

9.   **I I I I I**-She of Akhmim, whom God Engenders

10.   **I I I I I I**-She who Dominates in the Throat-Her name has Power

11.   **I I I I I I I**-She whose Love is Great-She who Protects in Life-She who is Parti-colored.[313]

12.   The Bull is: The Bull Who is their Husband[314]

13.   This teaching is about Seker-Asar[315] and Ra. Keep this book secret. Do not use imagination or memory when interpreting it. Read it only with the one who taught[316] it to you. Oh goddesses! Oh God! Save the reader of these words from all evils because they are your followers.

14.   If this is done, it means complete freedom, contentment, peace and serenity as well as immortality and unity with God.

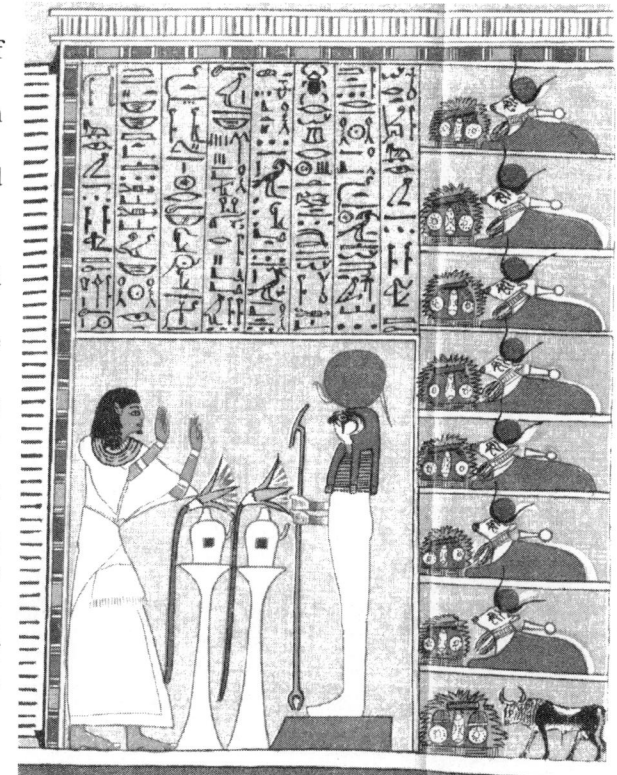

---

[310] Generally referred to as Chapter 148

[311] Maak-heru.

[312] Righteousness, truth, justice, order, etc.

[313] Having parts, sections, or areas colored differently from each other; pied.

[314] The god Asar Seker.

[315] Seker is the form of Asar as King of the Netherworld (Astral Plane experienced in the afterlife).

[316] The spiritual preceptor, guru.

Verse 1-2

In this Chapter there is a special reference to God not as the sundisk, but as manifesting in it. This is a highly advanced recognition of the difference between idol worship and a symbol used as a religious metaphor. There are many people in modern times who believe that the symbols used in their religion are true, and that they represent factual events, places and divine beings. They look at religions such as Hinduism or Kemeticism and see many gods and goddesses and immediately consider this as idol worship. Actually, mystical religions such as the Hindu and Kemetic never apply exclusive residence of the spirit in a particular icon or statue over another. These are always understood as *Bes* or images of the Divine, which manifests as the image as well as everything else. Actually, it is orthodox religion that practices idol worship because in believing that God is found only in one image, excluding others, they are actually worshipping the particular form of the Divine. In so doing, they are limiting their understanding and engendering the seeds of animosity and hatred against other religions, which they come to prejudicially consider as pagan or not real religious practice. By now the reader should have the understanding that true religion is any movement that leads one to spiritual enlightenment. Any movement of mental agitation, limitation and constriction is contrary to authentic religious movement.

Verse 3-5

A special propitiation is made here, that the initiate be given special divine food. This food is composed of the very body of God. It is to be likened to the sun and its rays. As the sun's rays proceed directly from it, imbibing the rays is equal to imbibing the sun itself. Likewise, tasting and ingesting the divine essence means knowing God intimately as the very basic nature of all that is. In other words, when a human being comes to the understanding that the air being breathed and the very food that is consumed is actually inhabited by God, then there is an instantaneous blessing and closeness with the Divine. Thus, the initiate asks that this blessing may continue in perpetuity. This is called supreme devotion to the Divine Self, which leads to the greatest, spiritual enlightenment.

A special reference is also made to the goddess Hetheru in her seven-fold form. Hetheru manifests as the seven cows of creation from which Creation arises. Just as on a farm a single bull can impregnate several cows and bring forth several progeny, these cows are impregnated by the Bull who is the Spirit of the Divine, Asar-Ra. This means that the one Spirit manifests as the multiplicity of Creation through the seven principles of Creation. Therefore, everything that exists in creation is a result of the union of spirit and the seven aspects of Creation which go to form the material universe and everything in it, including animate and inanimate objects, and sentient and non-sentient beings. Thus, everything in the universe occurs in sevens (rainbow colors, seven tones in music, and the seven psycho-spiritual consciousness energy centers-Serpent Power or Kundalini). These seven cows are related in the Kemetic mystical system, to destiny (ari, karma) and they were adopted by the Greek philosophers who related them in the form of the three *Fates*. The Fates, also called Parcae, were the daughters of Night. Clotho, the spinner, personified the thread of life. Lachesis was chance, the element of luck that a man had a right to expect. Atropos was inescapable fate, against which there was no appeal.

Verse 14-15

There is a special injunction within this text. The aspirant is admonished to read and study this text, and not deviate from the teaching that was received from the spiritual preceptor who originally taught it to {him/her}. Many times people like to believe that they can read and understand a spiritual text on their own without the benefit of being initiated into the mystical system. This is a form of subtle ignorance, which may affect even the most intellectual persons. The spiritual teachings are in a way like any other discipline that requires exacting detailed training and practice. You would not expect to use the services of a doctor who learned how to do an operation by just reading about it in a book, or an architect who learned how to design a building by reading about it at a library. If this was the best way to learn, society would not need universities, because people could learn just from books. But it is not so, because books cannot correct a person if they are straying from the correct understanding. Only a living person can do that. In the

same way, mystical spirituality is a highly evolved science of spiritual evolution that needs to be imparted by an authentic spiritual guide. This process is called Initiation. The initiatic way of education is a process through which spiritual knowledge is transferred from teacher to disciple in a long line stretching back in time to the original preceptor. In the Kemetic tradition, it is recognized that God, in the forms of Djehuti and Aset, is that original preceptor who taught the first human beings, and they passed on the wisdom through the Temple system and the wisdom of these spiritual texts.

There is a specific technique, which is prescribed by the scriptures themselves for studying the teachings, proverbs and aphorisms of mystical wisdom. The method is as follows: The spiritual aspirant should read the desired text thoroughly, taking note of any particular teachings which resonate with him or her. The aspirant should make a habit of collecting those teachings and reading them over frequently. The scriptures should be read and re-read because the subtle levels of the teachings will be increasingly understood the more the teachings are reviewed. One useful exercise is to choose some of the most special teachings you would like to focus on and place them in large type or as posters in your living areas so as to be visible to remind you of the teaching. The aspirant should discuss those teachings with others of like mind when possible, because this will help to promote greater understanding and act as an active spiritual practice in which the teachings are kept at the forefront of the mind. In this way, the teachings can become an integral part of everyday life and not be reserved for a particular time of day or of the week. The study of the wisdom teachings should be a continuous process in which the teachings become the predominant factor of life rather than the useless and oftentimes negative and illusory thoughts, devoid of spiritual truths. This spiritual discipline should be observed until Enlightenment is attained.

The text ends with a guarantee, that if these instructions are followed, the goal of spiritual realization will be secured. This is the difference between the science of mysticism and other forms of lesser evolved spirituality and limited religious practices. Yoga is an exacting science, which if followed correctly, through the correct guidance, will lead to a result that can be repeated by aspirants everywhere and at any time in history (today, 5,000 years ago or 5,000 years in the future). So there is proof of its benefits, and these are to be discovered by the aspirant. Lesser religions exhort its followers to go on faith alone. Mystical religion proclaims that faith is to be fulfilled with spiritual realization. This is therefore the path of a holistic spiritual movement, that is, religion encompassing all the steps which lead to enlightenment, and not just the lower stages which require faith, but lead nowhere else. Mysticism is the art and science of discovering God and although this journey begins with faith, it ends by transcending faith, for there is no need for faith in finding something once you have found it. Therefore, from this perspective, religions that profess that faith alone leads to spiritual evolution are promoting only the first step of authentic spirituality and religion.

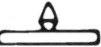

CHAPTER 21[317]

CHAPTER FOR WARDING OFF CROCODILE DEMONS THAT COME TO TAKE AWAY A PERSON'S WORDS OF POWER IN THE NETHERWORLD

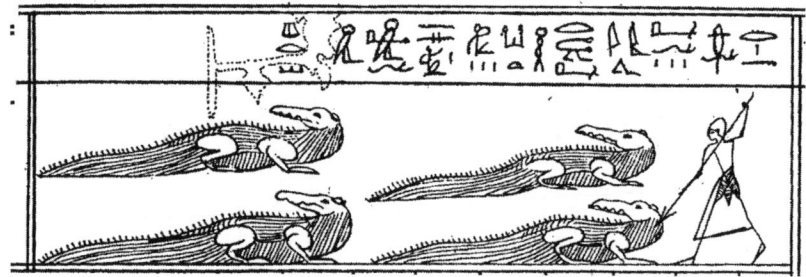

Plate 47: Vignette for Chapter 21- the initiate fights crocodiles, which symbolize the demoniac nature of the lower self when the lower self is uncontrolled.

1. Words to be spoken by Asar _____ maakheru.

2. Get back! Get away from me you slaying crocodile! Do not even come close to me for I am righteous and know the Hekau[318] within (myself).

3. Do not speak the name of the slaying divinity great who sent you. (I already know the names); one is "Messenger" and the other name is "Bedty"[319].

4. I traverse the heavens invoking my words of power. I eat with teeth as hard as rocks of the Viper Mountain.

5. I am the aged one.

6. I am that I am, Asar, the seal of my father Geb and my mother Nut.

7. I am Heru, the heir on the day of risings.

8. I am Anpu on the day of reckonings.

9. I am that I am, the god Asar.

10. I open the mouth of the gods and goddesses.

11. In silence I sit as a scribe and the words satisfy the heart.

12. There are thousands of loaves and thousands of drinks here at the altar of Asar. Heru stands up for Djehuti and I am as a scribe with a contented heart, living off the offerings to Asar in the city of Djedu (for they are offerings to me).

13. I am! I am! Existing upon the east wind and I control the west wind.

14. No crocodile can overcome my Words of Power!

---

[317] Generally referred to as Chapter 31.
[318] Words of Power.
[319] "The Physical One."

15. Anyone who knows this Chapter goes out into the light; (with this knowledge) one is able to walk among the living, on earth and one cannot be injured ever. This Chapter is infallible. Its teaching has been proven a million times over!

GLOSS ON CHAPTER 21: ITS MEANING AND MYSTICAL SIGNIFICANCE

The translation for this chapter was based primarily on the Papyrus of Auf-Ankh and others. It is included here as representative of a genre of teachings found in similar chapters dedicated to warding off the negative influence of demons and fiends that reside in the Netherworld. The demons are usually depicted as animal forms (crocodiles, serpents, scorpions, etc.). In a mystical sense these represent the dark forces which emerge in the mind of an unrighteous person (lust, greed, anger, hatred, jealousy, envy, etc.). This chapter was also selected for this book because it contains a short but powerful rubric. As stated earlier, it is representative of several other chapters. These are: Chapter 32[320]: Repelling Crocodiles, Chapter 33[321]: Chapter for Repelling any Reptile, and Chapter 35[322]: Not allowing oneself to be devoured by the reptile.

The use of animal symbols, especially reptiles, is a mystical way of denoting the type of energy that is being dealt with. Reptiles are symbolic of sexual energy, and also the animal instinct which is wanton and cruel. Attaining power over these energies means that the initiate has attained an advanced level of spiritual practice without which there can be no progress on the spiritual path. There must be control of the lower aspects of the personality, lust, desire and passion, in order for there to be reflection and peace of mind to understand the subtle spiritual teachings which lead to the Divine awakening.

As stated earlier, this Chapter is representative of several chapters in the genre of warding off unwholesome and unrighteous forces, which are presented in the form of vicious animals such as crocodiles and snakes. The idea is that an aspirant must actively assert {his/her} power to resist these forces (temptation, desire, aggression, etc.), and this is most effectively accomplished when the assertion is followed by the special hekau *Nuk pu Nuk* (I am that I am) which is included twice in this volume.

First there must be conviction and strong faith. Then there must be understanding, for uttering the words of power without understanding is not as effective. Therefore, the initiate asserts, I am that I am, implying that {he/she} is the existence which underlies all Creation and which cannot be destroyed. Then there is an association of this I am with the divinities Asar who represents the Spirit, Heru who represents the might of the spirit, and Anpu who represents the faculty of intellectual discernment, the power of not being deluded. The greatest delusion is the delusion of impotence, for the soul within every human being is magnanimous and supremely powerful. Only through delusion, the ignorance of the true Self, is it possible for a human being to fall under the spell of worldly desire and weakness in life on the Physical, as well as the Astral plane.

Thus, being relaxed in the comfort of knowing, and in knowing feeling secure and safe, the aspirant can sit in silence, deriving comfort and peace from the words of truth. When a spiritual aspirant truly understands the teachings being brought forth through the words of mystical wisdom, the spiritual scriptures evoke great peace and satisfaction. They are the greatest foods for the mind (heart), enlightening it, and are therefore considered as divine food for the heart. In this special peace there is a balance, and there is no coming or going, but a witnessing of the opposites of Creation (*existing upon the east wind and I control the west wind*). Living on what has come into being, in one's present lifetime, there is now control of the movement to the west, meaning that one has the power to end the struggle of life, that is, to go to the supreme abode, the west, as per one's choice. When one is secure about tomorrow, then one can relax, but when there is doubt and fear, there can be no relaxation, only frustration and anxiety. Spiritual enlightenment is the only true peace of mind. There is no higher state in life than peace of mind. However, people from time immemorial have sought peace of mind through

---

[320] This chapter designation is used by traditional Egyptology, but not in this volume.
[321] See previous note.
[322] See previous note.

possessions, relationships, fame and fortune, and history has shown, each and every time, that this is impossible to achieve, yet people strive and struggle due to ignorance. Enlightenment is equated with fearlessness because having attained the knowledge of Self, which is immortal, eternal and full, what is there to fear or desire in this world? In the absence of fear and desire there can be peace and bliss. This is the goal of life.

Section 3: The Movement of Transformations

𓏤𓂝𓊨𓉐𓈖 𓏤𓂝𓊨𓉐𓈖 𓏤𓂝𓊨𓉐𓈖 𓏤𓂝𓉐𓈖

Nuk ab, Nuk ab, Nuk ab, Nuk ab
I am Pure, I am Pure, I am Pure, I am Pure

nuk neter aa kheper tchesef
I am the great God, self created.

Nuk uab-k uab ka-k uab ba-k uab sekhem.
My mind has pure thoughts, so my soul and life forces are pure.

Nuk ast au neheh ertai-nef tetta.
Behold I am the heir of eternity, everlastingness has been given to me.

Nuk Anpu,
(I am Anubis)

Nuk Maat,
(I am Maat)

Nuk Aset,
(I am ASET)

Nuk Heru,
(I am Heru)

Nuk Asar
(I am Asar)

Nuk Neberdjerr
(I am all, transcendental, absolute!)

CHAPTER 22[323]

THESE ARE THE WORDS FOR MAKING THE TRANSFORMATION INTO THE SOUL OF TEM.[324]

Plate 48: Left: Vignette from Chapter 22 of papyrus Auf Ankh- The soul of the initiate and Tem (Atum) are one and the same. (symbol used- hawk with the head of the initiate.)

Plate 49: Right: Vignette from Chapter 22 of papyrus Ani- The soul of the initiate and Tem (Atum) are one and the same. (symbol used- Ram with burning incense.)

1. These words are to be said by Asar _____ who is Spiritually Victorious.[325] "There is no going into the place of execution. I do not perish; I do not experience this.
2. I am Ra, coming forth from Nun,[326] the Divine Soul, and Creator of his own body parts.[327]
3. Unrighteousness is an abomination to me; I do not see it, for my thoughts are with Maat exclusively. I live in it!
4. I am the God Hu, the one who does not perish in his name of 'Divine Soul.'
5. I myself created my own name, with Nun. My name is Khepri and in the form of the god Ra, I am All light."

GLOSS ON CHAPTER 22: ITS MEANING AND MYSTICAL SIGNIFICANCE

This chapter begins a series of chapters with the purpose of promoting the transformation of the spiritual initiate from having mortal (human) consciousness to discovering divine consciousness. In this chapter, the means of making the transformation is accomplished through the special discipline of the "I am formula" backed up by the practice of Maat.

First, the initiate is to assert {his/her} identity with Tem (Ra, Khepri) who symbolizes the fire of knowledge and the light of consciousness (enlightenment), and the absence of darkness (ignorance). The initiate then identifies with the soul. Hu, who symbolizes the experience of that enlightenment. This also implies the converse assertion, "I am not this mortal, limited personality; I am that same being who arose from the primeval ocean (Nun) and brought myself into being." Thus, an aspirant should learn all there is to know about Tem or any other divine form that is used for this practice. Then, there must be a subtle process of integration of that wisdom into the personality of the aspirant. This means that the wisdom

---

[323] Generally referred to as Chapter 85.

[324] Tem (Tmu) or Atum (Atem) is the ancient name of the Creator Divinity which emerged from the Primeval Ocean. Atum is also an aspect of the sun god Ra. Khepri is the morning sun, Ra is the noonday sun and Tem is the setting sun.

[325] Maak-heru.

[326] The Divine Primeval Waters.

[327] Referring to the objects of the world.

must be allowed to blossom in the mind (heart). This is promoted by living in accordance with the precepts of Maat. An aspirant must begin to feel and sense the truth of the higher nature. It is important to understand that just asserting the teaching is not enough. You must live it because living it allows you to work out the negative aspects of the personality and to cultivate the virtues. This is the glory of Maat. The assertion that "I am Hu" signifies control over the senses and awareness of the Divine because Hu is the divinity of divine taste. He is the sense as well as the principle of divine sustenance, which is beyond the physical senses.

Controlling the Senses

The following Ancient Egyptian Proverbs on the senses give insight into the senses and how they relate to the higher aspects of the personality.

"The senses give the meaning from a worldly point of view;[328]
see with the spirit and the true meaning will be revealed. This is the relationship between the object and its Creator, its true meaning."

"Knowledge derived from the senses is illusory; true knowledge can only come from the understanding of the union of opposites."

"Be not fooled, magic cannot alter the laws of nature; all must be according to Law; but an adept can, through control of thought and Law, alter the perception **of the spectators since the senses bring information not knowledge**."

"It is very hard, to leave the things we have grown used to, which meet our gaze on every side. Appearances delight us, whereas things which appear not, make their believing hard. Evils are the more apparent things, whereas the Good can never show Itself unto the eyes, for It hath neither form nor figure."

"To free the spirit, **control the senses**; the reward will be a clear insight."

Figure 99: Above-Relief showing the gods of the senses and their relationship to the Spirit (from the Temple of Heru at Edfu).

Most people do not ever have the conscious experience of being completely free from the senses in their lifetime, except in brief moments after they have fulfilled a longing or desire. They make the error of associating their fleeting short-lived peace or relaxation with the object or situation they acquired. They associate objects with the source of happiness because when they acquire objects of desire, there is a brief period of relaxation and expansion as the tension caused by the desiring subsides temporarily. Most people consider these brief periods of release to be happy or pleasurable times. They do not realize the

---

[328] Bold emphasis by the author.

"pleasure" and "happiness" actually came from temporarily resolving the egoistic struggle of desire which allowed the mind to relax and expand beyond the boundaries of the little me. So they strive to acquire more and more objects and situations of enjoyment, not realizing that they are promoting more tension in running after non-abiding situations and objects which therefore cannot, in the end, bring forth true abiding peace. Rather, they will become the source of more tension. Further, if there is not a satisfactory relief of tension, there will be dissatisfaction and frustration will be labeled as "unhappiness." The objects and idea of possessing them are sources of worry, distraction and burden for the mind. In this condition the mind degrades itself and wastes its energy looking after objects and longing for objects, and it never finds peace. It must be understood that as far as an individual person is concerned, other people are also "objects." In fact, everything outside of yourself is an object in reference to your individual point of view. Thus, a mind in this condition is considered to be a slave to objects rather than being their controller and master. A person under the control of their senses will not be able to control the movements of the senses even if their mind tells them not to look at or listen to a certain object. Coupled with the desires of the body, the senses are always searching for objects which are of interest to the desires of the body and of the ignorant mind which does not understand that objects cannot satisfy any desire, only multiply them to infinity. This is the plight of the *Distracted* mind. The relief of the Temple of Heru gives insight into the nature of the senses and their correct relationship to the Higher Self.

The Ancient Egyptian relief above from Edfu (Egypt - Africa) denotes the mystical understanding of the senses in relation to the Self. The boat of Ra depicts the sundisk with an image of the winged scarab (*Khepri* - the morning sun) in the center. Notice that there are certain gods inside and others outside. The ones inside are those which denote qualities which are innate to the Self, that is, those cosmic forces which are expressions of the Divine itself. These are *Heru-merti* (Horus of the two eyes), *Apuat, Maat, Hathor, Djehuti, Net,* and *Heru-khent-khathet* (the unborn Horus). The ones outside are, *Heru-pa-khart* (Horus the child - rising sun) directly in front of the boat, in front of him is Pharaoh Ptolemy IV offering *Maat* (truth and righteousness) to the Divine Company. Behind the king, outside of the boat, stand the gods of the senses of *Hu* (Taste and divine sustenance) and *Saa* (Touch, Feeling and Understanding). At the other end, also outside of the boat, stand the gods of the senses of *Maa* (Sight) and *Sedjem* (Hearing). As stated earlier, *Hu* and *Saa* were known to serve as bearers of the Eye of Horus (enlightened consciousness). They were also considered to be the tongue and heart of *Asar-Ptah* (the Self). Thus, they represent the vehicles through which human beings can understand and espouse the teachings of moral and spiritual wisdom. Thus, enlightened human beings can use these faculties to teach others, and spiritual aspirants must develop these faculties in order to understand the teachings.

The positioning of the gods and goddesses in the figure above is of paramount importance, because it points to the understanding that the neters within the boat itself are emanations of the Divine, while those outside of the boat are effects or reflections of the creative principles. Therefore, the occupants of the boat may be understood as *absolute attributes* of the Divine, while the characters outside of the boat may be understood as *relative manifestations* of the Divine in time and space. This is significant because it means that the senses are not real and abiding, but conditional and transient. Also their depiction in the *Ushet* (praise - worship) posture with upraised arms towards the Divine conveys the understanding that the senses are subservient. So just as the Self has senses, the human body has senses. These should be under the control of the soul and not the other way around.

There are two most effective methods of controlling and transcending the senses. First through the study, reflection and practice of mystical philosophy, the mind is to be rendered subtle. Through Saa, the faculty of understanding, the mind can realize at every moment that the objects which the senses are aware of are not absolute realities, but emanations from the Divine. Therefore, from an elevated spiritual-philosophical standpoint, there is really nothing to desire. This can occur even as the mind is perceiving the objects as a person practices daily reflection on the spiritual teachings. As this movement occurs in the mind, it becomes easier and easier to let go of the objects which interest the mind, but are not in line with Maat (correctness, truth, etc.). Secondly, through the practice of concentration, the senses can be controlled whether or not there is awareness of objects. Concentration increases will power. So the senses

can be controlled through understanding or through willpower. However, the integral practice of all of the disciplines of yoga will assist in the movement to control and transcend the mind and senses.

The senses can be transcended through any of the paths of yoga (Wisdom, Devotion, Action, and Meditation). However, the Yoga of Meditation specializes in this art, and the practice of all the yogas in an integral fashion enhances the practice of meditation and transcendence. When the control and transcendence of the senses occurs, the person may experience various kinds of psychic phenomena. This is the lower form of transcendence. In the advanced form, one goes beyond all concepts, thoughts and feelings, and encounters a region within, wherein there is no being or un-being, no life or death, no desires and no absence of desires. This region transcends all. It is called *Nrutef.* This is Asar (Osiris), the transcendental Self from which all souls (seer-subject), all objects (seen) and the awareness of objects (sight-senses) arise. Thus, having this experience over longer and longer periods of time, a human being discovers that {he/she} is that same transcendental, immortal, infinite, formless, objectless, genderless, etc., Supreme Self, and thereby merges with {his/her} own nature. When this occurs, a human being is said to have reached spiritual enlightenment or in Ancient Egyptian terminology, *Nehast,* to have achieved "resurrection."

The subject of controlling the senses is very important in the process of meditation. In the Yoga system of Sage Patanjali of India (200 B.C.E.), the process of withdrawing the senses was termed as *Pratyahara.* It means withdrawing the senses from the objects of the world so as to enable the mind to have an unhampered experience of consciousness when there is no awareness of objects. In Indian Yoga, this experience is called *Samadhi* or super-consciousness. In Ancient Egypt, the word *Seeh* (*Seh, Sihu*), meaning religious ecstasy, was used. When the senses are controlled and the mind begins to rise above them, a unique form of peace and happiness arises in the mind which is termed "bliss." This process of transcending the mind and senses and the planes of existence that are discovered has been dealt with at length in the gloss for Chapter 18.

PYRAMID TEXT UTTERANCE 261/ COFFIN TEXT 288: BECOMING FIRE AND AIR[329]

Words said by Asar_____, this person who makes the heart jump, the beloved son of the god Shu.
Expanding, stretching out in brilliance, powerful, shining forth, Asar _____ is a flame moving before the wind to the ends of the sky and to the ends of the earth.

PYRAMID TEXT UTTERANCE 332: ASCENDING IN A BLAST OF FIRE UNITING HEAVEN AND EARTH

I am the one who moved away from the *Mehen.[330]* I have ascended (to heaven) in a blast of fire, turning myself away from the world. The sky comes to me. The earth comes to me. I have walked the path over the green Kad plant that is below Geb's feet and I have stomped on the road of Nut.

GLOSS ON UTTERANCE 261/COFFIN 288, AND UTTERANCE 332: ITS MEANING AND MYSTICAL SIGNIFICANCE

These texts are included here to show the continuity from the earliest period of Kemetic scripture and some special teachings related to Creation and fire. The Mehen serpent is a giant coiled snake that churned in the primeval ocean and caused vibrations in it, bringing Creation into being. Moving away from it is symbolically a movement away from Creation (physical existence) and the earthly reality (which is an illusory reality), and a movement towards the spiritual reality, which is a higher truth. The *Pyramid Text* 261 and *Coffin Text* 288 are almost identical, and Utterance 332 closely follows them in meaning. Many people believe that Kemetic culture always believed in burial of the deceased. These passages present a different fate of the body and the soul. They show a preference for becoming fire and shooting forth in a blaze of fire. Becoming fire metaphorically relates to the body entering into the funeral pyre[331] and the soul entering into oneness with the spirit, Ra, who is fire. Ascending as fire refers to the transformation of the physical body from solid, to gas and ashes, and the soul's flight into eternity.

---

[329] This utterance appears, with some minor changes, as Coffin Text 288.
[330] The coiled serpent of the Primeval Waters.
[331] A heap of combustibles for burning a corpse as a funeral rite.

CHAPTER 23[332]

MAKING THE TRANSFORMATION INTO GOD AND FOR GIVING LIGHT TO THE DARKNESS.

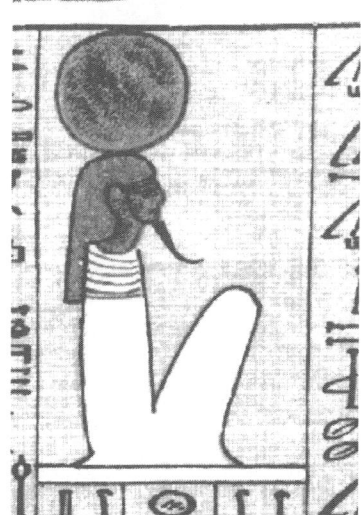

Plate 50: Vignette from Chapter 23 of Papyrus Ani, the divinity of light.

1.   These words are spoken by Asar _____ who is maak-heru.

2.   I am the weaver of the garments of Nun, shining and spreading light. I am the guardian of his chest, making light in the darkness and uniting the two goddesses within my body through the words of power on me and in my mouth. The enemies of he who is in the valley of Abdu[333] will not rise up. I am in peace now and I am remembering him (Asar). I have taken control of the god Hu in my city[334]. I found him in it and I have carried away the darkness, such strength I have! I repaired the Eye in its faltering at the arrival of the 15th day of the festival.

3.   I have weighed Set in the noble houses above with him. I have provided Djehuti in the house of the moon god and the 15th day had not yet come. I took control of the Ureret[335] Crown. Divine Righteousness is in my body as well as turquoise and faience of her[336] months. My field is lapis lazuli in his riverbank. I am the woman who lights up the darkness. I came to light up the darkness and brighten, to doubly light up the darkness.

4.   I put down unrighteous spirits. I adore those within the darkness. I have caused to stand up those who mourn, hiding their faces due to their spiritual weakness, and they see me.

5.   As far as you are concerned, I am the woman who has not allowed you to hear of her.[337]

---

[332] Generally referred to as Chapter 80
[333] Asar.
[334] Here the initiate affirms control of the divinity or cosmic principle symbolized by Hu in {his/her} own being (city).
[335] Crown of Upper and Lower Egypt together, worn by Heru-Mystical symbolism: one who has attained union of the lower and Higher Self, i.e. an enlightened human being.
[336] Goddess Maat is the cosmic principle of righteousness.
[337] The goddess Aset, a form of Net, is the divinity who remains veiled until the spiritual aspirant reveals the supreme wisdom of enlightenment.

Verse 1-3

This Chapter is dedicated to light. The vignette shows a god with a sundisk on his head, the universal symbol of light, but what kind of light? The sun's light is no ordinary light. It is a powerful conduit for the even more powerful force of the Pure Spirit. By this reckoning, the Spirit is the most powerful light, and it is within every human being, albeit, manifesting in a limited form due to refraction caused by impurities in the mind. Actually, the more subtle the light, the more powerful it is, and the light of Pure Consciousness is more powerful than a billion billion stars put together, because these are only emanations from that supreme light.

Weaving the garment of Nun is an allusion to the goddess Net who is known as the "weaver" who brought Ra, the light, into being. The garment of Creation is also to be understood as the patchworks which compose the day to day reality of life, that in turn deludes the mind. In fact, Creation is composed of atoms and molecules which interact and come together to compose elements. However, these atoms are in themselves composed of energy, but the limited mind and senses do not perceive this ocean of energy, which is an aspect of the Nun. This effect of not perceiving the most subtle essence of Creation is the veil of the goddess, and therefore, it is the goal of every aspirant to unveil her, that is, to see her true form, the pure light of consciousness devoid of the veil. The existence of this veil however, is not the fault of or an effect created by the Goddess. It is the fault of ignorance, which has deluded the mind of the individual. This is true because upon attaining enlightenment, a human being discovers the underlying essence of Creation, beyond the illusions they had made for themselves. This essence is there even now, but the deluded mind cannot perceive it because it is besieged by ignorance that is reinforced with desires, passions, mental agitations (anger, hatred, greed, lust, etc.) and egoism. The various paths of yoga science act to tear asunder the veil of illusion about the world. This chapter speaks about the yogic path of cultivating the Serpent Power.

The *two goddesses within me* refers to the two serpent goddesses, Uadjit and Nekhebet. They are forms of Aset and Nebethet, presiding over the Serpent Power Life Force and residing in the subtle spine in the form of the two serpents, meaning that the energy is serpentine-like (winding). When harmonized and cultivated, the energy uncoils. The goddesses transform themselves into the straight pillar (Asar), the light of the Spirit, eliminating all darkness in the personality as the upper psycho-spiritual consciousness centers open up.

The left Eye of Ra (Supreme Being) is the moon, and every month, after fourteen days of waxing, it begins to falter, i.e. wane. Symbolically, this (the 15th day) is when the force of righteousness and truth are necessary to fix or strengthen the Eye. This is symbolic of the mind in its movement towards spiritual enlightenment. Its movement needs to be waxing, that is, expanding with greater and greater fullness, but due to the ever-changing way of nature, the cycle of life dictates times of weakness and times of strength in the human personality (relative reality and the lower nature) in order to promote personality integration. At these times, the practice of the Maat Philosophy disciplines along with faith in as well as adherence to the wisdom teachings and their respective ritual practices (prayers, chants, meditations and other yogic disciplines) will carry the initiate through the waning period of consciousness, to become established in an expanding consciousness. This is the fullness of enlightenment wherein there is no longer any waning.

Verse 4-5

The initiate assumes the role of *the woman who lights up the darkness*. This is a mystical teaching with manifold implications. The idea of a female personality assuming a female role is understandable, but what of the male initiates? This identification with the female essence of the Divine, the goddess form, is an

256

example of the transcendental nature of mysticism. In reality the soul has no gender, this is a thing of bodies. What you are being asked to assume is the essential nature of a divinity, their principle, and not their sex-gender. Actually, every human being is composed of roughly 50% female and 50% male genes, and manifestation as a male or female is governed by karmic inclination and not by genes. The soul decides to create a male or female body depending on the lessons and experiences that need to be learned in that particular incarnation. If a human being is able to become free from the pressure of physical existence and the illusion of individuality, the pressure of gender and the sex desire are also lifted. In this peaceful state it is possible to perceive the genderless basis of the Spirit. This is called the unveiling of the goddess. All those who practice the disciplines of mystical religion and yoga are allowed by the goddess to see her true form. It is an illumination of momentous proportions wherein all darkness is destroyed. These verses as well as the allusion to the weaver aspect of the Divine all point to the goddess as the means to spiritual enlightenment. The Goddess form of worship constitutes the third major category of spirituality presented in the *Prt M Hru* when considered together with the Path of Aset and the Path of Ra. Therefore, it is appropriate here to give insight into the spiritual path of the Goddess and the glory of worshipping the Divine as the Goddess.

THE PATH OF THE GODDESS

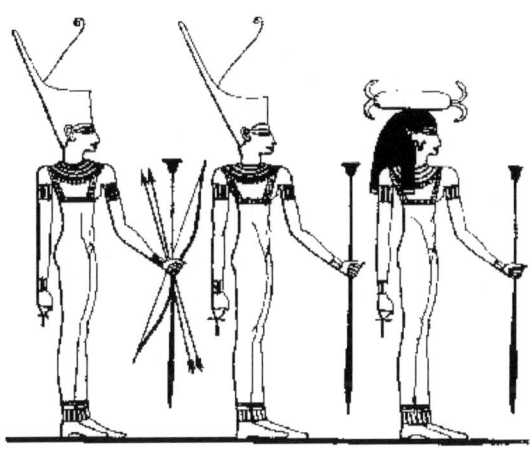

Figure 100: The Goddess Net

GODDESS NET

Net is the goddess of creation and war, as well as honor and decisive action. Her attributes are the bow, shield and arrows. She is androgynous (neither male nor female), and was known to watch over Asar's ceremonial bed when he lay dead, along with Aset and Nebthet. She assisted Djehuti in bringing justice for Heru in the Asarian myth. The goddess Net is the primordial Supreme Divinity with female aspect. She is the ancient form of the goddesses Aset and Hetheru, and her worship extended to the far reaches of antiquity, into the Pre-Dynastic period of Ancient Egyptian history. There are records from both priests and priestesses who served the temples of goddess Net. These show that worship of her was most popular, and expressed generally throughout the land of Egypt in ancient times. As we will see, the teachings related to goddess Net are profound and in every way as elevated as those of the Supreme Divinities of Ancient Egypt which portray the male aspect.

In *Pyramid Text* line 606, Net, together with Aset, Nebethet and Serqet, watched over the funerary bed of Asar. The bandages and shrouds used for the mummy of the deceased was given by goddess Net and through these she imparts her protection as well as her blessings in the form of spiritual power.

In *Pyramid Text* line 620-627, it is explained that the initiate is Sebek, the god who is the son of Net, and that the initiate rises like the son of Net. In the city of Net, Sebek is recognized as a form of Heru. Therefore, there is no conflict in finding that the goddess Aset was ascribed her attributes in the later dynastic period. The following speech of the goddess is also used by goddess Aset.

> "I am everything which has been, and which is, and which shall be and there has never been anyone who has uncovered my veil."

Of the goddess it is said that she:

"Created the seed of the gods and goddesses and men and women."

Net is the Goddess of Light, and thus her festival is characterized by the practice of lighting candles, torches and lamps. As light she gave birth to Ra, the sun divinity, who lights up the world.

Net is the:

"Divine Cow who gave birth to Ra."

Thus, Net is *Mehurt*, the primeval waters from which creation arose.

Her androgynous nature is related in the following epithet:

"Father of all fathers and mother of all mothers."

"Net-Menhit, the Great Lady, Lady of the south, the great cow who gave birth to the sun, who made the seed of the gods and goddesses and men and women, the mother of Ra, the one who raised up Tem in the primeval time,[338] who existed when nothing else had existence and who created that which exists after she came into existence."

The goddess gave birth to the gods and goddesses and to human beings, but she herself was not given birth. She brought herself into existence and gave birth without being impregnated. She was the primeval ocean and she emerged as herself out of herself and all has come forth through and from her. She is self-existent, and her nature is secret, a mystery to all.

shetat - deep mysterious nature of the goddess Net

Net is also referred to as:

"Ua-netert"
"Divinity One"

---

[338] At the time of Creation.

Thus, Net encompasses the non-dual, absolute, all-encompassing divinity, i.e., she is Neberdjer. This teaching is further illustrated through the hieroglyphic symbols of her name.

Her symbols are the bow, ⌒, two arrows, ←≪, the shield, ⋈, and the knitting spool, ☒ .

The name *Net*, ⌒ 𝄞, is a play on the word *nt*, ⌒ ,or *ntet*, ⌒ ⌒, meaning that which is, that which exists, i.e. that which is real, true, and abiding. The goddess provides *saa*, ∰, or protection for the spiritual aspirant. She uses a bow and arrow to shoot down the enemies of the righteous (anger, hatred, greed, jealousy, envy, lust, etc.).

In her name of *Net hetep*, ✕•⌒, the goddess is the abiding supreme peace.

Net is also known as Amentet, the hidden goddess and consort of the god Amen as well as Rat, the consort of the god Ra. Thus we are to understand that all the goddess forms are in reality aspects of Net.

Net is also known as *Mehenit*, ∿ 𝄞𝄞 ⌒ 𝄞, the weaving goddess. The material woven by the goddess is used for wrapping the mummy, but she also weaves her own clothing. This clothing is the outer appearance of the physical universe. The objective of spiritual movement within the *het Net*, 𝄞 ⌒ 𝄞 ⊗, the house of Net (Creation), is to propitiate the goddess to remove her clothing, to unveil herself, so that the initiate may see her true form...absolute existence.

Being the Goddess of Light and having the power to weave the intricate web of Creation wherein all is connected, the goddess allows herself to be disrobed by those who follow the path to her discovery. This path was given in the Temple of Aset, who is a later form of goddess Net. In the temple of Aset the path of spirituality (Shetaut Aset), known today as the Yoga of Wisdom, was taught. It is a spiritual discipline involving the following areas. The aspirant is to purify of the body through a vegetarian diet, control of the sex urge, engage in devotional practices and study of the wisdom teachings.[339] **Stage 1: Listening** to the teachings of the myth of the goddess and receiving mystical insights into these.[340] **Stage 2: Reflecting** on those teachings, and living life in accordance with virtue and truth (i.e. practice of the teachings in daily life). **Stage 3: Through Subtle One-pointed Mentation,** leading oneself to a meditative union with the Goddess who is the essence of light, which transcends mind, body, time and space.

How to Follow the Path of the Goddess

For those wishing more details on the path of Goddess Net and Aset, there are special materials that have been prepared to augment the teaching presented here as well as the practice of studying and living the mystic path of the goddess. These are: The book *The Wisdom of Isis,* the audio lecture *The Festival of Lights: Worship of Goddess Net,* the Audio Music and Chanting CD or Cassette *Glories of the Divine Mother.* Contact the Sema Institute for more information (305) 378-6253.

---

[339] Chanting, singing, prayer.
[340] See the book *The Wisdom of Isis* by Muata Ashby.

CHAPTER 24[341]

MAKING THE TRANSFORMATION INTO A LOTUS.

These words are said by Asar _____.

1. I am the lotus, pure, coming forth out into the day.

2. I am the guardian of the nostril of Ra and keeper of the nose of Hetheru.

3. I make, I come, and I seek after he, that is Heru.

4. I am pure going out from the field.

Plate 51: Vignette from Chapter 24 of Papyrus Ani, the initiate comes forth from the lotus of Creation as the Primeval Divinity arose from the Primeval Ocean for the first time to engender Creation in the form of Nefer-Tem.

---

[341] Generally referred to as Chapter 81A

GLOSS ON CHAPTER 24: ITS MEANING AND MYSTICAL SIGNIFICANCE

The Lotus is the Kemetic symbol for the number 1,000. It is also a symbol of detachment and the aroma of divinity. In mystical philosophy, the number 1,000 symbolizes manifold, and in Indian yoga it is used as the symbol for the psycho-spiritual energy center at the crown of the head, which contains 1,000 subtle petals, meaning transcendental experience.

The lotus grows in a pond of murky water, and yet it is untouched by the water. So too the aspirant must remain in the world of illusion, and yet be untouched by that illusion. Instead, it turns towards the sun during the day and closes up at night, turning away from the darkness. This is accomplished by daily application of a special ointment on the personality just as the lotus applies oils on itself to remain untouched by the murky waters of the pond. These oils used by aspirants are the fruits of practicing the spiritual disciplines. The treatment that the aspirant undergoes is increasing detachment from the world and increasing attachment to the Divine Self. Therefore, the more detachment one develops, the more insulated one becomes from the world and the more one is able to become attached to the Divine Self through one's spiritual disciplines.

When there is supreme detachment in the personality there is also power. The goddess Hetheru symbolizes the unfoldment of this power, in abundance, the power of Sekhem, the Life Force that sustains life through the breath. She is ever at the side of Heru, as in the Asarian Resurrection myth, and so too it is with the spiritual aspirant who has now assumed the role of Heru. Only those who possess such power over the world, the *field* of time and space, are capable of *going out* from it and coming back to it as they please. The fragrance of lotus is heavenly, containing medicinal purposes and spiritual significance. Thus, the smelling of lotus is symbolic of purity, detachment and the spirit.

CHAPTER 25[342]

MAKING THE TRANSFORMATION INTO PTAH

Plate 52: Vignette from Chapter 25 of Papyrus Ani, the divinity Ptah, in his shrine, standing on the pedestal of

Maat.

1. Words to be said by Asar _____. I eat bread, drink beer and put on the clothing. I fly as the falcon[343] and I cackle as the goose.[344] I have alighted through the way, through the mountains on the day of the festival of the Great God.

2. Evil doubly it is, detestable, I do not eat excrement; I do not eat it! It is abominable to my Ka. It does not go into my body. I live in accordance with the knowledge of the gods and goddesses and the glorious spirit beings. I live and am empowered through their bread.[345] Powerful am I by eating it. Under the hair[346], within Hetheru, my Lady, I make a great offering. I make bread in the city of Djedu[347] and oblations in the city of Anu.

---

[342] Generally referred to as Chapter 82.

[343] Heru.

[344] The goose is sacred to Amun-Ra. One of his sons, Geb, is the goose god. Ra is sometimes referred to as The Great Cakler. In one Ancient Egyptian Creation myth the cosmic egg was laid by the Goose Goddess Kenken-ur, The Great Cakler. In later times, Hindu mythology developed a cosmic egg creation myth as well.

[345] This is an allusion to divine sustenance, in some ways similar to the Christian eucharist bread. It is a metaphor referring to the divine light upon which spirit beings are sustained. When a human being consumes this divine food, they too become Akhu (glorious spirit beings). This food is devotion to God, righteous living and wisdom about one's divine nature (i.e. to Know oneself).

[346] Hair is a metaphor for tree branches; mystically it relates to the Tree of Life which is the body of the goddess, from which she imparts sustenance and nourishment (physical and spiritual).

[347] Where the pillar of Asar is found, i.e. establishment of the spiritual aspirant in the Self-God.

3. I dress myself in the clothing of goddess Matayt[348].
4. I stand and I rest wherever my heart desires in my being Ra. I complete myself as the god Tem and the four manifestations of Ra extending[349] as land.
5. I go out and my tongue is like Ptah's.
6. My throat is that of Hetheru.
7. I have remembered the words of Tem, my divine Father and I speak them.
8. He who compelled the priestess, the wife of Geb.
9. Destroyed are the heads by him and there is fear of him.
10. In repeating good words and in acts of strength I am accorded the legacy of the Lord of the earth, of Geb, the protector.
11. Libations, Geb gives to me at his risings.
12. Bow to me those within Anu with their heads.
13. I am their Ka, in their power from moment to moment, I am their sustainer.[350]
14. I copulate.
15. I am strong for eternity!

GLOSS ON CHAPTER 25: ITS MEANING AND MYSTICAL SIGNIFICANCE

Verse 1

The vignette and title which open this chapter are important because they establish at the outset that the Divinity who is being spoken of here, Ptah, is associated with the other main divinities of the *Prt M Hru* in an intimate way. Having already become the falcon, which is a symbol of Heru, and the goose, which is a symbol of Ra and Geb, the initiate has now made it to the festivity of the god Ptah. In Kemetic philosophy, the process of spiritual evolution is seen as a pilgrimage wherein one goes around discovering the various divinities and becoming one with them. When all of them have been assimilated, that is, their principles have been discovered and cultivated within the human personality, then one becomes whole and supremely powerful.

Verse 2

This verse continues an important symbol in Kemetic Philosophy which was introduced in Chapter 4, Verse 10 relating to "excrement." Excrement is used to symbolize everything that is detestable in life. Most people, due to their own ignorance, are forced to eat excrement in life in various ways. Whenever a person has to do something they would rather not do, this is eating excrement. Whenever a person cannot achieve their desires, this is eating excrement. Whenever a person is disappointed or frustrated in any way, this is eating excrement. Since ordinary human beings live their lives based on egoistic notions, desires and expectations, they are constantly stressed because they are constantly frustrated about something they desire, getting away from something they dislike, or in fear over something they achieved that they do not want to lose. Life is always unpredictable. Therefore, whatever one achieves is bound to

---

[348] Goddess who is the weaver of the embalming cloth-related to Goddess Net.
[349] Extending in four directions – north, south, east and west- i.e. all-pervading and all-encompassing.
[350] This section is extremely important as it reveals that God is the sustainer of life from moment to moment, i.e. from one time period to the next. Most human beings believe that once they are given life, they sustain that life on their own until the moment of their death. Actually, Divine Consciousness supports ALL existence from the minutest atom to the greatest star in the heavens. Just as a wave is sustained by the ocean underneath it, or as a human being sustains the dream world while dreaming, during every instant of the dream, so too, Divine Consciousness sustains the individual consciousness of the mind of every human being and when that consciousness (the individual soul) withdraws from the physical personality, the personality stops functioning. This is called death. Ab or individual human consciousness is like a wave in Ra Ab, the Divine Ocean of Consciousness.

be lost, if not due to theft or damage, then due to deterioration from normal wear and tear. Also, there is no guarantee that whatever one desires will be attained and ultimately all is left behind at the time of death. This is because the world is illusory and changeable. Thus, it is illogical to expect anything from the world and yet people run after the world pursuing objects and illusory goals with great zeal.

There is another aspect of excrement that is seldom discussed or understood. The real purpose of excrement in life is to remind us that the world is not all comfort and pleasure. From the perspective of the ego, there are some things that are liked and others which are disliked, but those things that occur against the ego's desires are in reality the chipping away processes of goddess Maat. She sends adversity and frustration to everyone in accordance with their previous actions. It is not meant to evoke frustration, anxiety or fear, but to cut the ego down to size, for it is impossible to have everything the way the ego wants it in the world. If the disappointments and frustrations are accepted and understood as reminders of the illusory nature of the world, then the disappointments will turn into real dis-illusionment. If this process moves on further, nurtured by sustained spiritual instruction, then the dis-illusionment turns into spiritual enlightenment. Disappointment is when you fail at acquiring your ego's desire, but still continue trying, even though the effort is a struggle and leads to further entanglements and suffering. This is the predicament of the masses that are uninitiated into the teachings. They are caught up in ignorance. Dis-illusionment is when you understand that even if you were to achieve the object of desire, it will not bring you the abiding happiness you are looking for so you give up your futile desires and place your energies in more worthy areas, such as the spiritual practices. This is the path leading towards spiritual enlightenment.

Therefore, an aspirant should develop the sensitivity to hear the messages that the goddess is sending through other people's actions as well as the disappointments, annoyances, nuisances, aggravations, provocations, the fiascoes, mistakes, misunderstandings and irritations of life. If this is done, the world will be viewed as a help, rather than a hindrance to spiritual enlightenment, because at every turn there is a disappointment waiting for you. Most people try to overlook these troubles of life. They look for the pot of gold at the end of the illusory rainbow of life, which can never be found, and therefore they suffer, while convincing themselves that "this is how life is, you win some and you loose some." In fact, there is no winning in the game of life when the ego is playing. Only God can defeat the world and an aspirant wins also when {he/she} becomes one with God. You should strive to remember that while things appear to be harmonious this moment, the next may see tantrums, upsetness, worry and anxiety from those around you or even from yourself, so you will be on guard not to allow the mind to fall into the delusion of the masses. You will be like the gatekeeper and watcher of the Netherworld, shielding your mind from illusory thoughts, feelings and memories. Being on guard is the practice of mindfulness wherein the discipline of remembering truth is a mainstay of life. The masses of people are constantly trying to forget the truth and get lost in the illusion of life. A strong aspirant will reject this way of life and thank the goddess instead of cursing the world, and thereby move relentlessly towards "Un-Maat," what is real. The prefix "Un" as in "Un-Nefer" relates to that which exists, that which abides, as the only reality, and that reality behind all creation is the Divine Self. Instead of wining and complaining about adversities and frustrations, an aspirant should learn to accept these and control the reactions to these by not expressing attachment or dislike for the situations that are presented in life. When prosperity comes, one should thank the Divine and when adversity comes, the same internal awareness should be there, that it is necessary on the path to self-discovery, and there should also be praise and thankfulness to the Divine. Further, when there is a rainy day, too much snow or stormy weather and an aspirant cannot go to the beach or other plans are "spoiled," there should be resignation and praise of God, for whatever happens in life needs to happen. The Divine plan unfolds thus, and spiritual enlightenment is advanced the more the plan unfolds and the more poise (balance, equanimity, patience, composure, endurance, etc.) that is developed by the aspirant through dealing with life's situations. An aspirant will never curse God by saying "this is a bad day" or this "bad thing happened to me today," etc. So too when your are having a bad day and you are asked how are you doing, as an aspirant you should at the very least reply "can't

complain," with this higher philosophical thinking behind it. In this sense God is "All Good." All arguments to the contrary are based on the egoistic and therefore, illusory understanding of life and should be abandoned forthwith.

> "Truth is but one; thy doubts are of thine own raising. It that made virtues what they are, planted also in thee a knowledge of their pre-eminence. Act as Soul dictates to thee, and the end shall be always right."
>
> —Ancient Egyptian Proverb

Verse 3-4

This verse once again reiterates the importance of having Maat in life. Putting on the clothing of a divinity means acting, feeling, talking and looking like the divinity. In this manner one is able to transform one's personality by retraining the mind to adopt the divine ways of the spirit. This practice may be seen as the earliest form of theater, not for entertainment, but for spiritual realization. Ritual is a highly evolved stage for transforming the mind and allowing the initiate to feel the principles of the divinity.

Verse 5-14

Here begin a series of affirmations, which make the transformation effective. The initiate first asserts that the tongue is Ptah's tongue. Ptah is the sustaining essence of Creation. The tongue is the means by which words are formed and the throat is where sounds are produced, through the power of breath, which is sustained by Life Force energy, which is Hetheru. The initiate's remembrance of the ancient wisdom allows {him/her} to receive the adoration of all divinities. This is because remembering the divine essence means that one becomes one with it and takes on all forms of Creation.

There is recognition here that one is the very essential nature of the gods and goddesses. In fact they emanate from the spirit and having understood one's true essential nature as spirit, one realizes that one is not a slave to the world, rather the world is dependant on one. This is the momentous occasion wherein one realizes that the spirit sustains this entire Creation at every instant. If the spirit were to withdraw from Creation even for an instant, this entire Creation would vanish into nothingness just like when a movie projector in a theater stops working there can be no movie projection on the screen. In this case, the projector of the movie, the movie itself and the screen onto which the movie is projected are all aspects of the spirit. This is called the Amun-Ra-Ptah Trinity teaching.[351] Neberdjer, or pure consciousness, transforms itself into the triad of mental experience, seer or witnessing consciousness, seen or the object, and the seeing instrument, which allows interaction between seer and seen. The importance of this teaching is the understanding that all the aspects are really parts of one essence. If they are dissolved there is no Creation, only Pure Consciousness, Pure Oneness and this vision is the goal of mystical wisdom and meditation practice.

---

[351] See the book *Egyptian Yoga Volume II: The Supreme Wisdom of Enlightenment* for more details.

CHAPTER 26[352]

MAKING THE TRANSFORMATION INTO A DIVINE BENNU.

1. Words to be said by Asar _____ who is maak-heru in peace:

2. I flew like the primeval gods and goddesses.

3. Khepri is my name, the god Khepri.

4. I grew in the form of plants.

5. I am hidden like the tortoise.

6. I am the substratum of all the gods and goddesses.

7. I am yesterday of the four[353] and the seven serpent goddesses[354] that came into being in the east.

8. I am the one who is great at making light through his body; I am Divine.

9. I am that god manifesting as Set.

10. Djehuti was among them as discriminator, separator, distinguishing between that one, foremost in the city of Sekhem with the spirits in Anu, sailing among them.

11. I come, rising!

12. I am glorified!

13. I am powerful!

14. I am Divine among all the divinities!

15. I am Khonsu[355], conquering all!

Plate 53: Vignette from Chapter 26 of Papyrus Ani, the Bennu bird, the divinity known to the Greeks and others as the Phoenix.

---

[352] Generally referred to as Chapter 83.
[353] Manifestations of Ra-see the previous chapter.
[354] Seven serpents of creation- also the seven psycho-spiritual energy centers-related to the seven cow goddesses- see Chapter #20 (The seven Cow Goddesses).
[355] Son of the god Amun. He is known as the traveler. He is the movement whereas his father is the immovable witnessing consciousness-See the book *Egyptian Yoga Volume II* by Muata Ashby.

GLOSS ON CHAPTER 26: ITS MEANING AND MYSTICAL SIGNIFICANCE

Verse 1-6

This is a beautifully poetic chapter, based on the glory of the mythological solar bird, which is symbolized by the bennu bird. It is the original teaching related to the idea of resurrection through fire, and it relates to the themes developed in Utterance 261/Coffin 288, Coffin 246, Utterance 332 and Chapter 23, in reference to the fire and the light. According to legend, the Phoenix is a bird that lived in Arabia. However, upon examination of Ancient Egyptian mythology, a more ancient origin emerges. The *Bennu* is a mythical bird in Ancient Egyptian Mythology. Its symbolism was transferred to Greece and Arabia in the form of the *Phoenix* by the early Greek and Asiatic philosophers who studied in Egypt. According to ancient tradition, the Phoenix would consume itself on a funeral pyre every 500 years, whereupon a new, young Phoenix sprang from its own ashes. In Ancient Egyptian mythology, the Benu represented the sun that dies at night only to be reborn in the morning. Early Christian tradition (as early as the first century) adopted the Phoenix as a symbol of both immortality and resurrection. St. Clementin related the legend of the Phoenix in the First Epistle to the Corinthians. This chapter epitomizes the high flying nature of spiritual enlightenment, likening it to flight and light, but also to some other very important symbols. The initiate asserts {his/her} identity with the gods and goddesses, and then there is a most profound teaching, that the true name of the initiate is Khepri, that aspect of divinity which brought Creation into being and created by becoming the Creation. Indeed the Spirit is within every object that exists and is hidden to all but to the initiates. They attain the realization that this Spirit is the essential nature of the gods and goddesses (cosmic forces which sustain the universe).

Verse 7-8

The four manifestations relate to the dimensions of the physical universe. The terms "yesterday" and the number "four" symbolize the being that brought all the directions into existence, i.e. all-encompassing. The seven serpent goddesses relate to the seven principles of Creation as described earlier.

In Chapter 23 we learned about the divinity of light. Here there is an allusion to this again, as if updating our knowledge, for nothing is left behind and each attainment is cumulative, that is, realizing one aspect of the Divine Self, one does not let go of other aspects which were acquired previously, in order to adopt this new identity. Rather, new identities are added to each other in order to make a complete composite being, the all-encompassing divinity.

Verse 9

Here we have an impressive teaching related to the god Set. The initiate asserts the identity with Set. Now, as you have already learned in the Asarian Resurrection myth, Set is the ego consciousness, the negative, lower aspect of the personality. So how can one be Set and also the Spirit? It must be understood that all-encompassing means exactly that, leaving nothing behind. The Spirit is like the sun, shining on good people as well as the unrighteous. So too the spirit manifests as all. However, the Spirit is not responsible for all. This is extremely important to understand. Individuals are responsible for their own fate, even while they use bodies, thoughts, ideas, etc. that are composed of spirit, the Nun. What one does with one's body, ego and personality is based on one's level of wisdom. So the ignorant are the ones who hurt, commit violence, engage in passion, etc., based on spiritual ignorance. Even when one is degraded and doing negative actions one is still part of the Spirit. Just as Set was redeemed, even though he was a murderer, liar, rapist, thief, etc., so too any individual can be redeemed by the power of spiritual realization, which washes away the ignorance and arrogance of egoism, that led one to the fall away from truth.

Verse 10-15

Here the text begins with a proclamation about the god Djehuti, who in the myth of the Asarian Resurrection, acted go between, advocate and mediator between Heru and Set. This implies that Djehuti, who represents cosmic mind, all-knowing and maker of peace, has acted as advocate for the initiate, making

peace between the Higher Self of the initiate and the Setian aspect which is all within the personality of the initiate.

Next a series of lofty affirmations begin, that lift up one's consciousness to heavenly levels, as one realizes (as these affirmations are repeated these with understanding and conviction) that {he/she} is glorious, exalted and magnanimous. This is the true nature of every human being, and it is the wondrous nature of the mystical texts such as the *Prt M Hru*, which carry the initiate to the knowledge of {his/her} Divine Essence!

CHAPTER 26B[356]
HOW TO COME INTO THE LIGHT: TAKING CONTROL OF ONESELF AND CREATION

Figure 101: From Papyrus Nu, The Initiate sits beside a tree and Goddess Hetheru Sits Nearby

1.   The words to be said by Asar _____.

2.   The doors of heaven are opened for me. The bolts and locks of Geb are opened for me.

3.   Behold, I was controlled and scrutinized but now I am free. His ropes had tied me down, his hand was holding me to the earth.

4.   Ra-hent[357] is opened for me. Ra-hent is opened for me. Now I will come forth in any place of my choosing.

5.   I have gained mastery over my heart.

6.   I have gained mastery over my chest.

7.   I have gained mastery over my hands.

8.   I have gained mastery over my feet.

9.   I have gained mastery over my mouth.[358]

10. I have gained mastery over my entire body.

11. I have gained mastery over the sepulchral offerings.

12. I have gained mastery over the waters.

13. I have gained mastery over the air.

14. I have gained mastery over the canal, the river and the land.

15. I have gained mastery over the ploughed lands.

16. I have gained mastery over my male and female workers in the Netherworld.

---

[356] Generally referred to as Chapter 68 from papyrus Nu.
[357] One of the entrances to the Netherworld.
[358] i.e. Speech and taste.

17. I will not live on what is an abomination. I will eat only the bread made with white grain and my wine will be made with the red grain from Hapi.[359] I will sit in the clean place, under the date palm tree of my goddess Hetheru, who dwells gloriously in the spacious disk[360] as it travels to Anu, containing within it the sacred books of divine words which were written by the god Djehuti.

GLOSS ON CHAPTER 26B: ITS MEANING AND MYSTICAL SIGNIFICANCE

Title and Verse 1

This chapter is a continued exaltation of the goddess aspect of the Divine. It relates how one must take control of one's life in order to attain spiritual realization. Many scholars have characterized this and the following chapters as "bullying" the gods and goddesses into submission of the will of the initiate, and rightly so. One cannot accomplish anything great without strong will, and the greatest will comes to a person when they realize they have it within themselves to accomplish the goal. However, spiritual enlightenment is no ordinary goal. It requires the greatest possible purity of heart and intellect in order to understand and feel the truth of the spirit. This strength comes from developing righteousness in life and insight into the mystical meaning of the teachings.

Verse 2

Geb is the earth, and it is the earthly aspect of a person that holds them as if prisoner, shackled to the lower nature. This passage states emphatically that the bonds of Geb have been loosened. We already learned in Chapter 25 that the initiate is now receiving the libations of Geb himself. In fact, the initiate has realized {his/her} identity with Geb, so how can one hold one's own self back? This is the advanced view of libations.

Figure 102: Above-left, the goddess Aset pours a libation for the soul of the Initiate. (From Temple of Aset)

Figure 103: Above-right, officiating priest pours libation for the initiate.

In fact, the ritual of pouring libations as a sacrifice or propitiation to the deity is the second stage of religion. This is practiced as a ritual of pouring water onto the ground. The first was developing devotion towards the deity and the desire to propitiate the deity. In the limited practice, some people pour libations for ancestors and minor gods and goddesses in the hopes of achieving some worldly objective. They want the deity or ancestor to intercede for them and help them secure some worldly goal. But why not go to the source of all power instead of to intermediaries, who themselves derive their existence and sustenance from the same source that is open to you, the Divine Self? However, the third stage of religious practice is

---

[359] The Nile river god.
[360] Sundisk of Ra.

pouring libations for the Supreme Spirit that is within oneself. In essence, the higher objective of libations is to discover the God. This is accomplished by pouring the libation of one's one-pointed thoughts inwards towards the Spirit and away from the world of desires and illusion. This is the magnanimous teaching behind the Hetep Ritual Table.[361]

Verse 3

In ordinary life, a human being is always controlled by nature, by laws of society, by family members, etc., and one is always looking over one's shoulder, worried about the next person watching. This is a state of bondage wherein a person {him/her} self, through ignorance, desire and weak will, renders themselves weak and impotent in life. They are caught in the day to day reality with no apparent escape to something better. This is because the feeling of meekness has led to constriction in their consciousness, and they see themselves as small, powerless and insignificant in the face of the grand universe. In view of the fantastic teachings of mystical spirituality, one can see that this pathetic condition is the worse fate that can befall a human being. In this state a person worries about the opinions of others, appearances, social status, etc. Also, this person is also thereby controlled by stronger personalities, the media with its repetitive negative hekau. This person is thus compelled to live life in contradiction with the true nature of the Spirit within; there is an internal conflict which leads to frustration and anguish. This is the bondage of ignorance that a person submits to because they hold a desire for something from the world. This desire may be for objects, approval, pleasures, etc., not realizing that these are as fleeting as the clouds in the sky and not worth the effort of one who is innately magnanimous and grand in {his/her} true nature.

Verse 4

For human beings that realize the truth of mystical philosophy, the world holds no restrictions. The body continues to exist but the mind easily flies high, as if soaring like a falcon. In this state, inspiration is like the never-ending flow of the Nile, and there is freedom of the Soul. Heaven is therefore open to such a person, and the means to achieve this is contained in the following verses.

Verse 5-16

Control is the key to all good things in life and the hereafter. Control here means the ability to direct one's own personality, every aspect of it, to whatever one desires. This means the ability to detach or attach from any thought, desire, object, etc., and the ability to be detached even from one's own body. Being in control of nature is the understanding that one is not susceptible to nature's whims like an animal that is directed by instincts and cannot control them. One becomes the master of oneself, and in so doing, one becomes the master of nature and the creator of one's own fate. This of course allows one to surmount any obstacle and attain any goal, foremost of these being ignorance and spiritual enlightenment, respectively.

Verse 17

Thus, there is a familiar affirmation, a vow, that having attained this power one will not stoop to accept anything less than what is pure, great and glorious. Anything else is an abomination, excrement. This lower form of existence can be avoided by seeking out the goddess who is the purveyor of wisdom, joy and spiritual strength. Then, having found her, one must sit at her feet and imbibe of her glorious teachings, which were set down by the god Djehuti. Henceforth one must never leave her side. When she is discovered and placed in the heart, wherever one goes, the goddess will always be there, carrying one through the challenges of life and keeping the eternal fire of wisdom burning brightly for all eternity.

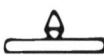

---

[361] See Part III, Chapter 1.

PYRAMID TEXT UTTERANCE 273-274: ASAR_____ EATS THE GODS AND GODDESSES AND ASSUMES THEIR POWER

It is Shesemsu who cuts them up for Asar_____ and cooked them for {him/her}.

Parts of them are in the cauldrons they are on fire.   Asar_____

Has   eaten   hekau*   theirs   consuming Akhu **   theirs

*words of power

** spirits

‡breakfast

†dinner

The great ones, they are for meal of morning, ‡ the midsized ones, they

Are for   evening meal † and the little ones, they are for the meal

Of the night   the old male ones   and the old female ones they are for the oven.

272

COFFIN TEXT INVOCATION 573: ASAR_____ EATS THE GODS AND GODDESSES AND ASSUMES THEIR POWER

1. The cauldrons are lit up for me.
2. Portions of the gods and goddesses are cooked for me.
3. I have eaten the hearts of the gods and goddesses.
4. I eat their hekau.
5. I swallow their power.
6. The powers of the gods and goddesses are within me.
7. The souls of the gods and goddesses are within me.

GLOSS ON UTTERANCE 273-274, COFFIN TEXT INVOCATION 573: ITS MEANING AND MYSTICAL SIGNIFICANCE

The *Pyramid Text* Utterances and *Coffin Text* Invocations presented here are direct Kemetic scriptural ancestors to Chapter 27, which is a text of the later period. They present, in graphic detail, the consumption of the gods and goddesses. They are boiled and cooked well done to serve as the meal of the morning and the evening (i.e. breakfast and dinner). Thus, they form the main staple of the diet of the initiate. Increasing wisdom is an ever-expanding aspect of an initiate. This expanding aspect is likened to a consumption of the world. The more an initiate learns about Creation, the more they devour it and in so doing, the mind assimilates it and transforms it, just as eating vegetables transforms them in the body. And just like the vegetables which are consumed and become part of the body, so too this entire Creation, which is a manifestation of the Spirit, through the neteru, the gods and goddesses or cosmic forces, becomes part of the mind. Rather, it is realized as already being part of the mind, an emanation of one's very own spirit. Thus, the ritual of cooking and eating the gods and goddesses is extremely profound in its greater implications.

CHAPTER 27[362]

THE REALIZATION OF THE HIGHER TRUTH

1. I am the child!
2. I am Ra!

3. I am one whose name is unknown[363], Lord of Eternity,
4. One of the celestial Judges. I judge like Khepri[364], Lord of the Ureret[365] Crown, dweller in the Udjat[366] and in the Egg[367], dweller in the Udjat when it closeth.[368]

5. I am Heru, traversing millions of years,
6. One whose forms are inverted.[369]
7. Un-Nefer[370], the Only One.[371]

8. I open the doors of heaven, the way for the births of today to occur.
9. I am yesterday and today and your protector of the future,[372] whether you may be inhabitants of heaven, earth, the south, the north, the east or the west!

10. I am "He who cannot be known."[373] I am the unveiled one.[374] My extension in the earth and progeny thereof cannot be calculated!

11. I am one who proceeds from an only One.[375] Not one day can pass without my being present in it!
12. I am the lotus[376] coming forth from Nu (Nun).

13. My mother is Nut.

---

[362] Excerpts from Papyrus Nu. Generally referred to as Chapter 42.

[363] One of the most ancient and mystical names to describe the transcendental Divinity, "Nameless One." This term also refers to the Primeval being who arose from the Primeval Ocean, bringing Creation into existence, i.e. Atum.

[364] See notes 25 & 33.

[365] Crown of Upper and Lower Egypt together, worn by Heru-Mystical symbolism: one who has attained union of the lower and Higher Self, i.e., an enlightened human being.

[366] Eye of Ra or Heru, depending on usage- Mystical symbolism: intuitional vision and creative life force.

[367] One Creation myth from Ancient Egypt holds that creation arose from a primeval egg laid by God.

[368] God is that spirit which is the creative Life Force behind existence in its manifest state as well as when creation dissolves back into the unmanifest state, i.e. Creation exists when God's eye is open and ceases to exist when God's eye is closed, but God exists transcendental of both states.

[369] This description of the Divine Self is similar to one which appears in the Indian Bhagavad Gita: Chapter 15 *Purushottam Yogah-- The Yoga of the Supreme Spirit* where Lord Krishna states that: 1. The Blessed Lord said: The scriptures speak of the imperishable Ashwattha tree (of the world-process) with its roots above and branches below; the Vedic verses (East-Indian scriptures) constitute its leaves. He who knows this Tree is the knower of the essence of the Vedas (East-Indian scriptures).

[370] Ever-existing reality and goodness.

[371] The Kemetic term "Only One" is an expression of the philosophy of the Divine Self as the singular or non-dual spirit from which all emanates. This confirms that Ancient Egyptian mystical philosophy did not promote duality and polytheism, but rather is an elaborate system of symbolism to explain the diversity through which the non-dual Self (God) manifests as Creation.

[372] This exceedingly important passage establishes the Divine Self as being the creator and sustainer of time in its three manifestations: past, present and future. Therefore, the Divine Self transcends these manifestations and thus the Transcendental Self is referred to as eternal, transcending time.

[373] The term God, the Spirit, is a metaphor for that which transcends the capacity of mental comprehension, i.e. God is beyond mind itself.

[374] While seemingly contradictory to the previous passage, this passage relates to the idea that while the Divine Self cannot be known with the mind and senses, it can be seen in its various manifestations as nature. This idea is explained further in the following passage.

[375] The Divine Self is the only cause of its own existence. God has brought herself into existence through herself, using herself as the raw material of which creation is composed. The Divine Self is the Absolute and there is nothing beyond. All the gods and goddesses with names and forms emanate from the Supreme Divinity.

[376] In one creation myth, creation (planets, stars, animals, human beings, etc.) is seen as the lotus which rises from the Primeval Ocean (Nun). The Primeval Ocean is a metaphor symbolizing the ocean of consciousness from which all forms emerged.

14. I am not known by you but I know you. I cannot be held in the hand but I am the one who can hold you in my hand.

15. I am the golden Baboon!

Chapter 27 Continued

THE DEIFICATION OF THE BODY OF ASAR _____.[377] [378]

Figure 104: Vignettes from Papyrus Nu

Chapter 27, Vignette 1: Becoming Nu, Ra, Hetheru, Apuat, Anpu, Serqet, and Aset.

Chapter 27, Vignette 2: Becoming Baneb Djeddu, Uadjit, Mert, Net, Set, Lord of Kheraha, Mighty One of Terror.

Chapter 27, Vignette 3: Becoming Sekhmet, Eye of Heru, Asar, Nut, Ptah, Orion, Living Urei.

---

[377] Each body part is blessed and sanctified by realizing it as an expression of a cosmic force, as part of one of the neteru (god or goddess). This chapter shows that the neteru are not deities, but expressions of the inner higher reality of a human being, yet to be realized by the ignorant and uninitiated, but discovered by advanced spiritual aspirants.

[378] The text is from Papyrus Ani.

Text of the Deification of the Body Parts

1- The hair of Asar _____ who is Maak-heru is Nu's hair.

2- The face of Asar _____ who is Maak-heru is Ra's face.

3- The eyes of Asar _____ who is Maak-heru are Hetheru's eyes.

4- The ears of Asar _____ who is Maak-heru are Wepwawet's.

5- The lips of Asar _____ who is Maak-heru are Anpu's.

6- The molars of Asar _____ who is Maak-heru are Serqet's.

7- The incisors of Asar _____ who is Maak-heru are Aset's.

8- The two arms of Asar _____ who is Maak-heru are those of the soul who is lord of Djedu.

9- The neck of Asar _____ who is Maak-heru is Uadjit's.[379]

10- The elbows of Asar _____ who is Maak-heru are Mert's.

11- The breasts of Asar _____ who is Maak-heru are those of the Lady of Sau.

12- The spine of Asar _____ who is Maak-heru is the spine of Set.

13- The chest of Asar _____ who is Maak-heru is that of the Lord of Kheraha.

14- The body of Asar _____ who is Maak-heru is that of Ashefit.

15- The belly and spine of Asar _____ who is Maak-heru are those of Sekhmet.

16- The buttocks of Asar _____ who is Maak-heru is the buttocks of the Eye of Heru.[380]

17- The phallus of Asar _____ who is Maak-heru is that of Asar.

18- The thighs of Asar _____ who is Maak-heru are those of Nut.

19- The feet of Asar _____ who is Maak-heru are those of Ptah.

20- The fingers of Asar _____ who is Maak-heru are those of Saah.[381]

21- The toes of Asar _____ who is Maak-heru are those of the Living Urei.[382]

---

[379] Serpent goddess-eye of Ra.
[380] Eye of intuitional vision in the form of the goddess.
[381] Divinity presiding of over the constellation of Orion, i.e. Asar (*Asar*).
[382] The eye of Ra as the life giving eye and serpent power.

COFFIN TEXT: INVOCATION 714

BECOMING NUN, THE PRIMEVAL OCEAN

1. I am Nu, The Only One, without equal and I came into being at the time of my flood.
2. I originated in the primeval void. I brought my body into existence through my own potency. I made myself and formed myself in accordance with my own desire.
3. That which emanated from me was under my control.

APPENDIX 1[383]

1. Grant that I may come forth[384] through your word, that I may see thy very own forms. Grant that I may come forth with spiritual strength over my own legs. May I be like Neberdjer upon his throne...
2. May I stand like the Lord of Life and may I be joined with Aset the Divine Goddess...
3. I supplicate, may I be with Neberdjer, that the gods and goddesses in the Netherworld may fear me and may they fight over me...
4. I am that I am[385], an Akhu[386] and I live in the light[387] and I came into existence through the limbs of God...
5. I have seen Asar and I have conversed[388] with him in reference to the things about his Soul.

APPENDIX 2[389]

1. The food and the altar are Heru.[390]
2. I go to become one with my father. The deliverance through my father is through my brother, is through my elders and through Heru who comes walking on the water[391] of his father.
3. He exists in decay. He is the ruler of Qamit.[392] He is thy soul.
4. The gods and goddesses have given to him the crown of millions of years and it causes him to live for millions of years in his Eye, the only one of the Lord, Neberdjer, the queen of the gods and goddesses.[393]

---

[383] Excerpts from Chapter 78 of The Papyrus of Ani.

[384] *perert m ra k-* enlightenment through the spiritual teachings.

[385] Literally, **Nuk Pu Nuk.** This passage is the prototype for the description of God in the Christian Bible (Exodus 3:14). It signifies that the Divine Self is transcendental of time and space and as such, is beyond naming, images and concepts. It means that the various words for God such as Amun, Aset, Asar, Jesus, God the Father, Allah, Krishna, Buddha, etc, are merely relative names, metaphors used by the limited mind. The Divine Self is in fact existence, being itself, unqualified, infinite and eternal. Creation is a limited manifestation of infinity through the keyhole we refer to as time and space-relative reality which is only applicable when the mind and senses are used. In order to experience pure existence, pure unqualified and transcendental being, it is necessary to go beyond the limitations of the human personality, which only operates within the confines of time and space of the physical creation (the waking world) and within the confines of time and space of the dream world when in the state of sleep.

[386] Glorious Shining Spirit Being- what spiritually enlightened human beings become upon attaining spiritual enlightenment.

[387] The light is the emanation of Ra, not the sun, but the Life Force of the Spirit. This light is what nourishes and sustains the *Akhus* or Glorious Shining Beings.

[388] This passage denotes the understanding that the initiate has beheld the Divine Self and as such, has obtained higher knowledge of the essence of that being, for seeing the Divine Self means knowing that Divinity. This is the kind of "knowing" (intuitional realization) that can only occur when one transcends the mind and senses and becomes one with Divinity.

[389] Excerpts from Chapter 78 of The Paris Papyrus.

[390] The Hetep offering table contains food items and these are the body and essence of Heru, the son of Asar, whose actions vindicated him and restored him to his divine station. Likewise, by making this offering and consuming it, the spiritual aspirant becomes like Asar, nurtured and resurrected and restored to the higher consciousness. This is a pre-Christian allusion to the teaching of the Eucharist. In Christianity the mass ritual consecrates the bread and wine, making it the "Body and blood of Christ." For more information see the section: A Gloss on Chapter 33.

[391] This is a pre-Christian allusion to the teaching of the walking on water of Jesus in the Gospels of the Bible. In most respects, the Ancient Egyptian god Heru is a precursor and prototype for the Christian Savior. See the book **Christian Yoga** by Muata Ashby

[392] Qmt (Kmt, Qamit, Kamit, Kemet) "the Black Land" i.e. Egypt.

[393] Here Neberdjer, the Supreme Being is referred to as a king (male) and as queen (female), i.e. transcending gender.

GLOSS ON CHAPTER 27, COFFIN TEXT 714, APPENDICES 1 AND 2: THEIR MEANING AND MYSTICAL SIGNIFICANCE

This chapter is very important because it gives insight into the teaching of assimilating the powers and mystical principles represented by the gods and goddesses and the entire Kemetic Philosophy as a whole. The refinement of the previous scriptures now bypasses the cooking and eating and now moves straight on to some bold and exalted statements related to the true nature and being one with the Higher Self. The following is an overview of the verses in this chapter.

1. The initiate first asserts identification with the solar child, Heru, who brought creation into being as Nefertem, the primeval Creator.
2. Now there is an assertion of being Ra, the Supreme Being and sustainer aspect of Tem.
3. The same Creator that is referred to by various names, Atum, Nefertem, Net, Ptah, Amun, etc., is actually originally referred to as the nameless one. This is the true and most ancient designation, because in reality that being transcends all names, and that is who you are essentially, beyond time and space and beyond names and forms.
4. Here there is an assertion of being not the judged, but the one who does the judging. This is similar to the teaching brought out in chapter 26B of controlling, as opposed to being controlled. Asar is the judge of souls. Once you become one with Asar, you too become the judge of souls and you are no longer judged.
5. This verse identifies the aspirant with Heru, the Higher Self, who moves through time without end.
6. The inverted forms of the Divine are the forms of creation themselves, since to the unenlightened mind they appear not to be God and yet they are.
7. This verse identifies the aspirant with UnNefer, Asar as the Supreme and singular essence of existence.
8. The opener of the door of heaven is God in the form of Meskhent, who is the goddess of future birth. She is the one who allows souls to leave the Astral plane (heaven) so that they may become embodied once more and experience human life again.
9. This passage is extremely profound because it states that the initiate now transcends the past, present and future, and even controls it and all beings therein. There is only one being that can do this ... the Self. So {he/she} has become one with the Self who is the controller of all.
10. This verse is a further explanation of Verse 3 in that it details the hidden nature of the Divine. It cannot be known and it is unveiled to the uninitiated and the unenlightened. Being so, it is the seed from which the tree of Creation grows as its progeny, and it is so vast that it is unfathomable. This is the glory of the Self.
11. In an ordinary sense, human beings proceed from other human beings, but anything that is born must die. God has no birth and that which proceeds from her is none different from her. This means that Creation and everything in it is not something separate from God. The Spirit is here now, in the words you are reading, the paper of this book as well as the ink. God is there, in your hands, your clothing, the walls in your room as well as the clouds in the sky, your relatives, friends and enemies. God is everywhere! This being so, Creation cannot exist without God for even a moment because God and Creation are one. If you take God away, you take Creation away at the same time.
12. The lotus is an elaboration on Verse 1 relating to the child who arose from the primeval ocean (Nun), sitting on a lotus, which became Creation itself.
13. Nut is the mother of Asar. In this understanding she is the queen who gives birth to the Spirit into Creation. She is also the one who receives the soul into Heaven, and having her as one's mother means that one's spiritual fate is secure.
14. This verse is an allusion to Verses 3 and 10. Not being known is an essential characteristic of the Divine. However, being everywhere and in all things, the Divine knows all, all the time.
15. The Golden baboon is an aspect of Djehuti as the solar manifestation of Ra in the form of pure mind.

The text of the Deification of the Body Parts is a set of Hekau designed to reinforce the teachings presented here. The idea is that the initiate is not the mortal body, but that even this human body is Divine. The statements from the *Coffin Text* and Appendices are highly advanced mystical philosophy. These statements not only deify the personality, but also relate the initiate to the transcendental essence beyond

even the gods and goddesses. The statements such as "I am Nu," "I am that I am," and "I go to become one with my father" are highly refined statements of spiritual realization on the highest order. Here the initiate is relating {him/her} self to the subtlest essence of existence, i.e. God herself. Appendix 2 is of particular importance because it relates the wisdom that as the initiate, one is in fact Heru, and Heru "comes walking on the water of his father." In later times this teaching was adopted by the Christians as the Bible relates that Jesus walked on water as well.[394] The significance of this statement is tremendous, because the water of Asar is the Creation itself, and assuming the identity of Heru, men and women are indeed walking in and on the Kingdom of Asar. Thus, the glory of life is in discovering one's divine nature and the nature of Creation.

---

[394] Matthew 14:26.

Section 4: The Mystical Union

Plate 54: The Initiate makes the greatest offering (Hetep) and is anointed, having discovered oneness with the Divine Self.

CHAPTER 28[395]

WORDS FOR COMING FORTH BY DAY AFTER WORKING THROUGH AND OPENING THE TOMB.

Plate 55: Vignette from Chapter 28 of Papyrus Ani. The initiate propitiates to the Divine Ram, the Divine soul within him which is also God.

1. These words are to be spoken by Asar _____.

2. Hail, soul great, and majestic! Verily, I have come to you! I see you.

3. I worked through the Netherworld to see my Divine Asar.

4. I have dispelled the darkness!

5. I am beloved by him!

6. I have come to see my father Asar.

7. I cut out the heart of this god Sety, as I am performing duties in service for my Divine Father Asar.

8. All the paths are opening for me in heaven and on earth.

9. I am the child, loved by my father Asar.

10. I am ethereal and glorified and fully equipped for the spiritual journey.

11. Hail, all you gods and goddesses! Hail, all you spirits!

12. Make a way for me, for I am Asar _____ maak-heru!

---

[395] Generally referred to as Chapter 9.

GLOSS ON CHAPTER 28: ITS MEANING AND MYSTICAL SIGNIFICANCE

This chapter was included in the collection because it contains a special teaching related to the subtlety of spiritual attainment. It begins with a devotional invocation to the Soul, the Divine Spirit, Asar, and his love for the initiate is proclaimed. This is akin to a long trek that has been undertaken to see a loved one, then finally arriving at the destination and being received with open arms. This is what it is like when egoism is left behind, that is, when one dispels the idea of individuality and has nothing left. This is when the soul receives one as if with open arms like the proverbial prodigal son who has been away on a long arduous journey, but who has finally come home.

Dispelling the darkness is dispelling the ignorance about the Self. The human personality has several aspects. It is a composite of gross and subtle elements. The initiate says in Verse 7 that Set or Sety's heart has been cut out. This refers to the grosser aspects of the personality, the Khat-body, Ren-name, that is, body consciousness and name consciousness, i.e., the belief in one's individuality-name and form.

In Verse 10, the newly discovered subtlety of the initiate is proclaimed. The subtlest parts of the body: *Khaibit, Individual - Ba, Sahu,* and *Khu or Akhu* are the deepest levels of the unconscious mind. The name and form of the personality cannot leave the grave or funeral pyre. Only the subtle aspects of the personality can soar like a bird, up to the heavens. One who is attached to the body and name cannot discover this subtlety. The mind of that person will constantly pull them down to worldly desires, thoughts and feelings, and these will effectively prevent the subtle aspects from leaving the lower forms of existence. This means that one will be compelled by one's own karmic entanglements, to come back to an embodied state. This process will continue until the subtle aspects of the personality are discovered, and identified with, instead of the lower, grosser aspects.

CHAPTER 29[396]

WORDS FOR NOT ALLOWING THE SOUL TO BE TAKEN AWAY.

Plate 56: Scene from the Papyrus of Ani. The Initiate holds his own Soul in his arms.

1. Words to be said by Asar _____. I am that I am[397], coming forth, through the floodwaters[398].

2. Given to me is Fullness, and Life Force Power within as the power of the river.

GLOSS ON CHAPTER 29: ITS MEANING AND MYSTICAL SIGNIFICANCE

This very short chapter was included because it contains the all-important hekau "I am that I am" and it is used in a special way. "I am" is the nameless Supreme Being of Existence. It is this principle of existence, also referred to as *The Absolute,* that emerges from the primeval waters of potential consciousness. This "I am" is undivided, eternal and all-pervasive, all-encompassing existence. It is this realization that protects one from the loss of one's soul. Loss of the soul means losing one's self, i.e. consciousness, as in falling asleep. The swoon of falling asleep makes one lose one's waking consciousness. When this happens, one is thrown into a world which seemingly comes out of nowhere. It appears to be real and yet it is not. But still the soul feels compelled to reside there as if all is correct and in order. This is a dreadful predicament, to lose control over one's identity and destiny, and yet people submit to this every day when they fall asleep without any guarantee they will wake up or where they may end up. They also submit to this state when awake when they accept the day to day "realities" of the world as abiding. The realization of the "I Am" is the realization that one is full and perfect, without need and without desire, and yet full of potential, joy, peace, vitality and strength of will (*power of the river*), love, and most of all, contentment.

---

[396] Generally referred to as Chapter 61.
[397] Literally: ***Nuk Pu Nuk.***
[398] Here the initiate is identified with the divinity of primeval times (Nefertem) who emerged in the beginning from the Primeval Ocean thereby bringing creation into being.

CHAPTER 30[399]

WORDS FOR NOT DYING A SECOND TIME IN THE NETERKHERT.
Plate 57: Vignette from Chapter 30 of Papyrus Auf Ankh. The initiate stands aside from the tomb.

1. Words to be said by Asar _____. Opened is my dwelling[400]; repeat twice.

2. Under the sanctified spirits in the depths of darkness, Heru sanctified me.

3. Wepwawet[401] blessed me.

4. I am hidden[402] among you.

5. The everlasting stars are on my neck as Ra.

6. My personality is open.

7. My heart and lungs are in my throne.

8. I speak the foremost wisdom teachings.

9. I am Ra! Behold I am he himself!

10. I am not ignorant of my self.

11. I am not one who looks after you.[403]

12. Lives for thee thy Father.

13. Son of Nut[404], I am thy eldest son, seeing your hidden mysteries.

14. It is my rising as sovereign of the gods and goddesses, not dying I, a second time in the Neterkhert!

---

[399] Generally referred to as Chapter 44.
[400] See also Chapter 17, line #1.
[401] Form of the god Anpu-"Opener of the Ways"- he led Asar to the land of the blessed.
[402] Amun is a member of the great trinity of Amun-Ra-Ptah. This word is a pun on witnessing consciousness (Amun), and amun meaning "hidden," i.e. hidden spirit among you.
[403] One does not look up to the gods and goddesses, but the other way around, they are looking to Asar _____.
[404] Asar.

GLOSS ON CHAPTER 30: ITS MEANING AND MYSTICAL SIGNIFICANCE

This Chapter contains some familiar themes, in Verses 1-6, already discussed in previous glosses. This is indicative of the manner in which spiritual teaching is to be imparted. Repetition is a tool used by the scriptures to drive home the spiritual teachings. This is because as a person living in the world, you are constantly being bombarded with sensations, thoughts, images, etc., that tantalize, arouse and distract the personality. The repetition of these impresses the world on the personality and leads the mind to delusion. The antidote for this is the repeated study and practice of the teachings until spiritual enlightenment has been attained.

The following verses contain a special statement. First it is stated that the personality is open. This may be seen as one of the primary requirements of a spiritual aspirant but what does it mean to be open? Being open is realizing one is ignorant and making oneself humble to listen to the teachings under the guidance of a qualified teacher. True listening is an art that cannot be practiced when there is egoism or desire in the heart. There are some special injunctions for spiritual initiates to follow. They are known as the Ten Virtues of the initiates.

> *(1)"Control your thoughts,"*
> *(2)"Control your actions,"*
> *(3)"Have devotion of purpose,"*
> *(4)"Have faith in your master's ability to lead you along the path of truth,"*
> *(5)"Have faith in your own ability to accept the truth,"*
> *(6)"Have faith in your ability to act with wisdom,"*
> *(7)"Be free from resentment under the experience of persecution"* (Bear insult)
> *(8)"Be free from resentment under experience of wrong,"* (Bear injury)
> *(9)"Learn how to distinguish between right and wrong,"*
> *(10)"Learn to distinguish the real from the unreal."*

Also, all of the 42 Precepts of Maat should be followed scrupulously in order to purify the personality and allow one to be open to the teaching, and thereby be able to understand it correctly. There are some special precepts from the injunctions of Maat that apply directly to this topic. They are 1, 11, 14, 18, 20, 22, 24, 33, 39, 40, and 41.

Following the precepts of the initiates serves to purify the heart and cleanse out the gross impurities of egoism (anger, hatred, greed, lust, arrogance, conceit, vanity, pride). When one is open, then one becomes a qualified aspirant and is able to listen to the wisdom teachings that act to cleanse out the subtle impurities of egoism (ignorance, desire, individuality, discontent, fear of death, etc.).

This wisdom is clearly defined in this chapter. In Verse 9 it is stated: *I speak the foremost wisdom teachings.* And what exactly is this foremost wisdom? The following verses explain in detail. The foremost wisdom is knowing one is God. Being ignorant of this momentous truth is the source of all troubles and human suffering. Living in a state of ignorance causes one to be in a subservient position in ordinary life, to other human beings, to one's own senses and desires and to the negative forces of the world as well as one's own demoniac qualities. Therefore, the initiate states emphatically that {he/she} does not look up to God, that is, {he/she} is not a follower, looking for something beyond. Rather, that same Divinity that others at the lower level of religion worship, has been discovered as the essential nature of the initiate. Thus, there is nowhere to go, nowhere to look for God since she is right here, now and forever. Therefore, the initiate is the one that is really being worshipped. It is the "I Am" in all that is being worshipped. This is the highest wisdom teaching.

CHAPTER 31[405]

THE CHAPTER OF KNOWING THAT IS TO BE KNOWN TO ATTAIN ENLIGHTENMENT: ALL IN ONE CHAPTER[406]

1. These words are to be said by Asar _____ .
2. I am yesterday and I know tomorrow. I have the power to give birth to myself again.
3. I am the hidden mystery from which the gods and goddesses arise, and the food which sustains those who reach the West.
4. I am the east rudder, the Lord of the two faces whose light illumines all.
5. I am the Lord of Resurrection, the one coming out of the darkness.
6. You two falcons who listen to all matters and lead the moored ones to the hidden sacred places, towing Ra, who follows from the place, the shrine above the shrine of the God who is in his shrine which stands in the center of the earth.
7. He is I and I am He.
8. It is I who produce the brilliant substance that Ptah emanates in the form of the physical world.
9. Ra, may your heart be filled with good truth of the present, which is your entering Heaven[407] and your going out on the Eastern side.
10. May the elders and the ancestors greet you. Make your roads and paths clear and pleasant for me so that I may cross the earth and heaven. May you shine your divine light upon me, oh, you three-fold hidden soul.
11. I am the one who comes close to the God whose words are heard by my ears in the Duat. There is no more sinfulness in my mother against you. May you rescue me and protect me from the one who closes the eyelids[408] at night; this is the restoration from the annihilation.
12. I am the inundation, the overflowing of life.
13. Great hearer is thy name.
14. I am the master of the soul, which wraps me in its bosom.
15. The fore-thigh is attached to the neck; the hind-thigh is on the head of the Amenti[409].
16. Adoration of this chief who is in his basin.
17. Delivered to me are those who belong to the chief of the two Great Ones.
18. Tears do not flow out of me.
19. May I sail from the dike, which is in Abdu, as the doorbolts move the doors and their faces are looking away.
20. Your image is provided with its arms... Your face is like that of a hound when smelling the shrine.
21. I make my legs to move like Anpu to start up before the going out of the smeller in Djedu towards the two lions. Therefore, I am healthy and safe.
22. I go out through the gate, which is illumination of the heart.
23. He who knows the depths of the waters is my name.
24. I act according to the faculties of the soul.
25. Hundreds of thousands and millions of things are on his altar.
26. I am the protector of these things, making hours run on the day of fitting the shoulders of the constellation Sahu.[410] The twenty four hours pass together coming one by one, as long as one-sixth of that which arrives in the Duat, which is the hour of overthrowing the rebels and foes by means of truth speaking and returning therefrom vindicated.
27. Those who are crossing over the Duat are like itself.
28. Thou requirest that I shine as a Lord of Life, true and radiant, making the seventh hour when he goes out.

---

[405] Generally referred to as Chapter 64.

[406] From the Turin Papyrus.

[407] i.e. at the West.

[408] When the eyelids close at night one falls asleep and loses consciousness as well as control over oneself as well as one's actions. One is at the mercy of whatever happens. This is a miserable predicament.

[409] The beautiful West (heaven).

[410] Orion, the stars of Asar (Osiris).

29. I have risen as a living being because of Maat from that day of coldness of blood, wounded at the burial.
30. I comply with the mysteries: I was brought forth to repel those who are upon their belly.
31. I go forth as a messenger of the Supreme Being, as an adviser of Asar.
32. There are seven steps in his ascent. My protection is in the words of power.
33. Do not let the Eye hold back its tears.
34. It is the god of the dwelling ... arriving from Sekhem towards Anu.
35. I make the Bennu acquainted with the things that are in the Duat: Oh the one who establishes that which is in me, producing the creations like Khepera going out in the form of the sun disk to light all.
36. I was conceived in the western side of heaven and I give light to the souls who are waiting in the Duat.
37. I move across heaven and pass through its walls and make light in it.
38. I fly away to illuminate the shades.
39. I prepare a good road towards the gates of the Duat;
40. I do so because he who is fainting is comforted by me, because he who is weeping is the one that I rescue among the people in the west whom I am also one.
41. Who is then a devourer in Amenti?
42. It is I who am in Restau. I enter in his name; I go out among the favorites of the Lord of the millions of years of the earth, the author of his own name.
43. I am Going Forth[411] By Day in the presence of Asar as a possessor of life.
44. The two snakes have opened the Duat for me so that I may come to behold the Uadjit[412] Eye.
45. The water is overturned on the back of the Bennu and the two lady confedcrates.
46. Heru is given the restored Uadjit Eye so that he may illumine at dawn. My name is his name.
47. There is not greatness above me, in my aspect as the god-lion.
48. The invocations to Shu are in reality to me.
49. My arms are pure in praising him.
50. I am the very one who gave birth to himself in ancient times and the same one who created my own name.
51. I am a Lord of Life, an adorer of Nun.
52. I go out of the great house of Asar.
53. I am protected against those who make evil successful.
54. I come to see him who is in the coils of the serpent Mehen[413], face to face, eye to eye.
55. I stand up, I make myself again, I fly up to heaven, and I rest on the earth.
56. I am brought forth by yesterday; I am master of transformations.
57. I create myself again at the appointed time.
58. The god who conceals his struggle is covered; his coverer moves behind me.
59. My will power imparts vigor to my flesh.
60. I am protected by the protection of my hands.
61. The Company of Gods and Goddesses rise up at my words.
62. Oh Lion of the Sun lifting up thy arm in Toser, thou are in me and I am in thee, thy shape is my shape.
63. "*I am the inundation, Rising From The Great Water*" is my name.
64. The transformations of Tmu, of Khepera, the terrestrial vegetation of Tmu are all me.
65. I enter Sekhem as an ignorant person and go out as an initiate, a pure spirit; I am Asar.
66. I see the forms of the men eternally.
67. *This Chapter assures spiritual enlightenment. Anyone who knows this teaching by his own will is victorious on earth as well as in the Netherworld and takes all forms desired due to the protection of the Great God.*
68. *This Chapter was found in the city of Khemenu[414] on a brick of burnt clay written in blue, under the feet of the god Djehuti. During the time of King Menkara, a prince named Hor-dada-f found it. This*

---

[411] Becoming spiritually enlightened.
[412] Wadjet.
[413] One Ancient Egyptian mythic relates the understanding of a giant serpent (Mehen) that lives in the Primeval Ocean. It is the energy and movement from this serpent which stirred up the Primeval Ocean and caused waves and forms to arise; thus, Creation came into being. The same teaching can be found in Hindu tradition (The Shesha Serpent). See the book *Egyptian Yoga Vol. 2* by Muata Ashby. The Fon Nation of Africa believes in a giant serpent as being the Creator and Sustainer of the universe through its 3,500 "coils."
[414] Per-Djehuti- the city of the god Djehuti.

teaching transported him into ecstasy. Then he brought it as soon as he realized that a great mystery was written upon the brick.

69. *This Chapter can be known by those who recite it and study it when they see no more, hear no more, have no more sexual intercourse[415] and eat no meat or fish[416].[417]*

70. *A scarab shall be placed on the breast of the person to whom shall be performed the ceremony of Opening the place of beauty and goodness, advancing over the period of sixty years into it. Favor not the stinking of my name in the presence of the sustainers of life. Favor not the speaking of lies about me around The God beautiful and good when listening to thee.*

Plate 58: Vignette from Chapter 31 of Papyrus Auf Ankh. The initiate comes out of the darkness of the tomb and into the light of the sun.

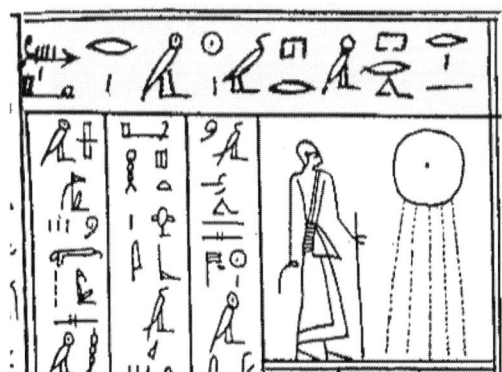

GLOSS ON CHAPTER 31: ITS MEANING AND MYSTICAL SIGNIFICANCE

This Chapter is remarkable in many ways. First, of all it is broad in scope and sublime in nature. It is one of the single most important chapters that should be studied repeatedly in order to draw from its profundity. It is boldly titled with words like *That Is To Be Known* and *All In One,* and these words give an indication that we are now going to move up to something great, to lofty levels of philosophy. If the teaching contained in this single chapter were known fully, it would lead to the understanding of the other chapters as well and of course, spiritual realization too. Like Chapter 4, this chapter is also so extensive that a full treatment would require a separate volume. This gloss will present the most important aspects of the chapter.

The Verses

1-13 This chapter opens with a bold declaration. Similar to the passage in Chapter 27, Verse 9, it states that the initiate is the controller of the past, present and the future, i.e., beyond time and space. The following verses augment this teaching, thereby leading us to understand exactly what is transcendental of time. What the teaching is really pointing to is eternity, but what is eternity? It is explained as the source and sustenance of the gods and goddesses, and in this sense, the neteru (gods and goddesses) are time and space, the manifestations or emanations of Pa-Neter, the Spirit. The Spirit does not exist in time and space, but these emanate from the Spirit. Essentially, time and space is a piece of eternity just as a drop of water is a piece of the whole ocean. The "I Am" formula is used here again, now to relate that the initiate is not identified with the small ego-personality. The

---

[415] Celibacy.

[416] Vegetarian Diet.

[417] Verses 67-69 is a variant of chapter 36 (30B).

"I Am" of the initiate is in reality the principle behind all, the ultimate cause and support for everything that has or will come into existence. This is an important quality of mystical religions such as the Kemetic and Indian Yoga/Vedanta, which affirm this kind of teaching. In ordinary, orthodox type of religions, this kind of statement would be considered blasphemous, but that assessment is based on a limited understanding of the nature of Creation. This is even now being exposed by quantum physicists. The essence behind all matter is intelligent energy. In mystical philosophy, this intelligent energy is the Self. In mystical religion, this principle would be referred to as the Spirit. In yoga science this principle is Universal Consciousness. Consider that when you have a dream, every object and situation in your dream is an emanation from you. You are the single, innermost principle sustaining the dream world. You are manifesting as the dream world and you are also everything in it as well. This entire universe is God's dream, and when she dreams, she dreams big. What is meant by this humorous statement is that the only difference between God and a human being is the level of creative power. However, if one were to realize one's essential nature as one with the Divine, then one also becomes a sublime dreamer and Creator with unlimited potential in God.

14 This verse is extremely important as it establishes the relative positions of the soul and personality. In ordinary worldly thinking, people believe that the soul is within the body, like a hormone that is secreted from the brain somehow. In fact, the grosser aspects of the personality, the Ka, the Ab, the Ren and Khat, are emanations from the soul, and the soul itself is an emanation from the Spirit, again, just as a drop of water is a piece of the whole ocean.

18 The initiate states that there are no longer any tears coming out of {him/her}. There are two types of people who do not shed tears over the world, implying caring over worldly events that affect one. The first group are those who are too sick (physically or mentally) to care, and the other group are those who have attained enlightenment and are thereby beyond caring over illusions and misunderstanding. One does not care over things that are not real or abiding. This does not mean that sages cannot show compassion or caring. In fact, only those who are detached and enlightened can truly care in a deepest sense, without prejudice or resentment of personal desire. This is the way God loves all, like the sun, supporting everything and in the midst of everything, and yet aloof and detached. Only those who are detached can give pure love because their love is given without expectation, greed, selfishness or egoistic desire for personal gain. For more on the teachings of detached love and supreme love see the books *Egyptian Tantra Yoga* and *The Blooming Lotus of Divine Love* by Muata Ashby.

22-24 Most people in life are content with what nature presents to them. The world they see is actually only the surface of a vast ocean of being. It is only the skin, as it were. However, initiates are not satisfied with this. They have a craving to know the truth of things, the depths below the surface. The personality is like that also. What we know of others and of our own depths, is actually only the surface. In fact there is a depth to the personality that people never know or understand. Beyond the functions of the mind, the thoughts, memories, desires, mental impressions, etc., there is a vastness that is frightening for most people to even consider and yet this is the domain of initiate, their area of specialty. This is what an aspirant needs to look forward to, the discovery of the Amentet, the Duat and the Djed, the ultimate abode of the innermost Self. Being in the level of consciousness of the Higher Self, one's actions are no longer egoistic or prideful, but magnanimous and for the universal good. This is acting *according to the faculties of the soul.*

28-32 Being One with the Divine Self, the initiates realize their true nature. Thus, when the sun rises, sustaining life on earth, it is actually one who is doing this, for the innermost Self of everyone is that same power which is manifesting in the sun. It is the practice of Maat, which has allowed this realization to occur. The resurrection from death (coldness of blood, wounded at the burial) is

achieved through Maat. Living by Maat means the practice of righteousness and truth in life, and there is no higher truth than the *mysteries,* the study and practice of this mystical philosophy. The practice of these mysteries allows one to climb the seven steps to the shrine of Asar (see Chapter 18), and the seven psycho-spiritual consciousness centers of the Serpent Power.

35-38 These passages are now dedicated to bringing home to us, the understanding that this true personality who we are innately, is not just the power which sustains the physical universe, but also the power which operates in the Netherworld as well. Khepri is the Creator aspect of the Divine. In this form as the sun, Creation is not only established, but also sustained daily. It is this same essence which originates in the Netherworld that illumines and enlivens all there and allows the physical world to come into being. The disembodied souls reside in the Duat (Netherworld), and when the sun passes through the Netherworld, it is their day and our nighttime. As explained earlier, the shades are the subtle reflection of the soul, which are not self-illuminating, and which therefore exist only due to the presence of light and an object. In this case, the object is the soul. If the soul were to merge with the light, there would be no more shadow because there is no longer an object for the light to reflect on and thereby produce a shadow.

39-48 In Verse 21, the divinity Anpu was introduced. Anpu is the god of intellectual discernment. He is the god with two faces, the one as the embalmer, the other as the knower of the ways, which lead through the Netherworld to the abode of the Divine Self. Thus, the initiate, having assumed the role of all divinities, now acts as Anpu, leading souls on the right path to enlightenment. As the Divine Self, the initiate is the comfort, the rest and refuge for all beings. Also, {he/she} is at the same time the devourer of souls, that power that consumes all as one consumes one's dream upon waking up. A similar teaching is presented in the Hindu Bhagavad Gita: Chapter 11, Verse 30 *Vishwarup Darshan Yogah*--The Yoga of the Vision of the Cosmic Form. There is a text wherein the initiate sees the true form of God and refers to it as a devourer:

> *You are devouring all the worlds by Your blazing mouths, and You are licking them up, O Vishnu! Terrible effulgence is scorching the entire world with its fierce flames.*

This magnanimous view occurs when the initiate neutralizes the opposites within {him/her} self. This means that the two serpents/ladies, a metaphor of the two serpents of the caduceus, have joined and become one, thereby allowing the non-dual vision of the Supreme Self (the restored Uadjit Eye). There is no higher reality or Divinity than this and therefore, having attained this realization, all forms of worship to the gods and goddesses are in reality worship of the initiate.

49-66 These verses are similar in many ways to ones we have already discussed in the glosses to previous chapters. What is special about them however, is the perspective from which they are told. It is as if God is speaking to you, about herself, describing her nature and her works. In doing so she describes the attributes of Asar, Ra, Khepri, etc., and as if says, "I am the one doing all of these things." This masterful set of passages establish the idea that God is One, and the gods and goddesses are like manifestations of that One Supreme Being. Therefore, Kemetic Mysticism is a non-dual philosophy and cannot be considered a polytheistic religion. The lack of this understanding is referred to as "ignorance," and the understanding of it is qualified as the wisdom of the initiates.

67-70 The concluding portion of this chapter is important for many reasons. Firstly, it contains an injunction proclaiming the infallibility of this spiritual knowledge, in leading one to awakening to the understanding that one is manifesting as all forms in Creation and to spiritual enlightenment.

The legend associated with this chapter is that it was found, as if from a lost period in the antiquity of Kemetic history, and that the finder, upon reading it, fell into a spiritual ecstasy. This is the desired effect

of these scriptures. If the mind is highly purified and there is devotion to God in the heart, the mere mention of God's names and glories should be enough to transport an initiate into an ecstatic feeling of communion with the Divine. The process of following the teachings (listening, reflection and meditation) under the guidance of an authentic teacher is the key to making this subtlety in the personality possible. However, if there is no proper preparation, even the most exalted text will be repudiated by the ignorant. This is why these teachings are not to be discussed with the masses, but only those who have been prepared. Preparation means those who are initiated, trained and purified through the practice of Maat. The practice of Maat makes a human being a qualified aspirant, and when a qualified aspirant meets an authentic teacher, Spiritual Enlightenment will surely follow. On the other hand, even if Asar, Buddha, or Jesus were to come from heaven to speak to an ignorant person, their teachings would fall on deaf ears. Therefore, even before meeting a teacher, the aspirant should work to follow the path of purification through righteous actions, thoughts, and speech.

The primary key to making the teachings in this chapter effective in life is given in Verse 69. It provides the specific Maatian concepts that lead to control of the ego-personality and thereby also to the development of concentration, will power and the faculty of Saa (understanding), for without control of the ego, there can be no understanding, since the ego and egoistic living is a distracting force which moves the mind towards ignorance and worldliness instead of wisdom. One must practice recitation of the teachings. This includes the practice of chanting. The teachings must be studied, preferably under the guidance of a spiritual preceptor. This is all to be done when one has abstained from engaging in worldly activities. In particular the text mentions sexuality, which implies any activity that excites the ego's desire for sense pleasures.[418] Also, the text mentions vegetarianism, for the sages of old discovered that gross foods make the physical body and the mind gross, thereby rendering a person worldly and incapable of understanding the teachings.[419]

---

[418] For more details on the Kemetic teachings related to sexuality, relationships and spiritual evolution see the book *Egyptian Tantra Yoga* by Muata Ashby
[419] For more details on the Kemetic teachings related to health and vegetarianism see the book *The Kemetic Diet: Food for Body Mind and Soul* by Muata Ashby

CHAPTER 32[420]

INVOCATION OF THE DJED PILLAR; THIS IS THE CHAPTER OF THE DJED OF GOLD.

1. These words are to be said by Asar _____ maakheru:

2. This is your backbone.[421]

3. Rise up thee for thyself, O weary one of heart, shine for thyself. O weary one of heart. Give thyself on your side. I have come and brought to thee a Djed of Gold, so rejoice thyself in it.

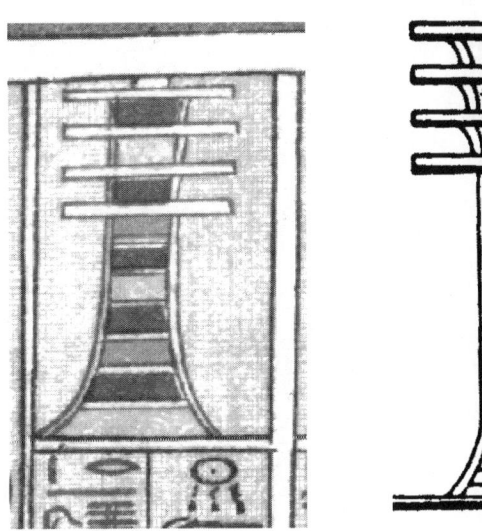

Plate 59: left- Vignette from Chapter 32 of Papyrus Ani. The Djed Pillar of Asar.

Figure 105: right- Alternate rendition of the Pillar of Asar now showing the eyes (symbolic of Asar, Hru and Ra).

---

[420] Generally referred to as Chapter 155.
[421] Referring to the Djed Pillar. An amulet is also used here. It is placed on the throat of the initiate, and when the Djed is raised and made upright, it symbolizes the resurrection of Asar in ancient times and concurrently the resurrection of the initiate.

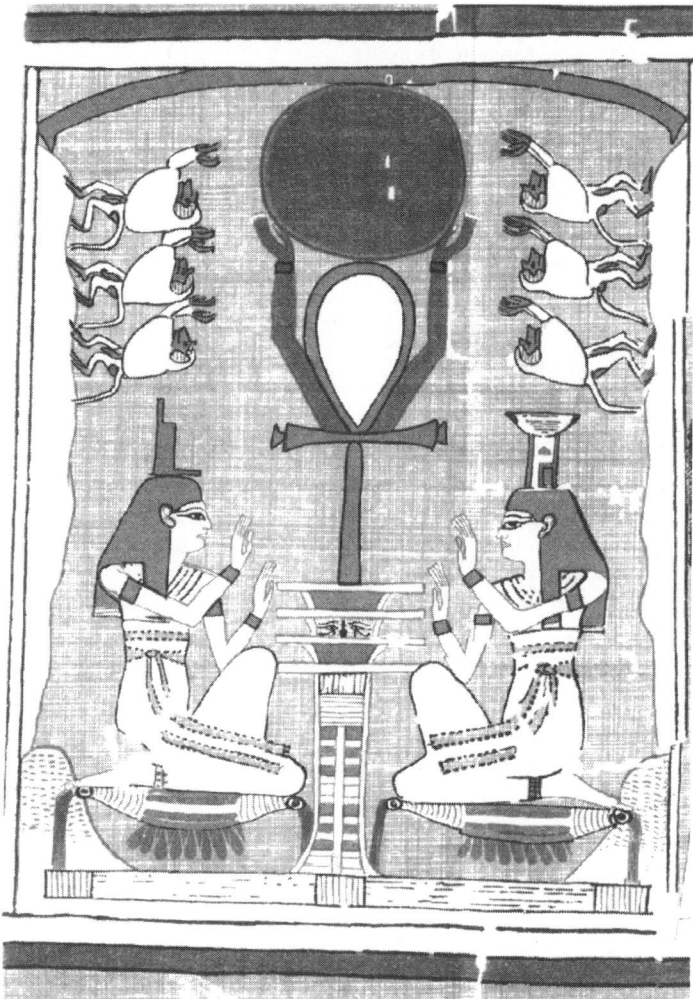

Plate 60: Left-Associated with the Hymn to Asar, this Vignette of raising the Djed is from Papyrus Ani.

The goddesses Aset and Nebethet adore the Asar (the Djed) and cause it to come alive (Ankh rising from the top of the Djed). The Ankh embraces (embrace symbolizes sustaining-nurturing with Life Force) the sundisk, suspended under the symbol of heaven, ⟋, while six baboons (the god Djehuti) dance and adore it.

Plate 61: Right-Associated with the Hymn to Ra, this Vignette is from a Chapter of raising the Djed. –from Papyrus Hunefer. Aset and Nebethet Adore the Djed with seven baboons as Herakti (Ra-Heru) rises.

294

GLOSS ON CHAPTER 32: ITS MEANING AND MYSTICAL SIGNIFICANCE

Figure 106: Asar as the embodiment of the Pillar.

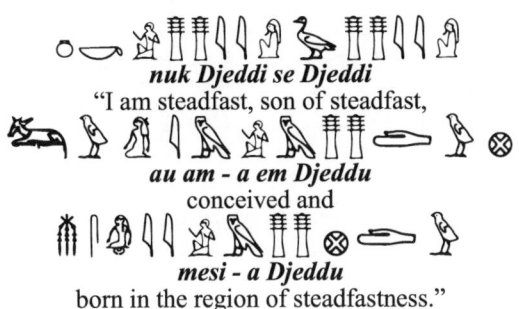

Many people mistakenly believe that the *Prt m Hru* is a book of rituals for people who have passed on, but as previously expressed, in reality it is a discipline for those who are alive. Having a physical body provides the best opportunity to carry out a spiritual program (the practice of Yoga and Mystical Religion), because it is then that the soul can experience an extended period of waking consciousness in which to consciously work on purifying the heart. The dream and dreamless sleep states relate to the subconscious and unconscious levels of the mind, and minimal spiritual progress occurs in these states of consciousness.

Human beings are different from all other forms of life in that they have the potential for reasoning and self-awareness. However, the animal instincts, the lower self in human beings in the form of desires, uncontrolled emotions, fears, hatreds, etc., cloud the intellect and cause them to think, feel, and act in unrighteous ways. Unrighteousness is seen as the primary cause of the inability to have peace, joy and spiritual realization in life. Therefore, the *Prt m Hru* is dedicated to showing the way in which a person should live in order to achieve material and spiritual prosperity. This means that a person's practical life needs to be controlled. This means controlling one's thoughts, desires, emotions and physical actions, etc.

In the after death state, the unresolved desires in the unconscious emerge to impel the soul to move on in the search for fulfillment of those desires, even though they are unreal and futile. Imagine if you could do whatever you wanted to do, but without restriction. If you wanted to eat pizza you could eat it continuously without getting overweight or sick. If you wanted to do violence against certain people you would be able to do so in an unrestricted manner. If you wanted to indulge in any pleasures of the senses such as sex, music, beautiful sights, etc., you could do so. In so doing, the intellect becomes overwhelmed and therefore unused. Thus the intellect becomes weak and atrophied. The senses take control and direct the path of the soul. At some point the astral experience is exhausted and then the soul, with its remaining unconscious impressions, returns to the physical realm in order to once again gain experiences as a living human being, or perhaps even some other life form (animal, plant, mineral, etc.). If enlightenment is not attained, this cycle of birth, death and astral experiences is repeated over and over again, indefinitely. This is why the process of yoga and mystical spirituality has as its primary goal to cleanse the unconscious impressions of the mind. In Ancient Egyptian terms this process, known as *Maak-heru* or "Purity of Heart," was the central mission presented in the *Ancient Egyptian Book of Coming Forth By Day*. This is what the following line from the Egyptian *Prt m Hru*, Chapter I (below) is referring to.

nuk Djeddi se Djeddi
"I am steadfast, son of steadfast,

au am - a em Djeddu
conceived and

mesi - a Djeddu
born in the region of steadfastness."

As discussed in Chapter 18 and the Gloss On Chapter 18, there is a special realm within the Duat which is the abode of Asar, as well as the ultimate destination of those who become enlightened. It is the realm of Supreme Peace, the *Sekhet-Yaru,* or in other times, as *Amentet.* As you recall, Amentet is a reference which unites the symbolism of Asar with that of Amun (Amen), because *tet* refers to the Djed Pillar of Asar, ∬. Asar is often depicted as a man with the body of a pillar containing four tears. The tears symbolize the four upper levels of

295

psycho-spiritual consciousness centers when awakened. The Djed symbolizes the awakened human soul which is well "established" in the knowledge of the Self. *Djeddu,* 𓊽𓊽 ⬭ 𓏤 ⊛, refers to the abode of Asar.

RAISING THE PILLAR

As stated earlier, the raising of the pillar or the Serpent Power, through the subtle psycho-spiritual energy centers of the vertebrae signifies the raising of consciousness. As consciousness is raised one is leading oneself to discover the Higher Self and immortality. This "raising" is accomplished by Aset and Nebethet in their serpentine aspects. Aset and Nebethet are identified as the "the two exceedingly great uraei" (serpents of higher consciousness). Also, in the myth of the Ausarian Resurrection it is said that Set tore the body of Asar to pieces and that Aset, Anpu, and Nebethet, with the help of the Serpent god Nehebkau, re-membered the pieces, all except the phallus which was eaten by the fish. In this way, assisted by the words of power of Aset, Asar was reconstituted. Following this, he (Asar) became the ruler in the realm of the dead, the beautiful West, the Amenta or Duat (Astral world).

The deeper mystical implications of the myth of Asar, Aset, Heru, Set and Nebethet involve the journey of the soul. Asar, as the symbol of the soul, experiences the passion of life and death as well as rebirth and resurrection. This is the ultimate fate of every human being when the "two ladies" as well as the psycho-spiritual qualities as represented by the other characters in the myth (Heru, Set, Anpu, Selket, Nehebkau, Sebek, Hetheru, Min, etc.) are harmonized and realized within one's own consciousness. In this sense, Serpent Power Yoga is a mythic experience wherein one can develop mystical insights through the understanding of the ancient myth, the practice of the rituals related to it as well as the psychospiritual discipline of meditation on the energy centers.[422]

Figure 107: The Goddess Aset and the King of Egypt raise the Pillar thereby resurrecting Asar. [From a bas relief in the temple of Asar at Abdu (Abydos) Egypt.]

---

[422] For the entire myth of the Ausarian Resurrection see the book ***The Ausarian Resurrection: The Ancient Egyptian Bible.*** For more on the Serpent Power see the book *The Serpent Power* by Dr. Muata Ashby.

CHAPTER 33[423]

PLATE 62: VIGNETTE FROM CHAP. 33. REGISTER (1)THE TWO MAATI GODDESSES PRESIDE AS (2)THE INITIATE PROPITIATES ASAR, (3)ANPU PREPARES THE SCALES OF MAAT, (4) DJEHUTI PREPARES (WRITES) THE FEATHER OF MAAT BY WHICH THE INITIATE WILL JUDGE {HIM/HER} SELF.

INTRODUCTION

1. These are the words to be said when going into the Hall of Maati. Adorations to Asar, the foremost being in Amentet.

2. These words are to be spoken by Asar _____ who is maak-heru.

3. "I come to you through the great path[424], to see thy beauties.[425] With my two arms I adore you in your name, Maa[426]. I have come through this exalted spiritual path and I find that it is a primordial path. The ash tree had not come into being, nor was the shed tree born yet; the ground was not yet created nor were there any plants or vegetation either. As to myself[427], I go into the abode of Hidden Existence.[428] I speak words with Set. I breathe in odors. Comes close to me the clothing which is upon those who prostrate upon the hidden things there.[429]"

4. He enters into the House of Asar. He sees his secrets, which are in him. The Divine Chiefs of the pylons are in the form of spirits.

5. These words are spoken by the god Anpu[430] for both of his aspects[431]. The words these of mine are coming from Tameri[432]. He knows the paths and locales. Offerings are made to me. I smell his odor through one among you. He speaks to me: I am Asar _____ who is maak-heru in peace, maak-heru. I come by the great path, to see the great gods and goddesses. I live by the offerings these of their Ka's and I have been to the limits of the soul who is the Lord of Djedu. He grants to me the great going forth[433] in the form of a bennu[434] bird according to my own words. I have been in the river. I have made offerings through divine incense. I have worked a way through the tree of human beings. I am in the city of Abdu, in the temple of the Satet

---

[423] Generally referred to as chapter 125- This translation is based on Papyrus Ani, Papyrus Auf Ankh, and Papyrus Nu.

[424] Initiation into the mysteries of Yoga and the spiritual path of practicing the yogic disciplines in life (meditation, study of the scriptures, righteous living and devotion to the gods and goddesses).

[425] Referring to the god Asar.

[426] From Maat-righteous One.

[427] Asar _____ (the initiate).

[428] The House of Asar.

[429] Secret Mysteries.

[430] Son of Asar and Nebethet-has two aspects: Embalmer (Anpu) and Opener of the Ways (Wepwawet).

[431]Physical personality and the spiritual essence of Asar _____.

[432] Beloved land-Egypt.

[433] Movement into spiritual enlightenment.

[434] Symbol of glorified or divine soul.

goddess[435]. I have submerged the boat of the enemies. I have journeyed to the lake in the neshemt boat and I have seen the Divine Ones of the Great Black[436]. I am in Djedu and I have made myself silent. I have given Life Force strength to the God on his two feet. I am in the temple and I am seen in the foremost divine abode. It is I who have entered into the house of Asar and I have clothed myself with garments of the one who is within. It is I who have entered into Rastau and I have seen the secrets which are within. Hidden was I but I found a way. It is I who went into Yanrutf. I put on the clothing, which was there, over my nakedness. Given to me was unguent of women by encompassing the earth of humankind. Truly, he has spoken to me about himself. I spoke about the idea of letting your equilibrium be through our innermost heart.

6.   These words were spoken by the majesty of Anpu: *Are you knowing the names of the door, this and can you speak these to me?*

7.   Spoken by Asar _____ who is maak-heru in peace, maak-heru this. *"Drive away thee the god Shu,"* is the name of door this.

8.   Spoken by the majesty of Anpu: As to this art thou knowledgeable about the name of the door part upper[437] and the door part lower[438]? The Lord of Truth, his personality is leading with his two legs in his name, door part upper and Lord Pehti[439], controller of cattle.[440] Pass thee, thou knower, Asar _____ maak-heru all venerable, reckoner of offerings divine of all the gods and goddesses of Waset.[441]

Plate 63: Vignette from Chapter 33 of the Papyrus of Ani. The initiate and spouse make offerings to the Divine.

---

[435] A form of the goddess Aset in which she spreads out fertility over the land.

[436] The Great Black is an epithet referring to the Divine Self in the form of the God Asar, who is known as the "Lord of the Perfect Black." Also, the Primeval Ocean can be seen as the "primordial blackness from which all things come into being."

[437] **lin·tel** (lĭn/tl) *n.* The horizontal beam that forms the upper member of a window or door frame and supports the structure above it.

[438] **thresh·old** (thrĕsh/ōld,' -hōld') *n.* **1.** A piece of wood or stone placed beneath a door; a doorsill.

[439] Mighty one, double strength.

[440] Name of the door part lower.

[441] The Ancient Egyptian city called Thebes by the ancient Greeks.

Plate 64: Vignette from Chapter 33 of Papyrus Ani.

Judgment of the Soul. Text: Ani addresses his heart. At top, the gods and goddesses presiding are (right to left: Ra, Atum, Shu, Tefnut, Geb, Nut, Nebethet and Aset, Heru Ur, Hetheru, Saa and Hu (Divine Taste). Far left, Ani enters the hall of Judgment. His heart (conscience) is being weighed by Anpu while the Divine principals Shai, Rennenet and Meskhenet look on. Ani's soul and his destiny also look on while Anubis measures Ani's heart against the feather of Maat. At far right Djehuti records the result while the Monster Ammit, the Devourer of the unjust, awaits the answer. The hands of Djehuti (God of reason) are "Shai" which means "destiny" and "Rennenet" which means "Fortune and Harvest (destiny)." The implication is that we reap (harvest) the result of our state of mind (heart). Our state of mind, including our subconscious feelings and desires, is weighed against cosmic order, Maat. If found to be at peace (Hetep) and therefore in accord with cosmic order (Maat) it will be allowed to join with the cosmos (Asar). Otherwise it will suffer the fate as dictated by its own contents (mental state of unrest due to lingering desires), which will lead it to Ammit who will devour the ego-personality. That soul will experience torments from demons until we learn our lessons or become strong enough through wisdom to know itself. Demons may be understood as negative cosmic energies which it has allowed itself to indulge in, in the form of mental anguish and torments people put themselves through, due to their own ignorance. Self-torment may be regret over some action or inaction while alive or a reluctance to leave the physical realm because of a lingering desire to experience more earthly pleasure. Therefore, one controls one's own fate according to one's own level of wisdom or reasoning capacity.

APPENDIX 4[442]

EXCERPTS OF CHAPTER 33 FROM CONTEMPORARY PAPYRI

1. I have lived by righteousness and truth while on earth. I live in righteousness and truth; I feed upon right and truth in my heart. I have done what is required to live in harmony in society and the gods and goddesses are also satisfied that I have worshipped rightly.
2. I have done God's will. I have given bread to the hungry, water to the thirsty, clothes to the clotheless and a boat to those who were shipwrecked. I made the prescribed offerings to the gods and goddesses and I also made offerings in the temple to the glorious spirits.

---

[442] Appendices are provided to show an expanded meaning of the utterances. They are taken from the same numbered utterances contained in different papyri.

3. Therefore, protect me when I go to face The God.[443]

GLOSS ON APPENDIX 4 TO CHAPTER 33: ITS MEANING AND MYSTICAL SIGNIFICANCE

There is one more important aspect of Chapter 33 which deserves special mention here. It is the teaching related to Selfless Service, included in Appendix 4. Here the initiate states {his/her} qualifications to be allowed into the inner shrine to see and become one with Asar. The initiate states that {he/she} helped those in need in various ways. This is one of the greatest and most secure methods of purifying the heart, because it makes one humble and it effaces the ego. Selfless Service is a vast area of spiritual practice as it forms the major part of the Yogic Path of Right Action. In a larger sense, the important teaching of right action is covered in Chapter 4, Part 1 of this volume. However, this particular section treats one of the essential elements of spiritual practice, Selfless Service. Every spiritual aspirant must understand the profound implications of Selfless Service and how to practice selfless service effectively in order to attain spiritual enlightenment.

First it must be understood that since God manifests as all Creation, she also is present in all human beings. This being so, one must realize that one is interacting in, with and through God in all actions, speech and thought. Since human interrelations have a most profound influence on the human mind, they are the most powerful means of effecting a change in the personality. However, if mishandled, they can be a most effective method of leading a human being to psychological attachment and suffering as well. An aspirant should understand that Maat comes to {him/her} in the form of human beings in need so as to give the aspirant an opportunity to grow spiritually by sublimating the ego through developing patience, dealing with difficult personalities without developing resentment, not taking attacks personally, and developing a keen understanding of human nature and human needs. Selfless Service allows a human being to discover caring for something greater than the little "me," and this leads to purity of heart from the gross fetters of anger, hatred, greed, lust, jealousy, envy, etc., and also the attachments based on blood relation and other filial relationships, for in order to serve in the highest order, one must serve all equally, without favorites. As a servant of God one's family becomes all humanity and nature itself. Therefore, the cause of environmental well being is also a high concern reflected in the following injunctions of the Prt M Hru.

    (15) "I have not laid waste the ploughed lands."
    (36) "I have never befouled the water." Variant: <u>I have not held back the water from flowing in its season.</u>
            —From Chapter 33 of the Ancient Egyptian Pert M Heru

When asked how she could stand to serve people and not feel disheartened, repulsed or depressed, Mother Teresa replied "I see only Jesus coming to me through people." This reply shows the saintly attitude towards humanity, and she displayed the highest level of spiritual practice through the path of right action, which is known as Selfless Service. Selfishness arises when a human being sees {him/her} self as separate from Creation and develops an egoistic selfishness, typified by the attitude of "I got mine you get yours." A spiritual aspirant must develop sensitivity to the fact that all Creation is inexorably linked at all levels (material, astral, and transcendental) and therefore, a true aspirant feels empathy and compassion for all humanity and will not rest until all human beings have the essential needs of life, those being food, shelter and opportunity to grow and thrive. All problems of the world can be traced to the selfishness and hoarding of precious basic necessities by certain segments of the population and the subsequent development of resentments, greed, hatred and violence which lead to untold social strife.

    (10) "I have not snatched away food."
            —From Chapter 33 of the Ancient Egyptian Pert M Heru

However, a spiritual aspirant does not pursue the betterment of the world in a sentimental manner, but with deep understanding of the fact that people's Ari (Karma) has led them to their current condition of

---

[443] Pa Neter-The Supreme Being from whom emanate the gods and goddesses. The goal of the Pert M Heru is to lead a person to an ultimate encounter to face God and become one with {her/him}.

suffering and therefore simply sending money or aid will not resolve the issue. Where food, clothing or funds are needed, they should be given, but in addition to these, one must undertake an effort to promote spiritual wisdom in humanity. Beyond the basic necessities of life, the world needs spiritual wisdom most of all. Technology, comforts of life, entertainments and other conveniences should come later. This is a well-ordered society along Kemetic-Maatian principles. Studying the teachings of yogic mysticism and their subsequent practice through selfless service will promote the enlightenment of humanity, which will end the cycle of egoism and disharmony. Therefore, the act of helping others is extremely important and should be pursued. It acts like soap and water to help an aspirant cleanse the gross impurities of the egoistic mind including the desire for praise, recognition, admiration and flattery from other human beings, which is fleeting, fickle and traitorous. Working in service of other human beings allows the aspirant to apply the teachings and experience the results. It allows the aspirant to develop the capacity to adapt and adjust to changing conditions of life and to other personalities, and still maintain the detachment and poise necessary to keep equal vision and awareness of the Divine. All of this promotes integration of the personality of the aspirant. Every aspect of the psyche, the intellect, the emotions, the action aspects (body, speech and thoughts) and the will aspect, are developed so as to produce a super-human being, who remains undisturbed by the world and though living in it, remains rooted in Divine Consciousness. In order to achieve this an aspirant serves God through {his/her} actions. These are to be seen as offerings to the Divine. Thereby an aspirant receives the recognition from God directly through inner peace and insight into the glory of life. Therefore, the results of one's selfless service actions are immediate and always good because no matter what the results of those actions are, the service itself is the goal of the aspirant. So while the aspirant should seek to act efficiently and qualitatively, the results of the actions are not {his/her} main goal. The fruits of actions are the purview of goddess Maat. The action itself is in the control of the aspirant. As the action of Selfless Service is performed and as the action itself is completed, the objective of the aspirant has been achieved and God is satisfied thereby.

The greatest act of service is to promote the dissemination of the philosophy of Maat so as to develop a consciousness of righteousness and virtue in all levels of society. Therefore, working in support of the cause of sages and saints and following in their footsteps or emulating them is seen as a highly advanced practice of Selfless Service. The dissemination of the teachings acts to promote subtlety of intellect and effacement of the subtle ego and thus, leads to spiritual enlightenment, the supreme goal of all aspirants. Thus, by serving humanity (God) and asking for nothing in return, one achieves the highest goal of life, the discovery of God in all. This is the glory of Selfless Service.

What are the disciplines of Selfless Service?

Service is an important ingredient in the development of spiritual life. From the earliest times the glory of service to humanity has been hailed as a means to promote purity of heart and thereby accelerate spiritual evolution. Service cures the disease of egoism because in order to be selfless, one must think of another first instead of self. This process draws grace to the spiritual aspirant because it opens up the heart, making it sensitive to the Divine presence. Selfless service is a mixture of the Yoga of Devotional Love where one adopts the attitude of seeing and serving the Divine in everyone and every creature, and the Yoga of Righteous Action (Maat) where one feels that they are an instrument in the Divine Hands, and thus it is God who is working through them performing the action. Thus, the ego gets no recognition, within oneself or externally in the world, and as a result, this process effaces the ego and leads immersion in divine awareness. When this process reaches its height, one can emphatically assert, as in Chapter 22, Verse 3, of Pert Em Hru scriptures, that: "Unrighteous (egoism) is an abomination to me; I do not see it, for my thoughts are with Maat (God) exclusively. I live in it." The following are some important points to keep in mind when practicing selfless service.

First, having controlled body, speech and thoughts, an aspirant should see {him/her} self as an instrument of the Goddess, being used by her to bring, harmony, peace, and help to the world. All human beings and nature are expressions of God; they (referring to their true essence) are God. Serving them is serving God. Therefore, act for their sake and not for the little "me." In a wider sense serving humanity is

like serving the big "Me" because in reality you are one with all Creation. However, one must be clear that one is serving God in that person, and not their ego. Their ego may want you to give them ten dollars so they buy alcohol, cigarettes or other kinds of drugs. In such a case, giving them the money serves the ego (lower self) in them and not the Higher Self, and thus is against the spiritual development of that person. So, by not giving them any money, you serve God in them best. This is how selfless service and the understanding of Maat philosophy purifies one's actions, because now instead of interacting with people in emotional and attached manner, oftentimes going against your conscience by giving into their egoistic whims, one has to constantly think of what the teachings prescribe in this or that particular circumstance, that is, does it serve the Divine in that person.

So, serving God in others sometimes requires discipline, which may be interpreted as harshness by the person you are serving, as in the situation above or when a parent scolds a child for playing with matches. Sometimes however, it requires the outward expression of gentleness and tenderness. One must realize that when one serves others holding the attitude of serving the Divine in others, regardless of if one is expressing outward harshness or tenderness, internally, in both situations, there should exist profound compassion and love flowing to the person being served, even if they can't recognize or appreciate it. So, in performing true service, serving without the expectation of needing to be thanked or feeling appreciated is of paramount importance (as will be discussed in more detail below in the second point about selfless service). Otherwise, when there is criticism and insults, these will create feelings of anger, frustration, being a martyr, etc., and one will become discouraged and stop their selfless service. Rather, a negative response of the part of the person being served gives one the opportunity to develop and/or perfect more spiritual qualities such as patience, perseverance, endurance, forbearance, and not getting caught up in the other person's egoism and lose one's focus on the Divine. In Chapter 34, Verse 10 of the Pert M Hru scripture, the initiates states that {he/she} has become a spiritual doctor: *There are sick, very ill people. I go to them, I spit on the arms, I set the shoulder, and I cleanse them.* Just as it would be inappropriate for a medical doctor to lose {his/her}patience with {his/her}patient because the person is complaining due to their illness, so too it is inappropriate for an initiate to lose their patience when dealing with the masses of worldly-minded people, suffering from the illness of ignorance of their true essence. So, it must be clearly and profoundly understood that in serving, you are serving, the true Self, not the ego.

Secondly, as discussed above, do not expect a result from your actions. In other words do not perform actions and wait for a reward or praises, and though working to achieve success in your project, do not develop the expectation that your efforts will succeed, because you may fail in what you are trying to accomplish. If you focus on the success of the project and failure occurs, the mind will become so imbalanced that it will negate the positive developments of personality integration, expansion and concentration which occurred as you were involved in the project. It will in effect, as the saying goes, throw the baby out with the bath water. That is, it will say that since the project was a failure, "I am a failure." This will intensify egoism, as it is contrary to the true essence of who you are, omnipotent (powerful beyond measure). Rather, if the work itself becomes the focus, and you work with the attitude that the very work is an offering to the Divine, first of all, you will only choose those works that are beautiful and fragrant, that is, spiritually uplifting and beneficial for humanity. Secondly, since God now becomes your focus, even if the project fails, you have gained spiritually, by thinking of God, since in mystical philosophy, adversity is defined as lack of remembrance of God, and prosperity, as constant remembrance of God. If this is achieved, regardless of whether the project outwardly succeeds or fails, there is inward spiritual success. Furthermore, if the project was of a worthwhile nature, you will try to see your errors and correct them, and continue to work for the outward success of the project so humanity can benefit, and will not stop working until you do succeed, promoting the feeling that it is God working through you, guiding you to eventual success. Therefore, your focus should be on you doing your part by performing the service, and letting God handle the results.

Thirdly, see yourself as being the goddess (Maat), working to alleviate suffering and uplift humanity. Adopt the attitude that she is in you as you perform actions and her presence brings with it glory, purity of heart, peace and universal love for all. If this is done, the action itself becomes the rewards and one's action

becomes an instant link with the Divine Self. Holding a dualistic vision in action causes mental agitation and engenders conflict and egoism. There is always a tendency for "looking out for number one" in one's egoistic actions. These types of actions are mixed with the impurities of vices and therefore one cannot serve perfectly in this capacity. Holding the vision of serving God in all is non-dualism in action. In this capacity one transcends the duality of action because one will not be elated or depressed over the results, but one will be fulfilled in the action itself, thereby transcending its result, and along with that, the egoistic expectations, worries, and entanglements of life. Transcending duality in action leads to transcendence of egoistic consciousness, allowing one to be free from actions (karma) and become immersed in God. These highly advanced and lofty teachings from Maat Philosophy of becoming one with God through righteous action is further augmented by the Hymn to Maat contained in the scripture now referred to as the Berlin papyrus.

> ***Maat Ankhu Maat***
> Maat is the source of life
> ***Maat neb bu ten***
> Maat is in everywhere you are
> ***Cha hena Maat***
> Rise in the morning with Maat
> ***Ankh hena Maat***
> Live with Maat
> ***Ha sema Maat***
> Let every limb join with Maat (i.e. let her guide your actions)
> ***Maat her ten***
> Maat is who you are deep down (i.e. your true identity is one with the Divine)
> ***Dua Maat neb bu ten***
> Adorations to goddess Maat, who is in everywhere you are!

Figure 108: Judgment Scene from Papyrus of Sutimes

Plate 65: Judgment Scene from Papyrus Hunefer

The following is a complete listing of the 42 precepts of Maat. Since there are various versions of the *Pert Em Heru* which have been discovered and no two have the same exact wording, variants will also be included to elucidate on the expanded meanings accorded to the precepts by different Sages.

The following is a composite summary of "negative confessions" from several Ancient Egyptian *Books of Coming Forth by Day*. They are often referred to as "Negative Confessions" since the person uttering them is affirming what moral principles they have not transgressed. In this respect they are similar to the Yamas or ethical restraints of Indian philosophy. While all of the papyri include 42 precepts, some specific precepts vary according to the specific initiate for which they were prepared and the priests who compiled them. Therefore, I have included more than one precept per line where I felt it was appropriate to show that there were slight variations in the precepts and to more accurately reflect the broader view of the original texts.

AFFIRMATIONS OF INNOCENCE: THE 42 PRECEPTS OF MAAT

(1) "I have not done what is wrong." Variant: I have not acted with falsehood.
(2) "I have not robbed with violence."
(3) "I have not done violence (to anyone or anything)." Variant: I have not been rapacious (taking by force; plundering.)
(4) "I have not committed theft." Variant: I have not coveted.
(5) "I have not murdered man or woman." Variant: I have not ordered someone else to commit murder.
(6) "I have not defrauded offerings." Variant: I have not destroyed food supplies or increased or decreased the measures to profit.
(7) "I have not acted deceitfully." Variant: I have not acted with crookedness.
(8) "I have not robbed the things that belong to God."
(9) "I have told no lies."
(10) "I have not snatched away food."
(11) "I have not uttered evil words." Variant: I have not allowed myself to become sullen, to sulk or become depressed.
(12) "I have attacked no one."
(13) "I have not slaughtered the cattle that are set apart for the Gods." Variant: I have not slaughtered the Sacred bull – (Apis)
(14) "I have not eaten my heart" (overcome with anguish and distraught). Variant: I have not committed perjury.
(15) "I have not laid waste the ploughed lands."
(16) "I have not been an eavesdropper or pried into matters to make mischief."
(17) "I have not spoken against anyone." Variant: I have not babbled, gossiped.
(18) "I have not allowed myself to become angry without cause."
(19) "I have not committed adultery." Variant: I have not committed homosexuality.
(20) "I have not committed any sin against my own purity."
(21) "I have not violated sacred times and seasons."
(22) "I have not done that which is abominable."
(23) "I have not uttered fiery words. I have not been a man or woman of anger."
(24) "I have not stopped my ears listening to the words of right and wrong (Maat)."
(25) "I have not stirred up strife (disturbance)." "I have not caused terror." "I have not struck fear into any man."
(26) "I have not caused any one to weep." Variant: I have not hoodwinked.
(27) "I have not lusted or committed fornication nor have I lain with others of my same sex." Variant: I have not molested children.
(28) "I have not avenged myself." Variant: I have not cultivated resentment.
(29) "I have not worked grief, I have not abused anyone." Variant: I have not cultivated a quarrelsome nature.
(30) "I have not acted insolently or with violence."
(31) "I have not judged hastily." Variant: I have not been impatient.
(32) "I have not transgressed or angered God."
(33) "I have not multiplied my speech overmuch (talk too much).
(34) "I have not done harm or evil." Variant: I have not thought evil.
(35) "I have not worked treason or curses on the King."

(36) "I have never befouled the water." Variant: <u>I have not held back the water from flowing in its season.</u>

(37) "I have not spoken scornfully." Variant: <u>I have not yelled unnecessarily or raised my voice.</u>

(38) "I have not cursed The God."

(39) "I have not behaved with arrogance." Variant: <u>I have not been boastful.</u>[444]

(40) "I have not been overwhelmingly proud or sought for distinctions for myself[445]."

(41) "I have never magnified my condition beyond what was fitting or increased my wealth, except with such things as are (justly) mine own possessions by means of Maat." Variant: <u>I have not disputed over possessions except when they concern my own rightful possessions.</u> Variant: <u>I have not desired more than what is rightfully mine.</u>

(42) "I have never thought evil (blasphemed) or slighted The God in my native town."

RUBRIC FOR CHAPTER 33: HOW TO MAKE THE PRESENTATION IN THE HALL OF MAATI.[446]

1. This Chapter shall be recited or chanted by the aspirant when {he/she} is cleansed and purified, and is arrayed in linen apparel, and is shod with sandals of white leather, with eyes painted with antimony, and the body is anointed with unguent made of myrrh. And an offering shall be presented, oxen and feathered fowl[447], and incense, and cakes and ale, and garden herbs.

2. And behold, thou shalt draw a representation[448] of this in color upon a new tile molded from earth upon which neither a pig nor any other animal hath trodden.

3. And if this book be chanted or written, the initiate shall flourish, and his children shall flourish, and {his/her} name shall never fall into oblivion, and he shall be as one who filleth the heart of the king and of his princes. And bread, and cakes, and sweetmeats, and wine, and pieces of flesh shall be given unto {him/her} from among those which are upon the altar of the Great God. And he shall not be driven back from any door in Amentet, and he shall be led along with the kings of the South and the kings of the North, and he shall be among the followers of Asar, continually and regularly forever. And {he/she} shall come forth in every form {he/she} pleaseth as a living soul forever, and ever, and ever.

4. This teaching is effective a million times!

---

[444] Bragging, pretentious, arrogant, egoistic.

[445] Selfishness, egoistically.

[446] Based on the Papyrus of Ani and other contemporary papyri.

[447] This refers to the Hetep offering which contains the leg of an ox and a goose symbolizing the male and female gender. This refers to the opposites of creation. The aspirant symbolically offers duality and in so doing affirms the non-duality between self and Divinity. Thus, the offerings are not of physical items, but of their symbolic principles. This offering principle comes from the mystical meaning of the Hetep Offering Table and the injunctions elsewhere in the *Prt M Hru* against initiates eating meat and drinking alcoholic beverages. Other food offerings contain additional symbolism as well, mainly referring to the essence of food, which is the source of life so as to promote the life of the Asar, the Higher Self.

[448] This important passage denotes the teaching of image in ritual worship. Ancient Egyptian mysticism holds that the invocation of an object requires only two things, the name and the image. Reality is not based on physicality but rather the idea and naming of it. For example, objects in a dream have no reality and yet they are created with the mind and one interacts with them and during the dream they are real in a practical sense. Like the modern quantum physicists of today, the Sages of Ancient Egypt recognized that matter has no abiding reality in and of itself. It is a creation of God's mind, the cosmic mind, out of the Primeval Ocean of consciousness. Thus, as God creates through her cosmic mind, so too a human being creates his or her own reality by means of the mind and its concepts, images and the names it gives to objects. These are only useful to the mind since objects have no awareness of their name or function. Therefore, creation is not an abiding reality, but a transient manifestation of names and forms sustained by the mind and will of God or the individual mind of a human being.

Chapter 33 treats a very important subject in Kemetic Philosophy, the concept of Maat. Maat is the concept that one's actions, while alive, direct one's fate here and in the hereafter. After death of the physical body, one is judged as to if one followed a righteous or unrighteous path in life and one's deeds lead one to spiritual enlightenment or to suffering and adversity. This is illustrated in the parable of Sa-Asar, introduced earlier in the gloss to Chapter18. The rest of the parable, included here, shows the teachings of the balance (scales) of Maat and the fate of the soul based on their actions in life. First though, we will present a proverb from the Instructions of Merikara which illuminates the concept of "ari" or actions.

1. The Court that judges the wretch, You know they are not lenient,
2. On the day of judging the miserable, in the hour of doing their task.
3. It is painful when the accuser has knowledge,
4. Do not trust in length of years; They view a lifetime in an hour!
5. When a man remains over after death, his actions are set beside him as treasure,
6. And being yonder lasts forever. A fool is who does what they reprove!
7. He who reaches them without having done wrong will exist there like a god, free-striding like the lords forever!

The following parable explains the teaching above in great detail, especially the teachings in lines 5-7 above, related to actions and their karmic consequences for the soul. One's actions follow one, and when it is time, they act as witnesses, as it were, before the Divine at the judgment and lead a human being either to prosperity or adversity. Together these parables and proverbs illuminate the teaching of Chapter 33 of the *Prt M Hru*. In Kemetic mystical philosophy the Netherworld is associated with sleep and dream. This is shown through the various Ancient Kemetic parable teachings such as those related to Sa-Asar. Sa-Asar was a Sage who incarnated to give spiritual teachings. One parable relates that:

A man and a woman wanted to have a child, but could not conceive so the woman, named Mehusekhe, went to a temple to sleep there in the hope that a god or goddess would come to her and tell her what to do. A spirit came to her in a dream and told her to go to the place where her husband was, and to eat from a melon vine and embrace her husband in love and that she would then conceive a child. She became pregnant and her husband, Setna, was very happy. In a dream, the spirit came to Setna and told him the child would be a boy and he is to be named "Sa-Asar," and that he will do great wonders in the land of Egypt. When the child was born Setna named him Sa-Asar and he grew up and was always mature for his years. When Sa-Asar was a boy of 10, but already respected as an enlightened Sage, one day he and his father, were looking at two funerals. One funeral was for a rich man, who had many mourners, attendants, and offerings to the gods and goddesses. The other funeral was for a poor man, who had no one to mourn him and no offerings for the gods and goddesses to be placed in his tomb. The father exclaimed, "When my time comes, may my funeral be like the one of the rich man." Sa-Asar looked at his father, and said "Oh no father I hope you die like the poor man." Setna looked at Sa-Asar with surprise. Then Sa-Asar asked "Would you like me to show you the fate of these two souls?" Sa-Asar led his father to the Netherworld and his father saw that the rich man was judged by the gods and goddesses and was found to be unrighteous, having committed more evil deeds, than virtuous deeds so his fate was to suffer. The poor man had led a virtuous life so all of the offerings of the rich man were accrued to the poor man, and the poor man was led into the presence of Asar, the Supreme Self, who was seated on his throne, with the goddesses Aset and Nebethet behind him and the gods and goddesses at his sides. Setna saw the evil rich man suffering. Others were reaching up to grasp at food that was dangling over them by a rope while under them, certain gods and goddesses were digging a pit so that they could not reach high enough. Still others were twining ropes while at the other end of the rope there were donkeys eating the rope. "Tell me Sa-Asar," Setna asked in amazement, "What is the meaning of these things I see? What happens to the people as they are judged?" Sa-Asar answered, "Those who are twining are the people who on earth labor everyday but their labors are fruitless for themselves because they do not perform the right actions, but the fruits of their actions benefit others. Those who

are reaching up to get their food in vain are those who in life on earth have their life before them, but do not make use of it. Those who are found to have more misdeeds than good deeds are made to suffer. Those who have an equal amount of misdeeds and good deeds are sent to be servants of Seker-Asar. Those who are found to have more virtuous deeds than misdeeds are allowed to be among the gods and goddesses as one of them, and their ba flies up to be among the glorified spirits.

At the end of the parable Sa-Asar explains his true identity. The name "Sa-Asar" means son of Asar (Osiris). Therefore, this teaching comes from Heru. He explains that he received permission from Asar to incarnate by placing his spirit in the vine and then becoming the soul in the womb of Mehusekhe. Thus, Sa-Asar is an "Avatar," the sun of God incarnate, who came down to the world to provide wisdom and enlightenment.

At the time of death or prior to death, the heart (consciousness, Ab) of the human being is weighed against truth, symbolized by the feather of Maat. Here our divine faculties of reason and moral rectitude and our ability to practice the precepts while on earth are judged.

The Significance of The Precepts of Maat

The profundity of the Precepts of Maat is of such an extensive nature that only an introduction has been provided here. Therefore, a full treatment of the Precepts of Maat and their individual teachings would require a separate volume due to the extensive teachings presented in them as they pertain to the righteous conduct of a spiritual aspirant which leads to enlightenment. However, the essence of the teachings contained in them are presented in this volume, but the teachings as they pertain to the specific issues mentioned in the precepts are discussed at length in an audio lecture series. In 1998, the author conducted a year long study of the philosophy contained in the Precepts of Maat. This lecture series was recorded. The books, *The Wisdom of Maati* and *The 42 Precepts of Maat and the Philosophy of Righteous Action,* by Dr. Muata Ashby, were used. Anyone interested in a thorough study of the precepts should consult these materials. The listing of subjects covered in the series is below.

Maat Philosophy Series 1998 Lectures Maat, the 42 Laws, the Ancient Egyptian Wisdom Texts   (each audio cassette $9.99)

4001 Class 1 - Introduction to Maat Philosophy
4002 Class 2 - Profound issues of Maat and its practice in life
4003 Class 3 - Profound issues and the Cycle of Vice
4004 Class 4 - Introduction to the Principle of Truth
4005 Class 5 - Principle of Truth Part 2
4006 Class 6 - Principle of Truth Part 3
4007 Class 7 - Principle of Truth part 4
4008 Class 8 - Introduction to the Principle of Non-violence
4009 Class 9 - Principle of Non-violence Part 2
4010 Class 10 - Principle of Non-violence Part 3
4011 Class 11 - Principle of Non-violence Part 4
4012 Class 12 – Principle of Non-stealing Part 1
4013 Class 13 – Principle of Non-stealing Part 2
4014 Class 14 – Principle of Non-stealing Part 3
4015 Class 15 – Principle of Selfless Service
4016 Class 16 – Principle of Right Action
4017 Class 17 – Principle of Right Speech Part 1
4018 Class 18 – Principle of Right Speech Part 2
4019 Class 19 – Principle of Right Speech Part 3
4020 Class 20 – Principle of Right Speech Part 4
4021 Class 21 – Principle of Right Worship Part 1
4022 Class 22 – Principle of Right Worship Part 2
4023 Class 23 – Principle of Right Worship Part 3
4024 Class 24 – Principle of Right Worship Part 4
4025 Class 25 – Principle of Right Worship Part 5
4026 Class 26 – Principle of Right Worship Part 6
4027 Class 27 – Principle of Right Thinking Part 1

The Precepts of Maat and the Judgment of the Aspirant

In life and at the time of death, the heart (consciousness, symbolized by the AB) of the human being is weighed against TRUTH, symbolized by the feather of MAAT. Here our godly faculties, symbolized by Anubis and Djehuti, and our ability to use them while on earth, are judged.

In the Hall of MAATI, 42 judges who are each in charge of one regulation judge the heart. All 42 regulations or virtuous guidelines for living make up the basis for the 42 "negative confessions." If one lives righteously, one will be able to say that one has <u>NOT</u> committed any offense. Maati means, "double Maat," referring to the two Maati goddesses, who are aspects of Aset and Nebethet. Aset is the goddess of transcendence, immortality and infinity. Nebethet is the goddess of the finite, phenomenal world. Thus, the Hall of Maati encompasses the idea of a place where all things are brought together, above and below, spirit and matter, i.e. the movement from ordinary human consciousness, which is beset with duality to the transcendental realm of non-duality.

Upon uttering these words, the deceased takes on a new name. Instead of John Wells, she is now Asar John Wells.   This signifies that the true nature is that of Universal Consciousness. What was separated only by ignorance is now re-united, re-membered. It is only due to ignorance and to distraction in the world of desirable objects that you think you are an individual human being with a body, which is mortal. In reality, you are an immortal and eternal being who is one with the universe and every one else.

To realize this even before death, it is necessary to live in a virtuous manner, learning the lessons of human existence and uncovering the veil of ignorance, which blinds us from the realization of our essential nature. We must therefore master the knowledge and wisdom of "EVERY" God.

In Chapter 33 of the *Ancient Egyptian Book of Coming Forth By Day,* it is stated that one should be able to declare one's innocence from wrong doing in order to see the face of God. How is this possible? Can a human being aspire to perfection and divine vision? The text of the *Prt M Hru* show how this to be accomplished by purifying oneself through Maat and understanding certain wisdom teachings about the nature of Self and the nature of the universe.

Through the practice of the precepts of Maat, mental peace and subtlety of intellect (purity of heart) arise. Purity of heart, meaning the absence or anger, hatred, greed, jealousy, discontent, covetousness, elation, stress, agitation, etc., is the means through which divine awareness is possible. When the mind is beset with agitation it is impossible to develop spiritual sensitivity. The mind in this state is as if caught in a web of illusion, based on the thoughts, desires and ignorance, which does not allow awareness of the Divine essence within the heart or in nature, but rather, intensifies the feelings of individualism, separation and individuality. These in turn open the door for egoistic feelings and personal desires to arise. Feelings of animosity, anger, hatred, greed, jealousy, lust, elation, depression, etc., can only exist when there is individuality or egoism.

Think about this. Can you feel jealousy in relation to your arm, your head, or your foot? No, because you accept these are part of you, that in essence they are you. In the same way, a perfected (righteous) Sage or Saint sees the entire universe as his or her body, and therefore, cannot feel jealousy, anger, greed, etc., towards anything or anyone. This is because the feeling of ignorance, individuality and separation has been replaced with truth and universality. It is a state where one has risen above the seeming contradictions of life. There is equal vision towards all and universal love for all that exists. This is the experience of an enlightened human being.

The objective of life is to become "light of heart," that is to say, one should live a life that is free of stress and which promotes mental peace. When this is possible, the mind relaxes and reveals the divine nature of the soul. If the heart is weighed down by egoism due to a life of worry, lies, frustration, and desire, the heart will be judged as heavier than the feather. If his acts were very unrighteous, instead of moving forward to join with Asar (the Divine Self), Asar John Wells is given over to a beast, an animal known as Ammit, and will experience hellish conditions. Then she will undergo reincarnation into a human form to again try to become "light of heart."

In several passages of the hymn, Asar Ani states emphatically "I have not spoken falsehood *wittingly,*[449] nor have done with deceit." This is a very important statement because it reflects recognition of the subtlety which spiritual life requires in relation to purity of heart. Many people do wrong things because they do not know any better. This does not excuse the error, and they will suffer some consequences due to the error. The consequences are nature's way of waking them up to their error. However, there are other people, who, due to the intensity of their egoism, greed and desires for objects and sense enjoyments, plan and scheme to do wrong. These people will suffer much worse consequences because they have done wrong, knowing that they were doing wrong. People in this category tend to delude themselves and even rationalize that they are justified in doing wrong. They may commit shoplifting because "the store has high prices and they rip people off anyway." They may get caught by the police and end up in jail and then they will experience mental unrest. Others may seem to get away with the offence, but they have also created a negative karmic impression in the mind, which will leave them full of mental agitation that will prevent them from experiencing true peace and joy. Consequently, they will not discover the deeper essence of their own being, and instead, those negative impressions will lead them to hellish conditions after death and future adversity in the next life, where perhaps they may become the victim of a heinous crime. The store may be unrighteous, but this does not justify your own unrighteousness. They too will suffer the consequences for their actions at some time in the future. Therefore, never do wrong wittingly, because you are leading yourself into deeper delusions, conflicts and egoism in the world which will lead you further away from divine realization. Every time you commit an error (sin), you are going against your own conscience, because deep down you are divine, and your divinity is righteousness itself (Maat, Ra). Therefore, when you go against your conscience, you are hurting yourself and leading yourself to hell.

---

[449] Italics emphasis by the author.

When you commit an error and it is pointed out to you, you should praise the source, which is bringing it to your attention. Then you will be able to understand the act you did and why it was wrong, and watch yourself so that it does not happen again. Every time you redress an error and eradicate it from your conscience you are gaining greater and greater purity of heart.

If the heart of Asar John Wells is found to be lighter than the feather or of equal weight, it signifies that he has lead a virtuous life and has mastered the *knowledge and wisdom of every god* (all of which are aspects of the one God, meaning he has mastered all 42 precepts). Asar John Wells is ready to transcend this world and move into the next realm of existence. He is ready to journey back to meet Cosmic Asar, who represents Cosmic Consciousness, his own Higher Self (God).

Asar John Wells, through his own virtuous life, is allowed to take or fashion a new, glorious body, to live in eternity as one with Asar (God). Thus, Asar John Wells, the individual human soul, meets and joins with Asar (God), the Supreme Being. This is the attainment of Enlightenment or the Kingdom of Heaven. This signifies that your own nature is that of Universal Consciousness. What was separated only by ignorance is now re-united, re-membered. It is only due to ignorance and to distraction in the world of seemingly desirable objects that people think they are individual human beings with bodies, which are mortal. In reality, humans are immortal and eternal beings who are one with the universe and each other. Through ignorance, fueled by egoistic desire, people have come to believe that the human existence is all there is. Through the process of living the teachings of Maat or in the case of Christianity, the Commandments and Beatitudes (given by Jesus), the mind can be lightened to such a degree that it allows the soul to behold its true nature, unclouded by the passions and desires of the mind.

The objective of all mystical religions and philosophies is to achieve this realization before the time of death. To realize this even before death, it is necessary to live in a virtuous manner, learning the lessons of human existence and uncovering the veil of ignorance which blinds us from the realization of our essential nature. We must therefore master the knowledge and wisdom of every "neteru," through the practice of every precept.

Anpu (god of discernment between reality and illusion) and Djehuti (god of reason and truth) oversee the scales of Maat. They judge the condition of the Heart (Ab) and determine its level of spiritual achievement. This is also symbolized by the Ammit monster, the devourer of hearts, who, according to the Ancient Egyptian *Kenna* papyrus, determines those who are the advanced spirits and worthy of salvation versus those who are not. They are those who have developed their higher consciousness centers or the virtues: selflessness, peacefulness, universal love, etc., as opposed to those who have not progressed beyond their base animal natures of the lower consciousness centers: fear, attachments, egoistic desires, anger, hatred, etc. The unrighteous are symbolically devoured by the Ammit monsters (demon). They will have to reincarnate in order to further evolve beyond this stage. Upon reincarnating, they will once again have the possibility of confronting situations which will afford them the opportunity to perform correct action and thus, to change. Correct action leads to correct feeling and thinking. Correct feeling and correct thinking lead to harmony and prosperity in life as well as to a state of consciousness, which is, unburdened. This is the goal— to unburden the mind so that consciousness, the soul, may be revealed in its true appearance. When this occurs the soul is discovered to be one with God and not individual and separate. One realizes that the Kingdom of Heaven is within oneself. This is the highest realization of all Mysteries, Yogas and Religious systems.

Table 14: Comparing The Indian, Christian and Kemetic Scriptures on Self-Knowledge

VEDANTA PHILOSOPHY IS SUMMED UP IN FOUR MAHAVAKYAS OR GREAT UTTERANCES TO BE FOUND IN THE UPANISHADS:	COMPARE TO THE CHRISTIAN BIBLE:	COMPARE TO THE PRT M HRU OF ANCIENT EGYPT
1- Brahman, the Absolute, is Consciousness beyond all mental concepts. 2- Thou Art That (referring to the fact that everyone is essentially this Consciousness). 3- I Am Brahman, the Absolute (I am God); to be affirmed by people, referring to their own essential nature). 4- The Self is Brahman (the Self is the essence of all things).	On the essence of God: "God is everywhere and in all things." (Deuteronomy 4:7) On the name of God: "I Am That I Am." (Exodus 3:14) Jesus speaks of his own origin and identity: "I and the Father (God) are ONE." (John 10:30)	Nuk Pu Nuk. ("I Am That I Am.") (Chapter 21 Verse 6) In reference to the relationship between God and humankind: Ntef änuk, änuk Ntef. "He is I and I am He." (Prt M Hru 31:7) I am that God, the Great one in his boat, Ra, I am. (Prt M Hru Chapter 1, Part 1, Verse 4) I am that same God, the Supreme One, who has myriad of mysterious names. (Prt M Hru 9:4)

The Egyptian *Prt m Hru* is a text of wisdom about the true nature of reality and also of *Hekau* (chants, words of power, Chapters) to assist the initiate in making that reality evident. These chants are in reality wisdom affirmations, which the initiate recites in order to assist him or her in changing the consciousness level of the mind. The hekau themselves may have no special power except in their assistance to the mind to change its perception through repetition with understanding and feeling in order to transform the mind into a still and centered state. Thus, the magical effect comes by their use and the force of will behind them when uttered by the purified mind. Through these affirmations, the initiate is able to change {his/her} consciousness from body consciousness ("I am a body") to Cosmic Consciousness ("I am God"). Indian Gurus also recognize this form of affirmatory (using affirmation in the first person) spiritual discipline as the most intense form of spiritual discipline. However, there must be clear and profound understanding of the teachings before the affirmations can have the intended result. It is also to be found in the Bible and in the Gnostic Gospels. Compare the statements in the first and second columns of the chart below from the Indian Upanishads and the Christian Bible to the following Ancient Egyptian scriptures (*Metu Neter,* Sacred Speech) taken from the *Egyptian Book of Coming Forth By Day* and other hieroglyphic texts:

The 42 declarations of purity have profound implications for the spiritual development of the individual as well as for society. They may be grouped under three basic ethical teachings, *Truth, Non-violence* and *Self-Control.* Under the heading of self-control, three subheadings may be added, *Balance of Mind or Right Thinking Based on Reason, Non-stealing* and *Sex-Sublimation.* The principles of Maat are very similar to the principles of Dharma of India.

Like the Ancient Egyptians their descendants, the early Coptic Christians also included a Book of the Dead in the burial tombs and mummified their dead in keeping with the Ancient Egyptian traditions. The book consisted of sheets of papyrus inscribed with Gnostic Christian texts such as the gospels. Many of these copies of the "Coptic" *Prt m Hru* can be found in the British Museum. One of the surviving books[450] contains a copy of the Apocryphal letter of King Abgar to Christ and the first words of each of the four Gospels.

---

[450] Oriental museum #4919 (2)

Table 15: Maat Philosophy Compared with Hindu Dharma Philosophy

Maat Principles of Ethical Conduct	Hindu Dharma Principles o Ethical Conduct (From the *Manu Smriti*)
<ul><li>**Truth** (1), (6), (7), (9), (24)</li><li>**Non-violence** (2), (3), (5), (12), (25), (26), (28), (30), (34)</li><li>**Right Action- Self-Control (Living in accordance with the teachings of Maat)** (15), (20), (22), (36)</li><li>**Right Speech** (11), (17), (23), (33), (35), (37)</li><li>**Right Worship** (13), (21), (32), (38), (42)</li><li>**Selfless Service** (29)</li><li>**Balance of Mind - Reason – Right Thinking** (14), (16), (18), (31), (39)</li><li>**Not-stealing** (4), (8), (10), (41)</li><li>**Sex-Sublimation** (19), (27)</li></ul>	<ul><li>Firmness.</li><li>Forgiveness, forbearance.</li><li>Control of Senses.</li><li>Non Stealing.</li><li>Purity of body and mind.</li><li>Control of mind.</li><li>Purity of Intellect.</li><li>Knowledge.</li><li>Truthfulness.</li><li>Absence of anger.</li></ul>

There is one more important factor, which is inherent in the Precepts of Maat, that must receive special mention. Generally when people are ignorant of the greater spiritual realities and caught up in the emotionality of human life, they tend to look for something on which to blame for their miseries. They want to find a cause for the troubles of life and the easiest way to do this is to look around into the world and point to those factors around them, which seem to affect them, be they people, situations or objects. In Chapter 33 of the *Book of Coming Forth By Day,* the use of the word *nuk* ("I") is emphasized with a special connotation. The spiritual aspirant says continually "I have..." He or she does not say "You have allowed me" or "The devil made me do it" or "I wanted to, but I couldn't," etc.

There is a process of responsibility wherein the spiritual aspirant recognizes that {he/she} has the obligation to act righteously and, in so doing, to purify their own heart. Spiritual practice can succeed only when you assume responsibility for your actions, thoughts, words and feelings. If you constantly blame your short comings or adversities on others or on situations, etc., you will be living life according to ignorance and weakness. True spiritual strength comes from leaning upon the Self within for spiritual support and well being, rather than upon external situations, people or objects, even though the help itself may come in the form of external situations, people or objects.

Thus, within the teachings of Maat can be found all of the important injunctions for living a life, which promotes righteousness, purity, harmony and sanctity akin to other great world religions and mystical philosophies. In Christianity, Jesus emphasized non-violence and in Vedantism and Buddhism, the discipline of *Dharma,* composed of *Yamas and Nyamas,* which are moral (righteous) observances and restraints for spiritual living, emphasizes non-violence.

The Ancient Egyptian, Vedantic and Buddhist mystical traditions were the first to recognize the power of non-violence to heal the anger and hatred within the aggressor as well as the victim. When this spiritual force is developed, it is more formidable than any kind of physical violence. Therefore, anyone who wishes to promote peace and harmony in the world must begin by purifying every bit of negativity within themselves. This is the only way to promote harmony and peace in others. Conversely, if there is anger within you, you are indeed promoting anger outside of yourself and your efforts will be unsuccessful in the end.

Chapter 33 of the *Book of Coming Forth By Day* is to be read, chanted or written daily. In this manner the precepts are to be studied and practiced so as to engender a mind that is peaceful and harmonious.

Non-dual Philosophy in the Scales of Maat

Notice that the scales of Maat are not depicted either in favor of Maat (righteousness) or in favor of egoism (actions in contradiction to Maat). This is because an imbalance either way signifies being caught up in the illusion of life. If a person is elated that person is just as deluded by the world as if they were depressed. In fact, when a person goes beyond elation or depression, desire or disgust, right or wrong, and the other opposites of creation which delude the mind and make them think that the world is abiding and that there is some true happiness, wealth, pleasure to be found, then they are not disturbed by the world and they can then transcend the world. The fact of death and the impermanence of the world signify, to the wise, that the best way to live in the world is to be detached and this allows a person to have control over the world and the world cannot control the mind. The world makes a person happy or sad only when that person is deluded about the world and a person becomes deluded about the world when they fall for the idea that the world is something other than God and that they are individuals in competition with other individuals and that happiness is to be found in the world through some action performed or object that can be acquired. This attitude leave a person stressed for there is in this way of understanding, always a fear, born of mental agitation and these can also lead to frustration, hatred, and anger. In short, this is the miserable predicament of the life of the uninitiated masses, living from day to day groping for happiness and finding, more often than not, disappointment and frustration. The dogging questions in the background of the mind are always pressuring a person to actions that lead to more stress and delusion. Will I find happiness? Will I lose my savings? When will I get my vacation? Will I have that pleasurable evening I have been planning for so long? These desires plague the mind constantly and force the mind to be move in the realm of time and space, the past or future, and this is the dualistic state of consciousness. When the mind realizes that the opposites only have a value in time and space, which is itself illusory, the mind turns away from the world and begins to be cleansed to the point where it too is discovered to be illusory itself. Then the person discovers the true essence of Self, the Soul essence, which is beyond time and space but experiencing these through the medium of the mind and senses and the body for the purpose of having experiences in the physical realm. This divine purpose is perverted by the delusion of love and hate, elation and depression. From the point of view of the spirit there is no good or evil, only experiences. All experiences are perishable and all situations are transient. Therefore, they have no meaning or validity in themselves. They are only experiences, like a dream, which have no abiding effect on the soul, so they are not real and not to be held on to, sought after, longed for or repudiated from an egoistic or sentimental point of view. One should live and desire what is in line with Maat and this will keep the mind free of delusion. This means that too much emphasis on virtue and too much emphasis on vice are both leading to illusion and duality. Maat allows for no extremes, only balance. This is the state of non-dual consciousness, the state of spiritual enlightenment, which is the goal of the mystic practices. Living by the 42 principles of Maat and having a deep-rooted understanding of these, as they are imparted by an authentic spiritual preceptor, paves the way for the development of non-dual consciousness, i.e. Sagehood. This is what it means to become "One with Maat," as stated in the Berlin Papyrus. Thus, Maat Philosophy is an extremely advanced mystical philosophy, which if practiced will allow the masses to lead a life of righteousness and order and lead them to a place in life wherein they will be able to practice the advanced teachings of Maat. If practiced by advanced aspirants it will lead them to the heights of spiritual enlightenment. The heart center, being at the middle or nucleus of the seven spheres of spiritual consciousness, in the discipline of Serpent Power Psychology, is understood as the seat of enlightened consciousness and therefore, an enlightened sage does not live by extremes but by a perfect balance between heaven and earth, the spirit and the body, but all the while transcending these. This is the glory of Maat Philosophy. When managed by sages it is a discipline designed for all levels of human evolution and the means through which leaders of society can promote order in society and spiritual evolution in humanity, at the same time.

(Utterance 28)

Utterance 28

O Asar _____, Heru has given you his Eye; complete yourself with it.

Utterance 41

O Asar _____, take the two Eyes of Heru, which are the black one and the white one. Place them on your forehead and your face will be illumined.

Utterance 57J

O Asar _____, I bring to you the two Eyes of Heru and these have the power to expand the heart.

Utterance 48

O Asar _____, take the Eye of Heru which was wrested from Set and which you shall take to your mouth, with which you shall open your mouth— WITH WINE OFFERING.

Utterance 51

O Asar _____, take the Eye of Heru which you shall taste— WITH CAKE OFFERING.

Utterance 89

O Asar _____, take the Eye of Heru which Set has pulled out—WITH A LOAF OFFERING.

Utterance 93

O Asar _____, take this bread of yours which is the Eye of Heru.

PYRAMID TEXT UTTERANCE 78: ASAR_____ RECEIVES THE EYE OF HERU

(Utterance 78)

O Asar _____, the Eye of Heru which he[451] took from your brow is brought to you.

PYRAMID TEXT UTTERANCE 87, EATING THE EYE

O Asar _____take the Eye of Heru and put it in your mouth and assimilate it.

Figure 109: Ancient Egyptian Eucharist: Sem Priest Offering Bread, and Wine.

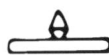

---

[451] The god Set.

PYRAMID TEXT UTTERANCE 210: TURNING AWAY FROM THE WORLD AND TOWARDS THE DIVINE BOAT

Awake, Oh Wepwawet! Raise on high, Djehuti! ...My mouth is pure and my tongue is pure. I despise feces! I loathe urine! Further, I find my own contemptibleness contemptible! I will never accept these two detestable things. Hail! You two Divine companions, you who are called Ra and Djehuti! Take me with you so that I may eat what you eat, drink what you drink, so as to live on what you live and sit where you sit. I want to be strong by living on what you live on and sail on that boat which you sail on. My food and drink offerings are with you and in the field of peace. My water is wine like Ra's, and I traverse the heavens like Ra and Djehuti.

CHAPTER 34[452]

ENTERING INTO THE DIVINE BOAT AND SAILING FOR ETERNITY

Plate 66: Left- Vignette from Chapter 34 of Papyrus Auf Ankh. The initiate boards the boat of Ra, the Supreme Being, and adores him.

Plate 67: Right- Vignette from Chapter 34 of Papyrus Nu. The initiate boards the boat of Ra as Ra journeys for eternity with Maat making the way.

1. These words are to be said by Asar _____ maakheru:

2. Oh Great One in His Boat! I bring myself to thee, into thy boat.

3. I am foremost[453] of those in your crew; these beings who are in the indestructible stars, not the weak stars.

4. Putrefied stuff, excrement, I detest these things and will not eat that, not shall I eat it! Filth and muck, that I shall not consume.

5. I am in peace and my Ka will not fall, destroyed, in me.

---

[452] Generally referred to as Chapter 102.
[453] Commander.

6. Not shall I go on the path touching filth with my hands nor shall I walk on it with my feet.

7. I eat white barley and my beer is made from red barley from Hapi.[454]

8. By the Sekhtet Boat let there be prosperity and the Amdet Boat let there be brought to me 1,000 quantities of Divine food, vegetables and grains, as offerings like those given to the souls in Anu.

9. I praise thee, Great Eye of Ra, and ask for your protection from the rebels who are in the heavens and within me, wherever. May I understand these things about that person who is me. I bring myself; I take up residence there as a Divinity within.

10. There are sick, very ill people. I go to them, I spit on the arms, I set the shoulder, and I cleanse them.

11. On the path, my personality does not come and go.

12. I make myself enter the Boat of Ra.

GLOSS ON PYRAMID TEXT UTTERANCE 210 AND CHAPTER 34: ITS MEANING AND MYSTICAL SIGNIFICANCE

In mystical Philosophy, the color gold is a symbol of the sun and the sun is a metaphor for that which is eternal as opposed to the moon which is temporal, as denoted by its phases. Getting into the boat of Ra means joining him on his eternal journey which transcends time and space. In the discipline of Geometry, is it accepted that a line which extends in opposite directions will join in infinity. The line extending into infinity is therefore nothing but a segment of a circle. This circle has cycles or stages which recur again and again without beginning and without ending. It is these cycles which human beings refer to as time and history. But how many histories have there been? How many cycles have there been? This is a mathematical interpretation of the most important teaching inherent in the symbol of the circle, O. What is normally called time is nothing but a piece of eternity. Thus, eternity is also symbolized in the sundisk of Ra, $\odot$, which also contains the source of creation itself, the primordial dot, $\bullet$.

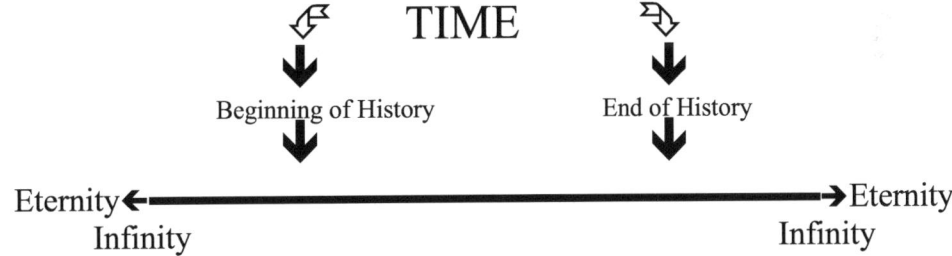

Where is the beginning of eternity and infinity? Where is the ending of eternity and infinity? Where is the beginning and ending of a circle? The concepts of beginning and ending, now and later, are merely concepts of the mind, which have no bearing on reality except from the point of view of an objective observer. These concepts are relative, and therefore illusory. Time is not experienced in the same way uniformly throughout the universe. Therefore, it is not stable or abiding and thus, unreal. A rock knows nothing of today and tomorrow. Where is the beginning and ending of a dream? These concepts are only valid for those who are ignorant of the eternal nature of the universe and the true nature of the Divine. Time is a concept that has relation only to the human mind. When the limiting factors of the mind (ignorance, egoism, desire, and agitation) are transcended, the transcendental nature of the universe and of the human soul is revealed.

---

[454] The colors white and red have special mystical significance. They symbolize the union of opposites, i.e. going from duality to non-duality and oneness with the transcendental Divine essence.

Due to the assimilation of the initiate into the Divine, in the form of Ra, the initiate is able to accept the sublime position of not only healer, but also purifier of people, the role of usually associated with Aset, Djehuti and Imhotep. Further, the next bold statement shows unwavering establishment in Divine Consciousness, as there is no longer any "coming and going of the personality." The established state of consciousness is contrasted from that of the ignorant, uninitiated masses in that the unenlightened human being's mind is in constant flux, wavering back and forth constantly between the past, present and future, desires, longings, prejudices, expectations, etc. In the midst of all of this confusion caused by the coming and going of the personality, which results ultimately in frustration, unrest and dissatisfaction with life, there is an ego concept which keeps the ignorant human being separate from awareness of the Divine. The pursuit of the ego's desires foments a constant disturbance and consequently, also a distraction of the mind. In this state the mind is constantly alternating in the realm of duality, between peace and agitation, understanding and misunderstanding, happiness and sorrow, virtue and vice, etc., that never allows a human being to "know" who they truly are. This is the coming and going of the personality, the affliction of spiritual ignorance and the predicament and degrading factor of unenlightened human existence.

The Essence of The Path of Divine Love

The cure for the adversity of possessing a personality that comes and goes is to practice the disciplines of yoga and mystical spirituality so as to discover and become established in the Higher Self. This chapter espouses the path of Devotion to God as a means to overcome the coming and going mind. This is the Path of Devotion wherein the spiritual aspirant is led to develop the understanding that what the personality is searching for can only be found in God and not in egoistic pursuits based on spiritual ignorance. Through the myth and the mystical teachings of the myth and *Ushet,* worship of the Divine through study of the stories of God, chanting and singing the Divine name(s) of God, the aspirant is able to develop a devotional feeling and intellectual understanding (wisdom) of God. If this intellectual understanding is firm with faith in the teaching, the teacher and in God, then the mind realizes that the true object of desire is God and all fulfillment is also in God. In the Kemetic Mystical Philosophy of Ushet, God is seen as the objet of love and as love itself, and the goal of life is to discover that love and to return it in kind. The path of Divine Love may be considered the easiest because love comes naturally to the personality. The only problem is in understanding what should be loved. Only that which is real and abiding should be loved and not that which is coming and going, transient, and therefore illusory, because it will always lead to pain and disappointment in the end. God is the reality behind everything a person loves. Therefore, it is that reality that should be loved as God and not the outer, illusory expression. So an aspirant must learn to love God in their family members, the objects they possess or desire, in humanity and in nature, and when this universal consciousness of love emerges, non-violence, peace, cooperation, sharing and all forms of virtues emerge from that personality. This is the divine treasure of authentic worship of the Divine, which benefits not only aspirants, but also humanity as a whole.

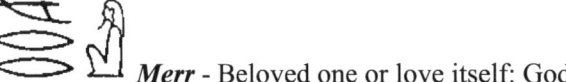

Merr - Beloved one or love itself: God

Now the world, the objects and personalities in it all are understood to be expressions of God, and therefore should be loved as God, even those who act unrighteously, for they are acting out of ignorance and therefore, should be forgiven and extended compassion. So devotional feeling and understanding of God increase to a point where the aspirant discovers universal love for humanity and Creation, growing beyond the limited forms of love, love of self (selfishness, vanity, narcissism), family, country, etc. The aspirant discovers the universal love of God, who sustains all (including the virtuous as well as the vicious), and thereby becomes one with God. This is the true goal of life, the majestic path of Self-knowledge through Devotional Love of God.[455]

Various Chapters of the *Prt M Hru* affirm the power and glory of Devotion to God, and do so expressing the teaching as a "two way street." This means that the goal is not just to develop love for God, but to understand that God loves one also, unconditionally. The following are excerpts from various chapters of the *Prt M Hru* highlighting the path of reciprocal love between the spiritual aspirant and the Divine.

---

[455] For more on the glorious path of Divine Love, see the book *The Path of Divine Love* by Muata Ashby.

Therefore, fulfillment comes from loving and being loved by God. Being loved by God is discovering one's very essential nature as being one with God and further, that one has been nurtured, and cared for throughout many lifetimes, regardless of the evil actions or thoughts one engaged in. The aspirant's feeling and understanding lead to surrender of the personality to God, and thereby it is freed from the clutches of egoism (going and coming nature). To love this way is to love as God loves and thus, by practicing forgiveness and universal love, a spiritual aspirant becomes godlike, spiritually enlightened. The power and glory of Devotion to God is the single most pervasive factor in Kemetic Spirituality, not just in the scriptures themselves, but also in temple inscriptions in the form of the Divine offering(s).

The Devotional Love verses of the *Prt M Hru* include:	The Devotional Love verses from assorted Ancient Egyptian Proverbs include:
Chapter 4, verse 20 **"That person is beloved by the Lord"** Chapter 8, Verse 15: **"It is Heru, who is now established on the Serek[456] for those who are beloved and who are attaining sturdiness"** Chapter 28, Verse 5: **"I am beloved by him! (God)"** Chapter 28, Verse 9: **"I am the child, loved by my father Asar."**	"Give thyself to GOD, keep thou thyself daily for God; and let tomorrow be as today." "Seekest thou God, thou seekest or the Beautiful. One is the Path that leadeth unto, It Devotion joined with Wisdom." "O ye gods who are in the service of the deep. We follow the Lord, the Lord of Love."

CHAPTER 35[457]

RAISING UP FROM THE HEADREST

Plate 68: Vignette from Chapter 35 of Papyrus Ani. A headrest containing a sundisk

1. This is the Chapter about the headrest that is placed under the head of Asar _____ maakheru.

2. It is for awakening from the calamity of death.

3. Lift up your head into the horizon. I have bound up and secured you in spiritual victory. Ptah has made to fall, your enemies. His enemies are fallen.

4. They will not exist. Oh Asar!

---

[456] Royal standard. This symbol was used in ancient times prior to the cartouche for inscribing royal names.
[457] Generally referred to as chapter 166.

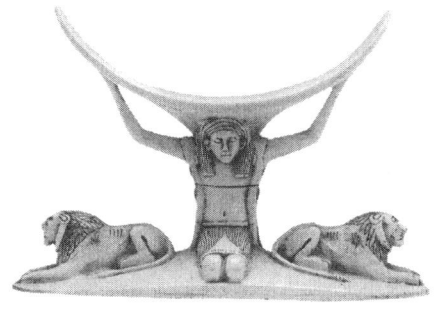

Figure 110: Left-An Ancient Egyptian headrest of King Tutankhamun with Aker lions and the god Heh (eternity).

Figure 111: Right-Akhet, the horizon, with the sundisk.

This chapter is about the sleep of death and the mystical awakening of spiritual enlightenment. All human beings who are not spiritually enlightened are as if asleep, even though they are awake to the world. Sages are actually truly awake because they perceive the reality beyond the physical world. Death is a form of sleep, and all human beings, therefore, undergo a process of death and rebirth everyday. The difference is that in death one does not wake up into the old body. In sleep, if consciousness is dull, however, a person also does not wake up. Rather, they fall into another level of dreaming which actually begins when they believe they have "woken up." Thus, the waking state of mind is in reality a dream for most people because they are caught up in the ignorance of their limited, individual existence.

The mystical symbolism of the headrest and its use as an amulet in the funerary proceedings is extremely profound. The symbols of the headrest, the horizon and the Divine boat are all related. In the Hymn to Ra, the horizon symbol is introduced as it is the valley through which the sun (Divine Boat) traverses to reach the "Beautiful West," the Netherworld. The mountains (Akeru) at either side of the valley are symbols of the past and the future. The sun itself represents non-duality and the mountains represent duality, i.e. non-duality = *eternity,* duality = *the past and the future.* Therefore, the sun boat must traverse through the eternal present in order to successfully enter into the Netherworld.

In the bottom of some coffins, the symbol of Akhet was used at the level of the head of the mummy. This is a clear linking of the horizon with the headrest. In Chapter 18 of the *Prt m Hru,* Sekhet-Hetepet-with Sekhet Yaru-Divine Boat (lower register)-Papyrus Nebseni (see the gloss on Chapter 18), there is a Divine Boat presented in the shape of a headrest. The initiate is exhorted to rise up from the headrest and death. Thus, through Chapter 34, *The Chapter of Rising Up From the Headrest,* the symbol of the horizon, the symbol of the guardians of the horizon, the Akeru (lion) god and goddess, we are provided the wisdom as to the path to spiritual resurrection. It is by maintaining presence of mind, identifying with the eternal journey of the boat, i.e. the eternal existence of the Divine Self.

The iconographic relationship between the headrest and the Aker points to the understanding that the movement of enlightenment occurs in the head, and more precisely, in the mind. Placing the symbol of Aker (horizon-non-duality) at the level of the head is a subtle way of synthesizing four mystical principles, (1) the concept of the *journey to eternity* from the movement of the sun boat, (2) *mind,* from the use of the symbol of the sun itself, (3) *head* (or brain), seat (residence) of individual consciousness, from the use of the symbol at the level of the head in the mummy casket and (4) duality-non-duality, the essence of creation, time and space, and the doorway to eternity. Therefore we have the following reading of the symbolism: *The movement into eternity through the oneness of mind.*

The teaching presented here may seen as a form of mindfulness meditation practice, in which the mind is not allowed to get lost in the past or the future by getting caught up in regrets, frustrations or nostalgia about the past or expectations, illusions or passions for the future. Rather, the mind of the initiate is trained to focus on and exist in the present moment, thereby discovering that time is only a mental concept which people have invented to explain changes in the world, changes that are ephemeral and illusory. In reality time has no existence, it is part of the relativity of the world. It is only a piece of eternity, and eternity is the deeper abiding reality. The deeper Self within every human being is eternal and transcendental. Living in accordance with this wisdom means following the precepts of Maat, the yogic disciplines leading to spiritual enlightenment and profound meditation on this great teaching.

Plate 69: Coffin showing the Aket symbol.

Ancient Egyptian Coffin showing Prt M Hru related texts and the symbols of goddess Nut with open arms, ready to receive her son Asar in the form of the mummy (the initiate), to take that person up to heaven with her. At the level of the head, the symbol of the horizon is placed above the symbol of heaven, that is transcending the physical sky.

Plate 70: Akeru, the lion gods of Yesterday and Tomorrow

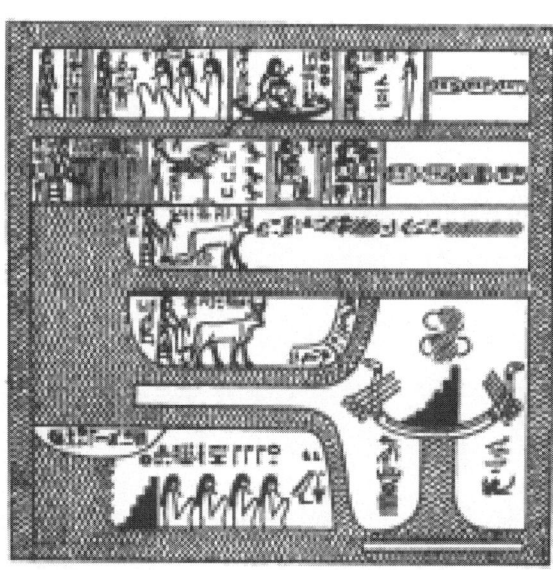

Plate 71: - Sekhet-Hetepet-with Sekhet Yaru-Divine Boat (lower register)-Papyrus Nebseni

321

Plate 72: - Sekhet-Hetepet-with Sekhet Yaru-Divine Boat (lower register)-Papyrus Anhai

322

CHAPTER 36[458]

ENTERING THE INNER SHRINE, MAKING THE OFFERING AND BECOMING ONE WITH ASAR

Plate 73: Vignette from Chapter 36 of Papyrus Ani.

The initiate is anointed, having become one with the Divine by entering the inner shrine. Asar, the initiate meets Asar, the Supreme Being. The illustration for this Chapter includes an offering with a Htp table containing the symbols of male and female.

Following the judgment, Asar Ani is taken by the androgynous Heru (note the female-left breast) and introduced to a mummified Asar who holds the Flail, Crook and Was staffs and is enthroned in a shrine surmounted by a Hawk - Heru. Asar wears a crown symbolic of Upper and Lower Egypt and is assisted by Nebethet and Aset. When Ani reaches the shrine, he is justified and glorified as symbolized by the anointment *"grease cone"* on his head, and kneels with upraised right arm, holding a Sekhem staff in the left. In front of him there is a table of offerings including flowers, fruit and a ***khepesh*** or "foreleg of ox." Above him there are vessels of wine, beer and oils, and at the topmost compartment of the register, there is another offering table with bread, cakes, a wreath and a *"set"* or *"aped"* or duck.

After being judged and having been found to be worthy (pure of heart), Ani is led by Heru, the Lord of Heaven and Earth (Upper and Lower Egypt), who is Ani's own androgynous soul, to Asar who is Ani's Higher Self. Ani has acquired the spiritual strength (Sekhem) to become one with Asar and thus will join Asar in Amenta. Ani's offering of the ***"khepesh and set"*** (symbols of male and female principles) represents Ani's relinquishment of his earthly - dualistic consciousness. Thus Ani is offering his ego-consciousness so that he may realize his non-dualistic - all-encompassing cosmic Higher Self in Asar.

---

[458] Generally referred to as chapter 30B.

323

Now Ani's name becomes Asar-Ani. The green Asar, who in this teaching assumes the role of the male aspect of Neter[459], being supported by Nebethet (death) and Aset (life), is the Supreme deity (Heru) representing *"that which is up there."* In this aspect, the green Asar's mummified form represents neither existence nor non-existence, neither life nor death, but that which lies beyond, the Life Force (green) which vivifies all things. He holds the power of leading one to absolute reality (Shepherd's Crook), the power to emanate Life Force (Was), and the power to separate the mortal human body from the eternal soul just as the winnowing whip or Flail separates the chaff from the seed. Aset and Nebethet (life and death) represent Creation, for only in the realm of creation can there be "life" or "death."

In the realm of Asar there is only eternal life. From the feet of Asar rises the World Lotus (symbol of creation) with the four sons of Heru (all directions of the compass - meaning all-encompassing) standing on it. Asar wears the Atef crown which is composed of the Hadjet crown (Upper Egypt), the Double Plumes crown (Amun) and a small solar disk at the top (Ra), not shown in scene above. Therefore, Asar incorporates the attributes of Heru, Amun and Ra. Thus, to join Asar in Amenta is to join with the attributes of Asar, since Amenta is Asar. In this way one's own soul is responsible for its own fate, either to be led by Apep (ignorance) into the jaws of Ammit (destruction, suffering, reincarnation) or to union with Asar (Hetep-eternal peace). Thus, it is one's own enlightened soul (Heru) who leads one (Ani) to union with one's true self (Asar).

Plate 74: Heru leads initiate into the inner shrine of Asar. From Papyrus Hunefer

Text of Chapter 36:

1. Words to be said by Asar _____.

2. Heart of mother mine– repeat twice –

3. The beginning of my coming into forms. May you stand up for me as a witness in the judgment. Side not towards rebuke of me. Side not towards making protests in reference to me to the controller of the judgment scales. Thou art my Ka in my body, keeping me whole and causing Life Force to flow in me, sustaining my limbs. Come forth thee to the place of beauty and goodness, advancing over the period of sixty years into it. Favor not the stinking of my name in the presence of the sustainers of life. Favor not the speaking of lies about me around The God beautiful and good when listening to thee.

4. These words are spoken by Djehuti, the truth opener of the primordial gods and goddesses who are in the presence of Asar:

---

[459] Other teachings concerning Asar describe an androgynous, omnipotent, hidden, all pervading being who supports all life. In various other texts, the same attributes are ascribed to Aset, Hathor, Heru, Amun, Ra, Ptah, and to other male and female Egyptian Creator divinities. Thus we are led to understand that there is one Supreme Being which is the basis of the Egyptian mysteries, in the same way as the Indian Gods and Goddesses Krishna, Rama, Brahma, Vishnu, Shiva, Saraswati, Kali, Parvati represent male and female aspects of the Supreme Divinity in Hindu mythology.

5. Hear you, words these, of existing truth. It is weighed, the heart of Asar _____ . {His/her} soul is standing up as a witness to {him/her} with a pronouncement of truth upon the great scales. Not has been found, unrighteousness any. Offerings in the temples have not been defrauded. Not damaged {he/she} any works or created things. Not move around {he/she} with low words, of evil while living upon the earth.

Plate 75: The initiate comes to the inner shrine of Asar as Goddess Serqet (Selket) looks on. From Papyrus Gaut-Sushen

6. Response: These words are spoken by the Pasedjed[460] of great gods and goddesses to Djehuti, who is in Khemenu[461]. It has been decreed, what comes forth through your mouth is truth straightforward.

7. Asar _____ who is maak-heru has not committed unrighteousness. {He/she} has not done evil in regards to us. It will not be allowed for Ammit[462] to prevail over Asar _____ . Let there be given to Asar _____ , cakes, the ability to come forth in the presence of Asar and a portion of land established in the field of supreme peace as it is given to all the followers of Heru.

8. These words are spoken by Heru, the son of Aset:

9. I come to thy presence, Un-nefer, and I have brought you Asar _____ [463] whose heart is righteous, going forth through the judgment. Not sinned, {he/she} against any god or goddess. Has judged {him/her} Djehuti and the transcripts of the case have been reported to the Ennead of gods and goddesses as being true and righteous, verily.

10. Grant that be given to {him/her} cakes, beer, and coming forth[464] in the presence of Asar. May {he/she} be like my followers[465] forever.

11. These words are spoken by Asar _____ :

12. Behold Lord[466] of Amentet! There is no failing in my body; not have I spoken lies knowingly; not have I acted with duplicity. Grant that I may be like the favored ones who are around thee Asar, the ones who are favored by the good God and are beloved by the Lord of the Two Lands. May I be loyal and true and beloved (I) Asar _____ who am maak-heru. Let this happen in thy presence of Asar.

---

[460] The Ennead, the nine primordial gods and goddesses who arose out of the Primeval Ocean as children of Ra.

[461] City of the god Djehuti.

[462] Devourer of unrighteous personalities who fail the judgment of the balance due to being found guilty of having committed unrighteousness while alive and living as a human being.

[463] In the beginning of the *Pert m Heru*, the initiate's first name had been changed to Asar in anticipation of this great moment when she is to meet and become one with the God Asar, the Supreme Being.

[464] Transcending death-spiritual enlightenment.

[465] Mythically, all followers of Heru are led into the inner shrine to discover Asar, their Higher Self as one with God.

[466] Having been introduced to God by Heru, the initiate speaks to God directly.

APPENDIX[467]

1. When this chapter is known it means spiritual victory on earth as well as in the Neterkhert. A person with this knowledge can perform actions and live through things[468] in the same way as the great God does.[469] Found, this chapter was, in city of Khemenu on a slab of iron of the south. It was inscribed with lapis-lazuli, truly and it was under the feet of the majestic one, God.

2. This was found in the time of the majestic one, the king of the north and south, Men-kau-Ra[470] by his royal son, Heru-dada-f[471] in spiritual victory. He found it while inspecting the temples. There had strength of mind[472] with him to allow him to understand what it said and realize its importance.

3. He brought it to the king and when he saw that is was a great mystery, it was previously unknown, unseen.

4. Henceforth, this chapter shall be recited by a person who is purified and washed; one who has not eaten animal flesh or fish.

5. And behold! A scarab shall be made and placed within the heart of a person and it will perform for that person the opening of their mouth, this is the anointing with the unguent.

Plate 76: Above-Vignette from Chapter 36 of Papyrus Auf Ankh. The initiate adores the scarab, the symbol of the Divine who presides over transformations, which is the god Khepri as well as the heart of every human being.

Figure 112: Green Heart-scarab amulet with opening words from Chapter 36.

"Heart of mother mine– repeat twice – The beginning of my coming into forms. May you stand up for me as a witness in the judgment..."

Opening text from Chapter 36

      In ancient times, the heart-scarab amulet was one of the most important artifacts associated with the *Prt M Hru*. Sections of the *Prt M Hru* were inscribed on the amulets, made of stone or some other precious material. It was believed, then as it is now, that remembrance of the teachings allows the mind to more easily flow towards the Divine. These amulets may be carried on one's person, placed on the altar or posted as signs in one's spiritual area to augment the spiritual practice.

End of the Mystical Chapters from the Ancient Egyptian Book of Enlightenment

---

[467] From Chapter 36 (30B) Rubric in papyrusat Paris (Naville, Todtenbuch, Bd. I., Bl. 167, ll. 14-27)
[468] objects.
[469] I.e. free and unencumbered by their actions.
[470] King of Ancient Egypt – name means "Established in all of the all of the astral bodies (minds of all living things) of Ra."
[471] This name means "Heru gives to him."
[472] Resoluteness, determination and stamina.

GLOSS ON CHAPTER 36: ITS MEANING AND MYSTICAL SIGNIFICANCE

The Ancient Egyptian Eucharist

From the Ancient Egyptian *Pyramid Texts* we receive the utterances, which show the ancient nature of the philosophy which later became known as the Christian Eucharist.

From the Christian Bible:

> Matthew 26:
> 26. And as they were eating, Jesus took bread, and blessed [it], and broke [it], and gave [it] to the disciples, and said, Take, eat; this is my body.
> 27 And he took the cup, and gave thanks, and gave [it] to them, saying, Drink ye all of it;
> 28 For this is my blood of the new testament, which is shed for many for the remission of sin.

The Eucharist is the central rite of the Catholic mass or church service. It re-enacts the Last Supper when Christ gave his disciples bread, saying, "This is my body," and wine, saying, "This is my blood." This sacrament is also known as the Holy Communion. However, there has been a controversy over what the communion is supposed to be since the rise in prominence of the Orthodox Roman Catholic Church. At the Lateran Council in 1,215, a doctrine called *Transubstantiation* was defined. It stated that there is a change in substance of the Eucharist elements after the consecration. This means that the substance of bread and wine changes to Christ's actual body and blood, respectively. This doctrine is opposed by that of *Consubstantiation,* which holds that after the words of consecration are uttered in Communion, the substances of bread and wine remain, along with the body and blood of Christ.

The important idea in the ritual of the Eucharist is that identification should go beyond rituals, prayers, austerities and penances. Identification implies a complete absorption into the Divine which completely excludes the ego self. Some mystery cults such as that of Asar and Attis went further in amplifying the identification of the initiate with the death, dismemberment and resurrection of the deity by having the initiate lay in a coffin for a period of time (meditation) and then rise up in triumph over death. The stigmata is another effect of strong psychic identification with the passion of Jesus, however, if the identification with the passion of the deity is not transcended, the experience remains at the level of the senses, mind and intellect. Even these still fall under the heading of egoism. What is required is that these be transcended and for the initiate to enter into an expanded consciousness as a result of the experience in the ritual. Thus, the Eucharist ritual was a long-standing ceremony, which Christianity adopted from Ancient Egyptian religion. It was first practiced in the mysteries of Asar and later in those of the Pythagoreans, Dionysus, Essenes, Mithras, and Attis who were initiated into the Asarian mysteries.

The ritual of eating the body and blood of the dismembered, reconstituted and resurrected deity, needs to be understood for its profound symbolic meaning. Whether or not actual bread or some other symbol is used is less important than the understanding of the underlying significance of the wisdom teaching behind it. When the world is understood as being composed of differently arranged atoms which are themselves composed of energy as modern physics has proven, the idea of consuming any kind of substance assumes a strong spiritual meaning. In this sense, keeping the metaphysical understanding in mind, every time food is consumed, the process should be viewed as an Eucharistic ritual, because all substances are composed of the same underlying essence. This essence may be called Asar, God, Brahman, Buddha, Amen, or energy. Therefore, every meal that is consumed is a communion with the Divine. Every breath is a communion as well because the body is consuming the necessary nutrients of life and in turn transferring its own essence into the environment. The environment itself is the body of God, the Divine Self. With this understanding, it is easy to understand that the body is constantly in communion with the ocean of energy for its survival. When there is conscious communion with that ocean as being one with it, then there is communion of the highest degree, Spiritual Enlightenment.

Part III

Chapter 1: The Ritual Uses of the *Prt m Hru*

Readings for the Guidance of the Dying Person and their Relatives

There were at least three recognized uses of the *Prt m Hru* Chapters that can still be effective in modern times. In ancient times, the scriptures of the *Prt m Hru* were used by priests and priestesses to officiate at burials, which were actually rituals related to the guidance of the deceased. The scriptures chosen by the departed were read as they were on their deathbed, and another formal performance would have also taken place. This one would have included the participation of the spouse of the deceased. For example, the wife of the deceased would assume the role of Aset, the resurrector.[473] In this capacity, a dying person should be read all the appropriate Chapters selected for that person, beginning with the passages from Chapter 1, Part 1, related to the commencement of the movement into the higher plane of existence. At the time of death, the deceased should be read the scriptures from Chapter 18, the movement through the Netherworld to discover the abode of Asar, and then Chapter 36, entry into the inner shrine. Here, the commentary (glosses) of the spiritual preceptor can also be read. Then at the time of death and immediately afterwards, the attendees at the deathbed and later, the funeral or wake, should recite Chapter 1, Part 2, Hymn 1 (Hymn to Ra) and Hymn 2 (Hymn to Asar). The reading of the scripture of *Prt m Hru* in this manner takes on a similar quality to the *Tibetan Book of the Dead*. The deceased would be guided by the readings to discover the abode of the Divine. Modern para-psychological experiments suggest the possibility that at the time of death, while an individual cannot move, they can still hear. Further, it is was believed in ancient times that the spiritual essence of a person, the astral body, would remain close to the body for a time and they would benefit from the readings.

The attendees should not be mourning at this time since the resurrection of the deceased's soul is a motive for rejoicing. The attendees should take comfort in the fact that the recitation of these verses is infallible for the person passing on if they had led a righteous life and turned their spiritual vision towards the Divine while they were still alive. The recitation will be helpful even if the person has not made these changes, but the help will be limited to experiencing less adversity in the Netherworld, and the next lifetime will be more propitious for attaining spiritual enlightenment. In any case, the attendees should by now realize that there is no real death. Therefore, mourning and fear are to be seen as irrational sentiments of those who are spiritually ignorant. The soul moves on, and they should free the soul by not regretting its passing and by wishing it a safe journey. This feeling helps the soul move on without the burden of attachments, and it allows the living to move on also in their own spiritual disciplines, leading up to their own passing.

In the case of those people who are in a coma or in a vegetative state, it must be understood that yogic philosophy holds that the soul is never in the body, but rather, it uses the body for a limited period of time. A person's death is determined by the soul's (Ba-Ka-Akhu) desire to move on even if the personality (Khat-Ren) of a person seems to be clinging to life. If there is clinging, then there is pain and sorrow for the dying person because they are going against the desire of the soul. Therefore, the family of the deceased should not try to hold on to the body and realize that the body is only an aggregate of elements that must go back to the elements where they came from (earth, air, water, fire). The soul is imperishable, and in this aspect we are all one and can never leave our loved ones. How can a wave leave the ocean? In deciding when to disconnect life support machines, the family should be guided by this wisdom along with the insight of health professionals, taking into account the factor of allowing other family members (those not initiated into this mystical teaching) sufficient time to grieve. It is degrading to the soul to be clinging to life in a limited state of health. Therefore, one should move on to the next life with a new body or on to self-discovery and oneness with the Absolute, God, the Self.

---

[473] See the Ausarian Resurrection Myth

The ideal of the practice of the *Prt m Hru* teachings is that by the time of the death of the physical body, the initiate should already have discovered that which is beyond. There should be no mystery about it, and the Divine should already have been discovered. This process of spiritual "awakening" is promoted through living in accordance with Maat Philosophy and practicing the rituals and meditations of the *Prt m Hru*.

In the Valley of the Queens in Waset, Kemet (Thebes, Egypt) and in various papyri, there are depictions of parents making the offerings and readings of the Prt M Hru for children who are too young to present themselves for judgment. Thus, in this manner, the parent or guardian should perform the rituals, meditations, chanting and offerings with the child or for the dead child.

The Body of the Deceased

Once a person dies, what should be done with the body? The body of the deceased was the instrument used by that person to perform actions in this realm. It is no longer needed now that the soul has flown away to continue its eternal journey. There are two possibilities prescribed by the Kemetic teachings. As there are two main paths to the Divine which are promoted in the *Prt m Hru*, the Asarian and the Atumian (Atum-Ra), so too there are different traditions for the disposal of the body of the deceased. In the case of the Asarian, there is a tradition of burial (see Utterance 261/Coffin 288, Coffin 246 and Utterance 332 and chapter 23 and 26) and in the case of the Atumian, cremation (see Coffin Invocation 246). Since Atum-Ra relates to the sun and to fire as well as to air, the indication for the disposal of the dead body is cremation. The body is to become one with the fire and as subtle as air, and the soul is to have power over these elements as it escapes their grasp and moves towards the ultimate abode of the Higher Self. The earliest known mummies are believed to date from the early dynasties of Ancient Egyptian Culture. This technique of mummification was adopted later by the Assyrians, Jews, Persians and Scythians. Early Christian Sarcophagi were decorated with biblical scenes. Christians forbade cremation because it was believed that the body would not be able to resurrect in the end times. Jews believed it was a desecration of the body and Muslims also forbade cremation.

As Asar is the god of vegetation, mythologically his body serves as fodder and fertilizer for all vegetation and since every human being is Asar, the indications for the disposal of the dead body is burial. The burial should take into account ecological issues and should not be done in such a way as to pollute the environment. Shrines or mausoleums can be created, but these should be in the form of temples wherein family and others may come to perform religious rites, worship, etc. In other words, ideally the tombs should be monuments not to the deceased, but sanctuaries exalting the teachings, containing segments of the scriptures in which the person believed, being displayed for all. Of course, the most profound teachings are to be reserved for the interior of the shrine. In Pre-dynastic times, the corpse of the deceased was not mummified. Mummification is defined as the maintenance of a corpse through artificial means. This practice grew out of a tradition attached to the practice of the Asarian religion. The idea was that if the images of life on earth were preserved, then the existence in the afterlife would be preserved as well. This idea is based in part on the teaching that everything in Creation is a form (image) and name. This great Ancient Egyptian teaching was the basis for much of Plato's work. If the form and name are given then, there is existence. Think about it. If you call an object to mind, you are giving it existence. This is what you do when you exercise the imagination, and even more so when you dream.

However, the extension of the idea into the conclusion that preserving the body guarantees existence in the afterlife with the image of the physical body, though true in part, is not the goal of the deeper aspects of Ancient Egyptian religion. This is only a tradition attached to a religion. It is not a mystical or spiritual ideal. Therefore, initiates and their families should be striving to release all attachments to mortal existence. Families should strive to release the deceased and not promote sentimental attachments to that which is not real. Also, the deceased should not leave this world in anguish over what will happen to their families without them and so on. Grieving over the loss of a loved one is indicative of a life lived in delusion, where the very basic truth of life, that everyone will die, was never reflected upon. Not facing up to one's own mortality is another manifestation of the same problem. Those with true faith and/or true insight into the teachings will release that form of ignorant thought, and will work earnestly towards the goal of life, to discover that which lies beyond death, but before death actually comes to them. This is the basis of the *Prt m Hru*.

Plate 77: Right- Pre-dynastic-Neolithic period Grave.

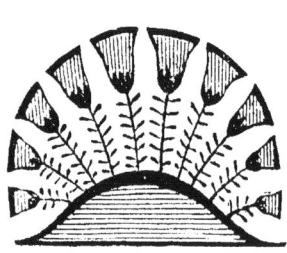

Figure 113: Left-Burial mound with lotuses growing from it, symbolizing the spiritual resurrection.

In ancient times (Neolithic period – beginning 10,000 B.C.E.), the deceased were wrapped in a reed mat and placed in simple graves with the body in a prenatal position, lying on its left side, and not stretched out on the back as in later times. They were buried with vessels (pottery) that were painted black and red. This pottery is almost identical to that which was found by archeologists in India, from the ancient period (Dravidian c. 2,500 B.C.E). While it is possible to be extravagant with funerals, it is not necessary or prudent in view of the mystical teachings. The use of coffins, tombs and elaborate structures came later in the Dynastic period. Many of the upper class began to think that they could "take it all with them," so they had slaves, food, jewelry, etc., buried with them only to have it robbed by grave-robbers or their tombs emptied by Egyptologists, museums, etc., and their mummified bodies destroyed. There is no security in this world or any other. Indeed, at any moment a passing comet or accidental nuclear war, or other possible disasters can destroy this world. It therefore behooves the wise aspirant to begin right away to exert effort in the spiritual disciplines so as not to fall prey to the world of illusions. There is no truth or security except in that Divinity which transcends Creation.

Figure 114: Pyramid tomb of the Old Kingdom Period.

Figure 115: Mastaba tomb of Giza area.

The term *Pyramid Text* is used because some of the kings from the Old Kingdom period inscribed *Prt m Hru* texts on the walls of their tombs. Mastabas (an Arab name for "low, long stone buildings") were used later, to the end of the 6th Dynasty. These structures were built to contain the body of the deceased, but also as places were friends and relatives could make offerings for the Ka of the deceased and utter Hekau for the well being of the deceased and themselves. After the Predynastic graves, wooden coffins were used. These wooden coffins were followed by the use of sarcophagi (a stone coffin, often inscribed or decorated with sculpture.)

Figure 116: (below left) Coffin of the Old Kingdom Period in the form of a square house with false doors.

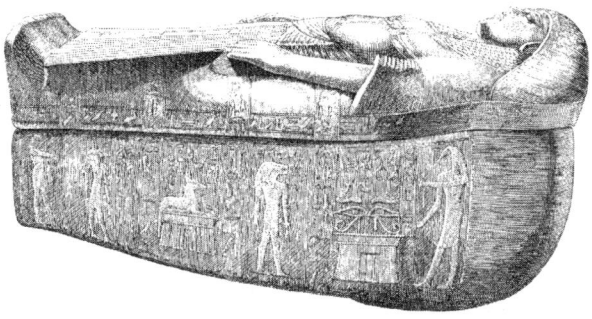

Figure 117: (right) Sarcophagus of the 19th Dynasty in Memphis now making use of (human form) anthropoid art.

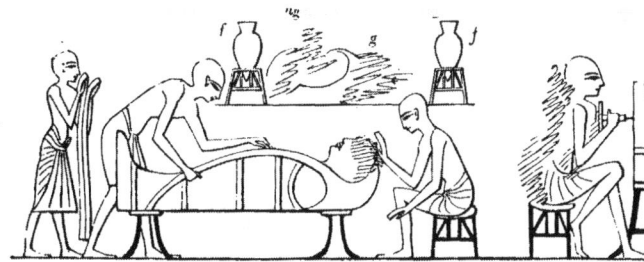

Figure 118: (above) The preparation of the mummy

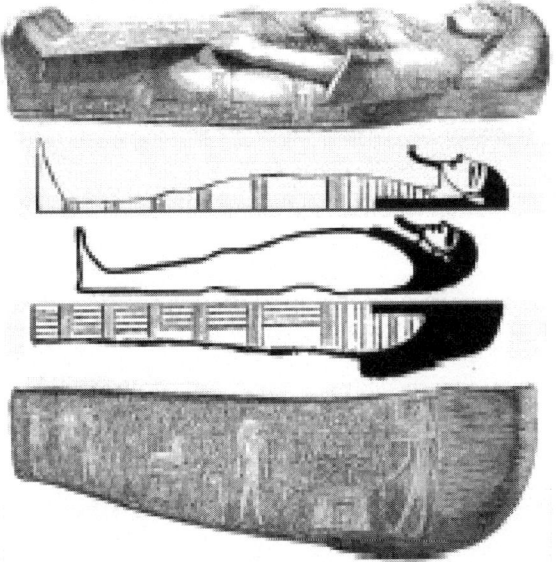

In later times, the body was prepared through an elaborate mummification and bandaging procedure (above left). Then it was placed in an anthropoid ornamented case, which in turn was placed inside the coffin (above right). The act of placing the mummy within a succession of containers within containers symbolizes the idea that the soul is encased within the elements or aspects of the personality. In mystical philosophy, these are likened to onion peels which surround the inner Self. This concept may be likened to the sheaths of Indian Yoga mysticism. If these outer layers of personality are peeled away, the inner Self is left unfettered. The initiate uttering the "I am" formula symbolizes this. It symbolizes the ability to take on any desired form, since God is all forms and one has discovered one's own identity as the Divine.

Figure 119: (Right) Elaborate burial containers: Mummy within gilded casket within a sarcophagus.

Mastaba architecture was oriented astronomically towards true north. The interior of a complete mastaba included an upper chamber, which serves as an entrance, a nook, which is a vaulted subterranean room with an opening in the north to admit air, and a pit, which leads to where the body is laid.

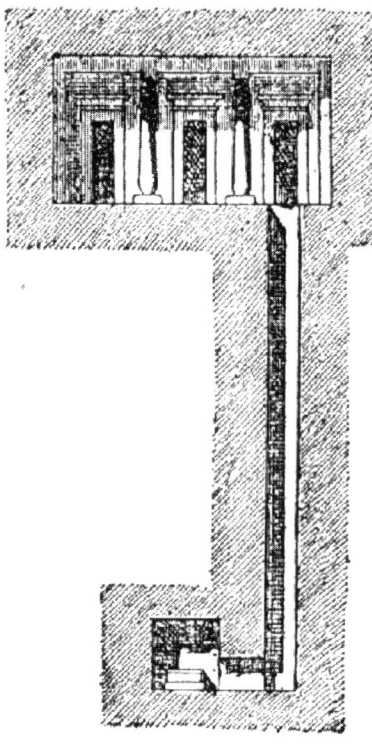

Figure 120: (right) Vertical section of a mastaba tomb showing the chambers.

Figure 121: (above) Section of the tomb of Seti I

Figure 122: Tombs in the cemetery-a lady is mourning in the distance-from a stele at Giza.

332

There is an Ancient Egyptian Proverb, which states, *"There are two roads traveled by humankind, those who seek to live MAAT and those who seek to satisfy their animal passions."* This means that there are two pursuits in human existence, worldly pleasures or spirituality. There are two pursuits in spirituality, heavenly pleasures or the supreme abode. It should be noted that just as in modern times there are those people who promote and practice religion with the expectation of a heavenly form of afterlife (not understanding that it is perishable and that they must reincarnate after a period of time), so too in ancient times there were those who practiced religion based on lower levels of understanding. However, also as in ancient times, there are always people who are advanced in the teachings of mystical spirituality who desire to seek the truth, and those who are qualified to lead others on this path to the ultimate truth. This is the path for those students of the mystical traditions from around the world. Initiates live their lives in such a way as to draw themselves closer to truth and the Divine and not to illusions, entanglements and sentimental attachments based on ignorance.

The "Hetep Slab" or Offering Table is another most important tantric symbol from Ancient Egypt associated with religious and funerary services. The Hetep Slab was used as an instrument for conducting ritual offerings to the Divine as well as to the deceased. It is composed of a stone slab ranging in dimensions from 6 inches to 3 feet in length, and 4 inches to 15 inches in width. The items placed on it are called *Hetepet*. Its basic items include special symbols. These are the male ⌒, thigh, and female ⌒, duck, symbols carved into the top, along with the symbol of Supreme Peace, ⌒, or Hetep, which consists of a loaf of bread, ϑ, and an offering mat, ⌒. The carving was of a mat that was composed of woven reeds (in Pre-dynastic times) and two libation vessels ⌒⌒. In ancient times the actual offering mat consisted of the articles themselves (loaf, thigh, duck and libation fluids (water, wine or milk), but in Dynastic times (5,500B.C.E-400 A.C.E) the table top or slab contained the articles as engraved glyphs. The top of the table has grooves, which channel the libations around the offering toward the front and center of the table, and then out through the outermost point of the protruding section. It would not be necessary to use actual items since the images carved into the stone slab call their essence into being for the purpose of the ritual.

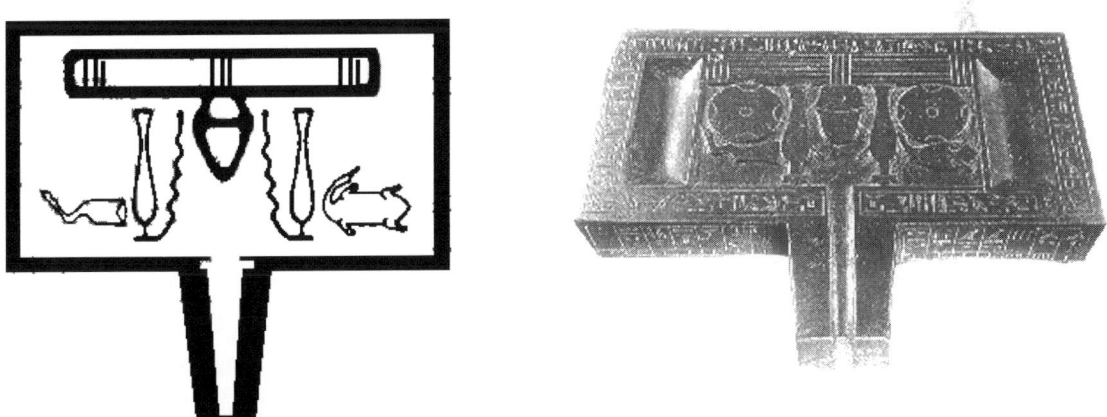

Figure 123: Line drawing of the Hetep (offering) Slab (table)

Plate 78: Actual Hetep offering Slab

The hetep symbol, ⌒, means "rest," "peace" and "satisfaction," and when it is used in the hetep offering ritual it refers to the satisfaction of the neters (gods and goddesses) which comes from uniting the male and female principles into one transcendental being. More specifically it refers to the union of the

male and female principle within the human heart, the opposites, and discovering the androgynous Supreme Spirit within. The Hetep Offering Table can be seen in the illustrations of the *Prt m Hru*. It is a propitiation of supreme peace, which comes when the opposites are unified in life. This means, offering one's dualistic feelings, one's individuality and egoistic concepts to the Divine. Thereby the soul is unified in God, and there is no more duality. This is a supreme mystical movement, a return to the primordial state. This is when an initiate feels "I am Tem."

Readings for the Guidance of the Spiritual Aspirant

Another other important use of the scriptures was as a ritual performance to fulfill the reenactment of the myth of Asar, Aset and Heru. In this capacity the recitation of the verses of *Coming Forth Into the Light* were used to educate and induct initiates into the spiritual order of *Shetaut Asar* (Mysteries of Asar) as well as to lead spiritual aspirants to achieve mystical experiences. Thus, a spiritual aspirant must study the scriptures carefully under the guidance of a spiritual preceptor, taking care to follow the precepts contained therein related to righteous living, including meditation on the teachings, and promoting a movement towards realizing their Asarian nature. The aspirant accomplishes this by first accepting the spiritual name Asar, and then by living life in the realization that Asar's passion, as well as his resurrection, are their own. This is the process, which will occur by means of the Yogic disciplines that the preceptor will prescribe.[474] In ancient times this process of spiritual enlightenment was achieved in the same manner in which it can be achieved today. It comes through living the life of Asar (according to the precepts of Maat), including fasting, vegetarian diet, celibacy, along with the practice of chanting the scriptures, meditation on them and their ritual performance. The idea is to experience the passion and death of Asar *in fact* by transcending one's ordinary human consciousness and thereby experiencing and consequently becoming one with Asar.

Figure 124: The image of Asar rising from grave, resurrected, is a powerful image to study. (from Papyrus Ani)

Initiates should also know that until they reach the higher levels of spiritual evolution they might experience some grief, anger, hurt, etc., even if they have knowledge of these high teachings. This is because the personality has not fully integrated the teachings at the deeper levels of the personality. This takes time and the process of personality integration should be allowed to continue until the practitioner reaches full dispassion and detachment from sentimental feelings about the world. This process occurs in degrees. An initiate should not think that there is no progress in their spiritual life since they are still affected by the world. In fact, even though initiates may experience sorrow or other emotions, they will not experience these in the same way that ordinary people will. The intensity and duration of psychological distress is reduced because deep down the teachings and one's positive actions of the present are at work relieving the ignorance and the stress caused by unrighteous beliefs and actions of the past. One is able to let go of the illusions about the world in degrees, so the process of spiritual evolution will be effective in degrees. In the meantime, an initiate should learn to be patient with the elements of

---

[474] See the book *Initiation Into Egyptian Yoga* by Dr. Muata Ashby.

their lower personality (Khat, Ren, Ka) and continue working towards the ideal, even if the lower nature continues to pull towards the world. So even if you cry, do so with this book in one hand, even as you have a handkerchief (for drying your tears) in the other.

A sane person does not mourn over a cloud that has taken the form of a cute puppy, only to disperse and move on. This is because a sane person has full understanding of the fact that the cloud formations are passing illusions. The mind suffers over death and the myriad miseries of life due to ignorance of the mind concerning the nature of life. In other words, there will be suffering in relation to death until there is full understanding (enlightenment dawns in the mind) as to the fact that nobody dies, and all of the problems of life are due to misunderstanding the nature of life and desiring things in the wrong way. They merely came for a while and must now move on, like the cloud. Especially in dealing with the question of death, initiates should look deep into their hearts and allow themselves to experience the paradox of life and death. Those people who turn away from this kind of reflection except when there is a sudden death in the family are living in a dream world which will be shattered one day. This is when the shock and dismay at the loss of a loved one, which is based on sentimental attachment to the deceased and a deep-rooted fear of death, hits hardest. It is a result of not facing truth. Allow yourself to think of life in terms of death. Ask yourself why am I doing this? This world is fleeting and illusory, so what can I or should I become attached to? What is my purpose in life? Who am I? etc. Your reflectiveness will lead you to transcend the grief and fear of death and to discover the Divine. You will find that relying on the teachings, especially in times of adversity, will lead you quickly to self-mastery and spiritual enlightenment. Therefore, adverse situations need not be viewed as negative, but as opportunities set up by goddess Maat to allows us the opportunity to practice the teachings and integrate the personality, i.e., to cleanse your heart of the illusions and egoism that lead one astray in life.

Death should not be shunned as most people in modern times do, as if they can escape its grasp. It should be viewed as a natural aspect of life. This idea is evident in the Ancient Egyptian manner of saying grace before meals, even by ordinary householders. Prior to consuming food or engaging in festive occasions, such as parties, etc., the host of an ordinary household would invite the guests to view an image of a divinity, principally Asar, the god of the afterlife. They would bring out and display for all, the figure of a mummy, usually one and a half to three feet tall, standing erect or lying down. This ritualistic act has the effect of reminding all about their own mortality, thereby showing the guests that life is fleeting, even as they are about to enjoy a sumptuous meal. In this manner, a person is reminded of the ultimate fate of life and a reflective state of mind is engendered rather than an arrogant, egoistic and deluded state. This theme is present in every aspect of Ancient Egyptian culture. In modern times, most people do not want to think about death, especially when they are "having a good time." This would have been considered a turning away from truth, a breach of one of the fundamental injunctions of Maat philosophy (precept #24: *I have not stopped my ears listening to the words of right and wrong.*). Thus, when death occurs, we should not turn away and act as if it does not exist or promote a "lets try to have a good time and not think about it" attitude. Drugs, worldly entanglements, and other distractions may soften the blow of death in the short term, but some day the issue will have to be dealt with through the death of close family members of oneself. If you are not ready, the experience will be harrowing and painful. If you are ready, it can be as smooth as silk. This is the prospect that initiates of the yogic sciences look forward to and discover.

Plate 79: Asar as figurine displayed at parties and dinners affairs

Facing death and uncovering its mystery is the most important task for every spiritual aspirant. This is because the fear of death and the sorrow caused by disease, old age and death typify the pain, misery and frustrations of life. Therefore, conquering death means conquering life. Initiates should strive to understand that since God is not only the author of this Creation, but also the essence of everything that exists in it, God is also the controller of everything that occurs. Therefore, initiates should accept all righteous situations as they arise, and not try to escape them due to a personal desire to avoid pain. You should not purposely create adversity to punish yourself for actions of the past, nor should you run from

it. You should strive to promote peace, harmony and understanding as well as forgiveness (of yourself as well as others), but this does not mean that you should evade dealing with negative Ari (karma) that you created for yourself, and which God has decreed should be part of your life experience to endure. Some Ari can be transcended through understanding the mistake alone. Other Ari must be worked through in dreams or in life situations in the physical world. The goddess (Maat) determines this. You created it and you must resolve it before you can move forward in your spiritual evolution. Otherwise you will need to confront the situation again later, in this life or the next, in order to resolve the issues causing you distress. God is there for you, to help you through this process, not to absolve you of your responsibility. Do not fool yourself into believing otherwise. If you try to escape your adversity, you are actually forsaking your own opportunity to attain enlightenment, and you are rebuffing the goddess and her efforts to help you on your spiritual journey, and thereby turning away from the process that will lead you to spiritual enlightenment. Thus, while prosperity, if used wisely, allows a person to turn towards the Divine, adversities too in the form of financial losses, deaths in the family, etc., are in reality God's way of leading you to the ultimate abode as well.

Readings for the Guidance of the Masses

While there were no public recitations of the mysteries, the very fact that the mythology related to them was re-enacted as plays (Ancient Egyptian Theater) in the outer courts of the temples made them known to the public and kindled spiritual aspiration in the masses. This activity served the purpose of holding society together by focusing their attention and aspiration towards someday holding closer consultation with the priests and priestesses, in order to discover the higher essence of life, once a full life in the world had been lived. In association with the mysteries, the myths were conducted as public performances which galvanized the mind of the masses and acted as a cultural adhesive which promoted interest in the spiritual teachings as well as the awareness of the Divine.

Chapter II: The Prt m Hru and Ancient Egyptian Theater and Music:

THE ANCIENT EGYPTIAN TEMPLE: THE THEATER OF RAU NU PRT M HRU

The Ancient Egyptian Temple was the place where the teachings of the *Prt m Hru* were developed, espoused and ceremonially reenacted. The Ancient Egyptian temple was constructed in such a way that every aspect of it is a symbolic representation of Creation, and as a reflection of Creation, it is a reflection of the Divine Trinity. Therefore, the Ancient Egyptian temple structure itself displays the wisdom of the Trinity for all who understand the mystic symbolism.

The rituals and invocations, Hekau, of the *Prt m Hru* are to be chanted, recited and/or enacted. This means that the ritual performance of the teachings of *Prt m Hru* is an important aspect of the spiritual practice. So what is theater and music?

Definition and Origin of: "Theater"

> A place or building in which dramatic performances for an audience take place; these include drama, dancing, music, mime, opera, ballet, and puppets.
>
> Theatre history can be traced to Egyptian religious ritualistic drama as long ago as 3200 BC. The first known European theaters were in Greece from about 600 BC.
>
> —Copyright © 1995 Websters Encyclopedia

Music as a Healing Force

Pythagoras, a student of the Ancient Egyptian Mysteries, learned from his Ancient Egyptian Masters, the teachings of mystical spirituality which included the art of music and how it affects the mind. He noted that certain music agitated the mind, and certain music did not. Music could be stimulating or pacifying if used properly. Therefore, there are certain forms of music that are conducive to peace, relaxation and harmony. This kind of music is suitable for promoting the healing and health maintenance process.

Figure 125: **Musicians in Ancient Egypt**

Ancient Egyptian Theater ➜ Greek Theater ➜ Roman Theater ➜ Christian Theater ➜ Modern Western Theater

Many people believe that the art of theater began with the ancient Greek theater. Thespis, a Greek actor-dramatist (about 560 B.C.E.), is considered to have been the first person to give the Greek drama its form and actors are still called "thespians." However, upon closer examination it must be noted that just as Greek philosophers such as Thales and Pythagoras learned their wisdom from the Ancient Egyptians and then set up their schools of philosophy in Greece. It is likely that the first Greek actors and playwrights learned their profession from the Ancient Egyptian teachings since the early theater was based on the mysteries of the gods and goddesses that was taught to the first Greek philosophers.[475] Actually, a great debt is owed to the Greek writers of ancient times because their records attest to many details, which the Ancient Egyptians did not record.

> Solon, Thales, Plato, Eudoxus and Pythagoras went to Egypt and consorted with the priests. Eudoxus they say, received instruction from Chonuphis of Memphis,* Solon from Sonchis of Sais,* and Pythagoras from Oeniphis of Heliopolis.*
>
> –Plutarch (Greek historian c. 46-120 A.C.E.)
> *(cities in Ancient Egypt where the main universities were located)

There was no public theater in Ancient Egypt, as the modern world knows theater at present. Theater in present day society is performed publicly for the main purpose of entertainment, but in Ancient Egypt the theatrical performances were reserved for the religious practice exclusively. This was because the performing arts, including music, were held to be powerful and sacred endeavors, which were used to impart spiritual teachings and evoke spiritual feeling, and was not to be used as frivolous forms of entertainment. The Greek writer, Strabo, relates that:

> *Multitudes of people would flock to festival centers (important cities and temples) where the scenes from myths related to the gods and goddesses would be acted out.*

Sometimes the main episodes of the religious dramas were performed outside the temple, in the courtyard or between the pylons and were the most important attraction of the festivals. The most esoteric elements were performed in the interior portion of the temple for initiates, priests and priestesses only. The priests and priestesses took great care with costumes and the decorations (direction and set design). The spectators knew the myths that were being acted out but never stopped enjoying their annual performance, being a retelling of the divine stories, which bring purpose and meaning to life. Thus, the art of acting was set aside for spiritual purposes and was not to be used for mindless entertainment, which serves only to distract the mind from reality and spiritual[476] truths. The spectators would take part by clapping, lamenting during the sad parts, and crying out with joy and celebrating when the ultimate triumph came. In this manner the spectators became part of the myth. The myth essentially represented the lives of the gods and goddesses not only as sustainers of the world, but also as leaders to better understanding the connection between the material and spiritual worlds. Further, the occasions were used as opportunities for enjoying life, though it was understood to be fleeting. Whenever there is joy in life, one's mind should be turned to the Divine. This has two benefits. First, it acknowledges that happiness comes from the inner Divine reality as opposed to external objets. Secondly, it prevents a person from developing egoism through the erroneous thought that they themselves are responsible for the happiness they experienced through their actions. Thus, the bridge between the mortal world and the eternal world was established, through mythological drama and the performing arts.

In the Ancient Egyptian view, life cannot be enjoyed without affirming the Divine, the Spirit. Further, theater, religion and mystical philosophy were considered to be aspects of the same discipline, known as "Shetaut Neter" or the "mysteries" or "Yoga Sciences." The awareness and inclusion of spirituality permeated every aspect of life in Ancient Egypt. For example, lawyers and judges followed the precepts

---

[475] see the book "From Egypt to Greece"

[476] The word "spiritual" here implies any endeavor, which seeks to bring understanding about the ultimate questions of life: Who am I? and What is life all about? So spirituality may or may not be related to organized religion.

of Maat and medical doctors followed and worshipped the teachings of the god Djehuti, who was adopted by the Greeks as the god Asclapius.

Music in Ancient Egypt

Shmai, to make music

Music was an integral part of the Ancient Egyptian Mystical Religious system. This fact is pointed out by inscriptions still surviving at present on the walls of the temples in Egypt. For example, in the temple of Hetheru at Denderah, the following inscription can be found: *The sky rejoices, the earth dances, the sacred musicians shout in praise!*

The Ancient Egyptian Sages instituted tight controls on theater and music because the indulgence in inappropriate entertainments was known to cause mental agitation and undesirable behaviors. The famous Greek Philosopher and student of the Ancient Egyptian Mysteries, Pythagoras, wrote that the Ancient Egyptians placed particular attention to the study of music. Even today, one can visit the temples of Ancient Egypt and note the prominently displayed musical instruments that were part of the temple rituals, where the rituals of the Prt M Hru were performed and also in the birthing houses. Another famous Greek Philosopher and student of the Ancient Egyptian Mysteries, Plato, states that they thought it was *beneficial to the youths*. Plato further reports that:

> *In the education of the youths they were particularly strict...they knew that children ought to be early accustomed to such gestures, looks and motions as are decent and proper; and not to be suffered either to hear or learn any verses and songs than those than those which are calculated to inspire them with virtue; and they consequently took care that every dance and ode introduced at their feasts or sacrifices should be subject to certain regulations.*

Strabo confirms that:

> *Music was taught to youths along with reading and writing, however, it was understood that music meant for entertainment alone was harmful to the mind, making it agitated and difficult to control oneself, and thus was strictly controlled by the state and the priests and priestesses.*

Like the Sages of India, who instituted *Nada Yoga*, or the spiritual path of music, the Ancient Egyptians held that music was of Divine origin and as such was a sacred endeavor. The Greek writer, Athenaeus, informs us that *the Greeks and barbarians from other countries learned music from the Ancient Egyptians*. Music was so important in Ancient Egypt that professional musicians were contracted and kept on salaries at the temples. Music was considered important because it has the special power to carry the mind to either elevated spiritual states or worldly states. When there is overindulgence in music for entertainment and escapism (tendency to desire to escape from daily routine or reality by indulging in fantasy, daydreaming, or entertainment), the mind is filled with worldly impressions, cravings, lusting, and uncontrolled urges. In this state of mind, the capacity for right thinking and feeling are distorted or incapacitated. The advent of audio and visual recording technology and their combinations in movies and music videos is even more powerful because the visual element, coupled with music, and the ability to repeat with intensity of volume, acts to intoxicate the mind with illusory and fantasy thoughts. The body is also affected in this process. The vibrations of the music and the feelings contained in it through the lyrics and sentiment of the performer evoke the production of certain bio-chemical processes in the mind and body. This capacity of music is evident in movies musicals, concerts, audio recordings, etc., in their capacity to change a person's mood. Any and all messages given to the mind affect it, and therefore, great care should be taken to fill the mind with the right kinds of messages in the form of ideas and feelings.

Those societies which produce and consume large quantities of audio and audio-visual entertainment for non-spiritual purposes will exhibit the greatest levels of mental agitation, violence, individual frustration, addiction, mental illness, physical illness, etc., no matter how materially prosperous or technologically advanced they may seem to become. So true civilization and success of a society should not be judged by material prosperity or technological advancement, but rather on how successful it is in producing the healthy development and inner fulfillment of its citizens. Being the creators and foremost practitioners of Maat Philosophy (adherence to the principles of righteousness in all aspects of life[477]), the Ancient Egyptians created a culture which existed longer (at least 5,000 years) than any other known society. Therefore, the real measures of civilization and human evolution are to be discerned by the quality and usage of the performing and visual arts in bringing forth spiritual philosophy, for these endeavors serve to bring harmony to the individual and to society. It should be clearly understood that art should not become stagnant or rigid in its expression since this is the means by which it is renewed for the understanding of future generations. Rather, the principle of right usage of the arts and the spiritual elements of Divine Music should be kept intact in the performance of the rituals, paintings, sculptures, music, etc., since these reflect transcendental truths which are effective today as they were 5,000 years ago in the Ancient Egyptian temple, and will be effective until the end of time. The loss of these is the cause of disharmony in society, but societal dysfunction is in reality only a reflection of disharmony in the individual human heart, which has lost its connection with the Higher Self within.

Dance was also an important part of Ancient Egyptian life. Dance, along with music, was used to worship the gods and goddesses, especially Asar and Hetheru. However, dance was also present in private dinner parties. Also, private parties were the scene for entertainments such as games (Senet-similar to modern day Parcheesi), juggling, mimes, music and limited theatrical performances. Men and women would dance together or alone and would improvise, more than in the dances of the temples and special ceremonies. As is the custom in modern day India and Japan, the Ancient Egyptians would take their shoes when entering a house or the temple as a sign of reverence for the host and a symbolic gesture of leaving the world outside when practicing higher endeavors.

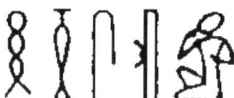

Hesi -Chant, sing repeatedly praises

Notice that the word for music and the word for chant or sing, all use the determinative sign, which means with the mouth. Therefore, the primary musical instrument is seen as the voice, and all other instruments are viewed as accompaniments to the voice.

Thus, the question of whether or not music and entertainment has an effect on youth and the mind of a person was resolved in ancient times. The Ancient Egyptians observed that the people from Greece and the Asiatic countries were more aggressive, and that their behavior was unstable. They attributed these problems to their lifestyle, which was full of strife due to life in harsh geographical regions, meat eating, overindulgence in sense pleasures or which resulted from their inability to control the human urges and consequent disconnection from the natural order of the universe as well as their spiritual inner selves. These observations of the psychology and lifestyle of the foreigners prompted the Ancient Egyptian Sages to refer to the Greeks and Asiatics (Middle Easterners) as "children," "miserable" and "barbarians." Their observations allowed the Ancient Egyptian Sages to create a philosophy of life and a psycho-spiritual environment wherein the Ancient Egyptian people could grow and thrive in physical, mental and spiritual health.

In ancient Greece, theater became a practice, which was open to the public. Later on in the Christian era, the passion plays gave way to theater of the masses. It deteriorated into mindless entertainment and corruption. In present times, it is a big business wherein its participants are paid excessive and disproportionately high salaries for their entertainment skills, or otherwise said, their ability to sell

---

[477] See the book "The Wisdom of Maati."

merchandise. In modern times, the almost unfettered creation and promotion of movies, videos, music and other forms of entertainment containing elements designed to promote sense pleasures and excitement, leads to mental agitation, with little true satisfaction of the inner need of the heart. Thus, while the entertainments may cause excitation, they do not lead to abiding fulfillment and inner peace, but to more desires for more excitement in a never ending cycle which is impossible to fulfill. This process leads to mental confusion and stress, which in turn lead to strife, conflict, and internal frustration. Corresponding with the emergence and development of Western and Middle Eastern culture, with its negative lifestyle elements that were noted by the Ancient Egyptians, the world has also seen an increase in wars, violence against women and children, environmental destruction, slavery, taking advantage of weaker human beings, drug abuse, crime, divorce, and overall personal dissatisfaction with life. In other words, the lack of restraints, in both individuals and societies as a whole, has led to a frustration with life, a kind of cultural depression and degradation, which has led to record numbers of people suffering from mental illnesses such as depression, schizophrenia, psychosis, as well as medical disorders of all kinds. Many of these problems were not present in ancient times, due to self-control and the direction of life being guided by spiritual pursuits as opposed to egoistic pursuits.

The Ancient Egyptian Mystery theater provided the means for allowing a human being to come into harmony with the spiritual reality (mental expansion and self-discovery), while frivolous entertainment serves to dull the intellectual capacity to discover and understand that which is beyond the physical world and the physical sense pleasures of life (mental contraction and hardening of the ego). This inability to go beyond sense pleasures and experiences in the world of human activity is what leads a person to mental stress, which in turn leads to mental and physical illness.

Therefore, understanding the message of Ancient Egyptian Theater is of paramount importance to human evolution. In Ancient Egypt, theater and music were used for spiritual education and to maintain harmony between the individual and the universe, the soul and the Divine. Thus, spiritual plays were enacted by the priests and priestesses, initiates, and sometimes by the relatives of the deceased, especially in the case of the *Prt m Hru* mysteries. The use of masks in theater did not originate in Greece. Their use already existed in Ancient Egypt. Unlike the Greek theater which placed great importance on tragedy in life, playing the characters of the mystery was for the purpose of understanding the mystery by becoming one with it, to embody the qualities of the divinity being portrayed and in so doing, ultimately becoming one with the Divine. Also, the purpose was to promote the well being of others by directing one's mind and heart towards what is righteous, beautiful and good in the world and beyond. This was the motivation and source of strength, which allowed Ancient Egyptian Culture, led by the priests and priestesses, to achieve a high degree of "civilization" and spiritual enlightenment.

Thus, the earliest religious rituals in Egypt were performed as plays, which were often part of festival periods. This tradition began in the early pre-dynastic period with the Ausarian Resurrection myth (5,000 B.C.E. or earlier), which surrounds the death and resurrection of the god Asar. The Asarian drama was the main play that was performed universally in Ancient Egypt. Then it was re-enacted in Greece and Rome in later times after the Greeks came to Egypt to learn the arts, sciences, and spiritual philosophy, which they used when they established their disciplines of philosophy. In Ancient Egypt, the story of Hetheru was so highly revered that an annual play and festivity was held in her honor which commemorated her saga (See the books *The Glorious Light Meditation* and *Mysticism of the Goddess)* and continued even down to the early Christian era. It was so popular that it was observed widely throughout the entire country of Egypt. Remnants of it and other Ancient Egyptian festivals survive even today in the rituals of the Muslims who live in Egypt as well as in some Jewish and Christian holidays, rituals, symbols and customs. Thus, theater emerged in ancient Africa and influenced Europe, and what would later develop into Greek and Christian Theater. The practice of the mystery play was done for the purpose of worshipping the gods and goddesses and also as a method of imparting some important mystical teachings. Therefore, anyone wishing to learn more about the teachings and practice of Ancient Egyptian philosophy could learn much from participating in the play and studying Ancient Egyptian Mystical Philosophy and Divine Music.

Chapter III: Meditation: Based on the Mystical Chapters of *Prt m Hru*

INTRODUCTION TO MEDITATION

Using The *Prt m Hru* texts for Rituals and Meditation

The *Prt m Hru* texts are designed to bring forth Rituals and Meditations which will lead any human being to turn their mind towards the Divine and transform their consciousness from ignorant and mortal to immortal and Divine. The following instructions constitute informal and formal meditation practice based on the *Prt m Hru* teachings.

NOTE: It is recommended that the aspirant should practice the informal meditation lifestyle outlined throughout this text and the simple meditation techniques, described below, until there is a good grasp of the philosophy, before entering into the practice of the *Prt m Hru* rituals as meditations for spiritual enlightenment.

What is Meditation?

Meditation may be thought of or defined as the practice of mental exercises and disciplines to enable the aspirant to achieve control over the mind, specifically, to stop the vibrations of the mind due to unwanted thoughts, imaginations, etc. Just as the sun is revealed when the clouds disperse, so the light of the Self is revealed when the mind is free of thoughts, imaginations, ideas, delusions, gross emotions, sentimental attachments, etc. The Self, your true identity, then becomes visible to the conscious mind.

The mind and nervous system are instruments of the Self, which it uses to have experiences in the realm of time and space, which it has created in much the same way as a person falls asleep and develops an entire dream world out of {his/her} own consciousness. It is at the unconscious and subconscious levels where the most intensive work of yoga takes place, because it is here that the conscious identification of a person creates impressions in the mind and desires based on those impressions develop. It is these desires that keep the aspirant involved in the realm of time and space or frees the aspirant from the world of time and space if they are sublimated into the spiritual desire for enlightenment. The desire to attain enlightenment is not viewed in the same manner as ego based desires; it is viewed as being aspiration which is a positive movement.

Externalized consciousness - distracted by egoism and worldly objects. ◄ ◄ ◄ 𝒞

The light of the Self (consciousness) shines through the mind, and this is what sustains life. The flow of consciousness in most people is from within moving outward. This causes them to be externalized, distracted and lose energy. Where the mind goes, energy flows. Have you ever noticed that you can "feel" someone looking at you? This is because there is a subtle energy being transmitted through their vision (which is an extension of the mind). Those who live in this externalized state of mind are not aware of the source of consciousness. Meditation as well as the other disciplines of yoga serve to reverse the flow of consciousness on itself so that the mind acts as a mirror which reveals the true Self.

Internalized consciousness of a yoga practitioner. ➤ ➤ ➤ 𝒞

Most people are unaware that there are deeper levels to their being, just as they are unaware of the fact that physical reality is not "physical." Quantum physics experiments have proven that the physical world is not composed of matter, but of energy. This supports the findings of the ancient Sages who have taught for thousands of years that the reality which is experienced by the human senses is not an "Absolute" reality, but a conditional one. Therefore, you must strive to rise beyond your conditioned mind and senses in order to perceive reality as it truly is.

"Learn to distinguish the real from the unreal."

Human beings are not just composed of a mind, senses and a physical body. Beyond the physical and mental levels, there is a soul level. This is the realm of the Higher Self which all of the teachings of yoga and the various practices of meditation are directed towards discovering. This "hidden" aspect of ourselves which is beyond the thoughts is known as Amun, Asar or Amenta in the Ancient Egyptian system of spirituality, and as Brahman, in Indian Vedanta philosophy.

Universal Soul

↙ ↓ ↘

Mind and Senses
(Astral Body and Astral World - the Duat or Netherworld)

↙ ↓ ↘

Physical Body and Physical World

When you are active and not practicing or experiencing the wisdom of yoga, you are distracted from the real you. This distraction which comes from the desires, cravings and endless motion of thoughts in the mind is the *veil* which blocks your perception of your deeper essence, the Supreme Self. These distractions keep you involved with the mind, senses, and body that you have come to believe is the real you. When your body is motionless and you are thinking and feeling, you are mostly associated with your mind. At times when you are not thinking, such as in the dreamless sleep state, then you are associated with your Higher Self. However, this connection in the dreamless sleep state is veiled by ignorance because you are asleep and not aware of the experience. In order to discover this realm you must consciously turn away from the phenomenal world which is distracting you from your inner reality. The practice of yoga accomplishes this task. Meditation, when backed up by the other disciplines of yoga, is the most powerful agent of self discovery. The practice of meditation allows one to create a higher awareness which affects all aspects of one's life, but most importantly, it gives the aspirant experiential knowledge of {his/her} true Self.

What is the Goal of Meditation?

Meditation may be thought of or defined as the practice of mental exercises and disciplines to enable the meditator to achieve control over the mind, specifically, to stop the vibrations of the mind due to unwanted thoughts, imaginations, etc.

Consciousness refers to the awareness of being alive and of having an identity. It is this characteristic which separates humans from the animal kingdom. Animals cannot become aware of their own existence and ponder the questions such as *Who am I?, Where am I going in life?, Where do I come from?,* etc. They cannot write books on history and create elaborate systems of social history based on ancestry, etc. Consciousness expresses itself in three modes. These are: Waking, Dream-Sleep and Dreamless-Deep-Sleep.

Ordinary human life is only partially conscious. When you are driving or walking, you sometimes lose track of the present moment. All of a sudden you arrive at your destination without having conscious awareness of the road which you have just traveled. Your mind went into an "automatic" mode of consciousness. This automatic mode of consciousness represents a temporary withdrawal from the waking world. This state is similar to a daydream (a dreamlike musing or fantasy). This form of existence is what most people consider as "normal" everyday waking consciousness. It is what people consider to be the extent of the human capacity to experience or be conscious.

The "normal" state of human consciousness cannot be considered as "whole" or complete because if it was there would be no experience of lapses or gaps in consciousness. In other words, every instant of

343

consciousness would be accounted for. There would be no trance-like states wherein one loses track of time or awareness of one's own activities, even as they are being performed. In the times of trance or lapse, full awareness or consciousness is not present, otherwise it would be impossible to not be aware of the passage of time while engaged in various activities. Trance here should be differentiated from the religious or mystical form of trance like state induced through meditation. As used above, it refers to the condition of being so lost in solitary thought as to be unaware of one's surroundings. It may further be characterized as a stunned or bewildered condition, a fog, stupor, befuddlement, daze, muddled state of mind. Most everyone has experienced this condition at some point or another. What most people consider to be the "awake" state of mind in which life is lived is in reality only a fraction of the total potential consciousness which a human being can experience.

The state of automatic consciousness is characterized by mental distraction, restlessness and extroversion. The automatic state of mind exists due to emotions such as desire, anger and hatred which engender desires in the mind, which in turn cause more movement, distractions, delusions and lapses or "gaps" in human consciousness. In this condition, it does not matter how many desires are fulfilled. The mind will always be distracted and agitated and will never discover peace and contentment. If the mind were under control, meaning, if you were to remain fully aware and conscious of every feeling, thought and emotion in your mind at any given time, it would be impossible for you to be swayed or deluded by your thoughts into a state of relative unconsciousness or un-awareness. Therefore, it is said that those who do not have their minds under control are not fully awake and conscious human beings.

Meditation and Yoga Philosophy are disciplines which are directed toward increasing awareness. Awareness or consciousness can only be increased when the mind is in a state of peace and harmony. Thus, the disciplines of Meditation (which are part of the Yoga) are the primary means of controlling the mind and allowing the individual to mature psychologically and spiritually.

Psychological growth is promoted because when the mind is brought under control, the intellect becomes clear and psychological complexes such as anxiety and other delusions which have an effect even in ordinary people can be cleared up. Control of the mind and the promotion of internal harmony allows the meditator to integrate their personality and resolve the hidden issues of the present, of childhood and of past lives.

When the mind has been brought under control, the expansion in consciousness leads to the discovery that one's own individual consciousness is not the total experience of consciousness. Through the correct practice of meditation, the individual's consciousness-awareness expands to the point wherein there is a discovery that one is more than just an individual. The state of "automatic consciousness" becomes reduced in favor of the experiences of increasing levels of continuous awareness. In other words, there is a decrease in daydreaming as well as the episodes of carrying out activities and forgetting oneself in them until they are finished (driving for example). Also, there is a reduced level of loss of awareness of self during the dreaming-sleep and dreamless-sleep states. Normally, most people at a lower level of consciousness-awareness become caught in a swoon or feinting effect which occurs at the time when one "falls" asleep or when there is no awareness of dreams while in the deep sleep state (dreamless-sleep). This swooning effect causes an ordinary person to lose consciousness of their own "waking state" identity and to assume the identity of their "dream subject" and thus, to feel that the dream subject as well as the dream world are realities in themselves.

This shift in identification from the waking personality to the dream personality to the absence of either personality in the dreamless-sleep state led ancient philosophers to discover that these states are not absolute realities. Philosophically, anything that is not continuous and abiding cannot be considered as real. Only what exists and does not change in all periods of time can be considered as "real." Nothing in the world of human experience qualifies as real according to this test. Nature, the human body, everything has a beginning and an end. Therefore, they are not absolutely real. They appear to be real because of the limited mind and senses along with the belief in the mind that they are real. In other words, people believe that matter and physical objects are real even though modern physics has proven that all matter is not "physical" or "stable." It changes constantly and its constituent parts are in reality composed of "empty spaces." Think about it. When you fall asleep, you "believe" that the dream world is "real" but upon waking up you believe it was not real. At the same time, when you fall asleep, you forget the waking world, your relatives and life history, and assume an entirely new history, relatives, situations and world systems. Therefore, philosophically, the ordinary states of consciousness which a human being experiences are limited and illusory. The waking, dream and dreamless-sleep states are only transient expressions of the deeper underlying consciousness. This underlying consciousness which witnesses the other three states is what Carl Jung referred to as the "Collective Unconscious." In Indian Philosophy this "fourth" state of consciousness-awareness is known as *Turia*. It is also referred to as "God Consciousness" or "Cosmic Consciousness." The corresponding terms in Kemetic philosophy are, *Nhast* spiritual resurrection or *Maak-heru* –spiritual victory.

The theory of meditation is that when the mind and senses are controlled and transcended, the awareness of the transcendental state of consciousness becomes evident. From here, consciousness-awareness expands, allowing the meditator to discover the latent abilities of the unconscious mind. When this occurs, an immense feeling of joy emerges from within, the desire for happiness and fulfillment through external objects and situations dwindles and a peaceful, transcendental state of mind develops. Also, the inner resources are discovered which will allow the practitioner to meet the challenges of life (disappointments, disease, death, etc.) while maintaining a poised state of mind.

When the heights of meditative experience are reached, there is a more continuous form of awareness which develops. It is not *lost* at the time of falling asleep. At this stage there is a discovery that just as the dream state is discovered to be "unreal" upon "waking up" in the morning, the waking state is also discovered to be a kind of dream which is transcended at the time of "falling asleep." There is a form of "continuous awareness" which develops in the mind which spans all three states of consciousness and becomes a "witness" to them instead of a subject bound by them.

Further, there is a discovery that there is a boundless source from which one has originated and to which one is inexorably linked. This discovery brings immense peace and joy wherein the worldly desires vanish in the mind and there is absolute contentment in the heart. This level of experience is what the Buddhists call *Mindfulness*. However, the history of mindfulness meditation goes back to the time of ancient India and Ancient Egypt. In India, the higher level of consciousness wherein automatic consciousness is eradicated and there is continuous awareness is called *Sakshin Buddhi*. From Vedanta and Yoga Philosophy, the teaching of the "witnessing consciousness" found even greater expression and practice in Buddhist philosophy and Buddhist meditation. Buddhi or higher intellect is the source of the word *Buddha*, meaning one who has attained wakefulness at the level of their higher intellect. The corresponding terms relating to "witnessing consciousness" in Kemetic philosophy is *Amun* -"witnessing consciousness" or "witnessing Self or Divinity" and *Shetaut Neter* – "Hidden innermost Divinity."

INFORMAL MEDITATION: THE MEDITATIVE LIFESTYLE

Meditation is not just an exercise that is to be practiced only at a certain time or at a certain place. In order for your meditative efforts to be successful, the philosophy of meditation must become an integral part of your life. This means that the meditative way of life, the yoga lifestyle, must become the focus of your life no matter what else is going on in your life. Most people who do not practice yoga cannot control the clamoring thoughts of the mind and because of this, do not experience inner peace or clarity of purpose in life; the teachings cannot help them. Others, beset by intensely negative thoughts, succumb to these and commit acts against their conscience and suffer the consequences of a self-defeating way of life wherein painful situations and disappointments in life are increased while happiness and contentment are decreased. The mind is weakened due to the mental energy being wasted in useless endeavors which only serve to further entangle one in complex relationships and commitments. Another source of weakening one's will to act correctly and promote situations of advancement and happiness is caused by the susceptibility to negative emotions. Negative emotions such as anger, hatred, greed, gloom, sorrow, and depression as well as excessively positive emotions such as elation, serve to create mental agitation and desire which in turn cloud the intellectual capacity to make correct decisions in life.

When life seems unbearable due to the intensification of negative emotions and the obscuring of intellectual capacity, some people commit suicide in an attempt to escape or end the painful onslaught of uncontrollable thoughts. Still others prefer to ignore the messages from the deeper Self which are beckoning them to move toward introspection. Situations of stress in life are motivators whose purpose is to turn us away from the outer world because we have lost our balance. There is a place for material wealth and sensual experience (outer experiences of the senses), however, when the inner reality is ignored or when inner needs and inner development is impaired due to excess concentration on worldly goals and desires, then experiences of frustration and disappointment occur. If these situations are understood as messages from nature to pull back and find the inner balance, then personality integration and harmony can be discovered. However, if these times are faced with lack of inner strength, then they lead to suffering. Sometimes there are moments of clarity wherein the Higher Self is perceived in an intuitive flash, but people usually tend to discount the occurrence as a coincidence or other curious event while others, in bewilderment, believe they are going mad. Others prefer to ignore the issue of spirituality altogether and simply shun any thoughts about death or the afterlife. This is a reverse-yogic movement that stunts spiritual evolution. Its root cause is fear of the unknown and fear of letting go. The practice of yogic meditation techniques can serve to counteract any and all negative developments in the mind if the correct techniques are used and the correct understanding is adopted.

There are four main components of meditation. These are: posture, breath-life force control, sound and visualization. In the beginning stages of practice, these components may be somewhat difficult to perform with consistency and coordination, but with continued effort, they become a pleasurable experience which will bring you closer to your awareness of your Self. It is difficult to control the mind in the beginning. Many aspirants loose heart because they have not obtained the results they had anticipated. They either quit prematurely or jump to different techniques without giving sufficient time for the exercises to work. They do not understand that although on occasion, profound changes will occur in a short time, for the most part it's a gradual process.

A meditative lifestyle should be developed along with one's formal meditation practices. This means acting in such a way that there is greater and greater detachment from objects and situations, and greater independence and peace within. This can only occur when there is a keen understanding of one's deeper Self and the nature of the world of human experience along with formal meditation practices and other activities which promote physical health (diet and exercise). Ordinarily, people "do" things in order to gain some objective or to derive some pleasure or reward. From a mystical perspective they are "doers of action." They act out of the unconscious and subconscious desires arising in the mind at any given time and are thus, beset with a perpetual state of unrest and agitation. The meditative way of life means that your actions are always affirmations of your higher knowledge and awareness and not based on the unconscious desires and emotions of the mind. The perfection in this discipline only comes with practice. When this art is perfected, the practitioner is referred to as a "non-doer." This is because even though they may be doing many things in their life, in reality they have discovered that the true rewards of life do not depend on the outcome of an activity, its fruit or reward.

Thus, true peace and inner fulfillment will never come through pursuit of actions when there is an expectation or desire for the fruits of those actions. The belief in objects or worldly activities as a source of happiness is therefore seen as a state of *ignorance* wherein the individual is caught up in the *illusions*, *fantasies* and *fanciful notions* of the mind. However, happiness and peace can arise spontaneously when there is an attitude of detachment and dispassion toward objects and situations in life. If actions are performed with the idea of discovering peace within, based on the understanding of the philosophy outlined above, and for the sake of the betterment of society, then these actions will have the effect of purifying the heart of the individual. The desires and expectations will dwindle while the inner fulfillment and awareness of the present moment will increase. There will be greater and greater discovery of peace within, a discovery of what is truly stable and changeless within as opposed to the mind and outer world which are constantly changing and unpredictable. Along with this there is greater effectiveness and perfection in one's actions.

Actions of any type will always lead to some result. However, this result is not as predictable as people have come to believe. In reality, the only thing a human being can control is the action itself and not the fruits (results) of the action. If there is concentration on the action without desire or expectation of the fruits of the action, then there can be peace and contentment even while the action is being performed. This is the way of the non-doer. Actions performed with expectations and desire are the way of the doer. The non-doer is free from the fruits because {he/she} is free from desires and expectations, while the doer is dependent on the actions and is bound to the results be they positive or negative. When desires and expectation in the mind are resolved, the mind becomes calm and peaceful. Under these conditions, the non-doer is free from elation or depression because {his/her} pleasure is coming from the present action in the present moment, promoting concentration of mind and expansion in consciousness. The actions are no longer based on memories of the past of pleasurable situations which are impelling a movement to repeat those activities, or on expectations for future activities which will somehow bring happiness. The non-doer, not being bound to the memories or to the expectations, is not bound by either the past or the future, and thereby discovers an eternal present. The doer is always caught up in the past or the present, and thereby loses the opportunity to discover peace and true happiness. This is the condition of most people in the world. Before they realize, it their entire life has gone by without their being aware of the passage of time. The art of true spiritual life leads one to detach from the world even while continuing to live in it, and thereby to discover the hidden inner spiritual dimensions of the unconscious mind and what lies beyond. The doer is always bound to a form of experience which is determined by and bound to the world of time and space, because only in time and space can there manifest the memories of the past and the expectations for the future. The non-doer eventually discovers a transcendental experience of expanding consciousness in the present moment.

The philosophy of meditation may seem foreign to you at first, but if you reflect upon it, you will discover that it holds great truth as well as great potential to assist you in discovering abiding peace and harmony in your life. When you begin to practice and discover how wonderful it is to be in control of your mind instead of being prey to the positive or negative emotions and desires, you will discover an incomparable feeling which goes beyond the ordinary concept of happiness. As with other human endeavors, in order to gain success you need to study the philosophy intensively with great concentration and then practice it in your day to day life. Treat it as an experiment. The world and your life will not go away. Just ask yourself: What would happen if I was to become less attached and more in control of my mind? Follow the teachings and discover the inner resources you need to discover true happiness and to overcome the obstacles of life.

The practice of meditation requires regular and sustained practice. Failure is assured if there is no effort. Likewise, success is assured if there is sustained, regular effort. This is the key to accomplishing any goal in life and, enlightenment, is a goal like any other, albeit the highest goal. With respect to attaining the goal of enlightenment, all other goals are like dust blowing in the wind. The following instruction will serve as guidelines for meditation and is not intended to be a substitute for a competent instructor. There are many techniques of meditation. Here we will focus on basic techniques of "moving"

meditations for initially calming the mind of the beginning practitioner. For more on the philosophy of non-doership see the book *The Wisdom of Maati.* For more on the philosophy of Kemetic meditation and meditation instructions see the book *Meditation: The Ancient Egyptian Path to Enlightenment* –both by Muata Ashby

FORMAL MEDITATION PRACTICE

Formal meditation practice means taking out a special time to turn away from the world, to sit in quiet contemplation and using special rituals such as the burning of incense, lighting a candle, uttering prayers, etc., in a special area chosen for this regular practice. In the formal practice of meditation, certain technical information must be understood. This section is an overview of these techniques as well as more advanced teachings of meditation based on the teachings of the *Prt m Hru*.

Proper Breathing

Most people in the modern world do not know how to breathe properly. Most people (especially males) have learned to breathe by pushing out the chest in a "manly" or "macho" fashion. This mode of breathing is harmful for many reasons. The amount of air taken in is less and vital cosmic energy is reduced and becomes stagnant in the subtle vital energy channels, resulting in physical and mental diseases. The stagnation of the flow of energy through the body has the effect of grounding one's consciousness to the physical realities rather than allowing the mind and body to operate with lightness and subtlety.

"Belly breathing" or abdominal breathing massages the internal organs and develops Life Force energy (Ra, Chi or Kundalini). It will be noticed that it is our natural breathing pattern when we lie down on our back. Instruction is as follows: A- Breathe in and push the stomach out. B- Breathe out and pull the stomach in. This form of breathing is to be practiced at all times, not just during meditation. It allows the natural Life Force in the air to be rhythmically supplied to the body and nervous system, and proper oxygen intake into the body. This process is indispensable in the achievement of physical health and mental-spiritual power to control the mind (meditation).

Alternate Nostril Breathing Exercise[478]

Prior to your practice of exercises and meditation you should practice *Alternate Nostril Breathing.* There are opposing forces (poles) of energy in all human bodies. These forces are related to mental energy, the emotions, mental and physical health. When these poles are out of balance, various mental, emotional and physical problems can arise. The study of these forces is related to the Uraeus Serpent of Egypt[479] and the Kundalini Serpent Yoga systems of India. For now simply follow the instructions below and you will begin to feel improved health and vitality. As you study the deeper implications of the breath, more teachings will be given to enhance your practice.

The opposing energy poles of the body: Uatchet (Udjat, Utchat) and Nekhebet (Ida and Pingala respectively) can be balanced by practicing a simple alternate nostril breathing exercise. This is accomplished as follows: Using the right hand, bend the index and middle finger toward the palm while leaving the thumb, fourth and fifth (pinkie) fingers extended. Using the thumb to close off the right nostril, breath out through the left nostril and then breath in (inhalation) through the left nostril while holding the right one closed, then close both nostrils using the fourth and fifth (pinkie) fingers to close the left nostril and leaving the other two fingers remaining bent. Release the thumb from the right nostril and exhale through the right nostril. Next breath in through the right nostril while holding the left one closed with the fourth and fifth fingers. Now close the right nostril with your thumb and retain the breath for a short time. Next, release your fourth and fifth fingers (while still holding the right nostril closed with your thumb), breathe out through the left nostril. This constitutes one cycle of the Alternate nostril breathing exercise. The ratio of inhalation: retention: exhalation should be 2:8:4 to begin, working up to 4:16:8.

---

[478] see *Egyptian Yoga Exercise Video*
[479] see the book *The Serpent Power* by Muata Ashby

You may repeat a hekau (mantra) while performing this exercise. Continue in this way for five minutes at the beginning, and then gradually building up to fifteen minutes or longer as needed. Then practice the desired form of meditation of your choice. The alternate breathing exercise is an excellent way to balance the body's energies. The energies may also be balanced in a variety of ways, such as controlling the emotions and remaining calm, and engaging one's self in activities that are in harmony with one's consciousness (hobbies, job, recreation).

Simple Meditation Technique

Modern scientific research has proven that one of the most effective things anyone can do to promote mental and physical health is to sit quietly for 20 minutes twice each day. This is more effective than a change in diet, vitamins, food supplements, medicines, etc. It is not necessary to possess any special skill or training. All that is required is that one achieves a relaxed state of mind, unburdened by the duties of the day. You may sit from a few minutes up to an hour in the morning and in the late afternoon.

This simple practice, if followed each day, will promote above average physical health and spiritual evolution. One's mental and emotional well being will be maintained in a healthy state as well. The most important thing to remember during this meditation time is to just relax, and not try to stop the mind from pursuing a particular idea, but also not trying to actively make the mind pursue a particular thought or idea. If a Hekau or Mantra (Prayer) is recited, or if a special hieroglyph is meditated upon, the mind should not be forced to hold it. Rather, one should direct the mind and when one realizes that one has been carried away with a particular thought, bring the mind gently back to the original object of meditation, in this way, it will eventually settle where it feels most comfortable and at peace.

Sometimes one will know that one has been carried away into thoughts about what one needs to do, or who needs to be called, or is something burning in the kitchen?, etc. These thoughts are worldly thoughts. Simply bring the mind back to the original object of meditation or the hekau. With more practice, the awareness of the hekau or object of meditation (candle, mandala, etc.) will dissipate as you go deeper. This is the positive, meditative movement that is desired. The goal is to relax to such a degree that the mind drifts to deeper and deeper levels of consciousness, finally reaching the source of consciousness, the source of all thought; then the mind transcends even this level of consciousness and there, communes with the Absolute Reality, Neter. This is the state of "Cosmic Consciousness," the state of enlightenment. After a while, the mental process will remain at the Soul level all the time. This is the Enlightened Sage Level.

Tips for Formal Meditation Practice

Begin by meditating for 5 minutes each day, gradually building up the time. The key is consistency in time and place. Nature inspires us to establish a set routine to perform our activities; the sun rises in the east and sets in the west every day, the moon's cycle is every 28 days and the seasons change approximately at the same times of the year, every year. It is better to practice for 5 minutes each day than 20 minutes one day and 0 minutes the next. Do a formal sit down meditation whenever the feeling comes to you, but try to do it at least once a day, preferably between 4-6 am or 6-8 pm. Do not eat for at least 2 hours before meditation. It is even more preferable to not eat 12 hours before. For example, eat nothing (except only water or tea) after 6 p.m. until after meditation at 6 a.m. the following morning. Do not meditate within 24 hours of having sexual intercourse, for this disruption of your hormones and energies will detract from the experience. Meditate alone in a quiet area, in a dimly lit room (candle light is adequate). Do light exercise (example: Chi Kung or Hatha Yoga) before meditating, then say Hekau (affirmations, prayers, mantras, etc.) for a few minutes to set up positive vibrations in the mind. Burning your favorite incense is a good way to set the mood. Keep a ritualistic procedure about the meditation time. Do things in a slow, deliberate manner, concentrating on every motion and every thought you perform.

When ready, try to focus the mind on one object, symbol or idea such as the heart or Hetep (Supreme Peace). If the mind strays, bring it back gently. Patience, self-love and self-forgiveness are the keys here. Gradually, the mind will not drift toward thoughts or objects of the world. It will move toward subtler levels of consciousness until it reaches the source of the thoughts and there commune with that source, Neter Neteru. This is the desired positive movement of the practice of meditation, because it is from Neter Neteru that all inspiration, creativity and altruistic feelings of love come. Neter Neteru is the source of peace and love and is who you really are.

Rituals Associated With Formal Meditation Practice

In the beginning, the mind may be difficult to control. What is needed here is perseverance and the application of the techniques described here. Another important aid to meditation is ritualism. You should observe a set of rituals whenever you intend to practice meditation. These will gradually help to settle the mind even before you actually sit to practice the meditation. They are especially useful if you are a busy person or if you have many thoughts or worries on the mind. First take a bath. Water is the greatest cleanser of impurities. In ancient times the practitioners of yoga would bathe before entering the temples and engaging in the mystery rituals. This practice has been kept alive in the Christian practice of baptism and the prayers using the Holy Water. In the *Gospel of Peace,* water is used as an external as well as internal cleanser of the body. In modern times, many Native American spiritual leaders and others use water as a means to transport negative vibrations in the body in the form of a restless mind, or other negative thoughts directed toward others or oneself out and away from the body. This may be accomplished by simply visualizing the negative feelings moving into the water as you bathe and then going down the drain and into the earth as the water is washed away. This is a very powerful means of purification because the mind controls the energies in the body. Therefore, if the mind is controlled, you will be able to control the energies of your body, your emotions, attitudes, etc. All of these must obey the command of your mind. Thus, through practice of this exercise you will gradually gain control of moods and other mental complexes. Eventually you will be able to control your mind and direct it to be calm according to your will.

Once you have bathed, put on clothing which you have specifically reserved for the practice of meditation. This will have a strong effect on your mind and will bring meditative vibrations to you because the clothing will retain some of the subtle essence of the meditation experience each time you use them. The clothing should be loose and comfortable. We recommend 100% Cotton or Silk because it is a natural material which will allow the skin to breath. Keep the clothing clean and use the same style of clothing for your meditation practice.

When you are ready, go to your special room or corner which you have set aside for meditation. Take the phone off the hook or turn off the ringer and close the door behind you, leaving instructions not to be disturbed for the period of time you have chosen. When you sit for meditation, light a candle and some incense of your choice, then choose a comfortable position maintaining the back straight either sitting on the floor in the cross-legged posture (Lotus), sitting in a chair with feet on the floor or lying on your back on the floor in the corpse-mummy pose (without falling asleep).

Words Of Power In Meditation: Khu-Hekau, Mantra Repetition:

The Ancient Egyptian words was spelled in various ways. It means "Words of Power."

The word *"mantra"* in Indian Yoga signifies any sound which steadies the mind. Its roots are: "man" which means "mind" and "tra" which means "steady." In Ancient Egyptian terminology, "hekau" or word formulas are recited with meaning and feeling to achieve the desired end.

Hekau-mantra recitation, (called *Japa* in India), is especially useful in changing the mental state. The sounds coupled with ideas or meditations, based on a profound understanding of the meaning can have the effect of calming the mind by directing its energy towards sublime thoughts. rather than toward degrading, pain filled ones. This allows the vibrations of the mind to be changed. There are three types of recitations that can be used with the words of power: 1- Mental, 2- Recitation employing a soft humming sound and 3- loud or audible reciting. The main purpose of reciting the words of power is somewhat different than prayer. Prayer involves you as a subject, "talking" to God, while words of power - hekau - mantras, are used to carry your consciousness to divine levels by changing the vibrations in your mind and allowing it to transcend the awareness of the senses, body and ordinary thought processes.

The recitation of words of power has been explored to such a degree that it constitutes an important form of yoga practice. Two of the most comprehensive books written on this subject by Sri Swami Sivananda were *Japa Yoga* and *Sadhana.* Swami Sivananda told his pupils to repeat their mantras as many as 50,000 per day. If this level of practice is maintained, it is possible to achieve specific changes in a short time. Otherwise, changes in your level of mental awareness, self-control, mental peace and spiritual realization occur according to your level of practice. You should not rush nor suppress your spiritual development, rather allow it to gradually grow into a fire which engulfs the mind as your spiritual aspiration grows in a natural way.

Hekau-mantras can be directed toward worldly attainments or toward spiritual attainment in the form of enlightenment. There are words of power for gaining wealth or control over others. We will present Ancient Egyptian words of power which are directed to self-control and mental peace leading to spiritual realization of the Higher Self. You may choose from the list according to your level of understanding and practice. If you were initiated into a particular hekau or mantra by an authentic spiritual preceptor, we recommend that you use that one as your main meditative sound formula. You may use others for singing according to your inclination in your leisure or idle time. Also you may use shortened versions for chanting or singing when not engaged in formal practice. For example, if you choose "Om Amun Ra Ptah," you may also use "Om Amun."

Reciting words of power is like making a well. If a well is made deep enough, it yields water. If the words of power are used long enough and with consistency, they yield spiritual vibrations which reach deep into the unconscious mind to cut through the distracting thoughts and then reveal the deeper you. If they are not used with consistency, they are like shallow puddles which get filled easily by rain, not having had a chance to go deeply enough to reveal what lies within. Don't forget that your movement in yoga should be balanced and integrated. Therefore, continue your practice of the other major disciplines we have described along with your practice of reciting the hekau-mantras. Mental recitation is considered to be the most powerful. However, in the beginning you may need to start with recitation aloud until you are able to control the mind's wandering. If it wanders, simply return to the words of power (hekau-mantras). Eventually the words of power will develop their own staying power. You will even hear them when you are not consciously reciting. They will begin to replace the negative thought patterns of the mind and lead the mind toward serenity and from here, to spiritual realization. When this occurs you should allow yourself to feel the sweetness of reciting the divine names.

As discussed earlier, HEKAU may be used to achieve control over the mind and to develop the latent forces that are within you. Hekau or mantras are mystic formulas which an aspirant uses in a process of self-alchemy. The chosen words of power may be in the form of a letter, word or a combination of words which hold a specific mystical meaning to lead the mind to deeper levels of concentration and to deeper levels of understanding of the teaching behind the words. You may choose one for yourself or you my use one that you were initiated into by a spiritual preceptor. Also, you may have a special hekau for meditation and you may still use other hekau, prayers, hymns or songs of praise according to your devotional feeling. Once you choose a hekau, the practice involves its repetition with meaning and feeling to the point of becoming one with it. You may begin practicing recitation out loud (verbally) and later practice in silence (mentally). At some point your level of concentration will deepen. You may use a rosary or "mala" (beads on a string) to keep track of your recitation. You will experience at some point, that the words of power drop from your mind, and there are no thoughts, but just awareness. This is the soul level where you begin to transcend thoughts and body identification. At that point your mind will disengage from all external exercises and take flight into the unknown, uncharted waters of the subconscious, the unconscious, and beyond. Simply remain as a detached witness and allow yourself to grow in peace. Listed below are several hekau taken from Ancient Egyptian texts. They may be used in English or in Ancient Kemetic according to your choice.

If you feel a certain affinity toward a particular energy expressed through a particular deity, use that inclination to your advantage by aligning yourself with that energy, and then directing it towards the divine within your heart. Never forget that while you are working with a particular deity in the beginning stages, your objective is to delve into the deeper mystical implications of the symbolic form and characteristics of the deity. These always refer to the transcendental Self which is beyond all deities. According to your level of advancement, you may construct your own Hekau according to your own feeling and understanding. As a rule, in meditations such as those being discussed now, the shorter the size of the hekau, the more effective it will be since you will be able repeat it more often. However, the shorter the hekau, the more concentration it requires so as not to get lost in thoughts. You may wish to begin with a longer hekau and shorten it as your concentration builds. Words of power have no power in and of themselves. It is the user who gives them power through understanding and feeling.

When practicing the devout ritual identification form of meditation, the recitation of hymns, the wearing of costumes and elaborate amulets and other artifacts may be used. Ritual identification with the divine may be practiced by studying and repeatedly reading the various hymns to the divine such as those which have been provided in this volume, while gradually absorbing and becoming one with the teachings as they relate to you. When a creation hymn is being studied, you should reflect upon it as your true Self being the Creator, as your true Self being the hero (heroine), and that you (your true essence) are the one being spoken about in all the teachings. It is all about you. "You" are the Creator. "You" are the sustainer of the universe. "You" are the only one who can achieve transcendence through enlightenment according to your own will. When you feel, think and act this way, you are using the highest form of worship and meditation towards the divine by constantly bringing the mind back to the idea that all is the Self and that you essentially are that Self. This form of practice is higher than any ritual or any other kind of offering. Here you are concentrating on the idea that your limited personality is only an expression of the divine. You are laying down your ego on the offering mat.

Simply choose a hekau which you feel comfortable with and sit quietly to recite it continuously for a set amount of time. Allow it to gradually become part of your free time when you are not concentrating on anything specific or when you are being distracted by worldly thoughts. This will serve to counteract the worldly or subconscious vibrations that may emerge from the your own unconscious mind. When you feel anger or other negative qualities, recite the hekau and visualize its energy and the deity associated with it destroying the negativity within you.

For example, you may choose *Amun-Ra-Ptah.* When you repeat this hekau, you are automatically including the entire system of all gods and goddesses. Amun-Ra-Ptah is known as *Nebertcher*, the "All-encompassing Divinity." You may begin by uttering it aloud. When you become more advanced in controlling your mind, you may begin to use shorter words. For example simply utter: *Amun, Amun, Amun...* always striving to get to the source of the sound. Eventually you will utter these silently, and this practice will carry your consciousness to the source of the sound itself, where the very mental instruction to utter is given. Hekau-mantras are also related to the spiritual energy centers of the subtle spiritual body (Uraeus-Kundalini).

The following Ancient Egyptian selections come from the *"Prt m Hru"* and other Ancient Egyptian scriptures:

*Nuk Neter**
I am the Supreme Divinity.

*Nuk Ast**
I am ASET

nuk neter aa kheper tchesef
I am the great God, self created.

Ba ar pet sat ar ta.
Soul is of heaven, body belongs to the earth.

Nuk uab-k uab ka-k uab ba-k uab sekhem.
My mind has pure thoughts, so my soul and life forces are pure.

*Nuk ast au neheh ertai-nef tetta.**
Behold I am the heir of eternity, everlastingness has been given to me.

Sekhem - a em mu ma aua Set.
I have gained power in the water as I conquered Set (greed, lust, ignorance).

*Rex - a em Ab - a sekhem - a em hati – a**
I know my heart, I have gained power over my heart.

Un - na uat neb am pet am ta
The power is within me to open all doors in heaven and earth.

Nuk sah em ba - f.
I am a spirit, with my soul.

*From the Prt M Hru

Procedure For Formal Meditation Practice Based on the Mystical Chapters of Prt m Hru

Having studied the teachings and taken care to purify the heart through righteous living (in accordance with Maat Philosophy principles), a spiritual aspirant should follow the instructions below.

The aspirant should be *ceremonially, physically and mentally pure*. This means that the area chosen to practice meditation should be clean and there should be an altar with the special articles related to the practice.

Articles Needed for Rituals and Meditation Based on the *Prt m Hru*

First, locate an area of your home where you can perform spiritual practices such as yoga exercises, prayers and meditations and not be disturbed. This area will be used only for yoga practice exclusively.

Now gather the basic materials needed to create your own altar. An altar is a place of worship which contains certain artifacts which hold specific spiritual symbolism that lead to spiritual awareness. The following items are to be considered as a basic listing of items. You are free to choose other items which resonate with your spiritual consciousness.

1- Small **table** to use as an altar.

2- **Candle** - The candle holds deep mystical symbolism. It contains within itself all of the four elements of creation: fire, earth (wax in solid form), water (wax in liquefied form), and air. All are consumed in the burning process and all of them come together to produce light. This singular light represents the singular consciousness which shines throughout the entire universe. This light is the illumination which causes life to exist and it is the reason and source of the human mind. This light is life itself and life is God. Therefore, God is ever-present in the candle, in the universe (nature) and in your heart and mind.

3- **Incense** - Incense invokes divine awareness through the sense of smell. When you perform spiritual practices and use a special incense consistently, every time that you smell the incense you will have divine thoughts and feelings even if you are not in the regular area of meditation. Therefore, select a fragrance which appeals to you and reflect within yourself that this is the fragrance of God in the same way as a flower emanates fragrance. Visualize that you are smelling divinity itself.

4- **Ankh** - The Ankh is one of the most universal symbols expressing eternal life, the union of opposites. It was, and is, used by the world religious traditions (Ancient Egyptian religion, early Christianity, Indian religion and others.)

5- **Sculpture**, picture or other symbol of a Deity (as a symbol of the Supreme Being). This may be an Ancient Egyptian Deity such as Heru, Aset, etc. Choose an icon according to your spiritual inclination. This will help you to develop devotion toward the Divine and will hasten your progress in yoga. This is called worship of God with name and form. As you progress, you will be instructed on how to worship the Divine in an abstract way without using any names or forms.

6- Small **audio cassette recorder** (to lead your spiritual sessions).

7- **Audio Recordings** of prayers, divine music, meditations, exercises, discourses from authentic Spiritual Preceptors.

Ancient Egyptian Music For Informal and Formal Meditation Practice

In Ancient Egypt, music was a powerful force, recognized by the priests and priestesses as a means to channel the energies of the mind towards a spiritual focus, and it is strongly recommend here as well. Divine music can open the heart and sublimate the feelings and emotions, turning them into a special form of worship of the Divine.

The sacred music of Ancient Egypt was so potent, inspiring and compelling that it has influenced Coptic and Arab culture in present day Egypt. It is believed by anthropologists that the primary characteristics of modern Coptic music were adopted from the music of the Ancient Egyptians. These characteristics include the use of triangles and cymbals, and a strong vocal tradition. The whole of the Coptic service is to be sung. The singing is alternated between the master chanter, the priest, and a choir of deacons. This technique of chanting was also used in Ancient Egypt during the processions and recitals of the mystery rituals.

Divine music can be used in informal religious practice as well as in festivities and also as a precursor[480] to formal meditation. In modern times, Dr, Muata Ashby has recreated the music and chanting of various texts from Ancient Egypt including selected portions of the *Prt m Hru*.[481]

8- After reading this book for the first time in its entirety, **select a Hekau** (words of power) which resonates with you. If you do not feel a special connection to a particular hekau or if you would prefer to wait for a period of time to allow yourself to become acquainted with the philosophy and the presiding deities of the hekau, simply use "Om" for now. Om is a universal word of power which was used in Ancient Egypt and is used extensively in India by yogis in our modern times. Om or Am[482] is related to the word Amun from Ancient Egypt, and Amun is related to the Amen of Christianity. Therefore, Om is generally useful for spiritual practice. Om is also not related to a particular deity but is common to all. It is also the hekau-mantra of the 6th energy center at the point between the eyebrows known as the Ancient Egyptian *Arat* or Uraeus serpent and the *Third eye of Shiva* in India. You will use hekau for chanting during your worship periods, and at idle times during the day. You will use it from now on to dig deeply into the unconscious regions of your mind as a miner uses a pick to cut into a mountain in search of gold. If you have difficulty selecting a Hekau, consult with your Spiritual Preceptor for assistance.

Procedure For The Formal Meditation and Rituals Based on the *Prt m Hru*

The following is a formal meditation for attaining spiritual enlightenment. For rituals you may add Divine music, anointing the head with the water or oil used in the libation.

---

[480] **pre·cur·sor** (prĭ-kûr′sər, prē′kûr′sər) *n.* **1.** One that precedes and indicates, suggests, or announces someone or something to come.

[481] For more information see the Egyptian Yoga Chant and Song book and the Egyptian Yoga Catalog at the back of this book or call for the latest releases from the Sema Institute of Yoga.

[482] see the book *Initiation Into Egyptian Yoga* or *Egyptian Yoga: The Philosophy of Enlightenment* for a more detailed description of AUM and Om.

Commencement

> Opening Recitations
> Lighting a candle
> Lighting incense
> Pouring libation

1- Recite the auspicious hekau for commencing your spiritual practice. These are given in Chapter 1 Part 1, Hymn 1 (Hymn to Ra), Hymn 2 (Hymn to Asar).

These prayers are directed toward the purification of the mind and body which will allow your spiritual practice to be unobstructed in earth as well as in heaven. It is a propitiation to the Divine that you should not be confined to the temporal world of time and space, and physical body and ego-self consciousness, so that you may go beyond the ignorance of ordinary human existence and thereby discover the truth of your true nature as one with the Supreme Self.

2- Select a Chapter from the *Prt m Hru* for your spiritual focus today, one that especially interests you. Recite your selected Chapter from the *Prt m Hru* one or more times in accordance with your feeling.

3-Closing the eyes, reflect on the teachings presented in it in accordance with your understanding. Visualize that the verses are speaking about you and your relationship with the Divine and allow yourself to be transported into an ecstasy as you view yourself as Asar.

4-Now, enter into repeated chanting (may be audible or silent in accordance with your feeling), using your chosen meditation technique. You may chant alone. You may coordinate the breath with the chant. You may concentrate on a candle or picture of your chosen deity as you chant.

You may play the audio chanting tapes[483]. These tapes help you to attune the mind toward the Divine through specific utterances, chants, prayers and songs which lead to Enlightenment. Asar and Aset of Ancient Egypt, are divinities whose main form of worship include the chanting and singing of devotional words of power (Hekau). Therefore, chanting the names of God and prayers which describe and glorify the attributes of God as well as the message of self-knowledge are most important elements in the practice of true mystical worship of the Divine.

5-After some time of practice (days, weeks, or months). At some point, after 20 minutes to an hour, your mind will become silent and you will automatically lose the chant and find yourself in a heightened state of consciousness. At this point allow the Divine to guide you to deeper and deeper levels of ecstasy and enlightenment. At some point during your spiritual practice you will gain entry into the Duat or Astral Plane. In the beginning, it is a scary proposition because you temporarily loose consciousness of your physical personality. At this time you should become an observer and allow your soul to unfold its desired plan. Allow Anpu, Djehuti and Aset, your purified mind, intellect and intuitional capacity, to lead you to Asar. Eventually you will discover the place which transcends even the Astral Plane and you will move to Asar, the Divine Self, and experience oneness with that glorious essence.

6-As you conclude the meditation or ritual practice, recite and reflect on the following teachings. They will lead you from understanding worship with form to meditation on the Divine without form, that is, transcending all forms.

Closing your Formal Ritual and Meditation Practice

Close here by reciting the auspicious hekau-mantras for commencing your meditation practice. The prayers should be recited four times. This quadruplicate format is a ritual-symbolic way to propitiate the divine forces, which control the four quarters of the phenomenal universe and the heavenly realms. There are four directions which the mind is aware of (East, North, West and South) in the physical plane as in

---

[483] available from C.M. Books, P.O. Box 570459, Miami Fl. 33257

the astral. The prayer is directed towards the purification of the mind and body, which will allow your spiritual practice to be unobstructed on earth as well as in heaven. It is a propitiation to the Divine that you should not be confined to the temporal world of time and space, physical body and ego-self consciousness, so that you may go beyond the ignorance of ordinary human existence and thereby discover the truth of your true nature as one with the Supreme Self. As you utter the following words of power, visualize that you embody the qualities of the neteru in the Ausarian Myth. See their virtues becoming your virtues and gain insight into their way. This is the deification of your personality, invoking your power within to transform yourself into a Neter.[484]

---

[484] One with the gods and goddesses.

Adorations to the forms of the Divine

Note: You may substitute the name of your chosen divinity after the word "Dua."

dua Asar
Adorations to
Asar

dua Asar
Adorations to
Asar

dua Asar
Adorations to
Asar

dua Asar
Adorations to
Asar

dua Aset
Adorations to
Aset

dua Aset
Adorations to
Aset

dua Aset
Adorations to
Aset

dua Aset
Adorations to
Aset

dua Heru
Adorations to Heru

dua Heru
Adorations to Heru

dua Heru
Adorations to Heru

dua Heru
Adorations to Heru

dua Hetheru
Adorations to Hetheru

dua Hetheru
Adorations to Hetheru

dua Hetheru
Adorations to Hetheru

dua Hetheru
Adorations to Hetheru

dua Ra
Adorations to Ra

dua Ra
Adorations to Ra

dua Ra
Adorations to Ra

dua Ra
Adorations to Ra

dua Anpu
Adorations to Anubis

dua Anpu
Adorations to Anubis

dua Anpu
Adorations to Anubis

dua Anpu
Adorations to Anubis

dua Djehuti
Adorations to Djehuti

dua Djehuti
Adorations to Djehuti

dua Djehuti
Adorations to Djehuti

dua Djehuti
Adorations to Djehuti

Affirmations of Oneness with the Divine

Nuk Anpu, Nuk Anpu, Nuk Anpu, Nuk Anpu,
I am Anubis, I am Anubis, I am Anubis, I am Anubis

Nuk Maat, Nuk Maat, Nuk Maat, Nuk Maat
I am Maat, I am Maat, I am Maat, I am Maat

Nuk Aset, Nuk Aset, Nuk Aset, Nuk Aset
I am ASET, I am ASET, I am ASET, I am ASET

Nuk Heru, Nuk Heru, Nuk Heru, Nuk Heru
I am Heru, I am Heru, I am Heru, I am Heru

Nuk Asar, Nuk Asar, Nuk Asar, Nuk Asar
I am Asar, I am Asar, I am Asar, I am Asar

Nuk ab, Nuk ab, Nuk ab, Nuk ab
I am Pure, I am Pure, I am Pure, I am Pure

Nuk Neberdjerr
I am all, transcendental, absolute!

Nuk Neberdjerr
I am all, transcendental, absolute!

Nuk Neberdjerr
I am all, transcendental, absolute!

Nuk Neberdjerr
I am all, transcendental, absolute!

Now relax in silence for a few moments. Allow the utterances to resonate in your mind and become a witness to whatever you see in your mind's eye. Take several deep breaths, and with each one, feel your body becoming lighter and more relaxed.

For the next five minutes, take deep breaths and hold them for five seconds. As you do so, visualize that Life Force energy from the universe is pouring into your body. This is the Hetheru breath for replenishing and accumulating mental energy. Feel revitalized and renewed. Slowly and softly exhale.

Visualize that your body is rising up into the air, above the clouds and into space. Now visualize that you are in an astral plane. It is a dark realm, but it is not empty. Visualize that your body is made of pure light and there are stars all about you. Experience the vast expanse of your surroundings and feel at ease in the realm. Relax every muscle in your body and discover the peace and joy of expansion.

Now take flight by simply willing yourself to move up and away. Travel to the far reaches of this plane. Visit the stars and the planets. There are worlds, galaxies and universes which expand to infinity. Behold the beauty and majesty of the Divine. Now relax and allow the feeling of joy, immortality, infinity and eternity to permeate every part of you.

Now see in the distance, a dark realm. It is the darkest place you have ever seen. No light emanates from or reaches this place. Nothing grows there. Come closer to this place and look into it. There is nothing to be seen but you feel a strange affinity to this place. It is beckoning to you, calling your soul to enter. You cannot explain it but somehow it feels warm, loving and complete. You attempt to go in but something prevents you, even as a glass door permits you to look within but not to enter.

You feel fearful because you know you are losing touch with the world that you have known. What prevents you from entering is your ego. The ego in you is what is causing you fear of letting go and losing yourself in the Divine. The deepest, darkest realm is the abode of the Supreme Self and none other can exist there. So if you wish to enter into the presence of the Divine, you will need to discard all notions of separation and all notions of individuality.

When you say "*I am Asar*," who is the "I"? You must forget the "ego-I" now and be Asar. Therefore, have faith and allow the mind and its thoughts of separation, worries, anxieties, etc. to subside as you discover the essence of who the "I" is referring to, deep down. Leave the mind behind; its thoughts cannot help you now. Feel and experience the silence of the quiet mind and allow yourself to melt into the cosmic mind. Reflect thus: This vast universe, these stars, this body, all this is me; I am the universe. I am the gods and goddesses. I am the Divine Self! Become one with the peace and emptiness. Now there is only awareness, pure consciousness. No thoughts reach you; this is perfect being. Now you are entering into the realm of absolute darkness, the realm of Asar.

Remain in this place of peace and tranquillity for as long as you like. When you are ready, gently return to normal body consciousness and slowly move your limbs as you rise. Paying your respects to the neters with upraised hands, utter the closing words of power and leave the meditation area feeling that divine grace has fallen upon you and will be with you throughout the rest of your day.

Om Asar Aset Heru,
Om Asar Aset Heru,
Om Asar Aset Heru,
Om Asar Aset Heru.

As you commune more and more with the Divine, your awareness will increase gradually and you will achieve greater and greater control of your thoughts, emotions, mind and senses, until you are in complete control and experience abiding spiritual awareness. This is the state of Enlightenment.

As you leave your altar or ritual area, visualize that the peace and enlightenment you have discovered is part of you now, and you will carry it forth into the rest of your day as you practice informal meditation at home, at work or wherever you may be. You are not just Asar when you are in deep meditation, but also at all other times as well.

Meditation on Peace

"Hetep": Supreme Peace

In Ancient Egyptian teachings, the word-symbol denoting supreme and transcendental peace is Hetep. What does it mean when yoga philosophy states that there is no true peace or happiness in the world of human experience?

Peace is a feeling of freedom and expansion. There are no worries when there is true peace. Also, true peace is not dependent on something that you need to do or acquire in order to have it. Usually people equate peace and happiness with things that must be done or acquired (money, big house, fame, vacation, movie, party) in order to achieve these feelings, but if you examine this mentality with the light of yogic wisdom, you will discover that this way of thinking is based on ignorance.

Supreme Peace, Hetep, is much like the peace which is experienced in the dreamless sleep state. In dreamless sleep there are no thoughts, just infinite awareness. However, because this form of experience occurs when you are asleep, your mind is veiled by ignorance and therefore, there is no transcendental awareness such as described above. The experience of Hetep transcends the most pleasurable dreams and events of the waking state. Advanced yogis can reach this level of consciousness through the practice of yoga. When they are able to abide in this state of awareness perpetually and spontaneously (without any effort), then they are considered to be fully enlightened. This state of supreme peace and transcendence of body consciousness and desires is called bliss and thus, God is known as "Bliss Absolute" and "Infinite Awareness" beyond thoughts and beyond duality. There is no more separation between you and me, the distant star, the blade of grass; there is Absolute oneness of identity with the Supreme within and Hetep. Thus meditate:

Remain seated or lying in a comfortable, quiet place. Reflect on the meaning of *htp (HETEP-Supreme Peace)* to sublimate your physical nature, to transform the ego-personality into the instrument of your Ba (individual soul) and to melt your individual soul into the Universal Soul of GOD, the *Neter NETERU,* to become "ONE" with GOD.

If the mind strays, gently bring it back to this central idea. When it strays, remind it that any ideas it may have, any notions to the contrary, are illusions because you now know that ALL the objects of the world, including your body, are really manifestations of GOD. You are a part of them and they of you. Therefore, there is no need to crave or desire them. You are them and ALL that is because your deep inner Self, your true Self, is ONE with GOD. Allow yourself to be filled with *htp* from this awareness. Try to maintain this sense of peace at all times, not just at meditation time.

Gradually, the mind will be less and less agitated and distracted and you will experience increasing levels of peace leading to enlightenment.

Allow your ego to ***htp***, to be sublimated and transformed. Submit your ego-will to the will of the Neters. *Do Maat, Live Maat, Speak Maat, Be Maat.* Maat is the way of the Neters; to be in harmony with the Neters is to achieve harmony, health and peace.

Practice these meditations or any others you feel work best for you and they will increase your awareness to such a degree that you will consciously realize that your Higher Self is and was always there awaiting discovery. You will leave your ignorant notions of yourself behind; you will be transformed into a oneness with GOD by leaving behind the misconceived notion (illusion) that you are a mortal personality.

ADVANCED RITUAL AND FORMAL MEDITATION

Prior to concluding your practice, utter, reflect and meditate on the following injunctions from the *Prt m Hru*:

I am Ra, I am Asar, I am Aset, I am Heru, I am Djehuti, I am Nut, I am Khepri, the Creator, I am Tem, the Dissolver of Creation, I am all the gods and goddesses. I am the Supreme One, I am Yesterday, Today and Tomorrow, I am the source from which all emanates. I am Neberdjer, all that is, has been and will ever be, I am all!

Assert within yourself:

I am not this mind and body with their negative thoughts and desires; I am the Self, who is like a bird that is free to roam the vast expanse of the sky; I am not this perishable body that is a conglomeration of earthly elements that will some day return to the earth; I am the spirit which is subtle and free of all associations of the body; I am free from all associations of the body, be they of family, country, etc.; these associations of the body may have a practical value in the world of time and space, but they do not in any way affect or hamper the real me.

Thus assert:

I have nowhere to go, nowhere to seek, nowhere to search for the greatest treasure of all existence because it is within me already, and it always was. Within my heart lies the source of all happiness. I am the abode of all fulfillment! All I need to do in order to discover this treasure is to open my heart by discarding the illusions and ignorance which cloud my mind; I look not to the world of time and space but to the eternity and infinity which is within me; I look not to the vanity of my body but to the peace of my innermost Self: I am That I am!

Assert boldly:

This world, this universe, my body, my loved ones, all human beings are manifestations of Divine consciousness! All this is a reflection of the innermost Self who is eternal and infinite! I (the innermost Self) am the sustainer of this reality as I sustain my dreams in the vastness of the mind; All that I see is a reflection of the innermost self. therefore, both internally and externally I have discovered the Transcendental Reality! I am all this!

Failure and Success in Formal Meditation

Seh Ecstasy, religious

The goal of all spiritual programs is to lead a human being to achieve an ecstatic experience. Religious ecstasy may be defined as a trance, or rapture associated with mystic or prophetic exaltation. It may be also thought of as a state of super-consciousness. This is the goal of all meditative efforts, be they informal or formal. But how is it possible to attain this state if the mind is constantly filled with thoughts and other distractions? It is very important to understand that in the early practice of formal meditation your mind will be very distracted. This is because of the un-maatian ways of thinking and acting of the past which have left impressions of mental agitation that rise to the surface of your mind. Just remember that you lived in un-maatian ways for years and lifetimes before, so you should not expect immediate results. However, if your practice of informal and formal meditation is regular and earnest, you may expect to see small changes very soon. Your personality will become virtuous, and this is a sure indication that you are on your way to discover the Higher Self. You will get angry less often and your egoistic desires will have less of a hold on you. You will begin to see the small but powerful miracles in everyday life as you discover how God is and always repeat has been with you, and is leading you in a mysterious way.

In order to deal with the restless mind, you should practice the rituals associated with meditation and you should practice your chosen hekau with higher volume and frequency as you work to coordinate the breath. Your sustained effort is the key to your success. Have faith in your teacher and your Higher Self that these will help you to overcome the demons of the mind, and also in your own ability to discover the Supreme Truth.

A Time-line of Major World Religions and Mystical Philosophies and Selected World Events

c. >36,766 B.C.E-10,858 B.C.E	Egyptian Pre-dynastic history
c. 10,000 B.C.E.	The Sphinx: Heru in the Horizon.
c. 10,500 - 5,700 B.C.E.	Egyptian Pre-dynastic history
c. 5,700 - 342 B.C.E.	Egyptian Dynastic History
c. 5,500 B.C.E.	Egyptian Philosophy (Yoga), *Pyramid Texts*, Egypt.
c. 2,500 B.C.E	Pre-Aryan Dravidian Religion -Yoga, India.
c. 1,700 B.C.E.	Invasion of Egypt, Europe, Persia and India by the Indo-Europeans (Aryans).
c. 1,400-900 B.C.E	Aryan Vedas, India.
c. 1,350 B.C.E.	Canaanite Religion.
c. 1,200-500 B.C.E.	Old Testament- Moses, Egypt.
c. 1,200 B.C.E.	Olmecs. Central America.
c. 1,200 B.C.E.	Jainism, India.
c. 1,030 B.C.E.	Druids.
c. 800 B.C.E.	Upanishads-Classical Indian Vedanta-, India.
c. 800 - 500 B.C.E.	Vasudeva - Krishna, India
c. 700 B.C.E.	Samkhya-Yoga philosophy, India.
c. 700 BCE-500 ACE	Greek mythology and Mystery religions, Greece-Egypt.[485]
c. 600 B.C.E.	Zoroaster, Persia.
c. 600 B.C.E.	Buddhism (Theravada), India.
c. 550 B.C.E.	Confucianism, China.
c. 500 B.C.E.	Taoism- Lao Tsu, China.
c. 500-51 B.C.E.	Celtic Religion.
c. 500-100 B.C.E.	Hinduism- Mahabharata, Bhagavad Gita, Patanjali- India.
c. 324 B.C.E.	Invasion of Egypt, Persia and India by Alexander the Great.
c. 300 B.C.E.-300 C. E	Gnosticism, Jewish Essene and Therapeut cults throughout: Egypt, Palestine, Greece and Rome. Buddhists send missionaries to Egypt, Persia, China Greece and Rome.
c. 200 B.C.E.	Roman composite and Mystery religions, Greece-Egypt-India.[486]
c. 100 B.C.E -100 A.C.E.	Hermeticism.
c. 100 B.C.E -100 A.C.E. to Present	Mahayana Buddhism develops becomes dominant religion in India. Missionaries sent to Egypt, Persia, China Greece and Rome.
c. 200 A.C.E.	Shaivism (Saivism)- Puranas and Agamas, Hindu scriptures in India.
c. 300 A.C.E.	Mayas (central America-decedents of the Olmecs).
c. 325 A.C.E.	Christianity accepted in Rome.
c. 400 A.C.E.	Theodosius of Rome decrees that Orthodox Christianity is the only form of Christianity allowed in the Roman Empire. All other forms of Christianity and all other religions and cults are outlawed. Dark ages of Europe begin. An exodus of religious leaders, artists, scientists out of increased contact with the Orient and the European renaissance.
c. 476 A.C.E.	Roman Empire overrun by barbarians from northern and northeastern Europe. Christianity almost dies out.
c. 1,000-1,500 A.C.E.	Invasion of India by Muslims.
c. 1,200 A.C.E.	Cabalism, Jewish.
c. 1,300 A.C.E.	European Renaissance.
c. 1,450 A.C.E.	Sikhism (combination of Islam and Hinduism), India.
c. 1,517 A.C.E.	Protestant Christian Movement.
c. 1,611 A.C.E.	King James Version of Old and New Testament.
c. 1,800 A.C.E. - Present	Modern Vedanta Attempts to integrate dual and non-dual philosophy, Buddhist psychology and yoga.
	The preceding dates are approximations. They represent the approximate date in which the religious precepts were first codified. Archeological and sociological history suggest that all of these systems undoubtedly existed for a long time before actually being "written down."

[485] Mystery religions based on the Egyptian mysteries of Aset and Asar and those of Buddha and Krishna (India).
[486] Mystery religions based on the Egyptian mysteries of Aset and Asar and those of Buddha and Krishna (India).

Appendix 1

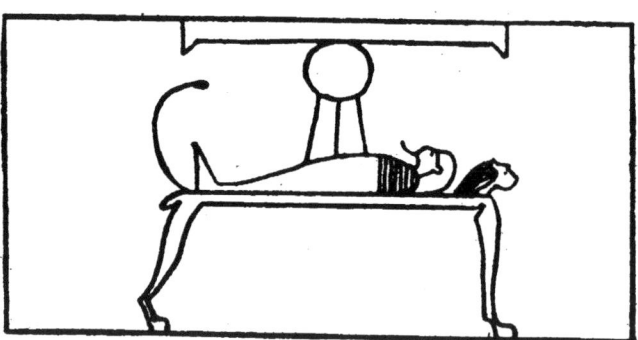

The image above relates to the vignette from the Per m Hru (Book of the Dead) chapter 154. This chapter relates to the renewal of the body through solar Life Force energy. The sun protrudes out from the sky and releases three rays that enliven the body, not allowing it to perish, I.e. the astral body revives and the personality moves on the path to meet the spirit (Ra). After paying homage to the divinity, there is a declaration of virtue and therefore worthiness of not being allowed to perish. Thus, the Divine is induced to revive the body and not allow it to perish in the netherworld.

The teaching of chapter 154 relates directly to the renewal of the body through infusion of the solar life force energy. This of course also relates to the cultivation of the Serpent Power. Much has been said about the serpent power throughout this book because it is an integral aspect of the overall program of spiritual enlightenment. Therefore, the theme of this chapter is inherent in any discussion of the Pert m Heru but it is also the subject of a vast discipline which is treated in a separate book called "The Serpent Power: The Ancient Egyptian Mystical Wisdom of the Inner Life Force." Therefore, the reader is urged to acquire this text and study it alongside the Pert M Heru teachings.

Bibliography

Egyptian Coffin texts
Egyptian Pyramid Texts
Excerpts from Chapter 78 of The Paris Papyrus.
Excerpts from Papyrus Nu. From the Turin Papyrus.
Hymns of Amun
Papyrus Anhai
Papyrus Ani
Papyrus Ankhwahibre
Papyrus Auf Ankh
Papyrus Gaut-Sushen
Papyrus Hunefer
Papyrus Kenna
Papyrus Nebseni
Papyrus Nekht
Papyrus Nu
Papyrus of Nesi-Khensu
Stele of Abu
Stele of Djehuti-nefer
The Ebers papyrus
The Greenfield papyrus
The Turin Papyrus
Various assorted Papyri
Various assorted Temple Inscriptions

Index

Other Books From C M Books

P.O.Box 570459
Miami, Florida, 33257
(305) 378-6253 Fax: (305) 378-6253

This book is part of a series on the study and practice of Ancient Egyptian Yoga and Mystical Spirituality based on the writings of Dr. Muata Abhaya Ashby. They are also part of the Egyptian Yoga Course provided by the Sema Institute of Yoga. Below you will find a listing of the other books in this series. For more information send for the Egyptian Yoga Book-Audio-Video Catalog or the Egyptian Yoga Course Catalog.

Now you can study the teachings of Egyptian and Indian Yoga wisdom and Spirituality with the Egyptian Yoga Mystical Spirituality Series. The Egyptian Yoga Series takes you through the Initiation process and lead you to understand the mysteries of the soul and the Divine and to attain the highest goal of life: ENLIGHTENMENT. The *Egyptian Yoga Series*, takes you on an in depth study of Ancient Egyptian mythology and their inner mystical meaning. Each Book is prepared for the serious student of the mystical sciences and provides a study of the teachings along with exercises, assignments and projects to make the teachings understood and effective in real life. The Series is part of the Egyptian Yoga course but may be purchased even if you are not taking the course. The series is ideal for study groups.

Prices subject to change.

1. EGYPTIAN YOGA: THE PHILOSOPHY OF ENLIGHTENMENT An original, fully illustrated work, including hieroglyphs, detailing the meaning of the Egyptian mysteries, tantric yoga, psycho-spiritual and physical exercises. Egyptian Yoga is a guide to the practice of the highest spiritual philosophy which leads to absolute freedom from human misery and to immortality. It is well known by scholars that Egyptian philosophy is the basis of Western and Middle Eastern religious philosophies such as *Christianity, Islam, Judaism,* the *Kabala*, and Greek philosophy, but what about Indian philosophy, Yoga and Taoism? What were the original teachings? How can they be practiced today? What is the source of pain and suffering in the world and what is the solution? Discover the deepest mysteries of the mind and universe within and outside of your self. 8.5" X 11" ISBN: 1-884564-01-1 Soft $19.95

2. EGYPTIAN YOGA II: The Supreme Wisdom of Enlightenment by Dr. Muata Ashby ISBN 1-884564-39-9 $23.95 U.S. In this long awaited sequel to *Egyptian Yoga: The Philosophy of Enlightenment* you will take a fascinating and enlightening journey back in time and discover the teachings which constituted the epitome of Ancient Egyptian spiritual wisdom. What are the disciplines which lead to the fulfillment of all desires? Delve into the three states of consciousness (waking, dream and deep sleep) and the fourth state which transcends them all, Neberdjer, "The Absolute." These teachings of the city of Waset (Thebes) were the crowning achievement of the Sages of Ancient Egypt. They establish the standard mystical keys for understanding the profound mystical symbolism of the Triad of human consciousness.

3. THE KEMETIC DIET: GUIDE TO HEALTH, DIET AND FASTING Health issues have always been important to human beings since the beginning of time. The earliest records of history show that the art of healing was held in high esteem since the time of Ancient Egypt. In the early 20th century, medical doctors had almost attained the status of sainthood by the promotion of the idea that they alone were "scientists" while other healing modalities and traditional healers who did not follow the "scientific method' were nothing but superstitious, ignorant charlatans who at best would take the money of their clients and at worst kill them with the unscientific "snake oils" and "irrational theories". In the late 20th century, the failure of the modern medical establishment's ability to lead the general public to good health, promoted the move by many in society towards "alternative medicine". Alternative medicine disciplines are those healing modalities which do not adhere to the philosophy of allopathic medicine. Allopathic medicine is what medical doctors practice by an large. It is the theory that disease is caused by agencies outside the body such as bacteria, viruses or physical means which affect the body. These can therefore be treated by medicines and therapies The natural healing method began in the absence of extensive technologies with

the idea that all the answers for health may be found in nature or rather, the deviation from nature. Therefore, the health of the body can be restored by correcting the aberration and thereby restoring balance. This is the area that will be covered in this volume. Allopathic techniques have their place in the art of healing. However, we should not forget that the body is a grand achievement of the spirit and built into it is the capacity to maintain itself and heal itself. Ashby, Muata ISBN: 1-884564-49-6 $28.95

4.   INITIATION INTO EGYPTIAN YOGA Shedy: Spiritual discipline or program, to go deeply into the mysteries, to study the mystery teachings and literature profoundly, to penetrate the mysteries. You will learn about the mysteries of initiation into the teachings and practice of Yoga and how to become an Initiate of the mystical sciences. This insightful manual is the first in a series which introduces you to the goals of daily spiritual and yoga practices: Meditation, Diet, Words of Power and the ancient wisdom teachings. 8.5" X 11" ISBN 1-884564-02-X Soft Cover $24.95 U.S.

5.   *THE AFRICAN ORIGINS OF CIVILIZATION, MYSTICAL RELIGION AND YOGA PHILOSOPHY* HARD COVER EDITION ISBN: 1-884564-50-X $80.00 U.S.   81/2" X 11"   Part 1, Part 2, Part 3 in one volume 683 Pages Hard Cover First Edition Three volumes in one. Over the past several years I have been asked to put together in one volume the most important evidences showing the correlations and common teachings between Kamitan (Ancient Egyptian) culture and religion and that of India. The questions of the history of Ancient Egypt, and the latest archeological evidences showing civilization and culture in Ancient Egypt and its spread to other countries, has intrigued many scholars as well as mystics over the years. Also, the possibility that Ancient Egyptian Priests and Priestesses migrated to Greece, India and other countries to carry on the traditions of the Ancient Egyptian Mysteries, has been speculated over the years as well. In chapter 1 of the book *Egyptian Yoga The Philosophy of Enlightenment,* 1995, I first introduced the deepest comparison between Ancient Egypt and India that had been brought forth up to that time. Now, in the year 2001 this new book, *THE AFRICAN ORIGINS OF CIVILIZATION, MYSTICAL RELIGION AND YOGA PHILOSOPHY,* more fully explores the motifs, symbols and philosophical correlations between Ancient Egyptian and Indian mysticism and clearly shows not only that Ancient Egypt and India were connected culturally but also spiritually. How does this knowledge help the spiritual aspirant? This discovery has great importance for the Yogis and mystics who follow the philosophy of Ancient Egypt and the mysticism of India. It means that India has a longer history and heritage than was previously understood. It shows that the mysteries of Ancient Egypt were essentially a yoga tradition which did not die but rather developed into the modern day systems of Yoga technology of India. It further shows that African culture developed Yoga Mysticism earlier than any other civilization in history. All of this expands our understanding of the unity of culture and the deep legacy of Yoga, which stretches into the distant past, beyond the Indus Valley civilization, the earliest known high culture in India as well as the Vedic tradition of Aryan culture. Therefore, Yoga culture and mysticism is the oldest known tradition of spiritual development and Indian mysticism is an extension of the Ancient Egyptian mysticism. By understanding the legacy which Ancient Egypt gave to India the mysticism of India is better understood and by comprehending the heritage of Indian Yoga, which is rooted in Ancient Egypt the Mysticism of Ancient Egypt is also better understood. This expanded understanding allows us to prove the underlying kinship of humanity, through the common symbols, motifs and philosophies which are not disparate and confusing teachings but in reality expressions of the same study of truth through metaphysics and mystical realization of Self. (HARD COVER)

6.   AFRICAN ORIGINS BOOK 1 PART 1 African Origins of African Civilization, Religion, Yoga Mysticism and Ethics Philosophy-Soft Cover $24.95 ISBN: 1-884564-55-0

7.   AFRICAN ORIGINS BOOK 2 PART 2 African Origins of Western Civilization, Religion and Philosophy(Soft) -Soft Cover $24.95 ISBN: 1-884564-56-9

8.   EGYPT AND INDIA (AFRICAN ORIGINS BOOK 3 PART 3) African Origins of Eastern Civilization, Religion, Yoga Mysticism and Philosophy-Soft Cover $29.95 (Soft) ISBN: 1-884564-57-7

9.   THE MYSTERIES OF ISIS: **The Ancient Egyptian Philosophy of Self-Realization** - There are several paths to discover the Divine and the mysteries of the higher Self. This volume details the mystery teachings of the goddess Aset (Isis) from Ancient Egypt- the path of wisdom. It includes the teachings of her temple and the disciplines that are enjoined for the initiates of the temple of Aset as they were given in

ancient times. Also, this book includes the teachings of the main myths of Aset that lead a human being to spiritual enlightenment and immortality. Through the study of ancient myth and the illumination of initiatic understanding the idea of God is expanded from the mythological comprehension to the metaphysical. Then this metaphysical understanding is related to you, the student, so as to begin understanding your true divine nature. ISBN 1-884564-24-0 $22.99

10. EGYPTIAN PROVERBS: TEMT TCHAAS *Temt Tchaas* means: collection of ——Ancient Egyptian Proverbs How to live according to MAAT Philosophy. Beginning Meditation. All proverbs are indexed for easy searches. For the first time in one volume, ——Ancient Egyptian Proverbs, wisdom teachings and meditations, fully illustrated with hieroglyphic text and symbols. EGYPTIAN PROVERBS is a unique collection of knowledge and wisdom which you can put into practice today and transform your life. 5.5"x 8.5" $14.95 U.S   ISBN: 1-884564-00-3

11. THE PATH OF DIVINE LOVE The Process of Mystical Transformation and The Path of Divine Love This Volume focuses on the ancient wisdom teachings of "Neter Merri" –the Ancient Egyptian philosophy of Divine Love and how to use them in a scientific process for self-transformation. Love is one of the most powerful human emotions. It is also the source of Divine feeling that unifies God and the individual human being. When love is fragmented and diminished by egoism the Divine connection is lost. The Ancient tradition of Neter Merri leads human beings back to their Divine connection, allowing them to discover their innate glorious self that is actually Divine and immortal. This volume will detail the process of transformation from ordinary consciousness to cosmic consciousness through the integrated practice of the teachings and the path of Devotional Love toward the Divine. 5.5"x 8.5" ISBN 1-884564-11-9 $22.99

12. INTRODUCTION TO MAAT PHILOSOPHY: Spiritual Enlightenment Through the Path of Virtue Known as Karma Yoga in India, the teachings of MAAT for living virtuously and with orderly wisdom are explained and the student is to begin practicing the precepts of Maat in daily life so as to promote the process of purification of the heart in preparation for the judgment of the soul. This judgment will be understood not as an event that will occur at the time of death but as an event that occurs continuously, at every moment in the life of the individual. The student will learn how to become allied with the forces of the Higher Self and to thereby begin cleansing the mind (heart) of impurities so as to attain a higher vision of reality. ISBN 1-884564-20-8 $22.99

13. MEDITATION The Ancient Egyptian Path to Enlightenment   Many people do not know about the rich history of meditation practice in Ancient Egypt. This volume outlines the theory of meditation and presents the Ancient Egyptian Hieroglyphic text which give instruction as to the nature of the mind and its three modes of expression. It also presents the texts which give instruction on the practice of meditation for spiritual Enlightenment and unity with the Divine. This volume allows the reader to begin practicing meditation by explaining, in easy to understand terms, the simplest form of meditation and working up to the most advanced form which was practiced in ancient times and which is still practiced by yogis around the world in modern times. ISBN 1-884564-27-7 $24.99

14. THE GLORIOUS LIGHT MEDITATION TECHNIQUE OF ANCIENT EGYPT ISBN: 1-884564-15-1$14.95 (PB) New for the year 2000. This volume is based on the earliest known instruction in history given for the practice of formal meditation. Discovered by Dr. Muata Ashby, it is inscribed on the walls of the Tomb of Seti I in Thebes Egypt. This volume details the philosophy and practice of this unique system of meditation originated in Ancient Egypt and the earliest practice of meditation known in the world which occurred in the most advanced African Culture.

15. THE SERPENT POWER: The Ancient Egyptian Mystical Wisdom of the Inner Life Force.   This Volume specifically deals with the latent life Force energy of the universe and in the human body, its control and sublimation. How to develop the Life Force energy of the subtle body. This Volume will introduce the esoteric wisdom of the science of how virtuous living acts in a subtle and mysterious way to cleanse the latent psychic energy conduits and vortices of the spiritual body. ISBN 1-884564-19-4 $22.95

16. EGYPTIAN YOGA *The Postures of The Gods and Goddesses* Discover the physical postures and exercises practiced thousands of years ago in Ancient Egypt which are today known as Yoga exercises. This work is based on the pictures and teachings from the Creation story of Ra, The Asarian Resurrection Myth and the carvings and reliefs from various Temples in Ancient Egypt 8.5" X 11" ISBN 1-884564-10-0 Soft Cover $21.95 Exercise video $20

17. EGYPTIAN TANTRA YOGA: The Art of Sex Sublimation and Universal Consciousness This Volume will expand on the male and female principles within the human body and in the universe and further detail the sublimation of sexual energy into spiritual energy. The student will study the deities Min and Hathor, Asar and Aset, Geb and Nut and discover the mystical implications for a practical spiritual discipline. This Volume will also focus on the Tantric aspects of Ancient Egyptian and Indian mysticism, the purpose of sex and the mystical teachings of sexual sublimation which lead to self-knowledge and Enlightenment. 5.5"x 8.5" ISBN 1-884564-03-8 $24.95

18. ASARIAN RELIGION: RESURRECTING OSIRIS The path of Mystical Awakening and the Keys to Immortality NEW REVISED AND EXPANDED EDITION! The Ancient Sages created stories based on human and superhuman beings whose struggles, aspirations, needs and desires ultimately lead them to discover their true Self. The myth of Aset, Asar and Heru is no exception in this area. While there is no one source where the entire story may be found, pieces of it are inscribed in various ancient Temples walls, tombs, steles and papyri. For the first time available, the complete myth of Asar, Aset and Heru has been compiled from original Ancient Egyptian, Greek and Coptic Texts. This epic myth has been richly illustrated with reliefs from the Temple of Heru at Edfu, the Temple of Aset at Philae, the Temple of Asar at Abydos, the Temple of Hathor at Denderah and various papyri, inscriptions and reliefs. Discover the myth which inspired the teachings of the *Shetaut Neter* (Egyptian Mystery System - Egyptian Yoga) and the Egyptian Book of Coming Forth By Day. Also, discover the three levels of Ancient Egyptian Religion, how to understand the mysteries of the Duat or Astral World and how to discover the abode of the Supreme in the Amenta, *The Other World* The ancient religion of Asar, Aset and Heru, if properly understood, contains all of the elements necessary to lead the sincere aspirant to attain immortality through inner self-discovery. This volume presents the entire myth and explores the main mystical themes and rituals associated with the myth for understating human existence, creation and the way to achieve spiritual emancipation - *Resurrection.* The Asarian myth is so powerful that it influenced and is still having an effect on the major world religions. Discover the origins and mystical meaning of the Christian Trinity, the Eucharist ritual and the ancient origin of the birthday of Jesus Christ. Soft Cover ISBN: 1-884564-27-5 $24.95

19. THE EGYPTIAN BOOK OF THE DEAD MYSTICISM OF THE PERT EM HERU $28.95 ISBN# 1-884564-28-3 Size: 8½" X 11" I Know myself, I know myself, I am One With God!–From the Pert Em Heru "The Ru Pert em Heru" or "Ancient Egyptian Book of The Dead," or "Book of Coming Forth By Day" as it is more popularly known, has fascinated the world since the successful translation of Ancient Egyptian hieroglyphic scripture over 150 years ago. The astonishing writings in it reveal that the Ancient Egyptians believed in life after death and in an ultimate destiny to discover the Divine. The elegance and aesthetic beauty of the hieroglyphic text itself has inspired many see it as an art form in and of itself. But is there more to it than that? Did the Ancient Egyptian wisdom contain more than just aphorisms and hopes of eternal life beyond death? In this volume Dr. Muata Ashby, the author of over 25 books on Ancient Egyptian Yoga Philosophy has produced a new translation of the original texts which uncovers a mystical teaching underlying the sayings and rituals instituted by the Ancient Egyptian Sages and Saints. "Once the philosophy of Ancient Egypt is understood as a mystical tradition instead of as a religion or primitive mythology, it reveals its secrets which if practiced today will lead anyone to discover the glory of spiritual self-discovery. The Pert em Heru is in every way comparable to the Indian Upanishads or the Tibetan Book of the Dead." Muata Abhaya Ashby

20. ANUNIAN THEOLOGY THE MYSTERIES OF RA The Philosophy of Anu and The Mystical Teachings of The Ancient Egyptian Creation Myth Discover the mystical teachings contained in the Creation Myth and the gods and goddesses who brought creation and human beings into existence. The Creation Myth holds the key to understanding the universe and for attaining spiritual Enlightenment. ISBN: 1-884564-38-0 40 pages $14.95

21.   MYSTERIES OF MIND Mystical Psychology & Mental Health for Enlightenment and Immortality based on the Ancient Egyptian Philosophy of Menefer -Mysticism of Ptah, Egyptian Physics and Yoga Metaphysics and the Hidden properties of Matter.   This volume uncovers the mystical psychology of the Ancient Egyptian wisdom teachings centering on the philosophy of the Ancient Egyptian city of Menefer (Memphite Theology). How to understand the mind and how to control the senses and lead the mind to health, clarity and mystical self-discovery. This Volume will also go deeper into the philosophy of God as creation and will explore the concepts of modern science and how they correlate with ancient teachings. This Volume will lay the ground work for the understanding of the philosophy of universal consciousness and the initiatic/yogic insight into who or what is God? ISBN 1-884564-07-0 $22.95

22.   THE GODDESS AND THE EGYPTIAN MYSTERIESTHE PATH OF THE GODDESS THE GODDESS PATH The Secret Forms of the Goddess and the Rituals of Resurrection The Supreme Being may be worshipped as father or as mother. *Ushet Rekhat* or *Mother Worship*, is the spiritual process of worshipping the Divine in the form of the Divine Goddess. It celebrates the most important forms of the Goddess including *Nathor, Maat, Aset, Arat, Amentet and Hathor* and explores their mystical meaning as well as the rising of *Sirius,* the star of Aset (Aset) and the new birth of Hor (Heru). The end of the year is a time of reckoning, reflection and engendering a new or renewed positive movement toward attaining spiritual Enlightenment. The Mother Worship devotional meditation ritual, performed on five days during the month of December and on New Year's Eve, is based on the Ushet Rekhit. During the ceremony, the cosmic forces, symbolized by Sirius - and the constellation of Orion ---, are harnessed through the understanding and devotional attitude of the participant. This propitiation draws the light of wisdom and health to all those who share in the ritual, leading to prosperity and wisdom. $14.95 ISBN 1-884564-18-6

23.   *THE MYSTICAL JOURNEY FROM JESUS TO CHRIST* $24.95   ISBN# 1-884564-05-4 size: 8½" X 11" Discover the ancient Egyptian origins of Christianity before the Catholic Church and learn the mystical teachings given by Jesus to assist all humanity in becoming Christlike. Discover the secret meaning of the Gospels that were discovered in Egypt. Also discover how and why so many Christian churches came into being. Discover that the Bible still holds the keys to mystical realization even though its original writings were changed by the church. Discover how to practice the original teachings of Christianity which leads to the Kingdom of Heaven.

24.   THE STORY OF ASAR, ASET AND HERU: An Ancient Egyptian Legend (For Children)   Now for the first time, the most ancient myth of Ancient Egypt comes alive for children. Inspired by the books *The Asarian Resurrection: The Ancient Egyptian Bible* and *The Mystical Teachings of The Asarian Resurrection, The Story of Asar, Aset and Heru* is an easy to understand and thrilling tale which inspired the children of Ancient Egypt to aspire to greatness and righteousness.   If you and your child have enjoyed stories like *The Lion King* and *Star Wars* you will love *The Story of Asar, Aset and Heru.* Also, if you know the story of Jesus and Krishna you will discover than Ancient Egypt had a similar myth and that this myth carries important spiritual teachings for living a fruitful and fulfilling life.   This book may be used along with *The Parents Guide To The Asarian Resurrection Myth: How to Teach Yourself and Your Child the Principles of Universal Mystical Religion.* The guide provides some background to the Asarian Resurrection myth and it also gives insight into the mystical teachings contained in it which you may introduce to your child. It is designed for parents who wish to grow spiritually with their children and it serves as an introduction for those who would like to study the Asarian Resurrection Myth in depth and to practice its teachings. 41 pages 8.5" X 11"   ISBN: 1-884564-31-3 $12.95

25.   THE PARENTS GUIDE TO THE AUSARIAN RESURRECTION MYTH: How to Teach Yourself and Your Child the Principles of Universal Mystical Religion.   This insightful manual brings for the timeless wisdom of the ancient through the Ancient Egyptian myth of Asar, Aset and Heru and the mystical teachings contained in it for parents who want to guide their children to understand and practice the teachings of mystical spirituality. This manual may be used with the children's storybook *The Story of Asar, Aset and Heru* by Dr. Muata Abhaya Ashby. 5.5"x 8.5"   ISBN: 1-884564-30-5 $14.95

26.   HEALING THE CRIMINAL HEART BOOK 1 Introduction to Maat Philosophy, Yoga and Spiritual Redemption Through the Path of Virtue   Who is a criminal? Is there such a thing as a criminal heart?

What is the source of evil and sinfulness and is there any way to rise above it? Is there redemption for those who have committed sins, even the worst crimes? Ancient Egyptian mystical psychology holds important answers to these questions. Over ten thousand years ago mystical psychologists, the Sages of Ancient Egypt, studied and charted the human mind and spirit and laid out a path which will lead to spiritual redemption, prosperity and Enlightenment. This introductory volume brings forth the teachings of the Asarian Resurrection, the most important myth of Ancient Egypt, with relation to the faults of human existence: anger, hatred, greed, lust, animosity, discontent, ignorance, egoism jealousy, bitterness, and a myriad of psycho-spiritual ailments which keep a human being in a state of negativity and adversity. 5.5"x 8.5"   ISBN: 1-884564-17-8 $15.95

27.   THEATER & DRAMA OF THE ANCIENT EGYPTIAN MYSTERIES: Featuring the Ancient Egyptian stage play-"The Enlightenment of Hathor' Based on an Ancient Egyptian Drama, The original Theater - Mysticism of the Temple of Hetheru $14.95   By Dr. Muata Ashby

28.   GUIDE TO PRINT ON DEMAND: SELF-PUBLISH FOR PROFIT, SPIRITUAL FULFILLMENT AND SERVICE TO HUMANITY Everyone asks us how we produced so many books in such a short time. Here are the secrets to writing and producing books that uplift humanity and how to get them printed for a fraction of the regular cost. Anyone can become an author even if they have limited funds. All that is necessary is the willingness to learn how the printing and book business work and the desire to follow the special instructions given here for preparing your manuscript format. Then you take your work directly to the non-traditional companies who can produce your books for less than the traditional book printer can. ISBN: 1-884564-40-2 $16.95 U. S.

29.   Egyptian Mysteries: Vol. 1, Shetaut Neter ISBN: 1-884564-41-0 $19.99 What are the Mysteries? For thousands of years the spiritual tradition of Ancient Egypt, *Shetaut Neter,* "The Egyptian Mysteries," "The Secret Teachings," have fascinated, tantalized and amazed the world. At one time exalted and recognized as the highest culture of the world, by Africans, Europeans, Asiatics, Hindus, Buddhists and other cultures of the ancient world, in time it was shunned by the emerging orthodox world religions. Its temples desecrated, its philosophy maligned, its tradition spurned, its philosophy dormant in the mystical *Medu Neter,* the mysterious hieroglyphic texts which hold the secret symbolic meaning that has scarcely been discerned up to now. What are the secrets of *Nehast* {spiritual awakening and emancipation, resurrection}. More than just a literal translation, this volume is for awakening to the secret code *Shetitu* of the teaching which was not deciphered by Egyptologists, nor could be understood by ordinary spiritualists. This book is a reinstatement of the original science made available for our times, to the reincarnated followers of Ancient Egyptian culture and the prospect of spiritual freedom to break the bonds of *Khemn,* "ignorance," and slavery to evil forces: *Sâaa* .

30.   EGYPTIAN MYSTERIES VOL 2: Dictionary of Gods and Goddesses ISBN: 1-884564-23-2 $21.95 This book is about the mystery of neteru, the gods and goddesses of Ancient Egypt (Kamit, Kemet). Neteru means "Gods and Goddesses." But the Neterian teaching of Neteru represents more than the usual limited modern day concept of "divinities" or "spirits." The Neteru of Kamit are also metaphors, cosmic principles and vehicles for the enlightening teachings of Shetaut Neter (Ancient Egyptian-African Religion). Actually they are the elements for one of the most advanced systems of spirituality ever conceived in human history. Understanding the concept of neteru provides a firm basis for spiritual evolution and the pathway for viable culture, peace on earth and a healthy human society. Why is it important to have gods and goddesses in our lives? In order for spiritual evolution to be possible, once a human being has accepted that there is existence after death and there is a transcendental being who exists beyond time and space knowledge, human beings need a connection to that which transcends the ordinary experience of human life in time and space and a means to understand the transcendental reality beyond the mundane reality.

31.   EGYPTIAN MYSTERIES VOL. 3 The Priests and Priestesses of Ancient Egypt ISBN: 1-884564-53-4 $22.95 This volume details the path of Neterian priesthood, the joys, challenges and rewards of advanced Neterian life, the teachings that allowed the priests and priestesses to manage the most long lived civilization in human history and how that path can be adopted today; for those who want to tread the path of the Clergy of Shetaut Neter.

32.   THE KING OF EGYPT: The Struggle of Good and Evil for Control of the World and The Human Soul ISBN 1-8840564-44-5 $18.95 This volume contains a novelized version of the Asarian Resurrection myth that is based on the actual scriptures presented in the Book Asarian Religion (old name –Resurrecting Osiris). This volume is prepared in the form of a screenplay and can be easily adapted to be used as a stage play. Spiritual seeking is a mythic journey that has many emotional highs and lows, ecstasies and depressions, victories and frustrations. This is the War of Life that is played out in the myth as the struggle of Heru and Set and those are mythic characters that represent the human Higher and Lower self. How to understand the war and emerge victorious in the journey o life? The ultimate victory and fulfillment can be experienced, which is not changeable or lost in time. The purpose of myth is to convey the wisdom of life through the story of divinities who show the way to overcome the challenges and foibles of life. In this volume the feelings and emotions of the characters of the myth have been highlighted to show the deeply rich texture of the Ancient Egyptian myth. This myth contains deep spiritual teachings and insights into the nature of self, of God and the mysteries of life and the means to discover the true meaning of life and thereby achieve the true purpose of life. To become victorious in the battle of life means to become the King (or Queen) of Egypt.Have you seen movies like The Lion King, Hamlet, The Odyssey, or The Little Buddha? These have been some of the most popular movies in modern times. The Sema Institute of Yoga is dedicated to researching and presenting the wisdom and culture of ancient Africa. The Script is designed to be produced as a motion picture but may be addapted for the theater as well. $19.95   copyright 1998 By Dr. Muata Ashby

33.   FROM EGYPT TO GREECE: The Kamitan Origins of Greek Culture and Religion ISBN: 1-884564-47-X $22.95 U.S. FROM EGYPT TO GREECE   This insightful manual is a quick reference to Ancient Egyptian mythology and philosophy and its correlation to what later became known as Greek and Rome mythology and philosophy. It outlines the basic tenets of the mythologies and shoes the ancient origins of Greek culture in Ancient Egypt. This volume also acts as a resource for Colleges students who would like to set up fraternities and sororities based on the original Ancient Egyptian principles of Sheti and Maat philosophy. ISBN: 1-884564-47-X $22.95 U.S.

34.   THE FORTY TWO PRECEPTS OF MAAT, THE PHILOSOPHY OF RIGHTEOUS ACTION AND THE ANCIENT EGYPTIAN WISDOM TEXTS ADVANCED STUDIES This manual is designed for use with the 1998 Maat Philosophy Class conducted by Dr. Muata Ashby. This is a detailed study of Maat Philosophy. It contains a compilation of the 42 laws or precepts of Maat and the corresponding principles which they represent along with the teachings of the ancient Egyptian Sages relating to each. Maat philosophy was the basis of Ancient Egyptian society and government as well as the heart of Ancient Egyptian myth and spirituality. Maat is at once a goddess, a cosmic force and a living social doctrine, which promotes social harmony and thereby paves the way for spiritual evolution in all levels of society. ISBN: 1-884564-48-8 $16.95 U.S.

Music Based on the Prt M Hru and other Kemetic Texts

Available on Compact Disc $14.99 and Audio Cassette $9.99

Adorations to the Goddess

Music for Worship of the Goddess

NEW Egyptian Yoga Music CD
by Sehu Maa
Ancient Egyptian Music CD
Instrumental Music played on reproductions of
Ancient Egyptian Instruments– Ideal for meditation
and
reflection on the Divine and for the practice of
spiritual programs and Yoga exercise sessions.

©1999 By Muata Ashby
CD $14.99 –

MERIT'S INSPIRATION
NEW Egyptian Yoga Music CD
by Sehu Maa
Ancient Egyptian Music CD
Instrumental Music played on
reproductions of Ancient Egyptian Instruments–
Ideal for meditation and
reflection on the Divine and for the practice of
spiritual programs and underline{Yoga exercise sessions.}
©1999 By
Muata Ashby
CD $14.99 –
UPC# 761527100429

ANORATIONS TO RA AND HETHERU
NEW Egyptian Yoga Music CD
By Sehu Maa (Muata Ashby)
Based on the Words of Power of Ra and HetHeru
played on reproductions of Ancient Egyptian
Instruments **Ancient Egyptian Instruments used:**
Voice, Clapping, Nefer Lute, Tar Drum, Sistrums,
Cymbals – The Chants, Devotions, Rhythms and
Festive Songs Of the Neteru – Ideal for meditation,
and devotional singing and dancing.
©1999 By Muata Ashby
CD $14.99 –
UPC# 761527100221

SONGS TO ASAR ASET AND HERU
NEW
Egyptian Yoga Music CD
By Sehu Maa
played on reproductions of Ancient Egyptian
Instruments– The Chants, Devotions, Rhythms and
Festive Songs Of the Neteru - Ideal for meditation, and
devotional singing and dancing.
Based on the Words of Power of Asar (Asar), Aset
(Aset) and Heru (Heru) Om Asar Aset Heru is the
third in a series of musical explorations of the
Kemetic (Ancient Egyptian) tradition of music. Its
ideas are based on the Ancient Egyptian Religion of

Asar, Aset and Heru and it is designed for listening, meditation and worship. ©1999 By Muata Ashby
CD $14.99 –
UPC# 761527100122

HAARI OM: ANCIENT EGYPT MEETS INDIA IN MUSIC
NEW Music CD
By Sehu Maa

The Chants, Devotions, Rhythms and Festive Songs Of the Ancient Egypt and India, harmonized and played on reproductions of ancient instruments along with modern instruments and beats. Ideal for meditation, and devotional singing and dancing.
Haari Om is the fourth in a series of musical explorations of the Kemetic (Ancient Egyptian) and Indian traditions of music, chanting and devotional spiritual practice. Its ideas are based on the Ancient Egyptian Yoga spirituality and Indian Yoga spirituality.
©1999 By Muata Ashby
CD $14.99 –
UPC# 761527100528

RA AKHU: THE GLORIOUS LIGHT

NEW
Egyptian Yoga Music CD
By Sehu Maa
The fifth collection of original music compositions based on the Teachings and Words of The Trinity, the God Asar and the Goddess Nebethet, the Divinity Aten, the God Heru, and the Special Meditation Hekau or Words of Power of Ra from the Ancient Egyptian Tomb of Seti I and more...
played on reproductions of Ancient Egyptian Instruments and modern instruments - **Ancient Egyptian Instruments used: Voice, Clapping, Nefer Lute, Tar Drum, Sistrums, Cymbals**
– The Chants, Devotions, Rhythms and Festive Songs Of the Neteru – Ideal for meditation, and devotional singing and dancing.
©1999 By Muata Ashby
CD $14.99 –
UPC# 761527100825

GLORIES OF THE DIVINE MOTHER
Based on the hieroglyphic text of the worship of Goddess Net.
The Glories of The Great Mother
©2000 Muata Ashby
CD $14.99 UPC# 761527101129`

Order Form

Telephone orders: Call Toll Free: 1(305) 378-6253. Have your AMEX, Optima, Visa or MasterCard ready.

Fax orders: 1-(305) 378-6253   E-MAIL ADDRESS: Semayoga@aol.com

Postal Orders: Sema Institute of Yoga, P.O. Box 570459, Miami, Fl. 33257. USA.

Please send the following books and / or tapes.

ITEM

_____Cost $_____

_____Cost $_____

_____Cost $_____

_____Cost $_____

_____Cost $_____

Total $_____

Name:_____

Physical Address:_____

City:_____ State:_____ Zip:_____

Sales tax: Please add 6.5% for books shipped to Florida addresses

_____Shipping: $6.50 for first book and .50¢ for each additional

_____Shipping: Outside US $5.00 for first book and $3.00 for each additional

_____Payment:_____

_____Check -Include Driver License #:

_____

_____Credit card: _____ Visa, _____ MasterCard, _____ Optima, _____ AMEX.

Card number:_____

Name on card:_____ Exp. date:_____/_____

Copyright 1995-2005 Dr. R. Muata Abhaya Ashby

Sema Institute of Yoga

P.O.Box 570459, Miami, Florida, 33257

(305) 378-6253 Fax: (305) 378-6253

16623042R00213

Printed in Great Britain
by Amazon